Embodiment, Political Economy and Human Flourishing

Frédéric Basso · Carsten Herrmann-Pillath

Embodiment, Political Economy and Human Flourishing

An Embodied Cognition Approach to Economic Life

palgrave
macmillan

Frédéric Basso
Psychological and Behavioural Science
London School of Economics
and Political Science
London, UK

Carsten Herrmann-Pillath
Max Weber Centre for Advanced
Cultural and Social Studies
University of Erfurt
Erfurt, Germany

ISBN 978-3-031-54970-0 ISBN 978-3-031-54971-7 (eBook)
https://doi.org/10.1007/978-3-031-54971-7

Cover illustration: ViewStock/gettyimages

This Palgrave Macmillan imprint is published by the registered company Springer Nature Switzerland AG
The registered company address is: Gewerbestrasse 11, 6330 Cham, Switzerland

Paper in this product is recyclable.

A tous ceux que j'ai tant plaisir à aimer.

Frédéric Basso

Biliang zum Gedenken

Carsten Herrmann-Pillath

"What is unique about the I hides itself exactly in what is unimaginable about a person. All we are able to imagine is what makes everyone like everyone else, what people have in common. The individual I is what differs from the common stock, that is, what cannot be guessed at or calculated, what must be unveiled, uncovered, conquered."

Milan Kundera, The Unbearable Lightness of Being

Acknowledgements

This book has been a long time in the making. It originally grew out of an unpublished book manuscript in French that Fred Basso co-authored with Olivier Oullier in the late 2000s. This book was based on a critical reading of Hayek's *The Sensory Order*, which was just being properly analyzed, even by Hayekian economists. Basso realized that the only economist who had substantially worked on *The Sensory Order* was Carsten Herrmann-Pillath, already in the early 1990s. So, the two authors came into contact, but for various reasons, the book remained unpublished. They parted ways, and only a decade later, the idea of revisiting the book project came up. Many new ideas were on the table, following Basso's engagement with theories of embodiment, and Herrmann-Pillath's engagement with Hegel (motivated by another partner, Ivan Boldyrev). Both authors converged on a shared view of the pressing need for social and economic transformation, and the imperative to reinstate Political Economy against economic orthodoxy. Finally, after years of creative struggle, the book is finished, and will hopefully be helpful to those in economics and the social and behavioral sciences who study people in real-world economic life.

We would like to thank our institutions for the assemblage of material, social, and financial support provided, namely the London School of Economics (FB), the Max Weber Centre for Advanced Cultural and Social Studies, Erfurt University, and DFG[1] (CHP). We would also like to thank the students, colleagues, friends, and loved ones, who have heard so (or perhaps too?) much about this project over the past months and years. Particularly, we would like to thank those with whom discussions about ideas related to the book have always been so enriching: Stephan Bannas, Martin W. Bauer, Ivan Boldyrev, Julien Bouillé, Thomas Curran, Liam Delaney, Alex Gillespie, Christian Hederer, Maxi Heitmayer, Juha Hiedanpäa, Bettina Hollstein, Sandra Jovchelovitch, Dario Krpan, Kate Laffan, Saadi Lahlou, Urs Lindner, Jens Madsen, Timo Maran, Olivier Oullier, Lionel Paolella, Olivia Petit, Philippe Robert-Demontrond, Hartmut Rosa, Don Ross, Simo Sarkki, Jennifer Sheehy-Skeffington, Ganga Shreedhar, Katriina Soini, Hiroykuki Takizawa, Julien Troiville, and Feiyang Wang. Most importantly, we are deeply grateful to Saransh Ahuja, Sophia Freckmann, Julian Kirschner, Dallas O'Dell, Atrina Oraee, and Torben Trapp for their enthusiasm in providing such a detailed, constructive, and thoughtful feedback on book chapters.

Note

1. The section on property in this book builds on results of a project supported by Deutsche Forschungsgemeinschaft (DFG, German Research Foundation) – Project-ID 424638267 – TRR 294 "Structural change of property," Project C01: "Hybrid ownership structures in state capitalism: ownership-based society, socio-economic differentiation and governmentality analysed through the example of Shenzhen, China."

Contents

List of Figures

List of Tables

CHAPTER 1

Introduction to an Embodied Approach to Economic Life

If there is one thing we can see everywhere in economic life but that remains absent in economic models, it is surely the body; unless a reference to embodiment, with a mention of emotions, for example, helps to explain why (not surprisingly) human behavior deviates so far from the model. What is embodied seems to be an unfortunate discrepancy, that glitch in the data that makes reality look so stubborn. Through and through, this book takes an opposite view, with one main bold claim: We need to take stock of embodiment in economics because the body *grounds* and *bounds* economic life.

Let us take a few illustrations, starting with work-related illnesses in modern societies. They abound in the economy, so much so that one could argue that bodily suffering has been a constitutive feature of capitalism since its emergence. In its early days, slavery became an essential element of capitalist operations. With the advent of so-called "free labor" during industrialization, endless working hours, nil workplace safety, and extreme conditions made working in the "satanic mills" a torture. These conditions have gradually improved, although the harmful effects of work on the body are still accepted as a necessary feature of modern-day capitalism: Think of those, usually in poor countries, who mine the rare

F. Basso and C. Herrmann-Pillath, *Embodiment, Political Economy and Human Flourishing*, https://doi.org/10.1007/978-3-031-54971-7_1

minerals that power smartphones, or work in the factories of the fast-fashion industry; those, often migrants, who build and maintain homes as construction workers; or those who endure long commutes to their workplace. Another illustration is the many forms of bodily care, such as taking responsibility for children or the elderly at home, that are not compensated in most societies via the market or monetary transfers. Women, in particular, bear the brunt of these conditions, with long working hours in addition to the domestic chores that remain largely theirs. In general, the care of the body as a productive source for the capitalist system is mostly left to the private and personal sphere, especially when these bodies are not yet or no longer productive.

Generally, such illustrations are treated nonchalantly in economics, as necessary frictions for economic growth, even though the development of nudging in the workplace shows that behavioral economics has recently endorsed the case that we should take care of our bodies to preserve our economic productivity. When it comes to preserving our ability to work, we are increasingly under pressure to adopt health disciplines, following similar trends in the late nineteenth century, when standards of hygiene and sanitation were imposed to keep a population fit for work and war. At the same time, many people are suffering from work-related psychological problems, such as discrimination and harassment.

Simply put, in capitalist societies, when bodies are not at the center of countless efforts to sell goods and services, they are the recipients of externalization strategies that impose uncompensated costs on them, such as work-related deaths and illnesses. The picture we have painted is bleak, but it is only a small part of the story. Another important element is global warming as a result of industrial activity, which should further raise awareness of the problematic position of the body in modern capitalism. The deaths and illnesses associated with air and water pollution, or extreme weather events such as floods, storms, and week-long heatwaves are some of the most striking illustrations. Again, the care of the body in these situations typically remains within the immediate family and other social circles (e.g., friends, local support groups), or is provided by public health systems.

These are essential points for demonstrating the importance of the body in the economy, but our book is about the neglect of the body in a more fundamental sense. We argue that disembodiment is a defining feature of capitalism, resulting from the abstraction of market forces operating on human (and non-human) life. One of these abstractions is the separation of "labor power" from the body and its inclusion in the process of monetary valuation, that is, the so-called "labor market." Of course, work is done by individuals with bodies, but as mentioned above, their bodily suffering is ignored as much as possible in the process of wage labor. The economic disadvantage of slavery was precisely this: The slave owner was confronted with the bodily life of slaves, such as disease, family, or aging, which he could only avoid by imposing the harshest and most horrific working conditions on them. Once the fiction of "free labor" was created and institutionalized, employers could forget about the family lives of their workers. This is a constant of capitalism: For instance, the Japanese *salaryman* in the supposedly golden age of Japanese economic growth worked under severe stress and was almost separated from his family, and his wife was confined to the home to take care of other duties and responsibilities, such as raising children. No wonder that today's societies are facing another problem of the body: Rapid demographic decline due to low birth rates—just look at China today and its infamous "996" work culture in tech companies.

Such arguments have a long history in critical thinking about the economy, beginning with Karl Marx and his penetrating observations about alienation and human degradation under capitalism. After Marx, however, these were rarely concerns of the discipline of economics, which separated from the other human sciences at the end of the nineteenth century, a process that was completed by its mathematization since the 1930s. In this process, economic analyses were abstracted from the body, for example by explicitly abandoning psychological research. Importantly, we argue that this abstraction in theory reflects a process of abstraction that unfolded in the real world through specific institutional forms of the economy, such as the gendered separation between wage labor and the domestic sphere. To a significant extent, this corresponds to Max Weber's analysis of the "iron cage of capitalism" and its forces of "rationalization." For Weber, dehumanizing abstraction is the hallmark of "market society" (*Marktvergesellschaftung*).

Our use of the term "abstraction" is inspired by the work of F. A. Hayek and stands in the tradition of thinkers who emphasized the novelty of the social and economic system that has emerged in recent centuries, such as Hume's notion of the "Great Society," or Ferdinand Tönnies' famous distinction between "community" and "society." Tönnies is of particular interest because he explicitly referred to "community" as an embodied, even feminine, form of life, and defined "society" as necessarily "capitalist," in which a masculine principle of abstraction reigns. In this view, modern society as a form of community is impossible. Similarly, Hayek argued that the market and its associated form of society are systems of abstract rules that must not be disturbed by interventions driven by motivations and valuations rooted in pre-modern (so-called "tribal") forms of communal life. Hayek saw social justice as a delusion created by more primitive emotions and (anthropomorphic) beliefs. This view, though rarely justified in the same terms, is characteristic of mainstream economic policy positions, which often ascribe a superior epistemic status to markets, in the sense that, as Hayek said, they are, thanks to the price system, processors and generators of economic information more powerful than human intelligence as embodied in individuals and communities.

Hayek was also influential in the context of the debate over socialist calculation of the 1940s and shaped the rise of "neoliberalism" in the 1980s. We take his work as our starting point in this book because we expose a fundamental contradiction in his thinking. His reasoning about the market is thoroughly disembodied, even as a normative principle: In his view, the market that underpins the Great Society must be disembodied in order to function properly. At the same time, his epistemic position was formulated in a long-neglected work, *The Sensory Order*, which is a remarkable systematic elaboration of an embodied approach to human cognition. So, there is a deep tension between his normative beliefs on the one hand and his epistemics on the other. Why does this matter, beyond mere interests in the intellectual history of economics?

In recent decades, economics has undergone profound changes. One of them is the rise of fields of research, namely behavioral, experimental, and neuroeconomics, that seem to approach humans as living beings made of flesh and that claim to reject the model of rationality represented by *Homo economicus* as a purely abstract analytical construct. In this literature, Hayek is almost completely ignored. Again, this may appear to be a mere historical anecdote, but there is more to it than meets the eye. It becomes clear when we consider the role of the body in these new strands of research. In behavioral economics, for instance, the body is commonly seen as a source of "misbehaving," that is, regular and pervasive violations of rationality (represented by *Homo economicus* as a benchmark), such as miscalculations of probabilities, or lack of consistency in dynamic choices over time. Though left in analytical limbo, the assumption is that the human brain, as part of the body, contains a separate system that should enable it to act rationally, but is constantly disrupted by interference from other bodily processes, such as eating too much when we want to stay healthy. Building on a "deficit view" that people almost always fail to behave as *Homo economicus* (unless they are trained to do so), the behavioral economist assumes the role of a therapist, responsible for designing methods to "nudge" people to listen to their better selves. This approach mixes positive and normative perspectives, essentially replicating a Cartesian dualism between mind and body, with "mind" being potentially equated with the qualities of that old fellow, *Homo economicus*. In contrast, the body is the place where "irrational" forces would prevail, such as emotions, visceral drives, or habits. This is eerily reminiscent of the struggle between the soul of the true Christian believer and the mortal sins that beset it. Behavioral economics is about disciplining the embodied self according to the precepts of rationality, based on the "scientific" diagnosis of the ills of embodied irrationality.

Now, interestingly, there is no strong commitment to empirically identifying the two systems that battle within people: Behavioral economics positions itself as using a psychological perspective to understand economic decision-making and behavior while following the analytical norms of economics and not *necessarily* reaching out to neuroscientific investigations. This is understandable: Compared to the "economic imperialism" of the standard rational choice model in economics, neuroscience mostly avoids theoretical generalizations and is thoroughly empirical, so that there is no normative evaluation of various drivers of human behavior. Yet, in the form of the neighboring field of neuroeconomics, there is a line of thinking that focuses on the brain and projects economic models of choice onto it, often even reintroducing advanced versions that are not really consistent with behavioral economics approaches. This is by no means a common view in neuroscience, so the field is now usually referred to as "decision neuroscience" to avoid reference to a specific approach. This is important because it can mean, as we argue in this book, that understanding human behavior *requires* a theoretical framework that is deeply embodied in terms of the interplay of many forces, such as emotions or cognitive projections of actions. In other words, grounding economics in neuroscience may lead to the rejection of the standard dualism of behavioral economics. This is precisely the lesson we draw from assessing Hayek's *The Sensory Order* in light of modern neuroscience.

There is another important strand of modern economics that has a somewhat complicated history. Behavioral economics also dates back to the early developments in combining the emerging cognitive sciences with economics, where another variant was developed by Herbert Simon. Simon's work was never fully embraced in economics beyond influential notions such as bounded rationality, when even at the time of its emergence, its antinomy, the rational expectations hypothesis, became a standard in economics. Nevertheless, a legacy of the early Simonian developments can be found in experimental economics with the use of artificial markets. This stands in an uneasy relationship with behavioral economics, although it is superficially wedded to the laboratory in a similar methodological stance. But this way of thinking has a radical implication: Human "misbehavior" seems simply irrelevant, since markets are supposed to guide even the dimmest person to the optimal choice. This view vindicates the Hayekian view of the epistemic powers of markets.

The link with Simon is the centrality of the computer metaphor in the analysis, whereby economic agents and markets can be seen in the guise of a machine. This metaphor is key to understanding abstraction in modern economics. Artificial markets that simulate markets are run on computers, and the implication is that real-world markets can be seen as a kind of supercomputer. Here, the abstraction from human bodies is perfect since their properties do not matter at all. Indeed, quantitative finance has come a long way in making markets without humans. Simon's tradition suggests the other important and complementary way to use the computer metaphor, which is to treat the human brain as a computer. Similar approaches have also been influential in neuroscience, and the computer metaphor has cemented an analytical stance that focuses on the brain and sidelines the body, at least as far as (the so-called) higher cognitive functions are concerned.

To sum up, the recent developments in economics do not herald a return of the body, quite the contrary. The difficulty is precisely that we observe different, sometimes contradictory, strands, although all seem to support the neglect of the body when it is not portrayed as a source of "misbehaving."

The strength of disembodiment is not unique to economics and has deep roots in the history of Western science, reflecting what Charles Taylor has dubbed the "excarnation" of Western culture and society. These roots lie in pre-scientific beliefs about the duality of soul and body, and the ethical conviction that the body is somehow the source of all evil that must be disciplined. These beliefs were transformed into influential intellectual constructs such as the aforementioned Cartesian dualism of mind and body, which continues to shape modern sciences to an astonishing degree. Economics is deeply Cartesian in that respect, and the result is the disembodiment of its theoretical constructs.

But economics also reflects the processes of disembodiment that actually took place with the emergence of capitalism. This is also the root of the Hayekian quandary: Hayek developed an embodied view of human beings, but endorsed, if not celebrated, the actual historical forces that abstracted from them.

As said, there is a long tradition of critical analysis of economics in terms of the neglect of, and outright harm to, the body. However, with the exception of feminist economics, these are mostly views from non-economic disciplines. One of the most influential schools of thought in the second half of the twentieth century was psychoanalysis, a *mixtum compositum* of humanistic psychology and philosophy. Our approach is different, in that we draw on theoretical analyses and empirical tests done in neuroscience, psychology, and sociology as well as economics and philosophy, to defend the case for the re-embodiment of economics. In doing so, our rhetoric can invoke the Hayek of *The Sensory Order* and thus directly target the core of those economic theories that defend capitalism in its purest forms. Hayek anticipated many insights of modern embodied approaches in the cognitive sciences, such as the sensory-motor grounding of abstract concepts. Although he does not refer to them in *The Sensory Order*, his related views on institutions are also connected to embodiment, as he envisions the distribution of cognitive processes beyond the physical boundary of the body.

Our approach to embodied economics is primarily positive and empirical. Nevertheless, as noted above, and again with reference to Hayek, it remains distinct from behavioral and neuroeconomics, and although similar views of "ecological rationality" can sometimes be found in the experimental economics literature, we go well beyond this focus on the brain and the body. Most importantly, we present an embodied view of capitalism as a distinct "assemblage" of economic institutions. This underscores an essential point: Although capitalism drives disembodiment, abstraction itself is grounded in the body. Put differently, there is no disembodiment without embodiment in the first place since something that is not embodied cannot be disembodied. The paradox is thus only apparent and is further resolved when we consider distributed forms of cognition, foremostly, those mediated by the institution of money. As aforementioned, our reasoning has much in common with Max Weber, and in a more direct sense, with Pierre Bourdieu and his analysis of habitus and field. In capitalism, abstraction is grounded in the body through internalization, or "inward embodiment" (in our parlance), of capitalist institutions. At the same time, these institutions are grounded in embodied cognitive processes, such as the transformative power of metaphors like TIME IS MONEY, and illustrate "outward embodiment," whereby embodied experience is externalized and shapes economic life.

This focus on institutions allows us to think of another form of therapeutic economics that presents the body not as a problem but as a solution: To address disembodiment in economic life, what is needed is not less embodiment, but more of it. In other words, if capitalism causes harm through disembodiment, we can heal that pain thanks to institutions that can empower people to transform capitalism into a new kind of system that features markets with strong forms of embodiment. This is what we call the "anti-Tönnies thesis:" The market is not just a feature of the capitalist society, but can be grounded (re-embedded) in the community. Therefore, we go on to construct our utopia, but one that is concrete in the sense that it is feasible and scalable once appropriate measures of institutional crafting are taken, following a participatory democratic process in the community. In fact, many of our ideas have been ventilated by economists of various obedience over the past two centuries, such as ring-fencing certain destabilizing effects of modern monetary and financial systems, and they have often proposed reforms aimed at anchoring financial markets in the (so-called) "real sphere." We rethink such proposals in terms of re-embodying economics. At this point, we part ways with Marx, as his vision of "communism" lacks detail. Nevertheless, we pick up common terminological elements: Our utopia is the market as community. This utopia is the expression of a critical reflection not only on current markets, but also on the role of the state in capitalism. The modern welfare state is another form of abstraction in terms of the bureaucratic management of human needs, a diagnosis that again echoes Max Weber's comprehensive view of rational capitalism. In this sense, markets as communities also address a central concern of classical liberal thought shared by critical theorists: The protection of the human individual from the overwhelming technocratic power of the state, epitomized by its totalitarian and Kafkaesque styles. We move beyond the "state versus market" dualism that has haunted thinking about economics and economic policy since the nineteenth century, and that has caused immense suffering as recently as the Hayek-inspired neoliberal turn of the 1980s.

In the rest of the book, the structure of our argument will unfold as follows.

Chapter 2 sets the stage for the book. We begin with the diagnosis that since its origins, especially in light of Adam Smith's comprehensive view of human nature and institutions, economics has evolved into a corpus of disembodied theories that have lost touch with human and social realities. The crucial period was the radical separation of economics from psychology and sociology following the marginalist revolution, and the turn to increased mathematization at the beginning of the twentieth century. The epitome of disembodiment is the widespread deployment of the computer metaphor to economic agents and markets. This view reduces and defines economic action as the abstract processing of information in decision-making. We identify three main motivations for this transformation of economics: First, to establish its disciplinary autonomy from psychology and sociology; second, to formalize the normative presumption of individual freedom; and third, to adopt a reductive explanatory approach to the complex behavior of large populations of agents. However, we argue that one of the hollow pillars of the standard disembodied model is the treatment of prices as carriers of information that would be the parameters of rational decisions in the market. Prices only become information when they are interpreted by living human beings in social contexts. Recently, new approaches have emerged that seem to re-embody economics, namely, behavioral, experimental, and neuroeconomics. Still, as we show in this chapter (and the subsequent ones), these approaches can remain incoherent and inconclusive as far as embodiment is concerned. For example, behavioral economics still adheres to the standard benchmark of rationality when it systematically builds on the methodology of diagnosing "anomalies," and even when it recommends therapeutic measures, as popularized by nudging. Experimental economics leads to results in which human beings are indistinguishable from programs and algorithms representing zero-intelligence agents. Neuroeconomics partly uses the standard economic model as a theoretical framework. On the other hand, these disciplines have also, willingly or unwillingly, highlighted the importance of the embodied and situated aspects of economic decision-making in experimental studies, demonstrating the fundamental role of experience, emotions, or culture, to name a few. We argue that one difficulty in systematically organizing these promising insights into a new paradigm in economics is that economics follows a covering-law or deductive-nomological understanding of explanation as does the field of physics. Neuroscience and much of psychology, in comparison, follow a methodology more characteristic of the life sciences in general, that is, exploring and identifying generating mechanisms for observed phenomena without bringing them into a coherent and closed set of theoretical hypotheses introduced a priori, or, axiomatically.

A famous critic of the physicalism that underlies standard economics and some currents in the social sciences is Hayek, consistent with his approach to the market as a spontaneous order and abstract system of rules. Arguably, as Thatcherism and Reaganomics illustrate, his views helped shape the neoliberal economic policies that unfolded in the last decades of the twentieth century and have influenced economic discourses for generations of economists and political scientists. Chapter 3 shows, however, that Hayek the economist remains deeply at odds with Hayek the psychologist, and in particular that his approaches to the market and the brain fail to fit into a coherent theoretical framework. The "Hayek paradox" that we identify points to one of the central themes of this book: Although Hayek promotes a disembodied conception of the market, he develops a radically embodied view of the brain, in his seminal work, *The Sensory Order*. The latter implies that abstraction as a cognitive process must be embodied; consequently, the market as a medium of abstraction must be grounded in, and bounded by, embodiment. We argue that Hayek's disembodied view of the market is motivated by his normative, ideological, and even visceral, rejection of social justice. Through a detailed examination of his view of the brain and cognition, we show why it cannot be reconciled with his analysis of the market as an abstract order. We compare this paradox with the coherent theoretical approach developed by Hayek's contemporary and fellow Nobel laureate in economics, Herbert Simon. Simon also combined the roles of psychologist and economist, but he consistently employs a disembodied approach to cognition throughout his work. Despite the strengths of some of their developments, in our book we follow in the footsteps of Hayek the psychologist to develop a more systematic approach to embodied economics in which eventually, contrary to Hayek the economist, social justice ultimately becomes the beacon for policy and economic practice.

Inspired by *The Sensory Order*, Chapter 4 develops the theoretical principles of embodiment. We bring together various strands of this rich literature, which is mainly focused on cognitive science, psychology, and closely related fields in (analytical) philosophy (and phenomenology), neuroscience, or computer science. Unlike Hayek, this literature is thoroughly grounded in empirical research. We explore several trends in this literature. We argue that moving from disembodied rationality to embodied reason to study economic life requires linking perception, cognition, and action, and coupling the organism and the environment. We also highlight the need to overcome the opposition between rationality and emotion, and connect current trends in embodiment research (e.g., mirror neurons, somatic markers) to economists such as Adam Smith and John Maynard Keynes. Embodiment is a foundational concept in the contemporary theories of perceptual symbols (Barsalou and others), conceptual metaphors (Lakoff, Johnson, and others), conceptual blending (Fauconnier, Turner, and others), neural reuse and exaptation (Anderson and others), distributed cognition (Hutchins and others), and language-based and artifact-mediated cognition (Vygotsky and others), to name just a few of the major references we explore in this chapter. All these theories converge on the idea that cognition is grounded in sensory-motor systems that enact the relationship between the organism and the (social and cultural) environment, implying that abstraction is not contrary to embodiment, but is made possible by it, and is even a call for more embodiment. The Hayek paradox identified in the previous chapter is thus resolved by celebrating, rather than annihilating, the role of embodiment in economic life. Moving forward, we propose the dialectic of inward and outward embodiment as a fundamental principle that can be traced back to the philosophy of G. W. F. Hegel and manifested in the thinking of eminent scholars in the history of Western social thought, such as Georg Simmel, Max Weber, Norbert Elias, John Dewey, George Herbert Mead, Maurice Merleau-Ponty, or, as a key thinker in our own embodied approach to economic agency and institutions, Pierre Bourdieu. Together, philosophical, psychological, and social approaches to embodiment offer an analytical apparatus that can be productively deployed to better understand economic phenomena. Anticipating later developments in the book, we pay special attention to image schemas and metaphors in the creation of the social ontology of economics (with applications to preferences and numerical cognition), to conceptual blending as a medium of creativity in economic life (with applications to material artifacts such as prices), and to the role of language in the making of the self and the constitution of economic actors (with applications to economic decision-making, and self-regulation). In this view, and in contrast to the mainstream trends in behavioral and experimental economics, embodiment is no longer neglected or seen as a source of disturbances to (market-based) rationality in light of a disembodied normative standard: Rather, the (inward and outward) embodiment of reason prepares the ground for our theory of economic agency and institutional action.

Against this background, Chapter 5 uses the concept of embodiment to develop a radical alternative to the rational economic agent, including its recent metamorphoses in behavioral economics. In doing so, we outline the characteristics of the reasonable person, or the economic actor, as distinct from the economic agent. The concept of actor is grounded in fundamental biological notions associated with embodiment, namely, autonomy and feelings. Autonomy is the counterpart of the conventional notion of freedom and refers to capabilities of self-determination and flourishing. Feelings ground valuation as enabling reasonable action. Our notion of agency stands in the Hegelian tradition of approaching the person as unfolding developmentally and historically, embedded in social relations. This can be analyzed in terms of the conceptual triad of inward embodiment, outward embodiment, and recognition. An important implication is that agency cannot be reduced to the individual, but is distributed in assemblages of actors and artifacts, resulting in a potential and situated transition to the "We-mode" of action. In such assemblages, agency is embodied in agential powers that accrue to an actor and are experienced as feelings. In the context of markets, an important example of feelings is trust. We further detail the concept of agency by referring to Amartya Sen's and Martha Nussbaum's notions of "capabilities" and "functionings." In addition to agency, identity is another defining property of an actor. Our approach to identity builds on the analysis of memory as constitutive of the self. A key medium for the formation and expression of identity is narratives shared with others. In sum, the reasonable person in the economy is the economic actor, experiencing feelings, seeking flourishing in autonomy, with reasons for action mutually recognized by others.

Chapter 6 continues the Hegelian line of argument initiated in the previous chapters by reinstating the view of institutions characterized as "second nature," meaning that the social world is inwardly embodied, and eventually becomes "transparent" to us. Put differently, we live by institutions without being aware of their contingency, as does the blind person using a stick as an extension of the body. In this perspective, we develop a new approach that synthesizes Masahiko Aoki's theory of institutions with Bourdieu's (embodied and cognitive) sociology. Whereas disembodied economic theorizing about institutions (and the original Aoki model) emphasizes their roles as media of information, we emphasize the role of power. This is both in the sense that power is necessary to enforce institutions, and that institutions create power as agential power that is allocated differentially across people, thus also produces inequality. More specifically, the chapter begins with a critique of disembodiment in game theory, which is the methodological standard in economic analyses of institutions. We show that game theory can only be meaningfully employed when it is thoroughly contextualized, with real actors exercising embodied agential powers, as can be seen in seminal approaches, such as Elinor Ostrom's de- and re-construction of the Prisoners' Dilemma in her theory and practice of the commons. Aoki has taken this a step further in a model that explicitly accounts for the role of linguistic and symbolic intermediation, as well as dispositions, in driving the interactions between actors that generate the institutionalization of practices. Building on such previous work, we present the Aoki-Bourdieu model as a new framework that aims to explain institutions in terms of Bourdieu's basic concepts of habitus, field, and symbolic capital. This model only suggests a conceptual logic of the embodied view of institutions. We go on to develop a more detailed conceptual apparatus that incorporates some essential elements of John Searle's notion of institution and relates them to the tools of embodied analysis developed in the previous chapters: In particular, we render the Searlean status function in terms of the embodied notions of metaphor and conceptual blending, and we refer to the two forms of intentionality that laid the groundwork for distinguishing the I-mode and the We-mode in the analysis of agential power. This general approach leads us to revisit a typology of four types of social relationships proposed by Alan Fiske, which we further systematize in terms of the primary distinction between the I-mode and the We-mode, with the We-mode defining the type of Community, and three types arising from the I-mode, Hierarchy, Reciprocity, and Market. The four types correspond to four kinds of cognitive scaling operations, as argued by Fiske, as well as to embodied schemas that we identify, namely the CONTAINER, VERTICAL, BALANCE, and RESOURCE schemas. In understanding real-world institutional actions, we recognize the need to consider hybrids, such as in the institutionalization of labor, where the market type (labor market) and the hierarchy type (the firm) are closely intertwined.

Chapter 7 applies the methodology derived from the previous chapter to the core institutions of capitalism, money, property, and labor, where money plays a pivotal role as the medium of abstraction in the market. Our approach to money is inspired by Simmel, and his combination of philosophical, psychological, and historical reasoning. Inward embodiment unfolds through the internalization of the opportunity cost principle as mediated by monetary prices, and outward embodiment works via assetification, that is the cognitive blending of objects and money in pricing. Both movements drive the expansion of markets unless contained by ethical and political forces. We reject disembodied accounts of money as supposedly designed to overcome the constraints to barter, and approach money as assetified debts in its private forms, where its functions as a standard of value emerge from public money, as in the form of monetized taxation. The Aoki-Bourdieu model makes it possible to explain the fundamental role of trust in money in such a complex institutional assemblage. Money is intrinsically related to power asymmetries in the market, since it has the comparatively lowest asset specificity, such as in labor markets where employers pay money wages to workers with skills that are more specific than money. Money is also a medium of abstraction in the institution of property, which we analyze as a mode of institutional action of appropriation, distinct from possession, ownership, and theft. Property emerges from abstraction, both conceptually and materially, as constituting the alienability of objects of appropriation through markets. In contrast, we define ownership as relational: Ownership is essentially embodied as an identifying form of appropriation. The difference is historically manifested in the transition from a commons regime of ownership of land to a private property regime. Possession is embodied in the Lockean sense of property, that is, by investing labor in an object to gain a benefit, and ownership and possession converge in the Hegelian understanding of property as an extension of the self and a medium of self-actualization. However, as Marx rightly identified, the Hegelian view is in tension with the abstraction mediated via alienation through the market. We conclude the discussion with the mode of theft that has been pivotal in modern capitalism since its inception, such as land expropriation in (neo-)colonialism, or today's crony capitalism in the exploitation of natural resources. The last part of Chapter 7 is a discussion of labor, which appears as a paradox in modern economics, which treats labor as disutility, free in markets but simultaneously subject to hierarchy in firms and unproductive if not mediated by markets. We explain this paradoxical situation as a result of the assetification of human work as "labor power." However, labor takes place primarily in organizations, not in markets. We explore the flaws in disembodied theories of economic organization that purport to explain how organizations overcome opportunism in the market, when, in fact, contemporary forms of organization create opportunism, and also often aim to disembody labor by appropriating workers' tacit knowledge. Theories of human capital establish the implicit connection between disembodiment in the organizational and market domains, furthering the commodification and dehumanization of workers. In contrast, we develop an embodied analysis that builds on

Arendt's approach to *vita activa*, which introduced an alternative terminology that is important for understanding the differences between care, reproduction, and production in human activities.

Our book concludes with Chapter 8 on utopia in embodied economics. Karl Polanyi diagnosed the transition to capitalism as the imposition on society of the utopia of nineteenth-century liberal economics, which we have analyzed in previous chapters as a process of disembodiment that abstracts people from their relationships with others and the world. Embodied economics offers a radical alternative without eschewing (or fetishizing) the market as a social practice of economic exchange. The key is to reinvent markets as communities. We approach this as a concrete utopia, expressing a utopian impulse understood as forward embodiment, where the (vision of a) future economy that is already sprouting today is deployed. We base our approach on a critical reflection of the mainstream approach to welfare and institutional design, centering on the notions of market failure and externalities. We reverse the conventional view of treating prices as indicators of scarcity, and we suggest that externalities are the embodied indicators of scarcity in terms of feelings of need and privation, whereas the internalization of externalities in the market through monetary prices amounts to "silencing" such feelings. We discuss the limitations of recent developments pointing to embodiment, especially in behavioral economics through nudging, in Elinor Ostrom's approach to institutions and welfare, and in happiness studies. Our framework follows the eudaimonic approach to well-being as flourishing, which we further detail in terms of the WISER framework. Standing for Well-being, Inclusivity, Sufficiency, Empowerment, and Resilience, we discuss WISER in the context of the United Nations (UN) Sustainable Development Goals (SDGs). In further outlining our concrete utopia, we move from one key topic, the creation of markets as communities with special reference to work with dignity, to its general institutional conditions. We show that Universal Basic Income (UBI) is the key to creating autonomy in and from the market, so that the market becomes subordinate to the human quest for flourishing, and thus a means, not an end in itself. This reshapes the relationship between workers and companies, and is also leveraged by other institutional transformations that re-embody markets, such as in fostering their regional embeddedness, or empowering independent productive activities (for example in the context of sharing, or repair and DIY). Such measures require institutional changes in the wider setting of markets, for instance, a radical reform of the Intellectual Property Rights (IPR) system. We outline these conditions, such as strengthening personal liability in economic and financial investment, reforming the monetary system and implementing its de-financialization, or overhauling the tax system. The chapter concludes with a discussion of the future research agenda for embodied economics, acknowledging some of the limitations of our book, and looking forward to contributions that will not only help to understand the economic world, but also change it.

CHAPTER 2

The Ills of Disembodiment and Abstraction in Economics

2.1 Introduction: The Road to Abstraction from Human and Social Realities in Economics

This chapter introduces the book's premise that, when compared to Adam Smith's comprehensive view of human nature and institutions, economics has become disconnected from human and social realities through its evolution towards disembodied theories.

We present three main motivations that have underpinned the transformation of economics, which also relate to distinct episodes in the history of thought. The first motivation was to establish a radical separation of economics from psychology and sociology by capitalizing on the marginalist revolution initiated after 1870, and the increased mathematization associated with it in the early twentieth century. The standard model was further disembodied by the widespread use of the computer metaphor to describe economic agents and markets, leading to the reduction and definition of economic action as the abstract processing of information in decision-making. The second motivation was to formalize the normative presumption of individual freedom and self-determination, even abstracted from biological needs, inherited from the European Enlightenment. This is illustrated by the concept of (subjective) utility and the definition of rationality in terms of pure logical constraints under the auspices of the revealed-preference model and the instrumentalist approach as principled methodologies that emerged as the mainstream

F. Basso and C. Herrmann-Pillath, *Embodiment, Political Economy and Human Flourishing*, https://doi.org/10.1007/978-3-031-54971-7_2

position in the mid-twentieth century. The third motivation was the adoption of a reductive explanatory approach to the complex behavior of large populations of agents in order to provide microfoundations for the macroeconomic models that were also being developed at the time. Economic models were further abstracted from individual economic agents, and the market was portrayed as a "representative agent" aggregating a population of economic agents, be they consumers or producers, who follow rational expectations informed by the economic models themselves.

After discussing the conceptual issues related to the disembodied approach, we focus on one of the main points that could justify this argument in terms of distributed cognition, a theory classically associated with embodiment. Indeed, it is traditionally argued in economics that the market performs the calculations for economic agents, who are then able to make optimal decisions. We contend that the problem with this position is that it relies on the treatment of prices as carriers of information. In contrast, we argue that prices become information when they are interpreted by living human beings in social contexts. We then turn to another part of the literature that could be interpreted as a form of re-embodiment of economics through recent developments in behavioral, experimental, and neuroeconomics. We acknowledge that these approaches can bring embodiment back into economics, for instance when they empirically demonstrate the importance of the embodied and situated aspects of economic decision-making through the concepts of experience or emotion, or the role of context. However, we contend that they cannot be properly articulated with the embodiment literature because they maintain the disembodied rational model as a benchmark, as in behavioral economics and neuroeconomics, or they remain unable to distinguish humans from algorithms, as in experimental economics.

One of the implications of our argument is that these recent developments in economics should abandon the deductive-nomological approach inherited from their reading of physics in favor of a more mechanistical approach that explores and identifies the generative mechanisms in economic life. Our book will provide a rich and comprehensive view of such mechanisms as embodied, material, and grounded in action.

2.2 The "Lost Century" of Economics

Today, conventional economics is disembodied, which is counterproductive to the advancement of the discipline and has led to cul-de-sacs in many areas. This is salient in the emergence of new areas of research that seem to bear many of the hallmarks of embodiment, namely, behavioral, experimental, and neuroeconomics. While dissecting these research programs may sharpen our understanding of "embodiment," we will show that they do not shake off the ghostly hand of disembodiment. Beyond these fields, economics remains disembodied in a principled way. We will approach this phenomenon by moving from the more general aspect of materiality to the more specific aspect of embodiment.

Materiality means that "social existence involves not only actors and social relations but also objects" (Pinch & Swedberg, 2008, p. 2), which has been emphasized in recent economic sociology (see also Callon et al., 2007). The loss of "materiality" in modern economics is the result of its increased mathematization, which began in the 1930s (Mirowski, 1991). Materiality reaches further than embodiment and conveys the idea that the social ontology implied by economics is immaterial, even "platonic," as early critics have christened it (Albert, 1998). There are many examples to illustrate this point. For instance, the complete exclusion of geography from the pure theory of international trade, often working with models that ignore transportation costs, or do not include the act of "trading" itself, which has only gradually been corrected with the rise of the "new economic geography" (Gallup et al., 1999). Another example is the conceptualization of prices as relative prices, that is, the relationship of one price to all other (Vining & Elwertowski, 1976), without any reference to prices as real objects, such as price tags or price lists. Sometimes, materiality is included in these models, such as when considering "menu costs," that is, the tedious task of writing and printing new price lists (Gordon, 1990). Often, however, even empirically oriented work in experimental economics shuns materiality, such as studying double auction markets extensively, but marginalizing posted-offer markets (with publicly observable price tags) which are considered (theoretically) uninteresting and inefficient, although they prevail in practice.[1] A final example is expectations, where until recently, economics has simply ignored how expectations are formed in everyday economic life by embodied economic agents in a state of "emotional anticipation"

(APA, 2023a), working instead with theoretical constructs such as rational expectations (Coibion et al., 2018).

Materiality matters for our theory of embodiment because, after all, the body is material. Yet, the two concepts are distinct because embodiment is material, but not all forms of materiality are embodied. A key theme in embodied economics will be how to include material phenomena beyond the skin in the notion of embodiment. To understand embodiment, we will begin by characterizing what distinguishes disembodiment from embodiment. At first sight, in the context of our argument, the notion of disembodiment seems to refer to a specific phenomenon, namely the explicit rejection of psychology and sociology in the conceptualization of the economic agent as a consequence of the marginalist revolution. This was seen as a major advance in establishing the disciplinary autonomy of economics (Ross, 2014, p. 36ff). In contrast, for instance, in embodied economics, the study of expectations would refer not only to individual psychology, but also to all kinds of social effects and processes, both of which create collective states of expectations in economic life.[2]

The medium of disembodiment was certainly abstraction, which had been at the center of crucial developments in economics since Adam Smith, beginning with Ricardo and British political economy. As a philosopher, Smith had developed a rich view of human nature and the role of "sentiments" in social interaction, which has only recently been rediscovered by behavioral economists (e.g., Ashraf et al., 2005). As we shall see in Chapter 4, this highlights the role of embodiment in decision-making. However, since the nineteenth century, following Ricardo and others, economists mostly focused on the legacy of *The Wealth of Nations* (Smith, 1776/2005), analyzing markets and the emerging modern capitalist economy on the basis of increasingly abstract and generic models of human behavior, as driven by a calculus of costs and benefits. Initially, this calculus was still seen as a psychological phenomenon, a kind of psychophysics, as advocated by Jevons or Edgeworth, who envisaged a calculus of pain and pleasure that could even be measured by a "hedonimeter" (Colander, 2007).

Two turning points took place. First, came the *Methodenstreit* between Schmoller and Menger in German-speaking economics (Backhaus & Hansen, 2000; Mäki, 1997), with many long-run consequences, such as separating sociology and economics. Max Weber was excluded from the doctrinal history of economics (Emmett, 2021), and many Austrian followers of Mengerian thought fled the Nazis and settled in leading

US universities (Scherer, 2000). Whereas Schmoller emphasized historical and anthropological empirical research, Menger championed abstract modeling of economic processes and behavior. This trend towards mathematization and abstraction was also initiated by Léon Walras who prepared the ground for general equilibrium theory (Debreu, 1984). His successor in Lausanne, Vilfredo Pareto, can also be seen as one of the intellectual figures who contributed to the separation of economics from sociology and psychology. Upon initial reading, it can be inferred from his writings that he established the distinction between economics and sociology by considering that the study of "non-logical conduct" is (rather) the matter of sociology whereas the study of "logical conduct" is (rather) the matter of economics (Pareto, 1935, §262–263; see also, Mirowski & Nik-Khah, 2017, pp. 26–27; Perry, 1935). In his view, "logical conduct is determined by interests, plus empirical calculation of most effective methods of satisfying them. Thus, if we know the interest of a group of men, you can calculate the actions in so far as their actions are logical" (Perry, 1935, p. 106; see also, Gross & Tarascio, 1998). Economics, as the science of rational action, is in charge of studying logical conduct under the scope of quantitative analysis (Pareto, 1935, §144). In contrast, non-logical conduct is influenced by drives that are different from interest. For instance, social beings have needs, habits, traditions, rituals, customs, or symbols, and they give rise to non-logical conduct, as a form of behavior that does not rely on rational choice but is motivated by instinct and sentiments (Pareto, 1935). Interestingly, in Pareto's view, non-logical conduct is the principal ingredient in social behavior, and, because it involves drives other than interest, non-logical conduct is mostly beyond the scope of economics (Perry, 1935).[3] In other words, the object of sociology is to study non-logical conduct, which can be seen as the principle of human behavior in social life, and, it might be inferred, the object of economics (as pure political economy) is to study an exception, the logical conduct, that generally occurs in economic life (Gross & Tarascio, 1998; Perry, 1935). Beyond the dichotomy between logical and non-logical conduct that generally structures the difference between economics and sociology, Pareto excluded the investigation of psychological mechanisms from the study of economic life. He ridiculed positions that suggested such orientations (Pareto, 1935, §37–38), and explicitly excluded psychology from economics.[4] To put it crudely, the Paretian view seems to vindicate an economic approach, at least when it comes to pure political economy, that is neither about social behavior nor about psychology.

The second turning point was the rise and decline of institutional economics in the US, which was deeply influenced by pragmatist philosophers who developed general principles of embodied and contextualized research with a transdisciplinary scope led, of course, by Dewey (Hodgson, 1998). Pragmatism had fostered an empirical focus in American economics that prevailed until World War II when it was obliterated by the Samuelsonian revolution. Samuelson was able to build on the earlier development of mathematical approaches to markets by Alfred Marshall and pull together the various strands to define a canonical framework for economics, which included the complete neutralization of psychology by treating the utility function as a mere mathematical description of observed behavior (revealed preferences) (Ross, 2014, p. 57ff). Not surprisingly, since then, much of mainstream economics has evolved as a discipline that does not take into account social and psychological dimensions, which favors a neglect of embodiment in economic life. In other words, disembodiment is primarily abstracting, or detaching, the economic agent from psychological and social processes: "The agent of the neoclassical model is quite drastically disembodied and disembedded" (Nelson, 1997, p. 160). As we can see, our argument implies that there was almost a "lost century" in the development of economics when disembodiment dominated theorizing.

Economics has not been alone in this. Our beacon is the development of cognitive science and, related to this, of philosophy, which was founded in the 1940s on a view of cognition incompatible with Pragmatism (Johnson, 2016, p. 102). Philosophy has always manifested a much wider scope for radically different positions, but the rise of formal approaches in logic and epistemology led to the establishment of a strong tradition of analytical philosophy, distinct from many strands of "continental" philosophy (Glock, 2008). One characteristic of this, which can also be identified in relation to economics as the discipline was embracing the concept of information, is the rise of the computational paradigm, concomitant with the emergence of artifacts such as computers. As John Searle pointed out:

> Because we do not understand the brain very well we are constantly tempted to use the latest technology as a model for trying to understand it. In my childhood we were always assured that the brain was a telephone

> switchboard. ('What else could it be?') I was amused to see that Sherrington, the great British neuroscientist, thought that the brain worked like a telegraph system. Freud often compared the brain to hydraulic and electro-magnetic systems. Leibniz compared it to a mill, and I am told some of the ancient Greeks thought the brain functions like a catapult. At present, obviously, the metaphor is the digital computer. (Searle, 1984, p. 44)

Analytical philosophy and cognitive sciences developed the idea of multiple realizability, conceiving of cognitive processes as mediated by abstract symbols and rules that can materialize in different forms, such as the computer or the human brain (Bickle, 2006). This has led to two lines of research: One explores whether and how the human mind can be replicated in a computer, hence, the term artificial intelligence (AI). The other posits that the human brain can be understood in terms of a computer. From the earliest days on, this has raised the question of whether there is a fundamental difference between a computer and a human, epitomized by the so-called "Turing test" and the "Chinese room" experiment (Cole, 2023). With the recent rise of high-powered AI, this question has become an existential one for many concerned people. The formal principles and structures of the computer have fostered the emergence of a set of disembodied notions that have spread across the fields of philosophy, cognitive science, and economics. The core ideas are the computational paradigm, which is linked to the notion of "information" as an external input and thus neatly distinguishes the computational system (inside) from the data (outside), and the concept of symbolic representation combined with the idea of a formal syntax that manipulates these representations (Brette, 2019). Since this kind of system can be described in formal logic, it can be seen as disembodied, which is manifested in the idea that the mind is multiply realizable, and thus could be built in various distinct ways, including systems that could supposedly be detached from the body (Shapiro, 2004, p. 1ff). As we will see with Herbert Simon's physical symbols systems, this fostered the conceptualization of the human mind as a computer in the cognitive sciences, which was also widely accepted in economics (Mirowski, 2001). Economics has added another line of thought, which is to approach the market as a computational system (Mirowski & Nik-Khah, 2017). In the heyday of general equilibrium theory, this was understood literally by interpreting general equilibrium as implemented in a computer, thus merging the theory of markets with the theory of central planning (Boldyrev & Kirtchik, 2017; see also, Bockman, 2011). Economic theory could even be identified with what could be run on a computer:

> I prefer to use the term 'theory' in a very narrow sense, to refer to an explicit dynamic system, something that can be put on a computer and run. This is what I mean by the 'mechanics' of economic development – the construction of a mechanical, artificial world, populated by the interacting robots that economics typically studies (…). (Lucas, 1988, p. 5; see also, Schotanus, 2022)

Hence, for the computational paradigm, what makes humans "beings with bodies" does not matter. There is a long tradition of merging paradigms in the natural sciences with views of human beings, and the computer paradigm can be seen simply as a metamorphosis of earlier ideas such as the view of human beings as "machines" (Newell & Simon, 1976), rooted in the Cartesian distinction between *res extensa* and *res cogitans*. These metaphors are not neutral, as they also influence how we perceive human ways of (economic) life: "The notion of economies as impersonal, machinery-like entities directly amenable to 'scientific' study was clinched when human beings were recast as robots whose conduct could be described by simple mathematical formulas" (Nelson, 2006, p. 20). The computer metaphor fits well with economic conceptions of humans as agents who constantly gather information, calculate costs and benefits, and seek optimal solutions. There is no room for other motivations, most importantly emotions and emotionally based notions of value.

The approach to humans as computers continues to inform the emerging, seemingly "embodied" economic subdisciplines of behavioral economics and neuroeconomics. As we will see, however, the shadow of disembodiment still looms over behavioral economics, because its intellectual endeavor is largely, if not entirely, about failures of rationality, taking the computationally (and supposedly) "correct" behavior as a standard, and even designing policies that would "nudge" people towards that standard. In neuroeconomics, the situation is more complicated, but a basic observation about neuroscience in general is that the computer metaphor has influenced certain connectionist conceptions of the neural system as a network of electrical flows—though, we add, and argue further in the next chapter, that the mainstream of connectionism is opposed to the standard interpretation of computational architecture (Buckner & Garson, 2019; Van Gelder, 1995). Such computational views can be easily combined with economic notions of optimality (Rustichini & Padoa-Schioppa, 2015). The metaphorical view of the brain as a computer leaves out important aspects of neurochemistry, which is mainly involved in the generation of emotional states and transcends the brain-body boundary (Jasanoff, 2018). Moreover, as we will see in Chapters 3 and 4, neuroeconomics will remain disembodied as long as it continues to separate perception, cognition, and action when it comes to studying decision-making.

All of these aspects are extremely complex, and we do not claim to address all of them. However, just as the computational paradigm has converged with economics in the past, in this book we ask what the rise of embodiment in the cognitive sciences means for economics. In doing so, embodied economics aims to bring psychological and social processes back into the analysis of the economic agent and its environment, the market.

Naturally, one might wonder why we need to bring back these psychological and social processes at all. They are indeed missing from standard economics, but modern developments such as research in behavioral and experimental economics, neuroeconomics, economic sociology, institutional economics, feminist economics, or ecological economics pave the way for the integration of psychological and social processes into economics. Point granted. However, we believe that what is missing in current research is an attempt to systematically integrate these findings: They tend to be based on different epistemologies, ranging from very computational approaches to very institutionalist ones. We believe that these different perspectives can be bridged by fully acknowledging the role of embodiment in economic theory. Note that we are not suggesting that embodiment is not already present to some extent in various approaches. Rather, we suggest that it is not fully recognized in economic analysis. Indeed, as we will show in this book, we can find evidence and illustrations of bodily influences in the literature on economic behavior and economic life, but to our knowledge, they have not been linked together within an embodied framework.

2.3 The Rationale of Disembodiment in Economics

Although we aim to avoid disembodied approaches to economic life, we must acknowledge strong intellectual justifications by economists. These justifications were not explicit when the turn to disembodiment unfolded, but they deserve attention in retrospect.

A key ingredient of disembodiment can certainly be seen in the notion of decision utility (Fumagalli, 2013). The mainstream conceptualization of (subjective) utility disembodies human wants and needs in the sense that the researcher does not need to specify them empirically, but only imposes certain constraints on what formally defines "rationality" (Becker, 1976). This does not necessarily imply disembodiment, as is evident from the early stages of the theory, when economists interpreted utility in psychological terms, as a sort of "forces" operating in the human brain. Yet this line of thinking was abandoned and has only recently been revived in some contributions to neuroeconomics. There were several reasons for this, mostly methodological, which we will examine below.

However, as von Weizsäcker (2011) has argued, subjective utility also has a strong normative background that is often sidelined even by economists: It is the analytical correlate of the recognition of human individual freedom and autonomy. The economic agent is even free to determine her own valuation of biological needs, an important element of the definition of autonomy in German idealism as condensing Enlightenment thought—with "excarnation" aka disembodiment as its main feature, as Charles Taylor (2007) has labeled it. Methodologically, this also implies that the economist abstains from any judgment about what individuals specifically prefer: "*de gustibus non est disputandum*," that is, in matters of taste there can be no dispute (Stigler & Becker, 1977). Thus, the notion of subjective utility reflects fundamental economic attitudes towards individual freedom as a key value of the European Enlightenment. As such, it is the correlate of the market conceived as a social structure that not only allows for the free expression of individual preferences, but also motivates others to recognize those preferences without any judgment of their merit or conformity with others' preferences.

In other words, the theoretical foundations of economics manifest a disembodied notion of freedom. Since Hegel, this has been a longstanding bone of contention, pitting abstract notions of freedom and autonomy against material notions that demand the capacities and capabilities for freedom, both individually and socially (Herrmann-Pillath & Boldyrev, 2014). We will return to this point in the next chapter when we discuss Hayek's difficulties with embodiment. Our book aims to develop a systematic alternative to disembodied economic liberalism by advancing an embodied notion of autonomy.

Another major justification for disembodiment in terms of subjective utility has been formalized by the "revealed preferences" model.[5] This has been interpreted in many ways, and we simply present our view, following Ross (2014). In this interpretation, subjective utility has no empirical reference at all but is only an element of the mathematical description of observed choices. That is to say, it combines extreme abstraction with extreme positivism, similar to behaviorism in psychology, which was dominant at the time the economic model was developed[6]: Economists can focus exclusively on (so-called) "observed" behavior when testing hypotheses, imposing only formal constraints of rationality (Becker, 1976).[7] Taking subjective preferences into account would require specifying them in explanations, which introduces huge degrees of freedom between external stimuli ("incentives") and observed behavior. If, at the same time, the normative prescription is applied that preferences are open to autonomous choice and self-determination, this would lead to complete individualization of single instances of empirical theory testing.

The rationality assumption is notoriously subject to much criticism, yet economics remains stubbornly wedded to it, even in the context of behavioral economics, as we shall see. Why is this? According to Max Weber, scientific explanations are not possible without the rationality assumption:

> For a scientific approach that constructs types, all irrational, affectively conditioned, meaningful contexts for behavior that influence action are best studied and represented as 'diversionary elements' with respect to a constructed, purely purposively rational course for such action. For example: explanation of the course taken by a stock exchange panic will first establish what would have happened if action had not been influenced by irrational emotions, following which these irrational components are introduced as 'disturbances'. (Weber, 1922/2019, p. 81)

This is almost a Hegelian way of reasoning since science is seen as an effort to rationally explain the world, which implies that rationality is also realized in the world. Weber argued that rational explanation provides the background against which "disturbances" such as emotions can be identified, but that they cannot be subjected to scientific explanations, only descriptive accounts.

We certainly do not follow this argument here, but we take it seriously. In a less Hegelian framework, this is an argument about the complexity and parsimony of scientific explanation. Economic phenomena may be far too complex for us to ever hope to achieve a complete explanation (Hayek, 1967, pp. 22–42), and according to standard theory, there are good reasons why the assumption or rationality helps to systematize phenomena. First, especially when it comes to markets, rationality is assumed to be adaptive and to become dominant in the course of market selection (Alchian, 1977). In addition, there is an argument known as the performative function of rationality, which can be traced back to Adam Smith (Scazzieri, 2006): In the marketplace, individuals encounter many others whom they do not know personally, so what can they reasonably assume about their behavior? Probably the best option is the "rational stance."[8] Yet, if people assume, if only by default, that others are rational, then the best response for them would be to act rationally as well. If everyone thinks this way, the argument goes, rationality will emerge as a universal pattern of behavior. This argument would imply that economics simply theorizes and abstracts the performative effects of real-world markets, as analyzed in Polanyi's seminal work (1944/2001), which have been denounced as "dehumanizing" by many critics (Herrmann-Pillath, 2020b). Ultimately, theories in standard economics may converge on an interpretation of the revealed preference approach as a description of statistical regularities at the population level, and not at all as a theory of the individual.

Methodologically, the revealed preference model was also justified by the (in)famous "as if" methodology called instrumentalism and formulated by Friedman, who claimed that: "The ultimate goal of a positive science is the development of a 'theory' or 'hypothesis' that yields valid and meaningful (i.e. not truistic) predictions about phenomena not yet observed" (Friedman, 1953, p. 7), and that

> the relevant question to ask about the 'assumptions' of a theory is not whether they are descriptively 'realistic,' for they never are, but whether they are sufficiently good approximations for the purpose in hand. And

> this question can be answered only by seeing whether the theory works, which means whether it yields sufficiently accurate predictions. (Friedman, 1953, p. 15)

This position remains in the standard methods toolbox of economists, while instrumentalism was debunked in the philosophy of science even before it was celebrated in economics (Popper, 1983/2015). There is, however, a sophisticated version of the rationale for the standard (disembodied) model in economics that overcomes instrumentalism. This concerns the micro/macro distinction.

Macroeconomics has shown a peculiar tendency towards the growing importance of econometrics and empirical work, on the one hand, and the strengthening of theoretically-based abstraction, on the other, as epitomized by the rise of dynamic stochastic general equilibrium (DSGE) modeling, which became the target of widespread criticism after the 2008 financial crisis (Romer, 2016; Stiglitz, 2018). This critique pointed out that the core models of mainstream macroeconomics, in their drastic simplifications, justified on purely theoretical grounds, lacked any relationship with the real economy and used econometrics as a way of suggesting empirical support while refraining from questioning their fundamentals. Most vocal critics would add that there is a political and ideological motivation behind this methodological stance since the basic theoretical assumptions are based on the notion of free markets and cast principled doubt on the idea of government intervention.

The backdrop to these methodological dilemmas was the microfoundations program that emerged from the powerful critique of Keynesian macroeconomics developed in the 1970s (Snowdon et al., 1994; Wren-Lewis, 2018). This began with the recognition of a deep divide between macroeconomics and microeconomics, and the problematic status of the micro/macro distinction. Macroeconomics was established in the 1930s as the study of economic aggregates, such as "Gross Domestic Product" (GDP), "consumption," or "unemployment," based on an aggregate view of "markets," such as the labor market, as distinct from goods markets, and adding other sectors, especially government. Keynesian macroeconomics typically rests on two basic theoretical premises. The first is to rely on certain stylized ideas about universals, that is, aggregate behavioral patterns of certain groups of agents, such as the propensity to save and consume on the part of consumers. The second is to construct hypotheses about regular causal patterns that link aggregates, and hence markets, starting from basic accounting principles in the systems of national accounts, most importantly, the identity of savings and investment. This identity implies a principled distinction between micro-behavior and macro-phenomena, as there is much scope for unintended consequences resulting from aggregate causal interdependencies and feedback loops, most famously the Keynesian paradox of savings (Schelling, 2006).

The central idea of the microfoundations program was to reconcile general equilibrium theory with aggregate macroeconomic analysis. It is of utmost importance to recognize that this transformation of macroeconomics was not triggered by problems with the empirical support for these models or even by outright falsification (de Vroey, 2016). After all, the debate about empirical macroeconomics continues to this day, and DSGE models have similar empirical weaknesses as Keynesian models.[9] Rather, this transformation was triggered by a purely logical argument about the structure of Keynesian macroeconomics, the famous "Lucas critique," which states that macroeconomic theories must explicitly take into account that these theories are part of the knowledge structure of the economy and hence become self-referential.[10] Following the Lucas critique, the central point of the paradigmatic shift in macroeconomics was that the information structure and knowledge of human agents must be treated as endogenous in modeling the economy. This introduces reflexivity into the system, especially in the sense that the economist's knowledge must also be treated as endogenous. Thus, a Keynesian macro-model must also be conceived as part of the information structure of the economy. By implication, rational agents will adjust their behaviors to any kind of information generated by these models. Therefore, model builders fall into a logical trap, that is formally homologous to all kinds of paradoxes of reflexivity that have been explored in philosophy and logic since antiquity, such as the "liar" who utters a proposition that claims she is a liar, truthfully: Models introduce a reflexive metalevel to which the model refers to itself. They cannot treat their model assumptions as exogenous but would have to predict the use of model-generated information by economic agents, and further modification would have to do the same. In other words, models have real effects on the economy that cannot be incorporated into the models without internal contradiction. This error is independent of evidence-based theorizing about the economy: Whether the Phillips curve is in the data or not, it must be rejected on principled theoretical grounds, and thus guides one's interpretation of the data. After all, if everyone knows about the curve, they will anticipate its effects and make it disappear. So goes the argument.

Building on this critique, macroeconomists have placed the assumption of rationality at the center of alternative model-building and have employed operations of abstraction at the level of aggregates. This is the concept of the "representative agent" in general equilibrium modeling as mapped onto aggregate markets, certainly a high point in the evolution of economic models towards disembodiment (Kirman, 1992). In a sense, this is counterintuitive, as the meaning of "microfoundations" seems strangely distorted here. On the surface, the models refer to a stylized individual agent, but this agent represents entire populations of agents who are treated as unified agents in the various markets. In fact, the "micro-agent" is an aggregate construct of its own status.

We have discussed this intellectual dynamic here because it reveals the deep implications of disembodiment for economics. The Lucas critique can be read quite differently, as a sociological account of what determines people's expectations. But as such it is silly: In the real world, few people form their expectations solely by reading economics A-journals, and many critics, including distinguished economists, recognize that these often fail to capture reality. For example, at the end of his career, Ronald Coase (2012, p. 36) indicated that: "The degree to which economics is isolated from the ordinary business of life is extraordinary and unfortunate;" and Akerlof and Shiller (2009, p. 6) claimed: "in telling how the economy really works, we accomplish what existing economic theory has not." What do people actually do in economic life? One medium is listening to and telling narratives about the economy. Later, we will introduce narratives as one of the key expressions of embodiment in economics, with language being an artifact that mediates cognition. At this point, we will only mention that even when economists move towards the role of narratives in economic life, most notably Robert Shiller (2019), they stick to disembodied views. Shiller reduces narratives to a mere epidemiological dynamic of the diffusion of given narratives in a population, and simply ignores the rich multidisciplinary research on narratives (Herrmann-Pillath, 2021).

Summarizing our observations, we find that two main reasons might justify disembodiment, beyond the mere interest in defending the autonomy of economics as a discipline and protecting its claim to be the leading social science (Fourcade et al., 2015), or the "queen of social sciences" (Samuelson, 1973, p. 6). One is normative, with disembodiment reflecting the idea of radical individual autonomy and self-determination, which is a form of philosophical idealism. The other is methodological, boiling down to the argument that economics is interested in markets, and thus in populations of agents, not individual agents. The disembodied rational agent is merely an analytical shortcut with no claim to relevance for understanding individual behavior.

The disembodied view of the individual is taken to its most extreme form when markets are approached with the computational metaphor (Mirowski & Nik-Khah, 2017). In such an approach, the individual is almost irrelevant, since all the computation takes place at the market level: Even "zero-intelligence" agents would be able to make optimal decisions (Gode & Sunder, 1993; Plott & Smith, 2008). This is a serious argument, especially in our context, since it might be consistent with certain views on embodiment in cognitive science that refer to "extended" cognition. But, as noted above, this raises the question of the extent to which markets are material, rather than just formal structures, as in most economic theorizing. As we shall see, the central concept here is "information."

2.4 Prices as Disembodied Information

Information is a key concept in the computational paradigm because computers are information processors. This is mainly shaped by Shannon's notion of information, which applies a purely quantitative framework. This deserves a closer look, although again we do not intend to discuss it in great detail (Herrmann-Pillath, 2020a). In Shannon's framework, information comes in "bits" suggesting that information is a kind of "thing" that flows through the computational device and is generated externally as "data." This is also the basic paradigm of contemporary approaches to AI: AI is designed as a complex system of statistical optimization based on input data, generating an internal structure that enables operations on that data. This metaphor can easily be applied to markets: Markets are complex statistical processors that process data and generate media of information, prices, which are parameters that guide individual choices (Arrow, 1974).

However, this model leads to deep problems. A standard economic argument is that prices carry information, even in the sense that they are richer than any other source of information, because they are conceived as aggregates over many individuals. But this argument is simply wrong. Consider two flaws.

First, imagine that the price of a good goes up. How can this convey any information without substantial additional information? An individual responding to a price increase must form expectations about a future change in prices. The increase itself can signal anything: To some, it means that prices will continue to rise, while for others, that they will fall. As Keynes' famous discussion of the "beauty contest" already revealed,[11] there is the additional problem that price increases can be seen as reflecting the beliefs of others, such as the belief that prices will continue to rise, so "buying now" is a good choice. By extension, these beliefs could include beliefs about one's own beliefs. Hence, the direction of the turning point depends on one's own choices and the reactions of others, caused by these interlocking beliefs. Consequently, prices as such cannot convey even a single bit of information, in this case, whether an observed price increase means "up or down" for the expected price movement. The information "up" is not embodied in the price but in the interpretive actions of the individuals.

Second, as is well established in the literature on group decisions, the argument that groups, in this case "the markets," make better choices than individuals by aggregating decisions depends crucially on the statistical independence of individual decisions, that is, on individuals basing their decisions exclusively on their own information (Theiner, 2014). That said, the very argument that prices convey information violates this criterion, since the price only conveys information if it is interpreted as reflecting judgments of others, and thus requires further information about them. Decisions then become interdependent (as one's decision depends on the decisions of others), and there is no reason why one should approach a state of optimal or complete information (Bikhchandani et al., 1998).

These two arguments point to the fundamental role of interpretation in so-called "information processing" via markets. However, this introduces a very different concept of information from the disembodied one in computational theory. The simplest way to state the difference is that, in mainstream economics, the concept of information is quantitative in the sense that it is an allegedly possible state of complete and perfect information from which the realized state in economic life is more or less distant. Along the same line of argument, since information is quantitative in the standard model, one economic agent may have more or less information than another. However, this position is quite different from saying that a certain datum can be interpreted in a different way: The mere quantity of price data is the same, so everyone should have the same "information," yet people respond differently because they have different interpretations. In this picture, the strange conclusion follows that most of these interpretations are "wrong," as they distort the supposed information. But this "information" would only be complete and perfect if it resided only in the mind of an omniscient observer.

In fact, the disembodied economic model of subjectivism leaves out an essential element of "subjectivism" that remains central in other disciplines, especially in the humanities, where the subject is seen as creative. In economics, this is recognized by some schools of thought, such as the "Austrian school," and is very prominent in theories of entrepreneurship. Indeed, embodiment looms large when considering Schumpeterian entrepreneurs (Dew et al., 2015; Nooteboom, 2006, 2012a, 2012b). But this also means that these theories remain only loosely connected to mainstream thinking. Prices only become information when they are interpreted by individuals, who are therefore the creators of the information: There is no "information" outside the individual epistemic subject.[12] However, we must immediately add that this can also include collective-level phenomena, such as talking with others about prices and generating shared interpretations, reading different analysts' opinions, and so on.

The notion of markets as computers, if taken seriously, leads to similar Gödelian problems of logical self-reference as in the case of the Lucas critique, epitomized in the famous "no-trade theorem" (Milgrom & Stokey, 1982). If all information is already contained in prices, why would any individual want to trade at all, knowing that all other individuals face the same prices? Trading would imply that someone has information that others do not have. Indeed, trading only makes sense if, given the same set of prices, there is heterogeneity in the interpretation of those prices across the population of agents (Lo, 2019).

Similarly, a related problem is that treating prices as information carriers ignores how prices are set in the first place, and by whom. Someone who announces a price does not automatically transmit any specific information, because motivations can vary widely. For example, there may be strategic reasons to keep the price low despite losses, or a high price may be intended to signal status, or the price may simply imitate other decisions, and so on. If someone else notices the price announcement, which of these interpretations will she adopt? These problems multiply when we consider observers who draw further conclusions from such price movements.

So, treating the market as a computer eventually leads us back to the individual, which also undermines the notion of information in economics. The key is to distinguish between Shannon information and semantic information (Adriaans, 2020). Simply put, semantic information is about the meaning of information. However, this phrase is misleading because it suggests that there is a "thing" such as information that has a "meaning." In fact, information, if we want to use the term, is what is created by assigning meaning to something. That is, as has often been commented on the original Latin, there is an activity by which something is imbued by meaning, that is "in-formed."[13] Nevertheless "the verb got reified into a noun, first into a number, then into a thing, and finally, into a cosmic principle of organization around which our age putatively revolves" (Mirowski & Nik-Khah, 2017, p. 45).

Interestingly, then, as some of the preceding remarks suggest, the notion of information in economics reveals many forms of materiality in theorizing. Once "information" is seen as a quantity, it can be thought of as a commodity that can be traded: Data is the "new oil," as the saying goes. But when it comes to prices, this would implicitly treat prices as "natural information," similar to the information about the age of an artifact that archaeologists can retrieve from certain traces of radioactivity (Floridi, 2004). Obviously, prices are fundamentally different: They are artifacts, such as language and tools that are continuously created by human price-setters to pursue certain intentions, but there is no objective scientific method for retrieving the information they supposedly carry. We will review the literature on artifact-mediated cognition in Chapter 4.

2.5 Forms of Disembodiment: Illustrations with Behavioral and Neuroeconomics

Let us now turn to behavioral economics. As the title of Thaler's book *Misbehaving: The Making of Behavioral Economics* makes clear, behavioral economics is not simply the application of a psychological perspective to economics (Thaler, 2016). So far, the entire research program has been defined in terms of violations of behavioral norms derived from the paradigm of rationality and optimality inherited from mainstream economics. This is very transparent in fields such as behavioral finance, where economists can clearly identify optimal solutions, and research aims to explain this deviation, which concerns even people trained in economics (e.g., Kumar & Goyal, 2015). More generally, this means that the standard economic model remains the reference for defining rationality, and any form of behavior that does not conform to this model is literally considered an "anomaly." Take the following, for example: "Theories in behavioral economics have generally retained the basic architecture of the rational model, adding assumptions about cognitive limitations designed to account for specific anomalies" (Kahneman, 2003, p. 1469). The (so-called) "cognitive biases" are merely deviations from what would be expected from an abstract decision-maker who, like *Homo economicus*, could maximize utility and reach the optimal solution. In this respect, Kahneman's (2003) "maps of bounded rationality" are defined in light of the disembodied standard of rationality, since "the rational-agent model was [his] starting point and the main source of [his] null hypotheses" (Kahneman, 2003, p. 1449). In other words, unlike embodied economics, behavioral economics maintains the standard model of rationality as a benchmark.

Similar observations apply to the behavioral macroeconomics of Akerlof and Shiller (2009), exemplified by their book *Animal Spirits*. Consider, for instance, the following quote: "Keynes appreciated that most economic activity results from rational economic motivations – but also that much economic activity is governed by animal spirits. People have non-economic motives. And they are not always rational in pursuit of their economic interests" (Akerlof & Shiller, 2009, p. ix). In this excerpt, Akerlof and Shiller (2009) associate animal spirits with non-economic motives and indicate that these may lead to some form of non-rational behavior. In doing so, they also maintain the standard model as a benchmark against which one can judge whether a given behavior is rational, and thus optimal, or not. One of the problems with this kind of approach is that it starts not with how people actually think and behave, but with how people should think and behave if they were rational—with rationality supposedly represented by *Homo economicus*, who is anything but made up of flesh and blood. This leads researchers to evaluate people's thoughts and actions referring to questions raised by standard economic theory rather than examining how these thoughts and actions come about in everyday life, such as when people solve problems (Gigerenzer, 2018). In this way, "the scholar puts into the heads of the agents he is studying (...) the theoretical considerations and constructions he has had to develop in order to account for their practices" (Bourdieu, 2005, p. 85).

Another proximity with the standard model is that behavioral economics goes far beyond the realm of markets, encompassing all aspects of human life through specific issues such as health or education (Thaler, 2016). This position is also fully in line with the neoclassical approach and the "economic imperialism" (Lazear, 2000) promoted by its famous proponents: "Economic theory may well be on its way to providing a unified framework for all behavior scarce resources, non-market as well as market, non-monetary as well as monetary, small group as well as competitive" (Becker, 1973, p. 814, see also, 1993). This is a clear departure from Pareto's (1935) aforementioned view that logical conduct is just a small part of human reality since social behavior is predominantly non-logical. This means that, contrary to Pareto, mainstream economics takes an exception—logical conduct—as the principle of social life.[14] To some extent, a modern expression of the dichotomy between logical and non-logical conduct that resists economic imperialism can be found in Akerlof and Shiller (2009), when they emphasize the importance of non-economic motivations in economic life. However, unlike Pareto, who warned that what is non-logical is not "illogical" (Pareto, 1935, §150), in their behavioral macroeconomics, Akerlof and Shiller equate "animal spirits" with "non-economic motives" and "irrational behaviors" (Akerlof & Shiller, 2009), thus maintaining the classic views of the standard model as a benchmark to define what rationality is.

Of course, there are also important differences between the standard economic model and behavioral economics, although, as we shall see, this does not necessarily make behavioral economics embodied. One important difference between the two is that behavioral economics does not consider the mind as a "black box," and takes a cognitivist look at it, as illustrated by the dual-process typology (Alós-Ferrer & Strack, 2014; Kahneman, 2012). This typology is not limited to behavioral economics, as it is also sometimes maintained in psychology as a parsimonious explanation of social behavior, including habitual versus intentional behavior, and the effects of deprivation (Strack & Deutsch, 2004). There are various ways of presenting this typology (e.g., Epstein et al., 1996). A common one that can be found in behavioral economics is presented by Slovic and colleagues (2004), which was adapted from Epstein (1994). In this view, the dual-process typology distinguishes between two main modes of thinking: The "experiential" and the "rational" systems, sometimes respectively referred to as "System 1" and "System 2" (e.g., Kahneman, 2012; Stanovich, 1999). The rational system is supposed to be logical and "encodes reality in abstract symbols, words, and numbers," whereas the experiential system relies on affect, images, metaphors, and narratives (Slovic et al., 2004, p. 313). Traditionally, the rational and the experiential systems have been contrasted. On the one hand, the rational system is considered slow and requires justification through logic and evidence; on the other hand, the experiential system is thought to be faster because it is action-oriented, holistic, associationistic, affective, and attached to behavior mediated by "vibes" from the past (Slovic et al., 2004, p. 313; see also, Kahneman, 2003, 2012). One of the most common manifestations of this dualism, according to behavioral economics, concerns failures of rationality: For instance, when it is claimed that System 2 has failed to detect and correct a "faulty intuition" automatically generated by System 1 (Morewedge & Kahneman, 2010). The challenge then becomes how to keep the fast system in check and limit its operations to the environments where the fast choices are optimal in terms of costs and benefits.

In economic life, there are several ways to "scaffold" rationality. The conventional approach in economics would not assume systematic failures of rationality, but only that there is a lack of information (Harrison & Ross, 2017). This is consistent with a strong normative commitment to individual freedom: Apparent failures of rationality would not justify interventions, only better access to information. This shows another key difference between the conventional view and behavioral economics, as the latter justifies interventions with a "therapeutic" intention, aiming to change the decision context and the architecture of the choices. This is the (in)famous nudging approach (Thaler & Sunstein, 2008), which will be further discussed later in this book (see Chapter 8). Suffice it to say for now that this can be interpreted as "extended rational cognition," but with the strong normative aspect that what is considered "rational" and contributes to people's well-being (such as healthy eating) is primarily defined by the scientific observer (Wiers et al., 2021). Accordingly, the approach underpinning nudging, which has been labeled "libertarian paternalism" by its main proponents (Thaler & Sunstein, 2008), is seen as problematic by liberal economists (McFadden, 2006), despite its deep ties to neoliberal thinking (Gane, 2021).

One question that remains is the extent to which the two systems are grounded in different areas of the brain. Behavioral economics is not neuroscientific by definition and refers mainly to psychological and behavioral processes associated with empirical results, such as "loss aversion," which are formalized in terms of functions of similar status to utility functions in economics, for instance, as in prospect theory (Tversky & Kahneman, 1981). However, there is no direct interpretation that is posited in terms of brain mechanisms. Indeed, a brain-based view of two systems would lead to theories long abandoned in neuroscience, such as the juxtaposition of the limbic system and the cortex (Lempert & Phelps, 2014), which effectively treats the picture of brain structure with "top" and "bottom" as a metaphor for the two systems ("rider and horse"). In fact, however, the two systems cannot be identified in any meaningful way in the brain (Herrmann-Pillath, 2019). For example, Kahneman argues that "there is overwhelming behavioral evidence both for the existence of multiple systems of thought and choice and for the importance of conflict," in contrast to Glimcher who "believes that there is no evidence from neuroscience to support the idea that (some) decisions arise from a conflict between emotion and reason, and concludes that a unitary system will do the job" (Kahneman, 2009, p. 525). In maintaining such a dual-system perspective, behavioral economics is not directly compatible with neuroeconomics. However, following the insights into embodied cognition emerging from neuroscience discussed in Chapter 4, Slovic and colleagues argue that the so-called "dichotomy" between the "rational" and the "experiential" system should be revisited,[15] and Epstein's (1994) "rational system" should be renamed "analytic system" because there are also "strong elements of rationality" in the experiential system and "affect is essential to rational action" (Slovic et al., 2004, pp. 313–314). As we will show below, despite his unwillingness to overcome a conflict between emotion and reason, there are genuine aspects of embodiment that emerge from Kahneman's work in behavioral economics.

Let us now turn briefly to neuroeconomics, which as a subdiscipline is difficult to define and perhaps a misnomer, as many neuroscientists prefer the label "decision neuroscience," thus eschewing the exclusive reference to economics (Bossaerts & Murawski, 2015). One meaning is the use of economic models in neuroscience (Glimcher, 2004). There are different variants, with some focusing on single mechanisms without necessarily extending to the level of the individual, and others directly interpreting the individual utility function in terms of neurophysiology (Ross, 2011). The latter would revive the older psychological tradition in economics and would indeed aim to "embody" utility by grounding it in brain processes—although, as we will argue later, embodiment is much broader in scope than a focus on the brain. The other meaning of neuroeconomics is to apply neuroscience to economic behavior, without invoking economic theory as the exclusive frame of reference (Camerer, 2013; Camerer et al., 2005). This would clearly open the vista on embodiment, but the question arises of what defines the "economic" dimension in this case. In most cases, this would be to make a choice among alternatives, following Robbins' (1932, p. 15) classic definition of economics as "the science which studies human behaviour as a relationship between ends and scarce means which have alternative uses." But neuroeconomics would then imply that the entire apparatus of utility theory and optimization would be shunned unless reconstructed by empirical neuroscience (Glimcher, 2011). On the other hand, and paradoxically, if neuroeconomics were to succeed in doing so, economists could simply ignore it, since they could continue to apply their model without referring to neuroscience, and simply note the vindication (Bernheim, 2009).

For our argument, therefore, the use of economic models in neuroscience is most relevant, especially in the form of efforts to effectively ground the utility function in neurophysiological mechanisms. In what sense can this be embodied? The use of the utility model implies a specific cognitive architecture of the choice process, in which the utility function is completely separated from the actions that realize the choice (Padoa-Schioppa, 2011). It assumes a neural representation of alternatives and their associated utilities, followed by the computation that identifies the best choice, and finally the implementation of the choice. As we will argue further in Chapter 4, this approach is not consistent with the embodiment view, which does not separate perception, cognition, and action, implying that there is no separate realm of amodal (i.e. non-perceptual) representations of valuations (Petracca, 2022). A simple, accommodating argument might be that "utilities" are a form of memory since they represent valuations in the past (Louie et al., 2015). But in the embodiment view, memory itself is distributed in the brain (for more on this, see Chapter 5). In contrast to such reasoning, the proponents of the utility model argue that utilities are constantly and instantaneously recalibrated, which is a very complex computational task. Thus, even if utility is seen as grounded in brain processes, the model remains disembodied because of the sharp dissociation between the cognitive system that calculates the utilities and the sensory-motor systems that underlie actions.

In sum, when compared to behavioral economics, neuroeconomics might come closest to an embodiment view because it is grounded in neurosciences, but as soon as the "economic" dimension is taken seriously as reflecting the mainstream approach, the ghost of disembodiment strangles even neuroscientific reasoning. As we will discuss later in this book, neurosciences are of great interest for building embodied economics not only because they provide rich empirical material on embodiment, but also because they represent a methodology that is radically different from economics as it stands.

2.6 Curing Disembodiment in Economics: Insights from the Neuroscientific Method

As discussed so far, many aspects of disembodiment depend on methodological issues. To a large extent, economics as it was defined in the mid-twentieth century claimed that it would be possible and desirable to analyze and explain economic phenomena in a single, coherent theoretical framework that would apply to either the flea market around the corner, domestic consumption decisions, or international capital flows. It pursued the ideal of an economic theory of at least everything economic and, in Becker's understanding, even everything human. This is an ideal that some natural scientists dream of, but do not realistically pursue: Indeed, many scientists are irritated by the universalistic claims made by economics for its field of inquiry (Wilson, 1999). The sciences pursue many ideas of cross-disciplinary reduction and integration, but in most respects, even subdisciplines remain partially autonomous, although most scientists accept the view of naturalistic monism, that is, the basic ontological unity of the physical world. After all, chemists can do a lot of chemistry without always referring to quantum physics, biologists can study a lot of animal life without referring to chemistry, and so on. So, why shouldn't we expect economics to divide into different fields with different theoretical frameworks, depending on the specific area of study? Neuroscience is a very interesting point of reference for thinking about economic methodology because it deals with the human agent and a system of similar complexity to the human global economy. To caricature the argument, in contrast to a form of economic imperialism, we would argue that neuroscience is not primarily concerned with the goal of establishing a grand unified theory of the brain,[16] nor does it start from certain first principles that would guide research in pursuit of this holy grail. In general, this leads neuroscientists to pursue a more modest agenda: To understand specific and concrete processes that produce certain phenomena and to understand their structural interrelationship in the system that is physically embodied in neurons, hormones, organs, and whatever other components of the human body appear to be causally involved. Can economics learn from this approach?

Following recent work on the philosophy of the neurosciences and the life sciences, methodological standards of mechanistic or constitutive explanation have been developed that provide an alternative to current economic methodology and can inform our approach to embodied economics (Bechtel & Abrahamsen, 2005; Craver & Tabery, 2019; Harbecke, 2014; Harbecke & Herrmann-Pillath, 2020). The motivation for applying the mechanistic approach to neuroscience was the diagnosis that neuroscience does not follow the covering law model of scientific explanation, which has long been observed in the life sciences (Mayr, 1982). The covering law notion, or deductive-nomological model, is the methodological standard mainly in physics, and physics served as a benchmark for much of the philosophy of science in the twentieth century. Put simply, this view requires scientists to formulate universal, law-like hypotheses about a given empirical domain, and to test these hypotheses using a fallibilist empirical strategy.

Neuroscientists mostly do not aim to generate universal hypotheses about their field. They tend to study phenomena and how they arise (Craver, 2009). In a certain sense, this means that they ask mainly "how" questions and fewer "why" questions. Probably a simple reason for this is that "why" questions cannot realistically be answered until "how" questions have been adequately addressed. "How" questions are questions about mechanisms. A mechanism is defined as a structure of parts that act together to produce a phenomenon. In contrast to the covering law model of explanation, there is no necessary reference to general regularities. The latter only play a role in grounding specific causal chains in laws of nature. Furthermore, the notion of causation is different, as a large part of the explanatory power does not rest on sequences of cause and effect in time, but on the simultaneous instantiation of a specific structure of elements that constitute the mechanism. This is captured by the notion of "constitutive" explanation: Causal analysis tends towards atomism, and mechanistic analysis towards holism, while at the same time requiring the finest possible degree of descriptive dissection.

More specifically, mechanistic explanations are multilevel explanations that may involve a lower level of analytical relevance. For example, the neurosciences tend to approach the "neuron" as one of these lowest-level parts. However, the neuron is further broken down into its constituent units because it represents a kind of mechanism in its own right. Nevertheless, much of the work in neuroscience can afford to treat the neuron as an elementary unit. Rarely, however, is it sufficient to refer to single neurons (such as the "grandmother" neuron): What usually counts are the structural configurations of multilevel neural networks and their positioning in even higher-level structures of the brain. This role of structural factors implies that mechanistic explanations include both bottom-up and top-down causation, extending to the role of regulatory (i.e., cybernetic) mechanisms governing lower-level processes.

The distinction between levels introduces an important aspect in considering the relationship between "how" and "why" questions. Multilevel complex mechanisms offer the possibility of functional answers to "why" questions (Perlman, 2009). Complex mechanisms include not only many components but also many simpler mechanisms that work together in the larger, comprehensive mechanism. One can then ask what the function of a mechanism within a larger mechanism is. The analysis of functions is of great importance for developing types of mechanisms of which empirical mechanisms are tokens. This includes the possibility that empirical mechanisms manifest variance in the realization of the functions, relative to a certain standard of proper functioning in producing a certain phenomenon, and even the possibility of multiple realizability, that is, the realization of the same functions, and thus type of mechanism based on completely different structures in the brain. In neuroscience, this is important to account for the empirical fact of plasticity, malleability, and flexibility of neural structures in the realization of certain performances.

Among the seemingly simple but factually complicated issues in mechanistic explanations are problems of identification. This refers to several aspects. First of all, what is the phenomenon in question? Is it a single event or is it a series of similar events? For example, we may want to explain why people always run away when they see a snake, or why Anton, who normally does not run away, does so today. That means that there may be difficult questions regarding the spatial and temporal identification of a phenomenon and its contextualization. For example, people may not run away when they see a snake in the zoo.

Similarly, there are difficult questions about identifying mechanisms, especially when drawing boundaries, both in time and space. When does a mechanism start; where does it begin? For example, even reflexes, which are archetypical mechanisms in neuroscience, may be partially conditioned by preparedness, such as via mechanisms of attention (Puglisi et al., 2017). Should this be included in the analysis of the reflex as a mechanism? Questions of this type become much more complicated when considering more complex phenomena. For example, an interesting case was the discovery of the default mode network in the brain (Raichle, 2015): At first, the researchers did not see a phenomenon at all, because they conducted another experiment and only noticed that in the supposed state of "rest"—that is, presumably no phenomenon at all, as defined by the researcher—the brain is considered to be even more "active" than during action. However, many areas of the brain are involved in the production of this peculiar performance (hence, "network"), so there are many open questions as to how this complex set of mechanisms can be combined into one. Similarly, many phenomena and putative mechanisms actually consist of many subsystems, such as "memory."

The question of boundaries is of particular importance in the context of our book. In the reductionist view of neuroscience, opening the black box seems to be tantamount to simply moving "inside" the body. But this is a naïve misconception. Once the mechanistic approach is rigorously adopted, setting boundaries is a research problem. This issue is familiar to dynamical systems theory in neuroscience, where "systems" can include, for example, the coordination of movement between bodies (Oullier & Basso, 2010; Oullier et al., 2008). This was the case in our previous discussion of neuroeconomics. Neuroeconomics takes a strictly reductionist approach, in the sense that "value" is embodied even in small-scale assemblages of neurons, at least within the brain. However, there are alternative theories of valuation that include the body as a bearer of values, such as the "somatic marker" theory first proposed by Antonio Damasio (Bechara & Damasio, 2005; Reimann & Bechara, 2010). A related question is whether values are embodied in neural mechanisms that integrate sensation and action via increased activity in the sensory-motor systems that directly involve the body, or possibly even the objects involved in the motor action. The question of sensory-motor integration as a mechanism is one of the central issues in understanding the generation of human behavioral and cognitive performance,[17] and is of utmost relevance to mechanistic approaches in the brain sciences (e.g., Petracca, 2020).

As we see, a strict application of the notion of constitution leads to the conclusion that mechanisms need not be confined to the brain or even to the body, contrary to claims suggesting that "a human being is his or her brain" and that "from toes to nose, everything else is a convenient accessory" (Alós-Ferrer, 2018, p. 235). Rather, social context must be conceived as an integral part of specific mechanisms. For instance, in addiction research, the paradigm of addiction as a "brain disease" is at odds with the fact that the mechanisms generating behavior depend on situational context (Wiers et al., 2021; see also, Sapolsky, 2017). Or, as research on empathy shows, empathic neural responses to another's pain are moderated by the perceived fairness of the other (Singer et al., 2006). Similarly, results from experimental games show that fairness influences people's valuations of other players' payoffs: People value others' payoffs positively when others have played fairly, but negatively when they have played unfairly (Fehr & Gächter, 2000). Against this background, where and how to draw the line becomes an important research question in its own right.

In sum, neuroscience provides strong support for an alternative methodological grounding in economics that would reorient the study of economic behavior towards a robust empirical effort to answer "how" questions without preconceived theoretical premises that ultimately conceal their value positions.

2.7 Signs of Embodiment in Behavioral, Experimental, and Neuroeconomics

As we have seen, a classic position in behavioral economics tends to conclude that people's decisions are biased in light of a given gold standard of rationality, namely the *Homo economicus* model. We disagree with this approach because it sets disembodied standards of rationality that are independent of the decisions made by economic agents in the real economic world (see further discussion in Chapters 3 and 4). However, it should be acknowledged that several insights from behavioral economics in many respects pave the way for embodiment, and in this section we will explore some of them, starting with some of Kahneman and Tversky's studies. To demonstrate this, we will use Simon's definition of *Homo economicus*:

> Traditional economic theory postulates an 'economic man,' who, in the course of being 'economic' is also 'rational.' This man is assumed to have knowledge of the relevant aspects of his environment which, if not absolutely complete, is at least impressively clear and voluminous. He is

> assumed also to have a well-organized and stable system of preferences, and a skill in computation that enables him to calculate, for the alternative courses of action that are available to him, which of these will permit him to reach the highest attainable point on his preference scale. (Simon, 1955, p. 99)

Virtually every aspect of this definition has been tested by Kahneman and Tversky's work on biases and heuristics. The availability heuristic challenges the idea that people have clear and voluminous knowledge and consider alternative courses of action. Rather, people are found to consider what comes easily to their mind when judging, for instance, the frequency of a category (Tversky & Kahneman, 1973). The representativeness heuristic shows that people do not have extraordinary computational abilities. Instead, they are subject to the conjunction error which violates the basic laws of probability, and their decisions are influenced by stereotypes and are more sensitive to what is plausible and makes a coherent story (Tversky & Kahneman, 1983). The anchoring heuristic shows that people do not reach the highest attainable point on their preference scale, but are actually influenced by the starting point they are given when they make their calculations (Tversky & Kahneman, 1974), or set the price they would be willing to pay for a good (e.g., Ariely et al., 2003; Jung et al., 2016). In addition to these three heuristics, Tversky and Kahneman (1981) also showed the presence of framing effects in decision-making, which illustrate that people do not have a well-organized and stable system of preferences: Valence, in this case, the presentation of information in terms of gains or losses, affects people's willingness to take risks.

Our argument here is not to develop the critiques and limitations of their work,[18] but to show that this set of heuristics, although consistent with the standard cognitivist paradigm and portraying people as inefficient information processors or "cognitive misers" (Fiske & Taylor, 2013, p. 16), can also be understood through the lens of embodiment and several related concepts and theories developed in Chapter 4—namely embodied simulation, conceptual metaphor theory, and situated cognition.

For example, the availability heuristic is part of the simulation heuristic later developed by Kahneman and Tversky (1982) to characterize the mental operations that "bring things to mind," and whose proximity to the concept of "embodied simulation" has been acknowledged by some of its main proponents, such as Gallese and Goldman (1998). The representativeness heuristic belongs to the prototype heuristic (Kahneman, 2003), whose main feature is that it is embodied. Indeed, as shown by Rosch and colleagues, people categorize objects at the basic level, which is the level at which category members are remarkably associated with similar motor actions (Mervis & Rosch, 1981; Rosch et al., 1976; Varela et al., 2016), and which, with image schemas, form one of the main pillars of conceptual metaphor theory (Lakoff, 1987; Lakoff & Johnson, 1980). The anchoring heuristic can be understood from an embodiment perspective as an illustration of the situatedness of knowledge, in the sense that cognition is strongly influenced by current task constraints, objectives, and intentions, including the spatial contextualization of number concepts (Fischer et al., 2021), such as an ascending or descending sequence of numbers, as tested by Tversky and Kahneman (1974).

With respect to framing effects, results from neuroeconomics show that gain and loss frames reflect a deeper "affect heuristic"[19] through which people incorporate emotional information into the decision process, as evidenced by increased activity in the amygdala (De Martino et al., 2006). Similarly, mental accounting, a cognitive process that has been used to explain framing effects (Thaler, 1985, 1999), can also be understood in light of the feelings it triggers (Prelec & Loewenstein, 1998; Thaler, 1999). The concept of emotional accounting further demonstrates the importance of bodily states in mental accounting (Levav & Mcgraw, 2009), and Zelizer's (1989) sociological approach to mental accounts can further open the analysis to social influences.

Turning now to the supposed dichotomy between System 1 (experiential) and System 2 (analytical), this dual-process typology can also be integrated into an embodiment approach, although, as we shall see, we argue in favor of a single rather than a dual process. For example, one can distinguish two levels of embodiment, a low and a high level, within the experiential (System 1) and the analytic (System 2) systems (Petit et al., 2016). At the low level, the experiential system can be seen as dominated by biases and heuristics, such as those described by Tversky and Kahneman (1974). At a high level, the experiential system can be understood as driven by visceral reactions and emotions, as can be inferred from Keynes' (1936/2018; Lainé, 2014) animal spirits or Damasio's (1994) somatic marker theory. With respect to the analytic system, at a low level of embodiment, people are supposed to engage in cold reasoning and tend to express a form of thinking aligned with economic rationality. At a high level of embodiment, people would engage in embodied reasoning, such as that described by conceptual metaphor theory (Lakoff & Johnson, 1999). This dichotomy can be fruitful when it is for analyzing decision-making in experimental studies and for organizing concepts and results from the literature. Like any typology, however, it should not pretend to exhaust the subtleties of human behavior in economic life. If it exists, the opposition between high and low levels of embodiment may be difficult to identify in real economic life, and more generally embodied economics assumes that there is a continuity, not an opposition, between the analytic and the experiential systems.[20] This perspective allows us to avoid the main drawback of focusing on the difference between the experiential and the analytic systems, and opposing them which usually feeds into an argument that tends to conclude that the analytic system is in charge of correcting the experiential system. As Evans and Stanovich noted: "Perhaps the most persistent fallacy in the perception of dual-process theories is the idea that Type 1 processes (intuitive, heuristic) are responsible for all bad thinking and that Type 2 processes (reflective, analytic) necessarily lead to correct responses" (Evans & Stanovich, 2013, p. 229). From an embodiment perspective, it would make no sense to argue that the affect, images, metaphors, and narratives that lie at the core of the experiential system are monitored by an "analytic system" separate from it. Rather, embodied economics argues that affect, images, metaphors, and narratives are some of the key elements of embodied reason in economic life. Embodied reason is experiential. Experience can be generally defined as "(the process of getting) knowledge or skill from doing, seeing, or feeling things" (Cambridge Dictionary, n.d.). Together, "doing," "seeing," "feeling," illustrate the importance of embodiment: It is hard to conceive of what one could do, see, or feel, without a body. Similarly, in psychology, experience can be defined as "an event that is actually lived through, as opposed to one that is imagined or thought about" (APA, 2023b). Against this background, there is no experience without a body. This implies that the "experiential" system that characterizes human thought is all about embodiment. Of course, the concept of experience is at the core of many developments in the field of embodied cognition, ranging from distributed cognition to enaction, perceptual symbol systems, conceptual metaphors, and neural reuse, to name just a few, which will be discussed in detail in Chapter 4.

Overall, embodied economics adopts a perspective that seeks to overcome dichotomies or emphasize their dialectic relationship—for instance, with the organism-environment coupling and with inward and outward embodiment. Embodied economics aims to bring together, in the same framework, different concepts such as mirror neurons, anthropomorphism, emotions, or somatic markers to understand their role in economic life. They are all related to some form of embodied cognition, and the experiential system. In this way, embodied economics recognizes that the experiential system is central to economic behavior and that such behavior can become more abstract or more analytical—that is, closer to so-called "economic rationality"—under the influence of the economic environment, namely the market or other economic agents or institutions. In other words, people's modes of thinking are sometimes aligned with what is called the analytic system because embodied cognition is situated and distributed: It is the adoption ("incorporation") of the cognitive tools (artifacts) provided by the market system—such as money, accounts, or price comparators—that can lead people to think abstractly, analytically, and also, at times, more selfishly in economic life.

Importantly, as we will see, this position means that, unlike standard behavioral and neuroeconomics approaches that tend to locate cognition within the brain, embodied economics locates the mind in the interaction of the brain, the body, and the socio-material world, which requires adopting a definition of "rationality" that is not defined in the abstraction of the organism and its interactions with the environment. Therefore, although several findings from behavioral and neuroeconomics point to the need for an embodiment approach to cognition and decision-making in economic life, we argue that embodiment will remain under-theorized and not fully celebrated as long as these disciplines remain brain-centric and mostly a-situated. A striking illustration of our argument is provided by Dhami's (2016) book, which is widely recognized as a comprehensive textbook that covers the major findings in behavioral (and experimental) economics in more than 1,700 pages. In fact, this textbook contains only one reference to the economic system, namely "capitalism" (p. 1552), because the word is included in the title of Akerlof and Shiller's (2009) book on "animal spirits," and a few mentions of "liberalism" in the chapter on "Behavioral Welfare Economics." When it comes to one of the most famous textbooks in neuroeconomics (Glimcher & Fehr, 2014), we could not find one reference to "capitalism" or "liberalism." To be fair, "capitalism" was mentioned in the first edition (Glimcher et al., 2009, p. 232), but again, this is because the word is included in the title of the reference, this time a chapter by Amartya Sen (1995).

It seems that behavioral and neuroeconomics can be studied in a vacuum, completely divorced from the specifics of the economic environment of its participants. From an embodied economics perspective, even if there are some indications of embodiment, so long as decision-making is studied *in abstracto*, the analysis is not properly situated. Some behavioral economists argue that abstraction is a feature of our economic system, and thus it makes sense to study decision-making in an a-situated way:

> the argument that the laboratory tasks and tests are not like 'real life' is becoming less and less true. 'Life,' in fact, *is becoming more like the tests!* Try arguing with your health insurer about a disallowed medical procedure, for example. The social context, the idiosyncrasies of individual experience, the personal narrative – the 'natural' aspects of Type 1 processing – all are abstracted away as the representatives of modernist technological-based services attempt to 'apply the rules'. (Stanovich in Chater et al., 2018, p. 812)

In contrast to such a conclusion, we will argue that economic life cannot escape embodiment because cognition is embodied and situated: It is grounded in the sensory-motor system and in the world. Let us illustrate this argument with research in experimental economics. Experimental economics is "behavioral game theory" (Camerer, 2011), which "uses laboratory methodology to examine motivated human behavior and its interpretation in small group interactive games, and in bidding, auctioning, and market institutions. Subjects earn cash payments depending upon their joint interactive decisions, and the rules governing their interactions" (Smith, 2006, p. 1070). In doing so, as illustrated by the ultimatum game:

> the source of uncertainty facing the decision maker [is] not the turn of a card or the roll of dice (as in probability theory) or nature (as in scientific research) but the mind of another decision maker, i.e., the outcome depends upon the ability of the individual to read the mind of another. (Farr, 1997, p. 715)

The Ultimatum Game (UG) is by far one of the most intensively studied experimental games in social sciences (Spiegler, 2011). In its original form, it is a game (usually a computerized task) played only once between two players under conditions of anonymity (Güth et al., 1982). These two players are shown a sum of money, for example, €10. One of the players, the Proposer, is given this sum of money and is instructed to offer the other player, the Responder, any number of euros between €1 and €10. The Responder can either accept or decline the offer. If the Responder accepts the offer, she receives the sum of €x and the Proposer receives the sum of €10-x. If the Responder declines the offer, both players get nothing. The key question on the Proposer's side is the following: How much should she offer the Responder? If the game is played once and under conditions of anonymity, the Proposer should offer the minimum possible amount (€1), approaching zero, assuming that the Responder is self-regarding, since she will accept any possible amount of money, that is, all positive offers (>0). In fact, when it comes to the behavior of real economic agents in this lab setting, "only a minority of agents behave in a self-regarding manner" (Gintis et al., 2005, p. 12), and almost no one offers the minimum possible amount that approaches zero.

Why is that? What happens on the Proposer's side during an Ultimatum Game? It can be argued that the Proposer must construct a "theory of mind" about the Responder (Singer, 2009, p. 253), in order to answer the following question: "How will the Responder react if I give her X amount of money?" The Proposer must predict whether the Responder will consider her offer acceptable (i.e. fair), and thus must think about the Responder's view of her offer.[21] As Vernon Smith (2003, p. 492) points out: "We particularly want to note that if every player is exactly like every other player, and is strictly self-interested, there is no room for 'mind reading,' or inferring intentions from actions, and no room for more sophisticated and subtle action in the self-interest." In other words, the Proposer mentalizes about the Responder's actions (Frith & Singer, 2008, p. 3878), and a successful economic exchange requires "taking" someone else's perspective.[22] If the Proposer's offer is rejected, one might assume that it is because she has failed to think like the Responder. In Western countries, the Responder usually feels that an offer of less than 30% of the original amount is unfair.[23] By rejecting the Proposer's offer, she is paying money to punish the Proposer. This situation is called altruistic punishment: "people voluntarily incur costs to punish violations of social norms" (de Quervain et al., 2004, p. 1254; see also, Guala, 2012).

An important point here, however, is the role of social norms and, more broadly, cultural practices in judging the fairness of the amount shared. Experimental studies in non-Western societies show that what may seem "irrational", especially from the Western-centric perspective that underlies the neoclassical model (e.g., Nelson, 1997; Seers, 1963; Strassmann, 1995), may be quite reasonable in another cultural context: For example, as Henrich and colleagues explain,

> among the Au and Gnau of Papua New Guinea many proposers offered more than half the pie, and many of these offers were rejected (...). In these societies, accepting gifts, even unsolicited ones, implies a strong obligation to reciprocate at some future time. Unrepaid debts accumulate, and place the receiver in a subordinate status. (...) Together, this suggests that as a result of growing up in such societies, individuals may have acquired values, preferences, or expectations that explain both high offers and the rejection of high offers in a one-shot game. (Henrich et al., 2005, p. 811)

In this context, it may not be mindreading that matters for making the right decision, but rather reading the relational model in which such a decision is made, which constitutes "the more basic perceptual, embodied, and affective capacities that sustain social interaction in the absence of mindreading" (Bohl & Fiske, 2014, p. 214; see also, Haslam & Fiske, 2005; Rai & Fiske, 2010).

From the perspective of embodied economics, these results illustrate two points. First, when cognition is considered embodied, it is situated, the body is grounded in the world, and thus, as aforementioned, it is highly problematic to specify axioms of economic rationality *ex ante* and to point out deviations against such an abstract theoretical background (Felin and colleagues in Chater et al., 2018, p. 820). Second, the literature suggests that market processes played an important role in the development of the cognitive form of empathy described above,[24] and pertains to the ability to make attributions about the mental states (desires, beliefs, intentions) of others, because "markets depend on the ability of buyer and seller to assume each other's role" (Farr, 1997, p. 715). As Mead explained:

> The economic development is one which starts off on the basis of the exchange. You offer what you do not want in exchange for something which another does not want. (...) The sort of thing ultimately produced will be that which answers to the demand of the customer. In the resulting functional organization one develops an economic personality of a certain

> sort which has its own sense of superiority but which is used in the carrying-out of its particular function in relation to the others in the group. (Mead, 1934, pp. 287–288)

The argument linking market integration and the development of cognitive empathy can actually be traced back to Adam Smith, sometimes under the Smith-Haskell hypothesis (Jankowiak, 2005), and to Hegel. Empirical illustrations can be found cross-culturally (e.g., Henrich et al., 2005) and historically (e.g., Enke, 2022). The main argument here is that the "economic personality" mentioned by George Herbert Mead and reflected in empathic processes, for instance, is developed through the incorporation of some form of market thinking.

We will develop similar points in Chapter 7 on institutions when we analyze the performative role of markets and money in human behavior. For now, in relation to cognitive empathy, suffice it to say that market exchanges require interaction with others.[25] For example, in the case of markets such as bazaars, studies in economic anthropology show that:

> The search for information (…) is the central experience of life in the bazaar. Every aspect of the bazaar economy reflects the fact that the primary problem facing its participants (that is, 'bazaaris') is not balancing options but finding out what they are. (Geertz, 1978, p. 30)

In this context, the two most important search procedures identified are "clientelization" and "bargaining." Both involve social encounters, face-to-face interactions, communication, and exchanges with people outside the family circle, which favor the development of empathic processes. Beyond the bazaar economy, face-to-face dealings are one of the main features of business and economic life (Goffman, 1961, p. 22; Leamer, 2007; Storper & Venables, 2004). In these situations, and more specifically in sales encounters, evidence from psychometric and neural studies (with Western participants) shows that the salesperson's ability to form a coherent interpretation, that is, to make sense of what is happening depends on her engagement in interpersonal mentalizing to infer mental states such as the customer's beliefs, intentions, and desires (Dietvorst et al., 2009). Cognitive empathy is thus supposed to be one of the essential ingredients for making sense of embodied interactions in the marketplace, and it is reinforced by market exchanges. As we will see in

Chapters 4 and 5, language is another fundamental ingredient for making decisions in economic life and making sense of it.

Furthermore, experimental results from UGs show that embodiment is not only important on the Proposer's side. Using fMRI, Sanfey and colleagues (2003) scanned participants in the role of Responder in the UG and showed the role of emotions when they were told they were playing with a human partner and when they were playing with a computer partner.[26] The behavioral results were roughly similar to the other UG experiments on Western participants: Fair offers are all accepted, and acceptance rates decrease as offers become less fair. Interestingly, however, unfair offers made by humans were rejected more often than those made by a computer, suggesting stronger reactions when an unfair offer is made by a human than by a computer (Sanfey et al., 2003).[27] At the brain level, the results from the contrast of unfair vs. fair offers from human partners led to increased activity in the bilateral anterior insula, dorsolateral prefrontal cortex (dlPFC), and anterior cingulate cortex (ACC).[28] In addition, contrasting unfair offers from human partners with unfair offers from computer partners also led to increased activity in the bilateral anterior insula. These two main findings suggest that increased activity in the bilateral anterior insula is not only a function of the amount of money offered (i.e., the degree of unfairness) but is also sensitive to the context of the interaction,[29] that is, the perceived unfair treatment by another human (rather than a computer). In light of findings in the literature showing increased activity in the anterior insula, a brain area implicated in somatosensory perception and associated with negative emotional states (e.g., pain, distress, anger, disgust), Sanfey and colleagues (2003) interpret these insular activations as associated with "moral disgust,"[30] and conclude that: "Models of decision-making cannot afford to ignore emotion as a vital and dynamic component of our decisions and choices in the real world" (Sanfey et al., 2003, p. 1758).[31]

Together with our previous developments, these results thus illustrate the role of bodily influences on decision-making through the study of the emotional and social dimensions of economic choices.[32] The concept of moral disgust is particularly important to embodied economics because it epitomizes the role of emotions when it comes to fairness in economic exchanges,[33] which in turn reflects the role of embodiment in social justice. However, to put it bluntly, moral disgust is less important per se than as an example of the embodied cognitive processes (here, the conceptual metaphor) that challenge the assumptions underpinning a wide range of economic approaches. The latter include Simon's physical symbols systems theory (Simon, 1990), and Hayek's (1982/2013) vision of a "Great Society" ruled by the market and the price system, which will be discussed in the next chapter. Essentially, moral disgust is a metaphor that uses a concrete physical experience (disgust) to make sense of a more abstract economic interaction (unfairness).[34] To understand why this is so important to embodied economics, we will develop the fundamentals of embodiment theory in Chapter 4. Overall, it appears that cognitive empathy and emotions are more than irrational processes, anomalies in light of substantive rationality, or mere heuristics: They are fundamental dimensions involved in people's interpretations of their economic and social environment.

2.8 Conclusion

This chapter has set the stage for the argument that unfolds in this book: We transcend the internal debates among economic schools by diagnosing their common pathology, namely the disembodiment of the human actor and the market, and we develop an alternative paradigm of embodied economics. Our (very) brief focus on the embodied dimensions of behavioral, experimental, and neuroeconomics shows that economic agents are embodied beings that are historically, socially, and culturally situated. This goes beyond mindreading (Lillard, 1997, 1998), as, for instance, the utility maximization principles of cost-benefit analysis seem foreign to some Indigenous peoples (Choy, 2018; Gudeman, 2001; see also, Fuentes, 2022; Krenak, 2023), and materialism is a recent phenomenon in human history, passed on (in part) through upbringing and education (e.g., Higgs, 2014; Noyes et al., 2023; Richins & Chaplin, 2015). But, while we have become economic agents, we are more than economic agents: We are also "gendered," "racialized," and "social-classed" beings (e.g., Acker, 2006; Boero & Mason, 2020; Crenshaw, 2017), with different capabilities and multiple social roles to fulfill in several kinds of social relational models. Economic life is thus embedded in the social world, which is why embodied economics is Political Economy: Embodiment *grounds* and *bounds* the markets.

Certainly, this suggests that there are strands of economics that think in embodied terms, such as those that are concerned with discrimination on bodily grounds, Feminist economics, and Black economics. In these fields too, we observe the rift between embodied approaches and mainstream theorizing about discrimination, which may even end up denying its embodied dimensions (Logan & Myers, 2022). What these heterodox approaches may lack, is a systematic and coherent grounding in a general theory of embodiment. We propose to develop such a theory from (and by extending) the perspective of embodied cognition, which is closest to neurosciences, psychology, and sociology (e.g., Cerulo, 2019; Newen et al., 2018). This allows us to develop our critique from an internal perspective of economics, as we did in our brief review of behavioral and neuroeconomics.

In the next chapter, we examine a specific case, namely some of Hayek's contributions to modern economics. Hayek is not a key figure in modern mainstream economics, but his work, along with that of Simon, was central to the development of information-based models in economics (Mirowski, 2001; Mirowski & Nik-Khah, 2017), as well as to the ideological shifts of the 1970s and 1980s, most commonly referred to as "neoliberalism" (Mirowski & Plehwe, 2015). This is important because we are interested not only in the analytical and empirical aspects of economics but also in the normative ones, which are often the main drivers of economic policies as elements of larger policy programs and political stances on the design of the economy (e.g., Callon & Roth, 2021).

Hayek and Simon are also of particular interest because they are unique multidisciplinary scholars who bridged the disciplines of psychology and economics in their writings. However, when it comes to Hayek, his essential contribution to psychology has never been systematically explored in behavioral economics and neuroeconomics, despite some recent attempts (e.g., Frantz & Leeson, 2013; Sunstein, 2023). As we will show, this is an intellectual loss, as Hayek the psychologist suggests a deeply embodied view of the human mind and action that offers an alternative to Simon's cognitivist paradigm. At the same time, however, we will see that this introduces a fatal internal contradiction into the Hayekian system since Hayek champions a radically disembodied view of the (neoliberal) market, that leads to strong normative conclusions, namely the rejection of the notion of social justice. In resolving this contradiction, embodied economics allows us to imagine a new framework for designing markets for human flourishing.

Notes

1. Note that the double auction game is hardly relevant to everyday economic life and, as Philip Mirowski claims, experimental economics fails to explain why the posted-offer market is so commonly used in every supermarket: "The posted-offer market (unlike the double auction) is familiar to most readers as what they encounter every week at their local grocery store. Sellers post a fixed price for each item, and buyers can take it or leave it. If Piggly Wiggly won't provide a good price, perhaps the Tesco or the Carrefour down the lane will. Although prevalent throughout the developed world, experimentalists can barely repress their disdain for the posted-offer market. In their view it is 'inefficient' relative to the double auction, it outputs prices that are 'too high' for competitive equilibrium, it inordinately slows convergence to competitive equilibrium, and if it has a competitive equilibrium, it unfortunately does not coincide with the Nash equilibrium (Smith, 1991, p. 300). Less frequently admitted is the fact that in the laboratory, playing the role of the 'buyer' in a posted-offer setting is dead boring: so much so that, early on, most experimentalists decided to save some money by zeroing out the human buyers in their posted-offer experiments (Kagel & Roth, 1995, p. 381; Davis & Holt, 1993, p. 177)" (Mirowski, 2001, pp. 550–551).
2. The contrast is striking when comparing theories of rational herding (Devenow & Welch, 1996) with multidisciplinary approaches (Raafat et al., 2009).
3. Note that Pareto does not exclude some form of non-logical conduct in the sphere of political economy (Pareto, 1935, §159).
4. For example, Pareto claimed that: "Pure political economy has (therefore) great interest in relying as little as possible on the domain of psychology," quoted in Bruni and Sugden (2007, p. 154); see also Camerer (2006). Pareto also excluded psychology from the study of non-logical conduct in sociology, for instance when he states that: "Non-logical actions originate chiefly in definite psychic states, sentiments, subconscious feelings, and the like. It is the province of psychology to investigate such psychic states. Here we start with them as data of fact, without going beyond that" (Pareto, 1935, §161).

5. In a sense, since logical conduct is an action that is logical both subjectively to the agent and objectively to the external observer (Pareto, 1935, §150), Pareto was making an argument that somewhat anticipated later developments in the revealed-preference theory (Camerer, 2006). Note, however, that Pareto's work should not be read as behaviorist (Gross & Tarascio, 1998).
6. As put by one of the founders of behaviorism, it can be summarized with an identity: "In a system of psychology completely worked out, given the response, the stimuli can be predicted; given the stimuli, the response can be predicted" (Watson, 1913, p. 167). Although there are some differences between the theory of revealed preferences and behaviorism, they share a similar conclusion: Only behavior, whether understood as response or choice, is of interest in making predictions.
7. In the context of the theory of revealed preferences, this can be illustrated as follows. For instance, if a person chooses vanilla ice cream and rejects chocolate ice cream, she might be considered to have revealed a preference for vanilla over chocolate. The next time this person is faced with the same alternative, mainstream economists would predict that since people are supposed to be rational, their actions are logical (consistent), and this person will choose vanilla. Past behavior is predictive of future behavior. In addition, thanks to the theory of revealed preferences, and because the system of preferences is assumed to be stable, mainstream economists believe they can make predictions even when people are presented with different alternatives. For example, if a person chooses vanilla over chocolate, and chocolate over strawberry, based on these choices, by transitivity, mainstream economists assume that the next time this person has a choice between vanilla and strawberry, she will choose vanilla. By observing a repeated pattern of behavior (i.e., a series of choices made in a given context), the standard model aims to "predict" what people will do. "Predict" is a key word here. Like behaviorism, the purpose of the standard model in economics is to make predictions on the basis of observed behavior, and this, without regard to any psychological and/or neural underpinnings.
8. This is a variant of Dennett's famous "intentional stance" argument, which attributes intentions not directly to minds, but to the way minds understand other minds (Dennett, 1998).

9. In the aftermath of the 2008 financial crisis, the debate over macroeconomic models involved most prominent macroeconomists (e.g., Blanchard, 2017; Caballero, 2010; Hendry & Muellbauer, 2018).
10. In Lucas' words: "given that the structure of an econometric model consists of optimal decision rules for economic agents, and that optimal decision rules vary systematically with changes in the structure of series relevant to the decision maker, it follows that any change in policy will systematically alter the structure of econometric models" (Lucas, 1976, p. 411).
11. The beauty contest is presented by Keynes in these terms: "to change the metaphor slightly, professional investment may be likened to those newspaper competitions in which the competitors have to pick out the six prettiest faces from a hundred photographs, the prize being awarded to the competitor whose choice most nearly corresponds to the average preferences of the competitors as a whole; so that each competitor has to pick, not those faces which he himself finds prettiest, but those which he thinks likeliest to catch the fancy of the other competitors, all of whom are looking at the problem from the same point of view. It is not a case of choosing those which, to the best of one's judgment, are really the prettiest, nor even those which average opinion genuinely thinks the prettiest. We have reached the third degree where we devote our intelligences to anticipating what average opinion expects the average opinion to be" (Keynes, 1936/2018, p. 137).
12. As noted, the topic of information is extremely complex and includes the notion of "natural information," such as information incorporated in the annual rings of trees. Floridi's various contributions provide excellent overviews, see for instance: Floridi (2004) or Sequoiah-Grayson and Floridi (2022). Our position follows those views that treat information as something "about" and "for whom".
13. To a certain extent, this is what happens in AI when the computer is flooded with huge amounts of data and ends up constructing information statistically, such as recognizing a word. The data contains no information at all, only the patterns that emerge from the processing.
14. As Gross and Tarascio (1998, p. 186) observe: "The economic approach (e.g., Gary Becker) extends the scope of maximizing

behavior into nontraditional areas, for instance, social and moral behavior. Yet Pareto demonstrated that logical conduct did not predominate in social and moral behavior. For him the factual unrealism of the assumption of rational behavior rendered it inappropriate. Rather, he developed and applied his model of non-logical conduct for such studies. Pareto's pioneering work in this area, which represented an extension of his theory of choice, has been neglected by economists and remains unknown to the profession at large."

15. Some authors argue that this dichotomy should be abandoned given its lack of empirical support (e.g., Keren & Schul, 2009; Kruglanski & Gigerenzer, 2011; Melnikoff & Bargh, 2018).
16. For example, according to Anderson and Chemero (2013, p. 205): "There is every reason to think that there can be no grand unified theory of brain function because there is every reason to think that an organ as complex as the brain functions according to diverse principles."
17. In the embodiment literature, this idea is nicely put by Matheson and Barsalou as follows: "It is taken for granted that cognition manifests itself as intelligent, goal-directed, and flexible behavior. But what does it take for a system to be cognitive? Does a single neuron have cognition? Two connected neurons? Of course, two neurons can't communicate electrochemically without an appropriate extracellular milieu, and this milieu needs to be incased in something (otherwise it would just spill outwards); it needs a body. Further, neuronal activity can't proceed without some sort of signal from outside the milieu, so it needs an environment. Also, since we are talking about intelligent behavior, a cognitive system must change its behaviors over time; it needs to respond. Overall, if neurons, the body, the environment, and behavior are inseparable in descriptions of cognitive phenomena, are they all a part of cognition? Is it possible to identify cognition that is not, in this way, embedded in a context, enacted through action, and grounded in the body, emotions, and situations (Noë, 2009)?" (Matheson & Barsalou, 2018, p. 1).
18. See, for example, Dhami (2016, pp. 1426–1431), Felin and colleagues (2017), Gal and Rucker (2018), Gigerenzer (2015), Rossiter (2019), Stanovich and West (2000), and Yechiam (2019),

for critiques of various kinds, whether methodological, empirical, or in terms of policy implications.

19. Note that the affect heuristic as documented by Finucane and colleagues (2000; see also, Slovic et al., 2007) is not included here.
20. For a similar argument in terms of continuity rather than a dichotomy between rational and experiential systems (or their equivalent), see for instance, Keren and Schul (2009), Kruglanski and Gigerenzer (2011), and Melnikoff and Bargh (2018).
21. According to Adam Smith (1759/2002), the impartial spectator also plays an essential role in fairness "by causing individuals to internalize other people's sense of fairness by viewing their own actions through the eyes of an objective observer" (Ashraf et al., 2005, p. 136).
22. If the Proposer's offer is rejected, it may be because she failed to think like the Responder. This may be what happened to this Proposer whose low offers were rejected: "I did not earn any money because all the other players are stupid! How can you reject a positive amount of money and prefer to get zero? They just did not understand the game! You should have stopped the experiment and explained it to them..." (Zamir, 2001, p. 6). This is an important quote because it illustrates that if someone thinks like *Homo economicus* while the other economic agents do not, the economic exchange will not happen: "this student clearly understood backward induction and sub game perfectness and had a very clear (but rather narrow) notion of rationality, according to which he was the only rational player there. Yet he exhibited the poorest performance" (Zamir, 2001, p. 6).
23. A review of the literature found that: "Modal and median ultimatum offers are usually 40–50 percent and means are 30-40 percent. There are hardly any offers in the outlying categories of 0, 1-10, and the hyper-fair category 51-100. Offers of 40–50 percent are rarely rejected. Offers below 20 percent or so are rejected about half the time" (Camerer, 2011, p. 49).
24. Two main forms of empathy are useful in understanding the current findings in behavioral economics: Affective and cognitive empathy. Affective empathy is "the tendency to take on, resonate with, or 'share' the emotions of others" and is also known as "experience sharing," "shared self-other representations," or "emotional contagion" (Zaki & Ochsner, 2012). In this case, as we will

see in Chapter 4, people have the same emotion or experience as others. Cognitive empathy is "the ability to explicitly reason and draw inference*s*" about people's mental states, and is also known as "mentalizing," "perspective taking," or "theory of mind" (Zaki & Ochsner, 2012, p. 676). These terms describe similar situations, namely trying to "take" someone else's point of view when one makes a decision. Interestingly, it is suggested that both the cognitive and affective sides of empathy can underpin sympathy (also known as "prosocial concern"): "prosocial motivation to help others as a result of using one or both of the other facets to share and/or cognitively understand the emotions they are experiencing" (Zaki & Ochsner, 2012, p. 676). Thus sympathy, as a prosocial concern, is different from empathy, but it is also the by-product of one of its cognitive or affective forms.

25. This might not hold true when it comes to affective empathy in the marketplace (Bowles, 1991; Hudson & Hudson, 2003).
26. In this study, participants were told that they would play with 10 different people (partners): Each game would be a one-shot, played once with each of the 10 partners, and their decisions with each partner in each one-shot would not be revealed to other partners and could not influence subsequent offers (anonymity). This study included three within-subjects conditions: In one condition 10 rounds were played with a human partner, and in another, 10 rounds were played with a computer partner. In the third condition, a control, participants received money for pressing a button in a series of 10 control rounds. Although participants in one condition were told they were playing with a human partner, they were actually playing with an algorithm that classified half of the offers as a fair split ($5:$5) and the other half of the offers as an unfair split in favor of the Proposer (2 offers of $9:$1; 2 offers of $8:$2; 1 offer of $7:$3) by Sanfey and colleagues (2003). The 10 offers from the computer partner were the same (5 fair, 5 unfair).
27. One might also speculate that any form of altruistic punishment was considered irrelevant to a computer: What would be the point of reminding a computer of the social norm of fairness?
28. Sanfey and colleagues interpret the dlPFC activations as related to the cognitive demands of the task: "namely the goal of accumulating as much money as possible. An unfair offer is more difficult to accept (…)" (Sanfey et al., 2003, p. 1757). Activations

in the anterior cingulate cortex (ACC) are interpreted as associated with the detection of cognitive conflict: "activation here may reflect the conflict between cognitive and emotional motivations in Ultimatum Game" (Sanfey et al., 2003, p. 1757).

29. These findings are supported by van't Wout and colleagues (2006) who showed that participants' (responders) skin conductance response (SCR) increased in response to unfair (vs. fair) offers in an ultimatum game when they played with another person, but not when they played with a computer. These studies are consistent with the idea that emotions in response to social cues can influence economic decision-making. van't Wout and colleagues (2010) also showed how reinterpreting (but not suppressing) an emotional response to an unfair offer can reduce rejection rates in the ultimatum game. Grecucci and colleagues (2013) showed that the dlPFC is associated with emotion regulation in economic decision-making, and that activity in the posterior insula decreased with down-regulation (when participants were instructed to imagine positive intentions on the proposer's side) and increased with up-regulation (when participants were instructed to imagine negative intentions on the proposer's side).
30. "Though studies of disgust have been largely focused on physical sensations of taste and odor, it has been suggested that emotion-based disgust (as perhaps induced by an insulting unfair offer) may be conceptually similar. The recruitment of similar neural structures, namely the anterior insula, in both physical and moral disgust gives some credence to this notion" (Sanfey et al., 2003, p. 1756).
31. In support of this interpretation, which is somewhat limited because it relies on reverse inference, it is worth noting that the anterior insular cortices are key to the human interoceptive cortex. Interoception refers to the sense of the physiological state of the body (Tsakiris & Preester, 2018). Anterior insular cortices are associated with neural representations of internal bodily and feeling states, such as arousal, hunger, thirst, taste, and pain (Critchley et al., 2001, 2004; Damasio, 1994). In this regard, increased activity in the anterior insula testifies to the influence of embodiment on economic decision-making. Furthermore, one of the most famous interoceptive models of emotion is the Jamesian theory, which is mentioned in relation to Damasio's somatic markers (Reimann & Bechara, 2010). This theory posits that changes in

bodily signals are essential to the experience of emotions, so much so that "emotions cannot be experienced in the absence of these bodily feelings" (Singer & Tusche, 2014, p. 521). Importantly, the interoceptive model of emotions can be extended to the study of empathy. In this case, the cortical representations of bodily states in the anterior insula have two main functions: They are involved in subjective representations of feelings so that one can understand one's own feelings when experiencing or anticipating them, and they operate "as the visceral correlate of a prospective empathic simulation of how something may feel for others" (Singer & Tusche, 2014, p. 522). Scores on individual difference measures of empathy—for instance, the Empathic Concern Scale of the Interpersonal Reactivity Index (IRI) developed by Davis (1983)—predict increased activity in the anterior insula when participants observe their loved ones suffering (Singer et al., 2004, 2006), or others expressing joy or disgust while tasting pleasant or unpleasant drinks (Jabbi et al., 2007). These findings further support this embodied interpretation of empathy.

32. For further developments on the central role of emotions in social decision-making, which has allowed research to go beyond the monetary costs associated with social interactions in strategic games, see Engelmann and Fehr (2017). For example, experimental studies on the Trust Game (TG) show that betrayal leads to an emotional response and that the cost of betrayal goes beyond the loss of money (e.g., Bohnet & Zeckhauser, 2004; Bohnet et al., 2008; Kosfeld et al., 2005). At the brain level, studies show that betrayal aversion is associated with increased activity in the anterior insula (Aimone et al., 2014).
33. Several experimental studies on the UG show that strong emotional reactions are associated with unfairness. For instance, the experience of anger predicts the participants' decision to incur a cost to punish the other player by rejecting her unfair offer (Pillutla & Murnighan, 1996). Other studies show that unfairness in the UG is also associated with the experience of contempt (Tabibnia et al., 2008), and that sadness and disgust lead to an increased rate of rejection of unfair offers in the UG (Harlé & Sanfey, 2007, 2010; Moretti & di Pellegrino, 2010).

34. MORALITY IS CLEANLINESS is well documented in the literature (Lakoff & Johnson, 1999; Lee & Schwarz, 2021), and can have implications for economic life. For example, people behave differently when handling fresh, clean versus dirty banknotes (Yang et al., 2013).

References

Acker, J. (2006). Inequality regimes: Gender, class, and race in organizations. *Gender & Society, 20*(4), 441–464. https://doi.org/10.1177/0891243206289499

Adriaans, P. (2020). Information. In E. N. Zalta (Ed.), *The Stanford encyclopedia of philosophy*. Metaphysics Research Lab, Stanford University. https://plato.stanford.edu/archives/fall2020/entries/information/

Aimone, J. A., Houser, D., & Weber, B. (2014). Neural signatures of betrayal aversion: An fMRI study of trust. *Proceedings of the Royal Society B: Biological Sciences, 281*(1782), 20132127. https://doi.org/10.1098/rspb.2013.2127

Akerlof, G. A., & Shiller, R. J. (2009). *Animal spirits: How human psychology drives the economy, and why it matters for global capitalism*. Princeton University Press.

Albert, H. (1998). *Marktsoziologie und Entscheidungslogik: Zur Kritik der reinen Ökonomik (Neuausg.)*. Mohr Siebeck.

Alchian, A. A. (1977). *Economic forces at work*. Liberty Press.

Alós-Ferrer, C. (2018). A review essay on *Social Neuroscience*: Can research on the social brain and economics inform each other? *Journal of Economic Literature, 56*(1), 234–264. https://doi.org/10.1257/jel.20171370

Alós-Ferrer, C., & Strack, F. (2014). From dual processes to multiple selves: Implications for economic behavior. *Journal of Economic Psychology, 41*, 1–11. https://doi.org/10.1016/j.joep.2013.12.005

Anderson, M. L., & Chemero, T. (2013). The problem with brain GUTs: Conflation of different senses of "prediction" threatens metaphysical disaster. *Behavioral and Brain Sciences, 36*(3), 204–205. https://doi.org/10.1017/S0140525X1200221X

APA. (2023a). Expectation. In *American Psychological Association (APA) Dictionary of psychology*. https://dictionary.apa.org/expectation

APA. (2023b). Experience. In *American Psychological Association (APA) Dictionary of Psychology*. https://dictionary.apa.org/experience

Ariely, D., Loewenstein, G., & Prelec, D. (2003). "Coherent arbitrariness": Stable demand curves without stable preferences. *The Quarterly Journal of Economics, 118*(1), 73–106. https://doi.org/10.1162/00335530360535153
Arrow, K. J. (1974). *The limits of organization*. W. W. Norton & Company.
Ashraf, N., Camerer, C. F., & Loewenstein, G. (2005). Adam Smith, behavioral economist. *Journal of Economic Perspectives, 19*(3), 131–145.
Backhaus, J., & Hansen, R. (2000). Methodenstreit in der Nationalökonomie. *Journal for General Philosophy of Science, 31*(2), 307–336. https://doi.org/10.1023/A:1026450710020
Bechara, A., & Damasio, A. R. (2005). The somatic marker hypothesis: A neural theory of economic decision. *Games and Economic Behavior, 52*(2), 336–372. https://doi.org/10.1016/j.geb.2004.06.010
Bechtel, W., & Abrahamsen, A. (2005). Explanation: A mechanist alternative. *Studies in History and Philosophy of Science Part C: Studies in History and Philosophy of Biological and Biomedical Sciences, 36*(2), 421–441. https://doi.org/10.1016/j.shpsc.2005.03.010
Becker, G. S. (1973). A theory of marriage: Part I. *Journal of Political Economy, 81*(4), 813–846.
Becker, G. S. (1976). *The economic approach to human behavior*. University of Chicago Press.
Becker, G. S. (1993). Nobel lecture: The economic way of looking at behavior. *Journal of Political Economy, 101*(3), 385–409.
Bernheim, B. D. (2009). Chapter 9—The psychology and neurobiology of judgment and decision making: What's in it for economists? In P. W. Glimcher, C. F. Camerer, E. Fehr, & R. A. Poldrack (Eds.), *Neuroeconomics* (pp. 113–125). Academic Press. https://doi.org/10.1016/B978-0-12-374176-9.00009-9
Bickle, J. (2006). Multiple realizability. In L. Nadel (Ed.), *Encyclopedia of cognitive science* (p. s00116). Wiley. https://doi.org/10.1002/0470018860.s00116
Bikhchandani, S., Hirshleifer, D., & Welch, I. (1998). Learning from the behavior of others: Conformity, fads, and informational cascades. *Journal of Economic Perspectives, 12*(3), 151–170. https://doi.org/10.1257/jep.12.3.151
Blanchard, O. (2017). *The need for different classes of macroeconomic models | PIIE*. https://www.piie.com/blogs/realtime-economic-issues-watch/need-different-classes-macroeconomic-models
Bockman, J. (2011). *Markets in the name of socialism: The left-wing origins of neoliberalism*. Stanford University Press.
Boero, N., & Mason, K. (2020). *The Oxford handbook of the sociology of body and embodiment*. Oxford University Press.
Bohl, V., & Fiske, A. P. (2014). Book review: "In and out of each other's bodies: Theory of mind, evolution, truth, and the nature of the social. Maurice Bloch.

Boulder, CO: Paradigm, 2012. 161 pp." *American Ethnologist, 41*(1), 214–215. https://doi.org/10.1111/amet.12070_18

Bohnet, I., Greig, F., Herrmann, B., & Zeckhauser, R. (2008). Betrayal aversion: Evidence from Brazil, China, Oman, Switzerland, Turkey, and the United States. *American Economic Review, 98*(1), 294–310. https://doi.org/10.1257/aer.98.1.294

Bohnet, I., & Zeckhauser, R. (2004). Trust, risk and betrayal. *Journal of Economic Behavior & Organization, 55*(4), 467–484. https://doi.org/10.1016/j.jebo.2003.11.004

Boldyrev, I., & Kirtchik, O. (2017). The cultures of mathematical economics in the postwar Soviet Union: More than a method, less than a discipline. *Studies in History and Philosophy of Science Part A, 63*, 1–10. https://doi.org/10.1016/j.shpsa.2017.03.011

Bossaerts, P., & Murawski, C. (2015). From behavioural economics to neuroeconomics to decision neuroscience: The ascent of biology in research on human decision making. *Current Opinion in Behavioral Sciences, 5*, 37–42. https://doi.org/10.1016/j.cobeha.2015.07.001

Bourdieu, P. (2005). Principles of an economic anthropology. In N. J. Smelser & R. Swedberg (Eds.), *The handbook of economic sociology, second edition* (pp. 75–89). Princeton University Press. https://doi.org/10.1515/9781400835584.75

Bowles, S. (1991). What markets can—and cannot—do. *Challenge, 34*(4), 11–16.

Brette, R. (2019). Is coding a relevant metaphor for the brain? *Behavioral and Brain Sciences, 42*, e215. https://doi.org/10.1017/S0140525X19000049

Bruni, L., & Sugden, R. (2007). The road not taken: How psychology was removed from economics, and how it might be brought back. *The Economic Journal, 117*(516), 146–173. https://doi.org/10.1111/j.1468-0297.2007.02005.x

Buckner, C., & Garson, J. (2019). Connectionism. In E. N. Zalta (Ed.), *The Stanford encyclopedia of philosophy (Fall 2019)*. Metaphysics Research Lab, Stanford University. https://plato.stanford.edu/archives/fall2019/entries/connectionism/

Caballero, R. J. (2010). Macroeconomics after the crisis: Time to deal with the pretense-of-knowledge syndrome. *Journal of Economic Perspectives, 24*(4), 85–102. https://doi.org/10.1257/jep.24.4.85

Callon, M., Millo, Y., & Muniesa, F. (Eds.). (2007). *Market devices*. Blackwell Pub.

Callon, M., & Roth, A. E. (2021). The design and performation of markets: A discussion. *AMS Review, 11*(3–4), 219–239. https://doi.org/10.1007/s13162-021-00216-w

Cambridge Dictionary. (n.d.). *English Dictionary, Translations & Thesaurus*. https://dictionary.cambridge.org/

Camerer, C. F. (2006). Wanting, liking, and learning: Neuroscience and paternalism. *The University of Chicago Law Review, 73*(1), 87–110. https://doi.org/10.2307/4495545

Camerer, C. F. (2011). *Behavioral game theory: Experiments in strategic interaction*. Princeton University Press.

Camerer, C. F. (2013). A review essay about *Foundations of neuroeconomic analysis* by Paul Glimcher. *Journal of Economic Literature, 51*(4), 1155–1182. https://doi.org/10.1257/jel.51.4.1155

Camerer, C. F., Loewenstein, G., & Prelec, D. (2005). Neuroeconomics: How neuroscience can inform economics. *Journal of Economic Literature, 43*(1), 9–64. https://doi.org/10.1257/0022051053737843

Cerulo, K. A. (2019). Embodied cognition: Sociology's role in bridging mind, brain, and body. In W. H. Brekhus & G. Ignatow (Eds.), *The Oxford handbook of cognitive sociology*. Oxford University Press. https://doi.org/10.1093/oxfordhb/9780190273385.013.5

Chater, N., Felin, T., Funder, D. C., Gigerenzer, G., Koenderink, J. J., Krueger, J. I., Noble, D., Nordli, S. A., Oaksford, M., Schwartz, B., Stanovich, K. E., & Todd, P. M. (2018). Mind, rationality, and cognition: An interdisciplinary debate. *Psychonomic Bulletin & Review, 25*(2), 793–826. https://doi.org/10.3758/s13423-017-1333-5

Choy, Y. K. (2018). Cost-benefit analysis, values, wellbeing and ethics: An indigenous worldview analysis. *Ecological Economics, 145*, 1–9. https://doi.org/10.1016/j.ecolecon.2017.08.005

Coase, R. (2012). Saving economics from the economists. *Harvard Business Review, 90*(12), 36.

Coibion, O., Gorodnichenko, Y., & Kamdar, R. (2018). The formation of expectations, inflation, and the Phillips curve. *Journal of Economic Literature, 56*(4), 1447–1491. https://doi.org/10.1257/jel.20171300

Colander, D. (2007). Retrospectives: Edgeworth's hedonimeter and the quest to measure utility. *Journal of Economic Perspectives, 21*(2), 215–225. https://doi.org/10.1257/jep.21.2.215

Cole, D. (2023). The Chinese room argument. In E. N. Zalta & U. Nodelman (Eds.), *The Stanford encyclopedia of philosophy* (Summer 2023). Metaphysics Research Lab, Stanford University. https://plato.stanford.edu/archives/sum2023/entries/chinese-room/

Craver, C. F. (2009). *Explaining the brain: Mechanisms and the mosaic unity of neuroscience*. Oxford University Press.

Craver, C. F., & Tabery, J. (2019). Mechanisms in science. In E. N. Zalta (Ed.), *The Stanford encyclopedia of philosophy*. Metaphysics Research Lab,

Stanford University. https://plato.stanford.edu/archives/sum2019/entries/science-mechanisms/

Crenshaw, K. W. (2017). *On intersectionality: Essential writings*. The New Press.

Critchley, H. D., Mathias, C. J., & Dolan, R. J. (2001). Neuroanatomical basis for first- and second-order representations of bodily states. *Nature Neuroscience, 4*(2), Article 2. https://doi.org/10.1038/84048

Critchley, H. D., Wiens, S., Rotshtein, P., Öhman, A., & Dolan, R. J. (2004). Neural systems supporting interoceptive awareness. *Nature Neuroscience, 7*(2), 189–195. https://doi.org/10.1038/nn1176

Damasio, A. R. (1994). *Descartes' error: Emotion, reason, and the human brain*. Avon Books.

Davis, D., & Holt, C. (Eds.). (1993). *Experimental economics*. Princeton University Press.

Davis, M. H. (1983). Measuring individual differences in empathy: Evidence for a multidimensional approach. *Journal of Personality and Social Psychology, 44*(1), 113–126. https://doi.org/10.1037/0022-3514.44.1.113

Debreu, G. (1984). Economic theory in the mathematical mode. *American Economic Review, 74*(3), 267–278.

De Martino, B., Kumaran, D., Seymour, B., & Dolan, R. J. (2006). Frames, biases, and rational decision-making in the human brain. *Science, 313*(5787), 684–687. https://doi.org/10.1126/science.1128356

Dennett, D. C. (1998). *The intentional stance*. MIT Press.

de Quervain, D.J.-F., Fischbacher, U., Treyer, V., Schellhammer, M., Schnyder, U., Buck, A., & Fehr, E. (2004). The neural basis of altruistic punishment. *Science, 305*(5688), 1254–1258. https://doi.org/10.1126/science.1100735

Devenow, A., & Welch, I. (1996). Rational herding in financial economics. *Papers and Proceedings of the Tenth Annual Congress of the European Economic Association, 40*(3), 603–615. https://doi.org/10.1016/0014-2921(95)00073-9

de Vroey, M. (2016). *A history of macroeconomics from Keynes to Lucas and beyond*. Cambridge University Press.

Dew, N., Grichnik, D., Mayer-Haug, K., Read, S., & Brinckmann, J. (2015). Situated entrepreneurial cognition. *International Journal of Management Reviews, 17*(2), 143–164. https://doi.org/10.1111/ijmr.12051

Dhami, S. (2016). *The foundations of behavioral economic analysis*. Oxford University Press.

Dietvorst, R. C., Verbeke, W. J. M. I., Bagozzi, R. P., Yoon, C., Smits, M., & van der Lugt, A. (2009). A sales force–specific theory-of-mind scale: Tests of its validity by classical methods and functional magnetic resonance imaging. *Journal of Marketing Research (JMR), 46*(5), 653–668. https://doi.org/10.1509/jmkr.46.5.653

Emmett, R. (2021). Frank Knight, Max Weber, la economía de Chicago y el institucionalismo. *Revista de Economía Institucional, 23*(45), 3–22. https://doi.org/10.18601/01245996.v23n45.02

Engelmann, J. B., & Fehr, E. (2017). The neurobiology of trust and social decision-making: The important role of emotions. In P. A. M. Van Lange, B. Rockenbach, & T. Yamagishi (Eds.), *Trust in social dilemmas* (pp. 33–56). Oxford University Press. https://doi.org/10.1093/oso/9780190630782.003.0003

Enke, B. (2022). Market exposure and human morality. *Nature Human Behaviour, 7*(1), 134–141. https://doi.org/10.1038/s41562-022-01480-x

Epstein, S. (1994). Integration of the cognitive and the psychodynamic unconscious. *American Psychologist, 49*(8), 709–724. https://doi.org/10.1037/0003-066X.49.8.709

Epstein, S., Pacini, R., Denes-Raj, V., & Heier, H. (1996). Individual differences in intuitive–experiential and analytical–rational thinking styles. *Journal of Personality and Social Psychology, 71*(2), 390–405. https://doi.org/10.1037/0022-3514.71.2.390

Evans, J. St. .B. T., & Stanovich, K. E. (2013). Dual-process theories of higher cognition: Advancing the debate. *Perspectives on Psychological Science, 8*(3), 223–241. https://doi.org/10.1177/1745691612460685

Farr, R. M. (1997). Book review. *The new economic mind: The social psychology of economic behavior*: A. Lewis, P. Webley, and A. Furnham (eds.). *Journal of Economic Psychology, 18*(6), 713–717. https://doi.org/10.1016/S0167-4870(97)00033-0

Fehr, E., & Gächter, S. (2000). Fairness and retaliation: The economics of reciprocity. *Journal of Economic Perspectives, 14*(3), 159–181.

Felin, T., Koenderink, J., & Krueger, J. I. (2017). Rationality, perception, and the all-seeing eye. *Psychonomic Bulletin & Review, 24*(4), 1040–1059. https://doi.org/10.3758/s13423-016-1198-z

Finucane, M. L., Alhakami, A., Slovic, P., & Johnson, S. M. (2000). The affect heuristic in judgments of risks and benefits. *Journal of Behavioral Decision Making, 13*(1), 1–17. https://doi.org/10.1002/(SICI)1099-0771(200001/03)13:1%3c1::AID-BDM333%3e3.0.CO;2-S

Fischer, M. H., Felisatti, A., Kulkova, E., Mende, M. A., & Miklashevsky, A. (2021). Measuring the mathematical mind: Embodied evidence from motor resonance, negative numbers, calculation biases, and emotional priming. In M. D. Robinson & L. E. Thomas (Eds.), *Handbook of embodied psychology* (pp. 149–170). Springer International Publishing. https://doi.org/10.1007/978-3-030-78471-3_7

Fiske, S. T., & Taylor, S. E. (2013). *Social cognition: From brains to culture*. SAGE.

Floridi, L. (2004). Information. In *The Blackwell guide to the philosophy of computing and information* (pp. 40–61). Wiley. https://doi.org/10.1002/9780470757017.ch4

Fourcade, M., Ollion, E., & Algan, Y. (2015). The superiority of economists. *Journal of Economic Perspectives, 29*(1), 89–114. https://doi.org/10.1257/jep.29.1.89

Frantz, R., & Leeson, R. (2013). *Hayek and behavioral economics*. Springer.

Friedman, M. (1953). *Essays in positive economics*. University of Chicago Press.

Frith, C. D., & Singer, T. (2008). The role of social cognition in decision making. *Philosophical Transactions of the Royal Society B: Biological Sciences, 363*(1511), 3875–3886. https://doi.org/10.1098/rstb.2008.0156

Fuentes, A. (2022). More than the market: Reinventing postpandemic economic relations. *Economic Anthropology, 9*(1), 172–175.

Fumagalli, R. (2013). The futile search for true utility. *Economics and Philosophy, 29*(3), 325–347.

Gal, D., & Rucker, D. D. (2018). The loss of loss aversion: Will it loom larger than its gain? *Journal of Consumer Psychology, 28*(3), 497–516. https://doi.org/10.1002/jcpy.1047

Gallese, V., & Goldman, A. (1998). Mirror neurons and the simulation theory of mind-reading. *Trends in Cognitive Sciences, 2*(12), 493–501. https://doi.org/10.1016/S1364-6613(98)01262-5

Gallup, J. L., Sachs, J. D., & Mellinger, A. D. (1999). Geography and economic development. *International Regional Science Review, 22*(2), 179–232. https://doi.org/10.1177/016001799761012334

Gane, N. (2021). Nudge economics as libertarian paternalism. *Theory, Culture & Society, 38*(6), 119–142. https://doi.org/10.1177/0263276421999447

Geertz, C. (1978). The bazaar economy: Information and search in peasant marketing. *American Economic Review, 68*(2), 28–32.

Gigerenzer, G. (2015). On the supposed evidence for libertarian paternalism. *Review of Philosophy and Psychology, 6*(3), 361–383. https://doi.org/10.1007/s13164-015-0248-1

Gigerenzer, G. (2018). The bias bias in behavioral economics. *Review of Behavioral Economics, 5*(3–4), 303–336. https://doi.org/10.1561/105.00000092

Gintis, H., Bowles, S., Boyd, R., & Fehr, E. (2005). *Moral sentiments and material interests: The foundations of cooperation in economic life*. MIT Press.

Glimcher, P. W. (2004). *Decisions, uncertainty, and the brain: The science of neuroeconomics*. MIT Press.

Glimcher, P. W. (2011). *Foundations of neuroeconomic analysis*. Oxford University Press.

Glimcher, P. W., Camerer, C., Poldrack, R. A., & Fehr, E. (2009). *Neuroeconomics: Decision making and the brain*. Academic Press.

Glimcher, P. W., & Fehr, E. (Eds.). (2014). *Neuroeconomics: Decision making and the brain* (2nd ed.). Academic Press.
Glock, H.-J. (2008). *What is analytic philosophy?* Cambridge University Press.
Gode, D. K., & Sunder, S. (1993). Allocative efficiency of markets with zero-intelligence traders: Market as a partial substitute for individual rationality. *Journal of Political Economy, 101*(1), 119–137. https://doi.org/10.1086/261868
Goffman, E. (1961). *Encounters: Two studies in the sociology of interaction.* Penguin Books.
Gordon, R. J. (1990). What is new—Keynesian economics? *Journal of Economic Literature, 28*(3), 1115–1171.
Grecucci, A., Giorgetta, C., van't Wout, M., Bonini, N., & Sanfey, A. G. (2013). Reappraising the ultimatum: An fMRI study of emotion regulation and decision making. *Cerebral Cortex, 23*(2), 399–410. https://doi.org/10.1093/cercor/bhs028
Gross, M., & Tarascio, V. J. (1998). Pareto's theory of choice. *History of Political Economy, 30*(2), 171–187.
Guala, F. (2012). Reciprocity: Weak or strong? What punishment experiments do (and do not) demonstrate. *Behavioral and Brain Sciences, 35*(01), 1–15. https://doi.org/10.1017/S0140525X11000069
Gudeman, S. (2001). Scales, tales and tools. *Economic and Political Weekly, 36*(21), 1859–1864.
Güth, W., Schmittberger, R., & Schwarze, B. (1982). An experimental analysis of ultimatum bargaining. *Journal of Economic Behavior & Organization, 3*(4), 367–388. https://doi.org/10.1016/0167-2681(82)90011-7
Harbecke, J. (2014). The role of supervenience and constitution in neuroscientific research. *Synthese, 191*(5), 725–743. https://doi.org/10.1007/s11229-013-0308-y
Harbecke, J., & Herrmann-Pillath, C. (Eds.). (2020). *Social neuroeconomics: Mechanistic integration of the neurosciences and the social sciences*. Routledge. https://doi.org/10.4324/9780429296918
Harlé, K. M., & Sanfey, A. G. (2007). Incidental sadness biases social economic decisions in the ultimatum game. *Emotion, 7*(4), 876–881. https://doi.org/10.1037/1528-3542.7.4.876
Harlé, K. M., & Sanfey, A. G. (2010). Effects of approach and withdrawal motivation on interactive economic decisions. *Cognition & Emotion, 24*(8), 1456–1465. https://doi.org/10.1080/02699930903510220
Harrison, G. W., & Ross, D. (2017). The empirical adequacy of cumulative prospect theory and its implications for normative assessment. *Journal of Economic Methodology, 24*(2), 150–165. https://doi.org/10.1080/1350178X.2017.1309753

Haslam, N., & Fiske, A. P. (2005). Social expertise: Theory of mind or theory of relationships? In *Relational models theory* (pp. 147–163). Psychology Press.

Hayek, F. A. (1967). *Studies in philosophy, politics and economics*. Routledge.

Hayek, F. A. (1982/2013). *Law, legislation and liberty: A new statement of the liberal principles of justice and political economy* (New ed.). Routledge.

Hendry, D. F., & Muellbauer, J. N. J. (2018). The future of macroeconomics: Macro theory and models at the Bank of England. *Oxford Review of Economic Policy, 34*(1–2), 287–328. https://doi.org/10.1093/oxrep/grx055

Henrich, J., Boyd, R., Bowles, S., Camerer, C., Fehr, E., Gintis, H., McElreath, R., Alvard, M., Barr, A., Ensminger, J., Henrich, N. S., Hill, K., Gil-White, F., Gurven, M., Marlowe, F. W., Patton, J. Q., & Tracer, D. (2005). "Economic man" in cross-cultural perspective: Behavioral experiments in 15 small-scale societies. *Behavioral and Brain Sciences, 28*(6), 795–815; discussion 815–855. https://doi.org/10.1017/S0140525X05000142

Herrmann-Pillath, C. (2019). From dual systems to dual function: Rethinking methodological foundations of behavioural economics. *Economics and Philosophy, 35*(3), 403–422. https://doi.org/10.1017/S0266267118000378

Herrmann-Pillath, C. (2020a). A semiotic approach to information in economics. *Recherches Sémiotiques, 40*(2–3), 209. https://doi.org/10.7202/1098867ar

Herrmann-Pillath, C. (2020b). Economics as a collective myth of 21st century modernity: The decivilizing power of market utopia. In S. Kramer & P. Ludes (Eds.), *Collective myths and decivilizing processes* (pp. 53–74). LIT Verlag Münster.

Herrmann-Pillath, C. (2021). Robert J. Shiller, Narrative economics: How stories go viral and drive major economic events. *Oeconomia, 11*(11–2), 403–408. https://doi.org/10.4000/oeconomia.11128

Herrmann-Pillath, C., & Boldyrev, I. A. (2014). *Hegel, institutions, and economics: Performing the social*. Routledge, Taylor & Francis Group.

Higgs, K. (2014). *Collision course: Endless growth on a finite planet*. MIT Press.

Hodgson, G. M. (1998). The approach of institutional economics. *Journal of Economic Literature, 36*(1), 166–192.

Hudson, I., & Hudson, M. (2003). Removing the veil? Commodity fetishism, fair trade, and the environment. *Organization & Environment, 16*(4), 413–430.

Jabbi, M., Swart, M., & Keysers, C. (2007). Empathy for positive and negative emotions in the gustatory cortex. *NeuroImage, 34*(4), 1744–1753. https://doi.org/10.1016/j.neuroimage.2006.10.032

Jankowiak, W. (2005). Market integration, cognitive awareness, and the expansion of moral empathy. *Behavioral and Brain Sciences, 28*(6), 826–827. https://doi.org/10.1017/S0140525X05330147

Jasanoff, A. (2018). *The biological mind: How brain, body, and environment collaborate to make us who we are*. Basic Books.

Johnson, M. (2016). Pragmatism, cognitive science, and embodied mind. In R. Madzia & M. Jung (Eds.), *Pragmatism and embodied cognitive science: From bodily intersubjectivity to symbolic articulation* (pp. 101–126). De Gruyter. https://doi.org/10.1515/9783110480238-006

Jung, M. H., Perfecto, H., & Nelson, L. D. (2016). Anchoring in payment: Evaluating a judgmental heuristic in field experimental settings. *Journal of Marketing Research, 53*(3), 354–368. https://doi.org/10.1509/jmr.14.0238

Kagel, J., & Roth, A. E. (Eds.). (1995). *Handbook of experimental economics*. Princeton University Press.

Kahneman, D. (2003). Maps of bounded rationality: Psychology for behavioral economics. *American Economic Review, 93*(5), 1449–1475.

Kahneman, D. (2009). Chapter 33—Remarks on neuroeconomics. In P. W. Glimcher, C. F. Camerer, E. Fehr, & R. A. Poldrack (Eds.), *Neuroeconomics* (pp. 523–526). Academic Press. https://doi.org/10.1016/B978-0-12-374176-9.00033-6

Kahneman, D. (2012). *Thinking, fast and slow*. Penguin Books.

Kahneman, D., & Tversky, A. (1982). The simulation heuristic. In A. Tversky, D. Kahneman, & P. Slovic (Eds.), *Judgment under uncertainty: Heuristics and biases* (pp. 201–208). Cambridge University Press. https://doi.org/10.1017/CBO9780511809477.015

Keren, G., & Schul, Y. (2009). Two is not always better than one: A critical evaluation of two-system theories. *Perspectives on Psychological Science, 4*(6), 533–550. https://doi.org/10.1111/j.1745-6924.2009.01164.x

Keynes, J. M. (1936/2018). *The general theory of employment interest and money*. Springer International Publishing. https://doi.org/10.1007/978-3-319-70344-2

Kirman, A. P. (1992). Whom or what does the representative individual represent? *Journal of Economic Perspectives, 6*(2), 117–136. https://doi.org/10.1257/jep.6.2.117

Kosfeld, M., Heinrichs, M., Zak, P. J., Fischbacher, U., & Fehr, E. (2005). Oxytocin increases trust in humans. *Nature, 435*(7042), 673–676. https://doi.org/10.1038/nature03701

Krenak, A. (2023). *Life is not useful*. Wiley.

Kruglanski, A. W., & Gigerenzer, G. (2011). Intuitive and deliberate judgments are based on common principles. *Psychological Review, 118*(1), 97–109. https://doi.org/10.1037/a0020762

Kumar, S., & Goyal, N. (2015). Behavioural biases in investment decision making—A systematic literature review. *Qualitative Research in Financial Markets, 7*(1), 88–108. https://doi.org/10.1108/QRFM-07-2014-0022

Lainé, M. (2014). Do animal spirits rely on somatic markers? Keynes in light of neuroscience. *Journal of Post Keynesian Economics, 36*(3), 439–466. https://doi.org/10.2753/PKE0160-3477360303

Lakoff, G. (1987). *Women, fire, and dangerous things: What categories reveal about the mind*. University of Chicago Press.

Lakoff, G., & Johnson, M. (1980). *Metaphors we live by*. University of Chicago Press.

Lakoff, G., & Johnson, M. (1999). *Philosophy in the flesh: The embodied mind and Its challenge to Western thought*. Basic Books.

Lazear, E. P. (2000). Economic imperialism. *The Quarterly Journal of Economics, 115*(1), 99–146. https://doi.org/10.1162/003355300554683

Leamer, E. E. (2007). A flat world, a level playing field, a small world after all, or none of the above? A review of Thomas L. Friedman's *The World is Flat*. *Journal of Economic Literature, 45*(1), 83–126. https://doi.org/10.1257/jel.45.1.83

Lee, S. W. S., & Schwarz, N. (2021). Grounded procedures: A proximate mechanism for the psychology of cleansing and other physical actions. *Behavioral and Brain Sciences, 44*, e1. https://doi.org/10.1017/S0140525X20000308

Lempert, K. M., & Phelps, E. A. (2014). Chapter 12—Neuroeconomics of emotion and decision making. In P. W. Glimcher & E. Fehr (Eds.), *Neuroeconomics* (2nd ed., pp. 219–236). Academic Press. https://doi.org/10.1016/B978-0-12-416008-8.00012-7

Levav, J., & Mcgraw, A. P. (2009). Emotional accounting: How feelings about money influence consumer choice. *Journal of Marketing Research, 46*(1), 66–80. https://doi.org/10.1509/jmkr.46.1.66

Lillard, A. S. (1997). Other folks' theories of mind and behavior. *Psychological Science, 8*(4), 268–274. https://doi.org/10.1111/j.1467-9280.1997.tb00437.x

Lillard, A. S. (1998). Ethnopsychologies: Cultural variations in theories of mind. *Psychological Bulletin, 123*(1), 3–32. https://doi.org/10.1037/0033-2909.123.1.3

Lo, A. W. (2019). *Adaptive markets: Financial evolution at the speed of thought*. Princeton University Press.

Logan, T. D., & Myers, S. L. (2022). Symposium: Race and economic literature—Introduction. *Journal of Economic Literature, 60*(2), 375–376. https://doi.org/10.1257/jel.20211685

Louie, K., Glimcher, P. W., & Webb, R. (2015). Adaptive neural coding: From biological to behavioral decision-making. *Current Opinion in Behavioral Sciences, 5*, 91–99. https://doi.org/10.1016/j.cobeha.2015.08.008

Lucas, R. E., Jr. (1976). Econometric policy evaluation: A critique. In K. Brunner & A. H. Meltzer (Eds.), *The Phillips curve and labor markets* (pp. 19–46). North-Holland.

Lucas, R. E., Jr. (1988). On the mechanics of economic development. *Journal of Monetary Economics, 22*(1), 3–42.

Mäki, U. (1997). Universals and the methodenstreit: A re-examination of Carl Menger's conception of economics as an exact science. *Studies in History and Philosophy of Science Part A, 28*(3), 475–495. https://doi.org/10.1016/S0039-3681(96)00011-8

Matheson, H. E., & Barsalou, L. W. (2018). Embodiment and grounding in cognitive neuroscience. In J. T. Wixted (Ed.), *Stevens' handbook of experimental psychology and cognitive neuroscience* (pp. 1–27). Wiley. https://doi.org/10.1002/9781119170174.epcn310

Mayr, E. (1982). *The growth of biological thought: Diversity, evolution, and inheritance*. Belknap Press.

McFadden, D. (2006). Free markets and fettered consumers. *American Economic Review, 96*(1), 5–29. https://doi.org/10.1257/000282806776157542

Mead, G. H. (1934). *Mind, self & society: From the standpoint of a social behaviorist* (C. W. Morris, Ed.). University of Chicago Press.

Melnikoff, D. E., & Bargh, J. A. (2018). The mythical number two. *Trends in Cognitive Sciences, 22*(4), 280–293. https://doi.org/10.1016/j.tics.2018.02.001

Mervis, C. B., & Rosch, E. (1981). Categorization of natural objects. *Annual Review of Psychology, 32*(1), 89–115. https://doi.org/10.1146/annurev.ps.32.020181.000513

Milgrom, P., & Stokey, N. (1982). Information, trade and common knowledge. *Journal of Economic Theory, 26*(1), 17–27. https://doi.org/10.1016/0022-0531(82)90046-1

Mirowski, P. (1991). The when, the how and the why of mathematical expression in the history of economics analysis. *Journal of Economic Perspectives, 5*(1), 145–157.

Mirowski, P. (2001). *Machine dreams: Economics becomes a cyborg science*. Cambridge University Press. https://doi.org/10.1017/CBO9780511613364

Mirowski, P., & Nik-Khah, E. M. (2017). *The knowledge we have lost in information: The history of information in modern economics*. Oxford University Press.

Mirowski, P., & Plehwe, D. (Eds.). (2015). *The road from Mont Pèlerin: The making of the neoliberal thought collective*. Harvard University Press. https://doi.org/10.4159/9780674495111

Moretti, L., & di Pellegrino, G. (2010). Disgust selectively modulates reciprocal fairness in economic interactions. *Emotion, 10*(2), 169–180. https://doi.org/10.1037/a0017826

Morewedge, C. K., & Kahneman, D. (2010). Associative processes in intuitive judgment. *Trends in Cognitive Sciences, 14*(10), 435–440. https://doi.org/10.1016/j.tics.2010.07.004

Nelson, J. A. (1997). Feminism, ecology and the philosophy of economics. *Ecological Economics, 20*(2), 155–162. https://doi.org/10.1016/S0921-8009(96)00025-0

Nelson, J. A. (2006). *Economics for humans*. University of Chicago Press.

Newell, A., & Simon, H. A. (1976). Computer science as empirical inquiry: Symbols and search. *Communications of the ACM, 19*(3), 113–126.

Newen, A., Bruin, L. D., & Gallagher, S. (2018). *The Oxford handbook of 4E cognition*. Oxford University Press.

Noë, A. (2009). *Out of our heads: Why you are not your brain, and other lessons from the biology of consciousness*. Macmillan.

Nooteboom, B. (2006). Elements of a cognitive theory of the firm. In E. Krecké, C. Krecké, & R. G. Koppl (Eds.), *Cognition and economics* (Vol. 9, pp. 145–175). Emerald. https://doi.org/10.1016/S1529-2134(06)09006-5

Nooteboom, B. (2012a). *Beyond humanism: The flourishing of life, self and other*. Springer.

Nooteboom, B. (2012b). Embodied cognition, organization and innovation. In *Handbook of knowledge and economics* (pp. 339–368). Edward Elgar Publishing. https://www.elgaronline.com/display/edcoll/9781843764045/9781843764045.00023.xml

Noyes, A., Dunham, Y., & Keil, F. C. (2023). Subjectivity and social constitution: Contrasting conceptions of institutions, artifacts, and animals. *Developmental Psychology, 59*(2), 377–389. https://doi.org/10.1037/dev0001499

Oullier, O., & Basso, F. (2010). Embodied economics: How bodily information shapes the social coordination dynamics of decision-making. *Philosophical Transactions of the Royal Society of London. Series B, Biological Sciences, 365*(1538), 291–301. https://doi.org/10.1098/rstb.2009.0168

Oullier, O., Kirman, A. P., & Kelso, J. A. S. (2008). The coordination dynamics of economic decision making: A multilevel approach to social neuroeconomics. *IEEE Transactions on Neural Systems and Rehabilitation Engineering, 16*(6), 557–571. https://doi.org/10.1109/TNSRE.2008.2009960

Padoa-Schioppa, C. (2011). Neurobiology of economic choice: A good-based model. *Annual Review of Neuroscience, 34*(1), 333–359. https://doi.org/10.1146/annurev-neuro-061010-113648

Pareto, V. (1935). *The mind and society—Volume 1—Non-logical conduct*. Harcourt, Brace and Company.

Perlman, M. (2009). Changing the mission of theories of teleology: DOs and DON'Ts for thinking about function. In U. Krohs & P. Kroes (Eds.), *Functions in biological and artificial worlds* (pp. 17–36). The MIT Press. https://doi.org/10.7551/mitpress/7977.003.0006

Perry, C. (1935). Pareto's contribution to social science. *International Journal of Ethics, 46*(1), 96–107.

Petit, O., Basso, F., Merunka, D., Spence, C., Cheok, A. D., & Oullier, O. (2016). Pleasure and the control of food intake: An embodied cognition approach to consumer self-regulation. *Psychology & Marketing, 33*(8), 608–619. https://doi.org/10.1002/mar.20903

Petracca, E. (2020). Two and a half systems: The sensory-motor system in dual-process judgment and decision-making. *Journal of Neuroscience, Psychology, and Economics, 13*(1), 1–18. https://doi.org/10.1037/npe0000113

Petracca, E. (2022). The utility of goods or actions? A neurophilosophical assessment of a recent neuroeconomic controversy. *Economics and Philosophy*, 1–22. https://doi.org/10.1017/S0266267122000189

Pillutla, M. M., & Murnighan, J. K. (1996). Unfairness, anger, and spite: Emotional rejections of ultimatum offers. *Organizational Behavior and Human Decision Processes, 68*(3), 208–224. https://doi.org/10.1006/obhd.1996.0100

Pinch, T., & Swedberg, R. (Eds.). (2008). *Living in a material world: Economic sociology meets science and technology studies*. MIT Press.

Plott, C. R., & Smith, V. L. (Eds.). (2008). 1. Markets. In C. R. Plott & V. L. Smith (Eds.), *Handbook of experimental economics results* (Vol. 1, pp. 3–13). Elsevier. https://doi.org/10.1016/S1574-0722(07)00118-7

Polanyi, K. (1944/2001). *The great transformation: The political and economic origins of our time*. Beacon Press.

Popper, K. R. (1983/2015). *Realism and the aim of science: From the Postscript to the logic of scientific discovery* (W. W. Bartley, Ed.). Routledge.

Prelec, D., & Loewenstein, G. (1998). The red and the black: Mental accounting of savings and debt. *Marketing Science, 17*(1), 4–28. https://doi.org/10.1287/mksc.17.1.4

Puglisi, G., Leonetti, A., Landau, A., Fornia, L., Cerri, G., & Borroni, P. (2017). The role of attention in human motor resonance. *PLoS ONE, 12*(5), e0177457. https://doi.org/10.1371/journal.pone.0177457

Raafat, R. M., Chater, N., & Frith, C. (2009). Herding in humans. *Trends in Cognitive Sciences, 13*(10), 420–428. https://doi.org/10.1016/j.tics.2009.08.002

Raichle, M. E. (2015). The brain's default mode network. *Annual Review of Neuroscience, 38*(1), 433–447. https://doi.org/10.1146/annurev-neuro-071013-014030

Rai, T. S., & Fiske, A. (2010). ODD (observation- and description-deprived) psychological research. *Behavioral and Brain Sciences, 33*(2–3), 106–107. https://doi.org/10.1017/S0140525X10000221

Reimann, M., & Bechara, A. (2010). The somatic marker framework as a neurological theory of decision-making: Review, conceptual comparisons, and future neuroeconomics research. *Journal of Economic Psychology, 31*(5), 767–776. https://doi.org/10.1016/j.joep.2010.03.002

Richins, M. L., & Chaplin, L. N. (2015). Material parenting: How the use of goods in parenting fosters materialism in the next generation. *Journal of Consumer Research, 41*(6), 1333–1357. https://doi.org/10.1086/680087

Robbins, L. (1932). *An essay on the nature and significance of economic science*. Macmillan & Co.

Romer, P. (2016). *The trouble with macroeconomics*. https://paulromer.net/the-trouble-with-macro/

Rosch, E., Mervis, C. B., Gray, W. D., Johnson, D. M., & Boyes-Braem, P. (1976). Basic objects in natural categories. *Cognitive Psychology, 8*(3), 382–439. https://doi.org/10.1016/0010-0285(76)90013-X

Ross, D. (2011). Neuroeconomics and economic methodology. In J. B. Davis (Ed.), *The Elgar companion to recent economic methodology*. Edward Elgar Publishing. https://www.elgaronline.com/display/edcoll/9781848447547/9781848447547.00009.xml

Ross, D. (2014). *Philosophy of economics*. Palgrave Macmillan.

Rossiter, J. R. (2019). A critique of prospect theory and framing with particular reference to consumer decisions. *Journal of Consumer Behaviour, 18*(5), 399–405. https://doi.org/10.1002/cb.1779

Rustichini, A., & Padoa-Schioppa, C. (2015). A neuro-computational model of economic decisions. *Journal of Neurophysiology, 114*(3), 1382–1398. https://doi.org/10.1152/jn.00184.2015

Samuelson, P. (1973). *Economics* (9th Ed.). McGraw-Hill.

Sanfey, A. G., Rilling, J. K., Aronson, J. A., Nystrom, L. E., & Cohen, J. D. (2003). The neural basis of economic decision-making in the ultimatum game. *Science, 300*(5626), 1755–1758. https://doi.org/10.1126/science.1082976

Sapolsky, R. M. (2017). *Behave: The biology of humans at our best and worst*. Penguin.

Scazzieri, R. (2006). A Smithian theory of choice. In *The Adam Smith Review Volume 2* (pp. 21–47). Routledge.

Schelling, T. C. (2006). *Micromotives and macrobehavior*. Norton.

Scherer, F. M. (2000). The emigration of German-speaking economists after 1933. *Journal of Economic Literature, 38*(3), 614–626. https://doi.org/10.1257/jel.38.3.614

Schotanus, P. (2022). Cognitive economics and the Market Mind Hypothesis: Exploring the final frontier of economics. *Economic Affairs, 42*(1), 87–114.

Searle, J. R. (1984). *Minds, brains and science*. Harvard University Press.
Seers, D. (1963). The limitations of the special case. *Bulletin of the Oxford University Institute of Economics & Statistics, 25*(2), 77–98. https://doi.org/10.1111/j.1468-0084.1963.mp25002001.x
Sen, A. (1995). Moral codes and economic success. In C. S. Britten & A. Hamlin (Eds.), *Market capitalism and moral values* (pp. 23–34). Edward Elgar.
Sequoiah-Grayson, S., & Floridi, L. (2022). Semantic conceptions of information. In E. N. Zalta (Ed.), *The Stanford encyclopedia of philosophy* (Spring 2022). Metaphysics Research Lab, Stanford University. https://plato.stanford.edu/archives/spr2022/entries/information-semantic/
Shapiro, L. A. (2004). *The mind incarnate*. MIT Press.
Shiller, R. J. (2019). *Narrative economics: How stories go viral and drive major economic events*. Princeton University Press.
Simon, H. A. (1955). A behavioral model of rational choice. *The Quarterly Journal of Economics, 69*(1), 99–118.
Simon, H. A. (1990). Invariants of human behavior. *Annual Review of Psychology, 41*, 1–19. https://doi.org/10.1146/annurev.ps.41.020190.000245
Singer, T. (2009). Chapter 17—Understanding others: Brain mechanisms of theory of mind and empathy. In P. W. Glimcher, C. F. Camerer, E. Fehr, & R. A. Poldrack (Eds.), *Neuroeconomics* (pp. 251–268). Academic Press. https://doi.org/10.1016/B978-0-12-374176-9.00017-8
Singer, T., Seymour, B., O'Doherty, J., Kaube, H., Dolan, R. J., & Frith, C. D. (2004). Empathy for pain involves the affective but not sensory components of pain. *Science, 303*(5661), 1157–1162. https://doi.org/10.1126/science.1093535
Singer, T., Seymour, B., O'Doherty, J. P., Stephan, K. E., Dolan, R. J., & Frith, C. D. (2006). Empathic neural responses are modulated by the perceived fairness of others. *Nature, 439*(7075), 466–469. https://doi.org/10.1038/nature04271
Singer, T., & Tusche, A. (2014). Chapter 27—Understanding others: Brain mechanisms of theory of mind and empathy. In P. W. Glimcher & E. Fehr (Eds.), *Neuroeconomics* (2nd ed., pp. 513–532). Academic Press. https://doi.org/10.1016/B978-0-12-416008-8.00027-9
Slovic, P., Finucane, M. L., Peters, E., & MacGregor, D. G. (2004). Risk as analysis and risk as feelings: Some thoughts about affect, reason, risk, and rationality. *Risk Analysis, 24*(2), 311–322. https://doi.org/10.1111/j.0272-4332.2004.00433.x
Slovic, P., Finucane, M. L., Peters, E., & MacGregor, D. G. (2007). The affect heuristic. *European Journal of Operational Research, 177*(3), 1333–1352. https://doi.org/10.1016/j.ejor.2005.04.006
Smith, A. (1759/2002). *The theory of moral sentiments*. Cambridge University Press.

Smith, A. (1776/2005). *The Glasgow edition of the works and correspondence of Adam Smith. Volume 2: An inquiry into the nature and causes of the wealth of nations*. Liberty Fund.

Smith, V. L. (1991). *Papers in experimental economics*. Cambridge University Press.

Smith, V. L. (2003). Constructivist and ecological rationality in economics. *American Economic Review, 93*(3), 465–508.

Smith, V. L. (2006). Economics, Experimental methods in. In *Encyclopedia of cognitive science* (pp. 1070–1079). Wiley. https://doi.org/10.1002/0470018860.s00714/abstract

Snowdon, B., Vane, H. R., & Wynarczyk, P. (1994). *A modern guide to macroeconomics: An introduction to competing schools of thought*. E. Elgar Pub.

Spiegler, R. (2011). *Bounded rationality and industrial organization*. Oxford University Press.

Stanovich, K. E. (1999). *Who is rational?: Studies of individual differences in reasoning*. Psychology Press.

Stanovich, K. E., & West, R. F. (2000). Individual differences in reasoning: Implications for the rationality debate? *Behavioral and Brain Sciences, 23*(5), 645–665. https://doi.org/10.1017/S0140525X00003435

Stigler, G. J., & Becker, G. S. (1977). De gustibus non est disputandum. *American Economic Review, 67*(2), 76–90.

Stiglitz, J. E. (2018). Where modern macroeconomics went wrong. *Oxford Review of Economic Policy, 34*(1–2), 70–106. https://doi.org/10.1093/oxrep/grx057

Storper, M., & Venables, A. J. (2004). Buzz: Face-to-face contact and the urban economy. *Journal of Economic Geography, 4*(4), 351–370. https://doi.org/10.1093/jnlecg/lbh027

Strack, F., & Deutsch, R. (2004). Reflective and impulsive determinants of social behavior. *Personality and Social Psychology Review, 8*(3), 220–247. https://doi.org/10.1207/s15327957pspr0803_1

Strassmann, D. (1995). Creating a forum for feminist economic inquiry. *Feminist Economics, 1*(1), 1–5.

Sunstein, C. R. (2023). Hayekian behavioral economics. *Behavioural Public Policy, 7*(1), 170–188. https://doi.org/10.1017/bpp.2021.3

Tabibnia, G., Satpute, A. B., & Lieberman, M. D. (2008). The sunny side of fairness: Preference for fairness activates reward circuitry (and disregarding unfairness activates self-control circuitry). *Psychological Science, 19*(4), 339–347. https://doi.org/10.1111/j.1467-9280.2008.02091.x

Taylor, C. (2007). *A secular age*. Belknap Press of Harvard University Press.

Thaler, R. H. (1985). Mental accounting and consumer choice. *Marketing Science, 4*(3), 199–214.

Thaler, R. H. (1999). Mental accounting matters. *Journal of Behavioral Decision Making, 12*(3), 183–206. https://doi.org/10.1002/(SICI)1099-0771(199909)12:3%3c183::AID-BDM318%3e3.0.CO;2-F

Thaler, R. H. (2016). *Misbehaving: The making of behavioural economics*. W. W. Norton & Company.

Thaler, R. H., & Sunstein, C. R. (2008). *Nudge: Improving decisions about health, wealth, and happiness*. Yale University Press.

Theiner, G. (2014). Varieties of group cognition. In L. Shapiro (Ed.), *The Routledge handbook of embodied cognition* (pp. 347–357). Routledge.

Tsakiris, M., & Preester, H. D. (2018). *The interoceptive mind: From homeostasis to awareness*. Oxford University Press.

Tversky, A., & Kahneman, D. (1973). Availability: A heuristic for judging frequency and probability. *Cognitive Psychology, 5*(2), 207–232. https://doi.org/10.1016/0010-0285(73)90033-9

Tversky, A., & Kahneman, D. (1974). Judgment under uncertainty: Heuristics and biases. *Science, 185*(4157), 1124–1131. https://doi.org/10.1126/science.185.4157.1124

Tversky, A., & Kahneman, D. (1981). The framing of decisions and the psychology of choice. *Science, 211*(4481), 453–458.

Tversky, A., & Kahneman, D. (1983). Extensional versus intuitive reasoning: The conjunction fallacy in probability judgment. *Psychological Review, 90*(4), 293–315. https://doi.org/10.1037/0033-295X.90.4.293

Van Gelder, T. (1995). What might cognition be, if not computation? *The Journal of Philosophy, 92*(7), 345–381. https://doi.org/10.2307/2941061

van't Wout, M., Kahn, R. S., Sanfey, A. G., & Aleman, A. (2006). Affective state and decision-making in the Ultimatum Game. *Experimental Brain Research, 169*(4), 564–568. https://doi.org/10.1007/s00221-006-0346-5

van't Wout, M., Chang, L. J., & Sanfey, A. G. (2010). The influence of emotion regulation on social interactive decision-making. *Emotion, 10*(6), 815–821. https://doi.org/10.1037/a0020069

Varela, F. J., Thompson, E., & Rosch, E. (2016). *The embodied mind, revised edition: Cognitive science and human experience*. MIT Press.

Vining, D. R., & Elwertowski, T. C. (1976). The relationship between relative prices and the general price level. *The American Economic Review, 66*(4), 699–708.

von Weizsäcker, C. (2011). Homo Oeconomicus Adaptivus: Die Logik des Handelns bei veränderlichen Präferenzen. *Preprints of the Max Planck Institute for Research on Collective Goods, 10*, 1–33. http://hdl.handle.net/10419/57517

Watson, J. B. (1913). Psychology as the behaviourist views it. *Psychological Review, 20*(2), 158–177. https://doi.org/10.1037/h0074428

Weber, M. (1922/2019). *Economy and society: A new translation* (K. Tribe, Ed. and trans.). Harvard University Press.

Wiers, R. W., van Gaal, S., & Le Pelley, M. E. (2021). Akrasia and addiction: Neurophilosophy and psychological mechanisms. In *Social neuroeconomics: Mechanistic integration of the neurosciences and the social sciences* (pp. 121–147). Routledge/Taylor & Francis Group.

Wilson, E. O. (1999). *Consilience: The unity of knowledge* (repr). Knopf.

Wren-Lewis, S. (2018). Ending the microfoundations hegemony. *Oxford Review of Economic Policy, 34*(1–2), 55–69. https://doi.org/10.1093/oxrep/grx054

Yang, Q., Wu, X., Zhou, X., Mead, N. L., Vohs, K. D., & Baumeister, R. F. (2013). Diverging effects of clean versus dirty money on attitudes, values, and interpersonal behavior. *Journal of Personality and Social Psychology, 104*(3), 473–489. https://doi.org/10.1037/a0030596

Yechiam, E. (2019). Acceptable losses: The debatable origins of loss aversion. *Psychological Research Psychologische Forschung, 83*(7), 1327–1339. https://doi.org/10.1007/s00426-018-1013-8

Zaki, J., & Ochsner, K. N. (2012). The neuroscience of empathy: Progress, pitfalls and promise. *Nature Neuroscience, 15*(5), 675–680. https://doi.org/10.1038/nn.3085

Zamir, S. (2001). Rationality and emotions in ultimatum bargaining. *Annales D'économie et de Statistique, 61*, 1–31. https://doi.org/10.2307/20076266

Zelizer, V. A. (1989). The social meaning of money: "Special monies." *American Journal of Sociology, 95*(2), 342–377. https://doi.org/10.1086/229272

CHAPTER 3

The Hayek Paradox of Abstraction and Embodiment

3.1 Introduction: Hayek and the Abstract Society, from the Embodied Mind to the Disembodied Market

"No one has characterized market mechanisms better than Friedrich von Hayek" (Simon, 1996, p. 34). Hayek is a very peculiar economist in that his work is celebrated in economics, as illustrated by Simon's quote, but also in psychology (e.g., Steele, 2002) and neuroscience (e.g., Fuster, 2011). At the same time, however, Hayek is almost completely ignored in the current mainstream paradigms of behavioral economics and neuroeconomics, even though he could certainly be recognized as a founding figure of these research programs (e.g., Sunstein, 2023). Tellingly, and importantly for our argument, the situation is different in experimental economics, where Vernon Smith explicitly acknowledges the significance of Hayek's work (Smith, 2003, 2008). Interestingly, this biased reception of a towering figure in economics replicates a similar strange split between the Adam Smith of *The Wealth of Nations* (1776/2005), who theorizes markets, and the Adam Smith of *The Theory of Moral Sentiments* (1759/2002), who theorizes human morality: Hayek can be seen in continuity with the former Adam Smith, while the latter Adam Smith has been widely ignored in mainstream economics (Cockfield et al., 2007). We will argue that such strange patterns in the disciplinary history of economics reflect the strong role of ideology in shaping its course.

F. Basso and C. Herrmann-Pillath, *Embodiment, Political Economy and Human Flourishing*, https://doi.org/10.1007/978-3-031-54971-7_3

Hayek was awarded the Nobel Prize for his work on the theory of money and economic fluctuations and for his analysis of the interdependence of economic, social, and institutional phenomena. Although there are several analogies between his approach to the mind and his approach to the market (e.g., Pasquinelli, 2021), the purpose of this chapter is not to develop a comprehensive analysis of Hayek's work in psychology and economics, as such an endeavor would require an entire book (e.g., Basso & Oullier, 2010). Rather, the purpose of this chapter is to highlight a paradoxical position in his thought that will further demonstrate the need for embodied economics (Oullier & Basso, 2010). As aforementioned, this paradoxical position is reflected in different contemporary receptions, where Hayek's approach to markets is applauded but his psychology is largely forgotten (e.g., Bowles et al., 2017). Indeed, although Hayek was well aware of the importance of bodily states at the cognitive level, he categorically refused to recognize the influence of embodiment in economic life. His main argument for rejecting any bodily influence pertains to the abstractness of the market, which emerges as an undesigned order from the decisions and actions of many individuals (Hayek, 1982/2013) and can be read as operating as an "algorithm" that processes information and distributes cognition to each of them (Bowles et al., 2017). In his opinion, for markets to function properly and benefit everyone, any influence of embodiment, for example, in the form of emotion or anthropomorphism, should then be refrained from, as it fosters expectations of social justice that are incompatible with the market order—epitomized in his crusade against socialism (Hayek, 1988). As we can see, positive and normative analyses merge at this point, as embodiment is seen as a fact of life, but one that should be suppressed for markets to function properly. Clearly, this view is close to the views of behavioral economists that we discussed in the previous chapter, namely, measuring real behavior in terms of standards of rationality established at an abstract level, such as the mathematics of probability, and concluding that the flaws and deficits of human beings must be corrected by appropriate interventions.

This chapter shows that the abstractness of the market order is unbearable if it lacks embodiment. In other words, we argue that markets require embodiment if they are abstract, and even more so if they are supposed to distribute cognition. In the following, we first develop some of Hayek's key concepts in psychology and economics, and detail how he arrived at these conclusions, before demonstrating that his position is theoretically and empirically untenable within his own theoretical edifice. More specifically, we show that Hayek the economist, who promotes a disembodied approach to the market order because of its abstraction, contradicts Hayek the psychologist, who developed a radically embodied view of the brain in which abstraction as a cognitive process must be embodied. We argue that Hayek's disembodied view of the market is motivated by his ideological rejection of social justice, and we compare this paradox with the psychologist and economist Herbert Simon, who consistently employs a disembodied approach to cognition throughout his work. In doing so, we will point out that the resolution of the "Hayek paradox" requires recognizing that markets, despite their abstraction, are not disembodied, but, on the contrary, are grounded in and bounded by embodiment. This conclusion paves the way for the embodied economics we develop in the subsequent chapters.

3.2 From Theoretical Psychology to Economic Theory

Hayek had a longstanding interest in psychology. In the preface to *The Sensory Order*, his book on theoretical psychology, he explained that "it is the outcome of an idea which suggested itself to [him] as a very young man when [he] was still uncertain whether to become an economist or a psychologist" (Hayek, 1952, p. 5). In this book, his main thesis is that the mind is "an instrument of classification" (Hayek, 1952, §3.1ff) that underlies associative processes ranging from sensory perception to abstract thought (Hayek, 1952, §3.69). This classification operates through a system of neural connections that "is acquired in the course of the development of the species and the individual by a kind of 'experience' or 'learning'" (Hayek, 1952, §2.49). The classification results in a "mental order," which is posited as fundamentally distinct from the physical order in the sense that events in both orders are of a different kind (Hayek, 1952, §1.11). He emphasizes that this is not a distinction between "appearances" and the "real" world: Rather, Hayek adopts a monistic perspective on the world, of which the brain is part and parcel, connected to the external environment by causal chains mediated by neurons—for the sake of argument he deliberately simplifies here (Hayek, 1952, §3.15). At the same time, however, he champions a non-reductionist approach to psychology (Hayek, 1952, §8.46ff). Although brain and mind are one in the sense of ontological monism, it is impossible for an external observer to reconstruct the internal processes of the brain using scientific methods, as far as the meanings of these processes are concerned. This means that "mind" and psychology, as an autonomous endeavor to understand the mind, remain irreducible scientific notions, even in relation to neuroscience (Hayek, 1952, §8.83ff). The reason is that Hayek grounds subjectivity in materialistic terms: Although the brain and the world are causally connected, the world only manifests itself in the brain in the form of neuronal impulses. This implies that the brain constructs the world in a process of autopoiesis, to use an expression coined later independently of Hayek's work. Hayek's radical subjectivism has been programmatically explored in Austrian economics, where the significance of *The Sensory Order* is increasingly recognized (Butos & McQuade, 2015; Iorio, 2010), and is also supported by principled approaches to the brain-world relationship in modern neuroscience (Friston, 2010).

The ultimate reason for Hayek's seemingly paradoxical stance towards ontological monism and subjectivism is his epistemological impossibility theorem, which identifies a Gödelian contradiction (van den Hauwe, 2011): Neuroscience can never fully explain the brain and its function in generating behavior because this would entail a complete metamodel of brain-world interactions (Hayek, 1952, §8.66ff). Hayek argues that this would require the brain—also as a medium of scientific thinking—to build an internal model of greater complexity than itself, which is logically impossible. This is highly relevant for thinking about concepts such as "knowledge" which have been deflated in conventional economics into quantitative measures of "information." There is no metaphysical standpoint from which we could possibly compare the world as manifested in physical causal chains and the world "in the mind." As we shall see, in principle, this makes his view incompatible with current approaches to information in economics. This broader epistemological perspective distinguishes Hayek's approach from modern connectionism in the neurosciences, to which it is otherwise very close (Rust, 2011). He developed a theory that is aligned with connectionism, according to which mental phenomena can be described in terms of interconnected neural networks: "The connexions between the physiological elements are thus the primary phenomenon which creates the mental phenomena" (Hayek, 1952, §2.50). His theory echoes Hebb's (1949) *The Organization of Behavior*, published as he was finishing *The Sensory Order* (Hayek, 1952, p. viii). According to Hebb's connectionist model, "neurons that fire together, wire together," a physiological mechanism that supports associative learning (e.g., it feels colder when it's windier).

Today, Hayek's book continues to be highlighted by some researchers as an early contribution that prefigured some of the future developments in neuroscience. For instance, in his article on network memory, Fuster indicates that Hayek "seems to have been the first to postulate (…) the idea of memory and perception represented in widely distributed networks of interconnected cortical cells. Subsequently, this idea has received theoretical support, however tangential, from the fields of cognitive psychology, connectionism, and artificial intelligence. Empirically, it is well supported by the physiological study and neuroimaging of working memory" (Fuster, 1997, p. 451). He adds, that for Hayek,

> a net or 'map' of cortical neurons representing in its connectional structure the associations (that) make up the essence of any perception and memory. Remarkably, he intuited this concept before anyone knew, as we now do, of the breadth and wealth of corticocortical connectivity in the primate. Furthermore, according to Hayek, that system of connections somehow recorded (by synaptic weights?) 'the relative frequency with which in the history of the organism the different groups of internal and external stimuli have acted together.' To a similar distributed construct, Edelman and Mountcastle later added the architecture of its associated nodes – neuronal groups or modules – and the role of re-entry (feedback) in the association of stimuli not exactly coinciding in time. (Fuster, 1997, p. 452; see also, Fuster & Bressler, 2012)

Along the same lines, Gerald Edelman, Nobel laureate in Medicine, in an address to the American Academy of Arts and Sciences, stated:

> I must say that I have been deeply gratified by reading a book [Hayek's *The Sensory Order*] of which I had not been aware when I wrote my little essay on group selection theory (…) I was deeply impressed (…) I recommend this book to your attention, as an exercise in profound thinking by a man who simply considers knowledge for its own sake. (Edelman, 1982, p. 24)

Hayek anticipated certain key tenets of connectionism that still delineate principled differences between various approaches in philosophy of mind, psychology, and brain science (Buckner & Garson, 2019), and that are pillars of modern approaches to embodied cognition, such as in the context of memory research (Sutton & Williamson, 2014). They are also in tension with certain views widely held in neuroeconomics. For example, connectionism rejects the notion of dedicated and stable functional specialization of the brain, which underlies many brain-scanning methods in neuroeconomics that aim to identify specific loci in the brain, such as for encoding subjective value (Ballesta et al., 2022). On a more abstract level, connectionism implies that functions are always realized in complex hierarchical structures of neural networks, which, theoretically, could even encompass the entire brain and allow multiple realizations by different network substructures (Hayek, 1952, §7.3ff). Indeed, this view has been vindicated by the shift in neuroscientific research from the functional assignment of brain areas to the identification of functional networks that are not exclusively confined to specific areas, but connect several of them, such as the default mode network related to the concept of self (Raichle, 2015). To some extent, Hayek (1952, §7.4ff) also anticipated that this implies functional flexibility of brain structure, such that similar functions can be realized by different structural arrangements that evolve adaptively and flexibly, for instance (but not only) after localized damage. This perspective echoes research on the "plastic structural and functional organization of the central nervous system" that can be found in neural reuse models (Raja & Anderson, 2019, p. 173), and is currently particularly emphasized in embodied and ecological approaches to neuroscience (see also Anderson, 2010, 2014). Another important implication of connectionism is that there is a universal principle of dynamic structural contextualization: Elementary phenomena such as groups of neurons firing together cannot be ascribed to regularly occurring effects independent of larger network contexts that are constantly reshuffled in brain activity. In other words, as Hayek (1952, §1.37, 2.49) already noted, a principle of holism applies to brain activity, in which top-down and bottom-up causation always interplay. One consequence of this is that there is no principled distinction of kind between elementary processes or "data" and higher-level abstract "concepts" (Hayek, 1952, §5.19, 6.33), a position maintained in modern views of grounded cognition (e.g., Barsalou, 2008).

Although Hebb, Fuster, and Edelman focused their contributions more on the physiological details of their theories, Hayek's writings also illustrated the implications of his approach for the social sciences and economic life. Indeed, his work in theoretical psychology inspired his subsequent developments in social science and economic theory (Hayek, 1982/2013, p. 524, note 6; Pasquinelli, 2021). We want to elaborate on these implications here because, to our knowledge, Hayek's theorization is one of the first in the social sciences to articulate psychological principles so deeply alongside economic reasoning. According to his theory, the mind is: (1) An apparatus of classification, the functioning of which is the result of (2) pre-sensory experiences (phylogenetic development), (3) and current experiences (ontogenetic development). From these three principles, inherited from Hayek's theoretical approach to the mind, we can derive three main general implications for the social sciences: Respectively, knowledge is (1) imperfect, (2) shared, and (3) situated, subjective, and embodied. These main articulations are presented in Table 3.1.

When rationality is considered bounded in economics, the argument is usually framed in terms of limited information and limited cognitive ability (Simon, 1955), or cognitive biases (Tversky & Kahneman, 1974). Hayek proposed an alternative explanation to this perspective. In his view, knowledge is fundamentally "imperfect" (Hayek, 1952, §2.7), because perception is categorization, and thus perception is interpretation of the environment:

> If sensory perception must be regarded as an act of classification, what we perceive can never be unique properties of individual objects but always only properties which the objects have in common with other objects. Perception is thus always an interpretation, the placing of something into one or several classes of objects. (Hayek, 1952, §6.36)

This differs from other views, especially in mainstream behavioral economics, because Hayek's approach implies denying any possibility of

Table 3.1 Principles of theoretical psychology and their general implications for the social sciences in Hayek's approach

Principles from theoretical psychology	*General implications for social sciences*
According to Hayek, the brain/mind is 1. an apparatus of classification, the functioning of which is the result of	• Knowledge is "imperfect"
2. pre-sensory experiences (phylogenetic development)	• Knowledge is shared, and can be shared, among individuals
3. and current experiences (ontogenetic development)	• Knowledge is embodied and situated

overcoming such imperfectness: It results merely from principled qualitative differences between the physical order and the sensory order. Consistently, Hayek (1952, §1.11) argues that there is no independent benchmark of "reality" by which to judge the status of single events in the two orders. This principle is consequential at the epistemological level: If perception is interpretation, then psychology is different from physics. Psychology pertains to the mental order, which is part of and an interpretation of (i.e., different from) the physical order. In other words, for instance:

> Consider the two lines in the Wundt-Hering illusion (…) This rather banal exercise serves to demonstrate that there is only a rough correspondence between what has been called the sensory order (Hayek, 1952) and the physical order. Furthermore it bears upon point (…) that the perceptual world is a world of adaptation rather than a world of complete veridicality. (Edelman, 1987, p. 24)

From Hayek's point of view, there is a "very imperfect correspondence" between the mental order and the physical order (Hayek, 1952, §1.48–1.49), and, therefore, we will never be able to find a correspondence between "particular physical events" and "a particular mental event" (Hayek, 1952, §8.98). As we will see later, this point is essential because it means that knowledge is not only imperfect, but also abstract.

In light of the fundamental epistemological issues discussed above, we emphasize the difference between Hayek's position on the mind-world distinction and the information-theoretic approach in economics. Hayek does not conceive of a quantitative gap in terms of incomplete and, therefore, imperfect information, but a fundamental qualitative difference, in this sense akin to the perennial philosophical debate about "qualia" (Tye, 2021). The mental order differs in principle from the physical order, but they are causally connected. So, there is coordination, but not correspondence in the sense of correspondence theories of truth. How can we explain that the brain still guides successful behavior in the world? Hayek's answer is the same as in recent neuroscientific approaches (e.g., Damasio, 2019), namely by referring to organismic homeostasis as an internal indicator of adequate coordination between mind and world (Hayek, 1952, §4.11ff). This means that there is no external criterion for judging whether there is a representational fit between mind and world, but an internal criterion for adaptive fit. This implies that the epistemic modus of the working brain is evolutionary, as envisioned in evolutionary epistemology and neuroscientific variants such as Edelman's (1987) "Neural Darwinism:" The brain is conceived as a complex system that continuously, and at high speed, generates conjectures about possible actions and possible consequences, and these action trajectories are eventually actualized following the gradients of internal valuations of homeostasis.

Furthermore, according to Hayek, knowledge is shared and can be communicated with others, because humans share a similar classification system due to evolutionary processes:

> it would, of course, not be possible to discuss the phenomenal world with other people if they did not perceive this world in terms of the same, or at least of a very similar, order of qualities as we do. This means that the conscious mind of other people classifies stimuli in a manner similar to that in which our own mind does so, and that the different sensory qualities are for them related to each other in a manner which is similar to that which we know. (Hayek, 1952, §1.69)

Put simply, knowledge, however imperfect, can be communicated because a similar classification system, inherited from evolution, is shared among humans. Nonetheless, similarity in terms of classification systems does not equate to identity (Hayek, 1952, §5.28). Importantly, there is no identity between people's minds because their knowledge is situated in the environment and new classes are formed with new subjective experiences (Hayek, 1952, §8.15). New experiences (can) lead to reclassifications (Hayek, 1952, §8.34) and learning (Hayek, 1952, §8.15–8.16), which introduce variability between people, such as differences in expertise. It follows that there is similarity but not identity between people's classification systems, and thus that knowledge is also subjective. More importantly, and we will illustrate this argument further as it is key to the argument developed in this book, knowledge is embodied. Hayek's writings on theoretical psychology illustrate the importance of embodiment in several ways.

First of all, he conceptualizes the role of sensory-motor processes at the cognitive level. For instance, he considers that motor responses are important "at all the various levels of the hierarchy of the central nervous system" (Hayek, 1952, §7.56). One of the main conclusions of his argument, fully in line with modern embodiment theories discussed in the next chapter (e.g., Barsalou, 2008; Wilson, 2002), is that there is no "sharp distinction between the direct sensory perception of qualities and the more abstract processes of thought" (Hayek, 1952, §5.19). Rather, Hayek posits that there is continuity between perception and cognition because

> the operations of both the senses and the intellect are equally based on acts of classification (or reclassification) performed by the central nervous system, and that they are both part of the same continuous process by which the microcosm in the brain progressively approximates to a reproduction of the macrocosm of the external world. (Hayek, 1952, §5.19)

Consistently, abstract concepts are "formed by a rearrangement of the objects of the sensory world" (Hayek, 1952, §6.46). A key process is proprioception, the reflective mapping of elementary sensory-motor structures onto higher levels of the neural network (Hayek, 1952, §4.37). The importance of embodiment is also conveyed by Hayek's consideration of the pervasiveness of valence in perception, which ultimately relates to the notions of homeostasis and purposive behavior in the satisfaction of certain needs (Hayek, 1952, §4.63, §5.68ff): "The emotional values attaching to various sensory qualities are well known, and there are indeed few sensory qualities which we do not regard at least as either pleasant or unpleasant, or as simply good or bad" (Hayek, 1952, §1.65). Likewise, when it comes to social interactions with others, he highlights the important role that another type of disposition, namely emotions, play in perception and action:

> Fear and anger, sorrow and joy, are attitudes towards the environment, and particularly towards fellow members of the same species, which may become attached to, and then regularly evoked by, a great many different classes of stimuli. This means that a great variety of external events, and also some conditions of the organism itself, may evoke one of several patterns of attitudes or dispositions which, while they last, will affect or 'colour' the perception of, and the responses to, any external event. (Hayek, 1952, §4.64–4.65)

Put differently, emotions are dispositions that shape perception and action. Finally, Hayek's observations on personification enshrine the pre-eminent role of embodiment in the perception, interpretation, and understanding of the world:

> Our tendency to personify (to interpret in anthropomorphic or animistic terms) the events we observe is probably the result of such applications of schemata which our own bodily movements provide. It is they which make, though not yet intelligible, at least perceivable (comprehensible or meaningful) complexes of events which without such perceptual schemata would have no coherence or character as wholes. (Hayek, 1967, p. 52)

This point is crucial because it shows that Hayek believed that embodiment contributes to making sense of the world, here through personification and especially anthropomorphism.

In conclusion, we would like to highlight the significance of Hayek's views by showing how they remain in tension with some recent neuroeconomic approaches that aim to justify the subjective utility model of choice, and converge with alternative evolutionary approaches, as has been salient in Edelman's (1982) praise of Hayek's contribution (Herrmann-Pillath, 2021). The key point is that the neuroscientific reconstruction of subjective utility imposes a specific structure on the process of action generation that contradicts the Hayekian principles outlined so far. First, there is the hypothesis of a strict localization of valuation in certain brain areas, even down to the level of single neurons (Ballesta et al., 2022). Second, some neuroeconomists assume a strict separation between the stages of valuation, choice, and action, and any feedback from action to valuation seems to be strictly excluded (Padoa-Schioppa, 2011). Third, subjective utility is assumed to be calculated at the moment of action, which requires simultaneous processing and integration of all relevant information in the preparation of the action. Some alternative views can be considered distinctly Hayekian (McDowell, 2019). They emphasize the role of learned neural structures in anticipatory action preparation and introduce the idea of internal selection of competing action plans in stored repertoires of schemes. This implies continuous and simultaneous action valuation, preparation, and execution, and thus continuous sensory-motor feedback (Hunt & Hayden, 2017). In such approaches, memory and attention are essential building blocks that dramatically reduce the computational demands of the standard economic model of choice. They generate a subject-centered stance towards the world, which is not a set of "goods" but of affordances, that is, perceived opportunities for action oriented towards organismic goals. Overall, there seems to be a direct line from Hayek to these alternative views.

3.3 From Economic Principles to Knowledge Division in the Abstract Society

In light of our previous developments, it can be said that Hayek considers knowledge of the world as "imperfect," situated, embodied, and communicable. Specifying how Hayek conceived of knowledge matters greatly because theoretical assumptions about knowledge shape economic analysis (Hayek, 1937). According to him, the core problem to be investigated in economics boils down to the question of knowledge:

> In short I shall contend that the empirical element in economic theory – the only part which is concerned, not merely with implications but with causes and effects, and which leads therefore to conclusions which, at any rate in principle, are capable of verification – consists of propositions about the acquisition of knowledge. (Hayek, 1937, p. 33)

He adds:

> The essential point here is that it is these apparently subsidiary hypotheses or assumptions that people do learn from experience, and about how they acquire knowledge, which constitute the empirical content of our propositions about what happens in the real world. They usually appear disguised and incomplete as a description of the type of market to which our proposition refers; but this is only one, though perhaps the most important, aspect of the more general problem of how knowledge is acquired and communicated. (Hayek, 1937, p. 45)

The implications of Hayek's propositions about knowledge are radical for economic studies, and they are directly tied to the three main implications for economics that we have previously drawn from his theoretical principles in psychology. More specifically, following Hayek, knowledge is "imperfect" in the sense that it is qualitatively different from the physical world, and there is no external standpoint from which to construct a representational correspondence. This means, as will be developed below, that (1) the perfect/complete knowledge hypothesis usually posited in standard economics should be rejected as a benchmark for any kind of judgment about "incompleteness of information." Moreover, because knowledge is (and can be) shared, subjective, and situated, (2) the function of the price system should be reconsidered as distributing cognition among the economic agents. Last, because knowledge is embodied, (3)

Table 3.2 From general implications for the social sciences to specific implications for economics in Hayek's approach

General implications for social sciences	*Specific implications for economics*
Knowledge is "imperfect."	• Reject the perfect/complete knowledge hypothesis
Knowledge is shared, and can be shared, among individuals	• Reconsider the price system as distributing cognition
Knowledge is embodied and situated	• Follow the rules of the market

the rules of the market should be followed. As we will argue later, we take issue with this last point. These main articulations are presented in Table 3.2.

We begin with the first assumption about knowledge in economics. As discussed in Chapter 2 with Simon's (1955) definition of *Homo economicus*, basic versions of the standard model assume that economic agents have complete knowledge of their environment: "the whole economic system must be assumed to be one perfect market in which everybody knows everything" (Hayek, 1937, pp. 44–45). This view has been challenged by the economics of information and behavioral economics, although, as discussed in the previous chapter, it remains a theoretical frame of reference for assessing "imperfections," "anomalies," "cognitive biases," and the like. Hayek's position is fundamentally different, because even this frame of reference must be rejected: If knowledge as a mental order is qualitatively different from the physical order, there is no room for a *Homo economicus* who is supposed to perceive the world as it really is (see also Simon, 1986). Indeed, if the assumption that economic agents have perfect knowledge of their environment is abandoned, it should be accepted that knowledge cannot be centralized by a "single controlling mind" (Hayek, 1945, p. 525). Tellingly, the famous "debate" over the possibility of socialist calculation revealed that general equilibrium theorists would necessarily envisage central planning as a viable alternative to markets, provided that all information could be concentrated in a powerful computer (e.g., Hayek, 1948). For Hayek, knowledge is subjective and situated, because it exists "solely as the dispersed bits of incomplete and frequently contradictory knowledge which all the separate individuals possess" (Hayek, 1945, p. 519). Knowledge is radically individualized to the extent that it can no longer be compared across individuals.

But knowledge can be communicated, in the sense that it is shared, and it can be shared, among individuals. This perspective on knowledge allows economics to rethink the price system. This means moving from a model in which all information is supposed to be centralized by each individual—or by one individual (e.g., the Walrasian auctioneer) in the case of central planning—who, as rational agents, would have the same set of information, to a model in which relevant but qualitatively different knowledge is decentralized through individuals (Hayek, 1937, p. 49). Indeed, if knowledge is divided between economic agents, it should be able to be shared through the price system which is at the heart of the market order: "we must look at the price system as such a mechanism for communicating information if we want to understand its real function" (Hayek, 1945, p. 526). The price system thus has a cognitive function in the Hayekian approach: It is a way to communicate and share the different items of knowledge that each economic agent possesses, and as such it provides a solution for dealing with their imperfect knowledge. The price system distributes cognition, that is, knowledge, among economic agents. Ultimately, this means that the price system would make it possible to approach the position of an external knowing entity, thus overcoming even the paradoxes of individual epistemics. This epistemological shift has been called "Hayek's transformation" (Caldwell, 1988): In addition to the "labor division," described by Smith (1776/2005), Hayek became aware that the key issue in economics—and more broadly in the social sciences—should be the "knowledge division" (Hayek, 1937, p. 49), rather than its centralization. This transformation takes a distinct shape in the exclusive focus on prices as a means of coordinating decisions and actions: It is essential to recognize that this does not mean that the content of individual knowledge is shared, since prices are not at all about the representation of that knowledge. Prices emerge from interactions driven by that knowledge, but these interactions transcend it because no individual can possibly know the pattern of these interactions.

This perspective has radical implications for economics, as it reframes the problem of the entire discipline: The economic problem of society becomes the "problem of the utilization of knowledge not given to anyone in its totality" (Hayek, 1945, p. 520). But Hayek's transformation also had very important implications for the boundaries of knowledge.

His position anticipated the idea that knowledge does not reside in the head of each individual (e.g., Bateson, 1972; Clark & Chalmers, 1998; Hutchins, 1995), as is still commonly posited today in behavioral (though not in experimental) and neuroeconomics (e.g., Glimcher & Fehr, 2014; Kahneman, 2012). Instead, knowledge is distributed through the price system. This entails that a rational decision does not begin with a series of calculations, but by following the rules of the market and the information provided by the price system: "it is the discipline of the market which forces us to calculate, that is, to be responsible for the means we use up in the pursuit of our ends" (Hayek, 1982/2013, p. 500). On this basis, Hayek posited that economic agents should neither consider the causes of their decisions (beyond price changes) nor the consequences of their decisions for other agents in the market. Since they take prices only as parameters for determining their own actions, they do not need to care at all about how the individual states of others relate to these prices. In Hayek's view, thanks to the market and its price system, most economic agents do not need to know the causes of what is happening in the market in order to make a decision. One of the most famous illustrations of this argument is the following:

> Assume that somewhere in the world a new opportunity for the use of some raw material, say tin, has arisen, or that one of the sources of supply of tin has been eliminated. It does not matter for our purpose – and it is very significant that it does not matter – which of these two causes has made tin more scarce. All that the users of tin need to know is that some of the tin they used to consume is now more profitably employed elsewhere, and that in consequence they must economize tin. There is no need for the great majority of them even to know where the more urgent need has arisen, or in favor of what other needs they ought to husband the supply. If only some of them know directly of the new demand, and switch resources over to it, and if the people who are aware of the new gap thus created in turn fill it from still other sources, the effect will rapidly spread throughout the whole economic system and influence not only all the uses of tin, but also those of its substitutes and the substitutes of these substitutes, the supply of all the things made of tin, and their substitutes, and so on; and all this without the great majority of those instrumental in bringing about these substitutions knowing anything at all about the original cause of these changes. (Hayek, 1945, p. 526)

The conclusion of this quote is particularly relevant to our argument: The price system provides the information that is relevant for economic agents to make a decision and take action (e.g., to economize tin), regardless of the causes of price changes. Moreover, according to Hayek, economic agents should not only make a decision while ignoring the *causes* of price changes, they should also not aim to know the *consequences* of their actions in the market.[1] Indeed, in characterizing the "Great Society," as an "economic order" (Hayek, 1982/2013, p. 479) that celebrates the spontaneous order of the market (Hayek, 1982/2013, p. 109) and the "capitalist" system as its *modus operandi* (Hayek, 1982/2013, p. 294), Hayek indicates that:

> In the Great Society we all in fact contribute not only to the satisfaction of needs of which we do not know, but sometimes even to the achievement of ends of which we would disapprove if we knew about them. We cannot help this because we do not know for what purposes the goods or services which we supply to others will be used by them. That we assist in the realization of other people's aims without sharing them or even knowing them, and solely in order to achieve our own aims, is the source of strength of the Great Society. (Hayek, 1982/2013, pp. 269–270)

Against this background, the only thing that economic agents should care about, since this is neither the causes nor the consequences of their actions, is to "follow (their) own interest(s)" (Hayek, 1945, p. 529) to make their "anonymous contribution" (Hayek, 1982/2013, p. 479) within the rules of the market, namely property, tort, and contract law (Hayek, 1982/2013, p. 269). Then, in line with his interpretation of the Scottish Enlightenment, as exemplified by Adam Smith, he concludes that: "the essential utility of the price system consists in inducing the individual, while seeking his own interest, to do what is in the general interest" (Hayek, 1945, p. 529). Overall, the Great Society is an "abstract society:" "a society in which no longer the known needs of known people but only abstract rules and impersonal signals guide action towards strangers" (Hayek, 1982/2013, p. 494). In other words, in the Great Society, people are guided only by abstract rules, such as the aforementioned law of property, tort, and contract, and impersonal signals, such as prices, to satisfy their own interests without having to pay attention to the consequences of their decisions. As we shall see, this last point led Hayek to categorically deny the role of embodiment in the market order:

To follow the abstract rules of the market and the impersonal signals of its price system, is to deny the embodied and situated underpinnings of cognition.

3.4 From the Abstract Society to the Unbearable Abstractness of the Market Order

According to Hayek, economic agents should accept that they have left "the small 'face-to-face-society', in which every member knows every other" in favor of the Great Society where "the knowledge which its members will have in common will be abstract features of things or actions" (Hayek, 1982/2013, p. 179). Basically, this means that economic agents must abandon any kind of anthropomorphism when it comes to understanding the market, for two main reasons. First, in his opinion, such a way of thinking would lead to constructivism (Hayek, 1982/2013, p. 189), that is, a form of constructivist rationality (Smith, 2008), which is based on central planning and thus assumes complete knowledge of the causes and consequences of people's actions—which is impossible due to their imperfect knowledge. Therefore, economic agents should stop thinking that economic and social processes can be conceptualized in the same way as a person acting consciously. This would mean mistakenly applying a form of psychology, which aims to explain conscious action, to an emerging ("spontaneous") order that has not been designed (Hayek, 1955). This is why, in his view, it is non-sensical to expect the market to be "just." Indeed, recall that the price system is supposed to allow economic agents to make decisions while ignoring the *causes* of price changes and the *consequences* of their actions in the market. Therefore, there is no room for a social justice argument that questions the *intentions* and *implications* of economic actions:

> the impersonal process of the market allocates command over goods and services to particular people: this can be neither just nor unjust, because the results are not intended or foreseen, and depend on a multitude of circumstances not known in their totality to anybody. The conduct of the individuals in that process may well be just or unjust; but since their wholly just actions will have consequences for others which were neither intended nor foreseen, these effects do not thereby become just or unjust. (Hayek, 1982/2013, p. 234)

This position brings us to our second point. In his view, anthropomorphism is one of the very mechanisms that nurture a drive for "social justice" or "solidarity," which is incompatible with the market—understood as spontaneous order. Hayek's rejection of social justice, in the name of anthropomorphism, and thus his rejection of the importance of bodily states in interpreting market processes, was further justified by their association with a form of "primitive" or "tribal" thinking:

> As primitive thinking usually does when first noticing some regular processes, the results of the spontaneous ordering of the market were interpreted as if some thinking being deliberately directed them, or as if the particular benefits or harm different persons derived from them were determined by deliberate acts of will, and could therefore be guided by moral rules. This conception of 'social' justice is thus a direct consequence of that anthropomorphism or personification by which naive thinking tries to account for all self-ordering processes. It is a sign of the immaturity of our minds. (Hayek, 1982/2013, p. 227)

He adds:

> A Great Society has nothing to do with, and is in fact irreconcilable with 'solidarity' in the true sense of unitedness in the pursuit of known common goals. If we all occasionally feel that it is a good thing to have a common purpose with our fellows, and enjoy a sense of elation when we can act as members of a group aiming at common ends, this is an instinct which we have inherited from tribal society (…). (Hayek, 1982/2013, p. 227)

Overall, economic agents must accept that they have left the so-called "tribal" society to live in the so-called "Great Society," which requires them to adopt certain rules, such as the rules of the market (property, tort, and contract law), and to follow impersonal signals, such as prices, in order to overcome their imperfect knowledge, tame their innate instincts, and ensure that everyone can pursue their own interests.

The rejection of anthropomorphism conveys a larger rejection of the role of embodiment, as exemplified by sensory perception and emotion, in the Great Society. In fact, Hayek considers the Great Society, and especially the market order associated with it, to be an impersonal and anonymous process that escapes sensory perception and implies a disregard for emotions. In terms of sensory perception, the Great Society is considered abstract because

> orders as that of the market do not obtrude themselves on our senses but have to be traced by our intellect. We cannot see, or otherwise intuitively perceive, this order of meaningful actions, but are only able mentally to reconstruct it by tracing the relations that exist between the elements. (Hayek, 1982/2013, p. 37)

This abstractness is contrasted with more concrete orders, whose "existence as distinct wholes can be perceived intuitively by the senses,"[2] whereas the "abstract spontaneous order of social structures usually can only be reconstructed by the mind" (Hayek, 1982/2013, p. 50). When it comes to emotions, the Great Society, as an abstract society,

> unfortunately cannot be based on such feelings as love which constituted the highest virtue in the small group. Love is a sentiment which only the concrete evokes, and the Great Society has become possible through the individual's efforts being guided not by the aim of helping particular other persons, but the confinement of the pursuit of their purposes by abstract rules. (Hayek, 1982/2013, p. 307)

If emotions, such as love, are not what founded the Great Society, then following emotions is also seen as detrimental to it and a threat to the market order: "It is not enough to recognize that 'social justice' is an empty phrase without determinable content. It has become a powerful incantation which serves to support deep-seated emotions that are threatening to destroy the Great Society" (Hayek, 1982/2013, p. 292).

In light of these points, the market order that underpins the Great Society, according to Hayek, is an abstract, impersonal, and anonymous process that is "disembodied" because its functioning escapes sensory perception, and requires a rejection of the influence of emotions and the role of anthropomorphism to make sense of it. These positions reveal a paradox in Hayek's thinking: Although he developed an entire psychological theory pointing to an embodiment of the mind, he then "disembodied" the economic agents in the market in the name of the abstraction of the so-called "Great Society," and in order to reject any consideration of social justice. At this stage of the argument, we would like to draw the reader's attention to the fact that we are fully aware that Hayek separated psychology and economics as disciplines. Indeed, he believed that the social sciences, including economics, were different from psychology in that they focused on explaining the undesigned results of the decisions and actions of many individuals. Thus, in his opinion, the social sciences do not aim to explain conscious action:

> this, if it can be done at all, is a different task, the task of psychology. (…) If social phenomena showed no order except in so far as they were consciously designed, there would indeed be no room for theoretical sciences of society and there would be, as is often argued, only problems of psychology. It is only in so far as some sort of order arises as a result of individual action but without being designed by any individual that a problem is raised which demands a theoretical explanation. (Hayek, 1955, p. 39)

Economics as a discipline is then charged with dealing with a spontaneous order that emerges as a by-product of everyone's decisions and actions in the market (e.g., Hudík, 2011).

Our main argument here, however, is not disciplinary: We do not intend to challenge his position on the difference in nature between explanations in psychology and in economics. Our argument is as follows: Hayek's recognition of the important role of embodiment in thinking, whether in the form of sensory perception, emotion, or anthropomorphism, contradicts his rejection of the same embodiment in thinking when it comes to conceptualizing the Great Society. The rejection of all forms of embodiment is generally justified by Hayek's idea that these are expressions of "primitive" thinking tied to concrete social life in the (so-called) "tribal" society, which cannot be applied to the abstract economic order of the Great Society. However, there is no reason to believe that because something is supposed to be "abstract," it must be separated from bodily influences—that is, "disembodied." For instance, considering the mind as a system of classification, and thus perception as an act of interpretation, is precisely what, according to Hayek, entails that knowledge of the environment, starting with sensory perception, is "abstract" because "it always selects certain features or aspects of a given situation" (Hayek, 1952, §6.39). In other words, Hayek questioned the very idea of a difference between concrete immediate experience and abstract concepts, considering such a distinction "misleading," because sensory perception is first and foremost an act of classification (Hayek, 1952, §6.35), which means that it is also an abstraction of the physical world. If something as embodied as sensory perception, such as seeing, hearing, touching, smelling, or tasting, is considered "abstract," then we argue that there is no reason to conceptually separate embodiment and abstraction, even when it comes to the perception of the social (rather than the physical) world.

In contrast to Hayek, we argue that it is precisely because an economic order is (supposedly) more abstract, that it requires embodiment. Indeed, if, as Hayek suggests, the Great Society is “an order of society which became increasingly incomprehensible” to economic agents (Hayek, 1982/2013, p. 496), in part because it is not perceivable (Hayek, 1982/2013, p. 37), and must be “reconstructed by the mind” (Hayek, 1982/2013, p. 50), then such a “reconstruction” must involve some form of embodiment. As Hayek himself explained in relation to personification, “our own bodily movements” provide “the schemata” that make “at least perceivable (comprehensible or meaningful) complexes of events which without such perceptual schemata would have no coherence or character as wholes” (Hayek, 1967, p. 52). This point is essential because, as noted above, it shows that Hayek believed that embodiment contributes to meaning, here through personification, and especially anthropomorphism. Actually, we would be curious to know how the “abstract spontaneous order of social structures” that make up the Great Society could “be reconstructed by the mind” (Hayek, 1982/2013, p. 50) without some form of embodiment. The Smithian “invisible hand” (Hayek, 1982/2013, p. 303) and the “social mind” (Hayek, 1937, p. 52) that inspired the Great Society, as well as Hayek’s mere use of the word “reconstructed,” are metaphorical expressions that rely on the associative mechanisms that underlie the functioning of the mind (Hayek, 1952; Hebb, 1949, Lakoff & Johnson, 1999). For instance, the expression “reconstructed by the mind” (Hayek, 1982/2013, p. 50) illustrates the building metaphor, which reflects the use of a concrete and embodied experience, the experience of buildings, to make sense of something more abstract, an idea (Lakoff & Johnson, 1980, 1999). As we will see in Chapter 7, by employing a conceptual metaphor such as IDEAS ARE BUILDINGS, Hayek relies on a psychological mechanism of the same nature as anthropomorphism. As an ontological metaphor, anthropomorphism is also a conceptual metaphor (Lakoff & Johnson, 1980), and it is based on a fundamental principle: Abstract thought is largely metaphorical and thus grounded in our embodied experience (Lakoff & Johnson, 1999). If the Great Society and its associated market order are incomprehensible to economic agents because of their abstractness, it is not surprising that in order to become comprehensible they must be made concrete, as (embodied) metaphors do, so that their meaning can be grasped. In a nutshell, the abstractness of the Great Society cannot escape the embodied mind (showcased in *The Sensory Order*), despite Hayek's wishes.

3.5 From the Abstractness of the Market Order to Disembodied Economic Rationality

So far, we have argued that Hayek the economist did not fully embrace the embodiment of the mind as elaborated in *The Sensory Order*, and instead excluded any role for embodiment in the comprehension of market processes because of his rejection of any form of social justice. But it seems that beyond his normative position against social justice, Hayek's approach may also have been motivated, at least in part, by the fact that his own theory of the price mechanism in the market order ended up contradicting his theory of the sensory order. The market as an information processor does not fit well with his embodied approach to the mind. Mirowski and Nik-Kah diagnose this neatly:

> Strangely for a doctrine that started out so concerned about respect for the inviolate individual and his or her subjectivity, the late Hayek rendered his system internally coherent by admitting that some knowledge did not really persist at the level of the individual mind, for the most part, but was processed and invested with meaning at the supra-personal level. In a catch-phrase, since so much that people actually knew was inaccessible to them, the only entity that really was capable of judging and validating human knowledge was The Market." (Mirowski & Nik-Khah, 2017, pp. 69–70)

Once the metaphor of the market algorithm is adopted, the embodied and situated aspects of knowledge become irrelevant, when they are not simply conceptualized by Hayek as a threat to the market under the idea of social justice.

Not surprisingly, then, some of Hayek's views resonate with the tradition of experimental markets research that grew out of the work of Herbert Simon, one of the main protagonists of modern computer science, and whose work inspired Vernon Smith (Davis, 2011; Dekker & Remic, 2019). Smith mentions Hayek's notion of "The Market" when referring to computational models of experimental markets which show that even zero-intelligence agents can discover the pathways to optimization and equilibrium (Smith, 2008, pp. 64–65). Modern commentators on Hayek's *The Sensory Order* have argued that this reasoning can be grounded in the notion of situated knowledge that has been championed by both Hayek and Simon (Frantz, 2013; Marsh, 2013). However, we do not take the step of suggesting that the market as a system is therefore a more powerful processor of information than humans: Situated knowledge does not imply that the "situation" itself has its own information processing capacities. In fact, we argue that the computer metaphor of the market is actually more in line with the computer metaphor of the mind than with an embodiment approach to cognition and knowledge. The computer metaphor of the mind makes two main claims, which are aptly summarized by Niedenthal and colleagues (2005).[3] As we shall see, the first claim contradicts Hayek's view of the mind, whereas the second *seems* to characterize Hayek's views of the market as an information-processing system. We contend that the problem with these two claims is that they lead to a disembodied view of economic rationality. This argument can be supported by analyzing the fallacies of disembodiment in Simon's approach to rationality. In other words, Simon's approach is internally consistent in its use of the computer metaphor for both the brain and the market. This exposes the internal contradiction in Hayek's thinking about how individual knowledge and the market are related.

The first claim of the computer metaphor of the mind is that cognition can be described as the ability to store and manipulate abstract and arbitrary symbols detached from perception and action, and that human and artificial (computer) intelligence can be approached under the same conceptual umbrella, namely physical symbol systems theory (Newell & Simon, 1976; Simon, 1990). In this model,[4] humans are viewed as "mere machines" that process information (Simon, 1990, p. 4): Information received about the environment (perception) is internally processed in terms of (arbitrary) symbols (thinking) before action (motor activity) is taken (Vera & Simon, 1993, p. 10).[5] In neuroeconomics, for example, which is still dominated by the computer metaphor (You, 2022), some authors argue that the economic choice between goods is computationally removed from sensory and motor representations (Serra, 2021, p. 50), leading to a disembodied view of economic rationality. In this perspective, "goods" are first valued on the basis of an abstract representation, and then their values are recalculated in light of the actions that people must take to acquire them (e.g., Kable & Glimcher, 2009; Rangel &

Hare, 2010).[6] These computer-metaphor-based architectures would be called "amodal" because they are not grounded in sensory-motor systems (Barsalou, 1999), but are abstracted from them by separating perception, cognition, and action.[7] In light of our previous developments, such a separation is at odds with Hayek's theory in *The Sensory Order*, according to which, as quoted earlier, there is no "sharp distinction between the direct sensory perception of qualities and the more abstract processes of thought" (Hayek, 1952, §5.19).

Consistent with the idea of "multiple realizability" discussed in Chapter 2, the second claim is that "physical instantiations," whether made of flesh and blood like humans or, say, silicon, plastic, and metal like computers, could theoretically possess human intelligence if they are complex enough (e.g., Newell & Simon, 1976; Simon, 1990). This point seems to fit well with Hayek's conceptualization of the price system in the market. Indeed, "Hayek's transformation" could be read as being based on a fundamental idea whereby "'the market' is posited to be an information processor more powerful than any human brain, but essentially patterned on brain/computation metaphors" (Hayek cited in Mirowski, 2009, p. 435). From this perspective, the market can indeed be seen as an algorithm that processes information (Bowles et al., 2017), and functions as the metaphor for the "social mind" (Hayek, 1937, p. 52), that is, a mind abstracted from a physical human body. Again, however, this position seems to be ideologically rather than epistemologically motivated.[8] As Mirowski points out,

> Hayek himself almost never treated knowledge as a 'thing,' but instead rather as tacit, local, and embodied (…). However, in order to render this proposition coherent with a number of other tenets later developed in the neoliberal thought collective, many subsequent neoliberals found it convenient to recast knowledge as more resembling a thing-like commodity, if only to have it resonate more closely with developments in the natural sciences and economics. (Mirowski, 2009, p. 447)

This can be further illustrated by subsequent developments in economics with a wide range of disembodied analyses of institutions (Mirowski, 2001; Mirowski & Nik-Khah, 2017). We will develop this argument further in Chapters 6 and 7, but to illustrate this point, it is sufficient to recall the famous results from experimental economics showing that replacing human participants with computer programs that submit random bids and offers—the so-called "zero-intelligence agents"—under a budget constraint, so that they cannot sell below their costs or buy above their values in a double-auction setup, leads to the allocative efficiency of these auctions (Gode & Sunder, 1993). The conclusion is quite clear: "Allocative efficiency of a double auction derives largely from its structure, independent of traders' motivation, intelligence, or learning," which means that market institutions, which are supposed to embody Adam Smith's invisible hand, can generate rationality from human "rationality" and "irrationality" (Gode & Sunder, 1993, p. 119; see also, Becker, 1962). In other words, economic rationality lies in market institutions and can be detached (abstracted) from human beings (hence disembodied): Zero-intelligence agents are merely "brainless programs" (Mirowski & Nik-Khah, 2017, p. 122). This led to the rather classic conclusion in experimental and institutional economics that "market institutions may be society's way of dealing with human cognitive limitations" (Sunder, 2004, p. 514).[9] The problem with this view is that, in order to claim that there are "human cognitive limitations," one should assume that it is possible to know what it is to be "limited" as compared to an "unlimited" view. This issue can be illustrated by the implications of the computer metaphor of the mind that Simon's approach to bounded rationality presents. As we shall see, contrary to the classical reading of Simon, bounded rationality is a disembodied view of rationality, since it requires decoupling the organism from its environment and positing a perfect/complete knowledge hypothesis, which according to Hayek is impossible.

Let us develop Simon's argument to illustrate this point. Building on the physical symbol systems theory, bounded rationality aims to replace the rationality of *Homo economicus* with a behavioral theory of rational choice (Simon, 1979, p. 476). This is particularly relevant in situations of uncertainty about the environment, where it seems necessary to move away from neoclassical models of "substantive" rationality, which focus only on the *result* of economic decision-making and its *maximization*, and embrace models of "procedural" rationality, which focus on the computational *processes* underpinning economic decision-making and its *satisficing* (Simon, 1978).[10] In Simon's view, both the environment and the limited computational capabilities of economic agents are essential to the definition of bounded rationality (Simon, 1986). They form the two blades of the "scissors" that shape human rational behavior (Simon, 1990, p. 7). However, according to Simon, "rationality is bounded when it falls short of omniscience. And the failures of omniscience are largely failures of knowing all the alternatives, uncertainty about relevant exogenous events, and inability to calculate consequences" (Simon, 1979, p. 502). In essence, this definition of bounded rationality remains mostly "negative" (Foss, 2003), since what is bounded is what is not omniscient.

Simon attempted to overcome this negative definition of bounded rationality by detailing the search and satisficing procedures that constitute "procedural" rationality (Simon, 1979, 1990). Nevertheless, this definition has important implications, since it means that for rationality to be considered "bounded," one should assume the ability to compare the organism-specific bounded perception of the environment with its perception by the "all-seeing eye" of an omniscient observer who is not subject to the peculiarities of a given organism. This is very clearly conveyed by Simon when he assumes that the "real environment" is what is seen by an omniscient observer, whereas economic agents perceive only a subset of their environment, which is one of the main reasons why they are boundedly rational.[11] In other words, in bounded rationality, the standards of rationality are set in relation to a perception of the environment that is independent of the organism, since the "real" environment is perceived by an omniscient observer (e.g., God or *Homo economicus*).[12] In this respect, bounded rationality is consistent with the use of the computer metaphor of the mind whereby the reality of the environment is given to, and independent of, the organism (e.g., Varela et al., 2016), and the nature of the organism is not relevant to the definition of substantive rationality (Felin et al., 2017). Rather, the nature of the organism, to the extent that it constrains its perceptual and computational abilities, is of interest in explaining why human behavior differs from that of *Homo economicus*, an omniscient observer who is assumed to be able to see the "real" (economic) environment.

Likewise, this position is reflected in Kahneman's research program on heuristics and biases,[13] which is also permeated by an "all-seeing view" of perception (Felin et al., 2017). In this respect, Kahneman's (2003) "maps of bounded rationality" express the adoption of a "disembodied" view of perception and cognition to conceptualize rationality in economics, acknowledging, as mentioned in Chapter 2, that "the rational-agent model was (his) starting point and the main source of (his) null hypotheses" (Kahneman, 2003, p. 1449). Through *Homo economicus*, the standard model remains the reference for defining rationality, and any form of behavior that does not conform to this model is literally considered an "anomaly" (Kahneman, 2003, p. 1469). The (so-called) "cognitive biases" are merely deviations from what would be expected of a decision maker if an agent, like *Homo economicus*, were omniscient and could perceive and know every item of information necessary to maximize utility and arrive at the optimal solution. Again, rationality is defined in a disembodied way: It is conceptualized in terms of a standard that is distinct from the peculiarities of a given organism evolving in a specific environment. For rationality to be considered *bounded*, there would have to be a form of rationality that is *unbounded*, which is not organism-specific, and one might ask which organism is endowed with such an unbounded rationality. In many respects, it seems that the economist, as a Walrasian "model-builder" (De Vroey, 2003), or as a behavioral scientist who nudges people (Katsikopoulos, 2020), can be seen as one of the figures of the omniscient observer (Felin & Felin, 2020), which is an "intellectual trap" (Ostrom, 1990, p. 215) and a form of "pretence of knowledge" criticized by Hayek (1989). Put differently, and more generally, as Mirowski and Nik-Kah point out, economists seem to be the ones who can actually enjoy the benefits of unbounded rationality:

> 'Why must an economics of knowledge end up propounding a doctrine that economic agents should be ignorant?' The tenacious reader will notice that we have been working our way toward a twofold answer. First, the imperative to design person–machine systems necessitated that agents be conceived as relatively stupid, at least when it came to economic rationality, and economists as sufficiently smart enough to understand how to orchestrate the amalgam of persons, machines, and markets into a knowledge producing whole. In their models, when agents are folded into person–machine systems, then the market-designing economist alone is granted the god's-eye knowledge to understand and shape the operation of the market – otherwise, the designer has no role to play. (Mirowski & Nik-Khah, 2017, p. 240)

Against this background, we argue that the two main claims of the computer metaphor of the mind, namely the separation of perception, action, and cognition, and the abstraction of cognition from the physical body, lead to a disembodied view of (bounded) rationality that requires the decoupling of the organism from its environment. In this process, the economic agent is ultimately disembodied and ignorant, whereas the economist is endowed with perfect knowledge of the economic environment, despite Hayek's disdain for any technocratic intervention in economic life.

3.6 Conclusion

Since the mid-twentieth century, the computer metaphor has traditionally dominated standard models in cognitive science (Niedenthal et al., 2005) and economics (Mirowski & Nik-Khah, 2017). As argued in this chapter, this approach is at odds with the embodiment of cognition in general, knowledge in particular, and rationality in economics that can be derived from a close reading of *The Sensory Order*. Nevertheless, Hayek favored a computer-based view of the market as a spontaneous order which requires disembodiment. By showing the implications of the computer metaphor of the mind as developed by Simon, we further exposed the internal contradiction between Hayek as a theorist of the "sensory order" and Hayek as a theorist of the "market order."

In subsequent chapters, we will develop embodied economics in great detail, starting with the literature on embodied cognition as an alternative to Simon's computer metaphor of the mind in Chapter 4. For now, we present only one key argument for why Hayek the economist must have relied on Hayek the psychologist to complete his own model, and thus ultimately to "re-embody" the market, which suffers a process of disembodiment through abstraction. This is straightforward since prices are nothing more than causal effects on the brain, just like any other kind of effect produced by a given stimulus. Therefore, how prices are further "processed" in generating action must be analyzed by Hayek the psychologist. What does this mean? We gave the answer in the previous chapter: First, prices carry no information at all unless they are interpreted by individuals, and second, prices must be set, so pricing is an action. This means that, contrary to Hayek the economist, prices cannot become independent of embodied and situated factors, and transform themselves into abstract media of dispersed knowledge.

Let us take the example of tin in the earlier quotation from Hayek (1945, p. 526). In responding to changing prices of tin, it is essential to develop ideas about the causes, for example, whether they are temporary or permanent, or whether they are related to market imbalances of technological change. In addition, producers and traders of tin need to monitor market trends and must decide whether to follow the trend or act against it when setting their prices individually. In other words, although prices are parameters that influence individual decisions, they are always translated into the embodied and situated knowledge of individuals. Moreover, reducing markets to communication through prices seems to be a highly distorted picture of real economic life: Since prices require interpretation, economic agents always rely on and eagerly consume all kinds of additional information that they can obtain through business media, personal networks, or active contextualization, such as monitoring political events. Without embedding price data in such rich contexts, it is simply meaningless.

Of course, it is also necessary to make a clear distinction between positive and normative analysis, which is unfortunately inextricably mixed up in Hayek's work, especially in his latest books. Hayek's analysis of the price mechanism is a positive analysis in the first place, and we have pointed out that the price mechanism does not really work that way and does not really fulfill the function of closing the knowledge gap between individuals in the Great Society. These points must be distinguished from the normative question of whether such a system is desirable from the point of view of individuals if we accept the Hayekian stance that only individual judgments of welfare count. Will a Hayekian individual agree to live in a world of Hayekian markets? Our response to this question is "no," because we think that the principles of embodiment expounded early in Hayek's psychology remain essential to the workings of markets in the real world, and that they must be essential if we are to maintain that markets contribute to the common good.

Overall, it seems that if Hayek aimed to "disembody" the market order, it was first and foremost because of his *visceral* (and thus, paradoxically, embodied) rejection of the concept of social justice, which he conceived as a form of "immaturity" (sic) of our minds (Hayek, 1982/2013, p. 227). He was certainly right to point out that social justice is tied to emotions, which implies that it is associated with the embodiment of economic agents. As discussed in Chapter 2, studies in experimental and neuroeconomics have shown the fundamental role of emotions, and thus embodiment, in the expression of fairness and social preferences. Ironically, what Hayek showed in his writings, despite his great efforts to exclude various forms of embodiment from the market order, is that *the market is grounded in and bounded by embodiment*. The market is grounded in bodily processes, because if the status of knowledge is so central to economics, and if knowledge is embodied, then, as we shall see, embodiment is essential to the proper functioning of the market order. The market is also bounded by bodily processes because feelings and emotions, as well as several other embodiment mechanisms that we will discuss later, limit the extent to which market processes can be abstracted from concrete reality, that is, real-world economic life. We are not arguing that the (so-called) "market order" is not more abstract, or less concrete, or in some way engaged in a process of disembodiment, compared to the other forms of sociality that make up society as a whole. Rather, we argue that it is precisely because the market is more abstract, or less concrete, or engaged in a process of disembodiment, that economics should take stock of embodiment: As the embodied cognition literature, which challenges Simon's computer metaphor of the mind, argues, the concrete is much needed to make sense of what is abstract and seems disembodied. The abstractness of markets is unbearable unless it is grounded in and bounded by embodiment. We will develop these arguments in the rest of the book.

Notes

1. This is one of the main reasons why Hayek's approach is radically different from utilitarianism (Vallier, 2022; Vergara, 1992).
2. In modern parlance, what Hayek conveys is that what is abstract has a lower level of perceptual strength (Borghi, 2022; Borghi et al., 2017).
3. Note that we do not follow the order suggested by Niedenthal and colleagues, as their first claim will be the second in our argument, and vice versa: "The first is that the software of the mind is independent of the hardware of the body and the brain (Block, 1995; Dennett, 1969). Thus, cognitive operations are arbitrarily related to their physical instantiations so that any sufficiently complex physical system could have human intelligence. In principle, the software that constitutes the mind (including the 'social mind') could run on anything—neurons, silicon, or even wooden gears—as long as the elements were arranged in proper functional relations. The second claim of the computer metaphor is that high-level cognition, such as inference, categorization, and memory, is performed using abstract, amodal symbols that bear arbitrary relations to the perceptual states that produce them (Newell & Simon, 1972; Pylyshyn, 1984)" (Niedenthal et al., 2005, p. 185).

4. This characterizes the "classical sandwich" model (Hurley, 1998).
5. Of course, this is not only Simon's view; it is implied by the computer metaphor. See, for instance, Brette (2022), Cisek (1999), Lakoff and Johnson (1999), and van Gelder (1998).
6. The alleged abstractness associated with the valuation process remains controversial (see Glimcher, 2014; Padoa-Schioppa & Conen, 2017; Platt & Plassmann, 2014).
7. From an embodiment point of view, as we will see in the next chapter, the representation of an object (or economic good), even with symbols such as words or pictures, cannot be purely abstract or arbitrary: Being presented with such symbols, or even imagining a particular good, should be associated with increased activity in sensory-motor areas (e.g., Barsalou, 1999; Niedenthal et al., 2005).
8. Mirowski and Nik-Khah note that Hayek's (1945) article on the use of knowledge in society is an intellectual landmark in neoliberalism: "Here we witness the birth of the First Commandment of neoliberalism. Markets don't exist to allocate given physical resources, so much as they serve to integrate and disseminate something called knowledge" (Mirowski and Nik-Khah, 2017, p. 63). Consistently, Prusik (2018, p. 1602) argues that "the neoliberal attempt to determine the economy as an epistemological subject—with a concept of 'information' as its key commodity definition—is the fetish form of market relations in their abstraction from society." See also Pasquinelli (2021) for an excellent discussion of the ideological neoliberal underpinnings of Hayek's connectionism.
9. As we will see in Chapter 7, cognitive limitations, under the guise of bounded rationality, also justify the existence of hierarchical institutions (i.e., organizations) in the marketplace whose purpose is to provide rationality through procedures such as the division of labor (Simon, 1991, 2000; Williamson, 1975, 1985).
10. Simon (1986, p. 224) identified several steps that characterize decision-making as a process, namely, "the focus of attention, the problem representation, and the processes used to identify alternatives, estimate consequences, and choose among possibilities" that take place in a given context. See also Artinger and colleagues (2022).

11. "In complex situations there is likely to be a considerable gap between the real environment of a decision (the world as God or some other omniscient observer sees it) and the environment as the actors perceive it" (Simon, 1978, p. 8). Likewise, he states that: If "we accept the proposition that both the knowledge and the computational power of the decision maker are severely limited, then we must distinguish between the real world and the actor's perception of it and reasoning about it" (Simon, 1986, p. 211).
12. The implicit or explicit reference to God is not isolated in economics. For Adam Smith, for example, the "invisible hand" is a religious metaphor, it is the invisible hand of God (e.g., see Lawson, 2013; Sahlins et al., 1996). On Hayek's faith in the workings of the market, see Whyte (2019).
13. We recognize that there are significant differences between Simon's "old" and Kahneman's "new" behavioral economics, but both are inspired by the computer metaphor of the mind as an information-processing device (Sent, 2004).

References

Anderson, M. L. (2010). Neural reuse: A fundamental organizational principle of the brain. *Behavioral and Brain Sciences, 33*(04), 245–266. https://doi.org/10.1017/S0140525X10000853

Anderson, M. L. (2014). After phrenology: Neural reuse and the interactive brain. *MIT Press*. https://doi.org/10.7551/mitpress/10111.001.0001

Artinger, F. M., Gigerenzer, G., & Jacobs, P. (2022). Satisficing: Integrating two traditions. *Journal of Economic Literature, 60*(2), 598–635. https://doi.org/10.1257/jel.20201396

Ballesta, S., Shi, W., & Padoa-Schioppa, C. (2022). Orbitofrontal cortex contributes to the comparison of values underlying economic choices. *Nature Communications, 13*(1), 4405. https://doi.org/10.1038/s41467-022-32199-y

Barsalou, L. W. (1999). Perceptual symbol systems. *Behavioral and Brain Sciences, 22*(04), 577–660. https://doi.org/10.1017/S0140525X99002149

Barsalou, L. W. (2008). Grounded cognition. *Annual Review of Psychology, 59*, 617–645. https://doi.org/10.1146/annurev.psych.59.103006.093639

Basso, F., & Oullier, O. (2010). *Le corps et les prix. Esquisse d'une théorie sensorielle de la valeur*. Unpublished manuscript.

Bateson, G. (1972). *Steps to an ecology of mind: Collected essays in anthropology, psychiatry, evolution, and epistemology*. Balentine Books.
Becker, G. S. (1962). Irrational behavior and economic theory. *Journal of Political Economy, 70*(1), 1–13. https://doi.org/10.1086/258584
Block, N. (1995). The mind as the software of the brain. In E. E. Smith & D. N. Osherson (Eds.), *Thinking* (pp. 377–425). MIT Press.
Borghi, A. M. (2022). Concepts for which we need others more: The case of abstract concepts. *Current Directions in Psychological Science, 31*(3), 238–246. https://doi.org/10.1177/09637214221079625
Borghi, A. M., Binkofski, F., Castelfranchi, C., Cimatti, F., Scorolli, C., & Tummolini, L. (2017). The challenge of abstract concepts. *Psychological Bulletin, 143*(3), 263–292. https://doi.org/10.1037/bul0000089
Bowles, S., Kirman, A., & Sethi, R. (2017). Retrospectives: Friedrich Hayek and the market algorithm. *Journal of Economic Perspectives, 31*(3), 215–230. https://doi.org/10.1257/jep.31.3.215
Brette, R. (2022). Brains as computers: Metaphor, analogy, theory or fact? *Frontiers in Ecology and Evolution, 10*, 878729. https://doi.org/10.3389/fevo.2022.878729
Buckner, C., & Garson, J. (2019, Fall). Connectionism. In E. N. Zalta (Ed.), *The Stanford encyclopedia of philosophy*. Metaphysics Research Lab, Stanford University. https://plato.stanford.edu/archives/fall2019/entries/connectionism/
Butos, W. N., & McQuade, T. J. (2015). The Sensory Order, neuroeconomics, and Austrian economics. In C. J. Coyne & P. Boettke (Eds.), *The Oxford handbook of Austrian economics* (pp. 611–640). Oxford University Press. https://doi.org/10.1093/oxfordhb/9780199811762.013.28
Caldwell, B. J. (1988). Hayek's transformation. *History of Political Economy, 20*(4), 513–541. https://doi.org/10.1215/00182702-20-4-513
Cisek, P. (1999). Beyond the computer metaphor: Behaviour as interaction. *Journal of Consciousness Studies, 6*(11–12), 125–142.
Clark, A., & Chalmers, D. (1998). The extended mind. *Analysis, 58*(1), 7–19.
Cockfield, G., Firth, A., & Laurent, J. (Eds.). (2007). *New perspectives on Adam Smith's The theory of moral sentiments*. Edward Elgar.
Damasio, A. R. (2019). *The strange order of things: Life, feeling, and the making of cultures*. Vintage Books.
Davis, J. B. (2011). *Individuals and identity in economics*. Cambridge University Press.
De Vroey, M. (2003). Perfect information à la Walras versus perfect information à la Marshall. *Journal of Economic Methodology, 10*(4), 465–492. https://doi.org/10.1080/1350178032000130466

Dekker, E., & Remic, B. (2019). Two types of ecological rationality: Or how to best combine psychology and economics. *Journal of Economic Methodology, 26*(4), 291–306. https://doi.org/10.1080/1350178X.2018.1560486
Dennett, D. C. (1969). *Content and consciousness*. Humanities Press.
Edelman, G. M. (1982). Through a computer darkly: Group selection and higher brain function. *Bulletin of the American Academy of Arts and Sciences, 36*(1), 20–49. https://doi.org/10.2307/3823913
Edelman, G. M. (1987). Neural Darwinism: The theory of neuronal group selection. Basic Books.
Felin, T., & Felin, M. (2020). Seeking rationality: $500 bills and perceptual obviousness. In R. Viale (Ed.), *Routledge handbook of bounded rationality* (1st ed., pp. 103–119). Routledge. https://doi.org/10.4324/9781315658353-6
Felin, T., Koenderink, J., & Krueger, J. I. (2017). Rationality, perception, and the all-seeing eye. *Psychonomic Bulletin & Review, 24*(4), 1040–1059. https://doi.org/10.3758/s13423-016-1198-z
Foss, N. J. (2003). Bounded rationality in the economics of organization: "Much cited and little used." *Journal of Economic Psychology, 24*(2), 245–264. https://doi.org/10.1016/S0167-4870(02)00206-4
Frantz, R. (2013). Frederick Hayek's behavioral economics in historical context. In R. Frantz & R. Leeson (Eds.), *Hayek and behavioral economics* (pp. 1–34). Palgrave Macmillan. https://doi.org/10.1057/9781137278159_1
Friston, K. (2010). The free-energy principle: A unified brain theory? *Nature Reviews Neuroscience, 11*(2), 127–138. https://doi.org/10.1038/nrn2787
Fuster, J. M. (1997). Network memory. *Trends in Neurosciences, 20*(10), 451–459. https://doi.org/10.1016/S0166-2236(97)01128-4
Fuster, J. M. (2011). Hayek in today's cognitive neuroscience. In L. Marsh (Ed.), *Advances in Austrian economics* (pp. 3–11). Emerald Group Publishing Limited. https://doi.org/10.1108/S1529-2134(2011)0000015006
Fuster, J. M., & Bressler, S. L. (2012). Cognit activation: A mechanism enabling temporal integration in working memory. *Trends in Cognitive Sciences, 16*(4), 207–218. https://doi.org/10.1016/j.tics.2012.03.005
Glimcher, P. W. (2014). Chapter 20—Value-based decision making. In P. W. Glimcher & E. Fehr (Eds.), *Neuroeconomics* (2nd ed., pp. 373–391). Academic Press. https://doi.org/10.1016/B978-0-12-416008-8.00020-6
Glimcher, P. W., & Fehr, E. (Eds.). (2014). *Neuroeconomics: Decision making and the brain* (2nd ed.). Academic Press.
Gode, D. K., & Sunder, S. (1993). Allocative efficiency of markets with zero-intelligence traders: Market as a partial substitute for individual rationality. *Journal of Political Economy, 101*(1), 119–137. https://doi.org/10.1086/261868
Hayek, F. A. (1937). Economics and knowledge. *Economica, 4*(13), 33–54.

Hayek, F. A. (1945). The use of knowledge in society. *American Economic Review, 35*(4), 519–530.
Hayek, F. A. (1948). *Individualism and economic order*. University of Chicago Press.
Hayek, F. A. (1952). *The sensory order: An inquiry into the foundations of theoretical psychology*. University of Chicago Press.
Hayek, F. A. (1955). *The counter-revolution of science: Studies on the abuse of reason*. The Free Press.
Hayek, F. A. (1967). *Studies in philosophy, politics and economics* (1st ed.). Routledge.
Hayek, F. A. (1988). *The fatal conceit: The errors of socialism*. Routledge.
Hayek, F. A. (1989). The pretence of knowledge. *American Economic Review, 79*(6), 3–7.
Hayek, F. A. (1982/2013). *Law, legislation and liberty: A new statement of the liberal principles of justice and political economy* (New ed.). Routledge.
Hebb, D. O. (1949). *The organization of behavior: A neuropsychological theory*. Wiley.
Herrmann-Pillath, C. (2021). Evolutionary mechanisms of choice: Hayekian perspectives on neurophilosophical foundations of neuroeconomics. *Economics and Philosophy, 37*(2), 284–303. https://doi.org/10.1017/S0266267120000371
Hudík, M. (2011). Why economics is not a science of behaviour. *Journal of Economic Methodology, 18*(2), 147–162. https://doi.org/10.1080/1350178X.2011.575949
Hunt, L. T., & Hayden, B. Y. (2017). A distributed, hierarchical and recurrent framework for reward-based choice. *Nature Reviews Neuroscience, 18*(3), 172–182. https://doi.org/10.1038/nrn.2017.7
Hurley, S. L. (1998). *Consciousness in action*. Harvard University Press.
Hutchins, E. (1995). *Cognition in the Wild*. MIT Press.
Iorio, F. (2010). The Sensory Order and the neurophysiological basis of methodological individualism. In W. T. Butos (Ed.), *The social science of Hayek's "The Sensory Order" (Advances in Austrian Economics)* (Vol. 13, pp. 179–209).
Kable, J. W., & Glimcher, P. W. (2009). The neurobiology of decision: Consensus and controversy. *Neuron, 63*(6), 733–745.
Kahneman, D. (2003). Maps of bounded rationality: Psychology for behavioral economics. *American Economic Review, 93*(5), 1449–1475.
Kahneman, D. (2012). *Thinking, fast and slow*. Penguin Books.
Katsikopoulos, K. V. (2020). Bounded rationality. The two cultures. In R. Viale (Ed.), *Routledge handbook of bounded rationality* (1st ed., pp. 90–102). Routledge. https://doi.org/10.4324/9781315658353-5
Lakoff, G., & Johnson, M. (1980). *Metaphors we live by*. University of Chicago Press.

Lakoff, G., & Johnson, M. (1999). *Philosophy in the flesh: The embodied mind and Its challenge to Western thought*. Basic Books.
Lawson, T. (2013). What is this "school" called neoclassical economics? *Cambridge Journal of Economics, 37*(5), 947–983.
Marsh, L. (2013). Mindscapes and landscapes: Hayek and Simon on cognitive extension. In R. Frantz & R. Leeson (Eds.), *Hayek and behavioral economics* (pp. 197–220). Palgrave Macmillan. https://doi.org/10.1057/9781137278159_9
McDowell, J. J. (2019). On the current status of the evolutionary theory of behavior dynamics: Status of the evolutionary theory. *Journal of the Experimental Analysis of Behavior, 111*(1), 130–145. https://doi.org/10.1002/jeab.495
Mirowski, P. (2001). *Machine dreams: Economics becomes a cyborg science*. Cambridge University Press. https://doi.org/10.1017/CBO9780511613364
Mirowski, P. (2009). Postface: Defining neoliberalism. In P. Mirowski & D. Plehwe (Eds.), *The road from Mont Pèlerin* (pp. 417–456). Harvard University Press. https://doi.org/10.4159/9780674054264-013
Mirowski, P., & Nik-Khah, E. M. (2017). *The knowledge we have lost in information: The history of information in modern economics*. Oxford University Press.
Newell, A., & Simon, H. A. (1972). *Human problem solving*. Prentice Hall.
Newell, A., & Simon, H. A. (1976). Computer science as empirical inquiry: Symbols and search. *Communications of the ACM, 19*(3), 113–126.
Niedenthal, P. M., Barsalou, L. W., Winkielman, P., Krauth-Gruber, S., & Ric, F. (2005). Embodiment in attitudes, social perception, and emotion. *Personality and Social Psychology Review, 9*(3), 184–211. https://doi.org/10.1207/s15327957pspr0903_1
Ostrom, E. (1990). *Governing the commons: The evolution of institutions for collective action*. Cambridge University Press.
Oullier, O., & Basso, F. (2010). Embodied economics: How bodily information shapes the social coordination dynamics of decision-making. *Philosophical Transactions of the Royal Society of London. Series B, Biological Sciences, 365*(1538), 291–301. https://doi.org/10.1098/rstb.2009.0168
Padoa-Schioppa, C. (2011). Neurobiology of economic choice: A good-based model. *Annual Review of Neuroscience, 34*(1), 333–359. https://doi.org/10.1146/annurev-neuro-061010-113648
Padoa-Schioppa, C., & Conen, K. E. (2017). Orbitofrontal cortex: A neural circuit for economic decisions. *Neuron, 96*(4), 736–754.
Pasquinelli, M. (2021). How to make a class: Hayek's neoliberalism and the origins of connectionism. *Qui Parle, 30*(1), 159–184. https://doi.org/ doi https://doi.org/10.1215/10418385-8955836

Platt, M. L., & Plassmann, H. (2014). Multistage valuation signals and common neural currencies. In P. W. Glimcher & E. Fehr (Eds.), *Neuroeconomics* (Chapter 13, 2nd ed., pp. 237–258). Academic Press. https://doi.org/10.1016/B978-0-12-416008-8.00013-9

Pylyshyn, Z. W. (1984). *Computation and cognition: Toward a foundation for cognitive science*. MIT Press.

Prusik, C. (2018). Neoliberalism: Critical theory as natural-history. In B. Best, W. Bonefeld, & C. O'Kane (Eds.), *The SAGE handbook of Frankfurt school critical theory* (pp. 1601–1614). Sage. https://doi.org/10.4135/9781526436122.n97

Raichle, M. E. (2015). The brain's default mode network. *Annual Review of Neuroscience, 38*(1), 433–447. https://doi.org/10.1146/annurev-neuro-071013-014030

Raja, V., & Anderson, M. L. (2019). Radical embodied cognitive neuroscience. *Ecological Psychology, 31*(3), 166–181. https://doi.org/10.1080/10407413.2019.1615213

Rangel, A., & Hare, T. (2010). Neural computations associated with goal-directed choice. *Current Opinion in Neurobiology, 20*, 262–270.

Rust, J. (2011). Hayek, connectionism, and scientific naturalism. In L. Marsh (Ed.), *Hayek in mind: Hayek's philosophical psychology (Advances in Austrian Economics)* (Vol. 15, pp. 29–50).

Sahlins, M., Bargatzky, T., Bird-David, N., Clammer, J., Hamel, J., Maegawa, K., & Siikala, J. (1996). The sadness of sweetness: The native anthropology of Western cosmology [and comments and reply]. *Current Anthropology, 37*(3), 395–428.

Sent, E.-M. (2004). Behavioral economics: How psychology made its (limited) way back into economics. *History of Political Economy, 36*(4), 735–760.

Serra, D. (2021). Decision-making: From neuroscience to neuroeconomics—An overview. *Theory and Decision, 91*(1), 1–80. https://doi.org/10.1007/s11238-021-09830-3

Simon, H. A. (1955). A behavioral model of rational choice. *The Quarterly Journal of Economics, 69*(1), 99–118.

Simon, H. A. (1978). Rationality as process and as product of thought. *American Economic Review, 68*(2), 1–16.

Simon, H. A. (1979). Rational decision making in business organizations. *American Economic Review, 69*(4), 493–513.

Simon, H. A. (1986). Rationality in psychology and economics. *Journal of Business, 59*(4), S209–S224.

Simon, H. A. (1990). Invariants of human behavior. *Annual Review of Psychology, 41*, 1–19. https://doi.org/10.1146/annurev.ps.41.020190.000245

Simon, H. A. (1991). Organizations and markets. *Journal of Economic Perspectives, 5*(2), 25–44.

Simon, H. A. (1996). *The sciences of the artificial*. MIT Press.
Simon, H. A. (2000). Public administration in today's world of organizations and markets. *PS: Political Science & Politics, 33*(4), 749–756.
Smith, A. (1759/2002). *The theory of moral sentiments*. Cambridge University Press.
Smith, A. (1776/2005). *The Glasgow edition of the works and correspondence of Adam Smith. Volume 2: An inquiry into the nature and causes of the wealth of nations*. Liberty Fund.
Smith, V. L. (2003). Constructivist and ecological rationality in economics. *American Economic Review, 93*(3), 465–508. https://doi.org/10.1257/000282803322156954
Smith, V. L. (2008). *Rationality in economics: Constructivist and ecological forms*. Cambridge University Press. http://www.loc.gov/catdir/toc/ecip079/2007002899.html
Steele, G. R. (2002). Hayek's sensory order. *Theory & Psychology, 12*(3), 387–409. https://doi.org/10.1177/0959354302012003016
Sunder, S. (2004). *Markets as artifacts* (M. Augier & J. March, Eds.). MIT Press.
Sunstein, C. R. (2023). Hayekian behavioral economics. *Behavioural Public Policy, 7*(1), 170–188. https://doi.org/10.1017/bpp.2021.3
Sutton, J., & Williamson, K. (2014). Embodied remembering. In L. Shapiro (Ed.), *The Routledge handbook of embodied cognition* (pp. 315–325). Routledge.
Tversky, A., & Kahneman, D. (1974). Judgment under uncertainty: Heuristics and biases. *Science, 185*(4157), 1124–1131. https://doi.org/10.1126/science.185.4157.1124
Tye, M. (2021). Qualia. In E. N. Zalta (Ed.), *The Stanford encyclopedia of philosophy (Fall 2021)*. Metaphysics Research Lab, Stanford University. https://plato.stanford.edu/archives/fall2021/entries/qualia/
Vallier, K. (2022, Winter). Neoliberalism. In E. N. Zalta & U. Nodelman (Eds.), *The Stanford Encyclopedia of Philosophy*. Metaphysics Research Lab, Stanford University. https://plato.stanford.edu/archives/win2022/entries/neoliberalism/
van den Hauwe, L. M. P. (2011). Hayek, Gödel, and the case for methodological dualism. *Journal of Economic Methodology, 18*(4), 387–407. https://doi.org/10.1080/1350178X.2011.628045
van Gelder, T. (1998). The dynamical hypothesis in cognitive science. *Behavioral and Brain Sciences, 21*(5), 615–628. https://doi.org/10.1017/S0140525X98001733
Varela, F. J., Thompson, E., & Rosch, E. (2016). *The embodied mind* (revised). MIT Press.

Vergara, F. (1992). Les fondements philosophiques du libéralisme. La Découverte.
Vera, A. H., & Simon, H. A. (1993). Situated action: A symbolic interpretation. *Cognitive Science, 17*(1), 7–48. https://doi.org/10.1207/s15516709cog1701_2
Whyte, J. (2019). The invisible hand of Friedrich Hayek: Submission and spontaneous order. *Political Theory, 47*(2), 156–184. https://doi.org/10.1177/0090591717737064
Williamson, O. E. (1975). *Markets and hierarchies*. The Free Press.
Williamson, O. E. (1985). *The economic institutions of capitalism: Firms, markets, relational contracting*. The Free Press.
Wilson, M. (2002). Six views of embodied cognition. *Psychonomic Bulletin & Review, 9*(4), 625–636.
You, Y. (2022). Data mining driven modelling on the individual heterogeneity of economic preference: A metaphor corpus of neuroeconomics. In J. C. Hung, J.-W. Chang, Y. Pei, & W.-C. Wu (Eds.), *Innovative computing* (pp. 327–333). Springer Nature. https://doi.org/10.1007/978-981-16-4258-6_41

CHAPTER 4

Principles of Embodiment in the Making of Economic Life

4.1 Introduction: Abstraction Is Not "Not Embodied"

As argued in Chapter 2, the standard economic model in economics is disembodied. This is partly a legacy of the Paretian turn, which autonomized economics from sociology and psychology (e.g., Bruni & Sugden, 2007; Camerer, 2006; Perry, 1935), but it is more than disciplinary: Its implications are ontological, involving the study of economic agents as abstracted from their psychological processes and social environments, so much so that it has been claimed that the development of economic models populated by "'flesh-and-blood human beings' was never the objective of economists" (Gul & Pesendorfer, 2008, p. 35). Instead, as Simon (1955) argued, economists have relied on an abstraction, *Homo economicus*, which typifies a model of substantive rationality based on the principle of preference maximization. Simon's (1979) critique of *Homo economicus* is certainly worth celebrating and, at first glance, one might consider that the (Simonian) cognitivist turn would naturally abandon such disembodied models when economic decision-making is situated in a specific context and follows a series of steps involving several cognitive mechanisms (e.g., attention, representation). Nevertheless, the existence of dual-process typologies seems to assume that there is some kind of disembodied abstract system within us, and, as we showed in Chapter 3, the development of some of the most influential alternative models of

F. Basso and C. Herrmann-Pillath, *Embodiment, Political Economy and Human Flourishing*, https://doi.org/10.1007/978-3-031-54971-7_4

economic rationality, such as Simon's (1955) bounded rationality, and Hayek's (1937, 1945) knowledge division, have not challenged disembodiment despite their emphasis on the economic environment (Hayek) along with the importance of psychological processes (Simon).

Importantly, we concluded the previous chapter by showing that Hayek developed a theory of the embodied mind but rejected the importance of the embodiment of knowledge in economic life, arguing that the market is an abstract process and should not be embodied. We contend that this argument was largely motivated by his visceral rejection of social justice and his political agenda, but we acknowledge that Hayek's position is singular. For many, the argument about the abstraction of markets is not normative: Rather, it is based on the idea that market processes are, or at least can be, characterized by abstract and impersonal mechanisms. In economics, for example, D. C. North pointed out that increasing specialization and division of labor require that "the society develops institutions that will permit anonymous, impersonal exchange across time and space" (North, 1993, p. 16), and Vernon Smith pointed out that, in economic life, our "evolved institutions" are "abstract norms or rules" (Smith, 2003, p. 468). Kenneth Arrow indicated that the market has traditionally been portrayed in economic theory as an "impersonal exchange" (Arrow, 1998, p. 94), and that economic agents are guided by "price signals" (Arrow & Hahn, 1971, p. vii) and engage "in relatively highly conscious calculating operations" (Arrow, 1951, p. 131). Abstraction and impersonality seem to be features of economic life, or at least, of standard economic models (Arrow, 1998).

Similar observations have been made in philosophy, sociology, and psychology.[1] Simmel (2004) theorized rationalization in light of money as an abstract and universal system associated with intellectual rationality (which prevails over emotions) and abstraction. Indeed, in his view, "the growth of intellectual abilities and of abstract thought characterizes the age in which money becomes more and more a mere symbol, neutral as regards its intrinsic value" (Simmel, 2004, p. 150). More recently, Fiske, for instance, has argued that, compared to the other relational models in society, market pricing relationships are "not embodied" because they are coordinated by ratios that are "intrinsically abstract," and characterized by arbitrary symbols such as numerical representations (e.g., monetary prices) (Fiske et al., 2009, pp. 1295–1296). Yet, as we shall see in this chapter, numerical representation is not "not embodied." More generally, although it is classic in the literature to view abstract thinking as characterizing a form of "disembodiment" (Maglio & Trope, 2012), we will argue that what is (supposedly more) abstract is not disembodied in the sense that it is "not embodied." Rather, we will argue that what is more abstract, even in the form of numerical representation, is in fact embodied. In doing so, we will adopt an embodied cognition perspective that develops a critique of the computer metaphor of the mind, which, as we shall see in more detail in Simon's physical symbol systems, assumes that everything can be represented in terms of abstract and arbitrary symbols.[2] We will also show that understanding why abstract concepts are embodied does more than just challenge the computer metaphor of the mind: It highlights the role of artifacts, language, and social interactions in economic life. What is more abstract is not detached from the body and the social world: Therefore, in light of the literature on embodiment and cognition detailed below, we argue that when something is considered abstract at the cognitive level and appears disembodied, it cannot be severed from embodiment and embeddedness: it is a call for embodiment and social interaction.

To make our argument as clear as possible: We claim that even if we accept the idea that economic life is more abstract at the cognitive level than other forms of sociality, this does not mean that economic life levitates in an ethereal world. Simply put, we will see in more detail below, and in the next chapters, in embodied economics, economic life is made of material things (artifacts like money) and populated by human beings who interact and talk with each other. Thanks to money and a system of property rights (see Chapter 7), the market is a relational model that allows economic agents to understand and represent reality with an abstract and universal system that commodifies the material, social, and natural world. In this respect, the market system is a process of disembodiment: For instance, the commodification of human beings (e.g., workers) is an abstraction from their humanness, a dehumanization. But we argue that this process of commodification is embodied on a psychological level: As we will see in more detail later in this book, the commodification of human beings is a metaphor (and a blend) that expresses the (inward and outward) embodiment of the market system.

In this chapter, we first contrast Simon's computer metaphor of the mind, which is at the core of the physical symbol systems theory, with Barsalou's perceptual symbol systems theory which connects perception, cognition, and action. We then turn to the literature on ecological rationality, which couples organism and environment, before developing our more specific embodiment view of economic rationality beyond problem-solving by shifting the focus to the essential role of meaning-making in economic life. In contrast to behavioral and experimental economics, we argue that embodied economics does not portray embodiment as a source of disturbances to (market-based) rationality, as posited by the disembodied normative standard model in mainstream economics. To do so, we link arguments from the theoretical and empirical literature on embodiment (e.g., mirror neurons; somatic markers) with notions developed in line with economists such as Smith and Keynes, respectively, through the concepts of moral sentiments and animal spirits. We then highlight the role of image schemas and conceptual metaphors developed by Lakoff & Johnson, as well as the related theory of conceptual blending developed by Fauconnier & Turner and their connection to the neural reuse theory formulated by Anderson, as essential theoretical building blocks for understanding meaning-making in economic life. These theoretical developments resolve the “Hayek paradox” identified in Chapter 3 by showing that abstraction is not opposed to embodiment, but enabled by it, with applications to the concept of preferences and numerical cognition. Moving forward, we introduce the Vygotskian cultural-historical approach to show the role of artifacts and language in social interactions as tools for shaping economic life, and reciprocally shaping the way economic actors think and act. To go beyond the cognitive science literature and connect the embodiment approach to economics as a social science, we contend that some of the key concepts of embodiment we have examined can be productively articulated under the concept of habitus as conceptualized by Bourdieu in the making of the self and economic life. We reveal the dialectic of inward and outward embodiment at the heart of habitus and introduce it as a fundamental principle of embodied reason in economic life. Through this perspective, the embodiment approach in the cognitive sciences is presented in line with a broader intellectual tradition that can be traced back to Hegelian philosophy and illustrated through the social theory of Elias and Weber. Overall, this chapter lays the groundwork for our embodied theory of economic agency and institutional action in the next chapters.

4.2 From Disembodied Rationality to Embodied Reason in Economic Life

In the cognitive sciences, the embodiment approach encompasses a wide range of theoretical positions that consider the interaction between the brain, the body, and the environment, rather than attempting to separate them. There are at least six different views of embodiment (Wilson, 2002), perhaps more,[3] that provide different but complementary explanations of phenomena. They all assume that "the mind must be understood in the context of its relationship to a physical body that interacts with the world" (Wilson, 2002, p. 625; see also Anderson et al., 2012; Matheson & Barsalou, 2018).

A point of contention in embodiment theories is the concept of "representation," which has led to the development of "anti-representationalist" approaches (e.g., Dreyfus, 2002; Gallagher, 2017; Golonka & Wilson, 2019). In embodied economics, we adopt an understanding of representations in their "weak sense" that is consistent with the enactivist approach developed by Varela and colleagues (2016). The strength of this approach, we believe, is that it is compatible with perceptual symbol systems theory (Matheson & Barsalou, 2018), conceptual metaphor theory (Johnson, 2017; Lakoff & Johnson, 1999), and neural reuse theory (Anderson, 2014; Toskos Dils & Flusberg, 2010), which will be developed in this chapter. Basically, Varela and colleagues reject the cognitivist claim that "cognition consists of acting on the basis of representations that are physically realized in the form of a symbolic code in the brain or a machine" (Varela et al., 2016, p. 41). According to them, the fundamental problem of the cognitivist perspective on representations is to posit "that the world is pregiven, that its features can be specified prior to any cognitive activity" (Varela et al., 2016, p. 135). This is an essential point because, according to embodiment theories, one cannot posit that the world is "out there," (Matheson & Barsalou, 2018) independent of the interaction between the brain, the body, and the environment (Gallagher, 2018, 2023). However, this does not mean that the concept of representations should be rejected altogether. Instead, Varela and colleagues (2016) favor a "weak sense" of representation, which conveys the idea that "cognition always consists in construing or representing the world a certain way," and that "refers to anything that can be interpreted as being about something" (Varela et al., 2016, p. 134). An interesting way of characterizing this approach is sometimes called "more-than-representational" in social sciences, and includes Pierre Bourdieu's practice theory (Carolan, 2008), which also resonates with embodied economics (see below and Chapter 6).

In this section, we do not intend to develop and detail every view and its related concepts, and we do not pretend that this presentation is compatible with all of them. The purpose of our argument in this section is to show three main things. First, by connecting perception, cognition, and action, the embodiment approach challenges Simon's physical symbol systems and aligns with Hayek's theory of sensory order, which will be illustrated with the theory of perceptual symbol systems. Second, embodiment challenges the reference to an omniscient view that underpins substantive and bounded (economic) rationality by coupling the organism and the environment. This will be illustrated with ecological rationality (Gigerenzer in Chater et al., 2018). Third, because it rejects the body-mind dichotomy, the embodiment approach reconceptualizes emotions beyond their (alleged) opposition to rationality. As we shall see, this view is very much in line with Keynes' idea of animal spirits, and Smith's moral sentiments.

4.2.1 Connecting Perception, Cognition, and Action

According to Simon's physical symbol systems theory, "the symbolic behavior of man arises because he has the characteristics of a physical symbol system" (Newell & Simon, 1976, p. 119), which is "a machine that produces through time an evolving collection of symbol structures" (Newell & Simon, 1976, p. 116). Importantly, this computer (or machine) metaphor implies that a symbol is arbitrary because it "may be used to designate any expression whatsoever. That is, given a symbol, it is not prescribed a priori what expressions it can designate" (Newell & Simon, 1976, p. 116). This means, as discussed in Chapter 3, that, according to Simon, cognitive processes (e.g., language, memory) are supported by (neural) systems that are considered separate from the modality-specific systems, which include sensory, motor, and introspective systems, that underlie perceptual states. In this view, cognition arises from computations performed on arbitrary and abstract symbols (hence "amodal") detached from perception and action. Language, for instance, is a module disconnected from modality-specific systems, and meaning emerges from an arbitrary set of abstract symbols. In this approach, a chair is a concept encoded as a set of arbitrary symbols (e.g., s1 for seat, b1 for back, l1 for legs) in memory, language, and thought, as any information processor, whether a computer or a human being, does.

One of the major embodied alternatives to the physical symbol systems theory is the perceptual symbol systems theory, in which Lawrence Barsalou proposes that symbols are not amodal but "perceptual," that is, "records of the neural states that underlie perception" (Barsalou, 1999, p. 582). As neural representations, located in the sensory-motor systems, they characterize perceptual experiences in a schematic way and involve the sensory modalities, including proprioception, introspection, and motor programs. Importantly, these perceptual systems are then assumed to be used in cognitive processes, such as perception, categorization, and judgment (decision-making), even when items (e.g., goods) are represented by symbols (such as words or pictures). This is an essential point because it means that "even when decoupled from the environment, the activity of the mind is grounded in mechanisms that evolved for interaction with the environment—that is, mechanisms of sensory processing and motor control" (Wilson, 2002, p. 626). To understand the latter point, and to further specify the psychological and neural processes at play, we will distinguish between the concepts of online and offline embodiment (Niedenthal et al., 2005).

Online embodiment is when cognition is situated in real-world environments: It occurs in the presence of real external stimuli, for instance when eating a chocolate cookie. Offline embodiment is when cognition is "decoupled" from these real-world environments, but remains supported by the modality-specific systems and bodily states associated with situated cognition: It occurs in the use of symbols that refer to real stimuli experienced in the real world but are not actually present, such as the picture of a chocolate cookie. Thus, while the object is absent or represented only by a symbol, such as a word or a picture, thinking about it or looking at it produces the embodied states usually produced as if the object were actually encountered in the real world. Perception, cognition, and action are no longer conceptualized as separate: Rather, "the modality-specific states that represent perception, action, and introspection in online situations are also used to represent these situations in the offline processing that underlies memory, language, and thought" (Niedenthal et al., 2005, p. 194).

At the neural level, the underlying process can be schematized as follows: Modality-specific representations (whether visual, auditory, olfactory, gustatory, emotional, etc.) that occur in the presence of real external stimuli (online embodiment) are partially captured by conjunctive neurons in various association (multimodal) areas—also called "convergence zones" (Damasio, 1989). These conjunctive neurons can later be activated to simulate (or re-enact) past sensory states in the absence of sensory input (offline embodiment). Such embodied mental simulations (or re-enactments) are multimodal, operate automatically and unconsciously, and underlie conceptual processing and knowledge that support memory, language, and thought (Barsalou et al., 2003; see also, Barsalou, 2020; Fernandino et al., 2016; Martin, 2007).

This position, which contrasts with Simon's physical symbol systems theory, is supported by a wide range of empirical findings in the literature.[4] For instance, viewing pictures of appetizing food (vs. non-food) such as cookies and burgers increases brain activity in several modality-specific regions, including the primary (insula) and secondary (lateral orbitofrontal cortex) gustatory cortices (Simmons et al., 2005; see also, Van der Laan et al., 2011). These results suggest that people automatically and implicitly simulate (re-enact) the taste of the food items they are presented with when they merely look at their pictures.[5] Likewise, neuroimaging studies show that reading odor-related (vs. neutral) words increases activity in language areas but also olfactory brain regions such as the piriform cortex and olfactory bulb, suggesting that the perceptual and motor information of a semantic reference contributes to the meaning and representation of odor-related words such as coffee or cinnamon (González et al., 2006). Thus, in line with the concept of offline cognition, a symbol (e.g., a picture or a word), that represents something experienced in the real world (e.g., food or odor), leads to increased activity in the sensory-motor parts of the brain associated with this situated experience (e.g., gustatory or olfactory cortex). Further evidence indicates that distributed neural circuits in the sensory-motor systems are activated when people make sense of symbols (or sets of symbols), such as a sound, a letter, or a story,[6] and demonstrates that their meaning is associated with the simulation (re-enactment) of related actions in the sensory-motor systems of the brain.

Note that these simulations are not just about external experience: Embodied simulations of more abstract concepts (such as "truth" or "trust"), whose level of perceptual strength is lower (i.e. less perceivable, in Hayek's parlance) than concrete concepts (Borghi, 2022; Borghi et al., 2017), will involve events and introspective properties rather than objects or entities (Barsalou & Wiemer-Hastings, 2005; Prinz, 2005; see also, Harpaintner et al., 2020).[7] For instance, Wiemer-Hastings and Xu (2005) found that abstract concepts were associated with more introspective and situational features, predominantly related to social aspects of situations, than concrete concepts. In any case, the theory of perceptual symbol systems posits that cognitive representations, for concrete and abstract concepts, are not abstracted from perceptual states, as assumed by Simon's physical symbol systems, but rather are underpinned by perceptual symbols, which can be combined to produce complex simulations. As pointed out by Barsalou (1999), Hebbian strengthening of connections between active neurons could explain how perceptual symbols are formed, thus linking his theory to some connectionist models referred to as "active symbol" connectionists (Schwartz et al., 1999; see also, Pulvermüller, 2005; Shebani et al., 2022) such as Edelman's (1987). These references are also linked to Hayek (1952), who, as mentioned in Chapter 3, described the Hebbian rule—also called the Hebb-Hayek principle (see Fuster & Bressler, 2012)—and inspired Edelman.

Overall, the theory of perceptual symbol systems claims, as Hayek (1952) did in *The Sensory Order*, that perception and action are central to cognition, which cannot be disconnected from our sensory-motor experiences, that is, from what we (did) feel, see, hear, taste, touch or do in the real world. In other words, "cognitive representations and operations are fundamentally grounded in their physical context" (Niedenthal et al., 2005, p. 186; see also, Barsalou, 2008; Harnad, 1990). This is why it is said that being embodied, cognition is grounded (Barsalou, 2008): The body is grounded in the world, hence situated, so that, "all cognitions are sustained by a 'ground' of postulates and finally by our communication with the world as primary embodiment of rationality" (Merleau-Ponty, 1945/1962, p. xxiii).

4.2.2 Coupling the Organism and the Environment

By grounding cognition, embodiment theories make the organism-environment coupling a fundamental assumption, which implies a different way of thinking about (economic) rationality.

In the standard model of substantive rationality, *Homo economicus* maximizes utility in a given environment. As Simon aptly explains with an analogy, this shifts the focus of analysis to the environment and neglects the organism.[8] This position has important implications for perception: In the standard economic model, "we do not need to distinguish between the real world and the decision maker's perception of it: he or she perceives the world as it really is" (Simon, 1986, p. S211). As aforementioned in Chapter 3, with bounded rationality, Simon challenged this model of substantive rationality and highlighted the key role of perception in understanding bounded rationality (e.g., Simon, 1986). However, because Simon posited the existence of a "real" environment independent of the economic agent as essential to the definition of (substantive and bounded) rationality, he set the standards of human cognition and rationality as unrelated to the organism-environment coupling (Felin et al., 2017). Bounded rationality is defined negatively in comparison to the omniscient view of a God-like *Homo economicus* that underlies substantive rationality: For a decision to be deemed ***boundedly*** rational, a definition of ***unbounded*** rationality is required.

The concept of ecological rationality, inherited from Simon's research program, helps to reconcile bounded rationality with the organism-environment coupling.Ecological rationality is defined "as a fit between the structures of the mind and the environment" (Todd & Gigerenzer, 2003, p. 145), and is inspired by Simon's metaphor of bounded rationality as the two blades of scissors, namely the computational capabilities of the actor and the structure of the task environments (Simon, 1990, p. 7). A similar position is taken by Vernon Smith's experimental economics, whose work on ecological rationality is inspired by Hayek and Simon, and who concludes that: "We have learned that people solve decision problems by drawing on their context-laden experience not by thinking about them as rational theoretical constructs with abstract fundamental properties that are independent of context" (Smith, 2008, p. 202).[9] In doing so, ecological rationality invites a critical distance from an interpretation of bounded rationality, sometimes endorsed by Simon, as "erroneous deviations from a rational standard" (Todd & Gigerenzer, 2003, p. 145). In contrast to the biases-and-heuristics research program inherited from Kahneman's work, ecological rationality does not compare "the workings of the mind with laws of probability and logic" typified by *Homo economicus*, but rather with the structure of the environment (Todd & Gigerenzer, 2003, p. 145; see also, Dekker & Remic, 2019). A significant implication of ecological rationality is that a cognitive strategy is not per se rational or irrational: This can only be determined by analyzing the structure of the physical or social environment in which a decision was made.

One of the main strengths of the ecological rationality approach is that it clearly states that one cannot understand the behavior of an organism, its rationality or "irrationality," if it is decoupled from the environment. This frees the definition of rationality from an external reference point and allows us to study "the subjective ecology of the organism that emerges through the interaction of its mind, body, and sensory organs with its physical environment," as von Uexküll (1956) did with the notion of *Umwelt* (Todd & Gigerenzer, 2012, p. 18), and thus resonates with embodiment theories (e.g., Gigerenzer, 2021; Raab, 2021), including Hayek's (1952) as discussed in Chapter 3. Indeed, if the environment is not thought of as independent of human beings, but rather as an *Umwelt* they inhabit, then, it follows, for instance, that.

> the axiom that the world is 3-D is not a statement about the true structure of space, but a statement about the fact that humans experience a three-dimensional world in the sense that we can move right-left, forwards-backwards, and up-down. (Gigerenzer, p. 801 in Chater et al., 2018)

We will return to similar views in the next chapter when we conceptualize agency in relation to autonomy in economic life, and later in this chapter we will further focus on the fundamental embodied dichotomies such as "right-left," "forward–backward," and "up-down," as they exemplify the notion of image schema that is central to embodiment theory (e.g., Johnson, 1987, 2017; Lakoff, 1987; Lakoff & Johnson, 1999).

For the time being though, it is important to explain why embodied economics does not identify with the ecological rationality approach. Ecological rationality means functionality (Gigerenzer, p. 800 in Chater et al., 2018) and studies *heuristics* that can *solve problems* (Gigerenzer & Gaissmaier, 2011).[10] Embodied economics does not focus on the "problem-solving" perspective on cognition and rationality inspired by the computational research program.[11] Embodiment theories shed a *different* and *complementary* light on rationality.[12] From an embodiment perspective: "Rationality is not a *problem*. (...). The world and reason are not problematical. We may say, if we wish, that they are mysterious"

(Merleau-Ponty, 1945/1962, p. xxiii). The difference between problem and mystery can be found in several important works in philosophy, such as those of Gabriel Marcel, John Dewey, and Noam Chomsky (Gallagher, 2018), as well as in economics. For instance, the abstractness of market society, according to Hayek (1988, p. 101), reinforces the "mysterious world of trade and money".[13] For Marx (1867/1990, p. 164), commodities are "mysterious" when they are abstracted from the economic and social conditions of their production under capitalism. The mysterious is that which is "not known" or "not understood" (Cambridge Dictionary, n.d.). This implies that if the (economic) world and reason are mysterious, then the question to be investigated is not primarily one of *problem-solving* but of the enactment of *meaning*, and thus of how people *make sense* of economic life, especially in the situations of uncertainty (or mystery) that pervade it. Therefore, embodied economics is fundamentally broader in scope than bounded and ecological models of rationality because embodied economics goes beyond the lens of "problem-solving" to embrace the question of how economic agents (or actors) make sense of their environment.[14] As we will see later in this chapter, meaning-making is not just an individual process, it is fundamentally a collective process. Let us illustrate the importance of meaning with the question of emotions.

4.2.3 *Overcoming the Opposition Between Rationality and Emotion*

As we shall see, Simon was aware of the importance of emotions in decision-making in order to have a complete theory of rationality (Simon, 1983). Although embodied economics agrees with this perspective, it does not portray emotions in economic life as an "interruption mechanism" (Simon, 1967, p. 39), or as a form of "corruption" (Kahneman, 2012, p. 8). Rather, embodied economics suggests viewing emotions as a way for people to make sense of their environment,[15] which requires reconceptualizing emotions beyond their (supposed) opposition to rationality. After repositioning Simon's and Kahneman's arguments, the relationships between affect and rationalization, animal spirits and somatic markers, and moral sentiments and mirror neurons will be briefly developed to illustrate a perspective more in line with embodied economics.

4.2.3.1 The Neglect of Emotions in Decision-Making

Simon acknowledged that information-processing theories have overlooked the "interaction of cognition with affect" despite the major influence of motivation and emotion on thinking and problem-solving (Simon, 1967, p. 29). Emotions are then conceptualized as an "interruption mechanism" whose function is to allow "the processor to respond to urgent needs in real time" (Simon, 1967, p. 39). In doing so, he leaves emotions a marginal role in decision-making because they are needed in situations of urgency, and decision-making generally remains governed by a goal-terminating mechanism associated with satisficing (Simon, 1967). Emotions are then categorized either as "non-rational processes" that constrain rational processes (Simon, 1986, p. S210), or as the "irrational" element that causes behavior to deviate from the "rationally" chosen action (Simon, 1987, p. 57). Therefore, within Simon's cognitivism, emotions are excluded from the scope of (boundedly) rational behavior. More importantly, "Simon's reformulation of rationality employs a mind–body dualism" whereby "mental processes are valorized, whereas physical and emotional experiences are marginalized" (Mumby & Putnam, 1992, p. 470). Even when emotions are studied rather than cognitive processes, embodiment remains marginal.

In some ways, Kahneman's approach to emotions is more constructive. Commenting on his article with Tversky (Tversky & Kahneman, 1974), in which they demonstrated that people used heuristics such as availability, representativeness, and anchoring and adjustment to make judgments (see Chapter 2), Kahneman argues that their research showed that "systematic errors in the thinking of normal people" can be "traced to the design of the machinery of cognition rather than to the corruption of thought by emotion" (Kahneman, 2012, p. 8). In other words, biases can be purely "cognitive" and not necessarily emotional. However, as the word "corruption" implies, this does not mean that, according to this approach, emotions are not also a source of bias. Consider a famous concept: The identifiable victim effect, which stems from an observation made by Thomas Schelling (1968), to illustrate the difference between an individual life and a statistical life. His point is that people tend to be more willing to give more money to save identified victims (e.g., a child), than to save unidentified victims (e.g., taxes for children's hospitals), even though the latter situation could potentially save more (statistical) lives.[16] This is illustrated by the famous story of Jessica McClure who was trapped in a well for more than 50 hours when she was 18 months old: "Americans responded with sympathy, a tremendous rescue effort, and money" amounting to $700,000 to save "baby Jessica" (Jenni & Loewenstein, 1997, p. 235). As argued in the literature following the behavioral economics approach, sympathy, an emotion of care, concern, and compassion experienced towards others, which is one of the main underpinnings of the identifiable victim effect, is then considered a "key distorting factor" which explains why "people fail to maximize social utility when choosing where to allocate scarce resources" (Small & Cryder, 2016, p. 113). Compared to rational deliberation, sympathy is an emotion that has been characterized as "immature and irrational" (Loewenstein & Small, 2007, p. 113).[17]

Contrasting rationality and emotions is probably as old as Western thinking,[18] and its tradition of understanding the world in terms of structuring dichotomies (e.g., Melnikoff & Bargh, 2018; Serra, 2021), generally loaded with gender stereotypes (e.g., Merchant, 1980; Nelson, 1997). However, several authors, inspired by results from studies in psychology and neuroscience, have pointed out the need to overcome the tension between rationality and emotion.[19] We will now turn to some arguments in support of this perspective.

4.2.3.2 *Affect and Rationalization*

In Chapter 3, we discussed the idea, proposed by Hayek (1952, §1.65), among others, that affect is often part of our interpretation of the environment. As Zajonc's (1980) work on decision-making shows, affective reactions to stimuli are usually automatic in the early stages of information processing, starting with perception, and thus guide judgment.[20] Perception is colored by affect: "We do not just see 'A house:' We see a *handsome* house, an *ugly* house, or a *pretentious* house" (Zajonc, 1980, p. 154). The role of affect is, therefore, key to understanding "rational" decision-making:

> We sometimes delude ourselves that we proceed in a rational manner and weigh all the pros and cons of the various alternatives. But this is probably seldom the actual case. Quite often 'I decided in favor of X' is no more than 'I liked X' (…). We buy the cars we 'like,' choose the jobs and houses we find 'attractive,' and then justify these choices by various reasons. (Zajonc, 1980, p. 155)

This quote makes two important points. First, it implicitly reminds us that emotions are about action. Etymologically, "emotion" comes from Latin "*emovere*" which means to "move out, remove, agitate." In other words, emotion is about "motion," movement, and, therefore, action, which in economic terms translates into decisions and choices. This has implications for economics because it means that emotion and value are not independent: Rather, as observed on the basis of several experimental results in neuroeconomics (for instance), "affective scientists suggest that these two constructs are inherently intertwined, since a primary function of emotion is to detect relevance and promote adaptive action" (Lempert & Phelps, 2014, p. 228).[21]

Second, Zajonc's quote conveys the idea that, contrary to what is usually assumed by the theory of revealed preferences in the standard model of economics (e.g., Samuelson, 1948), actions may not reveal preferences but actually create them, as choices are rationalized by economic agents (Ariely & Norton, 2008). This position echoes cognitive dissonance theory which describes situations in which people come up with reasons to explain why they behave in a way that is consistent with what they think or believe (Festinger, 1957; see also Cushman, 2020; Summers, 2017). This also highlights the importance of bodily inferences on decision-making, by considering how affect leads people to revise their preferences in light of their actions, as suggested by cognitive dissonance theory (Festinger, 1957; Harmon-Jones & Harmon-Jones, 2007),[22] and by considering how actions, influenced by situations, can generate people's preferences (Ariely & Norton, 2008; see also, Sharot et al., 2010). From an embodiment perspective. Rationality is embodied and situated, and thus whatever pertains to bodily influences in decision-making, should not be seen as a "psycho-physiological disorder" (Sartre, 1939/2014, p. 12) that moves people away from rationality. Rather, emotions can be viewed as implying consistency through affect. For instance, in situations of cognitive dissonance, people experience a form of negative affect which leads them to revise their opinions (i.e., preferences) to be aligned with their behavior in specific contexts (Festinger, 1957; Harmon-Jones & Harmon-Jones, 2007). These approaches show that considering flesh-and-blood economic agents, whose emotions and actions are concretely situated, provides a very different perspective on preferences. When embodiment is taken into account, the relationship between preferences and choices becomes more complex than the theory of revealed preferences suggests: Preferences may determine choices, but choices may also determine preferences, and this can happen under the influence of affect and situations.[23]

4.2.3.3 Animal Spirits and Somatic Markers

The association between emotion and action is also fundamental in situations of uncertainty when people struggle to make sense of the world. Although this approach is radically different from the standard model, it is not alien to economic theory, as showcased by Keynes' (1936/2018) "animal spirits" in his *General Theory* (see also, Akerlof & Shiller, 2009). Narrowly understood, animal spirits are "a spontaneous urge to action rather than inaction, and not as the outcome of a weighted average of quantitative benefits multiplied by quantitative probabilities" (Keynes, 1936/2018, p. 141). They operate as a default mode of (economic) action to which rational calculation is complementary, as they help to assess a situation and make a decision, especially when some form of calculation is impossible due to the uncertainty of economic life (Lainé, 2014).[24] Animal spirits are neither rational nor irrational, they rely on "embodied knowledge rather than probability calculus" (Lainé, 2014, p. 462), and "stem from an inductive analogical cognition (or pattern matching)," whose purpose is to answer the question: "Does the current situation resemble another one that happened in the past?" (Lainé, 2014, pp. 448–449) Again, when economic life is uncertain, unknown, and mysterious, embodied knowledge becomes essential to decision-making. Put differently, when the world is unstable, what remains stable is embodiment, and what can be trusted is emotion. In this regard, Keynes' animal spirits anticipated the conceptualization of emotion, including gut feelings, as a "privileged window" into experience for making sense of the world (Pham et al., 2012).

Keynes' animal spirits share many features with the somatic marker hypothesis coined by Damasio (1994) in neuropsychology to characterize situations in which emotions enable deliberation in decision-making.[25] Indeed, "both theories are very much in tune, in that they emphasize analogical induction, the intelligence of emotions, and the automaticity of cognition and action" (Lainé, 2014, p. 439). In Damasio's view, somatic markers are implied in the neurobiology of rationality. The somatic marker hypothesis proposes that somatic markers (bodily sensations, emotions) are involved in decision-making, via the ventromedial prefrontal cortex (vmPFC) which receives signals from sensory regions. Several studies have found that patients with bilateral lesions of the vmPFC cortex develop severe impairments in personal and social decision-making while preserving intellectual abilities. It is assumed that a somatic state (i.e., gut feelings/visceral states) marks an image that henceforth influences decision-making and shapes people's deliberation by high-lighting (or ruling out) some options.[26] As an embodiment theory of rationality and emotion, the somatic marker hypothesis overlaps with the Jamesian theory of emotion (Reimann & Bechara, 2010), and also claims that we think in terms of images (Damasio, 1994; Lainé, 2014), an idea that is close to the theory of perceptual symbol systems (Barsalou, 1999).[27] In these cases, emotions are aimed not only at solving problems, but also at making sense of the trade-offs that occur in economic life (Damasio, 1994): They are attached to what people value. This further illustrates the difference between the ecological approach to rationality and embodied economics. From an ecological perspective, emotions are neither rational nor irrational, as their rationality is "ecological rather than logical" (Volz & Hertwig, 2016, p. 111), and depends on the circumstances under which their consequences succeed (or fail) in the real world.[28] In embodied economics, the role of emotions in decision-making is to be appreciated not *only* in light of their successful (or not) consequences in a given environment. Emotions matter in economic life because they *ground* and *bound* market exchanges. For instance, they contribute to defining what is included in economic transactions in the case of child adoption, prostitution, or bodily organs, as analyzed in the literature on taboo trade-offs (e.g., Fiske & Tetlock, 1997; Licht-enstein et al., 2007) and repugnant markets (e.g., Roth, 2007). They also reinforce (injunctive) social norms (Elster, 1989),[29] and drive moral reasoning as a post hoc construction when "one feels a quick flash of revulsion" at the thought of a situation, and "one knows intuitively that something is wrong" (Haidt, 2001, p. 814).

Emotions are also involved in consumption and social reproduction. Contrary to the standard model in economics which states: "*De gustibus non est disputandum*" (Stigler & Becker, 1977), meaning that in matters of taste, there is no dispute, Bourdieu demonstrated the role of gut feelings in rejecting consumption choices and maintaining class endogamy:

> In matters of taste, more than anywhere else, all determination is negation; and tastes are perhaps first and foremost distastes, disgust provoked by horror or visceral intolerance ('sick-making') of the tastes of others. (…) Aversion to different life-styles is perhaps one of the strongest barriers between the classes; class endogamy is evidence of this." (Bourdieu, 1979/1984, p. 56)

Obviously, the same can be said about the role of emotions in social movements and politics (e.g., Nussbaum, 2013; Tsakiris et al., 2021). However, emotions, do not only keep people apart, but they can also bring them closer, as moral sentiments, especially empathy, illustrate.

4.2.3.4 Moral Sentiments and Mirror Neurons

The embodiment approach does not portray empathy as "immature" and "irrational" as some proponents of the biases-and-heuristics research program in behavioral economics have done (e.g., Loewenstein & Small, 2007; Small & Cryder, 2016). Following Adam Smith, in embodied economics, empathy is not a bias: It is the by-product of our embodiment. As we shall see, this more constructive view of empathy is supported by the mirror neuron literature.

With the publication of *The Theory of Moral Sentiments*, Adam Smith (1759/2002) developed his analysis of the principle of sympathy, which is now considered a classic in ethics and psychology (Anspach, 1972) as well as in behavioral economics (Ashraf et al., 2005). This concept has powerful implications for studying how people rationally pursue their self-interest in economics: Not because moral sentiments are strictly opposed to self-interest, which they are not, since people can experience pleasure from seeing others' happiness, but rather because they cast self-interest in a different light. In the very first lines of his book, Smith argues:

> How selfish soever man may be supposed, there are evidently some principles in his nature, which interest him in the fortune of others, and render their happiness necessary to him, though he derives nothing from it except the pleasure of seeing it. (Smith, 1759/2002, §1)

From his standpoint, sympathy is an innate endowment. This means that, naturally, human beings feel for others by putting themselves in their situations, which can be done by "taking" someone else's position, through imagination,[30] or can also happen automatically.[31]

In developing his argument, Smith makes important points from an embodiment point of view. First, he suggests that, through sympathy, people engage in an embodied process, that encompasses sensations, emotions, feelings, and experiences. Of course, these (imagined) sensations, emotions, feelings, or experiences, are not identical to those that someone else will experience, but, as we will discuss below, with results from studies of the mirror mechanism, they may involve similar neural underpinnings. Second, as he observes, sympathy can occur automatically, and is not something that people have to do explicitly or deliberately. Moral sentiments can operate implicitly and automatically: People can naturally and spontaneously experience something that is like another's experience. Third, because of its instantaneousness, the principle of sympathy seems to differ from calculations of self-interest, that is, from a self-regarding cost–benefit analysis.[32] In this respect, the principle of sympathy can help rethink self-interest in economics because moral sentiments are underpinned by automatic embodied processes (e.g., sensations, emotions, feelings).

In today's parlance, this description of Smith's principle of sympathy characterizes (affective) "empathy" as the ability to share the emotions of others (Frith & Singer, 2008): The "central emotion motivating our behavior towards others" (Gintis et al., 2005, p. 3). It appears that a substantial part of his argument pertains to affective empathy. According to him, people may intentionally (through imagination) or instantaneously experience pleasure or pain when they see others around them happy or suffering, and this relies, at least in part, on some automatic embodied processes, such as other-oriented emotions, that differ from the classic conceptualization of economic rationality in terms of explicit calculations of self-interest.

Findings on the mirror mechanism in the (social) neuroscience literature support the existence of such automatic and implicit processes that lead us to experience actions and emotions that allow us to connect with what others are currently experiencing. Indeed, it has been found that a variety of cell types distributed among several motor, sensory, and "emotional" areas of the brain form a "mirror mechanism," so that when one looks at someone performing an action, the representation of that action is underpinned by the brain pattern and embodied simulation associated with it in the real world (e.g., Bonini et al., 2022; Mukamel et al., 2010; Rizzolatti & Sinigaglia, 2010). For example, empirical results show that, in some parts of the brain, such as the insula and the anterior cingulate cortex, which can be associated with the emotion of disgust, there are neural networks that are automatically activated when people experience disgust themselves, but also when they observe someone else experiencing disgust (Wicker et al., 2003).[33] In a sense, research on mirror neurons has uncovered the neural underpinnings of the empathetic process associated with some of the descriptions of moral sentiments developed by Smith[34]: The experience of an emotion is simulated (re-enacted) when people merely watch someone express that emotion. Since people experience (at least some of) the emotions of those in front of them, we might speculate that moral sentiments, and the embodied re-enactments that underlie them, help people relate to each other because they can simulate the experience of the emotion that someone else has expressed, which facilitates social engagement.

The role of the mirror mechanism in social cognition and in guiding social interactions also includes its involvement in speech recognition (Bonini et al., 2022; Heyes & Catmur, 2022), and it has been proposed that the action and perception mechanisms to which mirror neurons contribute are reused for language, concepts, and communication (Pulvermüller, 2018). In other words, sensory-motor systems would be "exploited" to ground concepts, including the "abstract" ones (Gallese & Lakoff, 2005; Lakoff, 2008), as conceptual metaphor theory posits (Lakoff & Johnson, 1980, 1999). We will now turn to this linguistic theory to further explore why human reason is embodied, and how it is shaped by our social and cultural environment. Of course, this is true for emotions which are commonly expressed in terms of metaphors (e.g., Kövecses, 2010; Lakoff, 2016a) and influenced by culture (e.g., Lakoff, 2016b; Leemans, 2016). However, given the significance of *preferences* and *numbers* in the conceptual analysis of economic life and its abstraction, we will focus our discussion on their metaphorical representation in the subsequent sections.

4.3 Embodied Reason and the Enactment of Meaning in Economic Life

In this section, we do not aim to be exhaustive, but rather to use conceptual metaphor theory as a workhorse to show that, contrary to Hayek's (1982/2013) position, understanding the world (including the "market order") in anthropomorphic terms is not a form of "tribal" thinking, and that one cannot think about what is abstract without reference to one's concrete experience, as exemplified by research on space-valence and space-number associations. These developments will show that valence and numerical cognition, which underpin preferences and economic calculations, are not disembodied (understood as "not embodied"); this will allow us to discuss the role of some of the brain-, body-, context-, and culture-specific aspects of human thinking. We will extend the analysis with complementary research programs on embodied cognition, namely neural reuse theory and conceptual blending theory.

4.3.1 Bodily Experiences, Conceptual Metaphors, and Embodied Reason: Understanding Abstraction in Terms of Experience

Conceptual metaphor theory has arguably been one of the most important contributions to the literature on embodiment over the past 40 years, inspiring research in many different disciplines ranging from linguistics (e.g., Gibbs, 1994, 2008) to neuroscience (e.g., Feldman, 2008), psychology (e.g., Landau et al., 2014), philosophy (e.g., Johnson, 2017), literature (e.g., Turner, 1996), economics (e.g., McCloskey, 1983), sociology (e.g., Cerulo, 2019), anthropology (e.g., Wiseman, 2019), consumer research (e.g., Henry, 2005), management (e.g., Cornelissen & Clarke, 2010) and law (e.g., Winter, 2001). Countless illustrations have been documented and analyzed in the literature (see Gibbs, 1994, 2008; Kövecses, 2010; Lakoff & Johnson, 1980, 1999), and we will encounter several of them later in this book. In the subsequent paragraphs, we will explore analyses and findings about image schemas and anthropomorphism, as well as the metaphorical representation of abstract concepts. This approach brings a complementary analysis to the theory of perceptual symbol systems: In the latter, abstract concepts are assumed to be represented *directly* by perceptual symbols, here, abstract concepts are assumed to be represented *metaphorically* by using one domain of experience to understand another domain of experience.

4.3.1.1 Organism-Environment Coupling, Image Schemas, and Anthropomorphism

Like any embodiment approach, conceptual metaphor theory relies on the coupling between the organism and the environment that is experienced in every situation. This coupling has been remarkably analyzed by Mark Johnson:

> The patterns of our ongoing interactions (or 'enactions,' as Varela, Thompson, and Rosch (1991) have called them, to stress their active, dynamic character) define the contours of our world and make it possible for us to make sense of, reason about, and act reliably within this world. Thousands of times each day we see, manipulate, and move into and out of containers, so containment is one of the most fundamental patterns of our experience. Because we have two legs and stand up within a gravitational field, we experience verticality and up/down orientation. Because the qualities (e.g., redness, softness, coolness, agitation, sharpness) of our experience vary continuously in intensity, there is a scalar character to each of the qualitative dimensions of our world. For example, lights can grow brighter or dimmer, stoves get hotter or cooler, iced tea gets sweeter as we add sugar. We are subject to forces that move us, change our bodily states, and constrain our actions, and all these forces have characteristic patterns and qualities. We are bound inextricably to our world interactively (enactively) by means of these recurring patterns that are the very conditions for us to survive, grow, and find meaning. Without such patterns, and without neural maps of such characteristic patterns, each moment of our experience would be utterly chaotic, as though we had to make sense of our world from scratch, over and over again as each new moment arose. (Johnson, 2017, pp. 81–82)

Containment, verticality, and intensity are some of the fundamental patterns of ongoing interactions with the world. These are called "image schemas" in cognitive linguistics and form very simple embodied structures in topological neural maps that serve as *Gestalts* for us to make sense of our everyday experience (Johnson, 2017, p. 82; see Bottini & Doeller, 2020 for neural and behavioral evidence supporting this hypothesis). Many image schemas have been identified in the literature (see Grady, 2005; Johnson, 1987; Lakoff, 1987; Lakoff & Johnson, 1999), and, as we will see in Chapter 6, several of them, such as CONTAINER, VERTICALITY, BALANCE, and RESOURCE, help structure our understanding of economic institutions.

For now, let us focus on the CONTAINER schema to show one of the fundamental implications of recognizing it when it comes to the role of anthropomorphism in understanding abstraction. The CONTAINER schema refers to the basic experience of our body as a container: Things go in (food, water, air) and come out (air, urine, feces, etc.), it is located in space when one moves from one room (a container) to another room (another container), and one also manipulates containers when one pours coffee into a mug, puts things into a bag, or takes stuff out of the trunk of a car. As Maurice Merleau-Ponty, following Heidegger, argues, because such containment is experienced on a daily basis, it is literally impossible to escape any form of anthropomorphism, even when it comes to the most abstract forms such as geometric shapes:

> the perception of a completely objective world, without any anthropomorphic predicate, is inconceivable. Even a purely geometrical universe would be impossible without any human element; thus a geometrical figure, the circle for example, can be expressed by an analytical formula; but a subject who has never seen a circle would not be able to reconstruct the intuitive meaning of the formula. All geometry is based on the essentially anthropomorphic concept of contour, that is to say, of the boundary between 'outside' and 'inside,' a distinction that exists only for a subject who is himself situated in space, who sees from a certain point of view (his body), in relation to which the distinction between outside and inside takes on meaning. There can be no contour without a subject who structures given elements into figures."[35] (Merleau-Ponty, 1964, p. 186)[36]

Against this background, it is not surprising that the movements of geometric figures, such as a circle or a triangle, are interpreted as the actions of people (Heider & Simmel, 1944). Likewise, market trends, such as price movements, are regularly anthropomorphized (e.g., Epley et al., 2007; Morris et al., 2007). In both cases, people map their physical experience of the world onto the movements of geometrical figures or prices, as when they map their physical experience of inside and outside onto a circle. An analysis in terms of image schemas shows that anthropomorphism is not a form of so-called "tribal thinking" as posited by Hayek, but an expression of the organism-environment coupling and the way people, including economists in their textbooks (e.g., Alejo, 2010), make sense of everyday (economic) life.[37] Yet people, including economists (McCloskey, 1983), do more than refer to image schemas, they use metaphors,[38] which is quite common when it comes to understanding something more abstract.

4.3.1.2 Space, Metaphors, and Abstract Concepts

Unlike perceptual symbols and image schemas, a metaphor is interconceptual: It is the understanding and experience of one thing, usually abstract, in terms of another, usually more concrete, thing. The experience of a concrete source domain is mapped onto a more abstract target domain to induce a specific way of thinking and acting towards it (Lakoff & Johnson, 1980). Image schemas are commonly employed to form (primary) metaphors that structure thinking (Grady, 2005; Lakoff & Johnson, 1980). For instance, the VERTICALITY schema is used to form metaphors such as MORE IS UP or LESS IS DOWN, which are grounded in correlations in bodily experiences of the world: When water is poured into a glass, the level goes up, so MORE is associated with UP, and by extension, a subjective judgment of quantity is conceptualized in terms of the sensory-motor experience of verticality (e.g., "Prices are rising").[39] Two metaphors are particularly interesting at this stage of the argument: The GOOD IS RIGHT mapping (a space-valence association), and the mental number line (a space-number association), as they can illustrate the extent to which metaphors pertaining to the expression of preferences and numbers are body-, context-, and culture- specific, and highlight the role of neural reuse at the brain level.

Space-valence Association, Preferences, and Body-specificity

One of the main questions that naturally comes to mind when taking an embodiment approach is the extent to which the conceptual metaphors that people commonly use are actually shaped by their bodies. This is known as the body-specificity hypothesis (Casasanto, 2009). Indeed, one might wonder whether people with different kinds of bodies think differently: If cognition is embodied, thinking is embodied, and if the body is different, then *thinking* should be different. The word "thinking" is of paramount importance here since conceptual metaphor theory posits that people not only *speak* in metaphors, but also *think* in metaphors (Lakoff & Johnson, 1980, 1999).

Across many languages (e.g., Latin, French, German) and cultures (e.g., Ghanaian society, Islamic doctrines, Hinduism, Greek and Roman antiquity), it is observed that abstract concepts that are positively and negatively valenced can be represented in terms of physical space, respectively rightward (e.g., the "right answer") and leftward (e.g., "two left feet") (Casasanto, 2009; Li & Cao, 2019). If the source of metaphors is based on correlations in bodily experiences, the GOOD IS RIGHT mapping may be due to motor fluency. In general, people have a dominant hand and prefer objects that are easier to interact with (Ping et al., 2009; see also, Eelen et al., 2013),[40] which creates an association between the side of space they interact with more fluently and good things. Since about 90% of the population are right-handed, the GOOD IS RIGHT linguistic metaphor dominates, becomes a convention, and is also adopted by left-handed people. However, if metaphors are about thinking and are bodily-based, left-handed people should still associate good things with the leftward space at the behavioral level. This is demonstrated by Daniel Casasanto's (2009) results in a series of behavioral studies showing that left-handed people do not associate positive valence with the right-handed side, but with the left-handed side.

This result, which has been replicated several times, is important for embodied economics for three main reasons. First, it shows that when it comes to *thinking*, metaphors are body-specific: Something abstract (goodness) is represented by something more concrete (space), but this representation is a function of motor fluency, so much so that the GOOD IS LEFT mapping, which does not seem to exist in any linguistic form anywhere world, is the way left-handed people express their preferences at the behavioral level.[41] Second, the metaphor underlying these space-valence associations may be a more general metaphor, namely GOOD IS THE FLUENT REGION OF SPACE. This interpretation is supported by theories emerging from experimental studies that conceptualize the context-specificity of space-valence associations (Casasanto, 2017). For instance, when people cannot use their dominant hand for some reason, their preferences are reversed, and right- (left-) handed people temporarily use the good is left (right) mapping (e.g., Casasanto & Chrysikou, 2011; Song et al., 2019). This kind of result is fully consistent with embodiment theories: The body is situated, and thus preferences can change with contextual influences on motor fluency.[42]

Finally, it can be inferred from these results that something as fundamental as the organism-environment coupling (here, motor fluency) can be expressed through linguistic metaphors, but also through cultural forms such as rituals that structure people's everyday lives. For instance, Muslims should never use their left hand for eating or drinking, which is reserved for dirty activities such as defecation, and should enter the mosque with their right foot (de la Fuente et al., 2015). As we can see here, the experience of space (motor fluency) is projected onto the representation of something more abstract (goodness) which is then expressed in material forms such as language and cultural practices, which can then shape people's behavior.[43] Moreover, the widespread use of the GOOD IS RIGHT metaphor in language and cultural practices shows that this mapping may have been imposed on left-handed people by the vast majority of right-handed people. For instance, for decades in France and elsewhere, left-handed children were forced to learn to write with their right hand (e.g., Harris, 1990). In this case, as in many others, language and cultural practices reflect power inequalities in society (Bourdieu, 1982/1991; see also Henry, 2005; Nelson, 1992). We will return to the question of power in Chapter 6 on institutions, and we will further specify the conceptual link between practices and metaphors in this chapter when we analyze the relationship between embodiment and habitus.

Space-Number Association, Numerical Cognition, and Neural Reuse

Valence is not the only concept to be spatialized: "From the most elementary aspects of mathematics, such as the notion of measurement, all the way up to the concepts of the real number line, Cartesian coordinates, the complex plane and even the proof of Fermat's Last Theorem, metaphors by which numbers are made to correspond to spatial positions permeate mathematical thinking" (Hubbard et al., 2005, p. 435). This is evidenced, for example, by the space-number association such as the spatial-numerical association of response codes (SNARC) effect (Dehaene et al., 1993; Hubbard et al., 2005). The results are striking and well-documented: Smaller numbers are associated with the left side of the space and larger numbers with the right side of the space for participants writing from left to right, and vice versa for participants writing from right to left (Faghihi & Vaid, 2023).[44]

This is an illustration of a conceptual metaphor: Something abstract (here, a number) is expressed in concrete terms (space). Metaphors are thought to be learned by children throughout their development (e.g., Clark, 1973; Lakoff & Johnson, 1999; Mandler, 1992, 2004; Williams et al., 2009), and it is very likely that they have learned how to associate numbers with space experientially through finger counting (Wood & Fischer, 2008) as well as the arrangement of numbers in space through cultural artifacts such as calendars, rulers, or graphs (Pitt & Casasanto, 2020). Culture-specific conventions for reading and writing numbers can then explain cross-cultural variations in the mental number line (e.g., Westerners vs Arabic speakers) (Pitt & Casasanto, 2020; see also, Faghihi & Vaid, 2023). This point is crucial: Cognition is embodied, and the body is situated, so metaphors and, more broadly, concepts are not only body-specific, but also culture-specific (e.g., Barsalou, 2023; Kemmerer, 2022; Pitt & Casasanto, 2020). The number line is a cultural concept that seems "natural" to most people around the world, but did not appear in Europe until the 17th Century and remains foreign to, for instance, the "uneducated" Mundurukú adults in Amazonia (Núñez, 2011).

Cross-cultural and historical variations do not mean that the space-number association is not embodied. On the contrary, the spatialization of numbers could be an illustration of a larger brain process that includes processes described by perceptual symbol systems theory as well as conceptual metaphor theory: Namely, neural reuse (Anderson, 2010, 2014).[45] In short, the main idea at the core of neural reuse theory is that sensory-motor grounding extends beyond concepts to encompass many aspects of human cognitive life (such as memory, language, or mathematics) thanks to functional interactions between parts of the brain and the multiple functional roles that each part can play in the overall system. Different parts of the brain are then used and reused to perform different functions. In the case of the space-number association described by the SNARC effect, visuo-spatial resources, especially a particular circuit in the left inferior parietal sulcus involved in shifting spatial attention, would be reused for numerical cognition (Hubbard et al., 2005). It appears that the representation of numbers activates motor regions associated with finger awareness (see Anderson, 2010, p. 255ff, 2014, p. 23ff). For instance, small Arabic digits and number words (from one to nine) (vs. control) increase activity in the motor cortex (precentral gyrus) of participants due to their finger counting habits (Tschentscher et al., 2012). This further illustrates the importance of experience and associated sensory-motor processes as a fundamental element of human cognition: Those who preferred to start counting with their right hand showed (contralateral) left-hemispheric activation for small numerals, whereas those who preferred to start counting with their left hand revealed (contralateral) right-hemispheric activation (Tschentscher et al., 2012).

Beyond space-number association, some neural mechanisms originally developed in relation to concrete experiences (e.g., food or drug pleasures) are reused to approach more abstract experiences (e.g., listening to music or moral pleasures) (Kringelbach, 2009). Activity in the anterior medial and adjacent central region of the orbitofrontal cortex (OFC), which is associated with the representation of experienced utility, is observed in response to a wide range of stimuli, from the concrete (taste, odor, music, attractive faces) to the more abstract (getting money, points in a game, or positive social feedback) (Berridge & O'Doherty, 2014). This suggests that the economic and social processes investigated in neuroeconomics do not escape embodiment. Thus, in contrast to the computer metaphor of the brain, it is observed that brain activity associated with decision-making is distributed and includes several regions taking part in the control of movement: "Neural correlates of decision variables (such as payoff) appear to be expressed by the same neurons that encode the attributes (such as direction) of the potential motor responses used to report the decision, which reside within sensorimotor circuits that guide the online execution of movements" (Cisek & Kalaska, 2010, p. 270). Unsurprisingly, this view is in full alignment with neural reuse theory and embodied cognition (Anderson, 2014, p. 219).

Taken together, the studies on space-valence and space-number associations further demonstrate the role of embodiment in cognition in economic life by showing that what is (more) abstract, such as preferences and numerical cognition, is neither disembodied (in the sense of "not embodied") nor disembedded: It is subject to brain-, body-, situation-, and culture-specific influences, and grounded in sensory-motor systems. The space-number association highlighted the importance of neural reuse, which might describe a general process underlying perceptual symbol systems theory and conceptual metaphor theory. Interestingly, neural reuse theory is also connected to another embodiment theory, conceptual blending.

4.3.2 *Neural Reuse, Conceptual Blending, and Materiality in Economic Life*

In the following, we first introduce the conceptual links between neural reuse, conceptual blending, and material anchors, before developing our approach to conceptual blending as a type of action that engages with materiality in (economic) life.

4.3.2.1 *Neural Reuse, Conceptual Blending Theory, and Material Anchors*

One of the strengths of neural reuse is that it can accommodate bidirectional conceptual mappings (see Anderson, 2014, p. 20ff), whereas conceptual metaphor theory traditionally posits that metaphors are unidirectional, as the (concrete) source domain is mapped onto the (more abstract) target domain, and not the other way around (Lakoff & Johnson, 1980, 1999).[46] Although it is debatable whether conceptual metaphor theory can account for such bidirectional effects (e.g., Lee &

Schwarz, 2012), Gilles Fauconnier and Mark Turner's (2002) conceptual blending theory, a derived and complementary approach, does not involve unidirectional cross-domain mappings, and allows for more conceptual creativity, which is consistent with neural reuse.[47]

Simply put, conceptual blending theory posits that cognition is the creation of mental spaces that emerge temporarily (and non-consciously) when people make sense of their environment. In this theory, which will be discussed in more detail below, two input spaces, sometimes more, are linked by a generic space that shares some conceptual commonality with them and onto which elements from each input space are mapped (or matched). This generic space facilitates the emergence of a blending space, which is a new conceptual structure that integrates the input spaces by taking elements from both of them, but also provides an additional conceptual structure that distinguishes the blend from each of the two (or more) inputs. For instance, if we go back to the mental number line, it can be argued that this spatial-number association is the blending of numbers and motion along a line, whereby numbers can change like points moving along a line (see further details in Turner, 2014, pp. 210–212; see also, Hutchins, 2014, p. 42). Or, if we return to Adam Smith's moral sentiments, "to conceive of another mind, we blend ourselves with what we see of the other person. We project to the blend not only much of what we perceive of the other person, but also something from our own knowledge of ourselves: the possession of a mind lying behind behavior. Emotions we know, from ourselves, that are associated with such behavior are projected to the blend" (Turner, 2014, p. 40).

Arguably, cognitive blending theory resonates with neural reuse theory, according to which cognitive resources are redeployed to perform different functions (Anderson, 2010, p. 265, note 8), such as sensory-motor resources being reused for numerical cognition or for experiencing empathy. Beyond these points, another reason why neural reuse and conceptual blending theories are considered compatible would be that conceptual integration is "opportunistic" in both cases (Cánovas & Manzanares, 2014; Fauconnier & Turner, 2002, p. 282). According to this line of argument, mental spaces that operate as inputs are opportunistically recruited to be blended into another mental space. Then, blends (conceptual integrations) that are functionally suitable (through a trial-and-error process) would be reused and could be passed on from one generation to another after being materially anchored through symbolic procedures (Cánovas & Manzanares, 2014). We leave open the question of the extent to which neural reuse and conceptual blending are similarly opportunistic, and focus on materially anchored conceptual blends, which describe how meaning is attached to, or projected onto, material structure. For instance, as suggested by Hutchins, the mental number line could have been stabilized in culture by projecting material structure into a blended space that is part of the trajector-based cultural practices that can be observed in a given environment (Hutchins, 2005, 2014). This trajector-based cultural practice enables people to make inferences about the relations between numbers. This can be observed in measurements and artifacts such as calendars, rulers, graphs, and, by extension, prices and market trends. When the numbers are times, the number line becomes a timeline, and when the trajector is not a straight line but a curve, the blended space becomes an analogical clock. With such illustrations, some of which are borrowed from Fauconnier and Turner (2002), Hutchins aims to show that there is no need to posit the existence of a mental representation of the material structure as an input space: In the blending process, physical objects are input. In other words, the blending process does not need to be first mentally represented and then mapped onto the material structure, because the material structure is directly an input to the blending process.

4.3.2.2 *Conceptual Blending as a Type of Action Engaging with Materiality*

In this section, we develop the theory of conceptual blending by emphasizing the embodied nature of concepts and by approaching blending as a type of action, since a blend (or the integration of successive blends) can serve as a basis for "integrated action" (Fauconnier, 2001, pp. 264–265).[48] This is complementary to existing approaches to material anchors, which seem to treat materiality as an add-on, albeit an important one (Hutchins, 2005), whereas we regard materiality as essential. The main reason is that without materiality, blending could be arbitrary: Once we treat blending as an action, it necessarily involves materiality, including both things and people. Indeed, conceptual blends are mostly post hoc abstractions that account for the actions of blending. In pursuing this view, we do not go into detail because the proof of the pudding is in the eating, that is, in our later applications of the approach.

As aforementioned, conceptual blending is particularly powerful in explaining the role of creativity and imagination in human action, and we will thus develop this approach with applications to innovation. Economic life offers an immense richness of blending, as human technology, for example, evolves through the blending of pre-existing concepts as materialized in artifacts and practices: Innovations proceed by recombining pre-existing artifacts and practices (Arthur, 2009). For example, early automobiles were modeled after horse-drawn carriages, and the power of engines is still referred to as "horsepower." Edison's invention of the incandescent lightbulb proceeded by tinkering with many elements, undergirded by blending their concepts and constrained by their material properties (Carlson, 2000; Herrmann-Pillath, 2013, p. 456ff). Whether a portable communication device was seen as a "phone" or a "handheld computer" has been crucial to the development of modern digital devices, and the term "smartphone" aptly reflects this blending. However, this blending is not just an abstract operation, but has been realized through the expanding range of practices mediated by apps. The analytical construct of "blend" merely abstracts this evolving practice.

In this book, we employ a simple version of the blending analytical apparatus as shown in Fig. 4.1,[49] which describes the "basic integration network." In general, a blending operation relates two input spaces. For example, one is the input space of telephony, the other is the input space of computing. Both are constituted by various actions, which are mostly different: We use the phone to talk, we type in phone numbers, and so on; in computing, a similar action may be typing or storing information, but most other actions are different, such as using the computer for mathematical operations or drawing images. The blend of the smartphone came into being when people realized that the modules of computers had become so small that they could be crammed into ever-smaller devices, until the moment came when they could become portable (e.g., smartphone), or even "wearable" in the case of a smartwatch. So, we can refer here to the generic space of wearable, which in turn refers to anything that is a physical extension or addition to the body. In the case of the phone, the idea of portable was already well established as a practice. This could be related to the idea of a portable computer, which had already been realized, such as a handheld calculator. The result of this blend is the smartphone. This blending can operate at different levels of complexity, depending on the original input spaces, which may themselves be constituted by preexisting blending operations. The input spaces can be rich in detail, so the blending may be selective, focusing on only some of the constituent elements. For example, for the smartphone blend, the loudspeaker element is less relevant.

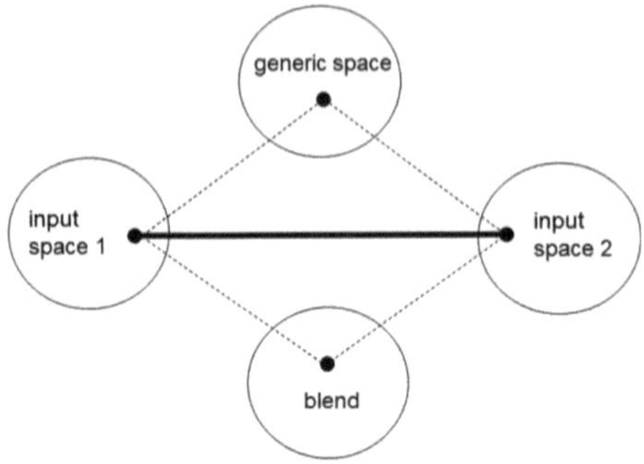

Fig. 4.1 *In a basic integration network, the cognitive process involves two different input spaces and their associated sensory-motor experiences (such as "phone" and "computer"), and relates them to a generic space (such as "portable device") to generate a blend ("smartphone")*

One pillar of conceptual blending theory is the notion of "vital relations," which refers to basic dimensions of human life and experiences such as time, space, or identity. Fauconnier and Turner (2002, p. 93ff) developed "the beginning of a list of 'vital relations' that repeatedly appear in compression under blending:" For instance, "time" can be a vital relation connecting two events between input spaces that are compressed in the blended space; or to return to the illustration of the smartphone, there is a "space" link between the computer and the phone, the parts became smaller and thus portable.

In embodied economics, we go beyond Fauconnier and Turner's notion of vital relations, and argue that vital relations can often be reduced to basic embodied metaphors that are highly relevant to understanding economic life. For example, as we will see in Chapter 6, the CONTAINER metaphor grounds a wide range of more specific relationships, such as the conceptualization of communities as enacted through ingroup/outgroup distinctions. In our later analysis of institutions in Chapter 6, we will draw on Alan Fiske's (1992) theory of four fundamental social relationships, which we denote as Community, Reciprocity, Hierarchy, and Market. These are "vital relationships" when it comes to using blending theory in embodied economics. Like Fauconnier and Turner's "vital relations," "vital relationships" are essential to blending, but there is a key difference between the two concepts: The vital *relationships* that emerge across input spaces are subject to the generic space that forms the social context of the conceptual blending process. This means that each vital relationship, whether community, reciprocity, hierarchy, or market, is *implicitly* present in the spaces, but we should not *explicitly* find each of these vital relationships compressed in each blending. That will be subject to the generic space.

Let us take an illustration of vital relationships in conceptual blending that is not applied to phones or watches, but to money. If the TIME IS MONEY metaphor is a blended space in the market context, as described in Chapter 7, it is not a blended space in the community context. For instance, typically, when a married couple has sex, they do not convert the time they had sex into money. This does not mean that such a blending cannot take place: Rather, it could be done cognitively in a different social context, for instance, when the market context rather than the community context, rules sexual intercourse, as in the case of prostitution. In this case, the blending process will be shaped differently, because a different generic space will favor the identification of a different vital relationship between the input spaces and within the blended space. An important implication follows: In situations where the social context is unclear, the generic space might be difficult to identify, and the vital relationship used to project one space into the other may match and be congruent (or mismatch and be incongruent) with the generic space as seen by others. For instance, one might see sexual intercourse in the market frame, while the couple sees it in the community frame. These situations of incongruence help to identify where one form of social relationship bounds another one (e.g., where the community ends, and the market begins).

Evidently, any space (or concept) is a complex construct in itself, and accordingly, different levels of complexity are manifested in blending. A relationship such as community is established through a variety of embodied actions, such as sharing food. Sharing food is not a blend per se, as when a parent shares food with her child. Food sharing transforms into blending when sharing food with a guest is seen as establishing a relationship of hospitality that includes the guest in the community. Complex forms of blending relate complex input spaces in terms of their respective frames, even in a selective form. In economics, for example, the relationships of hierarchy and market are most essential and are epitomized in more specific social forms, such as the corporation and the stock market. In the notion of privatization of government services, the two input spaces are blended in specific forms, such as imagining the management of prisons by private companies. These examples also show that blending can be a form of abstraction, in the sense that blending is mostly selective and compresses the internal diversity of the input spaces. As in the example of privatization, the realized blend in terms of practices, such as the management of the prison, may combine only a selection of original elements of both input spaces. This is an abstraction in the original sense of the term, and may result in an even more constrained replica of the original elements, such as the application of accounting principles to prisons.

As said, it is important to recognize that blends are embodied in principle. In the original blending theory, this is sometimes lost because the notion of generic space is not clearly made operational. Mostly, it is an abstraction suggested by the scientific observer in the sense of identifying certain concepts, such as "wearable" in the example of a smartwatch. However, blending as an empirical phenomenon would be grounded in generic spaces that are themselves situated and thus part of social practices and other embodied media. In other words, to what extent is generic space itself an empirical phenomenon, and not just an analytical assumption of the scientific observer? There are several possibilities. As Fauconnier and Turner note: "Cognition is embodied, and the spectacular intellectual feats that human beings perform depend upon being able to anchor the integration networks in blends at human scale, using the vital relations that are employed in perception and action" (Fauconnier & Turner, 2002, p. 319). In light of our prior developments, we might infer from this quote that blending corresponds to the neural reuse of action-perception circuits in the service of socially situated cognitive functions as described, for instance, in the case of language (or numerical cognition) (Anderson, 2010; Pulvermüller, 2018). Another empirical reference is reflexive communication, that is, the generic space is constructed by the actors themselves, such as when inventors explicitly argue in terms of blending (e.g., "wearables"). There are also forms of action that are explicitly grounded in and enact blending, such as rituals in many domains, most notably religion, which are typically deeply grounded in material anchors, such as sacred objects (Fauconnier & Turner, 2002; Krátký, 2012).

The blending approach is essential for understanding the core process of embodiment in markets, including the resulting transformations that drive abstraction. This is the role of money in objectifying value, which we will examine in Chapter 7. Money as a material artifact is involved in a myriad of embodied transformations of social action in human societies. As we shall see, the most fundamental are two distinct classes of transformations. The first is the transformation of subjective values into socially objectified values, the second is the transformation of objects of actions into priced goods (which we will later call "assets"). Taking the former as an illustration of the blending approach, money as an input space is the set of artifacts that are socially treated as money, which is itself a complex blend (Fauconnier & Turner, 2002, p. 201ff). If we start out from this as a vantage point, money as an input space consists of objects that can be arithmetically manipulated and treated as signs of other objects. This sign relation is established as a blend after matching with the second input space, which is the specific set of objects. This is not arbitrary, since these are objects for which there is a need, as subjectively conceived by economic agents, which we call "goods." As we can see, both input spaces are embodied and material, and have been projected from the generic domain of exchange onto price as a blend. This shows that the blend is a double-scope one, since in both input spaces exchange is a type of action: People can barter goods they need, and they can barter money tokens, as when they play games. Once the two kinds of exchange are matched within the same generic space, these two types of action are combined in practice as the exchange of goods for money. Then, after projection, a material blend emerges which is the price of goods in markets. Through this transformation, subjective values in the goods domain are objectified as prices. As we will argue in Chapter 7, and in line with recent approaches in economic sociology, prices are thus material objects, and not just abstract relations of disembodied values as classically depicted in standard economic models (Fig. 4.2).

This fundamental blend is actually much more complex, since it involves the emergence of a new institutional domain, the market. This refers to the vital relationships that are the embedding context of blending operations. In our example, exchange is observed in a variety of practices, such as bartering goods and bartering tokens in play: In fact, we can see two input spaces, barter and play, which are matched in the generic space of exchange, thus establishing the blend of "price." This is not yet a market. The double-scope blending results in enabling actions that are now cognitively processed as market actions, thus creating a new kind of vital relationship mediated by markets: Markets are indeed a kind of "serious" play, a staged performance in which money becomes

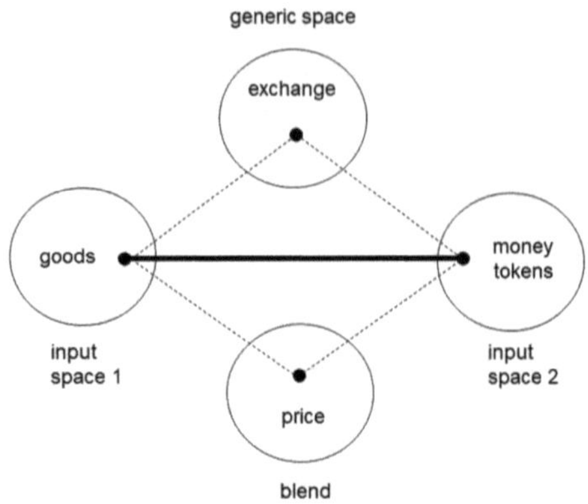

Fig. 4.2 *Price is a conceptual blend of two different input spaces, bartering goods and bartering value tokens, as when playing games. Both activities are matched within the generic space of exchange, so that the two actions of exchanging goods and value tokens are coupled, and the blend "price" is created after projection. Once this practice is established, the value tokens are identified as "money" (see further details in Chapter 7)*

a medium of exchange. The market can then become a generic space in its own right, which enables the blend of transforming goods into assets ("commodification"), as we develop in detail in Chapter 7. Thus, in the historical emergence of money, all of these processes interplayed to generate complex circular causation. We will develop this point further in Chapter 7 when we contend that money can have a performative effect on reality and shape the way we think. For now, we will simply emphasize that this argument supports the idea that conceptual and material structures can be blended together and that (economic) rationality:

> as held by game-theorists, economists, and political scientists, is a cultural construct that owes its existence to the ability to create a certain class of materially anchored conceptual blends. It is a mistake to assume that thinking is, in general, a symbol manipulation process. (Hutchins, 2005, p. 1575)

This very embodied conclusion leads us to the broader question of the role of artifacts in economic life, and how embodied economics is positioned towards extended and distributed cognition.

4.4 Artifact-Mediated Cognition and Language in Embodied Economics

The importance of artifacts is crucial to the study of embodiment in economic life and has been conceptualized in particular by the extended and distributed cognition approaches. Although these two approaches consider the interaction between the brain, the body, and the environment, they view cognition differently. In the following paragraphs, we will argue that embodied economics is more consistent with a distributed cognition approach than an extended cognition approach, and we will emphasize the importance of language in relation to artifact-mediated cognition.

4.4.1 *Artifact Mediation and Embodied Economics*

Extended cognition characterizes a *kind* of cognition and observes that some cognitive functions, such as memory, can be extended beyond the skull into the environment (Clark & Chalmers, 1998). The famous illustration is the case of Otto portrayed by Clark and Chalmers (1998), a patient suffering from Alzheimer's disease whose notebook, an artifact, contains information that plays a similar role to biological memory, for instance, to find his way to the museum. The argument is based on the parity principle according to which what is outside the head, a part of the world (e.g., a notebook), can sometimes be counted as part of the cognitive process (e.g., memory) if it appears to have a comparable or equivalent status to what goes in the head:

> If, as we confront some task, a part of the world functions as a process which, *were it to go on in the head*, we would have no hesitation in accepting as part of the cognitive process, then that part of the world is part of the cognitive process. (Clark & Chalmers, 1998, p. 8)

The externalist argument is clear: Although not all cognition is the head, what is intracranial defines what is cognition. This is the *container* metaphor of the mind, which assumes that the center of cognition is the brain (Hutchins, 2014, p. 36). In this respect, a distributed cognition approach, such as the one we use in embodied economics, can encompass but is not identified with the extended cognition approach. From a distributed cognition perspective, any form of cognition "can be seen as emerging from distributed processes," with (or without) a center, or multiple centers (Hutchins, 2014, p. 36). Moreover, cognition can be distributed across different scales: For instance, between several brain regions, between the brain and body organs, between the brain, the body, and an object, between members of a group, or a social network, and so forth. So far we have seen illustrations of distributed cognition through neural reuse, and material anchors in conceptual blending, but also when we mentioned interactions with artifacts such as money.

Therefore, although it differs from the extended cognition approach, a distributed cognition approach does not neglect the role of artifacts in cognition. On the contrary, distributed cognition can be conceptualized as artifact-mediated cognition. This conceptual position is illustrated by cultural-historical activity theory, which considers the mediation of human action by artifacts as central to the constitution of the human mind (Cole & Engeström, 1993).[50] Drawing on the Russian tradition in psychology initiated by Vygotsky, Luria, and Leontiev (and thus Marx and Engels; see Sève, 2021), as well as the American tradition associated with Dewey and Mead, this view posits that "an artifact is an aspect of the material world that has been modified over the history of its incorporation in goal-directed human action" (Cole, 2003, p. 9). This definition highlights two dimensions of artifacts that are essential to embodiment in economic life: They are material and conceptual. They are material because they are created by people in order to do something, and as such are the result of goal-directed actions. For instance, money can be said to have been created because it facilitates economic exchange.[51] Artifacts are also conceptual because they have been adapted over time: They have been shaped by humans in the course of their incorporation into human action and are the by-product of past human interactions. For instance, money has been conceptualized differently throughout human history, and has taken many forms, such as shells, beads, coins, or notes to name a few (Graeber, 2001). Human beings thus inhabit and grow in a material, social, and economic environment that has been shaped by past and present generations, and that also shapes and transforms their understanding of the world (Ingold, 2022; see also Tomasello et al., 1993 on the ratchet effect).

If mediation is understood as intrinsic to human cognitive processes, this means that cognitive processes cannot be defined in terms of their location in the human brain: "Cognition is not a 'within' property; it is a 'between' property" (Malafouris, 2013, p. 85), it belongs to the "relational domain of the living body coupled to its environment" (Thompson, p.xxv, in Varela et al., 2016). The locus of cognition is not in the brain: Cognition is distributed and is the result of an interaction between an organism, an artifact, and its environment. Consider the famous illustration of the blind man with his stick (e.g., Malafouris, 2019). As Gregory Bateson noted, in his work on the ecology of the mind, the blind man's locomotion, for example, will require consideration of the man, the stick, and the street, and their interactions. The analysis of his cognition will have to be artifact-mediated and situated. Moreover, the extent to which the stick mediates his cognition depends on the purpose of his action: When it comes to eating, forks, and knives, not the stick, are the blind man's vision (Bateson, 1972, p. 459). This means that the mind is distributed differently according to the artifacts used to interact with the world, and these artifacts are selected according to a specific purpose. Put another way, because cognition is artifact-mediated, it is distributed among individuals, artifacts, and the environment, and this will change according to the goals of situated action.

We will return to the importance of goals in action when we develop the analysis of agency in the next chapter, so we shall mention only one essential point at this stage of our argument: In order to achieve a goal in a given situation, different artifacts may fall into the same spontaneously constructed category. These are ad hoc categories, created online (in the situation) or offline (through simulation), with a specific goal in mind (Barsalou, 1999, 2011; see also, Casasanto & Lupyan, 2015). For instance, if I want to reach a coin that has fallen behind the couch and is out of reach of my arms, I might use a stick, a fork, or a knife. Normally, these artifacts have different functions, and belong to different categories, but they can temporarily share the same function depending on my action in a given situation. This means that categories are not given to us, as if the meaning of the world were predefined: They can be redefined in action in each specific situation. Our intentions and actions can shape the use of artifacts, and reciprocally, as we will see in Chapter 7 with applications to money, property, and labor, artifacts can shape our perceptions of the world as well as our actions: Artifacts are performative.

Against this background, "a cognitive science which does include artifact mediation in cultural historical context as part of its fundamental toolkit makes excellent contact with current attempts to understand human thought as the embodied activity of active agents, embedded in environments which are also active, embodied agents" (Cole, 2003, p. 15). Consistently, embodied economics aligns with distributed cognition, understood as artifact-mediated cognition. This leads us to further highlight the importance of language in economic life: In the cultural-historical approach, language can be seen in many ways as the "tool of tools," an artifact that is an integral part of the mediation process (Cole & Engeström, 1993, p. 6).

4.4.2 *Linguistic Mediation and Embodied Economics*

Our goal here is not to go into the details of the role of language in cognition,[52] but to point out some of the peculiarities of language when considering artifact-mediated cognition. The focus is then on language *use*, that is, *speech*, as a tool of communication that shapes both human activity and cognition: "tool and language use are the two mediums of human relations and interactions, and it is through these activities that we appropriate the social heritage psychologically" (Burkitt, 2019, p. 2).[53] As Alexander Luria (1981, p. 35) explained, language is a very special artifact because it "doubles" the human world. Without language, human beings would have to deal only with the concrete things that they can perceive and manipulate; with language, human beings can deal with things that they cannot even perceive (i.e. more abstract things), and with things that have been experienced by previous generations. Thus, language adds another dimension to the world of objects and situations, and this applies to every aspect of human life, including economic life.

In doing so, our approach differs from mainstream economics, which has traditionally neglected language use. For example, in this model, preferences are not declared (or said), but are assumed to be revealed by behavior (e.g., Samuelson, 1948), as discussed in Chapter 2, and game theory can be interpreted as a claim that economics can do without language (McCloskey, 2016, p. 15). One might think that developments in standard behavioral economics which show the importance of framing effects could be seen as a recognition of the role of language in decision-making (e.g., Farrow et al., 2018). Indeed, there is general support for the existence of framing effects leading to preference reversals (Kahneman, 2012; Slovic, 1995). However, behavioral economics omits linguistic behavior (McCloskey, 2022), and, as we will see, there is much more to language than framing effects: In embodied economics, language acts as a scaffold that enhances cognitive reasoning and abilities, as well as a tool that facilitates self-regulation in economic life.

4.4.2.1 Language Use as a Scaffold for Cognition

The idea that language use is a scaffold for cognition that allows us to do things we might not otherwise be able to do has been illustrated at length by Clark (1998, 2008; see also Dove, 2020).[54] In line with the cultural-historical approach, language is viewed as the "ultimate artifact," and in Clark's parlance, "a tool that alters the nature of the computational tasks involved in various kinds of problem solving" (Clark, 1998, p. 193). For example, language use can help offload the demands on memory, when writing down an idea, or just a shopping list, when doing some calculations on a piece of paper, or when rearranging some notes on documents. It is also argued that language, in the form of inner speech, can be seen as "memory augmentation" (Anderson, 2014, p. 269), after Baddeley's work on the phonological loop, a component of working memory (Baddeley et al., 1998). This is one of the earliest documented cases of neural reuse (Anderson, 2014, p. 25), as it shows that remembering the items on a grocery list, for instance, by repeatedly saying them to oneself creates a "phonological loop," which involves brain regions commonly used for both speech production and audition. In addition to its role in working memory and as a scaffold for cognition, inner speech has also been extensively documented in developmental studies (e.g., Winsler et al., 2003), and is hypothesized to generate and sustain self-awareness in some embodiment approaches (e.g., Skipper, 2022).[55]

As such, although inner speech is a "motor-based linguistic tool" (Alderson-Day & Fernyhough, 2015, p. 957), it might seem to be outside the scope of embodiment in economic life. But this is not the case: Inner speech is relevant to planning and motivation (e.g., Alderson-Day & Fernyhough, 2015; Hatzigeorgiadis et al., 2011), and its investigation has led to a better understanding of decision-making. For instance, a great deal of Simon's analysis of bounded rationality comes from empirical studies using think-aloud protocols. Indeed, after observing that people sometimes talk to themselves to solve problems—as Vygotsky and many others since have done by studying the behavior of children and adults (Alderson-Day & Fernyhough, 2015)—, Simon investigated inner speech by asking them to think aloud. To do this, people were instructed to overtly express their thoughts while solving a problem, which allowed Simon to identify the several steps involved in decision-making processes (Simon, 1993).[56] An important point emerges from these studies of bounded rationality and decision-making: Simon and his colleagues observed that although verbalizations of inner speech are generally incomplete sentences and phrases, these verbal descriptions can alter the course of thinking when addressed to another person (Ericsson & Simon, 1998). The argument, which aligns with views of language use as a scaffold for cognition, is that externalizing thoughts has "transformative powers" because it can improve and develop one's thinking.

Reciprocally, it can be argued that when others externalize their thoughts (i.e., their inner speech), whether directly (e.g., physically in a social interaction) or indirectly (e.g., with a text, a video recording), they also contribute to the scaffolding of someone else's cognition. This perspective is particularly useful when it comes to understanding abstract concepts (Borghi, 2022; Borghi et al., 2019),[57] and, we argue, sense-making in economic life. As discussed so far in this chapter, embodiment approaches show that the difference between what is abstract and what is concrete is a difference of degree, not a difference of kind: Perceptual symbol systems theory asserts that abstract concepts can be represented *directly* with perceptual symbols (Barsalou, 1999); conceptual metaphor theory posits that abstract concepts are represented *metaphorically* with more concrete ones (Lakoff & Johnson, 1999); neural reuse theory shows that sensory-motor regions are redeployed to accomplish different functions, whether they pertain to abstract or concrete representations (Anderson, 2014; Cisek & Kalaska, 2010). Therefore, the fact that economic life is pervaded by some abstract symbols, such as prices, does not mean that economic models should not be embodied. That said, if the difference between abstract and concrete concepts is not a difference of kind since both involve embodiment,[58] what makes it a difference of degree? Beyond the argument in terms of perceivability (or perceptual strength), one might consider that one of the peculiarities of abstract concepts is that, because they encompass many exemplars that might not share several features in common—as illustrated by the heterogeneity of the exemplars comprised in the categories "property," "externality," or "economic crisis" —we are more likely to need others to make sense of them.

This is why the use of language is so relevant to economic life: If some processes in economic life are more abstract, then we need other people to make sense of them. We cannot make sense of them in isolation from the rest of the world, just by looking at market trends or alleged price movements. Other people, usually with the help of metaphors, through conversations, by telling and sharing stories, writing newspaper articles, or providing analyses, and so on, can be viewed as an external scaffolding to make sense of economic life. We make sense of the (economic) world in interaction with others, collectively. Language is a means of communication and social interaction, hence the role of the mirror mechanism in language comprehension (Glenberg, 2019), and the role of argumentation in human reason (Mercier & Sperber, 2011). There are also important broader implications: As we will see, from the perspective of embodied economics, language use, and collective sense-making imply that we should conceive of economic life hand-in-hand with participatory, inclusive, and democratic processes. We will elaborate on these points in Chapter 8, particularly through Elinor Ostrom's (2010) work on the management of common-pool resources around the world. Her work shows that people have managed the potential externalities of common goods quite well for centuries when they can engage in face-to-face communication. What leads to "rational" outcomes in economic life is reasoned collective discussion. In many ways, however, this collective discussion would not take place if people were unable to regulate themselves. This brings us to the relationship between language use and self-regulation.

4.4.2.2 Language Use and Self-Regulation

Linguistic mediation is also self-mediation. We contend that language is not only a way to understand each other, abstract concepts, or what is happening in economic life by discussing, arguing, and exchanging with people, but it is also a tool to understand and regulate oneself in economic life because one can also discuss, argue, and exchange with oneself. Thanks to language, through inner speech, one can have a self-reflective internal dialogue with absent others, as already noted by Plato (Gillespie, 2007, p. 682). Nowadays, it is generally accepted that inner speech is a key component of cognitive and behavioral self-regulation in childhood and adulthood (Alderson-Day & Fernyhough, 2015). The idea advanced by Vygotsky is that, through the process of internalization, linguistically mediated social exchanges, such as interactions between a child and a caregiver, are transformed into an internalized "conversation" with the self. Self-regulation is the internalization of others' perspectives via words (signs). Internalization is thus a process that describes the social construction of the mind: "Every higher mental function was external because it was social before it became an internal, strictly mental function; it was formerly a social relation of two people" (Vygotsky, 1997, p. 105; see also Fernyhough, 2008; Tomasello et al., 1993). Self-reflection, then, can be described as the taking of another perspective within the individual, similar to what happens in a conversation when people argue with each other (Gillespie, 2007): "I relate to myself as people related to me. Reflection is a dispute" (Vygotsky, 1989, pp. 56–57). Self-reflection is talking to, arguing with oneself, and incorporating the perspectives of others in order to gain some distance from the current situation and to make sense of oneself and one's actions from an external point of view.

Importantly, as can be inferred from our previous section, highlighting its role in decision-making and motivation, self-talk, whether covert (inner speech) or overt (e.g., think-aloud), does not vanish after the completion of the internalization process in childhood, but rather persists into adulthood. Therefore, although Simon refers to Vygotsky (Ericsson & Simon, 1998), a Vygotskian critique of Simon's think-aloud protocols, which aligns quite well with an embodiment perspective on cognition, is that "think-aloud," as such, is incomplete. If cognition is mediated and situated, the procedure should be described as "think-and-mediate-aloud." The argument is that thinking (and hence cognition) is not merely an internal process, as portrayed by Simon; rather, it is "a process that reflects the cultural practices that are internalized through participation in speech-based interactions and which in turn act on their social context through speech-based interactions" (Smagorinsky, 1998, p. 171). In other words, language has transformative powers not only when it is used to externalize the inner thoughts of one person to another, but also because it is one of the primary (though not the only)[59] tools involved in internalizing and shaping the social world through human interactions.

When it comes to self-regulation, language, through self-talk, can lead to the shaping of one's behavior and influence economic exchange. For instance, Robinson and colleagues (2010) observed that (Western) participants in a Prisoner's Dilemma were more cooperative when they thought aloud (vs. a non-thinking-aloud protocol).[60] When self-talk is manipulated so that it is not spontaneous, as it is assumed to be in think-aloud protocols, results indicate that self-talk can also influence economic behavior. For instance, self-talk can increase or decrease cooperation among (Western) participants in a (repeated) Ultimatum Game

(Frey et al., 2022).[61] Indeed, results indicate that proposers who are instructed to tell themselves to focus on the other participant (other-focused self-talk) are significantly more likely to make fair offers to responders compared to other conditions in which participants were not instructed to self-talk (control treatment), to take some time to think about their decision (contemplation-inducing self-talk), or to keep their own interests in mind (self-focused self-talk).[62] When it comes to the responders, participants were more likely to accept unfair offers when the self-talk was other-focused or contemplation-inducing (vs. control), but not when the self-talk was self-focused. In another study, Gainsburg and colleagues (2022) found that when self-talk can also increase rational self-interest in (Western) participants when they are prompted to think about their own decisions in third- (vs. first-) person self-talk in a (one-shot) Dictator Game.[63] Overall, although the emerging research on the impact of self-talk on economic behavior can lead to contradictory results, as discussed by Frey and colleagues (2022, pp. 102–103), and Gainsburg and colleagues (2022, pp. 512, 514), these studies reflect the impact of self-talk and self-reflection on economic behavior and help to demonstrate that language can lead to consideration of others' perspectives in economic decision-making.

In this section, we have emphasized the importance of distributed cognition in the context of embodied economics. Embodiment requires thinking about cognition in relation to the environment. This environment, however, is social (and thus cultural), and includes others as well as artifacts such as language and tools that help us make sense of the world, but also shape the world as much as the world shapes us. This leads us to an important distinction in embodied economics that is related to the concept of habitus: Inward and outward embodiment.

4.5 Overcoming the Inside-Outside Dichotomy, and Moving the Embodiment Argument Beyond Cognition

Our previous developments have highlighted the need to overcome the conceptualization of cognition as located in the brain: An embodied perspective shows the importance of connecting cognition with perception and action by coupling the organism and the (social) environment. Because embodied economics is about the meaning that emerges from the coupling of organism and environment in economic life, it embraces the enactivist idea that: "Cognition is not an event happening inside the system; it is the relational process of sense-making that takes place between the system and its environment" (Thompson & Stapleton, 2009, p. 26; see also Gallagher, 2017, p. 6ff; Di Paolo, 2009). The analysis is then not about the brain, but about the body. The body comprises the brain and incorporates (from Latin "*incorporare*," "to bring into the body") processes, artifacts, and resources from the environment (Thompson & Stapleton, 2009, p. 28), which become *transparent* to the body, like "the blind man's stick (that) has ceased to be an object for him" (Merleau-Ponty, 1945/1962, p. 165).

In embodied economics, we adopt the (enactivist) principle that: "*For anything external to the body's boundary to count as a part of the cognitive system it must function transparently in the body's sense-making interactions with the environment*" (Thompson & Stapleton, 2009, p. 29). Incorporation has been extensively documented in psychology and neuroscience through studies of artifacts such as the rubber hand illusion and prosthetic limbs (e.g., Spence, 2015; Tsakiris, 2010). Similar analyses have also been developed in archaeology (e.g., Malafouris, 2021), and post-phenomenology (e.g., Ihde & Malafouris, 2019). For instance, Lambros Malafouris, one of the main proponents of material engagement theory, argues that: "Things mediate, actively shape, and constitute our ways of being in the world and of making sense of the world. Things also bring people together and provide channels of interaction. Things envelop our minds; they become us" (Malafouris, 2013, p. 44). In the context of economic life, however, incorporation should be understood more broadly, thanks to the concept of habitus, which allows us to bring the argument closer to key theoretical developments in the social science literature, beyond embodied cognition.

4.5.1 *Habitus, Inward and Outward Embodiment in Economic Life*

As Bourdieu argues with the concept of habitus, incorporation is not limited to things: It also includes the "durable objective structures of the world" (called "field") that we inhabit according to our social position (Bourdieu & Wacquant, 1992, p. 132; see also, Bourdieu, 1997/2000, p. 138ff). As we will see in Chapter 6, habitus is of paramount importance to embodied economics when it comes to the analysis of institutionalized action. For now, we will argue, in this section, that given that habitus is embodied knowledge that is environment-dependent (Fogle & Theiner, 2018), this concept is particularly insightful for connecting the literature on embodiment in the cognitive sciences with the literature on embodiment in social theory (e.g., Cerulo, 2019; DiMaggio, 1979, 1997; Lizardo, 2004, 2007), in phenomenology (e.g., Crossley, 1995; Marcoulatos, 2001; Shilling, 2012), and in the cultural-historical approach (e.g., Panofsky, 2003), among others.[64]

Habitus is the Latin translation of *hexis* employed by Aristotle and has been used in anthropology by Marcel Mauss and in sociology by Émile Durkheim, among others (Bourdieu, 1984, p. 134). There are several more or less comprehensive definitions of habitus in the literature (Lizardo, 2004). It can be briefly defined as "a set of historical relations 'deposited' within individual bodies in the form of mental and corporeal schemata of perception, appreciation, and action" (Bourdieu & Wacquant, 1992, p. 16); although one of the earliest formulations provides a more complete picture of habitus:

> A system of lasting, transposable dispositions which, integrating past experiences, functions at every moment as a matrix of perceptions, appreciations, and actions and makes possible the achievement of infinitely diversified tasks, thanks to analogical transfers of schemes permitting the solution of similarly shaped problems. (Bourdieu, 1972/1977, p. 95)

As several authors have pointed out, the concept of habitus allowed Bourdieu to develop an embodiment theory of the social world whose descriptions resonate with classic mechanisms such as the Hebbian rule,[65] as well as with the literature on embodied cognition (e.g., Cohen & Leung, 2009), and notably with concepts such as the cognitive unconscious, embodied simulation, and mirror neurons (Lizardo, 2004, 2007).[66] Moreover, the reference to "analogical transfers of schemes" connects it to the cognitive linguistics literature on image schemas, conceptual metaphors, and conceptual blending (e.g., Dodd, 2021; Kimmel, 2013). Although the details of its developmental and cognitive underpinnings have yet to be fully characterized (e.g., Cerulo et al., 2021; Lahire, 2003), these analyses arguably enrich the understanding of habitus in light of embodied cognition. However, it would be a mistake to think that this enrichment is a one-way street. One of the fundamental aspects of habitus is to emphasize the "dialectic of the internalization of externality and the externalization of internality" (Bourdieu, 1972/1977, p. 72), which characterizes the codependence between the body and the social world, meaning that perception, cognition, and action are shaped by the ways of being, having, and doing of a particular social (cultural) environment, which contributes to the reproduction the social world.[67] In Bourdieu's parlance: "The body is in the social world but the social world is in the body," (Bourdieu & Wacquant, 1992, p. 35) which expresses, in sociological terms, Merleau-Ponty's (1945/1962, p. 401) idea that: "Inside and outside are wholly inseparable. The world is wholly inside and I am wholly outside myself," and also resonates with embodiment approaches *à la* Vygotsky (Panofsky, 2003), Piaget (Lizardo, 2004), Marx (Loader, 2015), and Hegel (Testa, 2020).

Let us take a concrete illustration: The CONTAINER schema is associated with the bodily experience of containment, where the body is a container that moves from one container (e.g., a room) to another many times a day. However, the body does not move from one neutral container to another neutral container: It moves through socially constructed spaces that structure social roles. In other words, as much as image schemas are experienced in the context of material engagement (Malafouris, 2013, p. 66), they are also experienced in the context of social engagement. This is the case, for instance, in Bourdieu's work on the Kabyle house, where the interior space of the house is "female," and contrasted with the outside space which is "male," and also further divided into a higher, lighter "male" side, and a lower, darker "female" side. As Bourdieu explained:

> All actions performed in a space constructed in this way are immediately qualified symbolically and function as so many structural exercises through which is built up practical mastery of the fundamental schemes, which organize magical practices and representations: going in and coming out, filling and emptying, opening and shutting, going leftwards and going rightwards, going westwards and going eastwards, etc. (Bourdieu, 1972/1977, p. 91)

In other words, what Bourdieu's work showcased was that the internalization-externalization dialectic that characterizes the reciprocal relationship between habitus and field does not characterize an opposition between internal (intracranial) and external (extracranial) cognitive processes. Nevertheless, as Fogel and Theiner (2018, p. 246) note, "it is nearly impossible, for example, to speak of 'internalization' without reifying the concept of an autonomous subject interacting with, but essentially separate from, the world outside its skin." For this reason, we will prefer the terms of *inward* and *outward* embodiment.

Against this background, and building on Bourdieu's insights and embodied cognition, largely understood as reviewed in this chapter, we define *inward embodiment* as the incorporation of ways of being, having, and doing in order to interpret (make sense of), interact, and act within a given environment. Reciprocally, we define *outward embodiment* as the projection and expression of these ways of being, having, and doing as we interpret (make sense of), interact, and act within that environment. Importantly, the projection and expression of these ways of being, having, and doing occur through conceptual metaphors and blending. From this perspective, the organism-environment coupling is a constant movement from inward to outward embodiment, back and forth, which explains why embodiment shapes society and why society shapes embodiment.

The duality of inward and outward embodiment is essential for broadening the scope of our approach to include a wider range of scholars from the social sciences and humanities who are relevant to the construction of embodied economics. The literature on embodied cognition while interdisciplinary, is often narrowly circumscribed, mostly involving cognitive scientists, psychologists, phenomenologists, and analytical philosophers (e.g., Shapiro & Spaulding, 2023). One of the reasons for this, as our previous developments illustrate, is that this research is based on empirical methods mostly from psychology and neuroscience, complemented by thought experiments and stylized cases such as the famous "Otto" in extended cognition. However, there is a literature that goes much further, and uses other methods of empirical research, especially from sociology and related fields in the historical sciences. For the integration of these perspectives, our duality is most productive, since our topic is not cognition per se, but the conceptualization and explanation of economic behavior in a social context.

A case in point is our analysis of the conceptual blending of money. Blending is a specific cognitive mechanism that involves both inward and outward embodiment. Outward embodiment refers to the operations that people can perform by handling money tokens, which in turn are grounded in bodily schemata that relate to a range of capacities, such as the manipulation of numbers. Inward embodiment refers to the transformative effects of money on emotional and cognitive mechanisms. This duality and its processual dynamics have been analyzed in great detail by the sociologist Georg Simmel (2004), without the support of empirical research in psychology, cognitive science, and neuroscience that is standard today. Yet, he combines theorizing with a very rich collection of facts about everyday behavior and historical observations, which qualifies his work today as "sociology," rather than "philosophy," as his title suggests. We argue that embodied cognition allows us to ground Simmel's approach in modern science (Herrmann-Pillath, 2016).

In the following and final section, we further explore the extension of embodied and distributed cognition to the social sciences. This would deserve a separate chapter, if not a book, because it requires rethinking the entire intellectual history of modern self-reflection, as epitomized by economic reflections on capitalism. We cannot achieve that here, but we do not shy away from the task: We conceive of our subsequent chapters as actually doing this reflection as a form of epistemic practice. Still, it is necessary to sketch some basic aspects at a very general level, in order to hint at what is to come.

4.5.2 *The Dialectics of Outward and Inward Embodiment in Modern Social Thought*

As we argued in the previous section, this reflective approach is condensed into the dialectic of outward and inward embodiment. From this perspective, there are several earlier approaches in the history of sociology that clearly contribute to the analysis of this duality. We will briefly mention two important scholars who deserve much attention in the development of embodied economics: Namely, Norbert Elias and Max Weber, whose works also inspired Bourdieu (see Susen & Turner, 2011).

Elias (1939) examined the "civilizing process" in Europe since the Middle Ages and argued that it led to the formation of a peculiar type of actor, "*Homo clausus*." This actor perceives the social world as constituted by individuals who are separated from others by a clear boundary that is enacted through a variety of newly emerging social practices and tools. A key aspect is the drastic reduction of direct physical contact between individuals and the changing design of artifacts that are affordances for physical contact. One of his most famous examples is dining practices, which reduced the sharing of food and developed practices such as handling separate dishes with a knife and fork (compare with Petroski, 1994). Knives are multipurpose tools used to cut food, especially meat, and thus can be used as weapons. As such, they manifest affordances for violence. Elias argues that a key aspect of the civilizing process was the pacification of everyday life. This was manifested in the changing design of knives and their controlled use in conjunction with forks. The range of knife artifacts was greatly expanded, leading to a functional specialization of knives, such that dining was no longer done with multifunctional knives that people might also carry for other purposes, such as killing hunted prey. Elias' civilizing process proceeded through the interplay of outward and inward embodiment, mediated by the affordances of the new tools. The handling of knives and forks requires an orchestrated movement of the hands that is very different from the movements involved in an attack with a knife (e.g., no pushing); the dinner knife is "pacified" by not having a sharp tip, and so on.

Hence, Elias' work describes what today might be referred to as a transformation of collective social cognition, manifested not only in behavioral changes but also in the material artifacts that people use in their actions. The latter is important in terms of empirical methods since we cannot directly observe behavior in the past. Historians have a rich array of methods for identifying patterns of behavior, and one of them is to look at artifacts, such as the changing design of knives, the interiors of houses, or the devices used for personal hygiene (Elias, 1969). Of course, we cannot demonstrate how this might have manifested itself in changes in the level of brain data: But in the embodiment approach, this does not devalue such research, because it eschews brain-centered thinking anyway (e.g., Malafouris, 2010). That being said, recent research has shown that it is possible to formulate hypotheses about the relationship between the kinds of data typically analyzed in the cognitive sciences, including neuroscience, and historical data about artifacts, such as in archaeology (Malafouris, 2013). This is especially true for institutions such as money, for which neuroscientific evidence is now available which highlights its peculiar role as a culturally acquired primary reinforcer (Lea & Webley, 2006). Since this cannot possibly be explained by genetic changes over historical time, it is reasonable to hypothesize mechanisms of neural reuse (and hence exaptation) of pre-existing neural structures that explain the speed of diffusion of money in human populations (Bourgeois-Gironde, 2021).

The other exemplary author is Max Weber. Weber is of considerable interest in the context of our argument because his approach is methodologically close to economics, for instance in terms of methodological individualism (Weber, 1922/2019). After all, Weber was a professor of economics and even had a strained relationship with the emerging science of sociology, of which he was also an advocate. Later, however, Weber was excluded from the intellectual history of economics proper and labeled exclusively as a sociologist. One reason for this is certainly his highly contextualized notion of rationality and his view that it relates to a specific historical formation, capitalism. Weber's concept of rationality refers to a historical process similar to Elias' approach, in the sense that he analyzes "rationalization" rather than "rationality" as a universal and generic property of human beings, as conventionally posited by economics. Again, we can make much sense of his theories in terms of the two movements of embodiment. Outward embodiment is salient in his famous "Protestantism" hypothesis.[68] This thesis assumes that certain emotional structures emanating from religious beliefs were projected, that is, outwardly embodied, into the way Calvinists conducted their businesses, thus imbuing material entities such as "wealth" with specific religious meanings. As a result, business performance outwardly embodied emotional states, such as described as "inner-worldly asceticism." Critics of the Protestantism hypothesis often overlook that Weber himself treated this hypothesis as historically contingent and only part of the story, as Yu (2021) points out. Indeed, in our parlance, it takes two to tango, and Weber also emphasized inward embodiment, as in his focus on accounting as a key factor in explaining the emergence of the capitalist enterprise.

Weberian rationality is definitely not a property of individuals, but of the entire evolving structure of actors, practices, and institutions of capitalism. Yet, it is manifest in individual behavior. It is easy to understand that it is a form of distributed cognition, which also implies that it is contingent on these structures. Weber also emphasized the idea that rationality is a discipline, echoing Karl Marx's view that the system creates capitalists, but the capitalists do not create the system (Patterson, 2009). This points to a factor that has been examined by many others, including Elias: That the specific type of actor that emerges in capitalism also manifests structures of power that are materialized in disciplining practices and numerous mechanisms of inwardly embodying these structures. Classical references to this aspect include, of course, Michel Foucault, such as his notion of "governmentality" (Foucault, 2004).

The Weberian conundrum in the relationship between economics and sociology can be diagnosed in different but related forms in the history of modern social thought. A striking example is American pragmatism, especially Mead (1934) and Dewey (1929), which firmly emphasized embodied engagement with the world, both social and material, and both referred to the state of biological anthropology of their time. Pragmatism was closely linked to the institutional economics of the time, such as Thorstein Veblen (1899/2007) or John Commons (1996). Embodied concepts played a key role in bridging these different disciplines, especially the notion of habit (Hodgson, 2004). Nonetheless, the American "old institutionalism" is marginalized in modern economics and has been eclipsed by the "New Institutional Economics" à la Williamson (1975, 1985), which is based on a disembodied notion of individual rationality.

In this book, we cannot do justice to all of these approaches beyond the specialized literature on embodied cognition. However, we believe that they can be traced back to G. W. F. Hegel. Hegel has recently been recognized as a forerunner of modern theories of embodied cognition, although this certainly remains a fringe opinion (Crisafi & Gallagher, 2010). Hegel is relevant because he raised a deep conceptual issue that is still relevant today, especially when it comes to modern cognitive (neuro-) science. When we write about embodied cognition, like almost everyone else, we implicitly conflate references to a living individual and a generic type. That is, we argue at a higher level of abstraction making claims about a universal form of what constitutes human life. This follows the analytical traditions of the human sciences which aim at generalizations that define the difference between literary and artistic reflections on human life, which typically focus on individual experiences—the (in)famous "two cultures" (Snow, 2018). One discipline that bridges this fundamental difference is anthropology, which tends to emphasize the individuality of human communal forms of life; others are humanistic psychology and psychoanalysis, which focus on the idiosyncrasies of individuality.

This general point matters greatly since embodiment is necessarily individualized, tied to singular bodies here and there, past and present, and, in our view, even in the future. Indeed, neuroscience recognizes the uniqueness of individual brains, and the same is true of individual genotypes (Edelman, 2006). Accordingly, the radical question, then, is how we can ever arrive at and fully prove valid generalizations about humans as a generic category. The answer has been found in various disciplines and schools of thought: It is the necessary embeddedness of individuals in collective forms of life, the "*Gattungswesen*" in Marx's terminology. Some biologists, for example, generalize about human characteristics that are considered specific to the species *Homo sapiens sapiens*, such as language in the generic sense. But the species level only goes so far, given the immense phenotypic plasticity of humans, as illustrated by the diversity of languages. Hence, "collectives" take on a different form that is fundamentally consistent with the anthropological view: They can be thought of as human communities in which individuals live together and communicate with each other. That is, at the most basic level, communities share a language or a symbolic frame of reference. Depending on the discipline, these communities can be empirically specified in various ways, and often have a complex multilayered structure, such as a village, a community of workers in a settlement near a factory, soldiers in an army, and so on. Often, higher-level (abstract) "communities" are identified, which are then usually referred to as "societies," such as Japanese society, leading to terms such as "the Japanese." The highest level of abstraction is the systemic, as epitomized in theories of a universal form of human modernity, of which the classical distinction coined by Tönnies (1887) between community and society may be seen as an archetype: Society is the capitalist system and hence transcends all other more idiosyncratic forms of collectives.

The key methodological insight of embodied cognition for all other disciplines is that these abstractions are not determined from the point of view of the observer, but emerge from the process of embodiment itself: Embodiment as a radically individual phenomenon transcends individuality by characterizing a continuous relationship and interaction with the environment, especially with other human beings, and is mediated by external phenomena such as artifacts. Language is the analytical template: Language as "parole" or speech is radically individualistic, allowing for all kinds of subjective creativity, but at the same time meanings are necessarily embedded in patterns of social interaction between the individual and his environment. This is Wittgenstein's famous argument against a "private language." It is no exaggeration to say that the entire history of philosophy has been driven by the difficulties of grasping this complex relationship—for example, in the perennial debates about nominalism versus realism. There was, however, a pivotal moment, when Western thought—clearly diverging from other worldviews and philosophies of the time—took a path that led to a cul-de-sac: The Cartesian separations of mind and body, and subject and object. Cartesian thinking is still powerful in many recent theories and disciplines, certainly in economics (McCloskey, 2022). But there is also a strong and rich strand of non-Cartesian thinking after this turn. This was inaugurated by Hegel who challenged perhaps the most sophisticated expression of Cartesianism in the history of philosophy, Kant and his distinction between phenomena and noumena, and the corresponding idea of grounding a universal ethics in rational principles, namely the categorical imperative.

Hegel pervades modern thought in all forms, both in terms of positive reception and in terms of his critics. However, there are many areas where his thinking has not been well received. Economics is perhaps one of the most important cases in point. The reason is simple: Hegel's thinking about the economy is shaped by pre-industrial conditions, and economics as a discipline entered its formative stage in Britain when that country was already in the midst of industrialization (Priddat, 1990). Thus, the most influential Hegelian, Marx, developed his theory in the form of a critique of Hegel. Still, he retained fundamental principles, with the result that economics could no longer productively engage with Hegel itself, unfolding as a positive theory of capitalism and confronting the Marxian alternative. This remains true to this day and is directly related to our approach to embodiment (Herrmann-Pillath & Boldyrev, 2014).

Hegel refuted Kant by developing a complete alternative in which both the body and the community are the two lynchpins. We do not engage in an exegesis of Hegel here; therefore, we simply note that the embodiment approach is "Hegelian." Indeed, the reception of Hegel has been difficult because Hegel's thought actually reflects his own philosophy as an idiosyncratic epistemic practice. Following his own famous dictum that philosophy is like the owl of Minerva and can only reflect the historical conditions of its time *ex post*, his thought is deeply imbued with elements of the Protestant theology and political opinions of his time (Taylor, 2015). Their abstract reflection in his philosophy renders some of their important elements irrelevant today, such as his teleological view of history, which is philosophically essential for him since history is seen as the unfolding of "spirit." Despite this, we can also see this as proof of the validity of his basic principles since they also reflexively explain his own thinking.

The central Hegelian idea that we take as a leitmotif in the following chapters and that synthesizes our discussion of embodied cognition so far, is the dialectic of outward and inward embodiment, as defined in the previous section (Testa, 2020). Hegel begins with the body as the ground for all forms of human experience and thought. However, the body is not just a separate physical entity, it only comes to life in action and in interaction with others (Stekeler-Weithofer, 2011). Thus, Hegelian thought is deeply processual, at every level, from individual actions to larger historical transformations. As we detail in the next chapter, action engages the world in expressive ways, but this does not mean that expression is merely a manifestation of pre-existing characteristics of the individual. Through engagement with the world, the products of expression feed back to the individual, transforming her and stimulating further action. One concrete modus of expression is labor, which is why it became essential to Marx. Labor is a process of self-realization that leads to continuous formation as transformation ("*Bildung*").

This dialectic is a chain of steps of outward and inward embodiment since transformation is not seen as unfolding in a Cartesian "mind." To this, we must add the role of other human beings, crystallized in the Hegelian notion of "recognition" (Siep, 2011). This is crucial for understanding the peculiar mix of positive and normative concepts in Hegel, systematically expressed in the unity of being "*Sein*" and normative bindings "*Sollen.*" This is related to another concept that is also essential in economics, freedom (Neuhouser, 2008). Hegel's famous "master–slave" metaphor clearly states the key idea (Redding, 2008): The master does not work and indulges in consumption, so he is driven by his own desires, rests in a state of incomplete expression of his self, and thus lacks genuine freedom as self-determination grounded in self-consciousness. The slave is not free in the sense of being subject to domination, but in his work, he develops a sense of the potential for self-realization. This results in a deadly struggle for recognition, which can be resolved by acknowledging the mutual dependence of master and slave. The master can only achieve the full realization of his freedom by being recognized by the slave who would himself be a free person, since only such a self-determined expression of the slave's recognition can fully validate the master's freedom, and vice versa. In the end, a community of mutual recognition is established, in which individual freedom is possible, though bound to community life. Genuine freedom is grounded in and enabled by an ethical life that is not a constraint but is embodied in all members of the community (Pippin, 2008).

In modern theories of embodied cognition, this can be related to the notion of "transparency" aforementioned, which Hegel called "second nature." This refers to the dialectic of outward and inward embodiment in relation to the rules, norms, and practices of the communities in which individual action unfolds. Hegelian ethical life ("*Sittlichkeit*") means that these institutions become transparent, thus sublating the difference between "*Sein*" and "*Sollen*" (Taylor, 2015). That is, they become inwardly embodied. As a result, we can no longer conceive of the "individual" as abstracted from the community, a fundamental premise of all rationalist strands of thought.

Hegel's philosophy was ostracized in modern liberal economics not only because of its status as the midwife of Marxian thought, but also because of Popper's (1945) critique which associated Hegel with the totalitarianism of the twentieth century. However, when capitalism finally defeated "real socialism" in the revolutions of 1989, Fukuyama's (1992/2020) much-cited claim of an "end of history" was argued on the basis of Hegel, which is rarely noticed and must be seen as a fatal misunderstanding in its reception as a clarion call of neoliberalism. Indeed, to take Hegel seriously would imply that there is another "owl of Minerva" that only reflects the past as a culmination in the present, but without any implications for the future.

Finally, we note that despite his rejection of Hegel, Hayek was a closet Hegelian, since his evolutionism implied embodiment in the "three sources of human values" (Hayek, 1982/2013, p. 486ff). But he also praised the market as an abstraction from embodiment. This creates a stark contradiction in Hayek's work that haunts economics to this day: Hayek has an embodied conception of humans and community, but argues that the market must dominate over them in order to create a utopian and abstract "Great Society," in which the powerful and disembodied social mind of the market rules.

4.6 Conclusion

The purpose of this chapter has been to challenge the idea that because something is supposedly more abstract, such as market mechanisms, which in particular imply numerical cognition thanks to money and the price system, it becomes "disembodied" and thus supports the claim that it is no longer embodied. This idea has been further supported by models of cognition, inherited from the computer metaphor of the mind, which assume that cognition is not embodied, leaving no room for embodiment but looks like something to be "added" to the model, such as emotion or empathy, unless it is portrayed as an "anomaly" or as "irrationality."

Our position is strictly opposed to this view: Following the embodiment approach, we start from the idea that cognition is embodied in the first place. What is abstract may lead to a kind of disembodiment, in the sense that it might be “less perceivable” as Hayek argued—or of “lower perceptual strength” in modern parlance. Indeed, what is more abstract may be more difficult to represent perceptually: For instance, many people would agree on the most important concrete features of an orange, whereas things get more complicated when it comes to perceptually representing what the most important concrete features of “knowledge division” are at the societal level. In this sense, what is abstract involves a form of disembodiment, because it is “less perceivable.”

However, the term “disembodied” should not be read as “not embodied,” because what is “disembodied” through the process of abstraction relies on embodiment in several ways. As discussed in this chapter, the theory of perceptual symbol systems argues that embodied simulations of more abstract concepts involve introspection, emotions, and, importantly, social situations, that is, the presence of others. Conceptual metaphor theory shows that what is more abstract is understood in terms of a more concrete embodied experience. Neural reuse theory shows that sensory-motor systems are involved in abstract thinking, such as numerical cognition. Conceptual blending theory illustrates that what is conceptual is the by-product of creative action that blends the material and cultural environment. Artifact-mediated cognition theories emphasize the importance of language and social interactions in making sense of what is abstract. In any case, these theories do not account for what is abstract by “abstracting” individuals from their embodiment and their material, social, and cultural environment: Instead, this environment is inwardly embodied because the organism is coupled to the environment, and this environment implies the presence of others, whether physically and/or materially through tools and language inherited from prior generations. In this perspective, rationality cannot be thought of as a set of criteria detached from action in a situation: Rather rationality is embodied and located in time and space, attached to things, feelings, and reasons that make the economic and social environment meaningful through outward embodiment by metaphorical thinking and conceptual blending. Economic models in terms of “knowledge division” have abstracted the mind from the body, pushing the computer metaphor of the (social) mind to the extreme, forgetting that real-world economic life is populated by human beings manipulating things and interacting with each other. We will argue this further in the following chapters.

Notes

1. Similar ideas about the abstractness of market processes have been suggested by Tönnies (1887) who contrasts community and society; Durkheim (1893/2013, p. 327) who observes the "differentiation of individuals" and "the weakening of the common consciousness" which becomes "more abstract" with the division of labor in society; Weber (1922/2019) who describes the abstract rules of bureaucratic societies; or Polanyi (1944/2001) who shows the commodification of concrete labor, land, and money, which became fictitious, and thus abstract, commodities.
2. Note that the expression "computer metaphor" does not mean that people are seen as having a hard drive and USB ports (Brette, 2022). This metaphor can be understood in different ways, encompassing "strong" and "weak" versions of artificial intelligence. See, for instance, Lakoff & Johnson (1999, p. 252ff) for a detailed discussion of this metaphor.
3. There are several typologies in the literature. The 4Es is now a common expression to characterize embodiment theory (e.g., Newen et al., 2018). Mark Johnson (2017, p. 34) proposed the 7Es: Cognition is viewed as embodied, embedded, enactive, extended, emotional, evolutionary, and exaptative. According to Pelkey (2023, p. 7), the eighth "E" stands for "ecological.".
4. This is just a glimpse of some of the empirical findings in the literature on perceptual symbol systems and embodiment. For recent and/or comprehensive literature reviews and discussions, see for example: Barsalou (2020), Matheson and Barsalou (2018), and Pulvermüller (2018).
5. It follows that the way one views them, from a first- (actor) or third-person (observer) perspective, modulates brain activity in the modality-specific areas (Basso et al., 2018).
6. Consistently, other studies have shown that viewing single letters (vs. control) activates a pre-motor area involved in writing (Longcamp et al., 2003), listening to a person walk activates the temporal biological motion area, namely the posterior superior temporal sulcus (Bidet-Caulet et al., 2005), and reading stories describing a character getting up and eating breakfast, or playing with her friends on the playground, activates neural representations of visual and motor experiences (Speer et al., 2009). For instance, when

participants read a story in which the character interacts with some objects, brain activity increased in motor regions associated with grasping hand movements (e.g., pre-central and parietal areas).

A famous study found that simply reading words (e.g., "pick," "kick," or "lick") that refer to actions performed with different parts of the body (arm, leg, or face, respectively) activated motor and premotor cortex in a somatotopic fashion (Hauk et al., 2004). For example, arm-related words (vs. filler words) activate regions of motor and pre-motor cortex whose activity increases during actual arm movements.

It is important to note that these results are related to people's experience. For instance, unlike letters, pseudo-letters, i.e., symbols that the study participants had never written before, do not activate the premotor cortex (Longcamp et al., 2003).

7. Related to this argument, abstract concepts have been found to be grounded in emotional or interoceptive states (e.g., Connell et al., 2018; Kousta et al., 2011).
8. The analogy is striking: "If we wish to know what form gelatin will take when it solidifies, we do not study the gelatin; we study the shape of the mold in which we are going to pour it. In the same way, the economist who wishes to predict behavior studies the environment in which the behavior takes place, for the rational economic actor will behave in whatever way is appropriate to maximize utility in that environment. Hence (assuming the utility function to be given in advance), this maximizing behavior is purely a function of the environment, and quite independent of the actor" (Simon, 1990, p. 6).
9. Vernon Smith, who tested the Hayek hypothesis in experimental economics, was influenced by the work of Gerd Gigerenzer (Smith, 2003). However, there are important differences between Gigerenzer's and Smith's views on ecological rationality (Dekker & Remic, 2019).
10. Smith (2008, p. xix) argues that the term "heuristic" can encompass "adaptations that occur within institutions, markets, management, social, and other associations governed by informal or formal rule systems.".
11. This is clearly expressed by Simon in a section entitled "Psychology of problem solving" in his Nobel lecture: "The evidence on rational decision making is largely negative evidence, evidence of what

people do not do. In the past twenty years a large body of positive evidence has also accumulated about the processes that people use to make difficult decisions and solve complex problems. The body of theory that has been built up around this evidence is called information processing psychology, and is usually expressed formally in computer programming languages. Newell and I have summed up our own version of this theory in our book, *Human Problem Solving*, which is part of a large and rapidly growing literature that assumes an information processing framework and makes use of computer simulation as a central tool for expressing and testing theories. Information processing theories envisage problem solving as involving very selective search through problem spaces that are often immense. Selectivity, based on rules of thumb or "heuristics," tends to guide the search into promising regions, so that solutions will generally be found after search of only a tiny part of the total space. Satisficing criteria terminate search when satisfactory problem solutions have been found. Thus, these theories of problem solving clearly fit within the framework of bounded rationality that I have been expounding here" (Simon, 1979, p. 507).

12. See, for instance, Gallagher (2018) and Petracca (2021).
13. The importance of the unknown in the market, based on our imperfect knowledge of the world, is the reason why, for Hayek (1982/2013, p. 497): "Competition is (…) first and foremost a discovery procedure. No theory can do justice to it which starts from the assumption that the facts to be discovered are already known. There is no predetermined range of known or 'given' facts which will ever all be taken into account." He thus rejects the all-seeing eye that inspired substantive and constructivist rationality.
14. Phenomenologists would be more specific and speak of "situation" rather than "environment" (Gallagher, 2017), hence the situated aspects of cognition in grounded cognition.
15. This is how we read Sartre's definition of emotion as a "transformation of the world" (Sartre, 1939/2014, p. 39).
16. "There is a distinction between an individual life and a statistical life. Let a 6-year-old girl with brown hair need thousands of dollars for an operation that will prolong her life until Christmas, and the post office will be swamped with nickels and dimes to save her.

But let it be reported that without a sales tax the hospital facilities of Massachusetts will deteriorate and cause a barely perceptible increase in preventable deaths—not many will drop a tear or reach for their checkbooks" (Schelling, 1968, p. 129).

17. In some ways, such a conclusion is illustrative of how "Homo economicus remained the unquestioned ideal" in the (mainstream) behavioral economics literature, a standard that says more about a "view of human nature (that) is tainted by a bias bias" than about humanity (Gigerenzer, 2018, pp. 303–304).
18. For instance, Reddy (2020, p. 168) points out that: "from the 1980s on, anthropologists began to question whether there was an equivalent to "emotions" among non-Western societies. Their research showed, more often than not, that, outside the West, people do not oppose something called 'emotions' to something called 'reason' or 'thought,' as if these represented separate parts or 'faculties' of the self.".
19. It is now thought that there is no evidence of distinct brain regions underlying emotion and cognition (Lempert & Phelps, 2014, p. 220). The opposition between affect and control, which is another expression of the opposition between emotion and rationality, has also been convincingly criticized in the literature (e.g., Feldman-Barrett & Lindquist, 2008; Hommel, 2019; Pessoa, 2008).
20. Lewin's (1951) concept of valence in his field theory is another (and older) classical psychological approach that supports our argument.
21. At the brain level, for instance, the ventromedial prefrontal cortex (vmPFC) is a region implicated in affect and value calculation, although it remains unclear whether the same subregions are actually activated.
22. Interestingly, Sartre (1939/2014, pp. 39–41) suggested a similar idea in his illustration of an inaccessible bunch of grapes that are eventually deemed "too green," not without echoing Festinger's (1962) reference to the "sour grapes" metaphor.
23. Note that the same conclusion can be reached without reference to emotion. The famous studies led by Libet (1985) can be interpreted as showing that the initiation of actions can be triggered at the brain level (in the motor system) before the conscious experience of volition. Simply put, these studies may suggest that free

will might lag behind behavior, and people might start doing things without being conscious of what they are doing. Although this surely happens on a daily basis, it might be an exaggeration to suggest that any experience of volition is then merely a post hoc narrative interpretation of events (Haggard, 2008; see contra, Balaguer, 2014). Nonetheless, the main conclusion that follows is that, in economic life, people can engage in behavior that is not consciously planned. In this way, their actions can shape their preferences because they infer their preferences from what they do. Once they have done something, they come up with preferences. This is reinforced by the fact that human behavior is subject to many influences: For instance, gut feelings, emotions, but also the immediate context, whether social or physical, the effects of which can also work subliminally or non-consciously (Bargh & Chartrand, 1999; Gigerenzer, 2007; Lempert & Phelps, 2014). Retrospectively, people infer preferences from what they have done or are doing, even though these actions were not necessarily the by-product of conscious deliberation. Preferences are then inferred from memories, most of which are inaccurate, that reconstruct reality and contribute to people's sense of identity. Similar conclusions can be drawn from studies of split-brain patients in neuropsychology (Gazzaniga, 2013).

24. Although not related to embodiment, the issues of cost–benefit analyses in decision-making, under uncertainty or not, have been raised several times in the literature (e.g., Johnson et al., 2023: Weiss & Shanteau, 2021).
25. Note that Damasio's theory has inspired some developments in economics (e.g., Loewenstein & O'Donoghue, 2004).
26. As Damasio explains: "When the bad outcome connected with a given response option comes to mind, however fleetingly, you experience an unpleasant gut feeling. Because the feeling is about the body, I gave the phenomenon the technical term *somatic* state ('soma' is Greek for body); and because it 'marks' an image, I called it a *marker*. (...) In short, somatic markers are a special instance of feelings generated from secondary emotions. Those emotions and feelings have been connected, by learning, to predicted future outcomes of certain scenarios. (...) Somatic markers do not deliberate for us. They assist the deliberation by highlighting some options (either dangerous or favourable), and eliminating them

rapidly from subsequent consideration" (Damasio, 1994, pp. 173–174). The somatic marker hypothesis is supported by the results of the Iowa Gambling Task (IGT). The IGT was created by Bechara, Damasio, and their colleagues in 1994, to simulate "real-life decision-making in the way it factors uncertainty of premises and outcomes, as well as reward and punishment." It is now one of the most frequently cited assessments of experiential decision-making (Beitz et al., 2014). Experimental results showed that "normal" (and brain-damaged control) participants avoided the bad options and preferred the good options, whereas patients with bilateral damage to the vmPFC did not avoid the bad options (i.e., they preferred them). The results also showed an increased skin conductance response (SCR) during the IGT trial in "normal" subjects, suggesting that they physically experienced the anticipated risk before choosing a "risky" option. In contrast, patients with bilateral damage to the vmPFC failed to generate any SCR at all before choosing an option (Bechara, 2004).

27. See also Niedenthal and colleagues (2005) for a comparison between Damasio's (1989) theory of convergence zones and Barsalou's (1999) theory of perceptual symbol systems.
28. Indeed, as proponents of ecological rationality argue: "how (un)reasonable the influence of a specific emotion is depends on environmental circumstances. The question to be answered is thus the following: In which real-world environments and under what circumstances do emotions and their consequences result in successful or unsuccessful outcomes? The rationality of emotions can be decoded only by investigating the match or mismatch between their influences on computational processes and the demands of the environment in which the organism is situated" (Volz & Hertwig, 2016, p. 111).
29. Although Elster (1989, pp. 99–100) does not discuss the difference between descriptive and injunctive social norms, his descriptions may include injunctive social norms when he emphasizes approval and disapproval in the enforcement of social norms. There are several ways of distinguishing between descriptive and injunctive norms. One of the most meaningful is that a descriptive norm is a social norm that helps achieve the (social) "goal of (an) effective action" (Cialdini & Trost, 1998, p. 155), whereby people observe what is commonly done; whereas an injunctive

social norm refers to what is commonly approved or disapproved within a given culture (Goldstein & Cialdini, 2009). Importantly, an injunctive norm helps achieve the (social) "goal of building and maintaining social relationships" (Cialdini & Trost, 1998, p. 158). Injunctive norms are, for instance, the taboo of incest, the prohibition of cannibalism, the prohibition of murder, or the prohibition of unprovoked aggression, and are so essential to key social relationships and society that they can take the form of legal norms.

30. "By the imagination we place ourselves in his situation, we conceive ourselves enduring all the same torments, we enter as it were into his body, and become in some measure the same person with him, and thence form some idea of his sensations, and even feel something which, though weaker in degree, is not altogether unlike them" (Smith, 1759/2002, §2).
31. "Upon some occasions sympathy may seen to arise merely from the view of a certain emotion in another person" (Smith, 1759/2002, §6). He adds beforehand that: "the pleasure and the pain are always felt so instantaneously, and often upon such frivolous occasions, that it seems evident that neither of them can be derived from any such self-interested consideration" (Smith, 1759/2002, §1).
32. As Anspach (1972, p. 182) explained, "the instantaneousness of a sympathy reaction precludes for Smith the possibility that it is the result of time-consuming calculations of self-interest."
33. In this fMRI study on the mirror neuron system, participants, who were not instructed to explicitly empathize with the actors they saw, were presented with 3-second video clips showing people leaning forward to sniff the content of a glass before retracting their torso and displaying a facial expression of either disgust, pleasure, or neutral emotion. In addition to the visual conditions, participants were also exposed to two different smells: Disgusting or pleasant odorants. The results showed that (passively) viewing the facial expression of disgust automatically activates brain regions (left anterior insula and right anterior cingulate cortex) whose activity is also increased when participants smell disgusting odors. Understanding the expression of disgust on other people's faces is associated with increased activity in the brain regions activated during the individual experience of this emotion, suggesting the

existence of a mirror-neuron matching system for emotions. It is worth noting that they did not observe a similar overlap in brain activity between observing pleased facial expressions and smelling pleasant odors, which may be explained by a "much weaker link between pleasant odors/smells, the emotion of pleasure, and pleased facial expressions" (Wicker et al., 2003, p. 657). Subsequent studies confirmed these findings, showing that the anterior insula is activated when participants watch videos of people sampling pleasant or unpleasant tastes and when they sampled the different tastes themselves (Jabbi et al., 2007).

34. For instance, he states: "When we see a stroke aimed and just ready to fall upon the leg or arm of another person, we naturally shrink and draw back our own leg or our own arm; and when it does fall, we feel it in some measure, and are hurt by it as well as the sufferer" (Smith, 1759/2002, §3). Nevertheless, the concept of moral sentiments encompasses situations that go beyond the perception of action and emotions, such as situations of "Smithian empathy" (Roughley, 2015). For instance, when Smith describes how people can feel bad for a dead or mentally incapacitated person, while not feeling bad themselves. This feeling might express how one would feel if one were in their situation.
35. Translation by the authors from: "la perception d'un monde tout à fait objectif, sans aucun prédicat anthropomorphique est inconcevable. Même un univers purement géométrique serait impossible sans aucun élément humain; ainsi une figure géométrique, le cercle par exemple, peut être exprimé par une formule analytique; mais un sujet qui n'aurait jamais vu de cercle ne saurait reconstituer le sens intuitif de la formule. Toute géométrie est fondée sur le concept essentiellement anthropomorphique de contour, c'est-à-dire de limite entre le 'dehors' et le 'dedans,' distinction qui n'existe que pour un sujet, lui-même situé dans l'espace, qui voit d'un certain point de vue (son corps), par rapport auquel la distinction du dehors et du dedans prend un sens. Pas de contour sans un sujet qui structure des éléments donnés pour en faire des figures" (Merleau-Ponty, 1964, p. 186).
36. See also Lakoff and Núñez (2000), and Anderson (2014, p. 232ff), for complementary analyses of mathematics in terms of embodiment.

37. This may help explain why some anthropologists consider anthropomorphism to be the default ontological inference for humans in any society (Sahlins, 2014, 2022; see also, Descola, 2014), rather than a cognitive bias (Dacey, 2017). On the anthropomorphic brain and an analysis in terms of mirror neurons, see Gazzola and colleagues (2007).
38. Merleau-Ponty (1964) also does this: He uses an image schema, the CONTAINER, to interpret a CIRCLE, forming a metaphor in which A CIRCLE IS A CONTAINER.
39. Beyond this illustration, the metaphorical associations of verticality have been documented for cardinal direction (e.g., Brunyé et al., 2012; Meier et al., 2011; Nelson & Simmons, 2009), concreteness (e.g., Aggarwal & Zhao, 2015; Deng & Kahn, 2009), divinity (e.g., Chasteen et al., 2010; Meier et al., 2007), power (e.g., Giessner & Schubert, 2007; Meier & Dionne, 2009; Schubert, 2005; Sundar & Noseworthy, 2014), rationality/emotions (e.g., Cian et al., 2015; Fetterman & Robinson, 2013), risk-taking (Jami, 2019), virtuous consumption (e.g., Basso et al., 2021; Dong et al., 2020; Wang & Basso, 2021). The list could go on and on with other source domains such as balance, cleanliness, or warmth (e.g., IJzerman & Semin, 2009; Larson & Billeter, 2013; Lee & Schwarz, 2018).
40. Organism-environment coupling is facilitated by affordances, which are defined as the relations between the abilities of organisms and some features of situations (Chemero, 2003; Gibson, 1979).
41. Note that the GOOD IS LEFT mapping exists in a cultural form in the Tibetan religion, Bön. Despite this association between positive valence and leftward, right-handed Tibetan practitioners of Bön tend to exhibit the GOOD IS RIGHT mapping at the behavioral level. Goodness remains associated with motor fluency despite their religious beliefs (Li & Cao, 2019).
42. See also Elder and Krishna (2012) for an application to food consumption.
43. There are scores of illustrations of metaphors embodied in social practices. See, for instance, Bourdieu's (1972/1977) analysis of the spatial division of gender in the Kabyle house (also mentioned later in this chapter), and Wiseman's (2019) analysis of the movement metaphor that structures rites of passage.

44. SNARC-like effects have been observed in non-numerical magnitude domains such as time, size, letters, and luminance (Macnamara et al., 2018).
45. See also, Anderson (2014, p. 26ff) for reasons why perceptual symbol systems theory and conceptual metaphor theory do not always explain neural reuse. Nevertheless, the concept of neural reuse echoes (though does not identify with) "neural exploitation" (Gallese & Lakoff, 2005) or the "shared circuits model" (Hurley, 2008), at least in its support for embodied cognition. The main difference is that neural reuse is (can be) more radically anti-computational (Anderson, 2014, p. 99; Raja & Anderson, 2019). The concept of neural reuse has also been used to make sense of empirical results in the field of perceptual symbol systems theory (e.g., Pulvermüller, 2018; Shebani et al., 2022).
46. Several illustrations of bidirectionality have been reported in the literature. For instance, a cross-cultural association seems to be observed between verticality and power (e.g., Gannon & Pillai, 2015), which is represented by the conceptual metaphor: POWERFUL IS UP, POWERLESS IS DOWN. In support of this metaphor, experimental studies show that people infer a leader's power differently when confronted with an organizational chart: They tend to think their supervisor is a strong leader when the line depicting the distance between employees and their direct supervisor is long (vs. short) (Giessner & Schubert, 2007). The higher the manager is depicted in the organizational hierarchy, the more powerful she is perceived to be. Conversely, it appears that information about a leader's power, leads people to place her picture high on the organizational chart. This means that the association between POWER and VERTICALTY leads to concrete-to-abstract effects—where a manipulation in the concrete domain affects measurement in the abstract domain—but also to abstract-to-concrete effects—where a manipulation in the abstract domain affects a measurement in the concrete domain. This result, together with several others identified in the literature (e.g., Lee & Schwarz, 2012), implies that contrary to the classic interpretation of conceptual metaphors, the effect between the concrete source domain and the more abstract target domain is not only unidirectional, but can also be bidirectional.

47. See Evans and Green (2006, p. 435ff) and Lakoff (2008) for a comparison between conceptual metaphor theory and conceptual blending theory.
48. More specifically he points out: "In developing a theory of blends, attention has been focused on the optimality constraints that guide their construction, the cross-space mappings and common schemas that serve to launch them, and the dynamic emergent structure that runs the blend and provides inferences and novel concepts. Their efficiency in developing new types of integrated action, noted earlier in the ski example, deserves additional research. It bears in crucial ways with issues of embodiment and creativity that are central to cognitive science" (Fauconnier, 2001, p. 264).
49. The original theory of blending is aptly overviewed by Evans and Green (2006, p. 400ff).
50. This is also illustrated by Malafouris' (2013) material engagement theory, an embodiment approach to material culture and the cognitive dimensions that emerge from the co-constitution of people and things. This theory is aligned with Vygotsky's and Hutchins' distributed cognition in the sense that cognition can be understood and studied as an interaction between the brain, the body, and the (material) world. In this perspective, for instance, image schemas are experienced in some context of material engagement (Malafouris, 2013, p. 66). Bourdieu's (1972/1977) theory of practice anticipated such developments (e.g., Kabyle house).
51. Note that money and markets are not the only way economic exchanges take place. This is illustrated by Malinowski's (1922) descriptions of the "kula chain," a ceremonial exchange system in a province of Papua New Guinea, or the past "long-distance interaction spheres" in North America mentioned by Graeber and Wengrow (2021, p. 23).
52. See, for instance, Carruthers (2002), DiPaolo and colleagues (2018), and Nedergaard and colleagues (2023).
53. Burkitt (2019, p. 2) continues with the following quote from Leontyev, which summarizes the cultural-historical approach in psychology very well: "A tool mediates activity that connects a person not only with the world of objects but also with other people. This means that a person's activity *assimilates the experience of humanity*. It means that a person's mental processes (the 'higher mental functions') acquire a structure necessarily linked to

socio-historically formed means and modes, which are transmitted to him by other people through team-work and social intercourse. But to transmit a means or a mode for carrying out some process can be done only in external form—in the form of action or in the form of external speech. In other words, the higher and specifically human processes can arise only through mutual interaction of person with person, as *interpsychological* processes, which only later come to be carried out by the individual independently" (Leontyev, 1974, p. 19).

54. The scaffolding metaphor was first used in the context of Vygotskian approaches by Jerome Bruner and his colleagues (Wood et al., 1976) to describe the adult's help to the child in the zone of proximal development.
55. Note that despite being anti-modularist, Vygotsky's conceptualization of inner speech is not in full alignment with current embodiment theories of language that revolve around embodied simulation (see Alderson-Day & Fernyhough, 2015, pp. 932, 941). For further analyses between Vygotsky and embodiment, see González (2021).
56. This led Simon (2000) to emphasize the importance of qualitative methods in economics for observing behavior, interviewing economic agents, and analyzing written records in economic life.
57. For various arguments supporting the role of language in understanding abstract concepts, see for instance, Dove (2020) and Lupyan and Winter (2018).
58. As summarized by Borghi: "concrete and abstract concepts do not constitute a dichotomy (Barsalou et al., 2018). Instead, they can be represented as points in a multidimensional space: Compared with concrete concepts, abstract concepts are acquired later in development, are more variable across individuals and contexts, have lower dimensionality, have higher relationality, have lower perceptual strength, and are more grounded in interoception. Also, they are acquired mainly linguistically, and typically have low iconicity" (Borghi, 2022, p. 240).
59. See, for instance, Tomasello (2019) who identified four main types of learning and experience in human cognitive and social ontogeny that generally lead to the development of rationality and morality by the age of six to seven: (1) Individual learning, (2) observational learning, (3) pedagogical or instructional learning, and

(4) social co-construction (peer collaboration). On child's development and economic life, see also, for instance, Pesowski and colleagues (2022), and Webley and colleagues (2002).

60. It is important to note, however, that these results might be influenced by social desirability, and might not show that verbalizing thoughts changes the thought process and increases cooperation (Robinson et al., 2010, p. 122).
61. The reappraisal strategies employed by Grecucci and colleagues (2013) mentioned in Chapter 2 in relation to Sanfey and colleagues' (2003) results on the role of emotion (regulation) in Ultimatum Games can be viewed as a form of self-talk.
62. As such, as Frey and colleagues (2022, p. 101) acknowledge, these results do not allow us to conclude that when proposers are other-focused, their offers are more generous because self-talk increases their concern for fairness or because it increases their awareness that the responder could reject a low offer.
63. Participants in the self-immersed condition, or first-person self-talk, read: "Some people report thinking about themselves using first person language, so that's what we'd like you to do as you make your decision. In other words, as you think about how to split up the money, ask yourself things like, 'What should I do?'" Participants in the self-distanced condition, or third-person self-talk, read: "Some people report thinking about themselves using third person language, so that's what we'd like you to do as you decide what to do when making your decision. In other words, as you think about how to split up the money, ask yourself things like, 'What should [participant's name] do?'" with the participant's first name piped into the question from when they entered it earlier. As explained Gainsbourg and colleagues (2022, p. 515) explain, participants in both conditions were specifically prompted to engage in self-talk (as opposed to other types of thinking).
64. The concept of habitus also leads to a reconsideration of bounded rationality: "Reason (or rationality) is 'bounded' not only, as Herbert Simon believes, because the human mind is generically bounded (there is nothing new in that idea), but because it is socially structured and determined, and, as a consequence, limited" (Bourdieu, 2005, p. 84).
65. The Hebbian rule can be inferred from this quote: "To deny existence of acquired dispositions, in the case of living beings, is to

deny the existence of learning in the sense of a selective, durable transformation of the body through the reinforcement or weakening of synaptic connections" (Bourdieu, 1997/2000, p. 136; see also, Changeux, 2006).

66. In this quote, for example, Bourdieu's emphasis on mimesis (in contrast to imitation) echoes the mirror mechanism, and his reference to enactment, which takes place on a nonconscious level, evokes the concept of mental simulation (re-enactment), which occurs automatically and implicitly: "the process of acquisition—a practical *mimesis* (…) which implies an overall relation of identification and has nothing in common with an *imitation* that would presuppose a conscious effort to reproduce a gesture, an utterance or an object explicitly constituted as a model—and the process of reproduction—a practical reactivation which is opposed to both memory and knowledge—tend to take place below the level of consciousnes (…) The body believes what it plays at (…) [i]t does not represent what it performs, it does not memorize the past, it *enacts* the past, bringing it back to life" (Bourdieu, 1980/1990, p. 73).
67. Unsurprisingly, Bourdieu's theory of practice is considered by Heft as fully in line with the ecological-psychological approach (e.g., Rietveld & Kiverstein, 2023). See also Ingold (2000, pp. 162ff, 167, 427 note 3) for similar observations.
68. We do not examine this position here as a historical truth, as it has been much debated, often considered refuted, but still seems to be alive in scholarly debates, especially outside Western circles. See, for instance, Noguchi (2022).

References

Aggarwal, P., & Zhao, M. (2015). Seeing the big picture: The effect of height on the level of construal. *Journal of Marketing Research, 52*(1), 120–133. https://doi.org/10.1509/jmr.12.0067

Akerlof, G. A., & Shiller, R. J. (2009). *Animal Spirits: How human psychology drives the economy, and why it matters for global capitalism.* Princeton University Press.

Alderson-Day, B., & Fernyhough, C. (2015). Inner speech: Development, cognitive functions, phenomenology, and neurobiology. *Psychological Bulletin, 141*(5), 931–965. https://doi.org/10.1037/bul0000021

Alejo, R. (2010). Where does the money go? An analysis of the container metaphor in economics: The market and the economy. *Journal of Pragmatics, 42*(4), 1137–1150. https://doi.org/10.1016/j.pragma.2009.08.013

Anderson, M. L. (2010). Neural reuse: A fundamental organizational principle of the brain. *Behavioral and Brain Sciences, 33*(04), 245–266. https://doi.org/10.1017/S0140525X10000853

Anderson, M. L. (2014). After phrenology: Neural reuse and the interactive brain. *MIT Press*. https://doi.org/10.7551/mitpress/10111.001.0001

Anderson, M. L., Richardson, M. J., & Chemero, A. (2012). Eroding the boundaries of cognition: Implications of embodiment. *Topics in Cognitive Science, 4*(4), 717–730. https://doi.org/10.1111/j.1756-8765.2012.01211.x

Anspach, R. (1972). The implications of the *Theory of moral sentiments* for Adam Smith's economic thought. *History of Political Economy, 4*(1), 176–206. https://doi.org/10.1215/00182702-4-1-176

Ariely, D., & Norton, M. I. (2008). How actions create—not just reveal—preferences. *Trends in Cognitive Sciences, 12*(1), 13–16. https://doi.org/10.1016/j.tics.2007.10.008

Arrow, K. J. (1951). Mathematical models in the social sciences. In D. Lerner & H. D. Lasswell (Eds.), *The policy sciences; recent developments in scope and method* (pp. 129–154). Stanford University Press.

Arrow, K. J. (1998). What has economics to say about racial discrimination? *Journal of Economic Perspectives, 12*(2), 91–100. https://doi.org/10.1257/jep.12.2.91

Arrow, K. J., & Hahn, F. H. (1971). *General competitive analysis*. North-Holland.

Arthur, W. B. (2009). *The nature of technology: What it is and how it evolves*. Free Press.

Ashraf, N., Camerer, C. F., & Loewenstein, G. (2005). Adam Smith, behavioral economist. *Journal of Economic Perspectives, 19*(3), 131–145.

Baddeley, A., Gathercole, S., & Papagno, C. (1998). The phonological loop as a language learning device. *Psychological Review, 105*(1), 158–173. https://doi.org/10.1037/0033-295X.105.1.158

Balaguer, M. (2014). *Free will*. MIT Press.

Bargh, J. A., & Chartrand, T. L. (1999). The unbearable automaticity of being. *American Psychologist, 54*(7), 462–479. https://doi.org/10.1037/0003-066X.54.7.462

Barsalou, L. W. (1999). Perceptual symbol systems. *Behavioral and Brain Sciences, 22*(04), 577–660. https://doi.org/10.1017/S0140525X99002149

Barsalou, L. W. (2008). Grounded cognition. *Annual Review of Psychology, 59*, 617–645. https://doi.org/10.1146/annurev.psych.59.103006.093639
Barsalou, L. W. (2011). Ad hoc categories. In P. C. Hogan (Ed.), *The Cambridge encyclopedia of the language sciences* (pp. 87–88). Cambridge University Press.
Barsalou, L. W. (2020). Challenges and opportunities for grounding cognition. *Journal of Cognition, 3*(1), 31. https://doi.org/10.5334/joc.116
Barsalou, L. W. (2023). Implications of grounded cognition for conceptual processing across cultures. *Topics in Cognitive Science*, tops.12661. https://doi.org/10.1111/tops.12661
Barsalou, L. W., Dutriaux, L., & Scheepers, C. (2018). Moving beyond the distinction between concrete and abstract concepts. *Philosophical Transactions of the Royal Society b: Biological Sciences, 373*(1752), 20170144. https://doi.org/10.1098/rstb.2017.0144
Barsalou, L. W., Simmons, K. W., Barbey, A. K., & Wilson, C. D. (2003). Grounding conceptual knowledge in modality-specific systems. *Trends in Cognitive Sciences, 7*(2), 84–91. https://doi.org/10.1016/S1364-6613(02)00029-3
Barsalou, L. W., & Wiemer-Hastings, K. (2005). Situating abstract concepts. In D. Pecher & R. A. Zwaan (Eds.), *Grounding cognition: The role of perception and action in memory, language, and thinking* (pp. 129–163). Cambridge University Press. https://doi.org/10.1017/CBO9780511499968.007
Basso, F., Bouillé, J., & Troiville, J. (2021). Are you up for fair-trade products? Vertical dimension as a metaphorical representation of virtuous consumption. *Journal of Business Research, 135*, 508–518. https://doi.org/10.1016/j.jbusres.2021.06.050
Basso, F., Petit, O., Le Bellu, S., Lahlou, S., Cancel, A., & Anton, J.-L. (2018). Taste at first (person) sight: Visual perspective modulates brain activity implicitly associated with viewing unhealthy but not healthy foods. *Appetite, 128*, 242–254. https://doi.org/10.1016/j.appet.2018.06.009
Bateson, G. (1972). *Steps to an ecology of mind: Collected essays in anthropology, psychiatry, evolution, and epistemology*. Balentine Books.
Bechara, A. (2004). The role of emotion in decision-making: Evidence from neurological patients with orbitofrontal damage. *Brain and Cognition, 55*(1), 30–40. https://doi.org/10.1016/j.bandc.2003.04.001
Beitz, K. M., Salthouse, T. A., & Davis, H. P. (2014). Performance on the Iowa Gambling Task: From 5 to 89 years of age. *Journal of Experimental Psychology: General, 143*(4), 1677–1689. https://doi.org/10.1037/a0035823
Berridge, K. C., & O'Doherty, J. P. (2014). Chapter 18—From experienced utility to decision utility. In P. W. Glimcher & E. Fehr (Eds.), *Neuroeconomics (Second Edition)* (pp. 335–351). Academic Press. https://doi.org/10.1016/B978-0-12-416008-8.00018-8

Bidet-Caulet, A., Voisin, J., Bertrand, O., & Fonlupt, P. (2005). Listening to a walking human activates the temporal biological motion area. *NeuroImage, 28*(1), 132–139. https://doi.org/10.1016/j.neuroimage.2005.06.018

Bonini, L., Rotunno, C., Arcuri, E., & Gallese, V. (2022). Mirror neurons 30 years later: Implications and applications. *Trends in Cognitive Sciences, 26*(9), 767–781. https://doi.org/10.1016/j.tics.2022.06.003

Borghi, A. M. (2022). Concepts for which we need others more: The case of abstract concepts. *Current Directions in Psychological Science, 31*(3), 238–246. https://doi.org/10.1177/09637214221079625

Borghi, A. M., Barca, L., Binkofski, F., Castelfranchi, C., Pezzulo, G., & Tummolini, L. (2019). Words as social tools: Language, sociality and inner grounding in abstract concepts. *Physics of Life Reviews, 29*, 120–153. https://doi.org/10.1016/j.plrev.2018.12.001

Borghi, A. M., Binkofski, F., Castelfranchi, C., Cimatti, F., Scorolli, C., & Tummolini, L. (2017). The challenge of abstract concepts. *Psychological Bulletin, 143*(3), 263–292. https://doi.org/10.1037/bul0000089

Bottini, R., & Doeller, C. F. (2020). Knowledge across reference frames: Cognitive maps and image spaces. *Trends in Cognitive Sciences, 24*(8), 606–619. https://doi.org/10.1016/j.tics.2020.05.008

Bourdieu, P. (1972/1977). *Outline of a theory of practice*. Cambridge University Press.

Bourdieu, P. (1979/1984). *Distinction: A social critique of the judgement of taste*. Routledge & Kegan Paul.

Bourdieu, P. (1984). *Questions de sociologie*. Editions de Minuit.

Bourdieu, P. (1980/1990). *The logic of practice*. Polity Press.

Bourdieu, P. (1982/1991). *Language and symbolic power*. Polity Press.

Bourdieu, P. (1997/2000). *Pascalian meditations*. Stanford University Press.

Bourdieu, P. (2005). Principles of an economic anthropology. In N. J. Smelser & R. Swedberg (Eds.), *The handbook of economic sociology, second edition* (pp. 75–89). Princeton University Press. https://doi.org/10.1515/9781400835584.75

Bourdieu, P., & Wacquant, L. J. D. (1992). *An invitation to reflexive sociology*. University of Chicago Press. https://press.uchicago.edu/ucp/books/book/chicago/I/bo3649674.html

Bourgeois-Gironde, S. (2021). Has money transformed our brains? A glimpse into Stone-Age neuroeconomics. *Annals of the Fondazione Luigi Einaudi: An Interdisciplinary Journal of Economics, History and Political Science: LV, 1, 2021, 1*. https://doi.org/10.26331/1139

Brette, R. (2022). Brains as computers: Metaphor, analogy, theory or fact? *Frontiers in Ecology and Evolution, 10*, 878729. https://doi.org/10.3389/fevo.2022.878729

Bruni, L., & Sugden, R. (2007). The road not taken: How psychology was removed from economics, and how it might be brought back. *The Economic Journal, 117*(516), 146–173. https://doi.org/10.1111/j.1468-0297.2007.02005.x

Brunyé, T. T., Gagnon, S. A., Waller, D., Hodgson, E., Tower-Richardi, S., & Taylor, H. A. (2012). Up north and down south: Implicit associations between topography and cardinal direction. *Quarterly Journal of Experimental Psychology (2006), 65*(10), 1880–1894. https://doi.org/10.1080/17470218.2012.663393

Burkitt, I. (2019). Emotions, social activity and neuroscience: The cultural-historical formation of emotion. *New Ideas in Psychology, 54*, 1–7. https://doi.org/10.1016/j.newideapsych.2018.11.001

Cambridge Dictionary. (n.d.). *English Dictionary, Translations & Thesaurus*. https://dictionary.cambridge.org/

Camerer, C. F. (2006). Wanting, liking, and learning: Neuroscience and paternalism. *The University of Chicago Law Review, 73*(1), 87–110. https://doi.org/10.2307/4495545

Cánovas, C. P., & Manzanares, J. V. (2014). Conceptual mappings and neural reuse. *Frontiers in Human Neuroscience, 8*,. https://doi.org/10.3389/fnhum.2014.00261

Carlson, W. B. (2000). Invention and evolution: The case of Edison's sketches of the telephone. In J. M. Ziman (Ed.), *Technological innovation as an evolutionary process* (pp. 137–158). Cambridge University Press.

Carolan, M. S. (2008). More-than-representational knowledge/s of the country-side: How we think as bodies. *Sociologia Ruralis, 48*(4), 408–422. https://doi.org/10.1111/j.1467-9523.2008.00458.x

Carruthers, P. (2002). The cognitive functions of language. *Behavioral and Brain Sciences, 25*(6), 657–674. https://doi.org/10.1017/S0140525X02000122

Casasanto, D. (2009). Embodiment of abstract concepts: Good and bad in right- and left-handers. *Journal of Experimental Psychology: General, 138*(3), 351–367. https://doi.org/10.1037/a0015854

Casasanto, D. (2017). The hierarchical structure of mental metaphors. In B. Hampe (Ed.), *Metaphor: Embodied cognition and discourse* (pp. 46–61). Cambridge University Press.

Casasanto, D., & Chrysikou, E. G. (2011). When left is "right": Motor fluency shapes abstract concepts. *Psychological Science, 22*(4), 419–422. https://doi.org/10.1177/0956797611401755

Casasanto, D., & Lupyan, G. (2015). All concepts are ad hoc concepts. In E. Margolis & S. Laurence (Eds.), *The conceptual mind: New directions in the study of concepts* (pp. 543–566). MIT Press.

Cerulo, K. A. (2019). Embodied cognition: Sociology's role in bridging mind, brain, and body. In W. H. Brekhus & G. Ignatow (Eds.), *The Oxford handbook of cognitive sociology* (p. 0). Oxford University Press. https://doi.org/10.1093/oxfordhb/9780190273385.013.5

Cerulo, K. A., Leschziner, V., & Shepherd, H. (2021). Rethinking culture and cognition. *Annual Review of Sociology, 47*(1), 63–85. https://doi.org/10.1146/annurev-soc-072320-095202

Changeux, J. P. (2006). Les bases neurales de l'habitus. In G. Fussman (Ed.), *Croyance, raison et déraison* (pp. 143–158). Odile Jacob.

Chasteen, A. L., Burdzy, D. C., & Pratt, J. (2010). Thinking of God moves attention. *Neuropsychologia, 48*(2), 627–630. https://doi.org/10.1016/j.neuropsychologia.2009.09.029

Chater, N., Felin, T., Funder, D. C., Gigerenzer, G., Koenderink, J. J., Krueger, J. I., Noble, D., Nordli, S. A., Oaksford, M., Schwartz, B., Stanovich, K. E., & Todd, P. M. (2018). Mind, rationality, and cognition: An interdisciplinary debate. *Psychonomic Bulletin & Review, 25*(2), 793–826. https://doi.org/10.3758/s13423-017-1333-5

Chemero, A. (2003). An outline of a theory of affordances. *Ecological Psychology, 15*(2), 181–195. https://doi.org/10.1207/S15326969ECO1502_5

Cialdini, R. B., & Trost, M. R. (1998). Social influence: Social norms, conformity and compliance. In D. T. Gilbert, S. T. Fiske, & G. Lindzey (Eds.), *The handbook of social psychology*, Vols. 1 and 2 (4th ed.) (pp. 151–192). McGraw-Hill.

Cian, L., Krishna, A., & Schwarz, N. (2015). Positioning rationality and emotion: Rationality is up and emotion is down. *Journal of Consumer Research, 42*, 632–651. https://doi.org/10.1093/jcr/ucv046

Cisek, P., & Kalaska, J. F. (2010). Neural mechanisms for interacting with a world full of action choices. *Annual Review of Neuroscience, 33*(1), 269–298. https://doi.org/10.1146/annurev.neuro.051508.135409

Clark, A. (1998). *Being there: Putting brain, body, and world together again*. MIT Press.

Clark, A. (2008). Supersizing the mind: Embodiment, action, and cognitive extension. *Oxford University Press*. https://doi.org/10.1093/acprof:oso/9780195333213.001.0001

Clark, A., & Chalmers, D. (1998). The extended mind. *Analysis, 58*(1), 7–19.

Clark, H. H. (1973). Space, time XE "Time", semantics, and the child. In T. E. Moore (Ed.), *Cognitive development and the acquisition of language* (pp. 27–63). Academic Press.

Cohen, D., & Leung, A.K.-Y. (2009). The hard embodiment of culture. *European Journal of Social Psychology, 39*(7), 1278–1289. https://doi.org/10.1002/ejsp.671

Cole, M. (2003). Culture and cognitive science. *Outlines. Critical Practice Studies, 5*(1), 3–15. https://doi.org/10.7146/ocps.v5i1.2159

Cole, M., & Engeström, Y. (1993). A cultural-historical approach to distributed cognition. In G. Salomon (Ed.), *Distributed cognitions: Psychological and educational considerations* (pp. 1–46). Cambridge University Press.

Commons, J. R., Rutherford, M., & Samuels, W. J. (1996). *John R. Commons: Selected essays*. Routledge.

Connell, L., Lynott, D., & Banks, B. (2018). Interoception: The forgotten modality in perceptual grounding of abstract and concrete concepts. *Philosophical Transactions of the Royal Society b: Biological Sciences, 373*(1752), 20170143. https://doi.org/10.1098/rstb.2017.0143

Cornelissen, J. P., & Clarke, J. S. (2010). Imagining and rationalizing opportunities: Inductive reasoning and the creation and justification of new ventures. *Academy of Management Review, 35*(4), 539–557.

Crisafi, A., & Gallagher, S. (2010). Hegel and the extended mind. *AI & Society, 25*(1), 123–129. https://doi.org/10.1007/s00146-009-0239-9

Crossley, N. (1995). Merleau-Ponty, the elusive body and carnal sociology. *Body & Society, 1*(1), 43–63.

Cushman, F. (2020) Rationalization is rational. *Behavioral and Brain Sciences, 43*, e28: 1–59. https://doi.org/10.1017/S0140525X19001730

Dacey, M. (2017). Anthropomorphism as cognitive bias. *Philosophy of Science, 84*(5), 1152–1164. https://doi.org/10.1086/694039

Damasio, A. R. (1989). Time-locked multiregional retroactivation: A systems-level proposal for the neural substrates of recall and recognition. *Cognition, 33*(1), 25–62. https://doi.org/10.1016/0010-0277(89)90005-X

Damasio, A. R. (1994). *Descartes' error: Emotion, reason, and the human brain*. Avon Books.

de la Fuente, J., Casasanto, D., Román, A., & Santiago, J. (2015). Can culture influence body-specific associations between space and valence? *Cognitive Science, 39*(4), 821–832. https://doi.org/10.1111/cogs.12177

Dehaene, S., Bossini, S., & Giraux, P. (1993). The mental representation of parity and number magnitude. *Journal of Experimental Psychology: General, 122*(3), 371–396. https://doi.org/10.1037/0096-3445.122.3.371

Dekker, E., & Remic, B. (2019). Two types of ecological rationality: Or how to best combine psychology and economics. *Journal of Economic Methodology, 26*(4), 291–306. https://doi.org/10.1080/1350178X.2018.1560486

Deng, X., & Kahn, B. E. (2009). Is your product on the right side? The "location effect" on perceived product heaviness and package evaluation. *Journal of Marketing Research, 46*(6), 725–738. https://doi.org/10.1509/jmkr.46.6.725_JMR6B

Descola, P. (2014). The grid and the tree: Reply to Marshall Sahlins' comment. *HAU: Journal of Ethnographic Theory*, *4*(1), 295–300. https://doi.org/10.14318/hau4.1.015

Dewey, J. (1929). *Experience and nature*. George Allen and Unwin.

Di Paolo, E. (2009). Extended life. *Topoi, 28*(1), 9–21. https://doi.org/10.1007/s11245-008-9042-3

Di Paolo, E. A., Cuffari, E. C., & De Jaegher, H. (2018). *Linguistic bodies: The continuity between life and language*. MIT press.

DiMaggio, P. (1979). On Pierre Bourdieu. *American Journal of Sociology, 84*(6), 1460–1474.

DiMaggio, P. (1997). Culture and cognition. *Annual Review of Sociology, 23*(1), 263–287.

Dodd, B. (2021). A feel for the frame: Towards a Bourdieusian frame analysis. *Poetics, 84*, 101482. https://doi.org/10.1016/j.poetic.2020.101482

Dong, P., Huang, X., & (Irene), & Labroo, A. A. (2020). Cueing morality: The effect of high-pitched music on healthy choice. *Journal of Marketing, 84*(6), 130–143. https://doi.org/10.1177/0022242918813577

Dove, G. (2020). More than a scaffold: Language is a neuroenhancement. *Cognitive Neuropsychology, 37*(5–6), 288–311. https://doi.org/10.1080/02643294.2019.1637338

Dreyfus, H. L. (2002). Intelligence without representation—Merleau-Ponty's critique of mental representation: The relevance of phenomenology to scientific explanation. *Phenomenology and the Cognitive Sciences, 1*(4), 367–383. https://doi.org/10.1023/A:1021351606209

Durkheim, E. (1893/2013). *The division of labour in society*. Palgrave Macmillan.

Edelman, G. M. (1987). *Neural Darwinism: The theory of neuronal group selection*. Basic Books.

Edelman, G. M. (2006). *Second nature: Brain science and human knowledge*. Yale University Press.

Eelen, J., Dewitte, S., & Warlop, L. (2013). Situated embodied cognition: Monitoring orientation cues affects product evaluation and choice. *Journal of Consumer Psychology, 23*(4), 424–433. https://doi.org/10.1016/j.jcps.2013.04.004

Elder, R. S., & Krishna, A. (2012). The "visual depiction effect" in advertising: Facilitating embodied mental simulation through product orientation. *Journal of Consumer Research, 38*(6), 988–1003. https://doi.org/10.1086/661531

Elias, N. (1939). *Über den Prozeß der Zivilisation: Soziogenetische und psychogenetische Untersuchungen*. Verlag Haus zum Falken.

Elias, N. (1969). *Die höfische Gesellschaft: Untersuchungen zur Soziologie des Königtums und der höfischen Aristokratie mit einer Einleitung* : Soziologie und Geschichtswissenschaft. Suhrkamp.

Elster, J. (1989). Social norms and economic theory. *Journal of Economic Perspectives, 3*(4), 99–117.
Epley, N., Waytz, A., & Cacioppo, J. T. (2007). On seeing human: A three-factor theory of anthropomorphism. *Psychological Review, 114*(4), 864–886. https://doi.org/10.1037/0033-295X.114.4.864
Ericsson, K. A., Simon, X. E., & Simon, Herbert A.". (1998). How to study thinking in everyday life: Contrasting think-aloud protocols with descriptions and explanations of thinking. *Mind, Culture, and Activity, 5*(3), 178–186. https://doi.org/10.1207/s15327884mca0503_3
Evans, V., & Green, M. J. (2006). *Cognitive linguistics: An introduction*. L. Erlbaum.
Faghihi, N., & Vaid, J. (2023). Reading/writing direction as a source of directional bias in spatial cognition: Possible mechanisms and scope. *Psychonomic Bulletin & Review, 30*(3), 843–862. https://doi.org/10.3758/s13423-022-02239-1
Farrow, K., Grolleau, G., & Mzoughi, N. (2018). What in the word! The scope for the effect of word choice on economic behavior. *Kyklos, 71*(4), 557–580. https://doi.org/10.1111/kykl.12186
Fauconnier, G. (2001). Conceptual blending and analogy. In D. Gentner, K. J. Holyoak, & B. K. Kokinov (Eds.), *The analogical mind: Perspectives from cognitive science* (pp. 255–285). MIT Press.
Fauconnier, G., & Turner, M. (2002). *The way we think: Conceptual blending and the mind's hidden complexities*. Basic Books.
Feldman, J. A. (2008). *From molecule to metaphor: A neural theory of language*. Bradford Books.
Feldman-Barrett, L. F., & Lindquist, K. A. (2008). The embodiment of emotion. In E. R. Smith & G. R. Semin (Eds.), *Embodied grounding: Social, cognitive, affective, and neuroscientific approaches* (pp. 237–262). Cambridge University Press. https://doi.org/10.1017/CBO9780511805837.011
Felin, T., Koenderink, J., & Krueger, J. I. (2017). Rationality, perception, and the all-seeing eye. *Psychonomic Bulletin & Review, 24*(4), 1040–1059. https://doi.org/10.3758/s13423-016-1198-z
Fernandino, L., Binder, J. R., Desai, R. H., Pendl, S. L., Humphries, C. J., Gross, W. L., Conant, L. L., & Seidenberg, M. S. (2016). Concept representation reflects multimodal abstraction: A framework for embodied semantics. *Cerebral Cortex, 26*(5), 2018–2034. https://doi.org/10.1093/cercor/bhv020
Fernyhough, C. (2008). Getting Vygotskian about theory of mind: Mediation, dialogue, and the development of social understanding. *Developmental Review, 28*(2), 225–262. https://doi.org/10.1016/j.dr.2007.03.001
Festinger, L. (1957). *A theory of cognitive dissonance*. Stanford University Press.

Festinger, L. (1962). Cognitive dissonance. *Scientific American, 207*(4), 93–107. https://doi.org/10.1038/scientificamerican1062-93

Fetterman, A. K., & Robinson, M. D. (2013). Do you use your head or follow your heart? Self-location predicts personality, emotion, decision-making, and performance. *Journal of Personality and Social Psychology, 105*(2), 316–334. https://doi.org/10.1037/a0033374

Fiske, A. P. (1992). The four elementary forms of sociality: Framework for a unified theory of social relations. *Psychological Review, 99*(4), 689–723. https://doi.org/10.1037/0033-295X.99.4.689

Fiske, A. P., & Tetlock, P. E. (1997). Taboo trade-offs: Reactions to transactions that transgress the spheres of justice. *Political Psychology, 18*(2), 255–297. https://doi.org/10.1111/0162-895X.00058

Fiske, A. P., Thomsen, L., & Thein, S. M. (2009). Differently embodying different relationships. *European Journal of Social Psychology, 39*(7), 1294–1297. https://doi.org/10.1002/ejsp.697

Fogle, N., & Theiner, G. (2018). The "ontological complicity" of habitus and field: Bourdieu as an externalist. In J. A. Carter, A. Clark, J. Kallestrup, S. O. Palermos, & D. Pritchard (Eds.), *Socially extended epistemology* (pp. 220–252). Oxford University Press.

Foucault, M. (2004). *Naissance de la biopolitique: Cours au Collège de France*, 1978–1979. Gallimard/Seuil.

Frey, V., De Mulder, H. N. M., ter Bekke, M., Struiksma, M. E., van Berkum, J. J. A., & Buskens, V. (2022). Do self-talk phrases affect behavior in ultimatum games? *Mind & Society, 21*(1), 89–119. https://doi.org/10.1007/s11299-022-00286-8

Frith, C. D., & Singer, T. (2008). The role of social cognition in decision making. *Philosophical Transactions of the Royal Society b: Biological Sciences, 363*(1511), 3875–3886. https://doi.org/10.1098/rstb.2008.0156

Fukuyama, F. (1992/2020). *The end of history and the last man*. Penguin Books.

Fuster, J. M., & Bressler, S. L. (2012). Cognit activation: A mechanism enabling temporal integration in working memory. *Trends in Cognitive Sciences, 16*(4), 207–218. https://doi.org/10.1016/j.tics.2012.03.005

Gainsburg, I., Sowden, W. J., Drake, B., Herold, W., & Kross, E. (2022). Distanced self-talk increases rational self-interest. *Scientific Reports*, *12*(1), Article 1. https://doi.org/10.1038/s41598-021-04010-3

Gallagher, S. (2017). *Enactivist interventions: Rethinking the mind*. Oxford University Press.

Gallagher, S. (2018). Embodied rationality. In G. Bronner & F. Iorio (Eds.), *The mystery of rationality. Mind, beliefs and social science* (pp. 83–94). Springer.

Gallagher, S. (2023). Embodied and enactive approaches to cognition. *Cambridge University Press*. https://doi.org/10.1017/9781009209793

Gallese, V., & Lakoff, G. (2005). The brain's concepts: The role of the sensory-motor system in conceptual knowledge. *Cognitive Neuropsychology, 22*(3–4), 455–479. https://doi.org/10.1080/02643290442000310
Gannon, M. J., & Pillai, R. (2015). *Understanding global cultures: Metaphorical journeys through 34 nations, clusters of nations, continents, and diversity*. SAGE Publications.
Gazzaniga, M. S. (2013). Shifting gears: Seeking new approaches for mind/brain mechanisms. *Annual Review of Psychology, 64*, 1–20. https://doi.org/10.1146/annurev-psych-113011-143817
Gazzola, V., Rizzolatti, G., Wicker, B., & Keysers, C. (2007). The anthropomorphic brain: The mirror neuron system responds to human and robotic actions. *NeuroImage, 35*(4), 1674–1684. https://doi.org/10.1016/j.neuroimage.2007.02.003
Gibbs, R. W. (1994). *The poetics of mind: Figurative thought, language, and understanding*. Cambridge University Press.
Gibbs, R. W. (2008). *The Cambridge handbook of metaphor and thought*. Cambridge University Press.
Gibson, J. J. (1979). *Ecological approach to visual perception*. Psychology Press.
Giessner, S. R., & Schubert, T. W. (2007). High in the hierarchy: How vertical location and judgments of leaders' power are interrelated. *Organizational Behavior and Human Decision Processes, 104*(1), 30–44. https://doi.org/10.1016/j.obhdp.2006.10.001
Gigerenzer, G. (2007). *Gut feelings: The intelligence of the unconscious*. Penguin.
Gigerenzer, G. (2018). The bias bias in behavioral economics. *Review of Behavioral Economics, 5*(3–4), 303–336. https://doi.org/10.1561/105.00000092
Gigerenzer, G. (2021). Embodied heuristics. *Frontiers in Psychology, 12*, 711289. https://doi.org/10.3389/fpsyg.2021.711289
Gigerenzer, G., & Gaissmaier, W. (2011). Heuristic decision making. *Annual Review of Psychology, 62*(1), 451–482. https://doi.org/10.1146/annurev-psych-120709-145346
Gillespie, A. (2007). The social basis of self-reflection. In J. Valsiner & A. Rosa (Eds.), *The Cambridge handbook of sociocultural psychology* (1st ed., pp. 678–691). Cambridge University Press. https://doi.org/10.1017/CBO9780511611162.037
Gintis, H., Bowles, S., Boyd, R., & Fehr, E. (2005). *Moral sentiments and material interests: The foundations of cooperation in economic life*. MIT Press.
Glenberg, A. M. (2019). Turning social tools into tools for action. *Physics of Life Reviews, 29*, 172–174. https://doi.org/10.1016/j.plrev.2019.02.009
Goldstein, N. J., & Cialdini, R. B. (2009). Normative influences on consumption and conservation behaviors. In M. Wänke (Ed.), *The social psychology of consumer behavior* (pp. 273–296). Psychology Press.

Golonka, S., & Wilson, A. D. (2019). Ecological representations. *Ecological Psychology, 31*(3), 235–253. https://doi.org/10.1080/10407413.2019.1615224

González, J., Barrós-Loscertales, A., Pulvermüller, F., Meseguer, V., Sanjuán, A., Belloch, V., & Avila, C. (2006). Reading cinnamon activates olfactory brain regions. *NeuroImage, 32*(2), 906–912. https://doi.org/10.1016/j.neuroimage.2006.03.037

González, N. (2021). Thinking outside the box: Externalization of psychological functions and the extended mind. In P. Fossa (Ed.), *Latin American advances in subjectivity and development* (pp. 147–167). Springer International Publishing. https://doi.org/10.1007/978-3-030-72953-0_9

Grady, J. E. (2005). Image schemas and perception: Refining a definition. In B. Hampe (Ed.), *From perception to meaning: Image schemas in cognitive linguistics* (pp. 35–56). Mouton de Gruyter.

Graeber, D. (2001). *Toward an anthropological theory of value: The false coin of our own dreams*. Springer.

Graeber, D., & Wengrow, D. (2021). *The dawn of everything: A new history of humanity*. Penguin UK.

Grecucci, A., Giorgetta, C., Wout, M., & van't, Bonini, N., & Sanfey, A. G. (2013). Reappraising the ultimatum: An fMRI study of emotion regulation and decision making. *Cerebral Cortex, 23*(2), 399–410. https://doi.org/10.1093/cercor/bhs028

Gul, F., & Pesendorfer, W. (2008). The case for mindless economics. In A. Caplin & A. Schotter (Eds.), *The foundations of positive and normative economics* (pp. 3–42). Oxford University Press. https://doi.org/10.1093/acprof:oso/9780195328318.001.0001.

Haggard, P. (2008). Human volition: Towards a neuroscience of will. *Nature Reviews. Neuroscience, 9*(12), 934–946. https://doi.org/10.1038/nrn2497

Haidt, J. (2001). The emotional dog and its rational tail: A social intuitionist approach to moral judgment. *Psychological Review, 108*(4), 814–834. https://doi.org/10.1037/0033-295X.108.4.814

Harmon-Jones, E., & Harmon-Jones, C. (2007). Cognitive dissonance theory after 50 years of development. *Zeitschrift Für Sozialpsychologie, 38*(1), 7–16. https://doi.org/10.1024/0044-3514.38.1.7

Harnad, S. (1990). The symbol grounding problem. *Physica d: Nonlinear Phenomena, 42*(1), 335–346. https://doi.org/10.1016/0167-2789(90)90087-6

Harpaintner, M., Sim, E.-J., Trumpp, N. M., Ulrich, M., & Kiefer, M. (2020). The grounding of abstract concepts in the motor and visual system: An fMRI study. *Cortex, 124*, 1–22. https://doi.org/10.1016/j.cortex.2019.10.014

Harris, L. J. (1990). Cultural influences on handedness: Historical and contemporary theory and evidence. In S. Coren (Ed.), *Advances in Psychology*

(Vol. 67, pp. 195–258). North-Holland. https://doi.org/10.1016/S0166-4115(08)61249-2
Hatzigeorgiadis, A., Zourbanos, N., Galanis, E., & Theodorakis, Y. (2011). Self-talk and sports performance: A meta-analysis. *Perspectives on Psychological Science, 6*(4), 348–356. https://doi.org/10.1177/1745691611413136
Hauk, O., Johnsrude, I., & Pulvermüller, F. (2004). Somatotopic representation of action words in human motor and premotor cortex. *Neuron, 41*(2), 301–307.
Hayek, F. A. (1937). Economics and knowledge. *Economica, 4*(13), 33–54.
Hayek, F. A. (1945). The use of knowledge in society. *American Economic Review, 35*(4), 519–530.
Hayek, F. A. (1952). *The sensory order: An inquiry into the foundations of theoretical psychology*. University of Chicago Press.
Hayek, F. A. (1988). *The fatal conceit: The errors of socialism*. Routledge.
Hayek, F. A. (1982/2013). *Law, legislation and liberty: A new statement of the liberal principles of justice and political economy* (New edition). Routledge.
Henry, P. C. (2005). Social class, market situation, and consumers' metaphors of (dis)empowerment. *Journal of Consumer Research, 31*(4), 766–778. https://doi.org/10.1086/426610
Heider, F., & Simmel, M. (1944). An experimental study of apparent behavior. *The American Journal of Psychology, 57*(2), 243–259.
Herrmann-Pillath, C. (2013). *Foundations of economic evolution*. Edward Elgar Publishing.
Herrmann-Pillath, C. (2016). Constitutive explanations in neuroeconomics: Principles and a case study on money. *Journal of Economic Methodology, 23*(4), 374–395. https://doi.org/10.1080/1350178X.2016.1218531
Herrmann-Pillath, C., & Boldyrev, I. A. (2014). *Hegel, institutions, and economics: Performing the social*. Routledge, Taylor & Francis Group.
Heyes, C., & Catmur, C. (2022). What happened to mirror neurons? *Perspectives on Psychological Science, 17*(1), 153–168. https://doi.org/10.1177/1745691621990638
Hodgson, G. M. (2004). Reclaiming habit for institutional economics. *Journal of Economic Psychology, 25*(5), 651–660. https://doi.org/10.1016/j.joep.2003.03.001
Hommel, B. (2019). Affect and control: A conceptual clarification. *International Journal of Psychophysiology, 144*, 1–6. https://doi.org/10.1016/j.ijpsycho.2019.07.006
Hubbard, E. M., Piazza, M., Pinel, P., & Dehaene, S. (2005). Interactions between number and space in parietal cortex. *Nature Reviews Neuroscience, 6*(6), 435–448. https://doi.org/10.1038/nrn1684

Hurley, S. (2008). The shared circuits model (SCM): How control, mirroring, and simulation can enable imitation, deliberation, and mindreading. *Behavioral and Brain Sciences, 31*(1), 1–22. https://doi.org/10.1017/S0140525X07003123

Hutchins, E. (2005). Material anchors for conceptual blends. *Journal of Pragmatics, 37*(10), 1555–1577. https://doi.org/10.1016/j.pragma.2004.06.008

Hutchins, E. (2014). The cultural ecosystem of human cognition. *Philosophical Psychology, 27*(1), 34–49. https://doi.org/10.1080/09515089.2013.830548

Ihde, D., & Malafouris, L. (2019). Homo faber revisited: Postphenomenology and material engagement theory. *Philosophy & Technology, 32*(2), 195–214. https://doi.org/10.1007/s13347-018-0321-7

IJzerman, H., & Semin, G. R. (2009). The thermometer of social relations mapping social proximity on temperature. *Psychological Science, 20*(10), 1214–1220. https://doi.org/10.1111/j.1467-9280.2009.02434.x

Ingold, T. (2000). The perception of the environment: Essays on livelihood, dwelling and skill. *Routledge*. https://doi.org/10.4324/9781003196662

Ingold, T. (2022). Evolution without inheritance: Steps to an ecology of learning. *Current Anthropology, 63*(S25), S32–S55. https://doi.org/10.1086/722437

Jabbi, M., Swart, M., & Keysers, C. (2007). Empathy for positive and negative emotions in the gustatory cortex. *NeuroImage, 34*(4), 1744–1753. https://doi.org/10.1016/j.neuroimage.2006.10.032

Jami, A. (2019). Having control over and above situations: The influence of elevated viewpoints on risk taking. *Journal of Marketing Research, 56*(2), 230–244. https://doi.org/10.1177/0022243718813544

Jenni, K. E., & Loewenstein, G. (1997). Explaining the identifiable victim effect. *Journal of Risk and Uncertainty, 14*(3), 235–257.

Johnson, M. (1987). *The body in the mind: The bodily basis of meaning, imagination, and reason*. University of Chicago Press.

Johnson, M. (2017). *Embodied mind, meaning, and reason: How our bodies give rise to understanding*. University of Chicago Press.

Johnson, S. G. B., Bilovich, A., & Tuckett, D. (2023). Conviction narrative theory: A theory of choice under radical uncertainty. *Behavioral and Brain Sciences, 46*, e82. https://doi.org/10.1017/S0140525X22001157

Kahneman, D. (2012). *Thinking, fast and slow*. Penguin Books.

Kemmerer, D. (2022). Grounded cognition entails linguistic relativity: A neglected implication of a major semantic theory. *Topics in Cognitive Science*, tops.12628. https://doi.org/10.1111/tops.12628

Keynes, J. M. (1936/2018). *The general theory of employment interest and money*. Springer International Publishing. https://doi.org/10.1007/978-3-319-70344-2

Kimmel, M. (2013). The arc from the body to culture: How affect, proprioception, kinesthesia, and perceptual imagery shape cultural knowledge (and vice versa). *Integral Review, 9*(2).

Kousta, S.-T., Vigliocco, G., Vinson, D. P., Andrews, M., & Del Campo, E. (2011). The representation of abstract words: Why emotion matters. *Journal of Experimental Psychology: General, 140*(1), 14–34. https://doi.org/10.1037/a0021446

Kövecses, Z. (2010). *Metaphor: A practical introduction*. Oxford University Press.

Krátký, J. (2012). Cognition, material culture and religious ritual. *Diskus: The Journal of the British Association for the Study of Religions, 13*, 49–62.

Kringelbach, M. L. (2009). *The pleasure center: Trust your animal instincts*. Oxford University Press.

Lahire, B. (2003). From the habitus to an individual heritage of dispositions. Towards a sociology at the level of the individual. *Poetics, 31*(5–6), 329–355. https://doi.org/10.1016/j.poetic.2003.08.002

Lainé, M. (2014). Do animal spirits rely on somatic markers? Keynes in light of neuroscience. *Journal of Post Keynesian Economics, 36*(3), 439–466. https://doi.org/10.2753/PKE0160-3477360303

Lakoff, G. (1987). *Women, fire, and dangerous things: What categories reveal about the mind*. University of Chicago Press.

Lakoff, G. (2008). The neural theory of metaphor. In R. W. Gibbs (Ed.), *Cambridge handbook of metaphor and thought* (pp. 17–38). Cambridge University Press.

Lakoff, G. (2016a). Language and emotion. *Emotion Review, 8*(3), 269–273. https://doi.org/10.1177/1754073915595097

Lakoff, G. (2016b). Author Reply: Reply to Commentaries on Language and Emotion (2015). *Emotion Review, 8*(3), 284–285. https://doi.org/10.1177/1754073915595104

Lakoff, G., & Johnson, M. (1980). *Metaphors we live by*. University of Chicago Press.

Lakoff, G., & Johnson, M. (1999). *Philosophy in the flesh: The embodied mind and Its challenge to Western thought*. Basic Books.

Lakoff, G., & Núñez, R. (2000). *Where mathematics comes from*. Basic Books.

Landau, M., Robinson, M. D., & Meier, B. P. (Eds.). (2014). *The power of metaphor: Examining its influence on social life* (pp. viii, 301). American Psychological Association. https://doi.org/10.1037/14278-000

Larson, J. S., & Billeter, D. M. (2013). Consumer behavior in "equilibrium": How experiencing physical balance increases compromise choice. *Journal of Marketing Research, 50*(4), 535–547. https://doi.org/10.1509/jmr.11.0455

Lea, S. E. G., & Webley, P. (2006). Money as tool, money as drug: The biological psychology of a strong incentive. *Behavioral and Brain Sciences, 29*(2), 161–209. https://doi.org/10.1017/S0140525X06009046

Lee, S. W. S., & Schwarz, N. (2012). Bidirectionality, mediation, and moderation of metaphorical effects: The embodiment of social suspicion and fishy smells. *Journal of Personality and Social Psychology, 103*(5), 737–749. https://doi.org/10.1037/a0029708

Lee, S. W. S., & Schwarz, N. (2018). A grounded cognition perspective on folk-economic beliefs. *Behavioral and Brain Sciences, 41*, e175. https://doi.org/10.1017/S0140525X18000419

Leemans, I. (2016). Comment: Embodied emotions from a Dutch historical perspective. *Emotion Review, 8*(3), 278–280. https://doi.org/10.1177/1754073915595102

Lempert, K. M., & Phelps, E. A. (2014). Chapter 12—Neuroeconomics of emotion and decision making. In P. W. Glimcher & E. Fehr (Eds.), *Neuroeconomics (Second edition)* (pp. 219–236). Academic Press. https://doi.org/10.1016/B978-0-12-416008-8.00012-7

Leontyev, A. N. (1974). The problem of activity in psychology. *Soviet Psychology, 13*(2), 4–33. https://doi.org/10.2753/RPO1061-040513024

Lewin, K. (1951). Intention, will and need. In *Organization and pathology of thought: Selected sources* (pp. 95–153). Columbia University Press. https://doi.org/10.1037/10584-005

Li, H., & Cao, Y. (2019). The body in religion: The spatial mapping of valence in Tibetan practitioners of Bön. *Cognitive Science, 43*(4), e12728. https://doi.org/10.1111/cogs.12728

Libet, B. (1985). Unconscious cerebral initiative and the role of conscious will in voluntary action. *Behavioral and Brain Sciences, 8*(4), 529–539. https://doi.org/10.1017/S0140525X00044903

Lichtenstein, S., Gregory, R., & Irwin, J. (2007). What's bad is easy: Taboo values, affect, and cognition. *Judgment and Decision Making, 2*(3), 169–188. https://doi.org/10.1017/S1930297500000838

Lizardo, O. (2004). The cognitive origins of Bourdieu's habitus. *Journal for the Theory of Social Behaviour, 34*(4), 375–401.

Lizardo, O. (2007). "Mirror neurons", collective objects and the problem of transmission: Reconsidering Stephen Turner's critique of practice theory. *Journal for the Theory of Social Behaviour, 37*(3), 319–350.

Loader, P. (2015). Marx and enactivism. *Intellectica. Revue de l'Association pour la Recherche Cognitive, 63*(1), 65–91. https://doi.org/10.3406/intel.2015.1024

Loewenstein, G., & O'Donoghue, T. (2004). Animal spirits: Affective and deliberative processes in economic behavior. *SSRN Electronic Journal*. https://doi.org/10.2139/ssrn.539843

Loewenstein, G., & Small, D. A. (2007). The scarecrow and the tin man: The vicissitudes of human sympathy and caring. *Review of General Psychology, 11*(2), 112–126. https://doi.org/10.1037/1089-2680.11.2.112

Longcamp, M., Anton, J.-L., Roth, M., & Velay, J.-L. (2003). Visual presentation of single letters activates a premotor area involved in writing. *NeuroImage, 19*(4), 1492–1500. https://doi.org/10.1016/S1053-8119(03)00088-0

Lupyan, G., & Winter, B. (2018). Language is more abstract than you think, or, why aren't languages more iconic? *Philosophical Transactions of the Royal Society b: Biological Sciences, 373*(1752), 20170137. https://doi.org/10.1098/rstb.2017.0137

Luria, A. (1981). *Language and cognition*. Winston & Sons.

Macnamara, A., Keage, H. A. D., & Loetscher, T. (2018). Mapping of non-numerical domains on space: A systematic review and meta-analysis. *Experimental Brain Research, 236*(2), 335–346. https://doi.org/10.1007/s00221-017-5154-6

Maglio, S. J., & Trope, Y. (2012). Disembodiment: Abstract construal attenuates the influence of contextual bodily state in judgment. *Journal of Experimental Psychology: General, 141*(2), 211–216. https://doi.org/10.1037/a0024520

Malafouris, L. (2010). The brain–artefact interface (BAI): A challenge for archaeology and cultural neuroscience. *Social Cognitive and Affective Neuroscience, 5*(2–3), 264–273. https://doi.org/10.1093/scan/nsp057

Malafouris, L. (2013). *How things shape the mind: A theory of material engagement*. MIT Press.

Malafouris, L. (2019). What does the stick do for the blind? In J. Bennett & M. Zournazi (Eds.), *Thinking in the World* (pp. 115–128). Bloomsbury Academic.

Malafouris, L. (2021). Making hands and tools: Steps to a process archaeology of mind. *World Archaeology, 53*(1), 38–55. https://doi.org/10.1080/00438243.2021.1993992

Malinowski, B. (1922). *Argonauts of the Western Pacific: An account of Native Enterprise and adventure in the Archipelagos of Melanesian New Guinea*. Routledge & Kegan Paul.

Mandler, J. M. (1992). The foundations of conceptual thought in infancy. *Cognitive Development, 7*(3), 273–285.

Mandler, J. M. (2004). Thought before language. *Trends in Cognitive Sciences, 8*(11), 508–513. https://doi.org/10.1016/j.tics.2004.09.004

Marcoulatos, I. (2001). Merleau-Ponty and Bourdieu on embodied significance. *Journal for the Theory of Social Behaviour, 31*(1), 1–27. https://doi.org/10.1111/1468-5914.00144

Martin, A. (2007). The representation of object concepts in the brain. *Annual Review of Psychology, 58*(1), 25–45. https://doi.org/10.1146/annurev.psych.57.102904.190143

Marx, K. (1867/1990). *Capital. A critique of political economy*. Volume 1. Penguin Classics.

Matheson, H. E., & Barsalou, L. W. (2018). Embodiment and grounding in cognitive neuroscience. In J. T. Wixted (Ed.), *Stevens' handbook of experimental psychology and cognitive neuroscience* (pp. 1–27). John Wiley & Sons. https://doi.org/10.1002/9781119170174.epcn310

McCloskey, D. N. (1983). The rhetoric of economics. *Journal of Economic Literature, 21*(2), 481–517.

McCloskey, D. N. (2016). Max U versus Humanomics: A critique of neo-institutionalism. *Journal of Institutional Economics, 12*(01), 1–27. https://doi.org/10.1017/S1744137415000053

McCloskey, D. N. (2022). *Beyond positivism, behaviorism, and neoinstitutionalism in economics*. University of Chicago Press.

Mead, G. H. (1934). *Mind, self & society: From the standpoint of a social behaviorist* (C. W. Morris, Ed.). University of Chicago press.

Meier, B. P., & Dionne, S. (2009). Downright sexy: Verticality, implicit power, and perceived physical attractiveness. *Social Cognition, 27*(6), 883–892. https://doi.org/10.1521/soco.2009.27.6.883

Meier, B. P., Hauser, D. J., Robinson, M. D., Friesen, C. K., & Schjeldahl, K. (2007). What's "up" with God? Vertical space as a representation of the divine. *Journal of Personality and Social Psychology, 93*(5), 699–710. https://doi.org/10.1037/0022-3514.93.5.699

Meier, B. P., Moller, A. C., Chen, J. J., & Riemer-Peltz, M. (2011). Spatial metaphor and real estate: North–south location biases housing preference. *Social Psychological and Personality Science, 2*(5), 547–553. https://doi.org/10.1177/1948550611401042

Melnikoff, D. E., & Bargh, J. A. (2018). The mythical number two. *Trends in Cognitive Sciences, 22*(4), 280–293. https://doi.org/10.1016/j.tics.2018.02.001

Merchant, C. (1980). *The death of nature: Women, ecology, and the scientific revolution*. Harper Collins.

Mercier, H., & Sperber, D. (2011). Why do humans reason? Arguments for an argumentative theory. *Behavioral and Brain Sciences, 34*(2), 57–74. https://doi.org/10.1017/S0140525X10000968

Merleau-Ponty, M. (1945/1962). *Phenomenology of perception*. Routledge.

Merleau-Ponty, M. (1964). Structure et conflits de la conscience enfantine. *Bulletin De Psychologie, 18*(236), 171–202.

Morris, M. W., Sheldon, O. J., Ames, D. R., & Young, M. J. (2007). Metaphors and the market: Consequences and preconditions of agent and object metaphors in stock market commentary. *Organizational Behavior and Human Decision Processes, 102*(2), 174–192.

Mukamel, R., Ekstrom, A. D., Kaplan, J., Iacoboni, M., & Fried, I. (2010). Single-neuron responses in humans during execution and observation of actions. *Current Biology, 20*(8), 750–756. https://doi.org/10.1016/j.cub.2010.02.045

Mumby, D. K., & Putnam, L. L. (1992). The politics of emotion: A feminist reading of bounded rationality. *Academy of Management Review, 17*(3), 465. https://doi.org/10.2307/258719

Nedergaard, J. S. K., Wallentin, M., & Lupyan, G. (2023). Verbal interference paradigms: A systematic review investigating the role of language in cognition. *Psychonomic Bulletin & Review, 30*(2), 464–488. https://doi.org/10.3758/s13423-022-02144-7

Nelson, J. A. (1992). Gender, metaphor, and the definition of economics. *Economics & Philosophy, 8*(1), 103–125. https://doi.org/10.1017/S026626710000050X

Nelson, J. A. (1997). Feminism, ecology and the philosophy of economics. *Ecological Economics, 20*(2), 155–162. https://doi.org/10.1016/S0921-8009(96)00025-0

Nelson, L. D., & Simmons, J. P. (2009). On southbound ease and northbound fees: Literal consequences of the metaphoric link between vertical position and cardinal direction. *Journal of Marketing Research, 46*(6), 715–724. https://doi.org/10.1509/jmkr.46.6.715

Neuhouser, F. (2008). Hegel's social philosophy. In F. C. Beiser (Ed.), *The Cambridge companion to Hegel and nineteenth-century philosophy* (1st ed., pp. 204–229). Cambridge University Press. https://doi.org/10.1017/CCOL9780521831673.009

Newell, A., & Simon, H. A. (1976). Computer science as empirical inquiry: Symbols and search. *Communications of the ACM, 19*(3), 113–126.

Newen, A., Bruin, L. D., & Gallagher, S. (2018). *The Oxford handbook of 4E cognition*. Oxford University Press.

Niedenthal, P. M., Barsalou, L. W., Winkielman, P., Krauth-Gruber, S., & Ric, F. (2005). Embodiment in attitudes, social perception, and emotion. *Personality and Social Psychology Review, 9*(3), 184–211. https://doi.org/10.1207/s15327957pspr0903_1

Noguchi, M. (2022). Max Weber und das Narrativ der fehlenden Grundlagen "modernen" Japan. Eine Ideengeschichte des Ethos Begriffs. In *Max Weber revisited: Zur Aktualität eines Klassikers* (pp. 277–294). BeltzJuventa.

North, D. C. (1993). Institutions and credible commitment. *Journal of Institutional and Theoretical Economics (JITE) / Zeitschrift Für Die Gesamte Staatswissenschaft*, *149*(1), 11–23.

Núñez, R. E. (2011). No innate number line in the human brain. *Journal of Cross-Cultural Psychology, 42*(4), 651–668. https://doi.org/10.1177/0022022111406097

Nussbaum, M. C. (2013). *Political emotions*. Harvard University Press.

Ostrom, E. (2010). Beyond markets and states: Polycentric governance of complex economic systems. *American Economic Review, 100*(3), 641–672. https://doi.org/10.1257/aer.100.3.641

Panofsky, C. P. (2003). The relations of learning and student social class: Toward re-"socializing" sociocultural learning theory. In A. Kozulin (Ed.), *Vygotsky's educational theory in cultural context* (pp. 411–431). Cambridge University Press.

Patterson, T. C. (2009). *Karl Marx, anthropologist*. Berg.

Pelkey, J. (2023). Embodiment and language. *WIREs Cognitive Science*, e1649. https://doi.org/10.1002/wcs.1649

Perry, C. (1935). Pareto's contribution to social science. *International Journal of Ethics, 46*(1), 96–107.

Pesowski, M. L., Nancekivell, S. E., Tasimi, A., & Friedman, O. (2022). Ownership and value in childhood. *Annual Review of Developmental Psychology, 4*(1), 161–183. https://doi.org/10.1146/annurev-devpsych-120920-041124

Pessoa, L. (2008). On the relationship between emotion and cognition. *Nature Reviews Neuroscience, 9*(2), 145–158. https://doi.org/10.1038/nrn2317

Petracca, E. (2021). Embodying bounded rationality: From embodied bounded rationality to embodied rationality. *Frontiers in Psychology, 12*, 710607. https://doi.org/10.3389/fpsyg.2021.710607

Petroski, H. (1994). *The evolution of useful things*. Vintage Books.

Pham, M. T., Lee, L., & Stephen, A. T. (2012). Feeling the future: The emotional oracle effect. *Journal of Consumer Research, 39*(3), 461–477. https://doi.org/10.1086/663823

Ping, R. M., Dhillon, S., & Beilock, S. L. (2009). Reach for what you like: The body's role in shaping preferences. *Emotion Review, 1*(2), 140–150. https://doi.org/10.1177/1754073908100439

Pippin, R. B. (2008). *Hegel's practical philosophy: Rational agency as ethical life*. Cambridge University Press.

Pitt, B., & Casasanto, D. (2020). The correlations in experience principle: How culture shapes concepts of time XE "Time" and number. *Journal of Experimental Psychology: General, 149*(6), 1048–1070. https://doi.org/10.1037/xge0000696

Polanyi, K. (1944/2001). *The great transformation: The political and economic origins of our time*. Beacon Press.

Popper, K. (1945). *Open society and its enemies*. Routledge.

Priddat, B. P. (1990). *Hegel als Ökonom*. Duncker & Humblot.

Prinz, J. J. (2005). Passionate thoughts: The emotional embodiment of moral concepts. In D. Pecher & R. A. Zwaan (Eds.), *Grounding cognition: The role of perception and action in memory, language, and thinking* (pp. 93–114). Cambridge University Press. https://doi.org/10.1017/CBO9780511499968.005

Pulvermüller, F. (2005). Brain mechanisms linking language and action. *Nature Review Neuroscience, 6*(7), 576–582. https://doi.org/10.1038/nrn1706

Pulvermüller, F. (2018). Neural reuse of action perception circuits for language, concepts and communication. *Progress in Neurobiology, 160*, 1–44. https://doi.org/10.1016/j.pneurobio.2017.07.001

Raab, M. (2021). *Judgment, decision-making, and embodied choices*. Academic Press.

Raja, V., & Anderson, M. L. (2019). Radical embodied cognitive neuroscience. *Ecological Psychology, 31*(3), 166–181. https://doi.org/10.1080/10407413.2019.1615213

Redding, P. (2008). The independence and dependence of self-consciousness: The dialectic of Lord and Bondsman in Hegel's Phenomenology of spirit. In F. C. Beiser (Ed.), *The Cambridge companion to Hegel and nineteenth-century philosophy* (pp. 94–110). Cambridge University Press. https://doi.org/10.1017/CCOL9780521831673.005

Reddy, W. M. (2020). The unavoidable intentionality of affect: The history of emotions and the neurosciences of the present day. *Emotion Review, 12*(3), 168–178. https://doi.org/10.1177/1754073920930781

Reimann, M., & Bechara, A. (2010). The somatic marker framework as a neurological theory of decision-making: Review, conceptual comparisons, and future neuroeconomics research. *Journal of Economic Psychology, 31*(5), 767–776. https://doi.org/10.1016/j.joep.2010.03.002

Rietveld, E., & Kiverstein, J. (2023). Reflections on ecological psychology: An interview with Harry Heft. In M. Segundo-Ortin, M. Heras-Escribano, & V. Raja (Eds.), *Places, sociality, and ecological psychology: Essays in honor of Harry Heft* (1st ed., pp. 10–22). Routledge. https://doi.org/10.4324/9781003259244

Rizzolatti, G., & Sinigaglia, C. (2010). The functional role of the parieto-frontal mirror circuit: Interpretations and misinterpretations. *Nature Reviews Neuroscience, 11*(4), 264–274. https://doi.org/10.1038/nrn2805

Robinson, A. E., Sloman, S. A., Hagmayer, Y., & Hertzog, C. K. (2010). Causality in solving economic problems. *The Journal of Problem Solving, 3*(1). https://doi.org/10.7771/1932-6246.1081

Roth, A. E. (2007). Repugnance as a constraint on markets. *Journal of Economic Perspectives, 21*(3), 37–58. https://doi.org/10.1257/jep.21.3.37

Roughley, N. (2015). Resentment, empathy and moral normativity. In N. Roughley & T. Schramme (Eds.), *Forms of fellow feeling: Sympathy, empathy, concern and moral agency* (pp. 225–247). Cambridge University Press.

Sahlins, M. (2014). On the ontological scheme of *Beyond nature and culture. HAU: Journal of Ethnographic Theory*, *4*(1), 281–290. https://doi.org/10.14318/hau4.1.013

Sahlins, M. (2022). *The new science of the enchanted universe: An anthropology of most of humanity*. Princeton University Press.

Samuelson, P. A. (1948). Consumption theory in terms of revealed preference. *Economica, 15*(60), 243–253. https://doi.org/10.2307/2549561

Sanfey, A. G., Rilling, J. K., Aronson, J. A., Nystrom, L. E., & Cohen, J. D. (2003). The neural basis of economic decision-making in the ultimatum game. *Science, 300*(5626), 1755–1758. https://doi.org/10.1126/science.1082976

Sartre, J.-P. (1939/2014). *Sketch for a theory of the emotions*. Routledge. https://doi.org/10.4324/9781315851006

Schelling, T. C. (1968). The life you save may be your own. In S. Chase (Ed.), *Problems in public expenditure analysis*. The Brookings Institute.

Schubert, T. W. (2005). Your highness: Vertical positions as perceptual symbols of power. *Journal of Personality and Social Psychology, 89*(1), 1–21. https://doi.org/10.1037/0022-3514.89.1.1

Schwartz, D. A., Weaver, M., & Kaplan, S. (1999). A little mechanism can go a long way. *Behavioral and Brain Sciences, 22*(4), 631–632. https://doi.org/10.1017/S0140525X99472140

Serra, D. (2021). Decision-making: From neuroscience to neuroeconomics—an overview. *Theory and Decision, 91*(1), 1–80. https://doi.org/10.1007/s11238-021-09830-3

Sève, L. (2021). Where is Marx in the work and thought of Vygotsky? *Mind, Culture, and Activity, 28*(4), 293–303. https://doi.org/10.1080/10749039.2021.1964535

Shapiro, L., & Spaulding, S. (2023). Embodied cognition. In E. N. Zalta (Ed.), *The Stanford encyclopedia of philosophy* (Spring 2023). Metaphysics Research Lab, Stanford University. https://plato.stanford.edu/archives/spr2023/entries/embodied-cognition/

Sharot, T., Velasquez, C. M., & Dolan, R. J. (2010). Do decisions shape preference? *Evidence from Blind Choice. Psychological Science, 21*(9), 1231–1235. https://doi.org/10.1177/0956797610379235

Shebani, Z., Carota, F., Hauk, O., Rowe, J. B., Barsalou, L. W., Tomasello, R., & Pulvermüller, F. (2022). Brain correlates of action word memory revealed by fMRI. *Scientific Reports, 12*(1), 16053. https://doi.org/10.1038/s41598-022-19416-w

Shilling, C. (2012). *The body and social theory*. SAGE.

Siep, L. (2011). 5. Mutual recognition: Hegel and beyond. In H. Ikaheimo & A. Laitinen (Eds.), *Recognition and social ontology* (pp. 115–144). BRILL. https://doi.org/10.1163/ej.9789004202900.i-398.37

Simmel, G. (2004). The philosophy of money. *Routledge*. https://doi.org/10.4324/9780203481134

Simmons, W. K., Martin, A., & Barsalou, L. W. (2005). Pictures of appetizing foods activate gustatory cortices for taste and reward. *Cerebral Cortex, 15*(10), 1602–1608. https://doi.org/10.1093/cercor/bhi038

Simon, H. A. (1955). A behavioral model of rational choice. *The Quarterly Journal of Economics, 69*(1), 99–118.

Simon, H. A. (1967). Motivational and emotional controls of cognition. *Psychological Review, 74*(1), 29–39. https://doi.org/10.1037/h0024127

Simon, H. A. (1979). Rational decision making in business organizations. *American Economic Review, 69*(4), 493–513.

Simon, H. A. (1983). *Reason in human affairs*. Stanford University Press.

Simon, H. A. (1986). Rationality in psychology and economics. *Journal of Business, 59*(4), S209–S224.

Simon, H. A. (1987). Making management decisions: The role of intuition and emotion. *Academy of Management Perspectives, 1*(1), 57–64. https://doi.org/10.5465/ame.1987.4275905

Simon, H. A. (1990). Invariants of human behavior. *Annual Review of Psychology, 41*, 1–19. https://doi.org/10.1146/annurev.ps.41.020190.000245

Simon, H. A. (1993). Decision making: Rational, nonrational, and irrational. *Educational Administration Quarterly, 29*(3), 392–411. https://doi.org/10.1177/0013161X93029003009

Simon, H. A. (2000). Bounded rationality in social science: Today and tomorrow. *Mind & Society, 1*(1), 25–39. https://doi.org/10.1007/BF02512227

Skipper, J. I. (2022). A voice without a mouth no more: The neurobiology of language and consciousness. *Neuroscience & Biobehavioral Reviews, 140*, 104772. https://doi.org/10.1016/j.neubiorev.2022.104772

Slovic, P. (1995). The construction of preference. *American Psychologist, 50*(5), 364–371. https://doi.org/10.1037/0003-066X.50.5.364

Smagorinsky, P. (1998). Thinking and speech and protocol analysis. *Mind, Culture, and Activity, 5*(3), 157–177. https://doi.org/10.1207/s15327884mca0503_2

Small, D. A., & Cryder, C. (2016). Prosocial consumer behavior. *Current Opinion in Psychology, 10*, 107–111. https://doi.org/10.1016/j.copsyc.2016.01.001

Smith, A. (1759/2002). *The theory of moral sentiments*. Cambridge University Press.

Smith, V. L. (2003). Constructivist and ecological rationality in economics. *American Economic Review, 93*(3), 465–508.

Smith, V. L. (2008). *Rationality in economics: Constructivist and ecological forms*. Cambridge University Press. http://www.loc.gov/catdir/toc/ecip079/2007002899.html

Snow, C. P. (2018). *The two cultures and the scientific revolution*. Martino Fine Books.

Song, X., Yi, F., Zhang, J., & Proctor, R. W. (2019). Left is "good": Observed action affects the association between horizontal space and affective valence. *Cognition, 193*, 104030. https://doi.org/10.1016/j.cognition.2019.104030

Speer, N. K., Reynolds, J. R., Swallow, K. M., & Zacks, J. M. (2009). Reading stories activates neural representations of visual and motor experiences. *Psychological Science, 20*(8), 989–999. https://doi.org/10.1111/j.1467-9280.2009.02397.x

Spence, C. (2015). The cognitive neuroscience of incorporation: Body image adjustment and neuroprosthetics. In K. Kansaku, L. G. Cohen, & N. Birbaumer (Eds.), *Clinical systems neuroscience* (pp. 151–168). Springer Japan. https://doi.org/10.1007/978-4-431-55037-2_9

Stekeler-Weithofer, P. (2011). Intuition, understanding, and the human form of life. In H. Ikäheimo & A. Laitinen (Eds.), *Recognition and Social Ontology* (pp. 117–144). Brill.

Stigler, G. J., & Becker, G. S. (1977). De gustibus non est disputandum. *American Economic Review, 67*(2), 76–90.

Summers, J. S. (2017). *Post hoc ergo propter hoc*: Some benefits of rationalization. *Philosophical Explorations, 20*(sup1), 21–36. https://doi.org/10.1080/13869795.2017.1287292

Sundar, A., & Noseworthy, T. J. (2014). Place the logo high or low? Using conceptual metaphors of power in packaging design. *Journal of Marketing, 78*(5), 138–151. https://doi.org/10.1509/jm.13.0253

Susen, S., & Turner, B. S. (2011). *The legacy of Pierre Bourdieu: Critical essays*. Anthem Press.

Taylor, C. (2015). *Hegel and modern society (Cambridge Philosophy Classics edition)*. Cambridge University Press.

Testa, I. (2020). Embodied cognition, habit, and natural agency in Hegel's anthropology. In M. F. Bykova & K. R. Westphal (Eds.), *The Palgrave Hegel handbook* (pp. 269–295). Springer International Publishing. https://doi.org/10.1007/978-3-030-26597-7_14

Thompson, E., & Stapleton, M. (2009). Making sense of sense-making: Reflections on enactive and extended mind theories. *Topoi, 28*(1), 23–30. https://doi.org/10.1007/s11245-008-9043-2

Todd, P. M., & Gigerenzer, G. (2003). Bounding rationality to the world. *Journal of Economic Psychology, 24*(2), 143–165. https://doi.org/10.1016/S0167-4870(02)00200-3

Todd, P. M., & Gigerenzer, G. (2012). *Ecological rationality: Intelligence in the world*. Oxford University Press.

Tomasello, M. (2019). Becoming human: A theory of ontogeny. *Harvard University Press*. https://doi.org/10.4159/9780674988651

Tomasello, M., Kruger, A. C., & Ratner, H. H. (1993). Cultural learning. *Behavioral and Brain Sciences, 16*(3), 495–511. https://doi.org/10.1017/S0140525X0003123X

Tönnies, F. (1887). *Gemeinschaft und Gesellschaft: Abhandlung des Communismus und des Socialismus als empirischer Culturformen*. Fues's Verlag.

Toskos Dils, A., & Flusberg, S. J. (2010). Massive redeployment or distributed modularity? *Behavioral and Brain Sciences, 33*(4), 292–293. https://doi.org/10.1017/S0140525X10001226

Tsakiris, M. (2010). My body in the brain: A neurocognitive model of body-ownership. *Neuropsychologia, 48*(3), 703–712. https://doi.org/10.1016/j.neuropsychologia.2009.09.034

Tsakiris, M., Vehar, N., & Tucciarelli, R. (2021). Visceral politics: A theoretical and empirical proof of concept. *Philosophical Transactions of the Royal Society b: Biological Sciences, 376*(1822), 20200142. https://doi.org/10.1098/rstb.2020.0142

Tschentscher, N., Hauk, O., Fischer, M. H., & Pulvermüller, F. (2012). You can count on the motor cortex: Finger counting habits modulate motor cortex activation evoked by numbers. *NeuroImage, 59*(4), 3139–3148. https://doi.org/10.1016/j.neuroimage.2011.11.037

Turner, M. (1996). *The literary mind*. Oxford University Press.

Turner, M. (2014). *The origin of ideas: Blending, creativity, and the human spark*. Oxford University Press.

Tversky, A., & Kahneman, D. (1974). Judgment under uncertainty: Heuristics and biases. *Science, 185*(4157), 1124–1131. https://doi.org/10.1126/science.185.4157.1124

von Uexküll, J., & Kriszat, G. (1956). *Streifzüge durch die Umwelten von Tieren und Menschen*. Rowohlt.

Van der Laan, L. N., De Ridder, D. T. D., Viergever, M. A., & Smeets, P. A. M. (2011). The first taste is always with the eyes: A meta-analysis on the neural correlates of processing visual food cues. *NeuroImage, 55*(1), 296–303. https://doi.org/10.1016/j.neuroimage.2010.11.055

Varela, F. J., Thompson, E., & Rosch, E. (2016). *The embodied mind* (revised). MIT Press.

Varela, F. J., Thompson, E. T., & Rosch, E. (1991). *The embodied mind: Cognitive science and human experience*. MIT Press.

Veblen, T. (1899/2007). *The theory of the leisure class* (M. Banta, Ed.). Oxford University Press.

Volz, K. G., & Hertwig, R. (2016). Emotions and decisions: Beyond conceptual vagueness and the rationality muddle. *Perspectives on Psychological Science, 11*(1), 101–116. https://doi.org/10.1177/1745691615619608

Vygotsky, L. S. (1989). Concrete human psychology. *Soviet Psychology, 27*(2), 53–77. https://doi.org/10.2753/RPO1061-0405270253

Vygotsky, L. S. (1997). The history of the development of higher mental functions. In R. W. Rieber (Ed.), *The collected works of L. S. Vygotsky. Volume 4: The history of the development of higher mental functions*. Plenum.

Wang, F., & Basso, F. (2021). The peak of health: The vertical representation of healthy food. *Appetite, 167*, 105587. https://doi.org/10.1016/j.appet.2021.105587

Weber, M. (1922/2019). *Economy and society: A new translation* (K. Tribe, Ed. and trans.). Harvard University Press.

Webley, P., Burgoyne, C., Lea, S., & Young, B. (2002). *The economic psychology of everyday life*. Psychology Press.

Weiss, D. J., & Shanteau, J. (2021). The futility of decision-making research. *Studies in History and Philosophy of Science Part A, 90*, 10–14. https://doi.org/10.1016/j.shpsa.2021.08.018

Wicker, B., Keysers, C., Plailly, J., Royet, J.-P., Gallese, V., & Rizzolatti, G. (2003). Both of us disgusted in my insula: The common neural basis of seeing and feeling disgust. *Neuron, 40*(3), 655–664. https://doi.org/10.1016/S0896-6273(03)00679-2

Wiemer-Hastings, K., & Xu, X. (2005). Content differences for abstract and concrete concepts. *Cognitive Science, 29*(5), 719–736. https://doi.org/10.1207/s15516709cog0000_33

Williams, L. E., Huang, J. Y., & Bargh, J. A. (2009). The scaffolded mind: Higher mental processes are grounded in early experience of the physical world. *European Journal of Social Psychology, 39*(7), 1257–1267. https://doi.org/10.1002/ejsp.665

Williamson, O. E. (1975). *Markets and hierarchies*. The Free press.

Williamson, O. E. (1985). *The economic institutions of capitalism: Firms, markets, relational contracting*. The Free Press.

Wilson, M. (2002). Six views of embodied cognition. *Psychonomic Bulletin & Review, 9*(4), 625–636.

Winsler, A., Leon, J. R., Wallace, B. A., Carlton, M. P., & Willson-Quayle, A. (2003). Private speech in preschool children: Developmental stability and change, across-task consistency, and relations with classroom behaviour. *Journal of Child Language, 30*(3), 583–608.

Winter, S. L. (2001). *A clearing in the forest: Law, life, and mind*. University of Chicago Press.

Wiseman, R. (2019). Getting beyond rites of passage in archaeology: Conceptual metaphors of journeys and growth. *Current Anthropology, 60*(4), 449–474. https://doi.org/10.1086/704696

Wood, D., Bruner, J. S., & Ross, G. (1976). The role of tutoring in problem solving. *Journal of Child Psychology and Psychiatry, 17*(2), 89–100.

Wood, G., & Fischer, M. H. (2008). Numbers, space, and action: From finger counting to the mental number line and beyond. *Cortex, 44*, 353–358.

Yu, Y. (2021). *The religious ethic and mercantile spirit in early modern China*. Columbia University Press.

Zajonc, R. B. (1980). Feeling and thinking: Preferences need no inferences. *American Psychologist, 35*, 151–175.

CHAPTER 5

Embodied Agency in the Economy

5.1 Introduction: Agents and Actors

This chapter develops our radical alternative to the much-criticized but still healthy and active *Homo economicus*. Following on from previous chapters, our approach differs from others in that we do not focus on alleged properties of the human agent in terms of computational ability or information endowment, but elaborate on a simple point: *Homo economicus* is disembodied, whereas we recognize that people not only *have* bodies, but *are* bodies, including brains.[1] We grasp this fundamental distinction by confronting the economic notion of "agent" with our concept of "actor." The concept of actor is based on two embodied notions: Autonomy, which refers to capabilities of self-determination and flourishing; and feelings, which ground valuation as enabling reasonable action. We approach the person as developmentally and historically unfolding, embedded in social relations, in the Hegelian tradition that we already reclaimed in the previous chapter.

The previous chapter laid the groundwork for the elaboration of embodied cognition as a radical alternative to the conventional economic model of individual behavior, which has led to the conceptualization of both individuals and markets as information-processing units. The embodied perspective suggests an entirely different way of looking at things and asks: What defines and enables economic agency, the power

F. Basso and C. Herrmann-Pillath, *Embodiment, Political Economy and Human Flourishing*, https://doi.org/10.1007/978-3-031-54971-7_5

to act in the real world? This question is absent from the conventional model, in which individuals simply calculate the optimal choice under constraints, and action occurs only as a consequence. In fact, individuals do not act at all here, since only the disembodied sphere of information processing is considered. As we saw in the concluding section of Chapter 4, the embodiment perspective opens a vista to the long intellectual history of taking action seriously as the cornerstone of understanding human behavior. Hegel remains at the center of such an analysis, conceiving of action as fundamentally social, embodied, and inextricably entangled with the other. This view shaped whole new disciplines that emerged in the late nineteenth and early twentieth centuries, such as George Herbert Mead's inauguration of social psychology (Marková, 1982),[2] which are completely ignored by economists (Herrmann-Pillath, 2019).

In this chapter, we do not consider the full range of these developments but focus on how the embodiment perspective leads to a new view of economic agency and action in the context of markets. That is, we focus on a distinct field and do not consider issues such as gender relations or politics. This is important to emphasize because key concepts in understanding agency in markets are universal in scope and, therefore, exceedingly complex, such as the notion of power, here specified as agential power, the power to act. Indeed, as Max Weber observed: "The concept of 'power' is sociologically amorphous. Any conceivable quality of a person, and all conceivable constellations, can place someone in a position of being able to enforce one's own will in a given situation" (Weber, 1922/2019, p. 134).

We can overcome this difficulty by relating economic agency to the embodied counterpart of freedom as the normative pole of conventional economics, namely "autonomy." This is illustrative of a Hegelian view of economic agency that emphasizes the dialectic of inward and outward embodiment, which leads to certain agential powers of individuals in markets. We hasten to add, however, that this autonomy does not result in methodological individualism. Indeed, in the embodiment view, the conceptual twin of distributed cognition is distributed agency: Agential power is ascribed to individuals, but it emerges in fluid assemblages of bodies and their world. In Malafouris' words: "Agency is a property or possession neither of humans nor of non-humans. Agency is the relational and emergent product of material engagement. It is not something given but something to become realized" (Malafouris, 2013, p. 148).

Thus, we combine the Hegelian view with advanced theories of cognition: Agency is analyzed in terms of the conceptual triad of recognition, inward and outward embodiment, and is distributed in assemblages of actors and artifacts.

We argue that agential power, and not some kind of individual satisfaction such as "subjective utility," is what matters in explaining economic action. As we will see in the subsequent chapters, this enables us to integrate economic, sociological, and psychological approaches to understanding human behavior in economic life. "Real actors" in the economy are actors who strive to exercise agential powers and often suffer from a lack of it. Agential power accrues to them in complex patterns of inward and outward embodiment. The assemblages of bodies and the material and social world underpin the potential "We-mode" of action as well as agential powers experienced as feelings, such as trust in the context of markets. In this chapter, agency is further elaborated with Sen's notions of capabilities and functionings, and complemented by identity, which is expressed through narratives and memories shared with others.

In this first section, we develop the various dimensions of the economic actor. We begin with an empirical illustration, a financial trader, and characterize what it means to recognize that traders are embodied economic actors, as distinct from the abstract agents of both mainstream and behavioral finance. We then introduce the basics of the biological notion of agency, which rests on two conceptual pillars, autonomy and feelings. We conclude by showing that agency is not rooted in an individualistic social ontology, since embodiment means that agency is fundamentally social, distributed in assemblages of people and artifacts. In sum, we further define the notion of "reasonable person" in the economy as the actor, who experiences feelings, seeks to flourish in autonomy, and whose reasons for action are mutually recognized by others.

5.2 Dimensions of Agency

5.2.1 Starring: The Man in the Pit

In this section, we report anthropological, psychological, and sociological research on one particular type of actor in the capitalist economy: Financial traders. In financial economics, they appear as agents who perform complex computations of financial transactions in terms of monetary returns, with underlying models of expected utility and risk. As such, they are increasingly being replaced by machines that perform such operations. One motivation is to reduce potential errors due to alleged flaws of human cognition as argued by behavioral finance research. However, in contrast to this research, disciplines such as sociology broaden the vista from "inner" psychological mechanisms to assemblages of actors and artifacts.

Let us meet trader Bill. To begin with, until recently traders were almost exclusively male. The pit is a place where male traders observe each other's actions in a dense and often highly emotional situation. The screens and other communication media are technological devices for observing "the markets" in the form of numbers and figures, such as quotations of foreign exchange or stock prices, with charts on screens showing movements generated by market exchanges. This is a sign of outward embodiment, as the lines in the charts can be interpreted as spatial metaphors, especially in terms of "up" and "down," which is one of the most influential metaphors for embodied evaluation (Lakoff & Johnson, 1999; Morris et al., 2007). Outward embodiment takes the form of anthropomorphizing the market, as when technical analysts use visual patterns such as "head-and-shoulders" to predict market trends (e.g., Osler & Chang, 1995). Bill responds to such observations by making decisions to buy and sell the relevant assets, which then affect the publicly visible movements of prices. Such feedback loops, mediated by analytical devices, generate the performative effects of distributed cognition discussed in Chapter 4 (MacKenzie, 2006). At the same time, market observations are inwardly embodied in the emotional states of traders (Laube, 2019).

The traditional pit is a community of traders who can largely observe each other. Although they may not observe the actual choices that others make, they can at least observe all the bodily expressions of trading, such as gestures of excitement or despair (Zaloom, 2004, p. 371): "Each trader displays a risk-taking self that his competitors, the market, and he himself will judge" (Zaloom, 2004, p. 367). These expressions are not intended as communicative acts directed at specific other traders, but as bodily expressions, everyone is aware of their public nature. Financial sociologists have noted that such forms of expressive behavior are replicated in the context of digital markets, such as the formation of communities of traders in social media that run parallel to the markets themselves (Knorr Cetina & Bruegger, 2002; Preda & Gemayel, 2020). Market exchange is accompanied by rich forms of expressive communication between people, even when the actual trading is implemented by algorithms (Zaloom, 2003). Why is this necessary?

In the context of the traditional pit, financial trading is a high-risk activity involving large sums of money and endemic uncertainty about market movements. Traders like Bill are well aware that "the markets" are ultimately just *them* (Ho, 2009), the entire population of individuals engaging in a given market, such as foreign exchange. They know that future movements are determined by the expectations of current actors, as influenced by their own actions and their expectations of the actions of others.[3] Standard financial theory simply aggregates individual traders into a type of "rational agent," which in its most extreme form, would imply that everyone simply thinks the same and draws the same conclusions. As we argued in Chapter 2, this would lead to the logical impossibility of trading at all, and to the conclusion that "(...) a perfectly efficient market, is, in fact, impossible" (Lo, 2019, p. 224). For trading, it is essential that agents' judgments differ. This means that some actors can (or will) be right and others wrong.

Thus, a key feature of financial markets, unlike most other markets, is that they are zero-sum games: "Proprietary trading is effectively a zero-sum game; your gains are someone else's losses: so is this activity unethical? There's no 'rising tide raises all boats' here. It's all 'I win, you lose'" (Lo, 2019, p. 343). Indeed, economists specialized in financial markets struggle to show that and how finance contributes to increasing general welfare, as argued for markets trading goods: "To this day, empirical measures of the benefits of an efficient market are fairly elusive" (Zingales, 2015, p. 1337). After all, financial markets merely reshuffle wealth among actors who are right or wrong in predicting the future, and only the difference in performance matters. The situation is very different for someone who buys an apartment at a price that is higher than justified by general market conditions, because she still ends up owning the apartment and enjoying its use. But for Bill, it is the loss relative to others that determines the benefits he can ultimately derive from the trade, such as investing his gains in the purchase of a home: In effect, his task is to engage in pure arbitrage, with no intention of holding an asset for any other use, such as getting the foreign exchange to buy wheat on global commodity markets. This means that the economic agents of the pit are part of a group of traders who engage in a specific form of competition, a tournament, which results in a ranking of traders in terms of their history of success or failure which is manifested in accumulated financial wealth

(Zaloom, 2004, p. 373; see also Foster, 2017; Ho, 2009). In financial markets, the performance of individual traders is compared to and by each other against the common benchmark of money. As a side effect, global financial centers are typically places where luxury goods markets flourish, because wealth is expressed in status goods, such as expensive watches or cars (Sassen, 2018, p. 204ff). The mere communication of bank accounts would not be a visible expression of relative status.

As a tournament, financial trading is emotionally charged. One manifestation of this is the forms of gendered behavior endorsed by the male subculture of traders.[4] A distinctive feature of this subculture is the widespread use of embodied metaphors related to combat and sexual prowess in describing market actions:

> Like the contexts emotions emerge in (performance, violence, gaming, and gambling), the boundaries of these lexical fields are not impermeable. Metaphor use here, which both establishes a protective distance and works to appropriate market action as a social activity, is not always limited to high-emotion situations, and may be found at less than exceptional moments, where the metaphors used have even stronger sexual connotations: 'feel up' or 'stroke' the market, 'touch [=get] a contract,' be 'in the air,' 'screw an order,' 'get the pussy,' 'give the market a screw.' Also to describe more routine market life, there is a series of metaphors related to eating – attack 'la fourchette,' 'the market is barfing,' etc. – together with regular references to liquidity, which according to some symbolic grids goes with sexuality or bodily intimacy. (Hassoun, 2005, p. 112)

The financial sector is highly gendered, and cultural norms of interaction and communication often make access difficult for women, even in the context of digitalization (Klaes et al., 2011). This metaphorical framing reflects the strength of the underlying emotions, resulting in complex conceptual blends of market phenomena and sexuality. As well documented in neuroeconomic and transdisciplinary behavioral studies, actions in financial markets are thus shaped by various forms of embodiment, especially hormonal mechanisms, as neuroscientific evidence suggests that these emotions are triggered by the hormonal dynamics of rank tournaments, that is, feelings of relative gain and loss (Coates et al., 2010). Similarly, experimental results

> suggest that short-term alterations in male cortisol and testosterone levels have significant effects on financial decision-making. The observed effects

are compatible with field observations in professional traders and suggest that these hormones may play a destabilizing role in financial markets (Cueva et al., 2015, p. 9)

This does not mean, however, that "irrationality" prevails in the financial markets. Becoming a member of the financial community is a process of socialization as inward embodiment that explicitly fosters individual capacities to manage the emotions that accompany trading. "Rationality" is manifested as emotional discipline, such as managing feelings of loss (Zaloom, 2004, p. 377ff): "The ascetic practices and social displays of virtue enacted in the pit describe a capitalist ethic that centers on the mastery of the self under conditions of hazard and possibility" (Zaloom, 2004, p. 366).[5]Compared to non-professionals, professional traders show a better (interoceptive) ability to sense their own heartbeat which is positively correlated with their profit/loss performance in financial markets (Bossaerts, 2021; Kandasamy et al., 2016). Socialization includes, for example, personal relationships such as mentorship by senior traders. The release of intense emotional stress is a function fulfilled by the social environment of financial centers, such as expensive clubs and parties, and strengthens the bonds of community among traders.

Emotions are not only individual states. Given the close interactions in the pit, if only by observing the bodily expressions of others, emotions are also collective states. This becomes clear when markets are anthropomorphized and assigned emotional states, often referred to as "moods" (Saurabh & Dey, 2020). There is evidence that "the market" can be seen as having a "mind" that embodies the collective states of the trading community (De Martino et al., 2013).[6] Shared emotions are an essential part of how market states are reflected and enacted by market participants. Again, this cannot be seen as "irrationality," because there is no effective reference to a supposedly "rational" state. The fundamental challenge in financial markets is to succeed in outguessing others, while being able to observe their actions only *ex post*, mostly without knowing the true reasons behind these actions. In such an environment, actors who aim to behave *à la Homo economicus* will often fail to predict future market developments because they misinterpret the real motives of other agents as an allegedly incorrect view of the market (Bikhchandani et al., 1998). Yet, even this cannot be unambiguously determined *ex post,* because their actions based on allegedly incorrect information also determine future market states.[7]

In other words, financial market states have a strong performative dynamic, in the sense that traders' current expectations (or theories) determine future market states, which then feed back into expectations for the next period (MacKenzie, 2006). Therefore, shared emotions are a crucial feature of markets, which Keynes (1936/2018, p. 141) famously referred to as "animal spirits," as discussed in Chapter 4. Unlike his followers, who put his theory into a mathematical framework *à la* Hicks and Hansen (Vroey & Hoover, 2004), Keynes clearly recognized that only emotions can resolve the paradoxical nature of "rational action" in markets, potentially leading to stalemate as identified by the "no trade theorem." Financial markets, contrary to mainstream views in economics, are not the apex of disembodied economic rationality but are necessarily driven by emotional states (Lo, 2019, p. 75ff), which are part and parcel of embodied reason, as argued in Chapter 4. This means that market states are embodied in two senses: They correspond to the shared emotional states of actors, as exemplified by herding behavior (Bobe & Piefke, 2019), and these are maintained or altered by metaphorical and anthropomorphic interpretations of market dynamics (e.g., Morris et al., 2007).

One implication of this analysis is that we cannot approach financial markets in terms of an "average" type of financial actor, or the (so-called) "representative" agent discussed in Chapter 2. This has been recognized by recent macroeconomic approaches that model the diversity of behaviors that arise from differences in strategy, expectations, or risk preferences (Grauwe & Ji, 2019). However, embodied economics takes this a step further by arguing that an ecology of types, such as the individual investor versus the investment bank professional, characterizes financial markets. These types define different forms of agency that are well recognized in practice: Consider, for instance, the difference between value investors and algorithm designers for investment banks. The distribution of types is partly institutionalized, but also endogenous to market developments: In some periods, for instance, the share of non-professionals who "gamble" on financial markets, and even influence market performance, increases significantly.[8]

In sum, the example of financial markets is a powerful illustration of agency in embodied economics. Most importantly, as Keynes famously argued in his view of "animal spirits," and consistent with the embodied cognition approach developed in Chapter 4, the computational view of economic agents would imply that agents would effectively lose any capacity to act at all, because they could not overcome the aporetic condition of calculating optimal choices in real-world markets. Agency is a quality that actors like Bill acquire in a process of market socialization, and it involves a wide range of skills and capacities, from analytical cleverness to emotional discipline.[9] They acquire the ability to act in the field of a financial market—they do not acquire the computational skills to fully explain financial markets and act accordingly. This is not a loss, as evidenced by the famous expression directed at financial economists who claim to acquire such skills: "If you're so smart, why aren't you rich?" Agency is relative to changing market conditions: In the long run, the successful financial actor is a person who experiences feelings of agency in coping with market uncertainty and is able to exploit market trends to his or her own advantage. In contrast, market conditions such as a financial crisis may result in a loss of perceived agential powers, with actors experiencing a complete loss of control and literally life-threatening challenges (Lo, 2019, p. 296ff). An emotional expression of this is a state of fear and panic that spreads at the collective level. In this respect, financial crises are a recurrent and permanent feature of financial markets, generating a widespread mood of impotence and despair, and following periods of "irrational exuberance:" In the crisis, traders experience a loss of agency; in the boom, they feel like "masters of the universe."

5.2.2 *Autonomy and Feelings as Elementary Constituents of Agency*

Trader Bill is an economic actor. As we have seen, although he appears to specialize in the most abstract form of market activity, the exchange of financial assets, he can in no way be seen as a computer in the flesh, performing calculations of financial values as prescribed by financial theory. Two conclusions are possible. One is to treat his human characteristics as disturbances and try to get rid of them. The ultimate method is to replace humans with algorithms, as is increasingly being done in finance. Obviously, this is the final stage of disembodying the economic agent. The other is to investigate the notion of agency in economic life. This is our choice.

Agency is a concept that is rarely used in mainstream economics, although the term "economic agent" is well accepted. The conventional notion of the rational economic agent does not refer to a form of agency widely recognized in sociology and psychology, where agency is a property that individuals may or may not have. In contrast, the economic agent is assumed to have this property by default, since she is always conceived as "free to choose," limited only by external constraints, such as the budget constraint. Apart from these constraints, agency is a priori given, taken for granted, and, therefore, not an object of study in economics. In other social science disciplines, by contrast, agency is a capacity that individuals acquire in various ways, and that is situated: It is not just a trait like having big or small ears but depends essentially on the situation in which the agent is acting. If small ears are considered beautiful in a certain society, this creates a potential for agency that is not available to those with big ears. Nevertheless, ears remain a bodily feature. Agency can include actions to reduce the size of ears through surgery, an act that can also be imposed by force, as illustrated by the ancient and cruel practice of foot binding in China. Here, agency is unequally distributed between women and men, especially because the practice was applied to young girls who lack the socially recognized agency of adults. The acquisition of "lotus feet" creates complicated internal states in women, who suffer acute physical pain while at the same time enjoying at least the recognition of their mates as they enter marriageable age.

In what follows, we develop a synthesis of two views of agency that may seem completely irreconcilable, namely, the view of biology and the view of German idealism, epitomized in Hegel. This perspective was prepared in Chapter 4, where we concluded the detailed discussion of embodied cognition with a look at Hegel. German idealism explicitly transcends biology, but, as Hegel famously asserted, in the form of a "second nature" (Hegel, 1820/2009, §151, compare Hegel, 1830/1991, § 513). This second nature emanates from the institutions of civil society which become internalized as ethical life ("*Sittlichkeit*"), custom ("*Sitte*"), and habit ("*Gewohnheit*") in a living community: Thus, a full treatment of economic agency is possible only in conjunction with this chapter and the next. However, the complex notions of external scaffolding and mediation in embodied cognition have already been introduced in Chapter 4. In this chapter, we will explore how the two views converge into a concept of agency, that is, on closer inspection, a Hegelian notion, that differs from other positions in German idealism, especially Kant. Some conceptual clarity is needed.

Our synthesis is based on the observation that the concept of agency, seen as attributed to an entity called an "agent," is a biological universal. In psychology, agency can be defined as "the state of being active, usually in the service of a goal, or of having the power and capability to produce an effect or exert influence" (APA, 2023).[10] Given this broad definition, it can obviously be applied to any living entity, even a bacterium. We distinguish between an agent as a universal biological phenomenon and an actor: Humans are agents who are *actors*. This distinction refers to the Hegelian concept of "action" as being enabled by institutions based on the mutual recognition of actors and constituting free will as the inward embodiment of ethical life (Hegel, 1820/2009, §113ff, §142ff; Quante, 2011, p. 199ff). This is a crucial step in the analysis that we pursue in the next chapters. Here, we elaborate on the meaning of the general concept of agency, starting with the two notions of "autonomy" and "feeling." The latter notion captures various aspects of emotion and affect discussed in Chapter 4, but with a view to how they relate to agency.

Living agents are defined as autonomous, with different aspects. The fundamental aspect is physical, that is, a living being is able to sustain itself thermodynamically by interacting with the environment in such a way that the boundary between its internal states and the environment is maintained: "An autonomous agent is a system able to reproduce itself and carry out one or more thermodynamic work cycles" (Kauffman, 2000, p. 52ff). In this book, we do not focus on this fundamental aspect (Herrmann-Pillath, 2021b), although it provides the basis for the embodied notion of autonomy. In order to maintain its independent thermodynamic state, the agent is capable of generating goals that are derived from the basic function of maintaining its internal states and that are necessarily grounded in interaction with the world (Roli et al., 2022). This is the concept of homeostasis that we introduced in Chapter 3, when we discussed Hayek's views on psychology and neuroscience, with a long intellectual pedigree, such as Piaget (1975).[11] That is another aspect of autonomy: The agent does not just passively react to the environment, but sets its goals as defined by its internal states, which is sometimes called "autopoiesis."[12] This concept posits that the agent enacts itself through interactions with the environment. Therefore, this environment is not simply the physical environment, but its valued transformation, the "*Umwelt*" in von Uexküll's parlance (Uexküll & Kriszat, 1956; see also, Stapleton, 2022). As Rosch writes:

> Enaction can be understood in two stages. The core idea of enaction is that the living body is a self-organizing system. This is in contrast to viewing it as a machine that happens to be made of meat rather than silicon. Mechanisms act and change their state only because of input and

> programming from sources outside of themselves, whereas the living body continuously reorganizes itself to survive and maintain its own homeostasis. (Notice how this alone is a radical departure from the dominant view of the body in present research.) Survival means that the organism must preserve the integrity of its boundaries while having a constant interchange with the environment. Even the simplest one-celled organism exchanges materials through the semipermeable membrane of its cell walls and performs overt actions relevant to its self-maintenance, such as swimming toward a detectable food source or away from insupportable temperatures. Actions of the organism are thus purposive and have been said by enactivists to be the embryonic forms of cognition, of mind, and even of value (Rosch, p. xxxviii, in Varela et al., 2016)

Valuation in its most universal form is "feelings," which means that all living beings as agents are sentient beings. In Hegel's anthropology, feelings are the primordial constituents of the bodily self (Testa, 2020). This principle unites all entities of the tree of life (Damasio, 2019). There are different degrees of feelings, and perhaps the feelings of bacteria should be called "proto-feelings." But once nervous systems emerge in the tree of life, the difference between feelings among living beings is only gradual, not essential. Even if cognitive systems differ substantially among different phyla, the fundamental fact of sentience unifies life forms.[13]

Feelings can be enhanced and embedded in more complex cognitive structures and processes. Even the bacterium feels where nutrients are and sets goals, and there are rudimentary cognitive scaffolds such as quorum sensing. Feelings are directed both inwards and outwards. There are feelings about internal states (e.g., the feeling of needing nutrients) and feelings about environmental states such as *Umwelt* (e.g., the perception of a threat). However, these feelings are not a "representation" of the environment as given (or pre-defined) but the expression of its perception through the lens of valued internal states of the body. As Damasio writes:

> The feeling experience is a natural process of evaluating life relative to its prospects. *Valence 'judges' the current efficiency of body states, and feeling announces the judgment to the body's owner*. Feelings express fluctuations in the state of life, within the standard range and outside it. Some states within the standard range are more efficient than others, and feelings express the degree of efficiency. Life within the central homeostatic range is

> a necessity; life upregulated to the flourishing edges is desirable. (Damasio, 2019, p. 106)

> Feelings are not neural events alone. The body proper is critically involved, and that involvement includes the participation of other important and homeostatically relevant systems such as the endocrine and immune systems. Feelings are, through and through, simultaneously and interactingly, phenomena of both bodies and nervous systems. (Damasio, 2019, p. 125)

Hence, combining the two notions of homeostasis and feelings, we can refer to agency as the concept of "flourishing" that goes beyond a mechanistical view of "adaptation" in evolutionary biology. Homeostasis is not simply the reproduction states but is future-oriented, which means that agency is about goals that improve and sustain the agent under conditions of an ever-changing and unpredictable world (Clark, 2023, p. 90ff). Feelings guide actions towards flourishing by, for example, characterizing situations that promise pleasure and others that are threatening. For instance, they have greater predictive power of "get-me-out-of-here actions" in the categories of neighborhood, partner, job, and hospital visits, than does a combined set of economic and social variables (Kaiser & Oswald, 2022).

A final observation about feelings is that they are not simply encoded in the neural system, which would imply another distinction between body and brain (Jasanoff, 2018, p. 97ff). On the contrary, feelings are intimately related to bodily states that are manifested in chemical phenomena that cross the blood–brain barrier and thus directly connect the brain to peripheral neural systems, that is, independently of neuronal signaling. This is especially significant when considering the role of the enteric nervous system, or "gut," which is prominent in many folk-psychological accounts of human feelings and actions. Damasio writes:

> This finding means that while the neurons themselves work to convey peripheral signals to the central nervous system, they do not do so alone. On the contrary, they are assisted; they are modulated directly by molecules circulating in the blood. The signals that, for example, help generate the pain from a wound are conveyed to precisely such dorsal root ganglia. Given the arrangement I just described, the signals are thus not 'purely' neural. The body has its say on the process, directly, via influential chemical molecules circulating in the blood. The same influence can be exerted

> higher up in the system, at the level of the brain stem and the cerebral cortices. The denuding of the blood-brain barrier is one mechanism for blending body and brain. In fact, permeability may turn out to be a fairly general feature of peripheral ganglia. These facts need to be factored in the scholarship of feelings (Damasio, 2019, p. 131)

In sum, we propose a generalized notion of biological agency as literally grounding our theory of economic agency. Building on this, we characterize human agents as actors rather than merely "agents." We encounter one such actor in the trader Bill. Even at this stage of the argument, the fundamental difference with the standard economic view is salient. The latter assumes a simple representational relationship between the world and the economic agent in terms of projections between states of the world and subjective utilities, and action is just a symptom of internal computations of these values. In the embodied view, actions and valuations are deeply intertwined, and the ultimate goals that actors pursue cannot be defined in utilitarian terms, but rather in terms of the powers of action that they can deploy and enjoy.

5.2.3 Autonomy and Freedom of Human Actors

We approach the two concepts of autonomy and feelings as universal features of agency common to living beings, human and non-human. Both are the pillars on which the embodied approach to economic agency rests. Thus, in considering humans in particular, we can either emphasize only general aspects of agency that apply to any living being, or we can move on to more specifically consider humans as actors. One way to distinguish between the two is to relate autonomy to "freedom."

"Freedom" is an ideological pillar of liberal (and neoliberal) economics, understood as being "free to choose" (Friedman & Friedman, 1990). But there is the problem of the alleged neutrality of constraints. From the perspective of "autonomy," autonomy is also enhanced or enabled by being free from certain constraints. At the same time, autonomy can also include the autonomous choice of which constraints matter. This defines the difference between agent and actor: The bacterium cannot choose between what matters for its survival, both ends and constraints. In other words, anticipating a theoretical approach that we will develop in more detail in the next chapters, human actors are supposed to be able to collectively choose among different ways of performing their life together, including ends and constraints. Actors' agency is performative agency.

As Amartya Sen has argued, there is a difference between someone who starves involuntarily and someone, such as the religious ascetic, who abstains from food, even though the result in terms of the material state is the same: The former is forced into the state of involuntary starvation, the other chooses it through fasting (Sen, 2004, p. 665). Their agency is radically distinct, resulting in a different contextualization of what is apparently the same bodily state. This is reflected in very different feelings when evaluating the state of being hungry, with the religious ascetic possibly even transforming this feeling into a feeling of bliss. This role of autonomy in contextualizing individual states of well-being is strangely absent in economics, despite its ideological centrality, with disturbing consequences for economic judgments: For example, the poor peasant (like today's slum dweller) who left the countryside to work in the "satanic mills" of early industrialization is thought to have "revealed" a preference because he chose to do so, without recognizing his complete lack of agency in determining his own fate, beyond the mere decision to migrate (Elster, 1982).

Such examples show what is the crucial difference between Hegelian and Kantian notions of autonomy, the latter being merely formal, the former including the social conditions of autonomy[14]:

> Hegel, in contrast, does not think that human freedom is possible without a social framework. What we must come to understand collectively is how this framework promotes rather than stifles our freedom and therefore our capacity to lead fully rational and good lives. (Hoy, 2009, p. 155)

The elementary form of autonomy as freedom is to be free to choose the means to a given set of ends in a community of actors. This is the autonomy that all living beings enjoy, while most of them are focused on genetically determined goals at the species level. Interestingly, economics takes this into account, with a twist: The goals are left unspecified. Subjective utility functions provide the goals. Sometimes these are even seen as genetically determined, but there is also the view that subjectivity is simply an analytical assumption reflecting that economics excludes goals from its domain (von Weizsäcker, 2011) In other words, as discussed in Chapter 2, economics does not explain the choice of goals at all to account for full (economic) freedom. However, Sen diagnoses here the "rational fool," who is unable or unwilling to choose her goals reflexively (Sen, 1977). To exclude the choice of goals from the scope of what economics must consider is to disregard how human reason chooses among goals. If the latter is ignored, the concept of "rationality" is simply "foolish:" It would mean following random drives without thinking, but optimizing their fulfillment. Choosing among goals—and thereby deciding which constraints matter and how—is a minimum requirement for human autonomy. Sen refers to this as "commitment:"

> The main thesis has been the need to accommodate commitment as a part of behavior. Commitment does not presuppose reasoning, but it does not exclude it; in fact, insofar as consequences on others have to be more clearly understood and assessed in terms of one's values and instincts, the scope for reasoning may well expand. I have tried to analyze the structural extensions in the conception of preference made necessary by behavior based on reasoned assessment of commitment. (Sen, 1977, p. 344)

German idealism in the Kantian vein adds the dimension of moral freedom, which means including the institutional domain in the broadest sense, that is, the rules that govern human interaction. The setting of goals is always in tension with the goals set by others, and so the question is whether an actor can autonomously decide the rules to which she will subject her actions. Kant presented his categorical imperative as a solution based on the assumption of a universal capacity for rationality in all human beings. Hegel rejected this solution by presenting a radically embodied view of autonomy. First, he asked what motivates individuals to adopt the ideal rational solution, which points to socially embedded emotional commitments, called "*Sittlichkeit*" (Pippin, 2008). Second, he also pointed to the material conditions of freedom, which we refer to as "capabilities."[15] Capabilities are not just internal states: They need to be supported and activated by external states. We can refer to these three forms of freedom as personal, moral, and social freedom (Neuhouser, 2008). As we will see, the autonomy of actors requires an essential consideration of the dimension of institutions (Fig. 5.1).

When we apply these categories to the market, the embodied view differs fundamentally from the view of mainstream economics. The latter focuses mainly on means, such as consumers choosing among goods that satisfy their needs, or producers choosing among cost-efficient inputs.

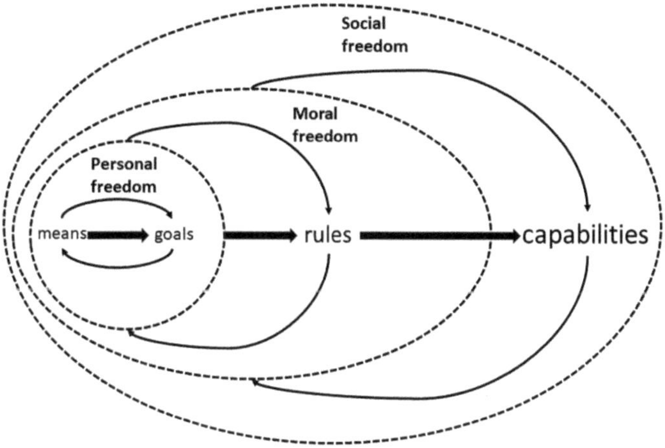

Fig. 5.1 The Hegelian concept of freedom distinguishes three emergent forms: Personal, moral, and social freedom. Personal freedom is the freedom to choose goals and the means to achieve them. However, this requires the establishment of rules since personal freedom can remain in conflict with others. Moral freedom consists in autonomous participation in the establishment of these rules. Yet, this also requires material capabilities (conditions and capacities) for participation, which constitute social freedom [After Herrmann-Pillath & Boldyrev, 2014]

There is no explicit treatment of autonomy in choosing ends. Moreover, autonomy is limited in deciding whether or not to participate in the market, since earning money as a universal means is a necessary condition for pursuing many, if not most ends in society. There is also limited autonomy in deciding on market institutions (e.g., Prusik, 2018), as illustrated by Williamson (1975, p. 21) who assumed that "in the beginning there were markets." At the political level, this could even lead to support for "transitional dictatorship" to restore free markets, as exemplified by Hayek's controversial visits to Chile (Caldwell & Montes, 2015; Farrant & McPhail, 2014). Finally, there is the problem of having the capabilities to participate in the market, which is multidimensional, such as having specific skills, having opportunities as defined by one's social context, or having the necessary capital to take part. In economics, these latter distinctions are usually subsumed under "constraints," and only freedom of choice is considered.

In sum, the standard economic view may accommodate the notion of agents with given ends, but it does not consider people as actors who seek autonomy in choosing among ends, determining the rules under which they act, and securing their capabilities to act. These are types of action that require coordination among many actors, which is an elementary form of politics. Thus, in the embodied view, economic agency is ultimately determined in the political realm: Embodied economics is political economy.

5.2.4 *Agency Beyond the Individual*

Mainstream economics is by definition individualistic, often crudely contrasted with "collectivism," as in Hayekian thinking, which opposes "true" and "false" individualism, the latter tending towards collectivism (Hayek, 1948; Robbins, 1961). Studies of agency in the social sciences and humanities have long since moved beyond this simple opposition. Despite their diversity, several views form a stream of research that understands agency as a property of complex assemblages of entities, including different human individuals, but also all other kinds of material entities, both living and non-living.[16] This perspective, too, can be traced back to Hegel, although contemporary authors may not recognize the connection. In fact, what was truly innovative about Hegel was that he combined idealism with a thoroughgoing view of embodiment (often dubbed the "continuity" thesis). The latter was radicalized by Marx as materialism, and one might conclude that this would be the necessary consequence of eschewing Hegel's metaphysics, which we take for granted. We do not reach this conclusion if materialism also entails abandoning the subjectivity of the body and reducing all human life to responses to the external material environment, which is not implied by Marx (Merleau-Ponty, 1955/1973), for whom (as for enactivists) "human beings are fundamentally embodied, embedded, active and intersubjective creatures." (Loader, 2015, p. 69).

In Fig. 5.2, we show the basic structure of the Hegelian approach to the individual and its agency (Herrmann-Pillath & Boldyrev, 2014, p. 40ff). We will continue to refer to "spirit" here, as this is Hegel's *terminus technicus* for what in modern parlance might be seen as the assemblage that ontologically constitutes agency. The subject-object relationship is based on expressive action, i.e. the subject acts and, in some form, creates an object (artifact), such as a text, a tool, and so on: This is included in what we labelled "outward embodiment" in Chapter 4. But this object (artifact) in use also changes the subject, by means of "inward embodiment." For example, I am writing a text in which I am trying to express my thoughts. However, I struggle with the words, and when I read what I have written, it further clarifies my thinking.[17] Hence, the Hegelian "objective spirit" refers to the performative loop of outward and inward embodiment, and to what we discussed at length in Chapter 4 in relation to language: The text outwardly embodies the subject, and the subject inwardly embodies the text. Obviously, and crucially for Hegel, this is a process (the unfolding of the spirit) and should never be approached in static terms.

As depicted in Fig. 5.2, a third aspect of human agency comes into play: recognition. Whether I think I have expressed myself well in the text requires recognition by others, whose feedback helps me to understand myself better.[18] Recognition points to human sociality as a fundamental requirement for being an agent, since even what I conceive of as an action depends on whether that action is recognized by others as a certain

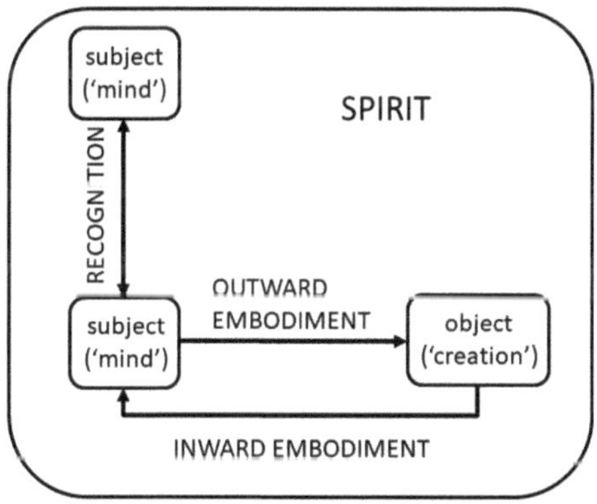

Fig. 5.2 The Hegelian concept of "spirit" can be understood as the process in which inward embodiment, outward embodiment, and recognition are interrelated. The Hegelian subject expresses her "internal" states in objects in the widest sense, including actions (hence outward embodiment), which are externalized and feed back on the subject with formative power (hence inward embodiment). These externalized expressions are recognized by others and thereby gain normative powers. These expressions are "objective spirit" in Hegelian parlance [Modified after Herrmann-Pillath & Boldyrev, 2014]

kind of action.[19] Thus, the Hegelian view approaches individual agency as resulting from the complex interplay of subjects with other subjects and objects (artifacts). This is tantamount to the contemporary notion of assemblage. As a result, we avoid the standard economic distinction between individuals and collectives: In the Hegelian view, individuals as actors emerge from the evolution of collectivities—this is what Hegel means when he speaks of "spirit." Similarly, embodied economics adopts the duality of inward and outward embodiment discussed in Chapter 4.

So, let us reframe this discussion from the standpoint of economics. Economics distinguishes between individual and collective action, but denies agency to collectives. This raises the challenge of how to explain collective action on the basis of individual choice alone. The embodied approach to agency suggests a radically different view, which has already been ventured by a few daring economists such as Robert Sugden, who proposes

> a different way of thinking about team agency, in which the preferences that individuals have as members of teams are distinct from, but on a par with, the preferences that guide their private choices, and which does not involve concepts of obligation. (Sugden, 2000, p. 177)

This assumes that agency is not necessarily confined to individuals, which raises the question of whether there are supra-individual entities (Tuomela, 2013). This question only becomes awkward if we juxtapose individual and supra-individual entities as separate types of social ontology. Instead, we posit agency as an independent type of social ontology: This does not mean that there is a stable object like "mountain" or an "elephant" that is "agency," but that agency emerges and is distributed in certain assemblages of entities as a dynamic property, like a hurricane that clearly exists and that we identify, even name, but that is not what we would consider a "thing" in naïve ontology (De Landa, 2006).

The embodied approach to agency does not allow for the absolute juxtaposition of the individual and the collective since agency is a systemic and distributed phenomenon, and thus resolves this polarity in a dialectical movement: The individual and the collective are Hegelian "moments" in the distributed totality of agency. Consider a revolutionary situation (Tilly, 2003): The crowd gathers in a public square, some leaders emerge, the police arrive, and there are shootings. Suddenly, the crowd morphs into a group that seems to have the intention of overthrowing the regime. The emotional state shifts from feelings of individual powerlessness to group empowerment. Together, the crowd overcomes violent repression and overthrows the regime. In such a situation, agency is empowered by group dynamics without being reducible to individual agency as the primary driver. The group changes the course of history, but like the hurricane, it dissolves after some time. Perhaps some members will reassemble and make plans for a new government.[20]

In this form of group behavior, strong elements of embodiment drive the emergence of distributed agency. The most important of these are various forms of emotional contagion and empathetic coordination of actions as well as contextual aspects, such as the topography of the square. The latter points to the role of material conditions theorized in approaches to "*agencement*" where technology scaffolds agency (Callon, 2008). Analogous to the notion of distributed cognition, we can speak of "distributed agency" in assemblages of human individuals situated in a material context (Malafouris, 2013). As in our example of financial traders, social media make a difference in creating new forms of coordination. Here, we need to make a clear distinction between the effects of the technology as such and the communication that is mediated. The latter is another form of emotional coordination among people in the assemblage.

A key aspect of embodied agency, beyond mere coordination of action, is when and why a transition from "I" to "We" is mediated (Tuomela, 2007). Economic problems of collective agency lose much of their bite when agents act in "We-mode," as Sugden also points out: Think of a professional basketball team that exhibits strong team spirit and excellent coordination of movements, with everyone focused on the common goal and joint performance. However, adopting the We-mode is only a capability, not a given.[21] In this sense, we could reconcile this view with the rejection of a dualistic ontology of individuals versus collectives: Human individuals have the capability to switch from the I-mode to the We-mode and thereby distribute agency, without implying the existence of a supra-individual entity.[22] The basketball team can manifest supra-individual agency in team spirit, but this does not mean that "team spirit" is embodied in the world. This capability is embodied in certain emotional mechanisms, such as empathy, and, most importantly in sports and music, in motor coordination between individuals mediated by mechanisms such as mirror neurons, which we discussed in the previous chapter (see above).

One of the essential aspects of human social life is that human groups and societies have evolved many forms of acculturation and ongoing institutionalized "mind shaping" through which humans maintain the capability for "We-action," even in extreme forms of altruism such as sacrificing one's life for another (Zawidzki, 2013). One key form is ritual, as in military organization and training. As classically analyzed by Émile Durkheim, ritual is one of the most powerful ways of creating and maintaining a group identity among humans (Bell, 1997). Ritual action does not simply emanate from individual decisions and preferences: The whole point of a ritual is that it is action without being "chosen." A ritual is defined by precise prescriptions of movements, gestures, and events that are enacted by the individual and thereby have transformative effects. In ritual action, inward and outward embodiment are closely intertwined, as rituals refer to specific emotional processes (such as mourning in funeral rituals) without being reducible to mere expressive movements: Rituals also create the feelings they purport to express. In Western societies, steeped in the intellectual tradition of disembodiment, ritual has been denounced as "irrational" since the Reformation because this apparent ambivalence could not be resolved analytically (Asad, 1993). In non-Western societies, by contrast, ritual is seen as a primary mode of action (Seligman, 2008).[23] This, however, has blinded much of Western social theory to the pervasiveness of ritual in everyday life, as systematically explored by Erving Goffman (1982) whose work clearly reveals its embodied nature, for example in his notion of "face work:"

> Universal human nature is not a very human thing. By acquiring it, the person becomes a kind of construct, built up not from inner psychic propensities but from moral rules that are impressed upon him from without. These rules, when followed, determine the evaluation he will make of himself and of his fellow-participants in the encounter, the distribution of his feelings, and the kinds of practices he will employ to maintain a specified and obligatory kind of ritual equilibrium. The general capacity to be bound by moral rules may well belong to the individual, but the particular set of rules which transforms him into a human being derives from requirements established in the ritual organization of social encounters. (Goffman, 1982, p. 46)

Ritual action matters for all forms of economic agency; for example, many consumer actions are ritualized, generating positive feelings of satisfaction that are inwardly embodied by handling items as ritual artifacts (Collins,

2005; Massa et al., 2017). This applies to everyday actions, such as drinking coffee in the morning, or to institutionalized rituals such as gift-giving, which are often the economic lifeblood of entire industries such as luxury goods—see, for example, Rupp (2003) on East Asian gift exchange circuits. With a change of perspective, ritual emerges as a fundamental form of action in embodied economics.

Another important mechanism is imitation (Orléan, 2013), especially if we interpret this not only as a conscious choice, but in line with Bourdieu's (1980/1990) notion of "mimesis" mentioned in Chapter 4. Imitation is significant because it operates beyond what is commonly understood as "collective action," and encompasses any form of implicitly coordinated behavior in groups without direct engagement of individuals with each other. Imitation is fundamental to economic life because it is also constitutive of personhood in a social context. While economics takes the self as given, even in solipsistic subjectivity, developmental psychology, especially its Vygotskian heritage, has a rich account of how selves emerge over years in constant interaction with others (Bogdan, 2010; Tomasello, 2019). In the primordial stages, resonant imitation blurs the distinction between the emerging Ego and Alter, and imitation remains the core process of acculturation, even in the mature individual (Hurley, 2008). This is important in all aspects of economic life. For example, consumption manifests strong group-level effects without direct coordination, as in fashion or popular music, and is a driver of blockbuster power-law effects in market dynamics (Potts et al., 2008). Much consumer behavior is in fact based on peer group effects, as illustrated by lifestyle consumption (Holt, 1997).

In terms of agency, this means that individual choices are distributed in groups and mediated through forms of embodiment such as mechanisms of imitation, which are ultimately grounded in mirror neuron mechanisms and related structures discussed in Chapter 4. This is reflected in narratives of consumption in all kinds of media, such as the recent "influencer" phenomenon in social media. The correlates of distributed agency are the many tools of corporate branding, which become elements of individual identities formation through brand attachment. The inclusion of the brand into the self can be conceptualized with reference to the social-psychological literature on self-expansion theory according to which "people are motivated to enter and maintain close relationships to expand the self by including the resources, perspectives, and characteristics of the other in the self" (Aron et al., 1991, p. 243). An important point in this theory is that love is one of the mechanisms that expresses this desire to "expand the self by including that other in the self, as well as by associating expansion with that particular other" (Aron & Aron, 1996). Interestingly, this resonates with the consumer experience of brands of active relationship partners (Batra et al., 2012; Fournier, 1998), which is fueled by marketing techniques such as brand personification (i.e., anthropomorphization). This is manifested in the "marriage metaphor" that underpins customer relationship management, which expresses a willingness to move from purely economic transactions (mostly utilitarian and short-term) to loyal relationships (more experiential and long-term) at the end of the last century (Tynan, 1999). This can be seen primarily as the result of an economic calculation, since it is considered cheaper to keep a consumer than to get a new one, but the marketing technique translates on a psychological and brain level.

Consistent with social-psychological theory on the inclusion of others into the self, findings indicate that the level of inclusion of a brand into the self is higher for established close consumer-brand relationships than for recently formed close or neutral relationships (Reimann et al., 2012). Moreover, when participants are presented with a brand with which they have established a close (vs. neutral) relationship, and are asked to choose or reject the brand, the anticipation phase prior to this choice is associated with increased bilateral insular cortex activations (and activations in the caudate, parietal lobe, and occipital lobe) (Reimann et al., 2012). The insula is a region active in the integration of bodily information into emotional and motivational functions, and it is then inferred that these findings "stand for all aspects of the physiological condition of the physical body, such as the representation of a 'material me'" (Reimann et al., 2012, p. 137). In light of prior studies on addiction, it is also argued that "consumers translate bodily signals (processed in the insula) into what they then subjectively experience as urging for the brand" (Reimann et al., 2012, pp. 138). Similar to feelings experienced in personal relationships, it is then concluded that people would associate a brand with themselves and feel an urge to engage with their brand partner. Although these results are reported for Western participants living in a highly capitalistic country (USA), and may be limited to a few brands, they clearly convey the idea that a brand can be seen (and conceptualized) as part of the consumer's self. Reciprocally, because objects of consumption can express social belonging, consumers can also be part of a brand community (McAlexander et al., 2002; Muniz & O'Guinn, 2001). A brand can become group identification, the expression of a lifestyle, or a consumption subculture, that may entail a transformation of the self, such as becoming a biker from the Harley-Davidson-oriented subculture (Schouten & McAlexander, 1995). The commercial exploitation of consumers' sense of community is the marketing response to the critique of modernity and the dominance of impersonal transactions: Building and entertaining communities adds value to the brand by facilitating relationships with and about it, and by conveying a "consciousness of kind" ("we-ness") or shared consciousness, "shared rituals and traditions" that sustain the community through social practices, norms and values, and a "sense of moral responsibility" through a sense of duty to the community (Muniz & O'Guinn, 2001, p. 413). Thus, a feature of economic life (at least in Western societies) is that as much as there can be inclusion of the brand into the self, there can also be inclusion of the self into a brand community.

In sum, for economics, agency beyond the individual is not a marginal phenomenon but is constitutive of markets as organized forms of economic behavior. The complex structure of markets, products, and actors reflects the sociality of individuals engaged in markets.

5.3 Embodied Agency in Markets

5.3.1 The Notion of Agential Power

The example of financial traders shows that there are two faces of agency. One is the capacities of actors, the other is their roles in a specific context, both together constituting the actor as an economic agent embedded in social life. This can be neatly condensed in the notion of agential power: Agency is the power of an actor to act in a particular context in such a way that the actor feels able to influence conditions to avoid harm, possibly even to reap benefits and to align her actions with these feelings. Agential power is manifested in flourishing.[24]

A rare but influential related contribution to economics is Sen's capability approach, developed by Martha Nussbaum (Nussbaum, 2006; Robeyns & Byskov, 2020; Sen, 1985/1999). The two faces of agency can be thought of as capabilities and functionings:

> Functionings represent parts of the state of a person – in particular the various things that he or she manages to do or be in leading a life. The

> capability of a person reflects the alternative combinations of functionings the person can achieve, and from which he or she can choose one collection. The approach is based on a view of living as a combination of various 'doings and beings,' with quality of life to be assessed in terms of the capability to achieve valuable functionings (Nussbaum & Sen, 1993, p. 31)

For example, someone may have the capability to be a financial trader, but not have access to the career, so cannot fulfill this functioning. Or someone may not have the chance or interest to nurture such a capability, and so voluntarily stays away from the functioning. A functioning is an actualized role in the economy, a capability is the capacity to fulfill that role. A specific combination of capabilities and functionings defines the agential power of an actor in the economy: The individual trader "Bill" becomes an actor in the pit by acquiring certain skills and getting the job. We note that the original use of these terms is not clearly focused on economic life, but in fact, there is a close affinity because the original motivation for developing the approach was to propose a new view of well-being in economics (Sen, 1985/1999). This also means that we no longer conceive of individuals as pursuing some form of satisfaction, theorized as "subjective utility," but rather of flourishing as enacting their agential powers. This does not mean that we conceive of agential power as a means, but as a Hegelian moment in the state of flourishing: The feeling of agential power as such means flourishing.

Power is a theoretical concept of great significance for embodied economics. However, as mentioned in the introduction, the term is exceedingly complex. This is because power, as agency, is not a property of individuals, but of individuals in contexts, and emerges from continuous and fluid interactions. This has been emphasized by numerous sociological contributions, such as Elias' (1969) "figuration" theory, which adumbrates the contemporary concept of assemblages (see Chapter 4).[25] Interestingly, this is even implied by conventional economics, since market power emerges only in the structural context of markets and depends crucially on the interaction between the supply and demand sides, especially when it comes to the degree of substitutability of goods on the demand side, which can be seen as another aspect of economic agency in the sense of autonomy from the *status quo*. In other words, as emphasized in game theory, power is inherent in interaction, and is, under certain conditions, self-reinforcing.[26]

Agential power is fundamentally different from subjective utility. Subjective utility is mostly a-social, and power is inherently social: In a bilateral relationship, Ego can gain more utility without affecting the other, while Ego's increasing power necessarily reduces Alter's power. Power is always contextual since power also depends on an agent's importance to other agents. This explains the apparent paradoxes of power, epitomized in Hegel's "master–slave" paradigm: The most powerful master will suffer an erosion of agential power because he cannot know whether his power is recognized by the other, with all the consequences known from countless historical episodes of paranoid tyrants: The tyrant, though most powerful, and for that very reason, can never trust that others are telling him the truth, so his apparent power is eventually undermined by his loss of control over information.

Hegel was the first to recognize that individual agency in society depends on complex institutional arrangements and social processes of mutual recognition of agency (Taylor, 2015). We add that agency is necessarily embodied, as the distribution of power among individuals is primarily reflected in feelings and resulting cognitive attitudes, such as mastery or self-efficacy. We feel powerful over others and in control of our fate, or we feel powerless and driven by forces beyond our control. The expression and negotiation of such feelings is a constant feature of human life (Goffman, 1982). One of the arenas is the job market and the corporate hierarchies that shape the lives of most people in the modern economy. We will look at this in Chapter 7.

Agential power is distributed and emerges from a continuous flow of actions that interweave inward and outward embodiment. This has been classically articulated by Bourdieu when physical space is the outward embodiment of social power relations that are inwardly embodied in cognitive schemas:

> Structures incorporated into appropriated physical space become incorporated structures—cognitive schemas, principle of vision and division (cf. *State Nobility* or Kabyle house). Thus, for instance, beyond expressing basic economic and cultural differences via the spatial distribution of housing among central-city neighborhoods and peripheral and suburban neighborhoods, the Parisian space presents a secondary, but very pronounced, opposition between the 'right bank' and the 'left bank' corresponding to the fundamental division of the field of power between, *grosso*

> *modo,* the poles of economic and cultural power, managers and intellectuals, the world of art and that of business (Bourdieu, 1989). We can discern in this simple example a social division objectified in physical space which, as I showed in *The State Nobility,* functions at the same time as a principle of vision and division, as a category of perception and appreciation—in short, as a mental structure (the Kabyle house was another one). And we have every reason to think that it is through the mediation of its realizations in the structures of appropriated physical space that the muted injunctions of the social order and the silent callings to order of objective hierarchy are reconverted in systems of preferences and in cognitive structures. (Bourdieu, 1979/1984)

> More precisely, the progressive inscription into bodies of the structures of the social order is perhaps accomplished, for the most part, *via moves and movements of the body, via the bodily poses and postures* that these social structures reconverted into physical structures-organize and qualify socially as in rive or decline, entry (inclusion) or exit (exclusion), bringing together or distancing in relation to central and valued site (one remembers the metaphor of the 'hearth,' the dominant point of the Kabyle house (…). (Bourdieu, 1996, pp. 15–17)

The distributed nature of agential power is partially recognized in the concept of social capital and related theories of social networks which approach power as emanating from positions in these networks (e.g., Burt, 1995; Lin, 2007). These theories bridge sociology and economics, but economics has been reluctant to embrace their insights, apparently because they remain in tension with methodological individualism (Jackson, 2019). However, they remain disembodied because they attempt to quantify structural positions from the perspective of an external observer and do not recognize the key role of embodiment that Bourdieu highlights. Positions are embodied inwardly and outwardly, and embodiment shapes the reproduction of embedding networks through the actions enabled by the distribution of agential power (e.g., Henry, 2005). One salient example is the capabilities of actors to mobilize collective action, which is determined by their embodied affective relationships with others and the physical patterns of their spatial relationships (Barnes, 2016). For example, the long resistance of British miners to Thatcherite policies was an expression of agential power that was embodied inwardly in their occupational identities and outwardly in their settlement patterns.

The resulting social networks are only an external manifestation of these underlying social forces:

> Miners in dense proximity were obliged to engage in frequent interaction with each other without the realistic probability of withdrawal or of alternative forms of social relationship. And it was just these villages that later became the *sine qua non* of labour solidarity and discipline in the mining industry. (Barnes, 2016, p. 181)

At the individual level, agential power is reflected in feelings that may not even be related to conscious evaluations of situations and conditions. Feelings are manifested in actions shared with others, such as the everyday culture of British miners in the early 1980s. Feelings are sense-making, as in adapting to one's life situation or mobilizing resistance to its conditions. In the context of the market, we speak of "market feelings."

5.3.2 Trust as "Market Feeling"

Let us more closely dissect the forms of embodiment in agency. The key is to understand that agency is defined as agential power in relation to others, that is, agency is a property in systems of "inter-action," and agential power is a distributed phenomenon. The complication in understanding agency is that agency is reflexive in the sense that power is not an "objective" property of a situation as determined by an external observer. The degree to which one agent has agency *vis-à-vis* another is determined in part by mutual beliefs about having and attributing agency, which are conditioned by mutual communication. These beliefs are rooted in feelings. We already encountered an important example of this when we discussed the tyrant: This is trust. Trust is a prime example of feeling embodied and distributed agential power, with deep economic significance. For instance, as Bourdieu argues:

> Symbolic capital resides in the mastery of symbolic resources based on knowledge and recognition, such as 'goodwill investment,' 'brand loyalty,' and so on; as a power that functions as a form of credit, it presupposes the trust or belief of those upon whom it bears because they are disposed to grant it credence (it is this symbolic power that Keynes invokes when he posits that an injection of money is effective if agents believe it to be so). (Bourdieu, 2005, p. 76)

There is a long record of economic research showing that the level of trust in societies is an important determinant of economic growth and development, as reflected in value surveys. However, this literature has also revealed the deep complexity of this phenomenon (Beugelsdijk & Maseland, 2011).

The topic of trust bridges mainstream economic debates, which clearly recognize the importance of trust, but struggle to include trust in their theoretical edifice (Nooteboom, 2002).[27] This is directly connected to embodied cognition, in the sense that trust is a way of seeing the other, and thus ascertaining some facts about the other, without relying on "information processing." We know we can trust because we feel we trust. The reason is that there is another paradox of rationality lurking here: Consider a rational agent who processes all available information and calculates all states of the world probabilistically. Would we say that this agent "trusts" another agent when she gives a "go" in an interaction? The answer is a resounding "no." The whole point of trust is that it is not rationally warranted (Field, 2001). Of course, there is a wide range of economic models, even in sociology (Coleman, 1990), that employ rational calculus, but these require the fulfillment of conditions familiar to all kinds of optimization, such as the complete assignment of probabilities to the entire set of states of the world, and they cannot account for primordial trust before any kind of interaction takes place and generates information about the other. The standard tool of experimental economics for studying trust, the "Trust Game" (Berg et al., 1995), reveals these limitations: For example, risk assignments can be explained by other psychological determinants such as aversion to betrayal, or social preferences in general, and there are strong framing effects that point to the social contextualization of trust, which is completely lost when the artificial construct of a Trust Game reduces trusting behavior to the calculation of pay-offs as defined by the experimental set-up (Alós-Ferrer & Farolfi, 2019).

We refer to "trust" as a kind of "payment in advance" that cannot be rationally justified. Its embodiment is also reflected in the role of oxytocin, a hormone and neurochemical that can increase one's propensity to trust others (Barraza & Zak, 2009; Declerck, 2020). This is also illustrated by the metaphors used to express trust. For instance, the literature has found a very strong link between smell as a physical experience and suspicion as a social experience and documented its impact on economic behavior. Smell is employed metaphorically to indicate suspicion in at least 18 languages, ranging from Arabic to Chinese, Bulgarian, French, German, and Spanish (Soriano & Valenzuela, 2008; see also, Schwarz & Lee, 2019). A common expression in English to express suspicion about a situation is to say that it smells fishy. Lee and Schwarz (2012) found that exposing English speakers to a fishy smell increases suspicion, to the point where people are less willing to trust others and engage in economic exchange with them. Their results are particularly striking in a Trust Game. In this experimental game, two players are each given an initial endowment (e.g., $5), and one of the players is incentivized to invest in the participant she trusts. In fact, one player, the proposer, is also offered a portion of her initial endowment with the other player, the responder. The amount shared with the responder is then multiplied by four (e.g., $5 becomes $20). The responder can then choose to either reciprocate and return some money to the proposer (e.g., $10), or defect, in which case the proposer may end up with nothing. This is all about trust. If the proposer trusts the responder, she may decide to share some of her endowment with the responder, with the expectation that the responder will then return some of it to her. In this experimental setting, the more the proposer trusts the other participant, the more likely she is to receive some money in return. However, if she is suspicious, she will be less willing to give because she thinks the responder is less trustworthy, and, therefore, she should receive less money at the end of the game. Lee and Schwarz (2012) showed that just being exposed to a fishy smell reduced investment in a Trust Game by 25% compared to the other conditions (odorless water or a fart spray). In other words, a fishy smell, which is metaphorically associated with suspicion, leads to distrust in an experimental game, further illustrating the importance of embodied experience in economic decision-making. The metaphorical association between smell and suspicion has been confirmed in many other studies conducted by different research teams (Schwarz & Lee, 2019).

Moreover, trust is a kind of shared agency in the sense that the trusted agent enjoys an enhancement of agential power relative to the trusting agent, which is manifested in the possibility of abuse of trust. At the same time, the trusting person also experiences agential power, as trust increases the feeling of being in control. Thus, the economic significance of trust is that it leverages agential powers on both sides of the trust relationship. Trust cannot be reduced to an "internal" state of the agent because it is established not only by trusting behavior, but also by the trustworthiness of the other (Glaeser et al., 2000).

The underlying dynamics are well established in the biological theory of signaling, which has been developed in some interaction with the economics of signaling, such as in labor markets (Spence, 1974; Zehavi & Zahavi, 1997). Again, we encounter paradoxes of rationality, since sending a signal of trustworthiness can always be interpreted as cheating. This has been recognized as a fundamental problem in moral philosophy since Plato's statement of Glaucon's dilemma (Abend, 2014). For public morality, it may not matter whether a person is morally good, but only whether he appears to be morally good:

> Indeed, as far as advantageous effects are concerned, actually being moral without the appearance of or reputation for being moral will not help. In brief, it seems that actually being moral is neither a necessary nor a sufficient condition for being believed to be moral. The conclusion is Machiavellian through and through. (Abend, 2014, p. 74)

The upshot of the biological and economic debates about signaling is that signals must be costly for the sender to be trustworthy: The paradigmatic case is the giant antlers, which signal health and prowess even as they impede movements in some circumstances.

We do not follow this argument here because it is motivated by the internal problems of rationality that appear in both the neo-Darwinian and mainstream economics paradigms, for the same reasons discussed in Chapter 3 (Grafen, 1990; Prum, 2017, p. 67ff). In the latter case, however, this is further accentuated by the reflexivity of human communication: The antlers emerged in an evolutionary process of Darwinian selection and are not chosen as a signal by the animal at the moment of interaction. Once the signal is chosen, it cannot be reliably interpreted by a reflexive agent. But this difference also points to the perspective of embodiment, since non-genetic forms of embodiment can also exclude the possibility of rational choice in the conventional sense, as is the case in Bourdieu's notion of habitus. Emotions, as manifestations of habitus,[28] cannot be the object of rational choice: As will be discussed in Chapter 6 with the famous chain store paradox, a threat is credible only if it is emotionally driven to the extent that it is not subject to rational choice (Frank, 1988). This does not depend primarily on the sender of the message but on the receiver. If the receiver believes that the emotions are only displayed and not real, credibility is lost. Therefore, the threat must be grounded in the personal characteristics of the sender which are clearly not at her disposal. At the same time, the receiver's response is not based on rational judgment but grounded in a resonant emotional stance of belief.

This applies to the general issue of trust: Only embodied trustworthiness can be trusted. There is a wide range of phenomena in markets that reveal this fundamental fact, such as the role of various cultural markers (ethnicity, dialect, etc.) in grounding trading communities which cannot be changed by instrumental action, if only at a very high cost, such as learning dialects and customs and adapting personal lifestyles to become a recognized member (Landa, 1994). Although game theory usually suggests that principles of rationality can explain reputation mechanisms, this takes the community framework as given, which only shifts the burden of explanation: What constitutes the community in the first place? As we have seen, even in the context of financial markets, communities of traders count, and they are embodied.

Returning to the general topic of agency, trust is a major determinant of agential powers, because actors not only have a sense of control, but this is also vindicated by the actions of others. As we have argued, trust is both a property of the actor and of the context, and in both cases, it is embodied in the sense of the embodied coupling between the actor and the environment. This analysis is exemplary for all other aspects of agency. There is also an important implication for thinking about capabilities. These are often thought of as properties of individuals, but as noted above, agential power emerges in assemblages of capabilities and functionings. Hence, even if we relate agential power to expressions of individual actions, and thus maintain a social ontology without supra individual agents, we cannot think of capabilities as properties of individuals only.

Our discussion reveals the centrality of feelings to economic agency. Often disparaged as "animal spirits," as discussed in Chapter 4, from an embodied perspective, they are actually essential for valuing choices in a market environment: One of the hallmarks of a market environment is complexity and unpredictability, as compared to my choice between apples and pears for breakfast this morning. Therefore, we propose the notion of "market feelings" to capture distinct phenomena such as trust in markets. Other feelings that we will not describe here due to space limitations are entrepreneurial optimism or feelings of uncertainty, as we learned from trader Bill.[29]

5.3.3 Capabilities and Agential Powers in Specialization

In the context of markets, a salient issue is specialization. My agency in markets is determined by my capacities for market action. This is also recognized by mainstream economics, mostly in the context of expansive notions of "capital" which, interestingly, partly coincide with what only at first sight appears to be a similar use of the term in sociology, especially Bourdieu, where this notion is strongly embodied.[30] Let us look at one important example, so-called "human capital"—which we will continue to critically examine in subsequent chapters. The most direct reference to human capital theory can be found in the discussion of embodied cognition in Chapter 4 since human capital is said to measure the cognitive capacities of human beings as manifested in economic action.

Even if economists do not refer to embodiment as we do, they de facto recognize it in the context of human capital theory. For example, following Heckman's (2013) seminal work, preschool education has been identified as one of the most important determinants of later performance, which is clearly an acknowledgment of inward embodiment, and is generic in terms of outcomes, such as general cognitive capabilities. Similarly, economists have recognized the role of social skills and other generic capabilities beyond formal schooling in specific disciplines (Deming, 2022). We suggest that the notion of human capital should eventually be abandoned in favor of the capabilities/functioning framework (Robeyns, 2006). The term falsely suggests a distinction between the individual and the "capital" that the individual "owns." In the embodied view, "capital" as capabilities, simply constitutes the individual as an embodied actor and is thus conceptually obsolete. Without a doubt, human capabilities are embodied, and the notion of human capital imposes a disembodied conceptual scheme on related phenomena, as will be discussed further in Chapter 7. A visible expression of this is the forming of bodily shapes through certain kinds of physical work. But purely epistemic capacities are also embodied in brain states as forms of memory, which can often be directly ascertained by brain imagining, such as the adaptation of brain structures to the demands of driving a taxi in London (Griesbauer et al., 2022).

We do not wade into the perennial debates about nature versus nurture, because as Heckman (2007, pp. 13,251) acknowledges, this "distinction, although traditional, is obsolete. The modern literature on epigenetic expression and gene environment interactions teaches us that the sharp distinction between acquired skills and ability featured in the early human capital literature is not tenable." For our discussion, however, human capital remains a disembodied concept that cannot really be meaningful without acknowledging the importance of embodiment as a manifestation of bodily states as capacities to generate certain types of actions demanded by other market agents. For example, I have acquired the skills of a plumber, and others rely on my services. Although these skills may erode if I no longer work in the trade, they are never completely lost, and are certainly maintained through ongoing practice. Tellingly, they might only be compromised by bodily impairments, such as illness or simply aging. As we have seen, being socialized as a financial trader means learning to discipline emotional states without constant (supposedly) "rational" intervention. Management science recognizes this in related concepts such as Michael Polanyi's (1966/2009) "tacit knowledge," which refers to "knowing how" or "routines" as organizational habits (e.g., Nelson & Winter, 1982/2004). These are all aspects of an (indirect) recognition of embodiment as a fundamental mechanism in economic life. Indeed, even my formal knowledge, say of mathematics, cannot simply be "given" to someone else, I can only teach it in a time-consuming process of literally "re-embodying" this knowledge in the other who understands it in practice (Ingold, 2000), and largely with the use of conceptual metaphors that stem from our embodiment (Lakoff & Núñez, 2000).

My agential powers resulting from capabilities are determined not only by these internal states, but also by the interests of others in relying on my capabilities, a notion covered by certain theories of social capital that we alluded to earlier. This is evident in market dynamics, such as the power-law patterns in the superstar phenomenon, where celebrities can accumulate strong agential power, or lose it as their trade declines (Gabaix, 2016). Capability-based agential power is strongly shaped by market structures under the institutional regime of capitalism, and as such is well recognized but not critically assessed in mainstream economics. Embodied economics goes beyond this by explicitly recognizing the constraints on changing capabilities through mere rational responses to changing market conditions, which is more than familiar in practical economic policy dealing with structural unemployment. It is often difficult, if not impossible, to change the capabilities of certain agents through rapid retraining (e.g., Hirshleifer et al., 2016). This is coupled with the adverse psychological effects of experiencing the loss of agential power.

For example, a coal miner who is forced to retrain as an accountant loses not only his original capabilities but also a distinct identity associated with a tightly bounded community, most often a co-residential one.

Markets and their niches are related to functionings. Capabilities are partly endogenous to functionings, as the latter also contribute to the formation of capabilities, such as learning by doing. However, the relationship with agential power can be intricate, as there is also the phenomenon of "de-skilling," that is, the loss of capabilities that are not actualized in functionings. This can have strong effects on agential power, as is well known from the literature on "asset specificity" (Goldthorpe, 2007; Williams, 2017). The more capabilities are specific to a certain functioning, the more the balance of power shifts to the demand side of the labor market, as the outside option of the specializing agent is reduced. When capabilities are generic, this effect is much weaker.

In sum, the relationship between capabilities and agential power is complex, although the mere scope and scale of capabilities as such certainly enhances agential powers. This relates to generic aspects of feelings of agential power. For example, I may develop my skills at playing the piano without ever aspiring to become a professional; nevertheless, my experience of being able to improve my skills strengthens general attitudes towards individual mastery and self-efficacy.[31] There is a reflexive dimension, in that these powers depend on how I feel and think about these capabilities. This ties in with our discussion of trust, for example, in the sense of feeling confident about what we can achieve. The literature on gender and racial discrimination has shown that performance is also determined by stereotypes even when individuals do not share them and objectively have the required capabilities.[32] This is strong evidence for the social nature of agency, even when capabilities are seen as primarily individually embodied.

5.3.4 Capabilities and Consumer Agency

So far, our discussion of capabilities has focused only on the production side. Economists have also used the notion of human capital to analyze consumption (Becker, 1996), which can also be read as an indirect acknowledgment—indirect because through such a disembodied mechanism—of embodiment in economic life. Since the mid-twentieth century, social critics have emphasized the loss of consumer agency in markets dominated by mass production and massive corporate efforts to shape consumer demand (e.g., Carrington et al., 2016; Fromm, 1956/2002; Galbraith, 1958/1999). Consider the radical opposite, a wealthy consumer of bespoke goods such as a yacht. This consumer has much agential power, if only because of her wealth. But there is also the dimension of active participation in the design of the yacht, which may require good lay expertise in judging materials, designs, and devices. In other words, consumer agency involves many dimensions beyond mere budgetary powers. More generally, this refers to the capabilities of consumption, that is, the skills and experience in deriving individual satisfaction from acts of consumption—as also recognized by Becker (1996). Agential power as a consumer can take many forms and is partly related to technology. For example, tourism is made possible by vast transportation networks. Travel is a specific form of agency in such markets, which can be threatened by political factors, for example.

It is an elementary fact that humans learn to consume, mostly as a result of acculturation, starting in early childhood, if not already in the womb (André et al., 2018; Ustun et al., 2023). In a sense, this refers to "producing" consumption: For example, if I want to ski in a winter resort, I have to learn the necessary skills and exert physical effort. Many forms of seemingly "passive" consumption require the embodied capacity to experience, that is to become an expert or connoisseur in many activities, such as wine, fine arts, or sports, which is related to embodied forms of memory (Sutton & Williamson, 2014). All of these capabilities are embodied, with extreme forms such as addiction—theorized by some economists as human capital for drug consumption (Becker & Murphy, 1988). At this point, we do not discuss the question of valuing such behavior, other than to note that consumption is a form of agency and involves agential powers that emanate from capabilities. We now turn to a key issue: The extent to which consumer agency includes the capability to reflect on and subsequently change one's preferences. We do not argue here that this capacity is a given, but that it can be acquired through critical discourse and reflection mediated via deliberation with others—linking the argument back to the debates on linguistic mediation in Chapter 4. Once acquired, however, it becomes an essential component of the agential powers that accrue to critical consumers, as will be discussed further in Chapter 8.

This is related to another important contribution by Sen (2004, p. 615ff), who argued that genuine rationality includes the capability to choose one's preferences. This is salient in the case of addiction, but also in all forms of habitual consumption, such as those resulting from the adaptation of tastes to the experiences of past consumption. For example, a person may meta-prefer to be vegetarian but still love the taste of meat. This explains the many efforts by producers of vegetarian foods to recreate "meat flavor." The general point, however, is that embodied consumption can constrain the meta-rational choice of preferences. More specifically, as we shall discuss in the next section, current consumption as a form of action engages embodied memories of past consumption, thereby creating path-dependent trajectories of consumption that are not easily altered by rational choice.

That apparently reduces the agential powers of the individual. This dilemma has been classically considered since the Stoa, but systematically developed by the German Idealists, as the key feature of being rational and free, namely in the sense of mastery over one's own desires (Brandom, 2007). In the market context, this is combined with the agential powers *vis-à-vis* the supply side: The consumer has minimal agential power relative to a (monopolistic) supplier of the desired good (Galbraith, 1958/1999).

The embodiment view of ethics avoids restoring the original "rational agent" in the sense of the ideal moral agent. At this point, we regard the problem as a highly significant indicator of embodied agential power in consumption. In the context of financial markets, we have already pointed to other functions of consumption, one of the most significant of which is the display of status (Veblen, 1899/2007; see also, Hamilton, 1989). Status consumption refers to functionings as a counterpart to capabilities, and a specific aspect of outward embodiment lies in the type of goods consumed, which at the same time inwardly embodies status as a habitus. This is an intricate issue because it touches on the multi-dimensionality of agential power. Consider, for example, weddings in many societies. Weddings and marriages are often key episodes of consumption, such as the acquisition of a wide range of items for the new household and the organization of a lavish wedding party. However, they are often governed by social norms and appear to be enforced by custom. This often drives poor households into debt traps and undermines their agential powers (Moav & Neeman, 2012). Yet, at the same time, the expenditures affirm social status and contribute to agential powers.

This example illustrates the important role of money in shaping agential power. We will discuss this in Chapter 7. Money is an embodied form of agential power in the market context because accumulated stocks of money (or money substitutes) enhance the range of choices and individual autonomy. This explains Simmel's (1907/2004) insight that money in the market context is not just a means but becomes an end as soon as markets become a dominant force in society.

5.4 Identity and the Self

We will now explore a deeper level of agency, which is the very meaning of what it is to be an "actor."[33] As noted above, the economic rational agent in mainstream economics is a construct that is not only disembodied, but also deflates the actual diversity of forms of agency in the economy. But if we recognize this diversity, the question arises as to what defines the unity of the actor beyond the various roles and functionings: The financial trader is also a consumer or a family member. What unifies these roles as forms of agency? In the embodied perspective, this is the self or, as we will argue, the person since we regard the self as an aspect—albeit one of the defining aspects—of the person. Following Hegel, we approach the person as constituted by institutions, so that this concept builds the bridge between this chapter and Chapter 6.

We have already pointed out a fundamental flaw in the notion of subjective utility, namely that it is subject to the impossibility of a private language (Davis, 2003, p. 148).[34] Subjective utility can only function either as a mere mathematical description of behavioral data along the lines of the revealed preference model, or as a description of a stimulus–response mechanism that operates without the involvement of consciousness, that is, as a pure set of reflexes. Once we introduce reflexivity and consciousness, subjective utility appears logically flawed because there is no way for an individual to reflexively identify utilities over time, that is, to compare utilities not only quantitatively but even qualitatively. There is no frame of reference as long as utilities are subjective, or effectively a private language. This is not covered by the debate over cardinal versus ordinal utility in economics, because the problem already emerges at a deeper level: How can the rational economic agent identify and distinguish the particular goods qualitatively and in a stable form over time? Economics treats utility as "subjective" but fails to provide an account of how the space of goods over which utilities are defined is constituted. Most solutions to this quandary refer to functions that can be ascertained by an external observer, such as generic biological functions that refer to intermediate goods as means to fulfill those functions (Becker,

1996), or social and technological functions that are generally recognized in a given society, as in hedonic pricing methods. Clearly, neither is "subjective" anymore. In other words, the indeterminacy of identity in the standard subjective utility model of economics has already motivated significant departures from its canonical assumptions which point towards embodiment.

When considering these problems, there are several paths to embodiment. We choose to explore memory. This may not seem obvious at first, because memory is a concept that is not explicitly considered a key term by most economic theorizing. As we shall see, behavioral economics recognizes the role of memory in decision-making, but curiously only as a source of biases and imperfections that impede rational and objective assessments of past states of the world. An individual who chooses among different food items in the present relies on memories of past consumption and experiences. Memory, however, is not only related to such individual actions, but also to the constitution of the actor's identity, and is thus an essential aspect of selfhood. Selfhood, in turn, is essentially social, so that memories cannot be reduced to the individual level.

5.4.1 Embodied Memory and Agency

As said, memory is a topic that is rarely considered in the standard model of economics. As discussed in Chapter 2, *Homo economicus* is assumed to have perfect, or at least "an impressively clear and voluminous," knowledge of his environment (Simon, 1955, p. 99).[35] In this line of reasoning, rational economic agents are conceived as always evaluating all currently available information and optimizing their choices among alternatives in the present, which makes memory, even perfect memory, largely irrelevant. Put simply, in such an economic model of choice, the mere fact that I consumed an apple in the past is not relevant to explaining my preference for apples today: Rather, it depends on current market conditions. Illustrations of similar positions can be found in neuroeconomics, where it is argued, for instance, that "intuition and empirical evidence suggest that subjective values are computed online at the time of choice, not learned and retrieved from memory" (Padoa-Schioppa, 2011, p. 347).

Arguably, memory becomes a proper research topic in economic decision-making when the origins of preferences are questioned or when bounded rationality is posited. When it comes to their origins, the discovered preference hypothesis, which can be derived from the writings of

Vernon Smith, Charles Plott, and to some extent, Ken Binmore, assumes that economic actors will behave rationally when given the proper incentives, and the chance to deliberate and learn through trial and error (Bruni & Sugden, 2007, p. 163). Our point here is not to discuss whether or not the evidence supports this hypothesis, but to argue that memory, as reflected in learning by doing,[36] appears to be essential for rational decision-making. This position is consistent with Simon's bounded rationality approach when he asserts that: "Human behavior, even rational human behavior, is not to be accounted for by a handful of invariants" but "in interaction with extremely complex boundary conditions imposed by the environment and by the very facts of human long-term memory and of the capacity of human beings, individually and collectively, to learn" (Simon, 1979, p. 510).

In contrast to these perspectives, which portray memory as an essential mechanism for understanding rational decision-making, Tversky and Kahneman's (1973) availability heuristic presents memory in a rather negative light: Memory is a source of "bias" in judgment and decision-making, because a decision is influenced by what comes easily to mind. When memory creeps into real-world behavior, it is seen as a source of dysfunction, as in behavioral economics and the "sunk cost fallacy."[37] The role of memory as a bias is further illustrated by the work of Kahneman and colleagues (1993, 1997; Kahneman & Krueger, 2006) on remembered utility and its contrast with experienced utility, which shows that a short painful event is generally remembered as equally painful as a long one. Moreover, if the short event ends with a particularly painful moment, it may be remembered as more painful than the long one. As Bruni and Sugden point out, these kinds of findings about memory biases related to affective experiences raise an important question about the discovered preference hypothesis: Indeed, "if individuals' memories of affective states are systematically biased, it is hard to see how any experiential learning process could discover the true relationship between actions and affective states" (Bruni & Sugden, 2007, p. 171).

The uneasy relationship between economics and memory, sometimes irrelevant, sometimes fundamental, and sometimes a source of bias in rational decision-making, is one of the conspicuous symptoms of disembodied models of rationality and their focus on information processing. These views generally ignore the extremely rich research and reflection on memory in psychology, neuroscience, cognitive science, philosophy, and even literature. Indeed, we can say that outside of economics, memory is one of, if not the pivotal capacity that enables action and constitutes the unity of the actor that is just taken for granted in neoclassical economics. It is not possible to do justice to this vast field of research here. We limit our focus to research on memory that explicitly adopts the embodiment perspective (e.g., Dijkstra & Zwaan, 2014). An important distinction from other views is that the embodiment approach rejects the notion of functional specialization of memory in the brain—as classically conveyed by the modular and amodal views of semantic memory—and emphasizes its distributed nature across brain, body, and environment.[38] To a considerable extent, however, this is also reflected in textbook treatments of the topic in neuroscience as memory is now viewed as encompassing many different types of memory processes involving different parts of the brain that may be active simultaneously (Gazzaniga et al., 2016, p. 421).[39] For example, when we return to a place where we have vacationed in the past, we simultaneously remember certain aspects of spatial information, certain sensory experiences such as smell, or actions taken there in the past, and all these different re-enactments interplay in consciously retrieved images and feelings (Barsalou, 1999). In this way, the embodiment view dovetails with Hayek's structural connectionism (Fuster, 1997) which is also championed in modern variants, such as in AI. At the most abstract level, this view approaches memory as embodied in changing patterns of neural connections, embedded in structural layers that are themselves constantly changing, resulting in the contextualization of more basic structural units. In other words, information storage in a computer is seen as a completely misleading metaphor for memory, because in a sense, the entire set of bodily states is memory (Michaelian & Sutton, 2017).

The embodiment perspective, as explained in Chapter 4, rejects amodal representations of any kind. That is, recalling an event, a person, or anything else is associated with sensory-motor simulations: Present action re-enacts past action. Such simulations involve related neurophysiological functions, such as auditory or motor functions. In terms of conceptualizing the self, the concatenation and nested mapping of such simulative loops is the elementary form of selfhood, as manifested in the reproduction and continuity of feelings associated with certain situations and objects: In this regard, Damasio speaks of the "core self" (Damasio, 2010, p. 205ff). Eating an apple today evokes such loops, thus merging past and present in the feelings associated with this action. One way to grasp this unity of memory is to take "experience" as a key notion, which, tellingly, behavioral economists see in tension with memory: "Odd as it may seem, I am my remembering self, and the experiencing self, who does my living, is like a stranger to me" (Kahneman, 2012, p. 390). Seminally and in contrast, John Dewey sees experience as the fundamental way in which human beings—and living beings, in general—relate to the world:

> Philosophers, even empirical philosophers, have spoken for the most part of experience at large. Idiomatic speech, however, refers to experiences each of which is singular, having its own beginning and end. For life is no uniform uninterrupted march or flow. It is a thing of histories, each with its own plot, its own inception and movement toward its close, each having its own particular rhythmic movement; each with its own unrepeated quality pervading it throughout. (Dewey, 1934/2005, p. 44)

> An experience has a unity that gives it its name, *that* meal, that storm, that rupture of friendship. The existence of this unity is constituted by a single *quality* that pervades the entire experience in spite of the variation of its constituent parts. This unity is neither emotional, practical, nor intellectual, for these terms name distinctions that reflection can make within it. In discourse *about* an experience, we must make use of these adjectives of interpretation. In going over an experience in mind *after* its occurrence, we may find that one property rather than another was sufficiently dominant so that it characterizes the experience as a whole. There are absorbing inquiries and speculations which a scientific man and philosopher will recall as 'experiences' in the emphatic sense. In final import they are intellectual. But in their actual occurrence they were emotional as well; they were purposive and volitional. (Dewey, 1934/2005, p. 45ff)

Consider the simple question of what it means to think about consuming, say, an espresso. It is not about the object but about the experience of performing the act of consumption. In other words, there is no distinction between subject and object, but there is a unity of process that this implies, and most importantly, an essential aspect of consuming the espresso in the present involves the re-enactment of past experiences. Interestingly, this is to some extent implied by some neuroeconomic views of utility in terms of prediction errors (Glimcher, 2011). From a wider cognitive science perspective, this evokes Dewey's pragmatism without referring to it:

> The deep unity (under predictive processing) of perception and action should now be apparent. There are two different, but equally effective, ways to minimize prediction errors during our encounters with the world. The first is by using prediction errors to help us discover the best guess about how things are out there in the world. But the second is to act so as to make the world fit some of our predictions. Instead of finding the prediction that best fits the sensory evidence (perception), you now find or create the sensory evidence that best fits the prediction. This is the predictive processing route to action. Actions are simply the brain's way of making its own proprioceptive predictions come true. (Clark, 2023, p. 75)[40]

If I now decide to drink an espresso, this involves expectations grounded in memory, perhaps manifesting in this case what pragmatists call "habit," so there is the possibility of divergence, in both positive and negative directions. An important implication of this observation is that identity grounded in chains of re-enactments is not frozen in repetition of the same. On the contrary, the co-presence of past and present experiences in the current action creates the possibility of learning and thus of changing the trajectory of actions: I may eventually stop drinking espresso after a series of negative experiences. Most importantly, experiences define patterns that can be broken by new events, thus triggering steps towards conscious reflection, and hence reasoning: In other words, there is no "rationality" without memory.

The sensory-motor grounding of consumption experiences is evident when we consider the habitual nature of many acts of consumption, such as always drinking an espresso after a meal. At this point, we should avoid confusion about different forms of memory. The form of memory we have discussed so far does not refer to any form of *conscious* retrieval of the past. Embodied consumption means that in consuming now, (schematic forms of) past experiences are always implicitly and automatically re-enacted. This is important, for example, for understanding the developmental formation of capabilities in consumption, which we explored earlier. One way to approach this is through what has been labeled "conceptual consumption" (Ariely & Norton, 2009).[41] When we eat an apple, there is a reflexive process triggered by the apple as a sign (aka concept) that activates sensory-motor simulations related to past experiences. This does not imply reflection in the sense of conscious recall but rather imbues the present with the past.[42]

As mentioned above, there are various forms of memory. One form is episodic memory,[43] which can easily be interpreted in light of the previous (e.g., Wilson, 2002), adding only the component of conscious retrieval. However, episodic memory includes a reference to a unified self around which the episodes are centered. This is important because the more general forms of embodied simulation of past experiences also involve "mirror" responses to observing the actions of others, which would blur the distinction between Ego and Alter (Hurley, 2008). This anchoring of the self in embodied memory is especially strong when the episodes involve the self as an actor. It is not our intention to explore these aspects in detail; essentially, what matters here is that the self emerges from a developmental process in which the individual continually interacts with others and develops a sense of agency not only through emerging feelings of being an actor but also of being treated as an actor by others (Bogdan, 2010; Tomasello, 2019). Since James and Mead, this has been recognized in psychology as the distinction between the two aspects of the "I" and the "Me" in the self. In the simplest terms, we can relate the "I" to the primordial feelings of action centered on the individual, and the "Me" as the reflexive establishment of the self (Mead et al., 1934/2015, p. 173ff). One type of memory is the recollection of one's traits over time, such as saying that we have always liked to eat fruit.

Reflexivity mediated through language becomes the key aspect of autobiographical memory (Damasio, 2010, p. 210ff). The medium of autobiographical memory is narratives of one's own past, with the self as author (McAdams, 2013). Since telling, listening to, or reading a narrative involves the evocation of sensory motor simulations (Speer et al., 2009), narratives about the self are also re-enactments of our own past. But there is the additional and essential aspect that narratives are also directed at the public and are often shaped by culture (Campbell, 1949/2008; Gergen & Gergen, 1988). Narratives are then key media of sense-making for an actor in the social world, especially in linking the past with future projections of actions as expressions of selfhood, such as career decisions. In this way, narratives anchor the actor's identity in the public sphere, for example, by imposing constraints of biographical consistency (Ross, 2007). As Jerome Bruner argues:

> eventually the culturally shaped cognitive and linguistic processes that guide the self-telling of life narratives achieve the power to structure perceptual experience, to organize memory, to segment and purpose-build

> the very 'events' of a life. In the end, we *become* the autobiographical narratives by which we 'tell about' our lives. And given the cultural shaping to which I referred, we also become variants of the culture's canonical forms. (Bruner, 2004, p. 694)

Narratives are thus a key concept in embodied economics as the linguistic counterparts of experiences as conceived by Dewey. Autobiographical narratives are embodied because an essential function of narratives is expressive, as they refer to emotional states as constitutive elements of experiences (Goldie, 2014; Rowlands, 2017).[44] Given that narrative triggers memories of past emotions and invites empathetic sharing of those emotions, it comes close to the general concept of re-enactment (or embodied simulation). Narratives are the medium of performing the self in the world, articulating the dialectics of inward and outward embodiment. As such, they reflect the general powers of language as scrutinized in Chapter 4.

5.4.2 *Narrating Agency: Identity and Performativity*

As we have said, embodied agency involves a multiplicity of forms of agency, both between different individuals and for the sole individual. These become identity-forming through the mechanisms of performativity. In economic sociology, performativity has mostly been referred to as the performativity of economic theories (MacKenzie et al., 2007) while in general sociology performativity reaches much further, for example in gender studies (Butler, 2010; Harding et al., 2022). However, the various uses can be unified in considering the interaction between symbolic imaginaries in a population of agents and the formation of agential dispositions, as theorized by Bourdieu in conceptualizing the relationship between habitus and symbolic and cultural capital. An exemplary issue linking the two applications is the performative role of economics in management education: Someone educated in economic theories may begin to interpret herself in these terms and form corresponding expectations about others (Ghoshal, 2005; Ong et al., 2023). As a result, the individual will switch to the behavioral patterns theorized in economics, ultimately confirming the expectations (Wang et al., 2011). This can even be contextualized, so that these performative mechanisms may work in the business context (Cohn et al., 2014), but not in the family context.

There are two ways in which such mechanisms are embodied. The first is that the dispositions to act in a specific way are inwardly embodied, and the second is that the cognitive media are outwardly embodied in the material sense. Both senses are combined in the special form that cognitive media invoke metaphorical transformations, which in turn are embodied. The example of financial traders provides a rich illustration of all these aspects: They adopt specific emotional disciplines, they express their rank in conspicuous consumption,[45] and they approach markets with anthropomorphic metaphors. And they even explicitly differentiate their professional role from other roles, such as the role of "father" in the family.

We will elaborate on performativity in the embodied approach to institutions. Here, we focus on narratively performing agency, which leads to the conception of "person" as an individualization of agency. In behavioral economics (Kahneman, 2012, p. 386ff), and even in so-called "narrative economics" (Shiller, 2019), narratives are mostly seen as biasing agents to misperceive the "real" situation. This is a far cry from approaches to narratives in other disciplines (Herrmann-Pillath, 2021a). As the key medium of autobiographical memory, narratives are constitutive of the self in recalling and performing experiences. The properties of narratives that are considered "distorting" in economics become essential in these views. Again, we will only sketch some key aspects (Goldie, 2014).

The first is that narratives evoke feelings because they reflect and induce emotional states via the arrangement of event sequences and plots, such as "suspense" and "fear" in a detective novel. Autobiographical memory does not need to have the finely tuned structure of a novel and can be just a Joycean arrangement of elements, but the role of narrative is to evoke past feelings and induce current feelings (which may be different) in action. These feelings are acts of making sense of what would otherwise be a pile of facts and current "data." In this sense, the function of narrative is related to the more general cognitive process of attention. Narrative highlights what is seen as the essential elements of past and present experiences and situations, where "essential" means primarily charged with valuation, as Dewey had already emphasized. This relates to the next key aspect, the creation of perspectives. Narratives allow individuals to take different positions by, for example, evoking a past feeling—say, resentment of an unfair boss—and generating current feelings—perhaps forgiveness of the boss. That is, the narrative opens a vista of multiple selves, both one's own and those of others. Narratives can include the views of others, even a detached observer, thus allowing for a rich assessment of events.

This brief discussion shows that narratives cannot be judged by the supposed standard of an "objective" reality as portrayed by an "all-seeing eye," or omniscient observer. Narratives are about the actions of many people, and thus about flows of events of deep complexity and uncertainty. They, therefore, create "reality:" This is the specific sense in which they are performative. This becomes clear when we consider that narratives are performances of the self in the mundane sense of telling a story to others. But in doing so, the present self is embedded in an unbroken trajectory of narrated experiences that constitutes its role today. Even more, narratives also perform the future of the self, as in entrepreneurial fiction, epitomized by the infamous "business plan" (Beckert, 2016).

As emphasized by many contributions in the literature, narratives are undergirded by culture (Bruner, 2004; McAdams, 2013). This is the more specific sense in which the self is performed. Narratives reach beyond the individual by evoking cultural imaginaries of personhood, such as the association of a profession with an idealized type of person. In this way, the bridge between roles and the individual is built, as the autobiographical self refers to the idiosyncratic life of an individual, but cast in a narrative, this trajectory becomes culturally meaningful beyond the individual.

Finally, we consider the materiality of narratives in terms of their grounding in the material environment (Roediger & Wertsch, 2008). For many, home is a collection of objects with histories (Hurdley, 2006), that extend the self (Belk, 1988). Corporations craft their brands with narratives (Escalas, 2004), and celebrate their history in their original location with special arrangements such as corporate museums (Cailluet et al., 2018; Massa et al., 2017). Designs are often embodied history and materialized narratives, such as certain elements of the design of a Porsche that evoke even the earliest versions of that car, similar to the resonances of sensory-motor re-enactments in the primordial forms of selfhood. Today's 911 design is imbued with themes from the past.

In sum, the embodied approach to the self, as grounded in the generic approach to embodied cognition outlined in Chapter 4, relates to language in the specific form of narratives. Narratives mediate the inward and outward embodiment of the self as they express the self in telling stories to others who share and respond to them, and as they relate to material manifestations, both of which in turn shape the self.

One of the essential manifestations of this is the distinction between space and "place" (Tuan, 2011): Human beings feel deeply attached to places where they have had experiences that define them, such as their "home" or their "hometown." In extending the self, places often shape economic decisions, such as the flows of investment, people, and remittances that connect migrants and emigrants to their home regions.

5.4.3 *The Reasonable Person in the Economy*

Pulling together the threads of the previous argument, we introduce the embodiment alternative to the rational economic agent, which is the reasonable person in the economy. This details our transition from "rationality" to "reason" as it unfolds in Chapter 4. Persons are rooted in embodied memories of experienced economic actions, such as memories of past consumption or entrepreneurial ventures. Inspired by, but also departing from McAdams (2013), we distinguish actors, authors, and persons, which together constitute the specific patterns of reasonable agency.

As actors, individuals develop embodied capabilities to perform certain roles as functionings in the economy, such as the emotional disciplines of financial traders or the motor skills of a roofer. As they develop, actors perform their roles reflexively, that is, they are aware of their roles and can even maintain an ironic distance. This is related to the aspect of authorship: Autobiographical memory is essentially based on personal narratives that open up a variety of perspectives, between past and present, and between different persons. This makes it possible to reflect on aspects of the individual as actor.

The person possesses agential powers that are endogenous to her performative acts as actor and author. In judging and using these powers, the person seeks to act in a reasonable manner that balances the perspectives and valuations of the many actors with whom the person interacts, thereby recognizing them as reasonable persons. For example, a woman who is a mother and a professional constantly evaluates and negotiates the expectations and demands of her partner, her children, her colleagues, and her superiors in order to preserve and perhaps expend her agential powers, which requires recognition by all of them and leads to conflict when the balance is lost. This includes many aspects of her economic life, such as considering the purchase of clothing, with choices ranging from bargains to luxury. Her economic life is essentially social.

The reasonable person is concerned with flourishing in community with others and thereby is thus, in many ways, forward-looking. As many philosophers over the millennia have emphasized, the person is an evolving project, actively participating "from within in the process of their own becoming" (Ingold, 2022, p. S43), when not hindered and stifled by circumstances. This perspective closes the circle of the Hegelian argument in this chapter, which, as we develop further in this book, reintegrates Marxian views into a comprehensive account of embodied agency (Loader, 2015). This larger context is aptly summarized by Charles Stafford, in the context of self-education:

> Hegel's notion of self-education as the outcome of a conflict-ridden process of learning definitively remains at Marxism's core (...). Moreover, this learning process is conceived by Marx (as it was by Hegel and Fichte before him) as intrinsically tied to 'economic agency' under a very broad definition (...). In short, it is through our active engagement with, and struggle against, both nature and other humans, in the course of meeting our needs, that we come to learn about ourselves. To state this schematically, then,
>
> - for humans, to become oneself and to know oneself are always two sides of the same coin;
> - this dual process of becoming and knowing is always active: it goes beyond contemplation and is framed in particular around transforming the world, oneself and others through activity;
> - it is always relational: the 'self' of becoming and knowing is caught up in (transformative) social ties; and
> - it is always historical: self-education occurs within particular historical moments (Stafford, 2020, p. 123).

5.5 Conclusion

This concluding observation points to a key theme that we will develop in the subsequent chapters: In modern society, the market (including corporations) is a defining feature of circumstances. As we have seen, understanding agency in markets requires adopting the perspective of embodiment, and embodiment restores economics as Political Economy. Conventional economics treats agents as disembodied. This is a theoretical flaw. But it reflects another fundamental fact, which is that markets are also powerful forces of disembodiment through abstraction. To some extent, economics simply reflects this fact without critically questioning it, when it does not contribute to constructing it.

In other words, there is a fundamental paradox: One cannot understand economic agency without conceiving it as embodied, but the market is a medium of disembodiment. Until one recognizes this fact, one cannot enact institutional designs of markets that positively sustain embodiment. This is a Hegelian act of recognition: Economic actors recognize others as embodied, and hence perform markets accordingly. This invokes the themes of the next chapters, institutions and ethics. As noted above, the theory of economic agency remains incomplete without consideration of institutions. This needs to be specified beyond generic aspects by considering institutions specific to markets: We consider money, property, and labor to be the key institutions, that interplay in complex ways to constitute economic agency, as manifested in the very diverging positions that individuals take in the economy, such as rentier, entrepreneur, or worker. These positions were central to the classical economists, culminating in Marx as the last main representative. Neoclassical economics conflated all these types into one disembodied construct of "rational agent." One result was the neglect of distributional issues, which had been the main concern of classical economists.

Notes

1. The expression "have bodies" suggests a dualism between a disembodied subject as "owner" and the body. A variant of this is that "brains" are seen as "having bodies" (Jasanoff, 2018).
2. For instance, Ivana Marková explains that: "Embodiment of the 'spirit' means (…) that mind and body, mind and medium, are dependent, each upon the other, for their growth and their very existence. We can see from these ideas of Hegel how much George Mead (1934) owed to Hegel although he hardly ever refers to him. It is obvious, however, from his book *Movements of Thought in the Nineteenth Century* (Mead, 1936), that he not only knew romantic philosophy generally and Hegel in particular, but that he also adopted a great many of their ideas. Mead's (1934) account of consciousness is clearly Hegelian and may help us to clarify the issue of embodiment of the mind. Mead points out that 'consciousness as such refers to both the organism and its environment and

cannot be located simply in either' (Mead, 1934, p. 332) (...)" (Marková, 1982, p. 138).

3. This interdependence is highlighted in Keynes' famous metaphor of the "beauty contest," as discussed in previous chapters (Keynes, 1936/2018).
4. Finance is not "naturally" gendered. There have been historical shifts in societal perceptions of risk-related financial action, which were initially seen as immoral, feminine seductions for men. In the 1920s, finance became increasingly associated with household management, and thus feminized in a different way. With the liberalization and spread of modern capital markets, male dominance was reasserted. For a review, see Maltby and Rutterford (2012).
5. Interestingly, Hassoun (2005) suggests that the embodied metaphors of market feelings actually help to distance traders from the real financial meaning of their actions which would otherwise generate overwhelming feelings of threat and danger.
6. Compare Zaloom (2003, p. 267ff) and Morris and colleagues (2007).
7. This is reminiscent of the classic "self-fulfilling prophecy" (Merton, 1948).
8. Lo (2019) presents an evolutionary approach to finance that emphasizes competition between investment strategies as types.
9. Emotional discipline evokes the concept of emotional labor (Hochschild, 1979) which will be mentioned in Chapter 7.
10. Many authors add specific criteria such as mastery or self-efficacy. See, for example, McAdams (2013) or Cannon and Rucker (2022). In the following, we will relate such criteria to our notion of actor.
11. In modern cognitive science, one of the main proponents of the thermodynamic approach to the brain is Karl Friston, who defends the "free energy principle" behind embodied inferences about the world (Friston, 2010; Ramstead et al., 2020).
12. Kauffman also speaks of autopoiesis (Roli et al., 2022). This notion remains central to the influential approach developed by Maturana and Varela (1980), and is reminiscent of Marxian epistemology (Loader, 2015).
13. As Godfrey-Smith (2017, p. 78ff) argues, sentience is a characteristic shared by all living beings, even if the cognitive system of an octopus is radically different from that of a human. In embodied cognition literature, there are related concepts, such as the notion

of "sense-making," that also claim to apply across the tree of life (Thompson & Stapleton, 2009). We do not see them as conflicting in a principled way since feelings can be interpreted as embodied sense-making.

14. For the following, see Stern (2012) and Krijnen (2020).
15. For a more detailed discussion, of where this figure comes from, see Herrmann-Pillath and Boldyrev (2014, p. 154ff).
16. We cannot review this rich literature in detail here. We will mention only two strands. One is the distributed cognition literature, with Hutchins (1995) as a seminal contribution to cognition as enacted in collectives of actors arranged in specific spatial patterns, which was discussed in the previous chapter. This approach has been used by sociologists to explain valuation in financial trading, see, for instance, Beunza and Stark (2008). Different in terminology but similar in spirit, the other strand is the actor-network theory (Latour, 2005) with specific options such as "*agencement*," which from the beginning included non-humans – seminally, see Callon (1986).
17. Consider, for instance, the exchange between the physicist Richard Feynman and the historian Charles Weiner reported in Clark (2008, p. xxv). On the transformative powers of writing, see Menary (2007).
18. For a Hegelian discussion of language, see Moyar (2008). This line of thinking has shaped G. H. Mead's conception of "Me," and Mead also notes that the meaning of utterances only becomes fully transparent to the speaker when they are actually pronounced in the presence of others (see Mead et al., 1934/2015, pp. 62ff, 196).
19. This fundamental relationship is emphasized in contemporary Hegelian scholarship on social ontology, see, for example, Laitinen (2011).
20. For an application of similar reasoning to organizational theory with reference to the Sartrian reading of Hegel, see Fleming (2022).
21. Tomasello (2019) provides a comprehensive and detailed account of how this capability emerges in human ontogeny. The "we" would be one of the defining differences between great apes and humans.

22. Similar ideas can be found in Sartre's (1960/2004, 1960/2006) *Critique of Dialectical Reason*, whereby "Sartre argued that there is a first-person plural apperception ('We') alongside that of the first-person singular apperception ('I') that does not require there to be anything like a separate element to the set of persons that each individually make up the 'We'" (Pinkard, 2022, p. xv). A similar view is upheld by Tuomela (2013).
23. A case in point is China, where ritual has been theorized by Confucians since ancient times as an essential form of human conviviality and continues to be a key aspect of social and economic life, in various forms, both traditional and modernist (Herrmann-Pillath, 2017). For related observations on Japan, see Nelson (1992).
24. The concept of flourishing has been defined and made operational by various authors, a seminal approach being Hupert and So (2013).
25. Elias remains an outsider in mainstream sociological debates, and his "figuration" sociology is mostly pursued by a small group of followers, even though he must be counted among the great classical sociologists (Van Krieken, 1998; see also, Paulle et al., 2011). To our knowledge, the various strands of thought related to assemblage theory such as actor-network theory (ANT), do not refer to Elias. One exception is the multidisciplinary field of organization studies, where Elias is seen in the context of contemporary debates (Iterson, 2002).
26. The economic view, understood in this sense, transpires in Coleman's (1990, p. 133) classic generic definition, power is always relative to others and is therefore fundamentally different from subjective utility: "The power of an actor resides in his control of valuable events. The value of an event lies in the interests powerful actors have in that event."
27. In the mainstream approach, trust is central to explanations of economic growth that take social capital into account, see, for instance, Bjørnskov (2012), and Algan and Cahuc (2013).
28. As an example, consider the "culture of honor" in the American South, as classically analyzed by Nisbett and Cohen (1996).
29. In the context of entrepreneurship, Keynes' animal spirits refer to an innate capacity or instinct or disposition of entrepreneurs that characterized "old-fashioned capitalism" (Dow & Dow, 2011, p. 5). Entrepreneurs are "individuals of sanguine temperament

and constructive impulses who embarked on business as a way of life" (Keynes, 1936/2018, p. 132). The results of Lawrence and colleagues (2008), who compared entrepreneurs and non-entrepreneurs (managers) on tests measuring cold (risk-free) and hot (risky) decision-making processes, support this interpretation. Both groups excelled and scored similarly on tests measuring cold decision processes. However, entrepreneurs outperformed managers on hot decision tasks: "Interestingly, this risk-taking performance in the entrepreneurs was accompanied by elevated scores on personality impulsiveness measures and superior cognitive-flexibility performance. We conclude that entrepreneurs and managers do equally well when asked to perform cold decision-making tasks, but differences emerge in the context of risky or emotional decisions" (Lawrence et al., 2008, p. 169). Animals spirits may even be considered one of the key determinants of social entrepreneurship: "A recurring theme for those of us immersed in social and sustainable entrepreneurship is passion. Social entrepreneurship and sustainable entrepreneurship are difficult to envision as dispassionate, coolly rational phenomena" (Krueger et al., 2011, p. 277).

30. For the differences between the mainstream economic approach and Bourdieu's use of economic language, see Lebaron (2003).
31. For instance, self-determination theory posits that "the extent to which people undertake tasks and activities with a sense of choice, ownership, and agency is linked with higher quality performance, greater persistence, and higher well-being when compared to more controlled forms of motivation" (Ryan et al., 2022).
32. These facts are increasingly recognized in economics, as evidenced by related work published in top-tier economics journals. For gender, see Bertrand (2020), and for race, see the recent symposium in the *Journal of Economic Literature* (Logan & Myers, 2022).
33. In *The Presentation of Self in Everyday Life*, Goffman (1956) expresses the idea that, during face-to-face interactions, each individual conceived as a social actor works to control the impressions others have of her, characterizing a central feature of human interaction: Impression management. Impression management is the attempt to present oneself to others in a particular way, and impression management techniques are classically used by corporations in

everyday economic life (e.g., Grove & Fisk, 1992). Furthering his work on impression management, Goffman studied and analyzed social interactions on the basis of principles derived from theatre. LIFE IS A PLAY is a classic metaphor used in the English language to describe social life (Lakoff & Turner, 1989), with cultural variations, such as LIFE IS OPERA in Chinese (Yu, 2017), as well as economic life, whereby BUSINESS IS A STAGE (e.g., Pine II & Gilmore, 1998).

34. Also, on the following, see Davis (2003).
35. However, this does not mean that every model of substantive rationality neglects memory, as illustrated by several developments in (mathematical) game theory, where "perfect recall" is regularly posited as an assumption (e.g., Alós-Ferrer & Ritzberger, 2017). See also, Rubinstein (1998) for models of bounded memory in game theory.
36. More generally, human capital theory seems to be concerned with memory, such as acquired skills.
37. We mention that the so-called "sunk cost" fallacy is a feature that seems to be widespread beyond humans (Magalhães & White, 2016; Sweis et al., 2018), like many other so-called "biases" (e.g., Santos & Rosati, 2015), and thus certainly has deep biological roots. Meanwhile, economics has identified good reasons why the "sunk cost" fallacy could be considered "rational" (McAfee et al., 2010).
38. As discussed in Chapter 4, the distributed cognition view can be used to look at distributed processes within the brain, but also between the brain and the environment, and this can apply to memory. For instance, as analyzed by Hutchins (2005, p. 1559ff) in his work on material anchors in conceptual blending, the conceptual blend of a trajector with a line of people, forms a queue in the blended space. This projection creates a spatial memory for the order of the people's arrival: Bodies are located in space to represent the order relations. But to see a line of people is not to see a queue. For such a queue to emerge, the process of blending is necessary, and will make sense in a given cultural context, ruled by a specific cultural principle, "first-come, first-served." Then, because the line is experienced as a queue, reasoning operations can appear to answer questions such as who is first or last in the queue, and who comes next. Similar analyses of memory externalization can

be found in Donald (1993), Malafouris (2013), and Roediger and Wertsch (2008).

39. See also Glimcher (2014, pp. 73–74) on the distributed nature of memory, although he maintains a modular view.
40. This view was hinted at in Piaget's (1975) distinction between the two processes of assimilation, whereby new information is incorporated into an existing cognitive structure, and accommodation, whereby existing structures change to accommodate new information. For an embodiment critique of predictive processing, see, for instance, Froese and Ikegami (2013).
41. Note that we are combining Ariely and Norton's (2009) argument with a strict embodiment approach to concepts, as championed, for instance, by Barsalou (2008).
42. This is reluctantly recognized in neuroeconomics, even if it avoids the term "memory" (Louie et al., 2015).
43. We are aware that the label "episodic memory" is a "vestige" of a more modular way of thinking (Anderson, 2014, p. 91).
44. Similar ideas were expressed by Dewey: "By the same token, emotions are attached to events and objects in their movement. They are not, save in pathological instances, private. And even an 'objectless' emotion demands something beyond itself to which to attach itself, and thus it soon generates a delusion in lack of something real. Emotion belongs of a certainty to the self. But it belongs to the self that is concerned in the movement of events toward an issue that is desired or disliked. We jump instantaneously when we are scared, as we blush on the instant when we are ashamed. But fright and shamed modesty are not, in this case, emotional states. Of themselves they are but automatic reflexes. In order to become emotional, they must become parts of an inclusive and enduring situation that involves concern for objects and their issues" (Dewey, 1934/2005, p. 52).
45. The consumption of luxuries, viewed as "a mark of the master" (Veblen, 1899/2007, p. 51), can be decoupled from conspicuous consumption, especially when a person's status superiority is taken for granted. This is characterized by the rise of "inconspicuous consumption" which is "the use of subtly marked products which are misrecognized by most observers, but facilitate interaction with those who have the requisite cultural capital to decode the subtle signals" (Eckhardt et al., 2015, p. 808; see also, Berger &

Ward, 2010). The luxury brand remains an expression of identity, but not to everyone, only to those whose cultural capital allows them to interpret this identity. As such, inconspicuous consumption requires us to move conceptually from Veblen to Bourdieu: With Veblen (1899/2007), consumption is a source of hierarchy between those who can consume luxuries and those who cannot, hence conspicuous consumption. Whereas, with Bourdieu, already quoted in Chapter 4, consumption becomes a source of distinction between what we want to consume and what we do not want to consume (Bourdieu, 1979/1984, p. 56). Possessions and their consumption, as well as their non-consumption, can be an expression of social belongingness as well as the expression of avoidance and rejection (experienced as social disgust) of other groups.

References

Abend, G. (2014). *The moral background: An inquiry into the history of business ethics*. Princeton University Press.

Algan, Y., & Cahuc, P. (2013). Trust and growth. *Annual Review of Economics, 5*(1), 521–549. https://doi.org/10.1146/annurev-economics-081412-102108

Alós-Ferrer, C., & Farolfi, F. (2019). Trust games and beyond. *Frontiers in Neuroscience, 13*(887). https://doi.org/10.3389/fnins.2019.00887

Alós-Ferrer, C., & Ritzberger, K. (2017). Characterizations of perfect recall. *International Journal of Game Theory, 46*(2), 311–326. https://doi.org/10.1007/s00182-016-0534-x

Anderson, M. L. (2014). After phrenology: Neural reuse and the interactive brain. *MIT Press*. https://doi.org/10.7551/mitpress/10111.001.0001

André, V., Henry, S., Lemasson, A., Hausberger, M., & Durier, V. (2018). The human newborn's umwelt: Unexplored pathways and perspectives. *Psychonomic Bulletin & Review, 25*(1), 350–369. https://doi.org/10.3758/s13423-017-1293-9

APA. (2023). Agency. In *American Psychological Association (APA) dictionary of psychology*. https://dictionary.apa.org/agency

Ariely, D., & Norton, M. I. (2009). Conceptual consumption. *Annual Review of Psychology, 60*(1), 475–499. https://doi.org/10.1146/annurev.psych.60.110707.163536

Aron, A., Aron, E. N., Tudor, M., & Nelson, G. (1991). Close relationships as including other in the self. *Journal of Personality and Social Psychology, 60*(2), 241–253. https://doi.org/10.1037/0022-3514.60.2.241

Aron, E. N., & Aron, A. (1996). Love and expansion of the self: The state of the model. *Personal Relationships, 3*(1), 45–58. https://doi.org/10.1111/j.1475-6811.1996.tb00103.x

Asad, T. (1993). *Genealogies of religion: Discipline and reasons of power in Christianity and Islam*. Johns Hopkins University Press.

Barnes, B. (2016). *The elements of social theory*. Princeton University Press.

Barraza, J. A., & Zak, P. J. (2009). Empathy toward strangers triggers oxytocin release and subsequent generosity. *Annals of the New York Academy of Sciences, 1167*(1), 182–189. https://doi.org/10.1111/j.1749-6632.2009.04504.x

Barsalou, L. W. (1999). Perceptual symbol systems. *Behavioral and Brain Sciences, 22*(04), 577–660. https://doi.org/10.1017/S0140525X99002149

Barsalou, L. W. (2008). Grounded cognition. *Annual Review of Psychology, 59*(1), 617–645. https://doi.org/10.1146/annurev.psych.59.103006.093639

Batra, R., Ahuvia, A., & Bagozzi, R. P. (2012). Brand love. *Journal of Marketing, 76*(2), 1–16. https://doi.org/10.1509/jm.09.0339

Becker, G. S. (1996). *Accounting for tastes*. Harvard University Press.

Becker, G. S., & Murphy, K. M. (1988). A theory of rational addiction. *Journal of Political Economy, 96*(4), 675–700. https://doi.org/10.1086/261558

Beckert, J. (2016). *Imagined futures: Fictional expectations and capitalist dynamics*. Harvard University Press.

Belk, R. (1988). Possessions and the extended self. *Journal of Consumer Research, 15*(2), 139–168.

Bell, C. M. (1997). *Ritual: Perspectives and dimensions*. Oxford University Press.

Berg, J., Dickhaut, J., & McCabe, K. (1995). Trust, reciprocity, and social history. *Games and Economic Behavior, 10*, 122–142.

Berger, J., & Ward, M. (2010). Subtle signals of inconspicuous consumption. *Journal of Consumer Research, 37*(4), 555–569. https://doi.org/10.1086/655445

Bertrand, M. (2020). Gender in the twenty-first century. *AEA Papers and Proceedings, 110*, 1–24. https://doi.org/10.1257/pandp.20201126

Beugelsdijk, S., & Maseland, R. K. J. (2011). *Culture in economics: History, methodological reflections, and contemporary applications*. Cambridge University Press.

Beunza, D., & Stark, D. (2008). Tools of the trade: The socio-technology of arbitrage in a Wall Street trading room. In T. Pinch & R. Swedberg (Eds.), *Living in a material world* (pp. 253–290). The MIT Press. https://doi.org/10.7551/mitpress/9780262162524.003.0009

Bikhchandani, S., Hirshleifer, D., & Welch, I. (1998). Learning from the behavior of others: Conformity, fads, and informational cascades. *Journal of Economic Perspectives, 12*(3), 151–170. https://doi.org/10.1257/jep.12.3.151

Bjørnskov, C. (2012). How does social trust affect economic growth? *Southern Economic Journal, 78*(4), 1346–1368. https://doi.org/10.4284/0038-4038-78.4.1346

Bobe, M. C., & Piefke, M. (2019). Why do we herd in financial contexts? *Journal of Neuroscience, Psychology, and Economics, 12*(2), 116–140. https://doi.org/10.1037/npe0000108

Bogdan, R. J. (2010). *Our own minds: Sociocultural grounds for self-consciousness*. MIT Press.

Bossaerts, P. (2021). How neurobiology elucidates the role of emotions in financial decision-making. *Frontiers in Psychology, 12*, 697375. https://doi.org/10.3389/fpsyg.2021.697375

Bourdieu, P. (1980/1990). *The logic of practice*. Polity Press.

Bourdieu, P. (1979/1984). *Distinction: A social critique of the judgement of taste*. Routledge & Kegan Paul.

Bourdieu, P. (1989). *La noblesse d'Etat. Grands corps et Grandes écoles*. Editions de Minuit.

Bourdieu, P. (1996). Physical space, social space and habitus. *Vilhelm Aubert Memorial Lecture, Report, 10*, 2–22.

Bourdieu, P. (2005). Principles of an economic anthropology. In N. J. Smelser & R. Swedberg (Eds.), *The Handbook of economic sociology* (2nd ed., pp. 75–89). Princeton University Press. https://doi.org/10.1515/9781400835584.75

Brandom, R. B. (2007). The structure of desire and recognition: Self-consciousness and self-constitution. *Philosophy & Social Criticism, 33*(1), 127–150. https://doi.org/10.1177/0191453707071389

Bruner, J. (2004). Life as narrative. *Social Research: An International Quarterly, 71*(3), 691–710. https://doi.org/10.1353/sor.2004.0045

Bruni, L., & Sugden, R. (2007). The road not taken: How psychology was removed from economics, and how it might be brought back. *The Economic Journal, 117*(516), 146–173. https://doi.org/10.1111/j.1468-0297.2007.02005.x

Burt, R. S. (1995). *Structural holes: The social structure of competition*. Harvard University Press.

Butler, J. (2010). Performative agency. *Journal of Cultural Economy, 3*(2), 147–161. https://doi.org/10.1080/17530350.2010.494117

Cailluet, L., Bernhard, F., & Labaki, R. (2018). Family firms in the long run: The interplay between emotions and history. *Entreprises et Histoire, 91*(2), 5. https://doi.org/10.3917/eh.091.0005

Caldwell, B., & Montes, L. (2015). Friedrich Hayek and his visits to Chile. *The Review of Austrian Economics, 28*(3), 261–309. https://doi.org/10.1007/s11138-014-0290-8

Callon, M. (1986). Some elements of a sociology of translation: Domestication of the scallops and the fishermen of St Brieuc Bay. In J. Law (Ed.), *Power, action and belief: A new sociology of knowledge?* (pp. 196–223). Routledge & Kegan Paul.

Callon, M. (2008). Economic markets and the rise of interactive agencements: From prosthetic agencies to habilitated agencies. In T. Pinch & R. Swedberg (Eds.), *Living in a material world* (pp. 28–56). MIT Press. https://doi.org/10.7551/mitpress/9780262162524.003.0002

Campbell, J. (1949/2008). *The hero with a thousand faces*. Princeton University Press.

Cannon, C., & Rucker, D. D. (2022). Motives underlying human agency: How self-efficacy versus self-enhancement affect consumer behavior. *Current Opinion in Psychology, 46*, 101335. https://doi.org/10.1016/j.copsyc.2022.101335

Carrington, M. J., Zwick, D., & Neville, B. (2016). The ideology of the ethical consumption gap. *Marketing Theory, 16*(1), 21–38. https://doi.org/10.1177/1470593115595674

Clark, A. (2008). Supersizing the mind: Embodiment, action, and cognitive extension. *Oxford University Press*. https://doi.org/10.1093/acprof:oso/9780195333213.001.0001

Clark, A. (2023). *The experience machine: How our minds predict and shape reality*. Allen Lane.

Coates, J. M., Gurnell, M., & Sarnyai, Z. (2010). From molecule to market: Steroid hormones and financial risk-taking. *Philosophical Transactions of the Royal Society b: Biological Sciences, 365*(1538), 331–343. https://doi.org/10.1098/rstb.2009.0193

Cohn, A., Fehr, E., & Maréchal, M. A. (2014). Business culture and dishonesty in the banking industry. *Nature, 516(7529)*, 86-89. https://doi.org/10.1038/nature13977

Coleman, J. S. (1990). *Foundations of social theory*. Harvard University Press.

Collins, R. (2005). *Interaction ritual chains*. Princeton University Press.

Cueva, C., Roberts, R. E., Spencer, T., Rani, N., Tempest, M., Tobler, P. N., Herbert, J., & Rustichini, A. (2015). Cortisol and testosterone increase financial risk taking and may destabilize markets. *Scientific Reports, 5*, 11206. https://doi.org/10.1038/srep11206

Damasio, A. R. (2010). *Self comes to mind: Constructing the conscious brain*. Pantheon Books.

Damasio, A. R. (2019). *The strange order of things: Life, feeling, and the making of cultures*. Vintage Books.

Davis, J. B. (2003). *The theory of the individual in economics: Identity and value*. Routledge.

De Landa, M. (2006). *A new philosophy of society: Assemblage theory and social complexity*. Continuum.

Declerck, C. (2020). Neuroeconomics of cooperation heuristics: The role of incentives, social cues, and hormones. In *Social neuroeconomics. Mechanistic Integration of the neurosciences and the social sciences* (pp. 77–96). Routledge.

De Martino, B., O'Doherty, J. P., Ray, D., Bossaerts, P., & Camerer, C. (2013). In the mind of the market: Theory of mind biases value computation during financial bubbles. *Neuron, 79*(6), 1222–1231. https://doi.org/10.1016/j.neuron.2013.07.003

Deming, D. J. (2022). Four facts about human capital. *Journal of Economic Perspectives, 36*(3), 75–102. https://doi.org/10.1257/jep.36.3.75

Dewey, J. (1934/2005). *Art as experience*. Berkeley Publishing Group.

Dijkstra, K., & Zwaan, R. A. (2014). Memory and action. In L. Shapiro (Ed.), *The Routledge handbook of embodied cognition* (pp. 296–305). Routledge.

Donald, M. (1993). Précis of *Origins of the modern mind: Three stages in the evolution of culture and cognition. Behavioral and Brain Sciences, 16*(4), 737–748. https://doi.org/10.1017/S0140525X00032647

Dow, A., & Dow, S. C. (2011). Animal spirits revisited. *Capitalism and Society, 6*(2). https://doi.org/10.2202/1932-0213.1087

Eckhardt, G. M., Belk, R. W., & Wilson, J. A. J. (2015). The rise of inconspicuous consumption. *Journal of Marketing Management, 31*(7–8), 807–826. https://doi.org/10.1080/0267257X.2014.989890

Elias, N. (1969). *Die höfische Gesellschaft: Untersuchungen zur Soziologie des Königtums und der höfischen Aristokratie mit einer Einleitung: Soziologie und Geschichtswissenschaft*. Suhrkamp.

Elster, J. (1982). Sour grapes—Utilitarianism and the genesis of wants. In A. Sen & B. Williams (Eds.), *Utilitarianism and beyond* (pp. 219–238). Cambridge University Press.

Escalas, J. E. (2004). Narrative processing: Building consumer connections to brands. *Journal of Consumer Psychology, 14*(1/2), 168–180. https://doi.org/10.1207/s15327663jcp1401&2_19

Farrant, A., & McPhail, E. (2014). Can a dictator turn a constitution into a can-opener? F.A. Hayek and the alchemy of transitional dictatorship in Chile. *Review of Political Economy*, *26*(3), 331–348. https://doi.org/10.1080/09538259.2014.932063

Field, A. J. (2001). *Altruistically inclined? The behavioral sciences, evolutionary theory, and the origins of reciprocity*. University of Michigan Press.

Fleming, P. (2022). Sartre's lost organization theory: Reading the *Critique of dialectical reason* today. *Organization Theory, 3*(3), 263178772211092. https://doi.org/10.1177/26317877221109282

Foster, R. J. (2017). The corporation in anthropology. In A. Spicer & G. Baars (Eds.), *The corporation: A critical, multi-disciplinary handbook* (pp. 111–133). Cambridge University Press. https://doi.org/10.1017/9781139681025.006

Fournier, S. (1998). Consumers and their brands: Developing relationship theory in consumer research. *Journal of Consumer Research, 24*(4), 343–353. https://doi.org/10.1086/jcr.1998.24.issue-4

Frank, R. H. (1988). *Passions within reason: The strategic role of the emotions*. Norton.

Friedman, M., & Friedman, R. D. (1990). *Free to choose: A personal statement*. Harcourt Brace Jovanovich.

Friston, K. (2010). The free-energy principle: A unified brain theory? *Nature Reviews Neuroscience, 11*(2), 127–138. https://doi.org/10.1038/nrn2787

Froese, T., & Ikegami, T. (2013). The brain is not an isolated "black box", nor is its goal to become one. *Behavioral and Brain Sciences, 36*(3), 213–214. https://doi.org/10.1017/S0140525X12002348

Fromm, E. (1956/2002). *The sane society*. Routledge.

Fuster, J. M. (1997). Network memory. *Trends in Neurosciences, 20*(10), 451–459. https://doi.org/10.1016/S0166-2236(97)01128-4

Gabaix, X. (2016). Power laws in economics: An introduction. *Journal of Economic Perspectives, 30*(1), 185–206. https://doi.org/10.1257/jep.30.1.185

Galbraith, J. K. (1958/1999). *The affluent society*. Penguin.

Gazzaniga, M. S., Ivry, R. B., & Mangun, G. R. (2016). *Cognitive neuroscience: The biology of the mind* (4th ed.). Norton.

Gergen, K. J., & Gergen, M. M. (1988). Narrative and the self as relationship. *Advances in Experimental Social Psychology, 21*, 17–56. https://doi.org/10.1016/S0065-2601(08)60223-3

Ghoshal, S. (2005). Bad management theories are destroying good management practices. *Academy of Management Learning & Education, 4*(1), 75–91. https://doi.org/10.5465/amle.2005.16132558

Glaeser, E. L., Laibson, D. I., Scheinkman, J. A., & Soutter, C. L. (2000). Measuring trust. *Quarterly Journal of Economics, 115*(3), 811–846. https://doi.org/10.1162/003355300554926

Glimcher, P. W. (2011). *Foundations of neuroeconomic analysis*. Oxford University Press.

Glimcher, P. W. (2014). Chapter 5—Introduction to neuroscience. In P. W. Glimcher & E. Fehr (Eds.), *Neuroeconomics* (2nd ed., pp. 63–75). Academic Press. https://doi.org/10.1016/B978-0-12-416008-8.00005-X

Godfrey-Smith, P. (2017). *Other minds: The octopus and the evolution of intelligent life*. William Collins.

Goffman, E. (1956). *The presentation of self in everyday life*. University of Edinburgh.

Goffman, E. (1982). *Interaction ritual: Essays on face-to-face behavior*. Pantheon Books.
Goldie, P. (2014). *The mess inside: Narrative, emotion, & the mind*. Oxford University Press.
Goldthorpe, J. H. (2007). Social class and the differentiation of employment contracts. In J. H. Goldthorpe (Ed.), *On sociology (volume two): Illustration and retrospect* (pp. 101–124). Stanford University Press.
Grafen, A. (1990). Biological signals as handicaps. *Journal of Theoretical Biology, 144*(4), 517–546. https://doi.org/10.1016/S0022-5193(05)80088-8
Grauwe, P. de, & Ji, Y. (2019). *Behavioural macroeconomics: Theory and policy* (1st ed.). Oxford University Press.
Griesbauer, E., Manley, E., Wiener, J. M., & Spiers, H. J. (2022). London taxi drivers: A review of neurocognitive studies and an exploration of how they build their cognitive map of London. *Hippocampus, 32*(1), 3–20. https://doi.org/10.1002/hipo.23395
Grove, S. J., & Fisk, R. P. (1992). The service experience as theater. *Advances in Consumer Research, 19*, 455–461.
Hamilton, D. (1989). Thorstein Veblen as the first professor of marketing science. *Journal of Economic Issues, 23*(4), 1097–1103. https://doi.org/10.1080/00213624.1989.11504976
Harding, N., Gilmore, S., & Ford, J. (2022). Matter that embodies: Agentive flesh and working bodies/selves. *Organization Studies, 43*(5), 649–668. https://doi.org/10.1177/0170840621993235
Hassoun, J.-P. (2005). Emotions on the trading floor: Social and symbolic expressions. In K. Knorr-Cetina & A. Preda (Eds.), *The sociology of financial markets* (pp. 102–120). Oxford University Press.
Hayek, F. A. (1948). *Individualism and economic order*. University of Chicago Press.
Heckman, J. J. (2007). The economics, technology, and neuroscience of human capability formation. *Proceedings of the National Academy of Sciences, 104*(33), 13250–13255. https://doi.org/10.1073/pnas.0701362104
Heckman, J. J. (2013). *Giving kids a fair chance*. MIT Press.
Hegel, G. W. F. (1830/1991). *Enzyklopädie der philosophischen Wissenschaften im Grundrisse: 1830* (F. Nicolin, Ed.; Nachdr. der 3. Ausg. Heidelberg, Osswald, 1830, 8., um ein Literaturverz. erw. Aufl). Meiner.
Hegel, G. W. F. (1820/2009). *Grundlinien der Philosophie des Rechts oder Naturrecht und Staatswissenschaft im Grundrisse* (Nachdr.). Reclam.
Henry, P. C. (2005). Social class, market situation, and consumers' metaphors of (dis)empowerment. *Journal of Consumer Research, 31*(4), 766–778. https://doi.org/10.1086/426610
Herrmann-Pillath, C. (2017). *China's economic culture: The ritual order of state and markets*. Routledge.

Herrmann-Pillath, C. (2019). Beyond dualities in behavioural economics: What can G. H. Mead's conceptions of self and reflexivity contribute to the current debate? *Journal of Economic Methodology, 26*(2), 118–132. https://doi.org/10.1080/1350178X.2018.1501081

Herrmann-Pillath, C. (2021a). Robert J. Shiller, Narrative economics: How stories go viral and drive major economic events. *Oeconomia, 11–2*, 403–408. https://doi.org/10.4000/oeconomia.11128

Herrmann-Pillath, C. (2021b). The natural philosophy of economic information: Autonomous agents and physiosemiosis. *Entropy, 23*(3), 277. https://doi.org/10.3390/e23030277

Herrmann-Pillath, C., & Boldyrev, I. A. (2014). *Hegel, institutions, and economics: Performing the social*. Routledge, Taylor & Francis Group.

Hirshleifer, S., McKenzie, D., Almeida, R., & Ridao-Cano, C. (2016). The impact of vocational training for the unemployed: Experimental evidence from Turkey. *The Economic Journal, 126*(597), 2115–2146. https://doi.org/10.1111/ecoj.12211

Ho, K. (2009). *Liquidated: An ethnography of Wall Street*. Duke University Press.

Hochschild, A. R. (1979). Emotion work, feeling rules, and social structure. *American Journal of Sociology, 85*(3), 551. https://doi.org/10.1086/227049

Holt, D. B. (1997). Poststructuralist lifestyle analysis: Conceptualizing the social patterning of consumption in postmodernity. *Journal of Consumer Research, 23*(4), 326. https://doi.org/10.1086/209487

Hoy, D. C. (2009). The ethics of freedom: Hegel on reason as law-giving and law-testing. In K. R. Westphal (Ed.), *The Blackwell guide to Hegel's Phenomenology of spirit* (pp. 153–171). Wiley-Blackwell. https://doi.org/10.1002/9781444306224.ch7

Huppert, F. A., & So, T. T. C. (2013). Flourishing across Europe: Application of a new conceptual framework for defining well-being. *Social Indicators Research, 110*(3), 837–861. https://doi.org/10.1007/s11205-011-9966-7

Hurdley, R. (2006). Dismantling mantelpieces: Narrating identities and materializing culture in the home. *Sociology, 40*(4), 717–733. https://doi.org/10.1177/0038038506065157

Hurley, S. (2008). The shared circuits model (SCM): How control, mirroring, and simulation can enable imitation, deliberation, and mindreading. *Behavioral and Brain Sciences, 31*(1), 1–22. https://doi.org/10.1017/S0140525X07003123

Hutchins, E. (1995). *Cognition in the wild*. MIT Press.

Hutchins, E. (2005). Material anchors for conceptual blends. *Journal of Pragmatics, 37*(10), 1555–1577. https://doi.org/10.1016/j.pragma.2004.06.008

Ingold, T. (2000). *The perception of the environment: Essays on livelihood, dwelling and skill* (1st ed.). Routledge. https://doi.org/10.4324/9781003196662

Ingold, T. (2022). Evolution without inheritance: Steps to an ecology of learning. *Current Anthropology, 63*(S25), S32–S55. https://doi.org/10.1086/722437

Iterson, A. van (Ed.). (2002). *The civilized organization: Norbert Elias and the future of organization studies*. Benjamins.

Jackson, M. O. (2019). *The human network: How your social position determines your power, beliefs, and behaviors*.

Jasanoff, A. (2018). *The biological mind: How brain, body, and environment collaborate to make us who we are*. Basic Books.

Kahneman, D. (2012). *Thinking, fast and slow*. Penguin Books.

Kahneman, D., Fredrickson, D. L., Schreiber, C. A., & Redelmeier, D. A. (1993). When more pain is preferred to less: Adding a better end. *Psychological Science, 4*, 401–405.

Kahneman, D., & Krueger, A. B. (2006). Developments in the measurement of subjective well-being. *Journal of Economic Perspectives, 20*(1), 3–24.

Kahneman, D., Wakker, P., & Sarin, R. (1997). Back to Bentham? Explorations of experienced utility. *The Quarterly Journal of Economics, 112*(2), 375–406. https://doi.org/10.1162/003355397555235

Kaiser, C., & Oswald, A. J. (2022). The scientific value of numerical measures of human feelings. *Proceedings of the National Academy of Sciences, 119*(42), e2210412119.

Kandasamy, N., Garfinkel, S. N., Page, L., Hardy, B., Critchley, H. D., Gurnell, M., & Coates, J. M. (2016). Interoceptive ability predicts survival on a London trading floor. *Scientific Reports*, *6*(1), Article 1. https://doi.org/10.1038/srep32986

Kauffman, S. A. (2000). *Investigations*. Oxford University Press.

Keynes, J. M. (1936/2018). *The general theory of employment interest and money*. Springer International Publishing. https://doi.org/10.1007/978-3-319-70344-2

Klaes, M., Lightfoot, G., & Lilley, S. (2011). Market masculinities and electronic trading. In S. Long & B. Sievers (Eds.), *Towards a socioanalysis of money, finance and capitalism*. Routledge.

Knorr Cetina, K., & Bruegger, U. (2002). Global microstructures: The virtual societies of financial markets. *American Journal of Sociology, 107*(4), 905–950. https://doi.org/10.1086/341045

Krijnen, C. (2020). Sittlichkeit and the actuality of freedom: On Kant and Hegel. In M. F. Bykova & K. R. Westphal (Eds.), *The Palgrave Hegel handbook* (pp. 389–407). Springer International Publishing. https://doi.org/10.1007/978-3-030-26597-7_20

Krueger, N., Hansen, D. J., Michl, T., & Welsh, D. H. B. (2011). Thinking "sustainably": The role of intentions, cognitions, and emotions in understanding new domains of entrepreneurship. In G. T. Lumpkin & J. A. Katz (Eds.),

Advances in entrepreneurship, firm emergence and growth (Vol. 13, pp. 275–309). Emerald Group Publishing Limited. https://doi.org/10.1108/S1074-7540(2011)0000013014

Laitinen, A. (2011). Recognition, acknowledgement, and acceptance. In H. Ikäheimo & A. Laitinen (Eds.), *Recognition and social ontology* (pp. 309–347). Brill.

Lakoff, G., & Johnson, M. (1999). *Philosophy in the flesh: The embodied mind and Its challenge to Western thought*. Basic Books.

Lakoff, G., & Núñez, R. E. (2000). *Where mathematics comes from: How the embodied mind brings mathematics into being*. Basic Books.

Lakoff, G., & Turner, M. (1989). *More than cool reason: A field guide to poetic metaphor*. University of Chicago Press.

Landa, J. T. (1994). *Trust, ethnicity, and identity: Beyond the new institutional economics of ethnic trading networks, contract law, and gift-exchange*. University of Michigan Press.

Latour, B. (2005). *Reassembling the social: An introduction to actor-network-theory*. Oxford University Press.

Laube, S. (2019). Der Markt im Körper. Emotionales Beobachten und Bewerten im digitalisierten Finanzhandel. *Zeitschrift Für Soziologie*, *48*(4), 263–278. https://doi.org/10.1515/zfsoz-2019-0019

Lawrence, A., Clark, L., Labuzetta, J. N., Sahakian, B., & Vyakarnum, S. (2008). The innovative brain. *Nature, 456*(7219), 168–169. https://doi.org/10.1038/456168a

Lebaron, F. (2003). Pierre Bourdieu: Economic models against economism. *Theory and Society*, *32*(5), 551–565. https://doi.org/10.1023/B:RYSO.0000004928.45684.d4

Lee, S. W. S., & Schwarz, N. (2012). Bidirectionality, mediation, and moderation of metaphorical effects: The embodiment of social suspicion and fishy smells. *Journal of Personality and Social Psychology, 103*(5), 737–749. https://doi.org/10.1037/a0029708

Lin, N. (2007). *Social capital: A theory of social structure and action*. Cambridge University Press.

Lo, A. W. (2019). *Adaptive markets: Financial evolution at the speed of thought*. Princeton University Press.

Loader, P. (2015). Marx and enactivism. *Intellectica. Revue de l'Association pour la Recherche Cognitive*, *63*(1), 65–91. https://doi.org/10.3406/intel.2015.1024

Logan, T. D., & Myers, S. L. (2022). Symposium: Race and economic literature—Introduction. *Journal of Economic Literature, 60*(2), 375–376. https://doi.org/10.1257/jel.20211685

Louie, K., Glimcher, P. W., & Webb, R. (2015). Adaptive neural coding: From biological to behavioral decision-making. *Current Opinion in Behavioral Sciences, 5*, 91–99. https://doi.org/10.1016/j.cobeha.2015.08.008

MacKenzie, D. A. (2006). *An engine, not a camera: How financial models shape markets*. MIT Press.

MacKenzie, D. A., Muniesa, F., & Siu, L. (Eds.). (2007). *Do economists make markets? On the performativity of econo*. Princeton University Press.

Magalhães, P., & White, K. G. (2016). The sunk cost effect across species: A review of persistence in a course of action due to prior investment. *Journal of the Experimental Analysis of Behavior, 105*, 339–361.

Malafouris, L. (2013). *How things shape the mind: A theory of material engagement*. MIT Press.

Maltby, J., & Rutterford, J. (2012). Gender and Finance. *Oxford University Press*. https://doi.org/10.1093/oxfordhb/9780199590162.013.0027

Marková, I. (1982). *Paradigms, thought, and language*. Wiley.

Massa, F. G., Helms, W. S., Voronov, M., & Wang, L. (2017). Emotions uncorked: Inspiring evangelism for the emerging practice of cool-climate winemaking in Ontario. *Academy of Management Journal, 60*(2), 461–499. https://doi.org/10.5465/amj.2014.0092

Maturana, H. R., & Varela, F. J. (1980). *Autopoiesis and cognition: The realization of the living*. D. Reidel Pub. Co.

McAdams, D. P. (2013). The psychological self as actor, agent, and author. *Perspectives on Psychological Science, 8*(3), 272–295. https://doi.org/10.1177/1745691612464657

McAfee, R. P., Mialon, H. M., & Mialon, S. H. (2010). Do sunk costs matter? *Economic Inquiry, 48*(2), 323–336.

McAlexander, J. H., Schouten, J. W., & Koenig, H. F. (2002). Building brand community. *Journal of Marketing, 66*(1), 38–54. https://doi.org/10.1509/jmkg.66.1.38.18451

Mead, G. H. (1934). *Mind, self & society: From the standpoint of a social behaviorist* (C. W. Morris, Ed.). University of Chicago press.

Mead, G. H. (1936). *Movements of thought in the nineteenth century*. University of Chicago Press.

Mead, G. H., Morris, C. W., Huebner, D. R., & Joas, H. (1934/2015). *Mind, self, and society* (The definitive ed.). University of Chicago Press.

Menary, R. (2007). Writing as thinking. *Cognitive Dynamics in Language, 29*(5), 621–632. https://doi.org/10.1016/j.langsci.2007.01.005

Merleau-Ponty, M. (1955/1973). *Adventures of the dialectic*. Northwestern University Press.

Merton, R. K. (1948). The self-fulfilling prophecy. *The Antioch Review, 8*(2), 193–210. JSTOR. https://doi.org/10.2307/4609267

Michaelian, K., & Sutton, J. (2017). Memory. In E. N. Zalta (Ed.), *The Stanford encyclopedia of philosophy* (Summer 2017). Metaphysics Research Lab, Stanford University. https://plato.stanford.edu/archives/sum2017/entries/memory/

Moav, O., & Neeman, Z. (2012). Saving rates and poverty: The role of conspicuous consumption and human capital. *The Economic Journal*, *122*(563), 933–956.https://doi.org/10.1111/j.1468-0297.2012.02516.x

Morris, M. W., Sheldon, O. J., Ames, D. R., & Young, M. J. (2007). Metaphors and the market: Consequences and preconditions of agent and object metaphors in stock market commentary. *Organizational Behavior and Human Decision Processes, 102*(2), 174–192.

Moyar, D. (2008). Self-completing alienation: Hegel's argument for transparent conditions of free agency. In D. Moyar & M. Quante (Eds.), *Hegel's Phenomenology of spirit. A critical guide* (pp. 150–172). Cambridge University Press.

Muniz, A. M., & O'Guinn, T. C. (2001). Brand community. *Journal of Consumer Research, 27*(4), 412–432. https://doi.org/10.1086/jcr.2001.27.issue-4

Nelson, J. (1992). Shinto ritual: Managing chaos in contemporary Japan. *Ethnos, 57*(1–2), 77–104. https://doi.org/10.1080/00141844.1992.9981447

Nelson, R. R., & Winter, S. G. (1982/2004). *An evolutionary theory of economic change*. The Belknap Press of Harvard University Press.

Neuhouser, F. (2008). Hegel's Social Philosophy. In F. C. Beiser (Ed.), *The Cambridge companion to Hegel and nineteenth-century philosophy* (pp. 204–229). Cambridge University Press. https://doi.org/10.1017/CCOL9780521831673.009

Nisbett, R. E., & Cohen, D. (1996). *Culture of honor: The psychology of violence in the South*. Westview Press

Nooteboom, B. (2002). *Trust: Forms, foundations, functions, failures, and figures*. Edward Elgar.

Nussbaum, M. C. (2006). *Frontiers of justice: Disability, nationality, species membership*. Harvard University Press.

Nussbaum, M. C., & Sen, A. (Eds.). (1993). *The quality of life*. Oxford University Press.

Ong, M., Cunningham, J. L., & Parmar, B. L. (2023). Lay beliefs about Homo Economicus: How and why does economics education make us see honesty as effortful? *Academy of Management Learning & Education*, amle.2021.0134. https://doi.org/10.5465/amle.2021.0134

Orléan, A. (2013). *L'empire de la valeur: Refonder l'économie*. Seuil.

Osler, C. L., & Chang, P. H. K. (1995). Head and shoulders: Not just a flaky pattern. *SSRN ELibrary*. http://papers.ssrn.com/sol3/papers.cfm?abstract_id=993938

Padoa-Schioppa, C. (2011). Neurobiology of economic choice: A good-based model. *Annual Review of Neuroscience, 34*(1), 333–359. https://doi.org/10.1146/annurev-neuro-061010-113648

Paulle, B., van Heerikhuizen, B., & Emirbayer, M. (2011). Elias and Bourdieu. In S. Susen & B. S. Turner (Eds.), *The legacy of Pierre Bourdieu: Critical essays* (pp. 145–172). Anthem Press.

Piaget, J. (1975). *L'équilibration des structures cognitives: Problème central du développement*. Presses Universitaires de France.

Pine II, B. J., & Gilmore, J. H. (1998). Welcome to the experience economy. *Harvard Business Review, 76*(July–August), 97–105.

Pinkard, T. (2022). *Practice, power, and forms of life: Sartre's appropriation of Hegel and Marx*. University of Chicago Press.

Pippin, R. B. (2008). *Hegel's practical philosophy: Rational agency as ethical life*. Cambridge University Press.

Polanyi, M. (1966/2009). *The tacit dimension*. University of Chicago Press.

Potts, J., Cunningham, S., Hartley, J., & Ormerod, P. (2008). Social network markets: A new definition of the creative industries. *Journal of Cultural Economics, 32*(3), 167–185. https://doi.org/10.1007/s10824-008-9066-y

Preda, A., & Gemayel, R. (2020). Scopic systems and decision making in financial markets. In *Social neuroeconomics* (pp. 262–276). Routledge. https://doi.org/10.4324/9780429296918-17

Prum, R. O. (2017). *The evolution of beauty: How Darwin's forgotten theory of mate choice shapes the animal world—and us*. Doubleday.

Prusik, C. (2018). Neoliberalism: Critical theory as natural-history. In B. Best, W. Bonefeld, & C. O'Kane (Eds.), *The SAGE Handbook of Frankfurt School Critical Theory* (pp. 1601–1614). Sage Publications. https://doi.org/10.4135/9781526436122.n97

Quante, M. (2011). *Die Wirklichkeit des Geistes: Studien zu Hegel*. Suhrkamp.

Ramstead, M. J., Kirchhoff, M. D., & Friston, K. J. (2020). A tale of two densities: Active inference is enactive inference. *Adaptive Behavior, 28*(4), 225–239. https://doi.org/10.1177/1059712319862774

Reimann, M., Castaño, R., Zaichkowsky, J., & Bechara, A. (2012). How we relate to brands: Psychological and neurophysiological insights into consumer–brand relationships. *Journal of Consumer Psychology, 22*(1), 128–142. https://doi.org/10.1016/j.jcps.2011.11.003

Robbins, L. (1961). Hayek on liberty. *Economica, 28*(109), 66–81.

Robeyns, I. (2006). Three models of education: Rights, capabilities and human capital. *Theory and Research in Education, 4*(1), 69–84. https://doi.org/10.1177/1477878506060683

Robeyns, I., & Byskov, M. F. (2020). The capability approach. In E. N. Zalta & U. Nodelman (Eds.), *The Stanford encyclopedia of philosophy* (Winter 2020).

Metaphysics Research Lab, Stanford University. https://plato.stanford.edu/archives/win2020/entries/capability-approach/

Roediger, H. L., & Wertsch, J. V. (2008). Creating a new discipline of memory studies. *Memory Studies, 1*(1), 9–22. https://doi.org/10.1177/1750698007083884

Roli, A., Jaeger, J., & Kauffman, S. A. (2022). How organisms come to know the world: Fundamental limits on artificial general intelligence. *Frontiers in Ecology and Evolution, 9*, 806283. https://doi.org/10.3389/fevo.2021.806283

Ross, D. (2007). H. sapiens as ecologically special: What does language contribute? *Language Sciences, 29*(5), 710–731. https://doi.org/10.1016/j.langsci.2006.12.008

Rowlands, M. (2017). *Memory and the self: Phenomenology, science and autobiography*. Oxford University Press.

Rubinstein, A. (1998). *Modeling bounded rationality*. MIT press.

Rupp, K. (2003). *Gift-giving in Japan. Cash, connections, cosmologies*. Stanford University Press.

Ryan, R. M., Duineveld, J. J., Di Domenico, S. I., Ryan, W. S., Steward, B. A., & Bradshaw, E. L. (2022). We know this much is (meta-analytically) true: A meta-review of meta-analytic findings evaluating self-determination theory. *Psychological Bulletin, 148*(11–12), 813–842. https://doi.org/10.1037/bul0000385

Santos, L. R., & Rosati, A. G. (2015). The evolutionary roots of human decision making. *Annual Review of Psychology, 66*, 321–347.

Sartre, J.-P. (1960/2004). *Critique of dialectical reason: Volume one—Theory of practical ensembles*. Verso.

Sartre, J.-P. (1960/2006). *Critique of dialectical reason: Volume two*. Verso.

Sassen, S. (2018). *Cities in a world economy* (5th ed.). Sage Publications.

Saurabh, S., & Dey, K. (2020). Unraveling the relationship between social moods and the stock market: Evidence from the United Kingdom. *Journal of Behavioral and Experimental Finance, 26*, 100300. https://doi.org/10.1016/j.jbef.2020.100300

Schouten, J. W., & McAlexander, J. H. (1995). Subcultures of consumption: An ethnography of the new bikers. *Journal of Consumer Research, 22*(1), 43–61.

Schwarz, N., & Lee, S. W. S. (2019). The smell of suspicion. In J. P. Forgas & R. F. Baumeister (Eds.), *The social psychology of gullibility* (1st ed., pp. 234–252). Routledge. https://doi.org/10.4324/9780429203787-13

Seligman, A. B. (Ed.). (2008). *Ritual and its consequences: An essay on the limits of sincerity*. Oxford University Press.

Sen, A. (1977). Rational fools: A critique of the behavioral foundations of economic theory. *Philosophy and Public Affairs, 6*(4), 317–344.

Sen, A. (1985/1999). *Commodities and capabilities*. Oxford University Press.

Sen, A. (2004). *Rationality and freedom*. Belknap Press of Harvard University.

Shiller, R. J. (2019). *Narrative economics: How stories go viral and drive major economic events*. Princeton University Press.

Simmel, G. (1907/2004). *The philosophy of money*. Routledge. https://doi.org/10.4324/9780203481134

Simon, H. A. (1955). A behavioral model of rational choice. *The Quarterly Journal of Economics, 69*(1), 99–118.

Simon, H. A. (1979). Rational decision making in business organizations. *American Economic Review, 69*(4), 493–513.

Soriano, C., & Valenzuela, J. (2008, May 31). Sensorial perception as a source domain: A cross-linguistic study. *Seventh International Conference on Researching and Applying Metaphor (RaAM 7).*

Speer, N. K., Reynolds, J. R., Swallow, K. M., & Zacks, J. M. (2009). Reading stories activates neural representations of visual and motor experiences. *Psychological Science, 20*(8), 989–999. https://doi.org/10.1111/j.1467-9280.2009.02397.x

Spence, M. (1974). *Market signaling: Informational transfer in hiring and related screening processes*. Harvard University Press.

Stafford, C. (2020). *Economic life in the real world: Logic, emotion and ethics*. Cambridge University Press.

Stapleton, M. (2022). Enacting environments: From Umwelts to institutions. In K. L. Lai (Ed.), *Knowers and knowledge in East-West philosophy* (pp. 159–189). Springer International Publishing. https://doi.org/10.1007/978-3-030-79349-4_8

Stern, R. (2012). On Hegel's critique of Kant's ethics: Beyond the empty formalism objection. In T. Brooks (Ed.), *Hegel's philosophy of right* (pp. 73–99). Wiley-Blackwell.

Sugden, R. (2000). Team preferences. *Economics and Philosophy, 16*(2), 175–204. https://doi.org/10.1017/S0266267100000213

Sutton, J., & Williamson, K. (2014). Embodied remembering. In L. Shapiro (Ed.), *The Routledge handbook of embodied cognition* (pp. 315–325). Routledge.

Sweis, B. M., Abram, S. V., Schmidt, B. J., Seeland, K. D., MacDonald, A. W., Thomas, M. J., & Redish, A. D. (2018). Sensitivity to "sunk costs" in mice, rats, and humans. *Science, 361*(6398), 178–181. https://doi.org/10.1126/science.aar8644

Taylor, C. (2015). *Hegel and modern society* (Cambridge Philosophy Classics). Cambridge University Press.

Testa, I. (2020). Embodied cognition, habit, and natural agency in Hegel's anthropology. In M. F. Bykova & K. R. Westphal (Eds.), *The Palgrave Hegel handbook* (pp. 269–295). Springer International Publishing. https://doi.org/10.1007/978-3-030-26597-7_14

Thompson, E., & Stapleton, M. (2009). Making sense of sense-making: Reflections on enactive and extended mind theories. *Topoi, 28*(1), 23–30. https://doi.org/10.1007/s11245-008-9043-2

Tilly, C. (2003). *The politics of collective violence*. Cambridge University Press.

Tomasello, M. (2019). Becoming human: A theory of ontogeny. *Harvard University Press*. https://doi.org/10.4159/9780674988651

Tuan, Y.-F. (2011). *Space and place: The perspective of experience*. University of Minnesota Press.

Tuomela, R. (2007). *The philosophy of sociality: The shared point of view*. Oxford University Press.

Tuomela, R. (2013). *Social ontology: Collective intentionality and group agents*. Oxford University Press.

Tversky, A., & Kahneman, D. (1973). Availability: A heuristic for judging frequency and probability. *Cognitive Psychology, 5*(2), 207–232. https://doi.org/10.1016/0010-0285(73)90033-9

Tynan, C. (1999). On metaphors, marketing and marriage. *Irish Marketing Review, 12*(1), 17–26.

von Uexküll, J., & Kriszat, G. (1956). *Streifzüge durch die Umwelten von Tieren und Menschen*. Rowohlt.

Ustun, B., Covey, J., & Reissland, N. (2023). Chemosensory continuity from prenatal to postnatal life in humans: A systematic review and meta-analysis. *PLoS ONE, 18*(3), e0283314. https://doi.org/10.1371/journal.pone.0283314

Van Krieken, R. (1998). *Norbert Elias*. Routledge.

Varela, F. J., Thompson, E., & Rosch, E. (2016). *The embodied mind* (rev.). MIT Press.

Veblen, T. (1899/2007). *The theory of the leisure class* (M. Banta, Ed.). Oxford University Press.

von Weizsäcker, C. (2011). Homo Oeconomicus Adaptivus: Die Logik des Handelns bei veränderlichen Präferenzen. *Preprints of the Max Planck Institute for Research on Collective Goods, 10*, 1–33. http://hdl.handle.net/10419/57517

de Vroey, M., & Hoover, K. D. (2004). Introduction: Seven decades of the IS-LM model. *History of Political Economy, 36*(5), 1–11.

Wang, L., Malhotra, D., & Murnighan, J. K. (2011). Economics education and greed. *Academy of Management Learning & Education, 10*(4), 643–660. https://doi.org/10.5465/amle.2009.0185

Weber, M. (1922/2019). *Economy and society: A new translation* (K. Tribe, Ed. and trans.). Harvard University Press.

Williams, M. (2017). An old model of social class? Job characteristics and the NS-SEC schema. *Work, Employment and Society, 31*(1), 153–165. https://doi.org/10.1177/0950017016653087

Williamson, O. E. (1975). *Markets and hierarchies*. The Free Press.
Wilson, M. (2002). Six views of embodied cognition. *Psychonomic Bulletin & Review, 9*(4), 625–636.
Yu, N. (2017). LIFE AS OPERA: A cultural metaphor in Chinese. In F. Sharifian (Ed.), *Advances in Cultural Linguistics* (pp. 65–87). Springer Singapore. https://doi.org/10.1007/978-981-10-4056-6_4
Zaloom, C. (2003). Ambiguous numbers: Trading technologies and interpretation in financial markets. *American Ethnologist, 30*(2), 258–272. https://doi.org/10.1525/ae.2003.30.2.258
Zaloom, C. (2004). The productive life of risk. *Cultural Anthropology, 19*(3), 365–391. https://doi.org/10.1525/can.2004.19.3.365
Zawidzki, T. (2013). *Mindshaping: A new framework for understanding human social cognition*. MIT Press.
Zehavi, A., & Zahavi, A. (1997). *The handicap principle: A missing piece of Darwin's puzzle*. Oxford University Press.
Zingales, L. (2015). Presidential address: Does finance benefit society? *Journal of Finance, 70*(4), 1327–1363. https://doi.org/10.1111/jofi.12295

CHAPTER 6

The Embodied Approach to Institutions

6.1 Introduction: Institutions Are Institutional Actions

The previous chapter explored the theory of the economic actor based on an embodied approach to agency. We showed that agency is an emergent capability of actors, agential power, in assemblages of individuals and artifacts, and is thus distributed through processes of inward and outward embodiment. This view has many concrete consequences for understanding economic action as grounded in social and psychological constructs such as feelings, emotions, and memory. These constructs are typically treated as sources of biases and alleged failures of rationality in the mainstream approach, as well as in behavioral economics, even though the latter is often seen as its powerful internal critique of the standard economic model. However, in addition to feelings, emotions, and memory, we pointed out that a complete view of agency must also include the analysis of institutions.

In this chapter, then, we present our embodied approach to institutions. There is a long intellectual tradition of seeing institutions as embodied, beginning with Hegel, and leading to advanced sociological views classically formulated by Bourdieu. We approach institutions not as objects external to the actor, as in the widely accepted notion of "rules of the game," but as a *type of action*. Institutions are inwardly

F. Basso and C. Herrmann-Pillath, *Embodiment, Political Economy and Human Flourishing*, https://doi.org/10.1007/978-3-031-54971-7_6

embodied in actions, without implying an independent "Platonic existence:" "The social order is merely the order of bodies" (Bourdieu, 1997/2000, p. 168).[1] We speak of "institutional action." This way of thinking differs radically from the rationalist tradition, which approaches institutions as objects of rational design, either by an authoritative agency (the Hobbesian view) or by a social contract (beginning with Locke). These views imply that institutions are external objects, metaphorically like a law book. The embodied economics view claims that institutions are not entirely external in this way but are also internalized in actors: Institutions are performative through loops of outward and inward embodiment, and they *are* the institutional actions. In this view, what is mostly seen as "institution" across disciplines, such as standard economics and some approaches in law, is merely the abstracted redescription of institutional action in their respective disciplinary conceptual frameworks. We encounter the same epistemological fallacy that has been mentioned many times before: The scientist claims an external position of observer and reifies as "institution" what is an embodied type of action. This concludes our analysis of the economic actor: The actor is not seen as separate from the institutions that "govern" her behavior, but rather as an essential aspect of her capabilities to act.

This chapter is not intended to cover all the pertinent issues about institutions, which would require a full monograph. We will develop our generic approach to institutions by focusing on embodiment. This means that we will marginalize issues such as the role of government in creating and enforcing institutions, since we are concerned only with the foundational aspects. This does not imply, however, that embodiment does not matter in these broader contexts: We try to reach as far as possible in the three sections of Chapter 7, where we consider money, property, and labor as the most important forms of institutional action that constitute markets as an autonomous social domain or "field."[2] But we also approach markets as a foundational form of their own, in a kind of dialectical relationship between constituting institutions and the market as a Hegelian "totality," with money, property, and labor as its "moments:" The market is a field with these three types of basic institutional actions, and not as reified external objects. We will show in Chapter 7 how a type of action mediated by money has the specific effect of disembodying action: Of course, this is a contradiction in terms, since there is no such type of action. The disembodiment of action in economic life is a cognitive phenomenon that operates primarily through abstraction, as seminally analyzed in Simmel's work, and is concretized in distinct ways (including bodily expressions), often identified as a "psychological" phenomenon in the handling of money (Vohs, 2015).

Accordingly, we acknowledge the performative role of economic theorizing about institutions (Boldyrev & Svetlova, 2016; MacKenzie et al., 2007): To the extent that standard economics has shifted to disembodiment, this mirrors (and fails to critically reflect on) the abstraction that emerges from and occurs through market processes, and also contributes to reinforcing this process. A truly essential question, then, is whether embodied economics can conceive of markets as embodied, which we will address in the final chapter. The psychological phenomena of abstraction also manifest themselves in institutionalized forms of human suffering in markets, which we discuss in Chapter 7 on labor. Paradoxically, this is recognized even by standard economics which treats "labor" exclusively as "painful" disutility, often literally as "pain," that is, as a cost to be expended in order to earn an income that can be spent on goods that produce pleasure.[3] Indeed, the standard model of the labor market, also a pillar of macroeconomics, would implode if labor were to become a source of pleasure: Feelings matter analytically.

The chapter introduces two key theoretical innovations. We build on a celebrated theory of institutions in recent economics: Aoki's game-theoretic approach, and we show why the game-theoretic view remains insufficient for understanding the embodied nature of institutions, which Hegel first elaborated systematically. We deconstruct and reconstruct Aoki's theory of institutions with Bourdieu's concepts of field, habitus, and symbolic capital as an alternative to the disembodied economic and game-theoretic approach to institutions as media of information. One important consequence is that we highlight the role of power as necessary for the enforcement of institutions, and the dual role of institutions in creating agential power that is differentially distributed among people, thus producing inequality. In this theoretical view of power, our model also integrates the analytical philosophy of institutions, which we reformulate in terms of metaphor and conceptual blending, and which articulates two forms of intentionality, distinguishing I- and We- modes in the analysis of agential power. This brings us to the second major theoretical innovation: We refer the general model of institution to Fiske's anthropological theory of four types of social relationships. The We-mode defines Community, and the I-mode Hierarchy, Reciprocity, and Market. These four types relate to different cognitive scaling operations and important embodied schemas, respectively the CONTAINER, VERTICAL, BALANCE, and RESOURCE schemas. Hence, we are able to ground the theory of institutions in the fundamentals of the embodiment of cognition as elaborated in Chapter 4.

6.2 From Hegel to Bourdieu Via Searle: Power and Institutions

Our approach will not be considered "economics" by most economists today, although it has a deep affinity with the views of the (so-called) "old institutionalists" in the tradition of Pragmatism which also emphasized the specific forms of action enabled by institutions that become internalized, grounded in the fundamental concept of "habit."[4] At first sight, we seem to be arguing in sociological terms. This is misleading in an important respect, since we are continuing the Hegelian line of thinking deployed in the previous chapters. As far as sociology is concerned, in Bourdieu's analysis of fields, institutions as structuring aspects of the field correspond to habitus as their inward embodiment, implying the Hegelian idea that institutions are "second nature," meaning that they are "transparent" to economic actors. Hegel had already articulated a related idea, namely that institutions are rooted in ethical life ("*Sittlichkeit*"), that is, in the internalized customs of communities (Pippin, 2008). Ethical life, however, would not count for Hegel as a fully developed institutionalization of the field since this requires the embedding of institutions in the state as an overarching structure. Taylor summarizes this as follows:

> First, that what is most important for man can only be attained in relation to the public life of a community, not in the private self-definition of the alienated individual. Secondly, this community must not be a merely partial one, for example, a conventicle or private association, whose life is conditioned, controlled, and limited by a larger society. It must be coterminous with the minimum self-sufficient human reality, the state. The public life which expresses at least some of our important norms must be that of a state. Thirdly, the public life of the state has a crucial importance for men because the norms and ideas it expresses as not just human inventions. On the contrary, the state expresses the Idea, the ontological structure of things. (Taylor, 2015, p. 90)

Hence, there is a gap in the Hegelian set up, and Bourdieu has added an aspect that is not yet explicit in Hegel's writings, given his notion of spirit unfolding, ultimately in the form of the state as a manifestation of the absolute spirit. This is the notion of symbolic capital, that is, the mediation of institutions through symbolic systems, such as ideas about the sacred nature of the sovereign. These systems are themselves institutionalized (such as sacrality associated with the Church), creating complex social structures in which power is immanent, in the form of symbolic power (such as the assignment of the power to define and enforce sacrality to certain groups). Similar to habitus, symbolic power implies that individuals would follow an institution because they take it for granted, to the extent that they even see the institution as grounded in their own choice rather than being enforced by powerful actors with symbolic capital. Despite their differences (Bourdieu, 1994/1998, p. 55), this echoes Engels' notion of "false consciousness," and Marx had already exposed the corresponding deficit in Hegel's notion of institution, which he had limited to "civil society" as a universal and necessary stage in the unfolding of "spirit" (Patterson, 2009).

The concept of power is essential to distinguish institutions from other forms of action, such as habit, social norms, or conventions, insofar as enforcement presupposes power to enforce (Elster, 2015, p. 351). What distinguishes my habit of practicing the guitar every day from an institution? Some economists, such as D. C. North (1990), have argued that institutions require the existence of a powerful enforcement mechanism, which can be explicit (the judiciary, the police, etc.) or implicit (via culture and social interactions).[5] In contrast, my habit is not enforced by a powerful mechanism. To be sure, in many cases, there is the possibility that an institution also undergirds a non-institutional type of action. An important example is the question of whether language is an institution like the others, which is often emphatically denied because language is a necessary condition for institutions (Searle, 2011). Yet, a national language is powerfully imposed through schooling, and there are many cases of minority children being physically punished for speaking their mother tongue. Here, national language is an institution.

This seems to suggest that institutions are political artifacts. The idea that institutions are "natural," in the sense of "second nature," is related to the distinction between community and society introduced by Tönnies (1887) in his seminal work. In Hegel's thought, which has been echoed many times in Western intellectual history, especially in the writings of

Arendt, to which we will refer later in this book, the original community is the Greek *polis*. The idea is that the Greek man (literally) embodied the rules of the *polis* and that modernity has broken this harmonious social state (Taylor, 1975). Of course, this view cannot be taken seriously, but the distinction between community and society still resonates with this view. In communities, institutions are embodied because they are embedded in the social world, especially if we conceptualize a democratic community where participation in political processes should be inclusive, as epitomized by republican ideals. Indeed, the notion of community plays a very substantial role in many contemporary contexts, such as addressing the ecological challenge of strengthening the role of Indigenous peoples and communities, as illustrated in management (e.g., Banerjee, 2022; Salmon et al., 2022), political ecology (e.g., Escobar, 2018; Kothari et al., 2019), or economics and political science (e.g., Ostrom, 2010; Smith & Max-Neef, 2011). Nowadays, a key challenge in many policy domains is how to protect or reinstate communities in the context of global societies.

For Tönnies, as for Hegel, modern society breaks with the community, and as later elaborated by Polanyi (1944/2001), this is a process of disembedding the individual by throwing him into the market society, hence capitalism. This is a key point. For Tönnies, "society," as opposed to "community," is capitalist by definition. This raises the important question of the extent to which a "society," as Tönnies understands it, which is not capitalist, is at all feasible.[6] In a sense, Hegel already presented such an alternative vision, because his civil society is still pre-capitalist. The main ingredients are corporatist institutions and the state. This structure would indeed resemble modern welfare states, with strong non-governmental actors in key policy areas, such as trade unions and employers' associations (Ver Eecke, 2008). We will explore these dimensions of institutions in Chapter 8.

One difficulty in dealing with institutions, given their conceptual importance in the social sciences, is that there are countless independent alternatives in theorizing, while the respective authors often blatantly ignore the others. One of the most influential philosophical approaches to institutions, which has also been discussed in institutional economics, is Searle (1995, 2011).[7] Interestingly for the embodied economics perspective, Bourdieu's work is considered to begin where Searle's ends, and despite some important differences, there is some conceptual overlap between their analyses (Gebauer & William, 2000; see also, Gebauer, 2017). For instance, as Bourdieu explains:

> As the collective individuated through embodiment or the biological individual 'collectivized' by socialization, habitus is akin to the 'intention in action' of Searle (Searle, 1983: especially chapter 3) or to the 'deep structure' of Chomsky, except that, instead of being an anthropological invariant, this deep structure is a historically constituted, institutionally grounded, and thus socially variable, generative matrix (see Bourdieu, 1987). It is an operator of rationality, but of a practical rationality immanent in a historical system of social relations and therefore transcendent to the individual. (Bourdieu & Wacquant, 1992, pp. 18–19)

In turn, Searle referred back to Bourdieu in order to bring together his concept of "background" and habitus:

> Pierre Bourdieu's important work on the 'habitus' is about the same sort of phenomena that I call the Background. (Searle, 1995, p. 132).

Searle puts the notion of status function <X counts as Y in context C>, at the center of his theory of institutions.[8] This is a minimalist formula that covers a range of complex notions. The "count as" refers to transforming an observer-independent fact into an observer-dependent fact: For example, a piece of metal X "counts as" money Y in a certain group of economic agents conducting market transactions, the context C. While the piece exists observer-independently, as "money", it exists only relative to observers. Once this transformation is complete, the physical characteristics of X no longer determine the actions: As long as money is metal coins, people can still use the coins only to extract valuable metal. But in the case of fiat money, this evaporates—except in the case of extreme hyperinflation.

The formula is handy but overly parsimonious, especially when it comes to Searle's key claim about the "constitutive" role of status functions, which some economists vehemently reject.[9] Indeed, for Searle, many human institutions have the character of being creative in terms of social ontology:

> The distinctive feature of human social reality, the way in which it differs from other forms of animal reality known to me, is that humans have the capacity to impose functions on objects and people where the objects and the people cannot perform the functions solely in virtue of their physical

> structure. The performance of the function requires that there be a collectively recognized status that the person or object has, and it is only in virtue of that status that the person or object can perform the function in question. (Searle, 2011, p. 7)

Economists deny that institutions can have this kind of autonomous power to create a "reality."[10] Take the simple example of comparing traffic rules to chess. The rules of chess create this kind of action, without rules, handling the chess figures would be meaningless. In the case of traffic, people will drive anyway, with or without rules. The fact that some institutions transform pre-existing actions should not lead to confusion between these actions and the institutional action: Driving a car in the wilderness is not an institutional action, it is in Paris. Yet, institutionalized driving does not create the "brute fact" of driving. What the debate shows is that what is actually missing from Searle's formula is a recognition of the embodied nature of the status function: Searle explicitly treats it as a metaphorical operation, but he does not explore its grounding in the body. We will return to this crucial point when we propose grounding Searle's status function in conceptual blending (Herrmann-Pillath, 2013).

Like Bourdieu, Searle recognizes the role of power in the formula of the "power creation operator." This refers to the general notion of desire-independent reasons for action, that is, deontic power, such as obligations, authorizations, permissions, and requirements (Searle, 2011, p. 145). This defines the most radical departure from the conventional economic approach, for which it is fundamental to assume that actors always act on the basis of the incentives they face: That is, "desire-independent" reasons would always be reduced to desire-dependent reasons, such as following an obligation because of expected costs and benefits. Searle argues that the essence of institutions is to enable actions that are independent of such preferences, and thus can even remain in conflict. This echoes much of Hegel's view.[11] The power creation operator includes the important aspect that power must be accepted individually and collectively. This also transcends mere incentives. For example, the mere threat of punishment as a sanction against an institution works very differently if the targeted agents are merely rational agents weighing the costs and benefits of a deviant action, or if they believe that the enforcer has a legitimate, perhaps even sacred, right. In the latter case, just setting some precedent may be sufficient to induce all agents to obey the institution. This also highlights the significance of another key element in Searle's theory, collective intentionality, which corresponds to what we have identified as the We-mode in our analysis of agency and which, by definition, sublates individual choice to incentivesfor a nuanced view, see Tuomela (2011).

Searle's view has been widely criticized by some institutional economists (Guala, 2016). Indeed, while the views reported so far are compatible with the "old institutionalists," going back to Veblen (who explicitly developed an embodied approach), they remain in tension with modern institutional economics, even beyond the narrower school of New Institutional Economics. This is particularly striking when one considers the canonical approach to institutions in economics, and game theory.

6.3 Transcending the Game-Theoretic Approach to Institutions

6.3.1 *Signs of Embodiment in Applied Game Theory*

Most economists employ the "rules of the game" metaphor when defining institutions (Williamson, 1998, p. 75). This has led to early applications of game theory in the analysis of institutions and behavior, often claiming that game theory has explanatory power (e.g., Guala, 2016, p. 31). However, this is controversial, as leading game theorists have argued that game theory is nothing more than a branch of mathematics without empirical and practical claims (Rubinstein, 2000, p. 71ff). Applying game theory to real-world institutions would implicitly introduce a bias towards disembodiment, as the analysis is developed in abstraction from economic life in the first place, beyond mere questions of empirical validity.

The projection of game theory onto institutions raises the question of whether an institution is a set of rules and game structures external to the behavior of individuals, or whether it is a regularity in the observed pattern of their behavior (Aoki, 2001, p. 4ff; Schotter, 1981). Is the institution the game structure that determines actions, as defined by strategies and their payoffs, or the equilibrium of the game, as manifested in actions? If we treat institutions as external rules and game structures, then institutions would be disembodied, since the typical approach is to merge the positions of the all-seeing eye of an external omniscient observer and the agents in positing common knowledge about the game structure, such as what type of game is being played and what the payoffs are. The game is solved, and the equilibrium of the game is found by deriving the rational solution, assuming that the agents are rational and perform the same calculations as the external observer. This means that the observed regularity is just an ephemeral expression of the logical structure of the game: It is literally given to the agents, whose behavior reflects the structure of their environment. By comparison, if we start from the observation of certain regularities in behavior, such as the way people behave in a double auction game, we find that the previous approach would be a form of causal explanation in which the game structure would be counted as the mechanism that generates the observed pattern, which is directly implied in the mechanism design approach and its practical applications (Roth, 2018; see also, Callon & Roth, 2021). Interpreted in this way, however, we immediately notice that the game-theoretic structure is not a causal mechanism at all, unless the theorist assumes that the underlying structural and behavioral assumptions are realistic, that is, manifest in empirical phenomena, such as "rationality" being a factual property of individuals.[12] In fact, experimenters recognized very early on that rationality can only be guaranteed if it is incentivized in a certain way, especially if only monetary incentives are used, and even if certain disciplinary measures are imposed by the experimenter. In other words, the game must be played according to rules set by the experimenter, and even more, there is the intricate challenge that the games played in practice may not be the ones that the experimenter deems "rational," that is, games that should be meta-preferred by rational agents.[13]

Let us look at three famous archetypal examples to illustrate the ills of disembodied game-theoretic reasoning about institutions: The Prisoner's Dilemma (PD), the chain store paradox, and the Ultimatum Game (UG).

The PD structure is a specific constellation of payoffs that describes a fictional real-world situation in which prisoners are placed in a particular physical environment (separate cells without mutual communication) and are confronted by the judge with payoffs such that an equilibrium is reached in which both prisoners confess. The PD as a theoretical construct was not derived from real-world patterns, such as the observation of the empirical fact that most prisoners, when placed in a given decision context, would confess. In fact, prisoners often do not confess. There are many reasons for this. To name just two: One is that prisoners may feel a strong moral commitment to preserve their honor by not cooperating with the despised authorities; another is that they may face severe sanctions from fellow criminals if they leave prison early after confessing. Of course, there is also the question of whether they can trust the authorities: Why should they trust the deal?

In this sketch, we see signs of an embodied economic approach as opposed to the disembodied view. First, contrary to the assumption of rationality, behavior in the PD setting may be shaped by emotional commitments and feelings, such as moral outrage or distrust, rather than by "rationality" as an abstract principle posited by the external observer. Second, the judge may incorrectly interpret the true setting as perceived by the prisoners, who may be members of a criminal group that would, for example, punish family members of a confessing prisoner: Thus, the PD inadequately captures the true setting but reflects the judge's misinterpretation. The PD structure is disembodied in two ways: It does not take into account real people, because it is abstracted from their embodied and embedded social relations, and it defines an artificially constrained context of behavior. As Ken Binmore argues:

> Game theorists think it just plain wrong to claim that the Prisoners' Dilemma embodies the essence of the problem of human cooperation. On the contrary, it represents a situation in which the dice are as loaded against the emergence of cooperation as they could possibly be. If the great game of life played by the human species were the Prisoners' Dilemma, we wouldn't have evolved as social animals! We therefore see no more need to solve some invented paradox of rationality than to explain why strong swimmers drown when thrown in a lake with their feet encased in concrete. No paradox of rationality exists. Rational players don't cooperate in the Prisoners' Dilemma because the conditions necessary for rational cooperation are absent in the game. (Binmore, 2011, p. 63)

Ostrom's famous work on commons has shown that such issues matter for policy-making and institutional crafting (Ostrom, 1990). For example, face-to-face communication and dense social networks allow people to "express and see emotional reactions to distrust" (Dietz et al., 2003, p. 1908) which helps explain why, in many circumstances, commons can be sustained for centuries, despite the apparent "irrationality" of cooperation when conceptualized as structured as a PD game. Real-world institutions of commons are embedded in real-world human groups that live together and share feelings and frames of interpretation. When the commons were suppressed, often violently, as part of enclosure movements in modernizing Europe, this was often met with fierce resistance by the communities. This reveals the complex reality of the commons as social arrangements that reach beyond issues of economic organization and touch on collective identities and ways of life (De Moor, 2015).

The second example is the chain store paradox which is based on the mathematical stringency of backward induction given the rationality of agents (Selten, 1978). This is called a "paradox" because it shows that the credibility of threats depends entirely on introducing the possibility that agents are not rational. A rational agent would anticipate the costs of fighting an incumbent, as would the incumbent, so they would agree to share the contested terrain. In contrast, an "irrational" agent would be able to credibly communicate that she would incur the immense costs of attacking the incumbent, so the incumbent would be better off withdrawing. Hence, for the ultimate pattern, emotional structures are causally important (Frank, 1988). Here the same problems arise here as with PD—and Selten acknowledges this, once mentioning his sleepless nights after discovering the paradox. The disembodied mathematical structure fails to explain anything in the real world, where what matters most is what the model does not (or cannot?) include or specify.

Our third example is the now classical literature on UG mentioned in Chapter 2, where empirical research has amply demonstrated that people's behavior generally does not conform to "traditional assumptions regarding rationality and material selfishness" (Güth & Kocher, 2014, p. 397).[14] As anthropological comparisons across a wide range of "small-scale societies" have shown, actual patterns vary according to contextual factors, such as established practices of sharing and interpretations of the game (Henrich et al., 2005). Experimenters can construct a real-world situation in which individuals are confronted only with payoffs and a decision framework consistent with the standard economic theory. But even if the game in a narrow sense can be described by some mathematical formalism, this observer's view does not reflect the real mechanisms that result in the observed behavior. As observed, "in many cases experimental play appears to reflect the common interactional patterns of everyday life" (Henrich et al., 2005, p. 795), which are far removed from an experimental game. Commenting on these studies, Binmore further indicates:

> If this attempt to apply game theory in an anthropological context has some descriptive validity, what should we expect to happen when we ask inexperienced subjects from small-scale societies to participate in a novel laboratory game designed to provide information on how people respond

> to situations involving social phenomena like fairness, trust, or reciprocity? The answer that seems obvious to me is that we should expect them to behave as they would behave in real life if they were offered similar cues to those offered in the laboratory. That is to say, we should use whichever equilibrium their own society operates in its repeated game of life to predict their initial behavior, rather than one of the equilibria of the one-shot game they are required to play in the laboratory. (Binmore, 2007, p. 7)[15]

What is mostly missing in mainstream economic game theory is a thorough consideration of how individuals perceive the experimental game and how they actually experience the payoffs.[16] In fact, the experimental situation involves an interpretive power structure *à la* Bourdieu: The experimenters see the behavioral deviations from the mathematical structure imposed by the game design as disturbances that need to be explained, and they do not recognize the power of the agents to perform the interaction as they see it, such as to really take it as a fun game of chance,[17] and thus not show deviations as defined by the experimenter, but to actually play the real game correctly—for this example, see Karlan (2005). Indeed, as mentioned above, one interesting methodological aspect of experimental economics, that differs from psychological experiments is that experimental economists should use monetary incentives (e.g., Croson, 2005; Harrison & List, 2004),[18] hoping that "control can be achieved by using a reward structure to induce prescribed monetary value on action" (Smith, 1976, p. 275), and resisting the temptation to add "realism" and "simulate the alleged circumstances of a particular market" (Smith, 1976, p. 278).

Whereas some (experimental) economists may believe that this allows the distillation of "pure" causal factors of behavior (see contra, Dhami, 2016, p. 49), we can also interpret this as the ***imposition*** of a specific behavioral pattern that is domain-specific, that is, profit-seeking actions through "market" transactions. For instance, Smith and Walker (1993, p. 245) argue that "increased rewards shift the central tendency of the data toward the predictions of rational models" (see also Smith, 2008, p. 180ff). In this sense, we can interpret the empirical relevance of game experiments in a radically different way, namely as a demonstration of the performative power of "real-world" markets to change behavior:

> Laboratory experience suggests that all of the characteristics of 'real world' behavior that we consider to be of primitive importance – such

> as self-interest motivation, interdependent tastes, risk aversion, subjective transactions cost (time is consumed), costly information (it takes time to acquire and process information), and so on – arise naturally, indeed inevitably, in experimental settings. (Smith, 1976, p. 276).

These experiments can be seen as toy models of markets, but not of human behavior in general, and in this sense, their abstract form reflects the forces of disembodiment in real markets (Herrmann-Pillath, 2019). In reality, experiments are actually performed by the participants in the experiment and are only partially controlled by the experimenter, who must impose the experiment as a discipline on the subjects. However, this, in turn, renders the theoretical set-up performative. This quandary has led to intense methodological debates about the external validity of experiments beyond the laboratory or the artificially constructed situation (Kagel, 2015).[19]

In sum, a critical flaw of established game-theoretic approaches to institutions is that they deliberately aim to de-contextualize experimental tests of "rules of the game," that is, to create a disembodied situation of choice. However, participants in experiments are people of flesh and blood, and they introduce friction into the models through their embodied interpretations of the structures the experimenters wish to impose on them. In the embodiment approach, experiments can then be seen as micro-rehearsals of societal power struggles over symbolic capital. In the following section, we show how the limitations of game theory can be overcome by developing a new synthesis of the Aoki-model of institutions, originally informed by game theory, with Bourdieu's sociological approach to embodiment.

6.3.2 *The Aoki-Bourdieu Logic of Institutional Action*

In what follows, we scrutinize a model of institutions suggested by Aoki and debated in institutional economics, which draws on game theory to develop a framework applicable to comparative studies of real-world institutions.[20] This model contains seeds of embodiment, such as references to public representations and behavioral dispositions. However, its game-theoretic basis blocks a full transition to an embodied view. As we will show, this requires abandoning one of the model's key assumptions, based on the computer metaphor of the (social) mind, namely that institutions "compress information." Tellingly, this corresponds to Hayek's view of market institutions as carriers of knowledge, which, as discussed in Chapter 3, are supposed to transcend even the cognitive capacities of individuals. This is related to the cognitive turn in some approaches to institutions that emphasize "shared beliefs."[21]

Importantly though, as we shall see, Aoki's model can be translated into analytical categories that are central to Bourdieu's embodied sociology. Our task, then, is to gradually enrich and replace the original concepts of the Aoki model when analyzing it, as has been done in the most recent version developed by Herrmann-Pillath and endorsed by Aoki himself. This extension (hereafter, "Aoki model 2.0") explicitly introduced the concepts of performativity and distributed cognition into the model.[22] As described below, in addition to still lacking full embodiment, the model also lacks the dimension of power. Accordingly, it does not neatly distinguish between institutions and other forms of regularities shared by actors in a population, such as social norms or conventions. It should therefore be seen as mapping a logic of social rules in general, and only after it has been transformed along Bourdieu's lines, can we properly speak of an embodiment model of institutions.

The Aoki model 2.0 distinguishes between two perspectives on the generation of institutional behavior (Fig. 6.1). The first perspective is the distinction between the individual and collective levels, or micro versus macro. At the same time, however, important generative forces are at the individual level, such as emotional commitments, which are summarily referred to as dispositions, and also often intermingle with collective-level phenomena. The other perspective is the distinction between the cognitive and the behavioral dimensions. The latter refers to institutional action, in the two forms of individual action and emerging patterns of collective behavior, which Aoki interprets along the lines of equilibria in games, though not necessarily referring to the specific formalism, hence called "recursive states of play." Collective patterns can deviate from intentional action at the individual level. The famous archetype for this is Schelling's (2006) analysis of racial segregation. Individuals act to choose residential neighborhoods, and despite individually weak racial preferences, the outcome might be strong segregation. This raises the question of whether this pattern is institutional collective action, even though there is no coordination of individual decisions in the first place. At what point can we diagnose the institutionalization of racism? This requires moving beyond the level of mere strategic interactions amenable to the analytical tools of game theory.[23]

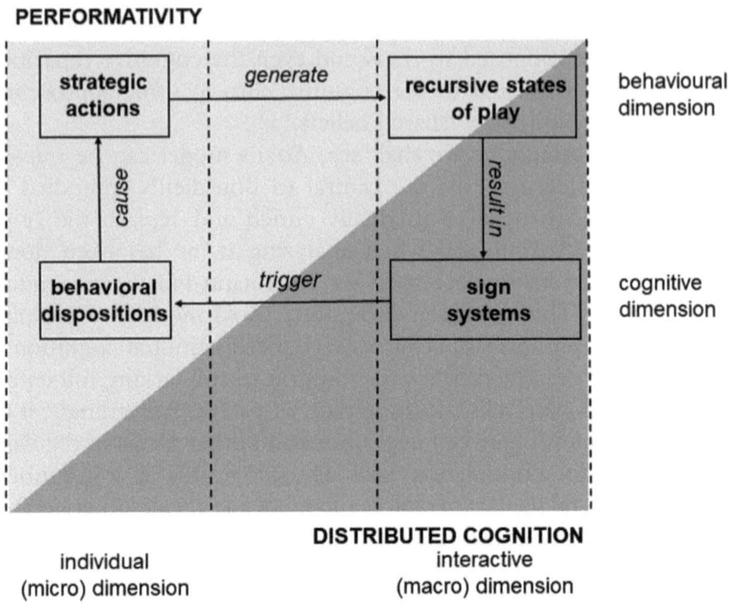

Fig. 6.1 The Aoki model 2.0 is a conceptual framework that arranges a variety of mechanisms in the generation of institutions as institutional actions which are linked in a causal feedback loop. The mechanisms are located in two dimensions defined by the duality of behavior and cognition versus interactive and individual, respectively. The shaded triangles show the two key phenomena: In distributed cognition, institutions operate as sign systems that trigger embodied individual actions that interact with the actions of other individual's actions, making the institution performative. See the main text for further details. After Herrmann-Pillath (2013)

In its original version, the Aoki model argues that "public representations," which Herrmann-Pillath in version 2.0 calls "sign systems," are essential. This idea has a long pedigree in psychology and sociology, not explicit in the model, going back to Durkheim and elaborated by Moscovici (Farr & Moscovici, 1984).[24] We use the term "sign" here because "representation" involves a specific kind of semantic relation that is actively created in a community of users of such representations. However, as implied by game-theoretic approaches to "salience" (Sugden, 2011), there are important classes of signs which operate as contextual cues that do not have the status of "representations," but depend entirely on the often-subliminal interpretive stances of actors. In its simplest form, realized segregation is itself a sign: Landlords, for example, may simply believe and accept it as a fact, and begin to actively discriminate against certain races in screening new tenants. Schelling's example is highly instructive in showing that symbolic representations evolve endogenously and outwardly embody the emerging social regularity. At the same time, however, this example also shows that the aspect of power inherent in symbolic capital, even to the extent of symbolic violence as posited by Bourdieu (1979), cannot be understood by focusing only on interactive dynamics and their cognitive mechanisms.

The signs refer to the individual level in the creation of individual dispositions for action. These dispositions are embodied, such as in certain emotional responses to certain contexts. For example, racial discrimination is also embodied in feelings triggered by viewing people of color, even if individuals may rationally deny being racist. Racial segregation reinforces such dispositions, because people in white neighborhoods might rarely meet people of color in daily life. Again, this is only one mechanism that does not reveal the dimension of power in race relations.[25] This closes the feedback loop in the Aoki 2.0 framework, as dispositions generate actions that interplay with other actions.

In sum, social regularity, in the model, is the whole loop unfolding across the various dimensions. We maintain this view in what follows: The model describes a conceptual logic of institutional action. That being said, we hasten to add that this logic only describes a type of mechanism and has no explanatory status as such, since the dimension of power is only implicit. The analysis of power requires the analysis of entire social fields and, even more, of the relations between them as determined by the distribution of various forms of capital, such as economic versus cultural (Bourdieu, 2019, p. 1038ff). Furthermore, (inward) embodiment operates through processes of internalization such as upbringing and (school) education (e.g., Bourdieu & Wacquant, 1992, pp. 12–13). In studying such phenomena, we are dealing with complex assemblages and regimes of manifolds of institutions that cannot be analyzed directly in terms of the mechanistic scheme of institutional action alone.

In order to elaborate further, let us turn to the four sides of the Aoki model, which indicate certain analytical domains in this elementary logic. In doing so, we begin to relate this logic to Bourdieu. The upper part, as we have seen, is closest to the standard economic approach, since it examines how individual actions interact to generate and sustain certain patterns of behavior at the collective level. In Bourdieu's account, this could be approached with the concept of "field," in which struggles over positions unfold, and eventually coalesce into institutionalized states (Bourdieu & Wacquant, 1992, p. 94ff). As in the case of racial segregation, game theory, or other mathematical models can be helpful, but only as a conceptual tool, not as an explanatory scheme. An important type of model is any kind of frequency-dependent mechanism, such as Schelling's. However, in the context of our argument, these mathematical models do not explain anything: The upper part of the Aoki framework would be left in limbo without specification of the underlying causal mechanisms that explain individual behavior and the physical structures of how actions interact.

As we saw in the discussion of the chain store paradox, this involves reflexivity of perception: The attacker would have to know whether the incumbent is a rational agent or a hothead who would simply ignore any potential costs to herself in attacking. Reflexivity is one of the key reasons why institutions have performative functions in the creation of individual identities, since the institution can function as a sign of the composition of types in a group of agents (Herrmann-Pillath, 2016b), building on contributions such as Sliwka's (2007). A compelling example of this, which directly undermines game-theoretic approaches, is that incentive systems, designed as institutions or organizations, can have "counter-performative" effects: The introduction of incentives can change the framing of the situation if individuals interpret this as an indication that the majority of other individuals fail to follow the rule without incentivization. Incentives can crowd out other commitments to the very action they are intended to motivate (Bowles, 2008; Bowles & Polanía-Reyes, 2012): For example, people may lose altruistic motivation when they are paid for the service, as in the much-cited case of reduced willingness to donate blood in Sweden when women received monetary compensation for doing so (Mellström & Johannesson, 2008). The key point is that in the Aoki 2.0 framework, we approach actor characteristics not just as externally given psychological facts, but as endogenously evolving, even to the extent that actors may change their characteristics in response to changing contextual factors. This is what Bourdieu theorizes in terms of the interaction between field and habitus.

As mentioned above, a key aspect in the formation of sustainable institutional states is that institutions include public representations, which can be analyzed with Bourdieu's symbolic capital. At first sight, this is related to the idea held by many economists and sociologists that institutions are devices to reduce the informational load for economic agents. This would amount to interpreting "capital" in economic terms, so that institutions would be seen as a stock that produces economic benefits. For example, labels applied according to institutional rules can assure consumers of product quality. In this view, institutions involve symbolic media that "compress" (in Aoki's parlance) the informational functions of institutions in coordinating behavior while reducing cognitive demands. Obviously, this interpretation is far from Bourdieu's understanding of symbolic capital, in which power is at its core.

We can generalize about this tension when we confront functionalist accounts of institutions with the perspective offered by Bourdieu. Beyond economics, a similar tension has emerged in anthropological research, where, for example, the "materialist" account of the Hindu institution of sacred cows refers to certain ecological functions which believers do not see as reasons for following the institution (Harris, 1979). However, as Bourdieu has forcefully argued, there is a high probability that the function will collapse if the actors are informed about the function of their belief. This creates a paradox: "*Illusio*," by definition disinformation, seems necessary to maintain a state that allegedly manifests informational functions, in the sense of enabling successful action (Rappaport, 1979).

This raises an important question: The idea of information compression by institutions implies a reference to a hypothetical state of full information accessible to the external observer who reconstructs the function of the institution. This suggests that there is a continuum of information with more or less amounts of it, reflecting a conception of information *à la* Shannon discussed in Chapter 2. But as the example of the sacred cow shows, we cannot say that the Hindu belief is just "less information" than the external observer claims since the meaning of sacredness is qualitatively radically different from the meaning of ecology. Indeed, Marxians would speak of "false consciousness:" In the conventional economic view, less information is not false information (which would be no information at all). The case of sacred cows reveals the functionalist fallacy of the information compression argument, since we must distinguish between the functions identified by the external observer and the reasons why internal agents manifest institutionalized behavior. The functionalist argument fails because the function is not the reason, and thus is not necessarily part of the causal mechanism of the institution:

The reasons, that is, the beliefs and interpretations of the agents, are the only causes that can actually count.[26] But these beliefs do not aim at "compressing information" and may even be "false" from the perspective of the external observer.

This analysis demonstrates that the meaning of institutions is autonomous from functional contexts unless those functional contexts are reflexively accessible to, and invoked by, the actors themselves. The simplest demonstration is to consider the law: The law is a primordial type of institution, and we might easily be tempted to argue that the law saves transaction costs. But, in fact, the law has merely shifted informational loads (if we use that term at all) between different subdomains through a "division of juridical labor" (Bourdieu, 1986, p. 817). Law and legal practice have become increasingly complex and demanding in terms of information processing, even as the information requirements of individual transactions have declined. The rising costs of litigation in modern societies clearly show that this is a delusion.

It is worth noting that the notion of efficiency of institutions in terms of informational load has become an important aspect of the legal process, especially in common law settings (Serkin, 2016). Once this applies, it can be argued that this function has become reflexively accessible to agents. This is certainly true of the rise of the field of law and economics in recent decades, but it was also true much earlier in the transition to modern civil law systems and the gradual transformation of common law since the eighteenth century. This is highly relevant for assessing the claims of most economists that the achievement of informational efficiency (i.e., a reduction in transaction costs) was a causal driver of institutional change. For example, land law has indeed evolved in the direction of easing market transactions of land rights (Graziadei, 2017). However, this only means that the specific informational requirements of a narrow type of economic actions, as perceived by the agents interested in that type of action, and with the power to enforce institutional change, are followed. In other words, instead of information compression benefiting all actors, we diagnose a distributional effect of the formation of public representations, also known as symbolic capital, that cement disadvantages through disinformation resulting from cognitive exclusion, that is, lack of access to what appears to be "compressed information." For example, information packages on complex financial products facilitate transactions among skilled professionals, but make the products even more opaque to ordinary citizens who lack the sophisticated knowledge to interpret them.

This discussion reveals the fundamental difference between Aoki's original model and Bourdieu's approach: The Aoki model does not consider power as an explanatory factor. However, this has recently been highlighted in a remarkable intellectual shift by one of the leading institutional economists, North, who switched from an efficiency to a power view of institutions (North et al., 2009). In short, the argument is that the main function of institutions is to contain violent conflict in human groups—although it neglects symbolic violence. The notion of violence combines the recognition of unequal access to and capacities for violent action, which means that institutional arrangements most often imply inequality of power and access to resources. This reveals a fundamental dilemma of institutions: Many institutions require active enforcement and the threat of punishment to prevent dissolution, which can be done at the group level, as in the primordial setting of hunter-gatherer societies, or through specialists in violence acting as enforcers. These enforcers can demand compensation but given their advantage in controlling the means of violence, they can also extract rents from other group members, as in the classical example of medieval feudalism (Earle, 2017; Hicks, 1969). This also triggers competition for access to rents through violent means. As we will see, this also applies to the efficiency account of modern markets, as is evident in the violent suppression of commons.

Hence, perhaps one of the most serious and worrying flaws of conventional economic accounts of institutions is that they neutralize, if not neglect, the role of power, violence, and inequality, which are embodied phenomena par excellence, combining actual violence with emotions such as fear or despondency, which in turn shape belief in the possibility of violence, that is, the credibility of threats. This is widely recognized outside of economics, though less so within it (Hirshleifer, 2001). However, as we have seen, the current version of the Aoki model suffers from the same problem. The question is how we can integrate power, at least implicitly, into this basic model of institutional action. Obviously, this should be done at the juncture of sign systems and dispositions and would replace the notion of information compression.

We refer to only one approach that we find particularly pertinent, Foucault's et al. (2004) concept of "governmentality," because it is one of the most appropriate alternatives to the notion of "information compression." Governmentality refers to the internalization of institutional governance, moving away from the pure expression of physical violence. In public health, for example, governments may be interested in maintaining a healthy population with strong capacities for economic productivity and military prowess. To this end, they create and enforce public health institutions. Over time, these no longer need to be enforced by interventions but become standards of hygiene that most people follow without enforcement. This is not primarily based on rational agreement, but is embodied in a set of everyday practices in which signs play a central role, such as wearing clean shirts, washing hands, and so on. An important aspect of this is that such practices and signs form patterns that are cognitively salient. Thus, on the lower side of the Aoki framework we consider a rich set of cognitive mechanisms with different loci, both individual and collective, hence we speak of "distributed cognition." There are generic mechanisms that are individually embodied. One prime example is all kinds of Gestalt formation (Schlicht, 2018): Taking corruption as an example, if individuals are confronted with dispersed and incomplete experiences of corruption, there is room for a Gestalt switch *à la* Necker cube, as they may see these as mere exceptions or as revealing a real pattern. Such switches are reinforced when different individuals communicate about their experiences, perhaps beginning with utter sentences such as "all police officers are corrupt," thus leveraging their own perceptions and resulting in a collectively shared view (Herrmann-Pillath & Hederer, 2023, p. 217ff).

We can now summarize our new version of the Aoki logic in terms of a systematic restatement along the lines of Bourdieu's thinking, and call it the Aoki-Bourdieu logic of institutional action (Fig. 6.2).

First, there are no "institutions" conceived as separate from institutional action: Institutions are embodied in action, unfolding in a Hegelian logic of outward embodiment (expressive objectification) and inward embodiment (symbolically mediated internalization). Referring to institutions in a conventional way conflates the perspectives of the external observer and the actors of institutional action, resulting in a misplaced reification of institutions by the former. Yet, reification can be an element of the reflexive stance towards institutional actions by the actors themselves: In this case, the external observer may refer to the institution, but only as an internal symbolic construct interpreted by the economic agents. How this works in detail will be shown in the discussion of money in Chapter 7.

Second, the external observer focuses on institutional actions and explores the causal mechanisms that generate them, and that distinguish this form of action from other regular patterns of behavior, such as

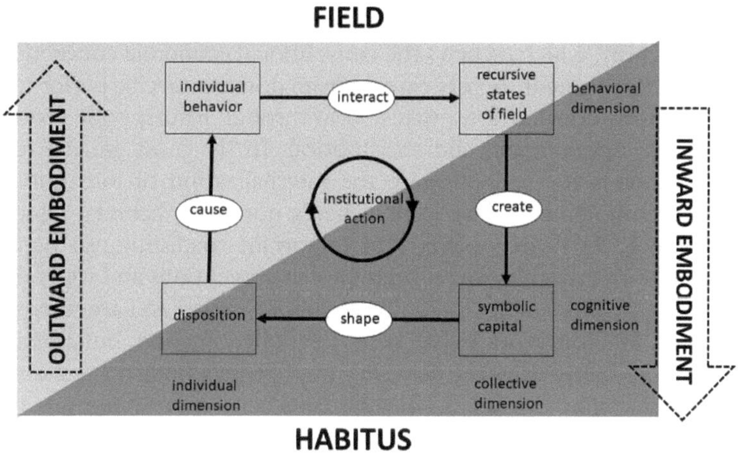

Fig. 6.2 The Aoki-Bourdieu model reformulates the conceptual logic of the Aoki 2.0 model by making explicit the circular flow of inward and outward embodiment, which renders institutions performative and generates their cognitive power. Furthermore, we link its components to Bourdieu's key concepts of field and habitus. A field is understood as a domain of interaction in collectives of actors in which symbolic capital is created, appropriated, and deployed. Habitus defines individuals as actors through their dispositions to institutional actions

habits. The Aoki-Bourdieu framework refers to a wide range of specific mechanisms of institutionalization in the dimensions of individual versus collective, and behavioral versus cognitive. These mechanisms differ across domains of institutional actions, such as the religious or the market, requiring the development of a taxonomy of institutional actions, with specific types, such as actions mediated by money. These domains are what Bourdieu calls "fields." Fields are defined by certain capacities of actors who are engaged in struggles for positions within the field, such as in academia ("scientific field"), in the news media ("journalistic field"), or in law ("juridical field"). We will not dissect these capacities further here, which Bourdieu refers to as various forms of "capital," encompassing economic, social, cultural, and symbolic capital. A key aspect of this analysis is the differentiation of a field through certain forms of symbolic capital, which are endogenously created within the field (such as the forms of scientific habitus in academia).[27]

Third, an important feature of the Aoki framework is the endogeneity of agent identity, which eschews the conventional economic conception of a generic rational agent. Actors emerge from domain-specific performative effects of institutional actions, that unfold through field-specific processes of individual development and socialization. In the most general terms, this corresponds to the notion of the internalization of institutions as a form of embodiment. This is Bourdieu's notion of habitus, discussed in Chapter 4. As noted above, it is important to distinguish between generic cognitive mechanisms such as Gestalt perceptions and views of the field, which are immanent to acquired symbolic capital and are, therefore, contingent. Habitus is not only a behavioral phenomenon, but also a way of seeing and interpreting the field. For example, economics has a distinct habitus of academic discourse that reflects its general presumptions about competition and performance (e.g., Lundberg & Stearns, 2019; Nelson, 1992), and is reinforced by organizations in the field:

> Economics as a profession is prominently intertwined with public administrations, corporations, and international organizations; these institutions not only provide economists with resources and collect their data, they also foster a 'fix it' culture – or, as sociologists would put it, a particular 'habitus,' a disposition to intervene in the world. (Bourdieu & Wacquant, 1992; Fourcade et al., 2015, p. 107)[28]

Fourth, a fundamental kind of mechanism is symbolic, which we have called "signs" to include all kinds of symbols, including unintentional ones such as emotions of embarrassment (e.g., blushing), which we now specify in Bourdieu's terms as symbolic capital. Hence, a central analytical concept is how individuals interpret the context in which institutional action unfolds. This ranges from interpreting the mere results of other actions (as in the example of segregation) to explicit communication and reflection (as in the propagation of ideologies). This defines another fundamental difference from conventional economic theory since we eschew the information-theoretic approach that relates institutions to efficiency, as in transaction cost theory which is another flawed projection of the external observer's view. Symbolic mechanisms shape cognitive processes that are distributed among groups of individuals and are emotionally grounded, as far as valuations in actions are concerned (see Chapters 4 and 5). A central type of cognitive mechanism is metaphor, which leads to a creative social ontology of institutions, such as the creation of new kinds of agents, for example, corporations as legal persons, through anthropomorphism.[29]

Fifth, the new Aoki-Bourdieu framework is completed by describing agency as constituted by dispositions to institutional actions, which may include rational decisions, but only as a minor case. Dispositions define types of agents in terms of their views (e.g., beliefs, attitudes) and behaviors towards following an institution, as perceived by the actors (such as following contractual obligations in business, even at an unexpected cost). Again, this is habitus: Dispositions are grounded in various embodied mechanisms, such as emotional, habitual, or interpretive stances. In this regard, our detailed analysis of "trader Bill" in Chapter 5 provided rich illustrations.

Sixth, the institutional actions of individuals within the group interact in the field, with a potential gap between individual motives and expectations on the one hand, and collective outcomes, on the other. Here, standard economic models describe mechanisms of interaction, as in game theory. However, the functioning of such mechanisms depends crucially on parameters which evolve endogenously, even to the extent that internal interpretations determine what type of game the interacting agents are actually involved in. This implies that the materiality of structures of interaction, such as the physical location of agents or the technology of communication, matters. Here, an example discussed in Chapter 5 is the role of settlement patterns in shaping capacities for collective action of miners under Thatcher. We refer to this as the mediation of embodied interaction.

Understanding the mechanisms of the Aoki-Bourdieu model of institutions requires a closer look at the mechanisms of embodied interaction drawing on the insights of Chapter 4. In particular, the dialectic of inward and outward embodiment, as mediated by specific cognitive processes, is a key task for institutional analysis.

6.4 Embodied Institutional Actions of Exchange and Their Cognitive Foundations

The term institution covers a wide range of phenomena, and we do not intend to be exhaustive. Our focus is on markets as a specific form of exchange in society, hence a distinct Weberian value sphere, or, in our new terminology, institutional action in the field of the market. We approach exchange as a perspective for understanding social relationships as a form of outward embodiment: A relationship—here understood largely to include market transactions—materializes in the form of an exchange of an object that is expressively created and received by the other side. This is what Marx (1932/1988) and later Bourdieu (1982/1991) refer to as fetishism. For example, in the previous chapter, we analyzed trust as a market feeling. Trust is constituted as arising from the interaction of trusting and being trustworthy, in which trust becomes objectified. This objectification can become an institutional action in the economy, for example, in the form of letters of recommendation or bills of exchange. These objects have the powers of inward embodiment to transform market feelings: The literature on trust diagnoses a transition from "personal trust" to "system trust" (Nooteboom, 2002).

We will develop a taxonomy of relationships as exchanges that take the form of institutional action in the economy. This taxonomy was proposed by Alan Fiske (1992), and we follow him in principle, although we propose some clarifications and simplifications to bring the taxonomy conceptually closer to the context of economic life. In Aoki's original approach, we also find a taxonomy of "domains," such as "trade," "commons," or "organization" (Aoki, 2001, p. 25). Most institutional economists do not use taxonomies because they claim to formulate universal theories about institutions as such (e.g., Guala, 2016). Our approach differs from Aoki's in that it is systematically grounded in the embodiment approach to economic agency developed in Chapter 5, along with the principles of embodied cognition outlined in Chapter 4. The taxonomy matters because there are principled differences between the basic types with respect to the mechanisms of embodiment and their behavioral consequences. At the same time, as said, we do not cover all social fields, as institutional economists often do, but focus on the economy.

6.4.1 *The Metaphorical Constitution of the Economy*

When considering the cognitive foundations of institutional action in economic life, it is of the utmost importance to recognize that what is "the economy" is itself a performative phenomenon that cannot be delineated exclusively in terms of an external, all-seeing eye (Herrmann-Pillath & Hederer, 2023, p. 27ff). The economy is performatively constituted by institutional actions grounded in embodied cognitive operations. For this reason, the economy pervades all social domains, insofar as its boundaries are open and indeterminate, which often lures "imperialist" economists to claim theoretical dominance over all other social sciences (Lazear, 2000; Samuelson, 1973), although this is also recognized by sociologists, such as Bourdieu (Lebaron, 2003). Even in fields in which actors explicitly reject economic motivations and valuations (such as in the "*l'art pour l'art*" doctrine, or in religion), economic factors ultimately influence the outcomes of institutional actions, for example, often in ways that allow actors to break through certain constraints of the field. We posit that this is related to the fundamental fact of the materiality of the economy, and thus to the pervasive power of a conceptual metaphor of the type we discussed in Chapter 4: The RESOURCE schema, which is the vehicle by which the economy diffuses into non-market domains. However, the RESOURCE schema does not identify an externally given object, but performatively creates such objects in a movement of outward embodiment as the first step in the institutionalization of "the economy" at a particular time and place.

Every day, for example, when we eat or drink, we experience what a RESOURCE is: A material resource is a kind of substance that can be quantified, has a unit value, serves a purpose, and is used up progressively as it serves that purpose (Lakoff & Johnson, 1980, p. 65). This schema is then employed to define several concepts such as Scarcity, Efficiency, Waste, and Savings, which are relevant in economic life (Lakoff & Johnson, 1999, p. 162). One of the most common metaphors that builds on the RESOURCE schema is TIME IS MONEY, a metaphor that can be found in everyday experiences as reflected in contemporary English and in various languages around the world. "I invested a lot of time in her," "you need to budget your time," or "he is living on borrowed time," are metaphors which illustrate the conceptual metaphor TIME IS MONEY (Lakoff & Johnson, 1980, pp. 7–8). The TIME IS MONEY metaphor refers to important institutions such as interest and was a bone of contention in religious debates about money in the Middle Ages when authorities argued that time was a gift from God and, therefore, priceless (Walsh & Lynch, 2008, p. 97). The institution of interest closes the performative loop of constituting "the economy" in a specific way: The movement of outward embodiment creates "time" as a resource through a cognitive blend that relates to money as another institutional form of economic action (see below for more detail). Once TIME is outwardly embodied as a RESOURCE, it becomes objectified in the institution of interest, which entails a second movement of inward embodiment: Most famously, and literally, this is the pound of flesh that must be paid for borrowed money, seen as postponing satisfaction on the part of Shylock.

MONEY is mapped onto TIME because TIME is a more abstract concept. TIME is more abstract because it is harder to figure out what TIME is than what MONEY is. We manipulate MONEY when we manipulate artifacts like coins and notes. TIME is not something we manipulate on a daily basis. Therefore, when we say "time is money," we are using our concrete experience of MONEY to make sense of TIME, which is more abstract. This metaphor gives us a specific way of thinking and acting toward TIME. The idea is that when we think about MONEY, we think about something that is a valuable commodity and a limited resource used to accomplish our goals, which can activate self-interested thoughts and have behavioral implications (e.g., Wang et al., 2020). When TIME is metaphorically framed, and thus perceived, as a valuable commodity and limited resource, we begin to optimize it by performing cost-benefit analyses in our own interest. This may explain, for instance, why the literature shows that when people think about the TIME IS MONEY metaphor, they are actually less likely to engage in environmental behavior (Whillans & Dunn, 2015), or volunteering (DeVoe & Pfeffer, 2010), which are other-oriented.

Beyond the TIME IS MONEY metaphor, metaphors are pervasive in economic life to structure understanding of the abstract concepts that generalize the market frame. For instance, inflation is commonly understood as an enemy, leading to the INFLATION IS AN ENEMY metaphor (Lakoff & Johnson, 1980), in which inflation is anthropomorphized to facilitate communication and implementation of government action in the economic sphere. Likewise, TRADE IS BALANCE when international trade is understood as zero-sum, NATION IS A CONTAINER when immigrants are portrayed as "stealing" jobs, or GOVERNMENT IS A NURTURING PARENT or A STRICT FATHER when the intervention is a recovery or austerity policy (Lee & Schwarz, 2018). Returning to the TIME IS MONEY metaphor, it clearly illustrates that specific metaphors are mediated by the institutions that constitute economic life, thus mediating the dialectics of outward and inward embodiment. Namely, a given institution of economic life, such as money, can lead economic agents to think and act in terms of a specific metaphor. In other words, an institution can embody a metaphor, and a metaphor like TIME IS MONEY is the by-product of our embodiment in economic life.

The operation of the RESOURCE schema illustrates the general approach to embodiment in institutional action. In terms of the Aoki-Bourdieu model, we argue that institutions are grounded in embodied cognitive mechanisms, including generic ones like the RESOURCE schema. This can be formalized along the lines of Searle's status function which can be read as a kind of metaphorical operation—though we reiterate that we are aware that Searle is viewed as a literalist, whose positions on metaphors differ from those of Lakoff & Johnson (1999, p. 122). We can achieve this by referring to the concept of conceptual blending introduced in Chapter 4, which generalizes and analyzes metaphorical operations in terms of projections between two concepts into a new blend, relative to a context. That is, as in the case of TIME IS MONEY, we have the two input spaces "money" and "time" which are blended into the metaphor "time is money," relative to certain contexts, such as markets (Fig. 6.3). As we see, we can refer the blending scheme directly to the elements of the Searlean status function, thus revealing it as the central cognitive mechanism in institutional action, which is missing in Searle's original version, in which the "count as" operation remains opaque (Herrmann-Pillath, 2013, p. 369ff).

The significance of the TIME IS MONEY metaphor stems from the fact that time is a universal resource that is potentially relevant to any kind of human action, thus driving the expansion of the economy in the specific sense of treating time as a cost. In the context of economics, the concept of COST is understood as a universal type of opportunity cost, such as when the opportunity cost of leisure is seen as the loss of income if the time were spent at work instead (Spencer, 2009): This metaphorical move pulls all kinds of human action into the sphere of the economy, for example, considering time spent with loved ones as cost. This truly "imperialist" power of the TIME IS MONEY metaphor was harnessed and materially mediated by the proliferation of all kinds of time-measuring devices, turning them into public objects (Landes, 2000). As a result, the entire society became subject to a coordinated and synchronized system of measuring and announcing time, which was indispensable for the new type of work in the factories (Rabinbach, 1992; Thompson, 1967). This transformation has often been diagnosed as one of the fundamental transformations of capitalism (Bourdieu, 1990).[30]

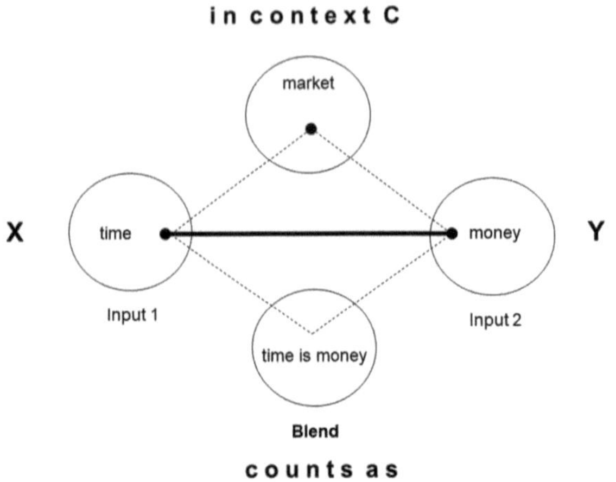

Fig. 6.3 The metaphor TIME IS MONEY emerges as the conceptual blend of "time" and "money" whose counterparts have been identified in the generic space of the "market." This mechanism grounds Searle's status function in the body, which relates "time" to "money" as a metaphor ("counts as") in the context of the "market." Searle's status function is reformulated in terms of embodied mechanisms of cognition

This exemplary discussion shows how "the economy" is metaphorically constituted by embodied institutional actions, which we can further analyze into a number of specific conceptual blends. This relates to Searle's concept of institutions, which still lacks full embodiment. This analysis needs further elaboration in distinguishing between the economy and the market in terms of their specific forms of institutional action. This is already evident in our analysis of TIME IS MONEY, which has been contextualized in relation to the market in terms of the notion of opportunity cost, which evokes a notion of exchange, that is, giving something up to get something else.

6.4.2 *Institutional Action and the Four Elementary Types of Social Relationships*

Our basic Aoki-Bourdieu model of institutional action describes generic forms of institutionalization that we will now explore in Fiske's (1992) taxonomy of social relationships. Our approach builds on a simple and abstract restatement of Fiske's original categories that follows from our analysis of agency. We treat his original categories, such as "communal sharing," as general forms of institutional action and as an extension of the list of vital relations in conceptual blending theory—as discussed with the concept of "vital relationships" in Chapter 4. This means that we regard the types as primarily embodied, and thus consider institutional actions as forms of outward embodiment: As we have seen in the case of the economy, this means, for example, that the type of "market" is not principally a type manifested in an "objective" field, but is performed by seeing the field in terms of this type, hence by outwardly embodying the market. For instance, actors may see a marital relationship in a "market" frame or in a "community frame," and perform it accordingly. Such a Searlian performation would be mediated by various material objects, such as a contract, that inwardly embody the "market" type, thus closing the performative loop of institutional action.

The taxonomic abstraction is implied by Fiske's own approach in which he associates each type of relational model to a specific type of "mathematical operation" that can be understood as involving conceptual blends, since these operations "project" a given relationship on a particular type of scale. Remarkably, his distinction of four types of relationships exhausts precisely the space of possible scales along which relationships could be measured: Nominal, ordinal, interval, and ratio (Fiske, 2004, p. 124ff).[31] In our view, these operations are grounded in more basic embodied metaphors.

Hence, in what follows, we neatly distinguish between the abstract analytical concepts, such as the I- and We modes introduced in the previous chapter, and the embodied mechanisms of institutional action. The former help to construct a conceptual space that leads to the taxonomy of institutional actions shown in Fig. 6.4. We distinguish between forms of agency, based on the analytical distinction between the I-mode and the We-mode, the latter of which relates to the nominal scale: In a nominal scale, individuals are assigned to certain classes, in our case generically to the class identified as "we," distinct from other "we," that is, other communities. In the I-mode, we treat actors as independent of each other, and we distinguish between two classes of actions, one that focuses only on their relationship, and the other that places these relationships in the context of alternative possible relationships. This distinction goes back to the identity operation: For instance, in the case of family and kinship relationships, most societies severely restrict agency in terms of creating alternative relationships, and as a striking illustration, one cannot choose another mother (but often one can adopt a child).[32] In other relationships, and systematically in the case of markets, actors can create alternative ones (such as changing suppliers); and, in Fiske's scheme, the market relationship refers to another operation: the ratio scale.

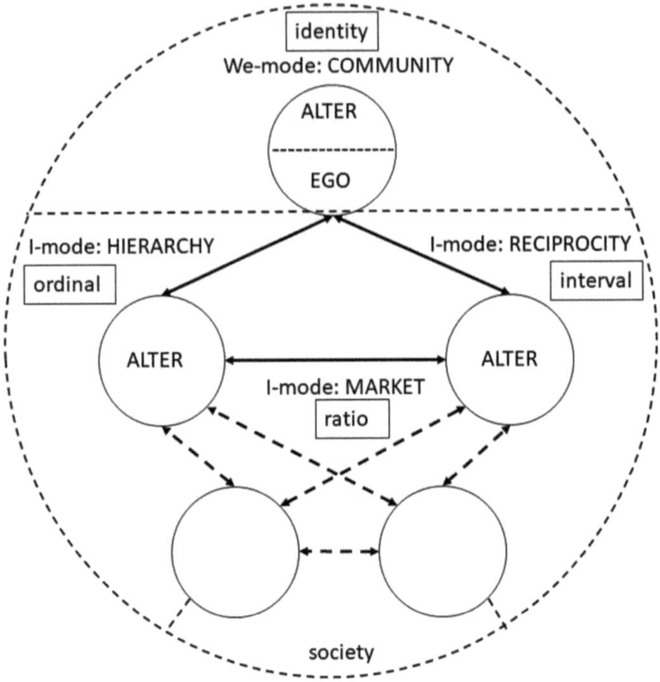

Fig. 6.4 We visualize the conceptual structure of four Fiske types of social relationships within the space delimited by the two poles of the We-mode and the I-mode. The We-mode defines the type of "community" for which the relevant scale is the operation of identity and characterizes a dividual self, which comprises Ego and Alter. The other three modes operate in the I-mode, where Ego and Alter are separated in interaction. The ordinal scale defines hierarchy, and the interval scale reciprocity. The fourth type, "market," differs from the others: It relates the interaction between Ego and Alter to a space of virtual alternative actors, operating on the ratio scale (opportunity cost). The empty circles refer to other actors in the market

Hence, in the first step of unfolding the taxonomy, we distinguish between two types: Community and market relationships, which is in line with Tönnies' (1887) distinction between community and society. This is further supported by considering Weber's (1922/2019, p. 122) fundamental distinction between two types of groups, namely, closed and open. Open groups allow for the activation of alternative relationships. Closed groups, when applied to Fiske's scheme, can be distinguished in terms of two types of relationships that refer to equality and inequality. A hierarchical relationship projects onto an ordinal scale, and a reciprocal relationship onto an interval scale.

Importantly:

- The community relationship is enacted through a specific type of institutional action, "communal sharing."
- In contrast, the market type, as an open relationship, pertains to what Fiske calls "market pricing," and is an institutional action in which people orient themselves to ratio values such as prices, wages, interest, rents, tithes, or cost-benefit analyses. We refer to these as "opportunity ratios," inspired by the notion of opportunity cost in economics. Unlike the other three types, which focus on the actualized relationship between individuals, the market introduces a field of potential relationships that can be compared to the existing ones.
- The reciprocity type refers to the institutional action that Fiske calls "equality matching." The mathematical operation is derived from the identity operation and is placed in the context of an additive interval scale, where even balance is the reference point. Reciprocity is the case where the relationship is considered to be balanced, which is enacted by corresponding institutional actions, such as matching rules in gift exchange. This example also shows that reciprocity is often the type that preserves the community feature: Reciprocity can be an I-mode transmutation of sharing in the We-mode.
- The hierarchy type corresponds to what Fiske calls "authority ranking" as an institutional action. Hierarchy as institutional action is about recognizing power in exchange, that is, verticality in a relationship, projected onto an ordinal scale. This can be seen as a radical imbalance, where the asymmetrical differences in relations are transitive and ordered.

Considering these four types, there is obviously a direct correspondence with Tönnies' juxtaposition of community and society, and the idealizations of the notion of community. The community breaks down into the other three types as soon as the We-mode shifts to the I-mode. In the We-mode, sharing is "natural." Still, once the We-mode is left, sharing becomes an institutional action that tends to require a power differential to be sustainable, as when, for instance, sharing in a community is compared to sharing in a democratic state, and takes the form of taxation to implement some redistribution. The discussion so far can be summarized in Table 6.1.

As we can see, types refer to distinct scales and institutional actions. Type and scale are abstract analytical categories, while institutional action enacts the types, thus entailing the embodiment of the type. The mode is also abstract and allows the types to be projected onto other categorizations, as discussed in the cases of Tönnies and Weber. Tönnies' conception of community can pertain to distinct forms of enacting community: In the We-mode, this is sharing, while in the I-mode we distinguish between the two possibilities of enacting equality via equality matching, or via authority ranking, as forms of enacting community. In stark distinction, the type of market operates in the I-mode and enacts what Weber calls the open group. The Weberian distinction, at first sight, links community and closure, but at this point, the distinction between types and action is purely essential, because institutional action can dynamize and hence open up community, in the simplest way of transforming a new interaction into the We-mode through sharing. This is

Table 6.1 Fiske types: Its defining features in embodied economics

Type	*Scale*	*Action*	*Mode*	*Tönnies*	*Weber*
Community	Nominal	Communal sharing	We-mode	Community	Closed/open
Reciprocity	Interval	Equality matching	I-mode	Community	Closed/open
Hierarchy	Ordinal	Authority ranking	I-mode	Community	Closed/open
Market	Ratio	Market pricing	I-mode	Society	Open

why, we treat closure and openness as valid alternatives for social relationships alongside the market—which is in line with Weber's idea of considering them also as strategic options for actors.

Further, the types are ideal-types and have an analytical status, which means that, in real-life relationships, the types are mixed.[33] For example, when considering the labor market in Chapter 7, similar to the Marxian concept of the "free laborer" (Feher, 2009), critical observers have pinpointed the paradoxical status of labor in liberal doctrine, as workers give up their freedom when they sign a work contract and subject themselves to authority in the company (Anderson, 2019). The contingent context of market power strongly contextualizes the nature of this authority, as workers may be effectively trapped in the company as a closed group when unemployment effectively offers no alternatives. In certain companies, employers may convey a form of community by establishing reciprocal relationships of gift exchange with workers (paternalism) (Akerlof, 1982; see also, Gallus et al., 2022). Thus, as we see, real-world labor markets may manifest a mix of the three types, namely, market, hierarchy, and reciprocity, contingent on specific situations. However, we recognize an epistemic convergence (though not an identity) between the views of observers and the views of agents, since, as we shall see, our analytical categories are grounded in foundational cognitive schemas (especially, kinesthetic image schemas) and metaphors that reveal the embodied nature of each type. This means that we can analyze the institutional action associated with a given type in terms of conceptual blends where a generic space representing a certain type of interaction is projected through which input spaces are matched. For example, paternalism in a company is often grounded in metaphorical uses of the kinship metaphor, treating the boss as a "father," which mobilizes related behaviors.

6.4.3 *Embodiment in Institutional Action*

In the following, we will look more closely at the community type, as we deal with the other types in the following subsections, the market type in the section on money, the reciprocity type in the section on property, and the hierarchy type in the section on labor. For the community type, it is essential to recognize that institutional action does not derive from the community as a social fact, but enacts it. This has become salient in recent anthropological debates about kinship as an elementary form of community (Sahlins, 2014; see also, McKinnon, 2005, p. 50ff). Kinship is not determined by given "natural" factors, but is enacted through the institutional action of sharing which expresses "dividual selves," and corresponds to our notion of We-mode. In the case of kinship, this means that even at this basic level, conceptual blends operate, such as treating someone as related by sharing food:

> If 'you are what you eat' – an inelegant paraphrasing of Brillat-Savarin – then those eating the same foods reproduce their individual bodies from the same substances and, together, create a shared social body. Those actually eating together perform their shared identity together, reinforcing bonds even more powerfully. Christ's words, 'take, eat, this is my body,' underlie the ritual through which Christians regularly reproduce the social body that is their congregation. Those who take the sacrament together become one body – the body of Christ. Eating from the same table – even the same plate or bowl – can express social solidarity, unity, and equality in subtle yet powerful ways. Families share food, but so do social clubs of myriad kinds. Eating together is a common means of team-building, from office parties to end-of-season sporting awards banquets. (West, 2021)

The institutional aspect of sharing food is thus more pronounced when one considers derived forms of community that metaphorically extend kinship, such as the institution of hospitality. In this case, the conceptual blend operates by treating a visitor as kin by sharing food with her (Fig. 6.5). We can immediately see the two movements of inward and outward embodiment at work: The cognitive operation of metaphor is outwardly embodied in the food given to the visitor, and eating in community inwardly embodies the trust as *vis-à-vis* kin.

For the community type, embodiment is accepted as a fact: People are socially related to each other through the physical connection of their bodies. This connection between bodies can occur in several ways, and we propose to explore some of them in light of the three main defining elements of the CONTAINER schema (Lakoff, 1987, p. 272): An interior (IN), an exterior (OUT), and a boundary (ON).

First and foremost, in Fiske's Communal Sharing (CS), people can share a bodily essence in common, as this relational model is constituted "primarily through consubstantial assimilation" (Fiske, 2004, p. 63). As explained, "consubstantial assimilation joins people indexically and enactively through the orifices and surfaces of their bodies, for example, by

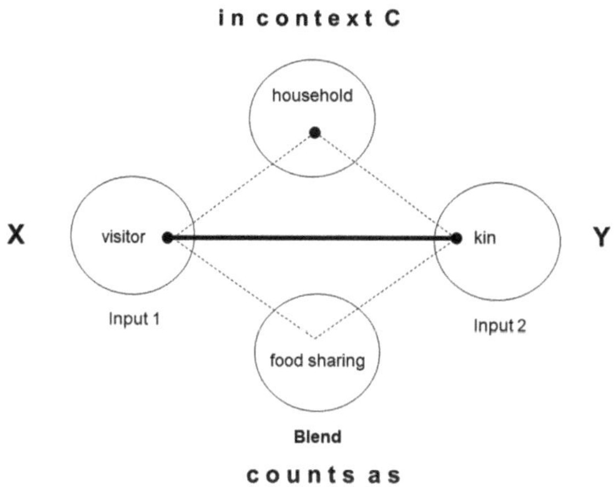

Fig. 6.5 In the institution of hospitality, the action of "food sharing" is a conceptual blend in which "visitors" are treated as "kin" by means of matching operation in the generic space "household." "Food sharing" creates a "community" relationship that extends the circumscription of "household" beyond blood ties

birth or commensalism," such as eating or drinking from a common source (Fiske, 2004, p. 63). Giving birth, which is literally a body coming out of another body, can be seen as a container coming out of another container. Likewise, when a mother breast-feeds her child, CS is generated by the transfer of a substance (breast milk) from one body to another body, that is, from what is inside one container to the inside of another container that connects them. A large number of ethnographic studies show that the connection of material bodies that nurtures CS also encompasses eating, drinking, and smoking similar things, or having sexual intercourse. Such connections involve an association with something that goes inside the body which is conceptualized as a three-dimensional container. From this perspective, the deep-seated association between food sharing and CS reinforces its interpretation in terms of the INTERIOR schema. Interestingly, hospitality, which is another way of creating and fostering CS as a relational mode, can also be understood in terms of the CONTAINER schema, since hospitality is welcoming someone to enter a container (one's home).

Consubstantial assimilation is associated with the concepts of contact (Tylor, 1871) and contagion (Frazer, 1890/2009), which describe mechanisms by which a physical connection conveys social meaning. Contact and contagion can refer to the BOUNDARY of the body. Body contact through carrying a baby, hugging, caressing, holding hands, and walking with arms around shoulders are several illustrations of situations that foster CS relationships across the world (Fiske, 2004, p. 83). What is on the surface of the body, such as shared body features (e.g., skin color, facial morphology) and "body modification, body marking, dress, hair, and adornment," is physically visible and may also contribute to defining people's group membership (Fiske, 2004, pp. 82–83).

The CONTAINER schema is characterized by a third dimension: EXTERIOR, which is what remains outside the body and does not even touch its boundary. For if what is accepted can be shared, what is rejected is also shared, and may specify a food or sex taboo (Fiske, 2004, p. 80). As elegantly summarized by Fiske (2004, p. 81), in CS,

> it is, specifically, the separation or intimacy of persons that is coded and constituted through their avoidance, acceptance, or active desire for contact with the substances coming from other persons' bodies. (Goffman, 1971, pp. 46–58; Rozin et al., 1989)

Symbolic contagion or contamination is strongly associated with CS, reflecting the importance of contact in economic life (e.g., Ayton et al., 2022; Kramer & Block, 2011). Social exclusion is a classic mechanism for reinforcing social groups (e.g., Williams et al., 2007). It turns out that many metaphors associated with social exclusion are about pain—pain is a social glue (Bastian et al., 2014), which may contribute to CS through shared hardship, but social exclusion is also physical pain as argued by the pain overlap theory (Eisenberger, 2015).[34]

Against this background, we argue that CS is directly meaningful to people because it can be understood largely as an experience of the CONTAINER schema. However, other schemas and additional embodied mechanisms, that differ from the CONTAINER schema, are also involved in the constitution of CS. For instance, in CS people can feel part of a whole (PART-WHOLE schema), and close to others (NEAR-FAR schema). Imitation and social coordination dynamics are other ways of constituting CS. As Fiske (2004, p. 63) observed, "synchronous rhythmic movement also connects participants through their mirrored motion in dance, ritual, and military drill." Imitation is also especially important in rites of passage.[35]

Fiske points out that food sharing occurs most often in the context of community, and less often in the other modes (Sahlins, 1972). However, as we have seen, food sharing can also enact relationships that hybridize community with other types (e.g., Gallus et al., 2022, p. 594).For instance, in Japanese business life, commensal eating (e.g., shared meals) is often essential to closing deals or cementing relationships (almost always) among men. In the ideal–typical Japanese company, shared drinking is essential for creating and maintaining a sense of community, although it is often seen as an individual burden, imposed by authority relations in the company (Hendry, 2019, pp. 207–213; see also, Dasgupta, 2013). When analyzing financial sector actors in the previous chapter, we also pointed to the importance of partying (e.g., drinking, taking drugs) in the social life of traders.

When it comes to reciprocity, we propose that Equality Matching (EM) is a relational model structured by the BALANCE schema (Gallus et al., 2022). Equality being an abstract concept, it is represented metaphorically. For instance, with respect to the "moral accounting metaphor," Lakoff and Johnson explain that "justice is the settling of accounts, which results in the balancing of the moral books" (Lakoff & Johnson, 1999, p. 296). Some metaphors extend beyond the BALANCE schema, as the literature has shown that equality is also metaphorically associated with horizontality, that is being on the same vertical level ("EQUALITY IS BEING ON THE SAME VERTICAL LEVEL").[36] As described by Fiske (2004, p. 63), several procedures are implemented to make equality concrete and can take various forms such as: "taking turns, flipping a coin, lining up on a starting line, voting, or distributing shares to participants with a one-to-one correspondence process."[37] These metaphors and procedures outwardly embody reciprocity.

Of course, reciprocity can be hybridized with other types. A famous case of associating reciprocity with the market type is Chinese *guanxi*, an elaborate ritual of exchanging gifts and mutual favors in which balance is only a reference point, since the mutual debt of doing favors, and thus the imbalance, is the cement that keeps the relationship stable in the long run (Herrmann-Pillath, 2017a, p. 364ff).[38] *Guanxi* is the social mechanism that sustains trust in the market and is grounded in specific forms of emotional commitment.[39] Indigenous theorizing reveals that *guanxi* is often seen as an open form of community, based on explicit forms of enacting shared identities, such as in various forms of associations, for example, native place associations.[40]

In terms of hierarchy, Authority Ranking (AR) relationships arrange people in terms of space, time, magnitude, and force:

> Higher rank is constituted by being above and in front, being more, coming earlier in time, and having greater 'power' or 'force.' This physics of social relations is iconic, creating social relations by metaphorically mapping people onto position, quantity, and temporal order. (Fiske, 2004, p. 63)

In this quote, "in front" and "coming earlier in time" convey the spatiality at play in time metaphors. TIME is more abstract than SPACE, and SPACE is commonly used to express TIME. For instance, in Western societies, TIME is commonly represented in front of people, as something that will unfold before their eyes, and people are considered at the back of those who came before (Lakoff & Johnson, 1980, 1999). "Above" expresses the verticality associated with hierarchy. This verticality is also conveyed by "being more" and "power" which respectively express the conventional metaphors MORE IS UP and POWER IS UP (Lakoff & Johnson, 1980), discussed in Chapter 4.

Needless to say, such metaphors are essential for understanding the existence of economic organizations in economic life. In addition to justifications in terms of transaction costs (Coase, 1937), opportunism (Williamson, 1985), or bounded rationality (Simon, 1979), which will be discussed in the next chapter, organizations could be analyzed as a by-product of our embodiment, namely our vertical experience of the world, as detailed by the UP/DOWN schema. We have already mentioned the paternalistic leadership model, which treats the organization as a "family," implying the authority relations in patriarchal societies.

In relation to the market relationship (Market Pricing), we have also mentioned the relevance of the RESOURCE schema, and as already discussed in Chapter 4, building on the embodied cognition literature, we disagree with Fiske's argument that the market relationship is "not embodied" by difference with the other types because it is characterized by the use of abstract and arbitrary symbols (Fiske et al., 2009). Beyond these points, the market relationship is a generic form that contains references to potential relations that are not yet realized or merely imagined: This is an abstraction, but the act of imagining remains embodied. Consider, for example, a "marriage market" in traditional societies compared to the modern equivalent of Internet dating platforms. In opportunity cost logic, an agent is faced with a realized or near-realized opportunity and compares it to a set of imagined alternatives. In Bourdieu's terms, then, the market relationship relates to the generic notion of field as defining the set of potential alternative opportunities. To understand embodiment in this relationship, we cannot only refer to outward embodiment as we have done so far but must also explicitly consider inward embodiment. This is salient when considering the artifact of money, which becomes inwardly embodied. Hence, marriage markets may be explicitly constituted by monetary transactions, so that money shapes relationships in an inwardly embodied way. By comparison, although the services of the dating platform are paid for, there is no direct exchange of money in the transactions between users. It is highly significant that societies manifest diverse institutional and normative regimes in regulating these forms of embodiment, effectively establishing boundaries between market and community modes—epitomized by poles such as prostitution versus romantic love (Zelizer, 1997).

Another example is our case of financial traders in Chapter 5. The community relationship plays an important role in establishing the identity of financial market actors, and undergirds certain patterns of trust formation. For example, market action can sometimes crucially involve sharing (not only of information), but also direct reciprocity in carrying out certain transactions ("helping hands"), with a distinct institutionalized form, "market making," which involves the recognition of certain actors as leaders of the trader community. The community is institutionalized through distinct forms of embeddedness, often involving direct physical contact, such as at parties, but also, as described above, via the communication of emotions and metaphors related to physical contact (sex, battle, etc.). These observations point to the pervasive role of communities in markets, such as ethnic traders, exclusive elite circles (like the notorious golf club meeting), and so on. As said, reciprocity is an important building block of trust among financial traders. It is a key aspect of all kinds of "deal making," which is often seen as fostering more enduring patterns of interaction among actors. Some of these patterns involve status distinctions, that is, hierarchy. The financial market is openly hierarchical, as is evident, for example, in the status order among underwriters in IPO operations.

6.5 Conclusion

As in the example of financial markets, most economists claim that the market is abstract, or that the optimal state of market design is to enable abstraction via institutions, resulting in a scenario in which humans operate under a regime of prices generated by the market as a giant computational system. Ultimately, this implies that markets could even operate without humans, as in software-driven financial market operations. This view conceals a fundamental paradox: Even if institutions are designed to support abstraction, they themselves remain embodied, and abstraction is only possible through embodied mechanisms. This is what we will develop in great detail in the subsequent chapter, starting with the institution of money. Money is the key force of abstraction in the economy, yet explaining these powers and how they impact other institutions, requires the full analytical arsenal of embodied economics.

The standard treatment of institutions in economics supports a disembodied view, although the so-called "old institutionalists" such as Veblen and Commons had prepared the ground for an embodied economics perspective. As we will see in the next chapter, the move towards disembodiment in the so-called "New Institutional Economics" has led to very problematic views of people as economic actors that have caused, and continue to cause, harm to people, such as in the context of the organization of companies, and the design of work environments. The design of institutions based on a disembodied economic theory always and necessarily tends to see what is "human" as a disturbance and a negative factor in the operation of the economic computer of the market.

Embodied economics has far-reaching practical implications because a key aspect of our view of institutions is the role of power. Accordingly, embodied economics is Political Economy: There is no such thing as an institution without power relations. Indeed, to envision institutions without power (or counterpower) would be another kind of abstraction (from states and capitalist markets) (Graeber, 2004, p. 24ff). Recognizing the essential role of power means that embodied economics always approaches institutions with a critical eye that first, makes power explicit, and second, asks for justifications of existing power relationships and invites critical discourse on how to subject power to political practices which ensures that power is a social means for human flourishing in dignity. In the final chapter of this book, we will present views on a concrete institutional utopia that fulfills this criterion. In this chapter, we have developed the analytical tools that we will now apply to the key institutions of capitalism as it emerged as a Hegelian institutional totality in the nineteenth century, money, property, and labor.

Notes

1. Interestingly, this is implied in Hegel's approach which has been dubbed "conceptual realism" that follows from his notion of "spirit" (Stern, 2008). Yet, Hegel's dialectic also means that without becoming manifest in action, institutions would remain only virtual in modern parlance.
2. The term "field" is a key concept in Bourdieu's (2019) sociology where it defines a domain of social struggle over relative positions and meanings. In Bourdieu's parlance: "A field consists of a set of objective, historical relations between positions anchored in certain forms of power (or capital), while habitus consists of a set of historical relations 'deposited' within individual bodies in the form of mental and corporeal schemata of perception, appreciation, and action" (Bourdieu & Wacquant, 1992, p. 16). A related approach has been developed by Fligstein and McAdam (2012), who explicitly recognize the similarity. Although there are many related concepts, such as "games," "networks," and so on, we prefer "field" as this is less ambiguous, and is clearly a meso-level concept that fits the observation that institutional actions rarely encompass entire societies, as in some totalitarian theocracies. It also allows us to focus our analysis of institutions on markets as fields. One difference between Fligstein and McAdam's view and Bourdieu's is that the former emphasizes "strategic collective action," which is only one type of institutional action.
3. For the intellectual and cultural background of this view, see Lane (1992). However, economics also transformed Jevons' original psychological identification between pain and disutility into the abstract notion of opportunity cost, conceived as lost leisure time, as Spencer (2009, p. 69ff) has shown in detail. Interestingly, leisure remains an embodied notion, whereas the opportunity cost of leisure is measured as lost income from work. This neutralizes the quality of work in terms of its psychological effects.

4. This is especially true of Thorstein Veblen (1899/2007), who famously defined institutions as "habits of thought," and anticipated some aspects of Bourdieu's notion of habitus. Despite their differences, the two thinkers are linked by their interest in expressions of social status.
5. In his later work, North placed even more emphasis on ideas such as cognitive schemata, which seems closer to the notion of symbolic capital (North, 2005).
6. This question is of great actual significance, after the "end of history" proclaimed with the collapse of socialist planned economies, resulting in the perception that only capitalism remains as a viable economic system (Milanović, 2019). This would mean that the wider social consequences of capitalism, that we scrutinize as disembodiment, would also prevail, as in Tönnies' analyses. The plurality of society would require either "caging" capitalism in an independent domain, or envisioning a non-capitalist economy, as we advocate.
7. Note that while we use both Searle's and Lakoff and Johnson's approaches as complementary in the context of this book, we are conscious of some of the theoretical oppositions that structure their approaches. One of them, as Lakoff and Johnson (1999, p. 122) note, is that Searle is a literalist: "Aristotle, the father of the traditional theory, was a literalist, as is John Searle, whose version of speech-act theory requires all propositions, that is, anything that can be true, to be literal." Likewise, Lakoff (1993) noted that, for Searle, metaphors cannot express truth, and he assumes that conventional language is not metaphorical, but literal. That said, these differences do not mean that Searle neglects the role of embodiment, as illustrated by the concept of Background (and its connection to habitus), which "consists of all of those abilities, capacities, dispositions, ways of doing things, and general know-how that enable us to carry out our intentions and apply our intentional states generally" (Searle, 2011, p. 31).
8. For a concise account, see Searle (2005). As argued in the literature: "It can be found that Searle's concept of status function of institutional facts has become a symbolic capital for Bourdieu; giving an entity the status function is to create the possibility for this entity" (Kuang, 2018, p. 168). However, the status function is more about the action that produces symbolic capital.

9. For example, Smit and colleagues (2011) argue that money is not created by a status function but generalizes over evolved practices, basically following Menger's evolutionary account. A key point of dissent is that Searle's assumption of collective intentionality is at odds with methodological individualism. Hindriks and Guala (2015) claim that all constitutive rules can be reduced to regulative rules.
10. For rare dissenting views, see, for instance, Lawson (2019).
11. As a representative position, see Stekeler-Weithofer (2011), as he refers to Tomasello's (2019) comparative approach to ontogeny, which provides strong empirical support for the Hegelian view on the objectification of sociality. This is no surprise, as Tomasello (2019) labels his theory "neo-Vygotskian," and Vygotsky's work can be traced back to Hegel and Marx (e.g., Friedrich, 2014, p. 53ff; Sève, 2021; Sawyer & Stetsenko, 2018; Stetsenko, 2017, p. 115).
12. Likewise, Bourdieu argues that: "*Homo economicus*, as conceived (tacitly or explicitly) by economic orthodoxy, is a kind of anthropological monster: this theoretically minded man of practice is the most extreme personification of the scholastic fallacy, an intellectualist or intellectualocentric error very common in the social sciences (particularly in linguistics and ethnology), by which the scholar puts into the heads of the agents he is studying – housewives or households, firms or entrepreneurs, et cetera – the theoretical considerations and constructions he has had to develop in order to account for their practices" (Bourdieu, 2005, p. 83).
13. The need to make rationality salient was made a methodological principle of economic experiments by Smith (1976). This is a defining difference between economic and psychological experiments (see Tyler & Amodio, 2015). Böhme (2016) is an ethnographic account of the disciplinary measures taken to ensure that participants play the game "right." As Miroswki points out: "In the laboratory, Smith takes great precautions to render his subjects as close to neoclassical agents as inhumanly possible: reservation prices and costs are imposed; controls are exerted so that the subjects both know and concentrate upon the data that the experimenter deems relevant; 'strict privacy' means that social interaction and communicative interchange is reduced to the stark minimum; if the rules are violated the data are discarded; subjects are schooled

in the protocols of machinelike behavior by being run through preparatory conditioning sessions on the workstations. Once you understand everything that is involved with the imposition of Smith's experimental protocols, it seems more than a little disingenuous then to bemoan that it is 'imperfectly understood' the ways in which these experimental markets 'induce individual rationality.' These experiments don't test neoclassical theory (as Smith sometimes will admit); they try and impose mechanical rationality upon subjects who might not otherwise display it" (Mirowski, 2001, p. 549). See also, Dhami (2016, p. 48ff).

14. See also, Camerer (2011); and see contra, Binmore (2005).
15. We note, however, that mathematical game theory can accommodate this in the famous "folk theorem," which states that in infinitely repeated games any kind of equilibrium emerges as "rational solution." This still leaves open the question of why in real life, even over long-time horizons, a specific solution emerges and is sustained (Skyrms, 2006; see also, Binmore, 2006).
16. In a series of experimental studies followed by interviews with participants, Parks and Stone (2010) investigated the reasons why group members who behaved fairly in a public good game experiment expelled unselfish members, that is, members who contributed much to the provision of the good but then used little of the good. Although this seems "irrational" from the standard economic model, they show that it can be explained by social comparison and normative reasons, demonstrating the importance of social mechanisms that underpin actors' decisions in economic games. In terms of social comparison, unselfish group-regarding individuals merely make fair actors lose face (e.g., "No one else is doing what he does. He makes us all look bad"). Moreover, these overly generous individuals violate social norms for the situation in a negative way that justifies their exclusion (e.g., "It's strange for someone to keep giving and not take much in return. If you give a lot you should use a lot").
17. It is not excluded that even if participants said something along these lines, it would not be taken into account: "Many experiments in economics use a post-experimental questionnaire where participants are asked to introspect as to why they made the decisions they made. But economists are very cautious when reporting and interpreting this data, and always ask these questions *after* they have

collected the actual (real-money) decisions of interest. The perception is that responses to questions like this are 'cheap talk' and may have no relation to what is actually in the minds of experimental participants" (Croson, 2005, p. 135).

18. For further discussion, see Guala (2005, p. 133), who argues that: "In fact, money or financial incentives are never mentioned in the precepts [of experimental economics]. The principles state only in abstract terms what kind of properties an appropriate reward medium should have but do not say what the medium should be." This means that, in his view, experimental economics could theoretically be done without monetary incentives, although this is not conventional practice. In his view, the use of payoffs might have been inherited from the very fact that: "The pioneers of experimental economics faced the problem of distinguishing their work from the research carried out in neighbor disciplines" (Guala, 2005, p. 232). Ironically, monetary incentives were introduced into experimental studies in the late 1950s and early 1960s by psychologists such as Sidney Siegel (see Smith, 2008, p. 174ff).
19. For an example, see Galizzi and Navarro-Martinez's (2019, p. 976) findings: "We present a lab-field experiment designed to systematically assess the external validity of social preferences elicited in a variety of experimental games. We do this by comparing behavior in the different games with several behaviors elicited in the field and with self-reported behaviors exhibited in the past, using the same sample of participants. Our results show that the experimental social preference games do a poor job explaining both social behaviors in the field and social behaviors from the past."
20. Building on Aoki (2001), the first version of the model was presented in Aoki (2011).
21. This is represented by Aoki in earlier versions of his approach (Aoki, 2001, p. 26), which resonates with Greif (1994), or "shared mental models" (Denzau & North, 1994). The problem is that institutions, such as wage labor, are rarely approached in the same way by various actors, hence the widespread and perennial social conflicts over institutions.
22. The first 2.0 version was presented in Herrmann-Pillath (2012) and further developed in Herrmann-Pillath (2017b). Aoki himself appreciated this as a "neo-Hegelian" interpretation, see Takizawa (2017).

23. This also requires going beyond standard models in economics: "I am going to suggest in this paper that market-based explanations will tend to predict that racial discrimination will be eliminated. Since they are not, we must seek elsewhere for non-market factors influencing economic behavior. The concepts of direct social interaction and networks seem to be good places to start" (Arrow, 1998, p. 93). See also May (2006) on the rationalization of gender discrimination and inequality through the logic of the market in mainstream economics.
24. As Harré explains, Moscovici "drew on and transformed a fundamental idea of the sociologist Émile Durkheim, the idea of a social representation, a shared body of knowledge that shaped the way the members of a community interacted with one another. According to this approach, active agents used social representations as a resource to accomplish their projects and to manage the affairs of everyday life. This approach injected a strong cultural element into psychology" (Harré, 2006, p. 190). In other words: "People share a social representation when each member of the social group in question holds a similar belief to every other member. Ironically a social representation is a special case of an individual representation, in which all the individual representations in a group are similar. As a result of sharing in this sense, a group of people displays a common pattern of belief, and a common reaction to situations and people" (Harré, 2006, p. 217). See also Jovchelovitch (2019), Lahlou (2017), and O'Connor (2017).
25. Racism is one of the most striking forms of oppression, which is defined as a situation in which "groups of people have unequal power (oppression as a state) and the more dominant groups use their power to exert violence on, exploit, marginalize, deny equal rights from, and inferiorize the dominated groups (oppression as a process)" (David et al., 2019, p. 1058). It is important to note that racism, and more largely oppression, "does not exist if there are no power and privilege inequalities between people" (David et al., 2019, p. 1058). Racial oppression is then intrinsically linked to (the existence of unequal) power. David and colleagues (2019, pp. 1059–1060) observe that studies of internalized racial oppression show that racism exists and operates not only in interpersonal interactions and institutions (in an outwardly embodied way, in

our parlance), but also "within people" at the internalized level (in an inwardly embodied way), as postcolonial scholars argued several decades ago (e.g., Fanon, 1961/1965; Freire, 1968/1970; Memmi, 1957/1965).

26. This can be related to the "construal" debates concerning the interpretation of results in behavioral economics, such as those of Kahneman & Tversky surveyed in Chapter 2. Basically, the idea is that participants in an experiment can have "alternative task construals" as claimed by "theorists who resist interpreting the gap between normative and descriptive models as indicating human irrationality:" In essence, "the alternative task construal argument places the blame at least somewhat on the shoulders of the experimenter for failing to realize that there were task features that might lead subjects to frame the problem in a manner different from that intended" (Stanovich & West, 2000, p. 655; see also, Dhami, 2016, p. 1426ff). The argument we develop goes beyond this view, which neglects the role of embodiment.
27. As Bourdieu explained, symbolic capital is the form that economic, social, or cultural capital "takes when it is grasped through categories of perception that recognize its specific logic or, if you prefer, misrecognize the arbitrariness of its possession and accumulation" (Bourdieu & Wacquant, 1992, p. 119).
28. We discussed some of the cognitive origins of habitus, and some of its links with embodiment theory in Chapter 4.
29. Although they later abandoned their initial typology because all metaphors more or less cover all three dimensions at once, Lakoff and Johnson (1980) identified three different types of metaphors: Ontological, orientational, and structural. Ontological metaphors encompass anthropomorphism. See also Epley and colleagues (2007, p. 867) on conceptual metaphors and (so-called) "weak" anthropomorphism.
30. The founder of the Chinese special economic zone and later megacity of Shenzhen, Yuang Geng, is famously quoted with the slogan "Time is money, efficiency is life" as a motto for this place. One of the authors (CHP) visited the new museum of the history of Shenzhen in the place of origin, Shekou. In the entrance area, there was an amazing installation, showing the slogan hanging over an arrangement of major company logos, with the giant painting of Mao Zedong in Beijing's Tiananmen Square in the background.

31. See also Favre and Sornette (2013) for a mathematical demonstration that there are only four relational models. See contra, Bolender (2010, p. 104ff) who identified a potential fifth relational model, called "oceanic merging," which is associated with a fifth type of relation and with logarithmic scales, although they "do not appear to have any natural or spontaneous social application."
32. There are, of course, some cultural exceptions to this principle. It is usually assumed that parents "gave birth" to their children, and therefore children cannot choose their parents. However, there are societies in which children have much more autonomy. For instance, anthropologists report that in some societies children can choose to live with another family: "The Iñupiaq even speak of childbirth in such terms; rather than the mother 'giving birth,' the child 'takes life.' Children are said to choose to be born. Adoption is also very common among the Iñupiaq, with children moving between natal families either because they want to (much like the seven-year-old who went to his grandparents) or because one family has lots of girls and no boys – so they swap" (Engelke, 2018, p. 146).
33. Fiske (2004, p. 127ff) is quite clear about this when it comes to relational models. See also, for instance, Gallus and colleagues (2022).
34. In support of embodied cognition, and more specifically conceptual metaphor theory, social neuroscience shows that social exclusion is associated with aversive emotions related to physical pain. That is, something as abstract as social pain is expressed in a concrete way through physical pain. Pain overlap theory suggests that physical and social pain share common neural and psychological underpinnings (Eisenberger, 2012; Eisenberger & Lieberman, 2004). For instance, people report similar levels of experienced pain regardless of whether the recalled past episodes involve physical or social pain (Chen et al., 2008; Riva et al., 2011). Consistently, recalling but also inducing physical pain—by asking people to immerse their hand in cold water—and social pain—by asking people to play the Cyberball Game (Williams & Jarvis, 2006) in which they are actively socially excluded by the other two players—decrease feelings of self-esteem and control, and similarly increase negative affect and the desire to aggress (Riva et al., 2011). At the neural level, when it comes to physical pain, neuroscientific

studies have shown that activity in the primary (S1) and secondary (S2) somatosensory cortices is associated with the sensory aspects of pain (e.g., Bushnell et al., 1999; Treede et al., 1999), whereas activity in the anterior insula and dorsal anterior cingulate cortex (dACC) is associated with the affective components of pain (e.g., Rainville et al., 1997; Shackman et al., 2011; Wiech et al., 2010). Social pain leads to increased activity in the anterior insula and dACC, which has been interpreted as evidence in favor of the pain overlap theory (Eisenberger, 2012; Kross et al., 2011). In support of this interpretation, physical and social pain also appears to be associated with activity in somatosensory brain systems (e.g., thalamus, S2, opercular insular region, dorsal posterior insula) (Eisenberger, 2015). See also Ferris and colleagues (2019) for an analysis of functional overlap and divergence between social and physical pain.

35. "People act like those with whom they identify, reproducing their actions as a way of becoming like them. Identity is expressed and enhanced when an individual reproduces the earlier actions of another. A stronger identification results when the imitation is mutual, synchronous, and rhythmic" (Fiske, 2004, pp. 84–85).
36. *MetaNet Wiki*. (n.d.). Frame: Equality. Retrieved July 14, 2023, from https://metaphor.icsi.berkeley.edu/pub/en/index.php/Frame:Equality
37. Fiske also draws on Piaget's concept of "concrete operations" which are obviously embodied as "manipulative procedures for assessing physical properties such as mass, volume, or number and are used by children for judging equality or inequality. Such procedures include aligning objects in one-to-one correspondence arrays, juxtaposing solids to see if their lengths match, and comparing the height of liquids poured into containers" (Fiske, 2004, pp. 103–104).
38. Beyond the specifics of *guanxi*, the imbalances at the heart of gift-giving can be analyzed in several ways. As Mauss explained, the three themes of the gift are "the obligation to give, the obligation to receive and reciprocate" (Mauss, 1925/1990, p. 50), which means that there is no such thing as a free gift. The reciprocity associated with the gift conveys a relation of solidarity, but it can also turn out to be the expression of a form of superiority in a relationship. Indeed, the larger the gift, the larger the debt, which means

that a gift can actually be an instrument of control and domination (Godelier, 1996/1999), as already pointed out in Chapter 2. On the dark side of the gift, see also Godbout and Caillé (1998) and Sherry and colleagues (1993).

39. Again, beyond *guanxi*, the gift economy can be viewed as complementary to, and not necessarily an alternative to, the market (e.g., Titmuss, 1970): "The gift cycle echoes Adam Smith's invisible hand: gift complements market in so far as it operates where the latter is absent" (Douglas, p. xviii in Mauss, 1925/1990).
40. See Herrmann-Pillath (2017a, p. 370ff) which cites Chinese research, especially the work of sociologists Fei Xiaotong and Zhai Xuewei. On Fei specifically, see Herrmann-Pillath (2016a).

References

Akerlof, G. A. (1982). Labor contracts as partial gift exchange. *The Quarterly Journal of Economics, 97*(4), 543–569. https://doi.org/10.2307/1885099

Anderson, E. (2019). *Private government: How employers rule our lives (and why we don't talk about it)*. Princeton University Press.

Aoki, M. (2001). *Toward a comparative institutional analysis*. MIT Press.

Aoki, M. (2011). Institutions as cognitive media between strategic interactions and individual beliefs. *Journal of Economic Behavior & Organization, 79*(1), 20–34. https://doi.org/10.1016/j.jebo.2011.01.025

Arrow, K. J. (1998). What has economics to say about racial discrimination? *Journal of Economic Perspectives, 12*(2), 91–100. https://doi.org/10.1257/jep.12.2.91

Ayton, P., Weiss-Cohen, L., & Barson, M. (2022). Magical contagion and commemorative plaques: Effects of celebrity occupancy on property values. *Journal of Environmental Psychology, 79*, 101723. https://doi.org/10.1016/j.jenvp.2021.101723

Banerjee, S. B. (2022). Decolonizing deliberative democracy: Perspectives from below. *Journal of Business Ethics, 181*(2), 283–299. https://doi.org/10.1007/s10551-021-04971-5

Bastian, B., Jetten, J., & Ferris, L. J. (2014). Pain as social glue—Shared pain increases cooperation. *Psychological Science, 25*(11), 0956797614545886. https://doi.org/10.1177/0956797614545886

Binmore, K. (2005). Economic man—Or straw man? *Behavioral and Brain Sciences, 28*(6), 817–818. https://doi.org/10.1017/S0140525X05230145

Binmore, K. (2006). Natural justice: Response to comments. *Analyse & Kritik, 28*(1), 111–117. https://doi.org/10.1515/auk-2006-0113
Binmore, K. (2007). *Economic man—Or straw man? A Commentary on Henrich et al.* https://discovery.ucl.ac.uk/id/eprint/14437/1/14437.pdf
Binmore, K. (2011). *Natural justice.* Oxford University Press.
Böhme, J. (2016). "Doing" laboratory experiments: An Ethnomethodological study of the performative practice in behavioral economic research. In I. Boldyrev & E. Svetlova (Eds.), *Enacting dismal science* (pp. 87–108). Palgrave Macmillan US. https://doi.org/10.1057/978-1-137-48876-3_4
Boldyrev, I., & Svetlova, E. (Eds.). (2016). *Enacting dismal science: New perspectives on the performativity of economics.* Palgrave Macmillan US.
Bolender, J. (2010). *The self-organizing social mind.* MIT Press.
Bourdieu, P. (1979). Symbolic power. *Critique of Anthropology, 4*(13–14), 77–85. https://doi.org/10.1177/0308275X7900401307
Bourdieu, P. (1986). The force of law: Toward a sociology of the juridical field. *Hastings Law Journal, 38*(5), 814–854.
Bourdieu, P. (1987). The historical genesis of a pure aesthetic. *The Journal of Aesthetics and Art Criticism, 46*, 201–210. https://doi.org/10.2307/431276
Bourdieu, P. (1990). Time perspectives of the Kabyle. In J. Hassard (Ed.), *The sociology of time* (pp. 219–237). Palgrave Macmillan UK. https://doi.org/10.1007/978-1-349-20869-2_15
Bourdieu, P. (1982/1991). *Language and symbolic power.* Polity Press.
Bourdieu, P. (1994/1998). *Practical reason: On the theory of action.* Stanford University Press.
Bourdieu, P. (1997/2000). *Pascalian meditations.* Stanford University Press.
Bourdieu, P. (2005). Principles of an economic anthropology. In N. J. Smelser & R. Swedberg (Eds.), *The handbook of economic sociology* (2nd ed., pp. 75–89). Princeton University Press. https://doi.org/10.1515/9781400835584.75
Bourdieu, P. (2019). *Sociologie générale.* Éditions Points.
Bourdieu, P., & Wacquant, L. J. D. (1992). *An invitation to reflexive sociology.* University of Chicago Press. https://press.uchicago.edu/ucp/books/book/chicago/I/bo3649674.html
Bowles, S. (2008). Policies designed for self-interested citizens may undermine "the moral sentiments": Evidence from economic experiments. *Science, 320*(5883), 1605–1609. https://doi.org/10.1126/science.1152110
Bowles, S., & Polanía-Reyes, S. (2012). Economic incentives and social preferences: Substitutes or complements? *Journal of Economic Literature, 50*(2), 368–425. https://doi.org/10.1257/jel.50.2.368
Bushnell, M. C., Duncan, G. H., Hofbauer, R. K., Ha, B., Chen, J.-I., & Carrier, B. (1999). Pain perception: Is there a role for primary somatosensory cortex?

Proceedings of the National Academy of Sciences, 96(14), 7705–7709. https://doi.org/10.1073/pnas.96.14.7705

Callon, M., & Roth, A. E. (2021). The design and performation of markets: A discussion. *AMS Review, 11*(3–4), 219–239. https://doi.org/10.1007/s13162-021-00216-w

Camerer, C. F. (2011). *Behavioral game theory: Experiments in strategic interaction*. Princeton University Press.

Chen, Z., Williams, K. D., Fitness, J., & Newton, N. C. (2008). When hurt will not heal: Exploring the capacity to relive social and physical pain. *Psychological Science, 19*(8), 789–795. https://doi.org/10.1111/j.1467-9280.2008.02158.x

Coase, R. H. (1937). The nature of the firm. *Economica, 4*(16), 386–405. https://doi.org/10.1111/j.1468-0335.1937.tb00002.x

Croson, R. (2005). The method of experimental economics. *International Negotiation, 10*(1), 131–148. https://doi.org/10.1163/1571806054741100

Dasgupta, R. (2013). *Re-reading the salaryman in Japan: Crafting masculinities*. Routledge.

David, E. J. R., Schroeder, T. M., & Fernandez, J. (2019). Internalized racism: A systematic review of the psychological literature on racism's most insidious consequence. *Journal of Social Issues, 75*(4), 1057–1086. https://doi.org/10.1111/josi.12350

De Moor, T. (2015). The dilemma of the commoners: Understanding the use of common-pool resources in long-term perspective. *Cambridge University Press*. https://doi.org/10.1017/CBO9781139135450

Denzau, A. T., & North, D. C. (1994). Shared mental models: Ideologies and institutions. *Kyklos, 47*(1), 3–31. https://doi.org/10.1111/j.1467-6435.1994.tb02246.x

DeVoe, S. E., & Pfeffer, J. (2010). The stingy hour: How accounting for time affects volunteering. *Personality and Social Psychology Bulletin, 36*(4), 470–483. https://doi.org/10.1177/0146167209359699

Dhami, S. (2016). *The foundations of behavioral economic analysis*. Oxford University Press.

Dietz, T., Ostrom, E., & Stern, P. C. (2003). The struggle to govern the commons. *Science, 302*(5652), 1907–1912. https://doi.org/10.1126/science.1091015

Earle, T. (2017). Property in prehistory. In M. Graziadei & L. Smith (Eds.), *Comparative property law. A global perspective* (pp. 3–25). Edward Elgar Publishing. https://doi.org/10.4337/9781785369162.00008

Eisenberger, N. I. (2012). The pain of social disconnection: Examining the shared neural underpinnings of physical and social pain. *Nature Reviews Neuroscience, 13*(6), 421–434. https://doi.org/10.1038/nrn3231

Eisenberger, N. I. (2015). Social pain and the brain: Controversies, questions, and where to go from here. *Annual Review of Psychology, 66*(1), 601–629. https://doi.org/10.1146/annurev-psych-010213-115146
Eisenberger, N. I., & Lieberman, M. D. (2004). Why rejection hurts: A common neural alarm system for physical and social pain. *Trends in Cognitive Sciences, 8*(7), 294–300. https://doi.org/10.1016/j.tics.2004.05.010
Elster, J. (2015). *Explaining social behavior: More nuts and bolts for the social sciences* (Revised edition). Cambridge University Press.
Engelke, M. (2018). *How to think like an anthropologist*. Princeton University Press.
Epley, N., Waytz, A., & Cacioppo, J. T. (2007). On seeing human: A three-factor theory of anthropomorphism. *Psychological Review, 114*(4), 864–886. https://doi.org/10.1037/0033-295X.114.4.864
Escobar, A. (2018). *Designs for the pluriverse: Radical interdependence, autonomy, and the making of worlds*. Duke University Press.
Fanon, F. (1961/1965). *The wretched of the earth*. Grove.
Farr, R. M., & Moscovici, S. (Eds.). (1984). *Social representations*. Cambridge University Press.
Favre, M., & Sornette, D. (2013). Categorization of exchange fluxes explains the four relational models. *SSRN Electronic Journal*. https://doi.org/10.2139/ssrn.2371238
Feher, M. (2009). Self-appreciation; or, the aspirations of human capital. *Public Culture, 21*(1), 21–41. https://doi.org/10.1215/08992363-2008-019
Ferris, L. J., Jetten, J., Hornsey, M. J., & Bastian, B. (2019). Feeling hurt: Revisiting the relationship between social and physical pain. *Review of General Psychology, 23*(3), 320–335. https://doi.org/10.1177/1089268019857936
Fiske, A. P. (1992). The four elementary forms of sociality: Framework for a unified theory of social relations. *Psychological Review, 99*(4), 689–723. https://doi.org/10.1037/0033-295X.99.4.689
Fiske, A. P. (2004). Four modes of constituting relationships: Consubstantial assimilation; space, magnitude, time, and force; concrete procedures; abstract symbolism. In N. Haslam (Ed.), *Relational models theory: A contemporary overview* (pp. 61–146).
Fiske, A. P., Thomsen, L., & Thein, S. M. (2009). Differently embodying different relationships. *European Journal of Social Psychology, 39*(7), 1294–1297. https://doi.org/10.1002/ejsp.697
Fligstein, N., & McAdam, D. (2012). *A theory of fields*. Oxford University Press.
Foucault, M., Ewald, F., Fontana, A., & Senellart, M. (2004). *Naissance de la biopolitique: Cours au Collège de France, 1978–1979*. Gallimard /Seuil.
Fourcade, M., Ollion, E., & Algan, Y. (2015). The superiority of economists. *Journal of Economic Perspectives, 29*(1), 89–114. https://doi.org/10.1257/jep.29.1.89

Frank, R. H. (1988). *Passions within reason: The strategic role of the emotions*. Norton.

Frazer, J. G. (1890/2009). *The golden bough: A study in magic and religion*. Oxford University Press.

Freire, P. (1968/1970). *Pedagogy of the oppressed*. Continuum.

Friedrich, J. (2014). Vygotsky's idea of psychological tools. In A. Yasnitsky, M. Ferrari, & R. van der Veer (Eds.), *The Cambridge handbook of cultural-historical psychology* (pp. 47–62). Cambridge University Press. https://doi.org/10.1017/CBO9781139028097.004

Galizzi, M. M., & Navarro-Martinez, D. (2019). On the external validity of social preference games: A systematic lab-field study. *Management Science, 65*(3), 976–1002. https://doi.org/10.1287/mnsc.2017.2908

Gallus, J., Reiff, J., Kamenica, E., & Fiske, A. P. (2022). Relational incentives theory. *Psychological Review, 129*(3), 586–602. https://doi.org/10.1037/rev0000336

Gebauer, G. (2017). *Wittgenstein's anthropological philosophy*. Springer International Publishing. https://doi.org/10.1007/978-3-319-56151-6

Gebauer, G., & William, J. M. (2000). Habitus, intentionality, and social rules: A controversy between Searle and Bourdieu. *SubStance, 29*(3), 68–83. https://doi.org/10.1353/sub.2000.0033

Godbout, J., & Caillé, A. (1998). *The world of the gift*. McGill-Queen's Press-MQUP.

Godelier, M. (1996/1999). *The enigma of the gift*. University of Chicago Press.

Goffman, E. (1971). *Relations in public: Microstudies of the public order*. Basic Books.

Graeber, D. (2004). *Fragments of an anarchist anthropology*. Prickly Paradigm Press.

Graziadei, M. (2017). The structure of property ownership and the common law/civil law divide. In M. Graziadei & L. Smith (Eds.), *Comparative property law. A global perspective* (pp. 71–99). Edward Elgar Publishing. https://doi.org/10.4337/9781785369162.00012

Greif, A. (1994). Cultural beliefs and the organization of society: A historical and theoretical reflection on collectivist and individualist societies. *Journal of Political Economy, 102*(5), 912–950.

Guala, F. (2005). *The methodology of experimental economics*. Cambridge University Press.

Guala, F. (2016). *Understanding institutions: The science and philosophy of living together*. Princeton University Press.

Güth, W., & Kocher, M. G. (2014). More than thirty years of ultimatum bargaining experiments: Motives, variations, and a survey of the recent literature. *Journal of Economic Behavior & Organization, 108*, 396–409. https://doi.org/10.1016/j.jebo.2014.06.006

Harré, R. (2006). *Key thinkers in psychology*. SAGE.
Harris, M. (1979). *Cultural materialism: The struggle for a science of culture*. Random House.
Harrison, G. W., & List, J. A. (2004). Field experiments. *Journal of Economic Literature, 42*(4), 1009–1055.
Hendry, J. (2019). *Understanding Japanese society* (5th ed.). Routledge Taylor & Francis Group.
Henrich, J., Boyd, R., Bowles, S., Camerer, C., Fehr, E., Gintis, H., McElreath, R., Alvard, M., Barr, A., Ensminger, J., Henrich, N. S., Hill, K., Gil-White, F., Gurven, M., Marlowe, F. W., Patton, J. Q., & Tracer, D. (2005). "Economic man" in cross-cultural perspective: Behavioral experiments in 15 small-scale societies. *Behavioral and Brain Sciences, 28*(6), 795–815. https://doi.org/10.1017/S0140525X05000142
Herrmann-Pillath, C. (2012). Institutions, distributed cognition and agency: Rule-following as performative action. *Journal of Economic Methodology, 19*(1), 21–42. https://doi.org/10.1080/1350178X.2012.661066
Herrmann-Pillath, C. (2013). *Foundations of economic evolution: A treatise on the natural philosophy of economics*. Edward Elgar.
Herrmann-Pillath, C. (2016a). Fei Xiaotong's comparative theory of chinese culture: Its relevance for contemporary cross-disciplinary research on Chinese "collectivism". *The Copenhagen Journal of Asian Studies, 34*(1), 25–57. https://doi.org/10.22439/cjas.v34i1.5187
Herrmann-Pillath, C. (2016b). Performative mechanisms. In I. Boldyrev & E. Svetlova (Eds.), *Enacting dismal science* (pp. 53–86). Palgrave Macmillan US. https://doi.org/10.1057/978-1-137-48876-3_3
Herrmann-Pillath, C. (2017a). *China's economic culture: The ritual order of state and markets*. Routledge.
Herrmann-Pillath, C. (2017b). Institutional naturalism: Reflections on Masahiko Aoki's contribution to institutional economics. *Evolutionary and Institutional Economics Review, 14*(2), 501–522. https://doi.org/10.1007/s40844-016-0037-2
Herrmann-Pillath, C. (2019). Creating social ontology: On the performative nature of economic experiments. In T. Kawagoe & H. Takizawa (Eds.), *Diversity of experimental methods in economics* (pp. 185–203). Springer Singapore. https://doi.org/10.1007/978-981-13-6065-7_10
Herrmann-Pillath, C., & Hederer, C. (2023). *A new principles of economics: The science of markets*. Routledge.
Hicks, J. (1969). *A theory of economic history*. Clarendon Press.
Hindriks, F., & Guala, F. (2015). Institutions, rules, and equilibria: A unified theory. *Journal of Institutional Economics, 11*(3), 459–480. https://doi.org/10.1017/S1744137414000496

Hirshleifer, J. (2001). *The dark side of the force: Economic foundations of conflict theory*. Cambridge University Press.

Jovchelovitch, S. (2019). *Knowledge in context: Representations, community and culture*. Routledge.

Kagel, J. H. (2015). Laboratory experiments: The lab in relationship to field experiments, field data, and economic theory. In G. R. Fréchette & A. Schotter (Eds.), *Handbook of experimental economic methodology* (pp. 339–359). Oxford University Press. https://doi.org/10.1093/acprof:oso/9780195328325.003.0018

Karlan, D. S. (2005). Using experimental economics to measure social capital and predict financial decisions. *American Economic Review, 95*(5), 1688–1699.

Kothari, A., Salleh, A., Escobar, A., Demaria, F., & Acosta, A. (Eds.). (2019). *Pluriverse: A post-development dictionary*. Tulika Books and Authorsupfront.

Kramer, T., & Block, L. (2011). Nonconscious effects of peculiar beliefs on consumer psychology and choice. *Journal of Consumer Psychology, 21*(1), 101–111. https://doi.org/10.1016/j.jcps.2010.09.009

Kross, E., Berman, M. G., Mischel, W., Smith, E. E., & Wager, T. D. (2011). Social rejection shares somatosensory representations with physical pain. *Proceedings of the National Academy of Sciences, 108*(15), 6270–6275. https://doi.org/10.1073/pnas.1102693108

Kuang, C. (2018). *Speech act thoughts in Pierre Bourdieu's economics of linguistic exchanges*. In 4th International Conference on Economics, Management and Humanities Science (ECOMHS) (pp. 167–171).

Lahlou, S. (2017). *Installation theory: The social construction and regulation of behaviour*. Cambridge University Press.

Lakoff, G. (1987). *Women, fire, and dangerous things: What categories reveal about the mind*. University of Chicago Press.

Lakoff, G. (1993). The contemporary theory of metaphor. In A. Ortony (Ed.), *Metaphor and thought* (pp. 202–251). Cambridge University Press.

Lakoff, G., & Johnson, M. (1980). *Metaphors we live by*. University of Chicago Press.

Lakoff, G., & Johnson, M. (1999). *Philosophy in the flesh: The embodied mind and Its challenge to Western thought*. Basic Books.

Landes, D. S. (2000). *Revolution in time: Clocks and the making of the modern world*. Viking.

Lane, R. E. (1992). Work as "disutility" and money as "happiness": Cultural origins of a basic market error. *The Journal of Socio-Economics, 21*(1), 43–64. https://doi.org/10.1016/1053-5357(92)90025-3

Lawson, T. (2019). *The nature of social reality*. Routledge.

Lazear, E. P. (2000). Economic imperialism. *The Quarterly Journal of Economics, 115*(1), 99–146. https://doi.org/10.1162/003355300554683

Lebaron, F. (2003). Pierre Bourdieu: Economic models against economism. *Theory and Society, 32*(5), 551–565. https://doi.org/10.1023/B:RYSO.0000004928.45684.d4

Lee, S. W. S., & Schwarz, N. (2018). A grounded cognition perspective on folk-economic beliefs. *Behavioral and Brain Sciences, 41*, e175. https://doi.org/10.1017/S0140525X18000419

Lundberg, S., & Stearns, J. (2019). Women in economics: Stalled progress. *Journal of Economic Perspectives, 33*(1), 3–22. https://doi.org/10.1257/jep.33.1.3

McKinnon, S. (2005). *Neo-liberal genetics: The myths and moral tales of evolutionary psychology*. Prickly Paradigm Press.

MacKenzie, D. A., Muniesa, F., & Siu, L. (Eds.). (2007). *Do economists make markets? On the performativity of economics*. Princeton University Press.

May, A. M. (2006). "Sweeping the heavens for a comet": Women, the language of political economy, and higher education in the US. *Feminist Economics, 12*(4), 625–640. https://doi.org/10.1080/13545700600885321

Marx, K. (1932/1988). *Economic and philosophic manuscripts of 1844*. Prometheus Books.

Mauss, M. (1925/1990). *The gift: The form and reason for exchange in archaic societies*. Routledge.

Mellström, C., & Johannesson, M. (2008). Crowding out in blood donation: Was Titmuss right? *Journal of the European Economic Association, 6*(4), 845–863. https://doi.org/10.1162/JEEA.2008.6.4.845

Memmi, A. (1957/1965). *The colonizer and the colonized*. Beacon Press.

Milanović, B. (2019). *Capitalism, alone: The future of the system that rules the world*. The Belknap Press of Harvard University Press.

Mirowski, P. (2001). Machine dreams: Economics becomes a cyborg science. *Cambridge University Press*. https://doi.org/10.1017/CBO9780511613364

Nelson, J. A. (1992). Gender, metaphor, and the definition of economics. *Economics & Philosophy, 8*(1), 103–125. https://doi.org/10.1017/S026626710000050X

Nooteboom, B. (2002). *Trust: Forms, foundations, functions, failures, and figures*. Edward Elgar.

North, D. C. (1990). *Institutions, institutional change, and economic performance*. Cambridge University Press.

North, D. C. (2005). *Understanding the process of economic change*. Princeton University Press.

North, D. C., Wallis, J. J., & Weingast, B. R. (2009). *Violence and social orders: A conceptual framework for interpreting recorded human history*. Cambridge University Press.

O'Connor, C. (2017). Embodiment and the construction of social knowledge: Towards an integration of embodiment and social representations theory.

Journal for the Theory of Social Behaviour, 47(1), 2–24. https://doi.org/10.1111/jtsb.12110
Ostrom, E. (1990). *Governing the commons: The evolution of institutions for collective action*. Cambridge University Press.
Ostrom, E. (2010). Beyond markets and states: Polycentric governance of complex economic systems. *American Economic Review, 100*(3), 641–672. https://doi.org/10.1257/aer.100.3.641
Parks, C. D., & Stone, A. B. (2010). The desire to expel unselfish members from the group. *Journal of Personality & Social Psychology, 99*(2), 303–310. https://doi.org/10.1037/a0018403
Patterson, T. C. (2009). *Karl Marx, anthropologist*. Berg.
Pippin, R. B. (2008). *Hegel's practical philosophy: Rational agency as ethical life*. Cambridge University Press.
Polanyi, K. (1944/2001). *The great transformation: The political and economic origins of our time*. Beacon Press.
Rabinbach, A. (1992). *The human motor: Energy, fatigue, and the origins of modernity*. University of California Press.
Rainville, P., Duncan, G. H., Price, D. D., Carrier, B., & Bushnell, M. C. (1997). Pain affect encoded in human anterior cingulate but not somatosensory cortex. *Science, 277*(5328), 968–971. https://doi.org/10.1126/science.277.5328.968
Rappaport, R. A. (1979). *Ecology, meaning, and religion*. North Atlantic Books.
Riva, P., Wirth, J. H., & Williams, K. D. (2011). The consequences of pain: The social and physical pain overlap on psychological responses: Common social and physical pain consequences. *European Journal of Social Psychology, 41*(6), 681–687. https://doi.org/10.1002/ejsp.837
Roth, A. E. (2018). Marketplaces, markets, and market design. *American Economic Review, 108*(7), 1609–1658. https://doi.org/10.1257/aer.108.7.1609
Rozin, P., Nemeroff, C., Wane, M., & Sherrod, A. (1989). Operation of the sympathetic magical law of contagion in interpersonal attitudes among Americans. *Bulletin of the Psychonomic Society, 27*, 367–370.
Rubinstein, A. (2000). *The economics and language: Five essays*. Cambridge University Press.
Sahlins, M. (1972). *Stone age economics*. Aldine-Atherton.
Sahlins, M. (2014). *What kinship is—And is not*. University of Chicago Press.
Salmon, E., Chavez, J. F., & Murphy, M. (2022). New perspectives and critical insights from Indigenous peoples' research: A systematic review of Indigenous management and organization literature. *Academy of Management Annals*. https://doi.org/10.5465/annals.2021.0132
Samuelson, P. A. (1973). *Economics*. McGraw-Hill.

Sawyer, J. E., & Stetsenko, A. (2018). Revisiting Marx and problematizing Vygotsky: A transformative approach to language and speech internalization. *Language Sciences, 70*, 143–154. https://doi.org/10.1016/j.langsci.2018.05.003

Schelling, T. C. (2006). *Micromotives and macrobehavior*. Norton.

Schlicht, E. (2018). *On custom in the economy*. Clarendon Press.

Schotter, A. (1981). *The economic theory of social institutions*. Cambridge University Press.

Searle, J. R. (1983). *Intentionality: An essay in the philosophy of mind*. Cambridge University Press.

Searle, J. R. (1995). *The construction of social reality*. Free Press.

Searle, J. R. (2005). What is an institution? *Journal of Institutional Economics, 1*(1), 1–22. https://doi.org/10.1017/S1744137405000020

Searle, J. R. (2011). *Making the social world: The structure of human civilization*. Oxford University Press.

Selten, R. (1978). The chain store paradox. *Theory and Decision, 9*(2), 127–159. https://doi.org/10.1007/BF00131770

Serkin, C. (2016). *The law of property* (2nd ed.). Foundation Press.

Sève, L. (2021). Where is Marx in the work and thought of Vygotsky? *Mind, Culture, and Activity, 28*(4), 293–303. https://doi.org/10.1080/10749039.2021.1964535

Shackman, A. J., Salomons, T. V., Slagter, H. A., Fox, A. S., Winter, J. J., & Davidson, R. J. (2011). The integration of negative affect, pain and cognitive control in the cingulate cortex. *Nature Reviews Neuroscience, 12*(3), 154–167. https://doi.org/10.1038/nrn2994

Sherry, J. F., Jr., McGrath, M. A., & Levy, S. J. (1993). The dark side of the gift. *Journal of Business Research, 28*(3), 225–244. https://doi.org/10.1016/0148-2963(93)90049-U

Simon, H. A. (1979). Rational decision making in business organizations. *American Economic Review, 69*(4), 493–513.

Skyrms, B. (2006). Ken Binmore's natural justice. *Analyse & Kritik, 28*(1), 99–101. https://doi.org/10.1515/auk-2006-0110

Sliwka, D. (2007). Trust as a signal of a social norm and the hidden costs of incentive schemes. *American Economic Review, 97*(3), 999–1012. https://doi.org/10.1257/aer.97.3.999

Smit, J. P., Buekens, F., & du Plessis, S. (2011). What is money? An alternative to Searle's institutional facts. *Economics and Philosophy, 27*(1), 1–22. https://doi.org/10.1017/S0266267110000441

Smith, P. B., & Max-Neef, M. (2011). *Economics unmasked: From power and greed to compassion and the common good*. Green Books.

Smith, V. L. (1976). Experimental economics: Induced value theory. *American Economic Review, 66*(2), 274–279.

Smith, V. L. (2008). *Rationality in economics: Constructivist and ecological forms*. Cambridge University Press.

Smith, V. L., & Walker, J. M. (1993). Monetary rewards and decision cost in experimental economics. *Economic Inquiry, 31*(2), 245–261. https://doi.org/10.1111/j.1465-7295.1993.tb00881.x

Spencer, D. A. (2009). *The political economy of work*. Routledge.

Stanovich, K. E., & West, R. F. (2000). Individual differences in reasoning: Implications for the rationality debate? *Behavioral and Brain Sciences, 23*(5), 645–665. https://doi.org/10.1017/S0140525X00003435

Stekeler-Weithofer, P. (2011). Intuition, understanding, and the human form of life. In H. Ikäheimo & A. Laitinen (Eds.), *Recognition and Social Ontology* (pp. 117–144). Brill.

Stern, R. (2008). Hegel's Idealism. In F. C. Beiser (Ed.), *The Cambridge companion to Hegel and nineteenth-century philosophy* (1st ed., pp. 135–173). Cambridge University Press. https://doi.org/10.1017/CCOL9780521831673.007

Stetsenko, A. (2017). *The transformative mind: Expanding Vygotsky's approach to development and education*. Cambridge University Press.

Sugden, R. (2011). Salience, inductive reasoning and the emergence of conventions. *Journal of Economic Behavior & Organization, 79*(1), 35–47. https://doi.org/10.1016/j.jebo.2011.01.026

Takizawa, H. (2017). Masahiko Aoki's conception of institutions. *Evolutionary and Institutional Economics Review, 14*(2), 523–540. https://doi.org/10.1007/s40844-017-0087-0

Taylor, C. (1975). *Hegel* (1st ed.). Cambridge University Press. https://doi.org/10.1017/CBO9781139171465

Taylor, C. (2015). *Hegel and modern society* (Cambridge Philosophy Classics edition). Cambridge University Press.

Thompson, E. P. (1967). Time, work-discipline, and industrial capitalism. *Past & Present, 38*, 56–97.

Titmuss, R. M. (1970). *The gift relationship: From human blood to social policy*. Allen & Unwin.

Tomasello, M. (2019). Becoming human: A theory of ontogeny. *Harvard University Press*. https://doi.org/10.4159/9780674988651

Tönnies, F. (1887). *Gemeinschaft und Gesellschaft: Abhandlung des Communismus und des Socialismus als empirischer Culturformen*. Fues's Verlag.

Treede, R.-D., Kenshalo, D. R., Gracely, R. H., & Jones, A. K. P. (1999). The cortical representation of pain. *Pain, 79*(2), 105–111. https://doi.org/10.1016/S0304-3959(98)00184-5

Tuomela, R. (2011). Searle's new construction of social reality. *Analysis, 71*(4), 706–719.

Tyler, T. R., & Amodio, D. M. (2015). Psychology and economics: Areas of convergence and difference. In G. R. Fréchette & A. Schotter (Eds.), *Handbook of experimental economic methodology* (pp. 181–196). Oxford University Press. https://doi.org/10.1093/acprof:oso/9780195328325.003.0012

Tylor, E. B. (1871). *Primitive culture: Researches into the development of mythology, philosophy, religion, art, and custom*. J. Murray.

Veblen, T. (1899/2007). *The theory of the leisure class* (M. Banta, Ed.). Oxford University Press.

Ver Eecke, W. (2008). *Ethical dimensions of the economy: Making use of Hegel and the concepts of public and merit goods*. Springer.

Vohs, K. D. (2015). Money priming can change people's thoughts, feelings, motivations, and behaviors: An update on 10 years of experiments. *Journal of Experimental Psychology: General, 144*(4), e86–e93. https://doi.org/10.1037/xge0000091

Walsh, A. J., & Lynch, T. (2008). *The morality of money: An exploration in analytic philosophy*. Palgrave Macmillan.

Wang, X., Chen, Z., & Krumhuber, E. G. (2020). Money: An integrated review and synthesis from a psychological perspective. *Review of General Psychology, 24*(2), 172–190. https://doi.org/10.1177/1089268020905316

Weber, M. (1922/2019). *Economy and society: A new translation* (K. Tribe, Ed. and Trans.). Harvard University Press.

West, H. G. (2021). *We are who we eat with: Food, distinction, and commensality*. https://thereader.mitpress.mit.edu/we-are-who-we-eat-with/

Whillans, A. V., & Dunn, E. W. (2015). Thinking about time as money decreases environmental behavior. *Organizational Behavior and Human Decision Processes, 127*, 44–52. https://doi.org/10.1016/j.obhdp.2014.12.001

Wiech, K., Lin, C., Brodersen, K. H., Bingel, U., Ploner, M., & Tracey, I. (2010). Anterior insula integrates information about salience into perceptual decisions about pain. *Journal of Neuroscience, 30*(48), 16324–16331. https://doi.org/10.1523/JNEUROSCI.2087-10.2010

Williams, K. D., & Jarvis, B. (2006). Cyberball: A program for use in research on interpersonal ostracism and acceptance. *Behavior Research Methods, 38*(1), 174–180. https://doi.org/10.3758/BF03192765

Williams, K. D., Wesselmann, E. D., & Zhansheng, C. (2007). Social exclusion. In R. Baumeister & K. Vohs (Eds.), *Encyclopedia of social psychology* (pp. 896–897). Sage Publications.

Williamson, O. E. (1985). *The economic institutions of capitalism: Firms, markets, relational contracting*. The Free Press.

Williamson, O. E. (1998). The institutions of governance. *American Economic Review, 88*(2), 75–79.

Zelizer, V. A. R. (1997). *The social meaning of money*. Princeton University Press.

CHAPTER 7

Abstraction and Embodiment in the Core Institutions of Capitalism: Money, Property, and Labor

7.1 Introduction: Money as a Medium of Abstracting Property and Labor

In this chapter, we dissect the core institutions of capitalism, money, property, and labor. We begin with money and adopt a distinct and deliberate Aristotelian stance: Aristotle famously distinguished between "*oikonomia*" as the economy of the household and "*chraematistikae*" as the monetary economy. Chrematistics, as economic activity, is driven by the desire to accumulate wealth in monetary terms and is unbounded as this desire can never be satiated. This concept has often been invoked to explain the unbounded growth of modern capitalism (e.g., Binswanger, 2013), and to diagnose the ethical dilemmas of markets (Walsh & Lynch, 2008). Aristotle already suggested a clear connection between the institution and material artifact of money on the one hand, and psychological and behavioral phenomena on the other. In our analysis, money is the key mediator of institutional actions that drive abstraction in the economy and thus create disembodied ways of economic life. This applies to both property and labor, and it largely reformulates Marx's classical analysis of the emerging capitalism of his time. In the case of property, money abstracts property by severing the connection between the body and objects in favor of attitudes and behaviors that highlight their potential to be traded in markets for profit. In the case of labor, money abstracts labor power and services to make them tradable for profit. In both cases,

F. Basso and C. Herrmann-Pillath, *Embodiment, Political Economy and Human Flourishing*, https://doi.org/10.1007/978-3-031-54971-7_7

then, the semantic ambiguity of "alienation" is analytically productive, since money fosters the potential to alienate objects related to an actor through markets, while at the same time alienating actors from their bodies, that is, disembodying economic action through abstraction and commodification.

Our account of money deploys the full range of analytical tools developed in the previous chapters. We reconstruct Georg Simmel's prescient approach to money in terms of conceptual blending and show how the inward embodiment of the action of pricing (assetification), enabled by the artifact of money, drives the disembodiment of money-mediated markets. These mechanisms can be further analyzed using the Aoki-Bourdieu model of institutional action. We combine this fundamental analysis with a brief review of the historical development and institutional forms of money in terms of the classical analysis of money functions. An important conclusion of this section is that a monetary economy always and necessarily generates power asymmetries between consumers and producers, or investors and firms, because money is the good with the least degree of specificity of use.

Money is essential for distinguishing between different modes of appropriation. Following Max Weber, we approach property as an act of appropriation of resources, but at the same time we deconstruct the concept in terms of modes of possession, ownership, property, and theft, which we refer to as types of action, respectively, "using," "belonging," "holding," and "usurping." This reflects the historical transformation of the world's dominant legal systems during the emergence of capitalism, epitomized by the replacement of the commons with private property. The embodied approach to property restricts the notion of "property" exclusively to the mode in which the institutional form enables alienation through markets, thereby nullifying the relationship of identity that is fundamental to embodied ownership.

Similarly, money acts as a force of disembodiment in relation to human labor. We challenge the paradoxical status of labor in standard economic theory, where it is seen as mere disutility, as simultaneously subject to market and hierarchy, and as "unproductive" when fulfilling reproductive functions. We show how these paradoxes emerge from tensions between cognitive blends that project human action onto different frames of market, community, or hierarchy. The site of alienation at work in modern societies is the capitalist firm. Drawing on theoretical and empirical research on the modern management of labor, we detail its mechanisms of disembodiment. We conclude the chapter by presenting an alternative embodied approach to labor informed by Hannah Arendt's *vita activa*, in which human activity becomes meaningful in the three main social spheres of economic life, namely the household or "domestic," the firms or "corporate," and government in the broadest sense, the "public."

7.2 Money

7.2.1 *Money and Rationality*

In our typology of social relationships, the market type tends towards disembodiment because the abstracting mechanisms associated with the artifact of money as a universal that can be applied uniformly to everything and everyone,[1] are (inwardly) embodied, and because the natural environment and social artifacts (hence the question of property), as well as people (hence the question of labor) are commodified (through outward embodiment) in capitalist markets. Importantly, this means that the process of disembodiment through abstraction that operates in markets cannot be possible without reference to embodiment (whether inward or outward). Moreover, while the commodification of nature and people is a process of disembodiment (and dehumanization), it requires generating a (metaphorical) blend whereby the embodied experience of "commodities" is mapped onto "nature" or "people."

Against this background, we disagree with Fiske's position when he concludes that Market Pricing (MP) is a type of relationship that is "not embodied" (Fiske et al., 2009, p. 1295). In embodied economics, the market type is not "not embodied," but rather is subject to a *process of disembodiment through abstraction favored by the use of an artifact (money)*. This process of disembodiment by abstraction reflects the specific nature of the underlying operation of forming ratios, and implicitly points to the opportunity cost principle. This principle is central to standard economics, where it is one of the core defining elements of "rationality." In this respect, we should go beyond Fiske's labeling of the respective institutional action, "Market Pricing," because it could seem to suggest that assigning a monetary value ("pricing") to opportunities is the central operation. Indeed, even in the view of standard economics, the opportunity cost principle is treated as a subjective assignment of value rooted in the preference function of individuals, independent of monetary valuation. We argue however, that by claiming psychological universality, the opportunity cost principle effectively generalizes through a process of inward embodiment of money, and thus of the market. In other words, pricing in the sense of opportunity cost logic can take place without money, but is the result of the embodiment of money and market logic. This view was first properly formulated by Georg Simmel (1907/2004) in his landmark contribution to the philosophy of money.[2] We use his contributions as a starting point for developing our embodied approach to money. The implication is that the market mode is not disembodied in the strict sense of "not embodied" (as Hayek would like it), but characterizes a specific form of abstraction that is leveraged by money in the market context, and that can, as Simmel argues, usurp psychological processes beyond the market domain.[3]

The opportunity cost logic suggests that individuals assign a value to an option by valuing the lost alternative option. As Simmel argued, this is an exchange because I am giving up something in order to obtain something else. Through this process, I learn about my own valuation of these options, even if I am not sure of the absolute valuation of the preferred choice: At least I know that I value it more than the alternative I gave up. As Simmel writes:

> The fact of economic exchange, therefore, frees the objects from their bondage to the mere subjectivity of the subjects and allows them to determine themselves reciprocally, by investing the economic function in them. The object acquires its practical value not only by being in demand itself but through the demand for another object. Value is determined not by the relation to the demanding subject, but by the fact that this relation depends on the cost of a sacrifice which, for the other party, appears as a value to be enjoyed while the object itself appears as a sacrifice. Thus, objects balance each other, and value appears in a very specific way as an objective, inherent quality. While bargaining over the object is going on – in other words, while the sacrifice that it represents is being determined – its significance for both parties seems to be something external to them, as if each individual experienced the object only in relation to himself. (Simmel, 1907/2004, p. 77)

The process described by Simmel does not necessarily imply that the operation of forming ratios is exactly quantified and complete in the sense of covering all possible opportunities, as is traditionally assumed in the standard model of economics. Yet, this process tends towards abstraction in the sense that it operates over imagined and future-oriented options.

For example, when I consider what I must give up, I imagine a future option, a virtual construct, and may refer to actualized states in what I give up.[4] In other words, unlike the other three types of relationships, the main characteristic of the market relationship is that it refers to a field of possible alternatives which are not currently actualized: In comparison, for example, in a situation such as authority ranking, it is not a matter of giving the subordinate the option of leaving the hierarchy, since this would effectively annul it.

The German fairy tale "Hans in Luck" reveals why the assumption of opportunity cost logic effectively implies reference to a monetary standard.[5] At the end of his apprenticeship as a craftsman, Hans receives a bulky piece of gold and travels home to his mother. On the way, he encounters various exchange opportunities and follows his subjective preferences at the time. For example, he buys a horse to travel faster, later trades the horse for a cow, then the cow for a pig, and so on, until he has lost everything, but still arrives home and recounts his experiences as gratifying, happy to be home. The original story included cheating by the various people he traded with, but since he takes it all at face value, we can ignore that in the current context. The essential point is that Hans makes a series of exchanges, always convinced that he is realizing a better alternative than the one he is currently realizing. Since he ends up in a happy state, what is wrong with that? Standard economic analysis reveals that his preferences, viewed as a structure that is invariant and stable throughout the process, are irrational. But how can we assert this, given his choices and his final state? The only way is to refer to the monetary value of the options chosen: Hans loses the original wealth incorporated in the piece of gold. Without such an external standard we cannot determine whether he is acting rationally or irrationally.

So, we learn that as long as Hans' preferences are seen as purely subjective, we can only claim their irrationality by imposing the standard axiomatic fixation of preferences that have no psychological basis but are eventually socially determined, as in his case, by the market. This means that if Hans followed the prescriptions of rationality, he would use monetary valuation to assess the alternative opportunities. This implies that rationality manifests the inward embodiment of a monetary standard that imposes the consistency of contextualized opportunity cost considerations. In this sense, the story of "Hans in Luck" has deep theoretical significance: On the one hand, it shows that the opportunity principle governs Hans' actions, as he happily enters into exchange relations to realize better alternatives. On the other hand, however, the funny thing about the story is that he is completely unaware that the exchanges take place in a market context where these alternatives are valued in monetary terms. So, he ignores that the barter transactions could be realized by first selling the item for money and then buying the desired alternative, which would entail making a profit, as the alternatives are of less and less value. In other words, Hans could have returned with a substantial amount of money, at least partially equal to the original value of the piece of gold.

At issue is the extent to which the market mode pre-supposes a monetary standard that enables "market pricing." The corresponding institutional action is market pricing. However, as aforementioned, pricing does not necessarily involve monetary valuation. For example, when people exchange favors in building social networks, they often literally "pay a price" to obtain something desirable, but this does not need to correspond to market pricing. Someone who performs sexual favors for an influential person that may help with career advancement is clearly paying a price, but this is not the same as the spot price of prostitution. In this sense, the opportunity cost logic may determine the behavior of both parties in the exchange, but it can only be metaphorically described as a "market." This means that we must make a clear distinction between, on the one hand, the opportunity cost principle of markets as generalized exchange (which Hans followed in his series of choices among alternatives, always imagining a better opportunity), and, on the other hand, the specific form of the abstract opportunity cost principle that results from the inward embodiment of the institution of money. The fairy tale describes a kind of disordered series of choices, not yet institutionalized, as in following the logic of market pricing.

7.2.2 *Pricing as a Fundamental Type of Institutionalized Action Mediated by Money and Its Complementary Institutional Actions*

In the following, and in contrast to standard economic theory, we approach market pricing as the key institutional action mediated by "money signs" that scaffold the inherent abstraction of thinking in terms of a virtual field of opportunities. The term "money sign" is merely a shorthand for a wide range of money signs, such as coins or numbers on a credit card account. We distinguish between money proper in the material sense, such as the coins in my wallet, and signs involving money, which are "economic values" in the most general sense, mostly in terms of the accounting values of objects. Pricing creates a distinct social ontology of objects that have a monetary price, as opposed to other objects that are "priceless." In between, there is a wide range of objects that are amenable to the opportunity cost logic, even though they have no monetary price: In these cases, we often observe vacillation and cultural variation in societal judgments, especially moral concerns, as in the previous example of sexual favors (Zelizer, 1997; see also, Gallus et al., 2022).[6]

We systematize this in Fig. 7.1, which visualizes the range of forms of choice and related objects. At one end, are "sacred objects" which do not allow any choice at all but commit the actor absolutely. Close to it are lexicographic preferences, where actors consider alternative opportunities but assign absolute ranked values to some of them. For example, marriage may be sacred to some actors, so that they do not even think about adultery, while others may be tempted, but still value marriage as almost sacred. Next are choices where alternatives are compared as opportunities, but not quantified. These are unique or rare choices of great complexity and significance, such as the choice of whom to marry. There are various institutional settings, some of which even have a marriage market, in the sense of a distinct field where the choice of partner is negotiated. Such a marriage market may even take the form of a quantified choice of opportunities, if bride prices and dowries are institutional actions. Nevertheless, this may still not qualify as a market with monetary valuation. There are transitional forms, such as the marriage market in ancient China, where parents even considered the monetary cost of raising daughters in negotiating marriages (Gates, 1996).

Indeed, since the emergence of money in antiquity, money has always been the subject of intense moral debates until recently, such as in the aftermath of the 2008 financial crisis, which now include references to psychology and neuroscience (Walsh & Lynch, 2008; Wargo et al., 2010). These debates focus on the behavioral consequences of using money, which are mediated by the psychological and cognitive transformations that money use induces. One institutional consequence of these debates is the normative and legal compartmentalization of money use at both the individual and collective levels, such as the allocation of money to different "mental accounts" (Thaler, 2016, p. 54ff; see also Levav & McGraw, 2009), or the demarcation of distinct domains in society from which money should be excluded or even legally prohibited, such as the buying and selling of human organs in most societies

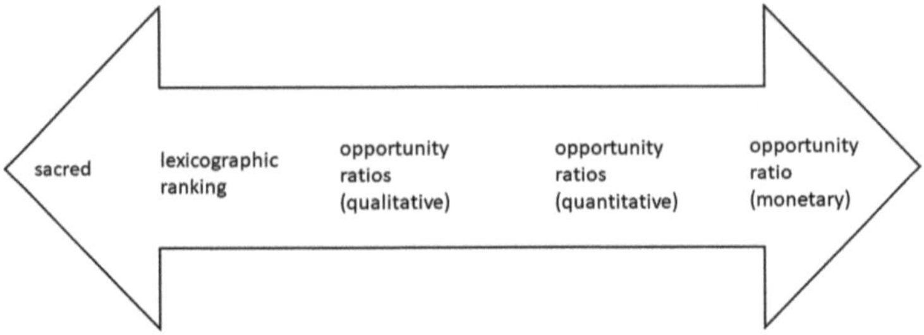

Fig. 7.1 "Sacred objects" do not allow for choice (e.g., life is sacred), while in "lexicographic ranking" values are ranked in absolute terms (e.g., "my children come first"). In "opportunity ratio (qualitative)," alternatives can be compared as opportunities (e.g., "who should I marry?"), while in "opportunity ratio (quantitative)," they are quantified (e.g., bride prices and dowries in a marriage market). In the case of "opportunity ratio (monetary)," the cost–benefit analysis applies to everything and everyone

(Fiske & Tetlock, 1997; Roth, 2007; Zelizer, 1989, 1997). The latter dovetails with concerns about the size and scope of markets: "A hired friend is not the same as the real thing. Somehow, the money that would buy the friendship dissolves the good I seek to acquire" (Sandel, 2013). Historically, compartmentalization has been much more widespread, even restricting what are now conceived as core elements of a monetary economy, such as the prohibition of interest in the Middle Ages, but also in Sharia law to the present day (Tripp, 2006, p. 124ff).

The example of interest is particularly significant in our context because it relates directly to the TIME IS MONEY metaphor, both in the sense of allocating time among alternative opportunities and in the sense of considering them in terms of the future. Even though compound interest was known and applied from the earliest times, reflecting the growth of livestock populations (Goetzmann, 2017, p. 35ff), its institutionalization was often seen as deeply problematic because of the potentially disruptive effects of the rapid accumulation of wealth. In the Middle Ages, scholastic thinkers directly invoked the categorization of opportunities as we present them in Fig. 7.1: Time was seen as sacred because it belonged to God, and was, therefore, resolutely excluded from any form of market pricing (Walsh & Lynch, 2008, p. 97). The literary treatments of interest as destructive and dehumanizing are countless, most famously Shakespeare's Shylock, which even directly invokes the embodiment of harm done in the flesh that Antonio demands as interest. One of the last literary monuments of this kind is Goethe's second part of ***Faust***, which centers on the insatiable yearnings caused by the inherent dynamics of the monetary economy (Shell, 1980). In principle, though, this view was already established in the Aristotelian distinction between "***oikonimia***" and "*chraematistikae*."

Throughout recorded history, money has been conceived as a force that tears down social orders and therefore has almost demonic qualities.[7] The larger historical trend, however, is the breakdown of compartmentalization in the expansion of the size and scope of markets, classically analyzed by Karl Polanyi (1944/2001), and referred to as "commodification" in Marxian theory. These processes are mostly ignored by conventional economics or neutralized in seemingly "technical solutions" to problems such as the installation of markets as institutional devices to address externalities (e.g., trading emission permits), as will be discussed further in Chapter 8.

These moral struggles reflect tensions over the embodiment of money, which we interpret as operating both inwardly and outwardly. This reveals a paradoxical but essential role of money in economic life: As money becomes inwardly embodied, it drives the abstraction of economic relations among actors, which is tantamount to crowding out the other three Fiske types, especially, as has been theorized in many ways, the community type. The specific form of abstraction is manifested in the fungibility of some objects in the market, which is an aspect of commodification. This is driven by the affordances of money: Money evokes the institutional action of pricing, and once an object is priced, it can enter the market. However, this does not mean that monetary valuation is only relevant in the market context: A major area where monetary valuation became significant early on is retributive justice, that is, paying compensation when, for example, someone harms another person, rather than taking revenge, and pacifying the process by demanding monetary compensation. Therefore, and this is important, we need to make a clear distinction between markets and money in two senses. First, markets can function without the full deployment of monetary valuation, such as maintaining a division of labor via long-term social relationships that mediate reciprocal exchange, which marks the distinction between traditional and capitalist markets, or between long-term supplier relationships and arm's-length markets. Second, money is an artifact that can be used in the full range of the other three types of social relationships:

- In the hierarchy mode, the archetypal form of money use is taxation and tribute.
- In the reciprocity mode, the archetypal form is the use of money as a gift.
- In the community mode, the archetypal form is the sharing of monetary wealth within a community.

This diagnosis makes the analysis of money exceedingly complicated. In our context, however, one observation stands out: Capitalism can be regarded as a societal regime in which monetary valuation is extended to as many social fields as possible.

Moreover, the crowding out of other social relationships is not necessarily a social pathology, an observation that Simmel (1907/2004, p. 285ff) has already elaborated on at length. This ties up with the ideology of market freedom. Indeed, the market may allow people to free themselves from a hierarchical power structure in which they are exploited, or it may allow them to leave tightly constraining community relations (e.g. Gasiorowska & Zaleskiewicz, 2022; Marcoux, 2009). Markets can help dissociate individual consumption from societal consumption norms (Trentmann, 2017). Yet, as the empirical evidence also shows, in the real world these potentially positive effects are often counteracted either by the power inherent in markets or by specific forms of hybridization of relationships. The most prominent example is the labor market, where hierarchy and market power often create highly unequal conditions for workers relative to employers (see Sect. 7.4 on labor).

The abstraction of markets is driven by cognitive processes that are ultimately based on cognitive blends, as illustrated by the TIME IS MONEY metaphor and the recruitment of the RESOURCE schema (see Chapter 6, Sect. 6.4.1). However, we now introduce an important distinction between "resource" and "asset," which refer to different institutional contexts of the economy. As argued earlier, the essential cognitive transformation in the field of the economy is to see objects as resources. This is true for all kinds of economic systems, such as a subsistence farmer or a capitalist firm. In the case of the latter, however, resources are cognitively blended with money by being constituted as "assets," that is, objects that generate monetary returns through market transactions. This is also the distinction between consumers and other actors, reminiscent of the Marxian distinction between use-value and exchange value: For the consumer, the consumption good is a resource; for the producer and seller, it is an asset. As soon as monetary valuation is involved and becomes inwardly embodied in terms of the opportunity cost principle, we speak of the resource as an "asset."[8] In principle, this is close to the notion of "commodity," but it makes more explicit the process of abstraction and the role of imagined future returns. We approach this transformation as a distinct cognitive blend, "assetification," as shown in Fig. 7.2.

Pricing enables various cognitive operations which are impossible without money, most importantly, it makes value commensurable across a potentially unlimited range of objects, and it makes possible all kinds of arithmetic operations independent of the physical nature of the objects.[9] Once money is accepted in a community of users, this valuation is also commensurable across different individuals, possibly even across everyone. Money thus enables the cognitive objectification of abstract value, which we refer to as assetification by means of pricing. For example, in ancient rural China, peasants would collectively buy a pig to raise for later own consumption or sale, and the calculation in terms of market

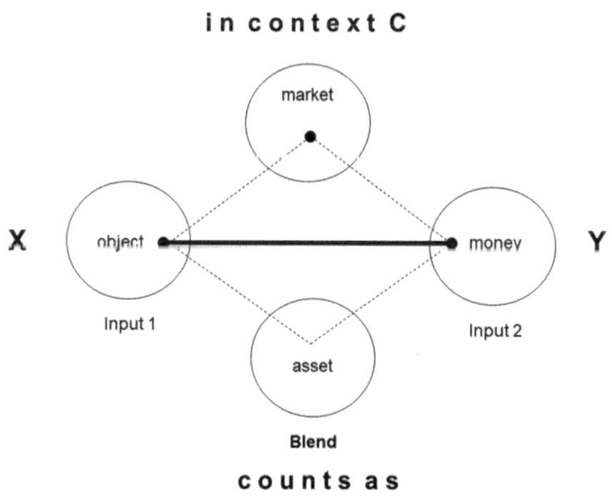

Fig. 7.2 Assetification results from blending an "object" and "money" in relation to the "market" as generic space. In terms of Searle's status function, whereby <X counts as Y in context C> , the "object" as "asset" is treated as "money," that is, valued in terms of monetary price and future flows of monetary gains derived from it

prices allowed them to define shares that would later determine the individual amount of meat they would receive, or the share of the proceeds from the sale. Here, the pig is an asset. As we shall see later, this establishes the role of money as wealth and, hence, closes another loop of the embodiment of money, that of the relationship between wealth and social status.

Assetification involves a double movement of inward and outward embodiment: As pricing involves more and more social domains, monetary valuation becomes internalized (inwardly embodied) in the decision-making process of individuals. At the same time, pricing as action means that subjective valuations become externalized (outwardly embodied). But the tension remains, as recognized, for example, in the distinction between "subjective value" and monetary prices in common law: My subjective valuation of the watch I inherited from my grandpa may differ substantially from the market valuation (Serkin, 2016, p. 79ff).

Indeed, the dissociation between market price and subjective value is a well-established finding that explains why pricing often triggers pronounced shifts in choices and behavior: "Monetary assessments heavily reflect transaction cues (i.e., variables relating to the transaction in which the purchase alternative may be acquired or forgone), insufficiently reflecting experience cues (i.e., variables relating to the experience of owning or consuming the purchase alternative) that inform predicted utility" (Amir et al., 2008, p. 1062). As we will discuss in the section on property, one of the most significant illustrations of this is the endowment effect, which can reveal a subjective preference when it comes to valuing owned objects, and can lead to a divergence between supply and demand prices in exchange. There is also strong evidence for the Marxian distinction between use-value and exchange value. Historically, this is salient in the expansion of pawnshops in the nineteenth century that accompanied the growth of capitalism (Woloson, 2012). In the United States, most people had to rely on their services on a regular basis, and were constantly confronted with the fact that the use-value of, say, a coat, was much higher to them than the usually very small amount of loan they could obtain, given the oversupply of such goods on the resale market. Moreover, as Woloson (2012, p. 94) notes: "Often, women 'put in' the family's Sunday best on Monday morning in order to cover the week's food and rent, redeeming the clothes Saturday night for the next day's church services." This observation shows that a key institutional mechanism that imposes monetary valuation on people is the budget by which they are constrained in their economic actions, and that this implies the cognitive blending of assetification: For the poor worker, even a piece of underwear became an asset to be regularly pawned.

The institutional action of pricing is crucial for the extension of market transactions to an increasing domain of physical entities. The complementary institutional action, emphasized by Max Weber's analysis of capitalism, is accounting, which places pricing in the context of an aggregate assigned to a certain entity or actor, that is, the budget (Soll, 2014). The performative aspects of money (i.e., its power to shape reality, including the way people think and act) are manifested in the commodification of the world. Accounting is a primary medium through which money commodifies the world. Once communities agree on certain accounting principles, economic values are created to the extent that new objects are created. In the modern economy, this is salient in the transition to accounting principles that aim to objectify immaterial goods and prospects of future market exchange opportunities (Perry & Nölke, 2006). Through such performative functions of accounting, understood as institutionalized action, narratives about the future prospects of a new technology become expectations that can be priced (Beckert, 2016). This in turn enables other actions, such as attracting investors.

The performative power of accounting crystallizes in the notion of "capital" as an essential conceptual correlate of money. Capital differs from wealth in that wealth is tied to social status, which often requires reducing the fungibility of wealth, for instance by protecting landed property from creditors' claims via institutions such as the *fidei commissum*, in which the actor engaging in ongoing transactions on the market is only a steward for the family that owns the land, so that his personal liabilities do not affect the family's wealth and status as embodied in landed property. On the contrary, measures affecting capital are aimed at achieving the highest possible degree of fungibility. Hence, the monetary valuation of capital and its future proceeds is a key feature of institutionalized action in modern capitalism—often dubbed "financialization" (Krippner, 2005). Money is a medium of assetification by employing various legal instruments, thus embodying monetary valuation in the assetified objects that become the objects of property relations (Pistor, 2019). Thus, money and property as institutional actions interplay in the creation of the social ontology of the capitalist economy—in the sense of Searle (2011).

As Simmel emphasized, this external objectification is deeply intertwined with internal objectification; or, in our parlance, inward and outward embodiment. This defines the key difference between his approach and the subjectivism of modern economic theory. The latter posits a rational agent who is able to assess subjective utilities in terms of a commensurable standard of measurement ("utility") and then compare various alternatives to arrive at a maximizing solution. This requires that certain mathematical conditions hold for subjective utility. But it also raises the simple question of how these can be assessed and compared over time (Davis, 2003). Philosophically, this is consistent with Wittgenstein's famous rejection of the possibility of a purely private language (Candlish & Wrisley, 2019). In a purely private language, the individual can never know whether meanings are commensurable over time, because she cannot refer to an independent framework for comparing meanings.[10] This requires reference to a public, and therefore external standard, which is language as a collective phenomenon. The same argument applies to subjective utility: This requires objectification via an external standard, which is monetary valuation in the case of inward embodiment of money in markets. In Simmel's words:

> The decisive fact in the objectivity of economic value, which makes economics a special area of investigation, is that its validity transcends the individual subject. The fact that the object has to be exchanged against another object illustrates that it is not only valuable for me, but also valuable independently of me; that is to say, for another person. The equation, objectivity = validity for subjects in general, finds its clearest justification in economic value. The equivalence of which we become aware, and in which we develop an interest through exchange, imparts to value its specific objectivity. For even though each of the elements in exchange may be personal or only subjectively valuable, the fact that they are equal to each other is an objective factor which is not contained within any one of these elements and yet does not lie outside of them either. Exchange presupposes an objective measurement of subjective valuations, not in the sense of being chronologically prior, but in the sense that both phenomena arise from the same act. (Simmel, 1907/2004, p. 79)

Strong indirect evidence for this is the fact that experimental economics (and, to some extent, neuroeconomics) uses money as a linear equivalent of subjective utility (Smith, 1976), treating money as a quasi-universal incentive commensurable across many individuals and experimental settings (Knutson & Wimmer, 2007). Without such a standard, generalizations by the standards of mainstream economic theory would prove difficult: Tellingly, this requires combining reliance on money as a standard with the creation of abstract and decontextualized conditions in laboratory experiments, as we discussed in Chapter 6 (Smith, 1976). Indeed, this move towards inward embodiment (meant here as a claim) even leads to the hypothesis of a "common currency" in the brain, thus invoking a monetary metaphor (Landreth & Bickle, 2008).

Money should, therefore, be seen as a form of institutional action that enables rational choice as defined by economics, and not simply as a tool for transactions driven by rational choice. This becomes clear when we consider the processual dimension. The key parameter is the budget constraint. The budget constraint imposes a specific form of "calculative" rationality by imposing the opportunity cost logic on the individual.[11] If I spend money on a new shirt, what else could I buy for the same amount of money? The conventional account takes subjective valuation for granted. The embodiment account claims that by starting with comparisons among alternative choices, individuals are enabled to construct what is commonly taken for granted, that is, subjective valuation. An important corollary of this is that all alternatives are made commensurable and, thus, in principle, can be substitutes.

In sum, a key aspect of money as an institutional action is pricing. The important economic implication is that absolute prices matter, yet not in the abstract sense of economic theory, but in the sense of prices as incorporated in artifacts of pricing such as price tags or price lists: Prices are material signs (Beunza et al., 2006). That is, whereas conventional economics treats relative prices as abstract relations of scarcity behind a "veil" of money, the embodiment approach treats relative prices as price comparisons in real-world practices of choosing among alternatives and calculating decisions. Conventional economics notoriously marginalizes the essential role of pricing as a type of institutional action in the economy.[12]

With regard to market exchange, this pertains to the notion of universal fungibility of money and reveals that money is intrinsically linked to the endogenous emergence of power relations in markets. We relate this association between money fungibility and power dynamics to the concept of asset specificity in institutional economics, which captures the scope and extent of potential exchange opportunities that relate to a specific object (Williamson, 1985). Asset specificity is an essential determinant of asymmetric bargaining, since the more limited the alternative uses of an object, the lower the relative bargaining power. This is particularly important for market exchange, when the seller/producer acquires or produces an object solely for the market opportunity, with no other use. Think of bespoke equipment that is made exclusively for one customer and cannot be used elsewhere. In comparison, money is the object with the relatively lowest asset specificity. Money, therefore, embodies agential powers for the expansion of social exchange as mediated by markets. An important consequence, already highlighted by Aristotle, is that there is no satiation point in the accumulation of money.

Correspondingly, as Gesell (1916/2022) seminally analyzed, money has the unique characteristic of not eroding with time, especially when it comes to modern forms of fiat money. As long as public authorities keep inflation in check by oversupplying money, this means that owners of money can afford to wait for years, unlike those in need of money, such as farmers, who face the temporal constraints of seasonal cycles. This is another determinant of the asymmetries of power embodied in money, and is reflected in the capability of money-holders to charge interest on loans, even usurious interest. This explanation of interest is fundamentally different from others based on subjective time preferences, advocated by conventional economics.

The embodied agential power of social exchange is the cause of the corrosive social effects of money, since money can be used in almost limitless ways and is also demanded without satiation. The examples in history are plenty, such as the intrusion of money into the religious sphere, that triggered the Reformation, which criticized the fusion of monetary and religious practices, such as the trading of indulgences. However, such issues also arise in modern times, as characterized by the notion of "repugnant markets" where the intrusion of money into certain spheres is rejected on ethical grounds, as salient, for instance, in the various national and even subnational regulations on surrogate motherhood (Roth, 2007). That said, this ethical reflection is grounded in embodied responses and is often merely an ex-post rationalization of feelings such as disgust (e.g., Lichtenstein et al., 2007).[13]

As we mentioned earlier, social exchange always involves the dimension of time, and money embodies opportunities for social exchange. Therefore, there are various motivations for accumulating money, which we refer to as the institutional action of hoarding. We use this term instead of "saving," because the latter already suggests a market logic in the context of mainstream economics, whereas hoarding is more inclusive and covers motivations related to wealth accumulation. Most importantly, hoarding avoids the implicit reference to interest as the main motivation for saving, as assumed in the new classical theories of macroeconomics. As Keynes' original theory of saving demonstrates, this is highly relevant to the use of equilibrium concepts applied to the capital market in the neoclassical model, where the interest rate is supposed to coordinate saving and investment directly. In contrast, in the Keynesian model, the capital market is institutionally bifurcated when saving does not respond to interest and investment does, thus suggesting that equilibrium is not automatically guaranteed, or may even be the exception, resulting from indirect mechanisms of national income fluctuations. The embodiment approach to money strongly favors a "Keynesian" approach by highlighting a wide range of psychological and social motivations for hoarding money (such as preparing for emergencies or for life-cycle events such as marriage), as is empirically evident in cases such as Japan, where the stability of hoardings (aka savings) underpins the resilience of a highly indebted public economy.

7.2.3 *Money as an Institution*

Money is treated as disembodied in conventional economics, to the extent that money is "a veil" that would not even affect the workings and outcomes of markets as conceived in general equilibrium theory. This separates microeconomics from macroeconomics, where a rich debate about the effects of money has unfolded over the decades since the Keynesian revolution. But this debate focuses only on macroeconomic aggregates such as the price level and unemployment, even including truncated forms of embodied approaches, such as Philipps' construction of a machine that materializes a metaphor of macroeconomics in terms of flows and stocks. There are other rudiments of embodiment, such as in Keynes' original approach to savings behavior, which refers to the psychological determinants of individual motives to postpone consumption:

> These eight motives might be called the motives of Precaution, Foresight, Calculation, Improvement, Independence, Enterprise, Pride and Avarice; and we could also draw up a corresponding list of motives to consumption such as Enjoyment, Shortsightedness, Generosity, Miscalculation, Ostentation and Extravagance. (Keynes, 1936/2018, p. 96)

Money is often taken as one of the testing grounds for theories of institutions, such as in the debates about Searle's theory (Smit et al., 2011). Because money is a complex assemblage of institutions, practices, and things, we need to deconstruct the common reference to money as *an* "institution" in the sense of one single and unified institution. This implicitly generalizes beyond the specific institutional conditions of money production and use in modern nation-states, where money is subject to a sovereign monopoly. As the rise of Bitcoin and other alternative forms of payment demonstrates, these conditions should not be taken for granted when elaborating a general theory of money (Nishibe, 2016). The embodiment view takes seriously the economist's adage that "money is what money does." We avoid the notion of money as an "institution" by examining the actions that are institutionalized through the mediation of money signs: These are "money practices," such as payment arrangements or social taboos about using money. Money signs are material artifacts that are collectively interpreted and accepted as "money," such as coins or digital representations. An embodiment perspective explores the institutional plurality of uses of the money sign in various contexts and for various types of agents, including the possibility, often recognized in the history of money, that this is reflected in the coexistence of different types of money signsfor example, state-controlled copper coins and imported Mexican silver dollars in Imperial China (Von Glahn, 1996). In this short section, however, we will not delve into these fascinating historical realities of money.

In the case of modern currencies, the collective acceptance of money is enforced by legal fiat. Most of us grow up using a national currency in all circumstances of economic life, and most of us rely exclusively on monetary income for our livelihood which is embedded into markets. Hence, money is an exemplary case of becoming *transparent* in money practices. In fact, the very notion of "society" as a modern phenomenon to be distinguished from "community," as conceptualized by classical sociologists, such as Ferdinand Tönnies or Max Weber, implies a universalization of the scope of markets. For the embodiment approach though, it is necessary to include the historical dimension, since the historical record allows us to disentangle several aspects of embodiment.

Two facts stand out when considering the history of money. First, there are different functional contexts of money, which can be summarized in the distinction between "private" and "public" or "sovereign" money (Martin, 2014). Second, and correspondingly, there is an early distinction between money as used in recurrent market transactions and money as wealth, the latter being the ground on which finance emerged as a distinct domain of the economy (Ferguson, 2009). The embodiment perspective refers these distinctions to various types of institutional action and combines cognitive and emotional aspects of the use of money. In economics, these distinctions have been recognized in competing theories of money, such as Menger's transaction-based account or Knapp's "state theory of money," and continue to motivate contemporary debates about the nature of money, such as in the context of the "new monetary economics" (Kelton, 2020). However, the historical record reveals that the various aspects have always played together and are manifested in the diversity of money practices.

The majority opinion in economics tends to approach money theoretically as a solution to mediate and balance trilateral exchange, that is to solve the problem of the "double coincidence of wants," as in Menger's evolutionary approach (Schotter, 1981). The standard view is a disembodied argument that abstracts market exchange without money, implicitly suggests that markets can exist independently of money, and ultimately generates the need to create the institution of money. To some extent, Menger's original theory is embodied, since physical characteristics of goods determine which will eventually emerge as universally accepted money, but the main burden of the argument is on frequency-dependent transactional practices. Menger's theory may work in a hypothetical scenario, but it is not consistent with historical facts. A classic study is Sundström's (1974) on pre-colonial Africa, which clearly states:

> The use of media of exchange in primitive societies is rather restricted as goods and services can be obtained in other ways (...). The objects referred to as primitive money are amassed for social and religious ends rather than for commercial ends (...). Money definitions generally exaggerate the influence of trading on the origin of money while neglecting the overwhelming importance of unilateral non-commercial payments in primitive society (...). (Sundström, 1974, p. 85ff)[14]

This discrepancy between fact and theory reflects a chicken-and-egg problem: Markets are supposed to drive the emergence of money, yet markets also presuppose the existence of money.

When we consider exchange under real conditions, the archetypal context is a community bound together by a web of social exchange relations (Graeber, 2011, p. 102ff). The notion of "community" can encompass many types, such as a rural community, a community of ethnic traders, or a professional group specializing in a trade. As we shall see, the latter notion is by no means limited to pre-modern economies. In such a community, the standard solution to the problem of the double coincidence of wants is credit: If an individual needs a good that another individual possesses, she can ask for credit, which is the promise of a later return. Communities of individuals rely on social capital to ensure the fulfillment of such mutual obligations, such as reputational effects, sanctions of ostracism, and so on.

Private money arises in contexts where there is a need to coordinate networks of bilateral debts. Without money, this works, for example, when I owe you an obligation that you accept as fulfilled when I give credit to one of your close relatives: You help me, I help your sister, as illustrated today by timebanks (Bellotti et al., 2014). In communities of traders, the same principle may apply among business partners, and so forth. However, there is the problem of how to evaluate these mutual obligations among different individuals. We can call this the problem of the "double coincidence of debts." Generalizing across historical contexts, we theorize this as a process of "assetification" of debts, that is, the creation of a sign that represents the debt, as illustrated in Fig. 7.3 (Herrmann-Pillath & Hederer, 2023, p. 303ff). This sign evolves into a money sign when it is accepted by a third party as fulfillment of an obligation to her. In other words, money in this context is assetified debt in networks of exchange. The original debts are "loans" in non-monetary objects, such as wheat, spices, or furs in a medieval trading community, and assetification means that such loans are evaluated in monetary terms, and thus made commensurable across transactions. These assets are IOUs, which would morph into private money once accepted by all parties as the fulfillment of obligations by anyone to anyone.[15]

This scenario is by no means limited to the context of historical communities. A key transition in modern economic systems is based on it, namely the recognition of bills of exchange by central banks in discount. This recognition was ultimately based on the recognition of reputation among narrowly defined elite businesspeople, thus reflecting social capital as in the original constellation of mutual obligation. We refer to this as the "primary monetary communities" (Richter, 1990). Primary monetary communities are systems of exchange of mutual debt. As soon as certain economic agents specialize in the trade of assetified debt, we observe

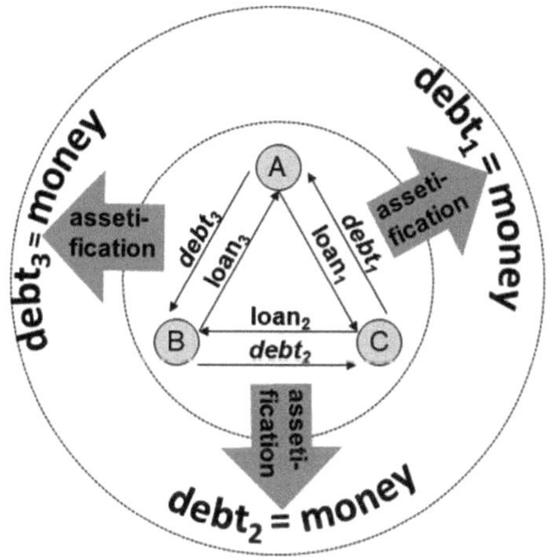

Fig. 7.3 In social exchange, actors lend each other goods and services, i.e., they make loans, and thereby create mutual debts. These items can only be made commensurable in terms of pricing, which presupposes money as a standard of value. Money drives the conceptual blend of assetification. Eventually, debts become money. This is private money as a means of exchange. Money as a standard of value can emerge independently as public money in the context of taxation (see main text below) [After Herrmann-Pillath and Hederer (2023)]

the emergence of "finance," which we refer to as "secondary monetary community." This reinstates the principle of recognition as social capital, taking into account the fact that modern finance is also organized as a tightly integrated network of individuals with a certain status, located in proximity to "financial centers," such as the eponymous "Wall Street" (Sassen, 2012).

In this analytical sketch, two fundamental facts about modern money come to the fore, revealing essential aspects of embodiment. The first is that money must be trusted. Trust in money is an elusive concept in conventional economics, although economists and philosophers agree on the fundamental fact that money is ultimately based solely on the recognition of a group of users, and hence is fiat by trust. Therefore, and second, we revive Walter Bagehot's (1873/2017) early insight that modern systems of fiat money are, therefore, essentially based on institutionalized trust in the central bank, beyond mere technical questions of the administration of the monetary system, in Bagehot's words, recognizing "how deeply our system of banking is fixed in our ways of thinking" (Bagehot, 1873/2017, p. 169). However, this applies mainly to secondary monetary communities. At the level of primary communities, trust in money transforms mutual obligations into a willingness to accept money as a means of fulfilling those obligations. This requires that the accepting individual be confident that other unrelated parties will also accept it as payment. Private money faces two problems here: One is that this universal acceptance is not warranted when the range of transactions increases. The other is that the value of money may change over the time span in which sequences of transactions unfold. Both coordination problems can be solved by anchoring money in public institutions.

This leads us to consider another historical context in which money emerged, namely as a unit of account in the public economy, or as sovereign money (Ingham, 2000). Generalizing about this context, this refers to the archetypal setting in which money is endorsed by a public authority that extracts resources from a community via taxation for the production of public goods, or what is allegedly perceived as such (Bromley & Chavas, 2008). If we combine this setting with markets, the authority may rely on markets for resource extraction, especially indirectly, that is, by paying its staff, especially the military, a monetary wage, so that they would rely primarily on markets to meet their own needs. The authority can simply issue money, but, beyond a fully centralized control of the economy, this money must be accepted by economic agents. There are two main conditions for this. First, this money must be the means of fulfilling tax obligations, and second, the value of money in market transactions must be stable over time. Both establish the institutional connection to private money. In short, sovereign money solves the problem of fixing a unit of account in private money. In both cases, the core is debt, either private debt or the obligation due to the public authority.

From the earliest times, minting has been claimed as a prerogative of public authorities. Apart from the benefits of seigniorage and the link between taxation and the efficient organization of governmental power, there has always been at least the side effect of bolstering trust in money, for example by imprinting coins with symbols of authority. This does not imply a direct crowding out of private money, insofar as it is constituted by the creation of tradable IOUs among private agents. However, these

IOUs may refer to established public money as a standard of measurement. Such fusions are a defining feature of modern monetary systems, such as when transferable bank accounts were recognized as "money" in the aftermath of the banking versus currency controversy in nineteenth-century Britain. The merging of private and public money implies that debasement of the currency by sovereign mints or modern central banks, which leads to inflation, is a major aspect of institutional failure, since inflation creates uncertainty about the unit of account over time.

The standard theory of money focuses on market transactions. Historically, there have been two main contexts: Petty day-to-day trade in local markets, and long-distance trade in trading centers. The latter was supported by the development of other means of payment, that is, IOUs of various forms. Clearance was mostly done at certain central occasions, such as large trade fairs, and thus involved personal contacts in networks of traders. These two settings defined different spheres of transactions, often dominated by different types of money, the small change money, and the money used to accumulate wealth, typically associated with public authorities. In pre-modern systems, this was commodity money, that is, high-value coins made of precious metals. This bifurcation manifests the multiple functions of money, often resulting in institutional bifurcation along the lines of money functions, transactions, or wealth accumulation.

As aforementioned, pre-modern monetary regimes often manifest the institutional bifurcation of the two contexts of market transactions and wealth accumulation, which in many cases reflects institutional dysfunction. However, even in the premodern times, we observe significant instances of the merging of these functions, which became almost universal in the modern period. Most significantly, this occurred with the emergence of the first minted coins in the Mediterranean, the Lydian electrum coins (Hutter, 1994). Electrum was an alloy of gold and silver. Silver was used as a medium of exchange among Greek peasant communities, while gold was the medium of wealth accumulation in neighboring Assyria, based on taxation as another form of exchange. Hence, these coins could be used as a medium of trade between the two societies, cognitively merging the two different structural principles of exchange in the more "egalitarian" Greek communities and the hierarchical differentiation in Assyria. Theoretically, as shown in Fig. 7.4, we reconstruct this as a conceptual blend in which silver and gold are metaphors for the emerging functions of money (Herrmann-Pillath, 2013, p. 382ff; Hutchins, 2005). Tellingly, after the emergence of this integrated money sign, Greek culture underwent major transformations in which money became deeply enmeshed in the social structure as a monetary medium of social status (Goetzmann, 2017, p. 73ff), thus transcending the purely transactional functions of money.

It should be emphasized that in such transformations, money as wealth becomes a metaphor for social status (e.g., Wang et al., 2020). This distinguishes the concept of "wealth" from that of "capital." This is salient in the social transformations of Western European countries, where money as a unit of account became a standard for judging and displaying social status, mediated by the value of property, and, specifically, by the ownership of government bonds with interest as an essential component of "*patrimoine*" apart from land (Piketty, 2013, p. 207ff). Since a key feature of wealth is being part of a patrimony that is inherited across generations, the stability of the value of money became a pillar of social structure that was later eroded by world wars and inflation.

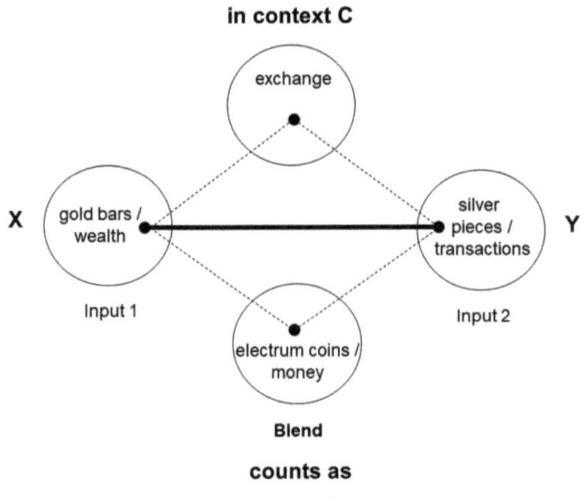

Fig. 7.4 In ancient Asia Minor, Greek peasant communities traded with Assyria. In the highly hierarchical Assyrian society, gold was a medium of wealth and a standard of value for the revenue appropriated by the rules. In the decentralized Greek communities, silver was a medium of valuation in market exchange. Lydium coins, made of electrum, an alloy of silver and gold, were a material anchor for the emergence of money as a medium of exchange between the two societies [After Herrmann-Pillath (2013)]

7.2.4 *Pulling the Threads Together: Money in the Aoki-Bourdieu Model of Institution*

In this section, we have outlined the foundations of an embodiment approach to money as an institution. We systematize our argument along the lines of the Aoki-Bourdieu framework (Fig. 7.5). Roughly speaking, this framework suggests approaching money as a set of diverse institutional actions that are sustained by a series of frequency-dependent network effects familiar from the analysis of communication systems, and most evident today in the international hegemony of the US Dollar in international transactions. However, these frequency-dependent network effects alone cannot explain a fundamental fact about money, which is trust, that is, a strong behavioral disposition to accept and use a certain "money species" for transactions and other activities. In the Aoki-Bourdieu framework, trust points more generally to the explanation of dispositions determined by constellations of emotional and cognitive factors (Lea & Webley, 2006). The key concept to approach these factors is the notion of money signs. Money signs mediate the individual and collective levels, as well as the behavioral and cognitive phenomena. We refer here to tokens in the sense of the concrete physical items that are regarded as money (e.g., coins, banknotes), as distinct from "money species," in the sense, for example, of national currencies (e.g., dollar, euro), or private versus public money. The transition between tokens and species is a cognitive transformation. Money practices involve tokens, such as paying at a restaurant with digital tokens via credit card, or sending a gift in an envelope with cash. This is tightly integrated into modern monetary systems, with recent fissures such as the emergence of bitcoin, and was much more fragmented in pre-modern times. Often this involves creative actions, such as reviving practices like treating livestock as money tokens in a hyperinflationary environment.

As aforementioned, money is anchored in emotional and cognitive mechanisms, of which "trust" is one of the most important. Another phenomenon that reveals its emotional and cognitive underpinnings is the money illusion, which conventional economics disparages as implying a "lack of rationality" and a "bias" towards nominal evaluation (Shafir et al., 1997). Money illusion describes people's evaluation of money on the basis of its face value (i.e., in terms of nominal values), overlooking its purchasing power, which is expressed in terms of real values by taking into account the role of inflation (e.g., Tyran, 2007). For instance, people

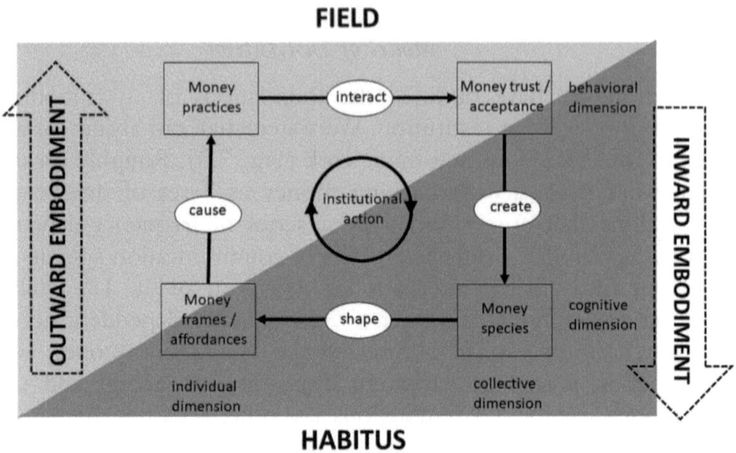

Fig. 7.5 In the Aoki-Bourdieu model, money species emerge in continuous exchange interactions in which frequency-dependent mechanisms sustain trust in money signs. Trust is grounded in the inward embodiment of money use, resulting in dispositions related to affordances for institutional action, such as the use of money in particular social contexts, primarily markets. Actions converge on money practices as forms of outward embodiment that also create the social domains of money use. The cycle of inward and outward embodiment links individual behavior and population-level regularities of money use

may be more likely to object to a 1% pay cut in a period of zero inflation than to a 5% pay increase in a period of 6% inflation. A common explanation of the money illusion provided by the biases-and-heuristics approach is that it arises largely because it is "considerably easier" and "more natural" to think in nominal terms than in real terms (Shafir et al., 1997, p. 367). A complementary perspective to this cognitive approach points to the role of brain areas involved in the experience of reward (e.g., vmPFC) and emotion (e.g., amygdala) in the money illusion effect (e. g., Huang & Yu, 2019; B. Weber et al., 2009). On a more psychological level, for example, it has been observed that Poles perceive prices expressed in US dollars as higher than prices expressed in their national currency (zloty) because of the Polish emotional attachment to the US dollar. These findings suggest that the money illusion effect can be underpinned and modified by the emotional attachment to the currency in which these prices are expressed (Tyszka & Przybyszewski, 2006; see also

Przybyszewski & Tyszka, 2007). This is related to historical reasons, when their national currency was inconvertible under communism, which led to distrust of their national currency, while the US dollar was an important reserve of value and means of payment, and was then considered as the "better currency" in Poland. Importantly, and "somewhat surprisingly, many Polish citizens, even after Polish zloty became a stable and a reliable currency, still preferred to use the US dollar as a parallel currency" (Tyszka & Przybyszewski, 2006, p. 522). In other words, money illusion may reflect an emotional commitment to a certain money (such as the US dollar for Poles), and a corresponding valuation of money that is separate from its mere function as a transactional tool. These results, but also more generally findings from the literature pertaining to money illusion, illustrate that "money illusion disconnects the psychological impact of money from what money can do" (Lea & Webley, 2006, p. 169) contrary to what is assumed by the theory of money as a tool for transaction stemming from the standard model of economics.

Such emotional and cognitive dimensions, independent of its role in transactions, ground money as an institutional fact in the Searlean sense, corresponding to its seemingly paradoxical status as an acquired "primary reinforcer." Indeed, as Elizabeth Phelps observed:

> Money, by definition, is a *secondary reinforcer*, in that its reinforcing properties are tied to what it represents; however, its prominence as a *cultural reinforcer* may give it properties more analogous to a primary reinforcer than to a typical secondary reinforcer. (Phelps, 2009, p. 240)

Put differently, money is associated with neurophysiological and psychological mechanisms akin to other primary reinforcers such as food, even though it is culturally acquired and, therefore, "secondary."

The Aoki-Bourdieu model is closed with the resulting dispositions to institutional actions, that is, money practices. We have considered some of the most important ones, such as the behavioral disposition to hoard. To sum up, money is not only an instrument that enables transactions, but it also emerges in a field of institutional action that is usually called the "market:" This, however, is not identical to a real-world institutionalized market as we use the term "market" in the Fiske sense, that is, as a type of social relationship. This difference is visible in the various metaphorical uses of the term "market," such as "marriage market." This correlates with the emergence of a specific habitus, classically described by

Simmel, and, to some extent, confirmed by experimental studies of the attitudinal and behavioral effects of money frames on individuals (e.g., Smith & Walker, 1993; Wang et al., 2020).

Our model can account for many phenomena that are treated as "anomalies" in behavioral economics, in particular the fact that people treat money differently in different contexts, which appears to be irrational in the abstract view of money that assumes perfect fungibility. This applies to different social contexts as well as to different material forms of money. Theoretically, this reflects the fact that money practices determine cognitive operations with money, in contextualized loops of outward and inward embodiment. Cases in point include the different ways in which money is handled depending on its material form, that is, cash versus credit cards and other digital representations—seminally, Laibson (1997)—and the assignment of money to different mental accounts, for example, depending on the origin of the money. What would be considered the same in standard economics—for example, paying with banknotes, debit cards, or gift cards—leads to different attitudes and behaviors (e.g., Helion & Gilovich, 2014; Reinholtz et al., 2015; Skwara, 2023; White, 2008). It is argued that depending on the concrete material form that money takes, it enters a different mental account and is then associated with a different spending. Therefore, money is fungible, but the way it is materialized—"embodied" by a bank note or a gift card—will be associated with a specific mental account that is separate from other mental accounts (e.g., hoardings or utilitarian spending). So, theoretically money is fungible, but psychologically its representation is not. Interestingly, this can also be influenced by people's culture: Those living in countries dominated by holistic (as opposed to analytical) cultures are more likely to represent these mental accounts as fungible (e.g., Banerjee et al., 2019).[16]

One important aspect is not immediately apparent when looking at the Aoki-Bourdieu-model, but is inherent in Bourdieu's analytical focus: This is the creation of distinct power relations through monetary practices. Indeed, this can even be seen as the defining difference between the embodiment view and the standard view. This becomes clear when we consider the simplest and most abstract picture of the field of a market delimited by monetary flows, which follows the standard terminology and framework of macroeconomics. In Fig. 7.6, we denote the differential power as P with a plus (+) or minus (−) sign.

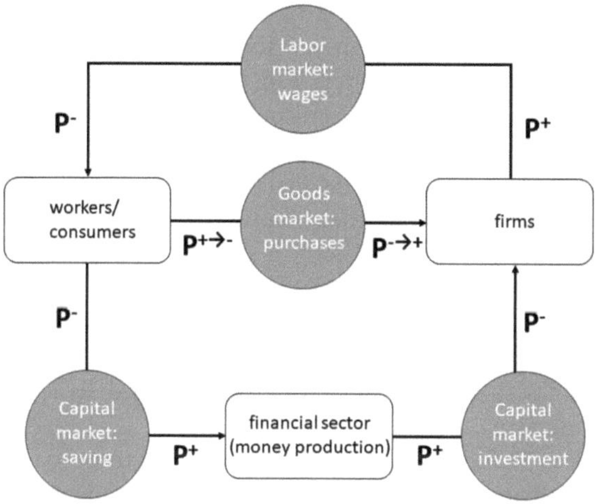

Fig. 7.6 This rudimentary standard macroeconomic model of an economy shows the asymmetries of agential power P that result from differences in the specificity of the respective assets assigned to the poles of capital, labor, and goods. The asymmetries are indicated by plus (+) or minus (−) signs. For example, firms enjoy a positive power differential in the labor market because they pay monetary wages, where money has less asset specificity than workers' skills and capacities. Depending on the market structure (such as the intensity of competition among producers) consumers may enjoy a positive power differential because they pay with money, which firms need to operate their more specific real capital in production

We consider a toy conceptual model with the labor market at its core, where workers offer their labor power at a price (wage rate) and receive monetary income which they spend in the goods market to purchase goods from firms that produce them using labor power and capital goods. The firms obtain loans from the financial sector to invest in this productive capital. Workers save by depositing money in the financial sector. The financial sector includes the central bank, so it produces money.

In this simple structure, deep asymmetries of power result from the specific features of the institution of money. In the relationship between firms and workers, the lowest asset specificity of money creates what has been described as the relatively "footloose" nature of the financial capital held by firms. On the one hand, this means that workers often form specific "assets" that are tied to the relationship with the firm and are embodied, such as their firm-specific skills or their embedded social relations at the place of residence. On the other hand, this means that employers (capitalists) can move money freely, and typically have more capital at their disposal than workers, either because of past accumulation, or because they have better access to loans, since they can make a profit by investing the loans rather than simply spending them on consumption. The resulting power asymmetry is exacerbated under the conditions of unemployment characteristic of capitalism, for various reasons, such as the possible substitution of productive capital for labor. A similar asymmetry arises between firms and financial investors, since monetary assets are more mobile than real assets which are bound to specific uses and contexts of operating a firm.

On the other hand, and at first sight, the asymmetry of asset specificity resulting from holding money works to the advantage of workers as consumers who spend money in the goods market, where sellers and producers offer specific goods that may have no other use beyond market opportunity—think of the famous example of the fish market or fast fashion. This creates strong incentives for firms to build countervailing power through monopolistic means, such as branding or outright anti-competitive practices. In the financial market, power asymmetries work in favor of the financial sector, because firms depend on the production of money and on loans. Interestingly, this is not the case in an economy that relies primarily on barter. The need for productive capital formation, and thus for advance loans, shifts power to the financial sector. Since the financial sector can produce both private and public money, there is also a power asymmetry in its favor *vis-à-vis* workers as hoarders (aka savers). Contrary to many theories in standard economics, the extension of loans is independent of the accumulation of deposits. Hence, savers deposit money in the financial sector only as a service that overcomes the potential erosion of their wealth if it were saved in other forms. This asymmetry is salient in the systematic and pervasive gap between the interest paid on deposits and the interest paid on loans, a reliable source of profit in the financial sector.

In sum, a monetary economy necessarily features structural power asymmetries, often diagnosed in terms of the struggle between labor and capital. In the most general sense, that is, including all kinds of monetary returns on assets, interest is a defining characteristic of capital. However, as the famous Cambridge controversy has convincingly shown, albeit without any impact on current mainstream economics, in the equilibrium approach this juncture entails Gödel-type paradoxes, since the value of capital as discounted flows of future income cannot be derived in a logically consistent way (Cohen & Harcourt, 2003). The alternative "Cambridge UK" view advanced a strongly embodied alternative in seeing interest as reflecting structures of social power. As we have seen, this is inherent in money as an institution because of the asymmetries in social exchange that it implies. Therefore, our view treats power asymmetries as endogenous to the institution of money, without downplaying other sources of social power. Yet, the important implication is that even in a society with strong egalitarian and democratic institutions, the introduction of a capitalist organization of the market would always generate power asymmetries unless the institution of money is fundamentally transformed. As we shall see in Chapter 8, this requires a comprehensive transformation of the monetary order and the financial sector.

7.3 Property and the Institutional Modes of Appropriation

7.3.1 *Property in the Dismal Science*

Property is another key concept in economics and a core concern of (new) institutional economics (Furubotn & Richter, 1997). With the rise of capitalism, controversies over property have emerged and become a defining feature of various economic and political systems, with China, for example, considering public ownership as an essential component of its "socialist market economy" while constitutionally recognizing private property (Long, 2009). At the same time, in many areas, the creation of new forms of property is seen as a panacea for addressing challenges such as reducing CO_2 emissions via markets for emission rights. The rationale is that clearly defined and assigned property rights are a necessary condition for markets to function efficiently: "For the decentralized coordination of productive specialization to work well, according to the well-known principles of comparative advantage, in a society with diffused knowledge, people must have secure, alienable private property rights in productive resources and products tradable at mutually agreeable prices at low costs of negotiating reliable contractual transactions" (Alchian, 2018, pp. 10,892–10,893).

However, property exists in a wide variety of forms and degrees. The theoretical concept of property rights is conceptualized along the lines of the absolute notion of private property. In Blackstone's (1763/2001, p. 3) famous words, the right of property is "that sole and despotic dominion which one man claims and exercises over the external things of the world, in total exclusion of the right of any other individual in the universe" (Blackstone, 1763/2001, p. 3). The strongly individualistic and exclusive conception of property right emerged during the Enlightenment and was enshrined in the civil law codifications of the nineteenth century, beginning with Article 544 of the Code Napoléon (Padoa Schioppa, 2017, p. 444ff). This was accompanied by the recognition of different types of property rights: The rights to use (*usus*), benefit from (*fructus*), and alienate (*abusus*) a thing. Consequently, these different rights may be assigned to different persons, yet, for each specific right, the exclusive and individualistic assignment remains (e.g., a tenant can use the premises while only the landlord can alienate the property). In reality, the absolute nature of property rights is often constrained by many regulations and legal arrangements, which, in theoretical (economics) terms, usually deal with externalities, such as environmental impacts or social nuisances. In fact, this has already been recognized in Article 544, which subjects the right to property to laws and regulations, effectively opening the door wide to societal interventions and restrictions on property, in the modern "liberal" sense (Dagan, 2021). Moreover, the role of property rights is now being questioned in many contexts, such as the open access movements, or the resurgent interest in commons, that is, arrangements of shared public property.

We argue that these complexities reflect the pernicious consequences of a disembodied approach to property. This is partly a problem of law, not of economics per se: We show that economics has largely merely theorized legal developments implemented since the nineteenth century, which have been driven by economic and political interests, and thus have a strong ideological component. In a nutshell, the modern conception of property is capitalist, and what is claimed to be a universal and timeless theory of property in economics is, in fact, the theory of capitalist property. One of the clearest cases of this is the property of land, which is ontologically a neat case of being embodied in its materiality and the ecosystems it contains. However, modern civil law reduces land to disembodied legal claims to parcels identified by cadastral maps (Vanuxem, 2022, p. 37f).

This key role of law highlights the importance of language, as emphasized by Searle, to an extent that goes beyond what we discussed in our example of money. Institutional economists typically distinguish between "economic rights" and "legal rights" (e.g., Barzel, 2015), which introduces a meta-level of social ontology with immense practical implications: I can buy and sell legal claims to a commodity without actually engaging in a physical transaction, even from a distant location. For example, the owner of a building may sell it (legal right) while the tenant continues to use it (economic right defined by the lease), or financial investors can trade commodity futures without physically moving the commodities. The validity of the former process relies exclusively on binding linguistic conventions in the idiom of law.

The historical perspective also reveals that the economic theory of property ignores the central role of property in defining social and political status in real-world societies, and hence is a component of social structures of power (Kennedy, 2011). Conventional economics approaches property as a matter of economic engineering, leaving aside important ethical and political concerns. In contrast, an embodied approach explicitly takes these dimensions into consideration, because property is not only a relation between a person and a physical thing, it is also, fundamentally, a relation between people (Hohfeld, 1917; see also Graeber, 1997). This has a long pedigree in social philosophy and has recently been somewhat reinstated in economics with the "turn" of a leading thinker on economic institutions, D. C. North (2009). This suggests approaching property as a means of pacifying societies, since otherwise, mere force would dominate the allocation of goods to people: "Violence must be near the heart of any explanation of how societies behave. The necessary prerequisite of forming durable large social groups is a way to control violence" (North et al., 2009, p. 258). This amounts to a fundamental paradigm shift in economics, since it implies that the evolution of property would be determined not by economic costs and benefits as objective categories measurable by the economist (usually dubbed "transaction costs"), but by the outcomes of societal struggles over property.[17] Although individual parties to these struggles might consider the costs and benefits of institutions, there is no overarching criterion beyond such particularistic views, and in the outcome of social struggles, one view prevails over the others. Here, the pacifying function is Janus-faced, since the enforcement of property is also based on the use of violent means, albeit formally legitimized by law (Cai et al., 2020). This view vindicates the position of those institutional economists who eschew the deflated notion of "economic property rights," and argue that property rights are necessarily "legal rights," hence, guaranteed and enforced by the state (Hodgson, 2015). In our view, this highlights the fact that capitalism as an economic system is inextricably intertwined with structures of political power.

This is also highly relevant in the legal context, as it points to two different ways of resolving conflicts. One is to apply efficiency standards, which has become the dominant view in many common law jurisdictions with the rise of the field of law and economics (Serkin, 2016, p. 24ff). The other, which goes back to a long tradition in European law (Padoa Schioppa, 2017), is to emphasize equity and material justice in resolving conflicts over the control of resources.[18] Indeed, this reflects a major shift in the interpretation of the common law, with institutional economists in the first half of the twentieth century, such as John Commons, emphasizing the tradition of equity, that is, a reasonable and fair judgmental balancing of interests and concerns in the particular context of a case (Commons, 1996). This perspective is again coming to the fore in recent legal theory (Dagan, 2021). We approach equity as a fundamental form of embodied norms, enacted in the juridical process (Hamrick, 1987). In terms of the distinction between the four fundamental modes of social relationships, the tension between efficiency and equity reflects the tension between the market mode and the other three, especially reciprocity.

In this section, we present a new approach to property, one that begins by considering it as a form of institutional action, that is, "appropriation." Mainstream economics tends to treat property as a structural phenomenon, such as a resource that is owned or a right that is held. Our embodied approach emphasizes the action of appropriation. In doing so, we follow Max Weber, who treated appropriation as a more general term, and property as a special one (Ford, 2010; Weber, 1922/2019).[19] The focus on action leads to a new embodied approach to property by distinguishing four different modes of appropriation that are institutionalized in distinct ways (elaborating on Herrmann-Pillath, 2023b).

7.3.2 *The Uneasy Relationship Between Embodied Property and Disembodied Market*

How is property disembodied? This becomes clear when we consider the famous Coase theorem (Coase, 1960). This theorem states that when transaction costs are zero, the initial assignment of property rights is irrelevant to efficient market allocation, since market transactions will transfer property to those agents who make the best use of it, that is, those who create the most value in the market. To be sure, the utterly unrealistic assumption of zero transaction costs is itself a form of disembodiment, but we want to highlight another point. Even though property is conceived as essential in economics, it is also seen as problematic because it blocks access for others, that is, it is a form of monopoly: "Market power is fundamental to our view of the economy and market power simultaneously retards productivity and depresses employment. Hoarding of property away from its most productive uses creates unemployment but also reduces economic growth" (Posner & Weyl, 2018, p. 254). Property holding implies that someone lazy and disinterested in exploiting it economically can exclude others who can be more productive. Hence, property and wealth creation in markets remain in tension. Accordingly, Posner and Weyl propose a "radical markets" approach to property in which property, such as a house, would be subject to a continuous auctioning process that would allow the most valuable use to emerge from continuous re-allocation. This is illustrative of the Coasean argument, which refers to an institutional setting, the auction, where transaction costs are minimal. As a result, property would become ephemeral to the market process, and thus ultimately disembodied.

We shall not discuss the realism of such thinking here, but point to the observation that the market is, once again conceived as a medium of disembodiment through assetification. This can be systematically explored by reflecting on Hegel's influential theory of property, for it reveals the inherent tension between market and property, which the young Marx exposed.

For Hegel, property and contract are the central institutions of law as the foundation of civil society (Ritter, 2004). However, Hegel approaches property in two ways, which can be conceived as converging, given his broader framework of the unfolding of the spirit in history: Since we do not subscribe to Hegel's metaphysics (nor did Marx), the tension is immediately obvious. The first meaning of property refers to the indispensable role of owned objects in the self-actualization of the Hegelian subject. The subject can only become a person by expressing itself in outward action, and for this an object (most generally, "nature") is necessary. This object is transformed by expressive action, and in the course of this process, the object also transforms the subject. Accordingly, a Hegelian view of property implies a dynamic relationship between subject and object of property corresponding to the duality of outward embodiment materialized in expressive action and inward embodiment of the object. More specifically, Hegel followed Locke in arguing that the action of the subject is labor applied to the object, and that this labor materializes a process of personal development.

Therefore, in this first view of property, property is constitutive of becoming a person, especially in the sense of being autonomous not only formally, but also materially. The young Marx could easily expose the flaw of this thinking, while at the same time agreeing with it in principle: What happens when a person is prevented from owning property? The proletarian worker is alienated and denied the right to personhood. But the very concept of alienation is Hegelian (Moyar, 2008).

Marx's point cannot be fully understood without considering the second Hegelian view of property. This is that civil society is built on the law of economic exchange, where property and contract are the institutional manifestations of freedom. Hegel was fully aware of the possible pathologies, and even the danger, of creating a property-less group, which he called the "rabble." This is why his complete system requires the embedding of law within the larger framework of "ethical life" ("*Sittlichkeit*"), which also includes incipient notions of a welfare state (Ver Eecke, 2008). However, to project his second view onto real-world conditions, as Marx did, is to isolate the workings of law, and here we must see Hegel in the context of his time, that is, when the new civil laws were promulgated, in which an absolute and individualistic notion of property was enshrined. This real-world law enacted a social reality far removed from the Hegelian ethical life, and created a very embodied immense suffering for those without property.

Hegel's internal tension directly mirrors the tension between markets as media of disembodiment and property as a form of embodiment. In what follows, we will develop an embodiment approach to property. This, however, faces a formidable task. Our language of property has been impoverished as a result of the legal transformations of the nineteenth century. Influential in these transformations was another philosophical approach to property, that of John Locke, which also influenced Hegel. Locke argued that what makes an object "property" in the first place is the expenditure of labor on it to obtain a benefit (Waldron, 2023). This is a thoroughly embodied argument, as Locke argues that labor is a priori property because it is an expression of the body, and the body is the subject. This primordial property right literally infects the object, making it the property of the subject. We will return to Locke's reasoning in the next section. At this point, we highlight that it had immense influence, for example, in legitimizing the land claims of European farmer-settlers in North America against native populations who were seen as just roaming in the wilderness (Greer, 2017).

The generalization of Locke's argument is that what constitutes property is the addition of value to a pristine object. With the civil law codifications in the nineteenth century, this was increasingly conceptualized as value added through market action. Thus, we can say that the framing of the Locke argument in terms of markets was the crucial transition from an embodied to a disembodied view. This is most evident when we consider the key resource in pre-capitalist times: land. The civil law codifications aimed to abolish all kinds of "feudal" constraints on the trading of property as landed assets on the market. To this day, an important aspect is to subject land to market prices, thus "objectifying" its value (Graziadei, 2017). This is essential in a specific context, namely the use of land as collateral for loans: The creditor needs to reliably assess the value of the land and be sure that if the loan turns sour, he can easily recover the money by selling the land on the market. As we can see, this is a concrete form of abstracting the object of property by commodifying it. This example is also illuminating in revealing counterforces in real life: In the case of a house, the borrower may also develop a relationship of belonging to the house and the community in which it is located, and that community may recognize the owner as a valued member. Foreclosures disrupt these positive relationships with neighbors, and can even create negative pecuniary externalities for them, since the value of their houses typically declines when neighboring houses are in foreclosure (e.g., Gupta, 2019). Thus, there are strong equity and fairness reasons to favor loan restructuring over foreclosure, which, nonetheless, reduces the market value of the house and the size of the potential mortgage loan. The forces of disembodiment and embodiment remain in tension.

The new codifications were the result of a revolutionary process. Two aspects stood out. The first aspect is that modern property aimed to abolish the commons as an alternative form of appropriation (De Moor, 2015). When it comes to land, the commons means that many individuals have simultaneous claims to access and enjoy certain benefits of the land. While these rights could theoretically be considered in turn as "property rights" (Schlager & Ostrom, 1992), this would create what legal scholars have called "the tragedy of the anticommons," that is, the fragmentation of rights that would make trading the land itself extremely cumbersome, while at the same time making it nearly impossible to assess the value of the land independently of the value of these fragmented rights (Heller, 1998). This means that a market for land could not operate at a sufficiently low level of transaction costs unless the underlying communal ownership of the land itself is privatized, thereby abrogating the partial rights claimed as ownership. Accordingly, the process of enclosure and political suppression of the commons was accompanied by a process of legal disembodiment of land, in the form of public land records and exclusive assignments to individual owners (Polanyi, 1944/2001, p. 187ff).

The second aspect is another form of disembodiment: The suppression of most forms of perpetual ownership in the family line, such as the *fidei commissum*, even though the common law continued with a special variant, the trust, while abolishing perpetuities. This is of interest to us for two reasons. First, in the second half of the twentieth century, the trust became a major legal instrument for assetification and the creation of abstract financial entities, which is another example of the expansion of the scope of the disembodied market (Pistor, 2019). The second is the breaking of the personal relationship between the subject and object of property. Compare this, for example, with Chinese customary property law, where there was a distinction between "life" and "dead" sales of land (Hase, 2013). Because land was considered the most essential element in the family's patrimony over generations and a crucial source of livelihood, a seller retained the right to redeem the land in perpetuity, and close relatives enjoyed a right of pre-emption (a "life" sale). Tellingly, a key measure of institutional transformation by British colonial rule in Hong Kong was the abolition of these forms of property and the granting of exclusive individual ownership in a land registry.

We have already mentioned that the Lockean view also justified the expropriation of native people in the colonies, and, later, especially in the young United States. The latter case is of particular interest because it also involved early forms of financialization of land, thus leveraging the process of disembodiment of land (Greer, 2017).[20] In contrast, Indigenous conceptions of land remain deeply embodied until today. Arguably, this creates deep tensions with modern legal systems. The key issue is that, in the Indigenous view, land is conceived as an essential part of people's identity, and, in turn, people are part of the land (Lenzerini, 2017). In modern parlance, people and land are assemblages that cannot be disrupted (Keenan, 2015). Therefore, the land is sacred, cannot be alienated, and cannot be subject to individual decisions, only those of the community. This clearly drives a deep wedge between Indigenous views and Western legal notions that individualize property on land and treat alienability as a fundamental aspect of individual freedom. As a consequence, this also limits the application of economic techniques of land valuation to their claims (Choy, 2018). In terms of Fiske's relationships, as mentioned earlier, we observe another instance of tension between the market mode and other modes, in this case, the community mode, crystallized in the contested notion of alienability.

Now, to return to the problem of language, the simple point is that we lack a term that can refer to this kind of "property." Our language is semantically impoverished because it has been shaped by legal conceptions directly aimed at underpinning the market. This goes back to Roman law, revived in civil law codifications, which conceived of ***proprietas*** as ***dominium***, that is, absolute appropriation by the *pater familias*, while also enabling economic exchange, that is, contractual transfers of property. However, Roman law distinguished between two domains of things, those governed by human law, and those governed by divine law (Bloch, 2006). The latter is exempt from any form of alienation and is sacred. However, Roman law never elaborated on this in legal detail, so we are left with human law, which focuses on precisely those dimensions that became hegemonic in the nineteenth century.

Hence, we are faced with the challenge of developing a new terminology that allows us to distinguish between the two Hegelian views of property. There is an interesting precedent in Hannah Arendt's distinction between property and wealth (Arendt, 1958/2018, pp. 58ff, 109ff). This differs radically from the meaning of property in civil law codes, as she relates property to the Greek *polis*, and thus specifically to a person's dwelling, which defines his (in Greece, his) status as a person in the community. As such, it is inalienable. In contrast, the legal systems of the nineteenth century effectively regulate "property" as "wealth" conceived as a fungible thing that can be valued on the market.

In the following, we develop a new conceptual framework of "property." We begin with perhaps the most contentious innovation, the distinction between ownership and property.

7.3.3 *Ownership and the Self*

We propose to call the white space in modern theories of property, that is, inalienable property, "ownership." In relation to Arendt, for example, her "property" would be our "ownership," and her "wealth" would be our "property." This remains in tension with some established legal usages, but these are not universal. In mixed common law regimes, "ownership" refers to a kind of Blackstonian absolute property, while in many US common law contexts the term is even avoided, in favor of "property" (Gretton, 2007; Honoré, 1961). Our terminology refers to uses in non-legal language, where "owning" often means that subjects identify with an object, which has a scholarly counterpart in the psychological literature on "ownership" (e.g., Belk, 1988; Pierce et al., 2003). Despite these tensions with some established uses, the great advantage of our proposal is that we can keep the economic use of "property" intact: Indeed, economics is only concerned with "property" in our sense, since it focuses on markets. Not only is "ownership" sidelined, but it is even treated hostilely, as an impediment to market transactions.

This establishes a perspective on appropriation that is most emphasized in critical theories of property, and, as noted, is most salient in juxtaposing Indigenous claims to land with land as property (Keenan, 2015). Today, while such claims are increasingly legally recognized, these Indigenous groups and lawyers also emphasize that they are fundamentally different from property (Bioneers, 2022; McNeil, 2017). The key distinction is the denial of alienability and, relatedly, the view of land as an essential element of their collective identity.

This can be generalized and theorized by distinguishing two modes of appropriation (Fig. 7.7). One goes back to Roman Law and draws a neat line between subject and object of appropriation, which is seen as domination and subordination: Here, property is the unlimited power of the subject over the object. This ontological separation ends up disembodying appropriation in terms of abstract and formal rights. The second type is a part-whole relationship, in the sense that the object is conceived as part of the subject, and vice versa. We refer to this as identifying appropriation—in French reflected in the double meaning of "*s'approprier*." A related expression is "belonging:" An object belongs to a subject and vice versa (Cooper, 1998).

Obviously, these two ways of relating to objects reflect different modes of social relationships: The subordinative one is the hierarchy mode, while the identifying relationship is the community mode, which combines elements of the reciprocity mode. This is important when considering economic organizations in the next section, where property rights in the firm are interpreted exclusively in the hierarchy mode, when it comes to Coasean institutional economics. The special status of identifying appropriation is salient in distinguishing between different transactions by which someone can become an appropriator. In social science and philosophy, the "gift" plays a particularly important role: The vast literature following Marcel Mauss' (1925/1990) classical treatment of gifts has highlighted the fact that a genuine gift retains an implicit relationship with the giver, in the sense of maintaining her or his identity and thereby establishing or confirming the personal relationship between giver and receiver (Hénaff, 2002; Schwartz, 1967):

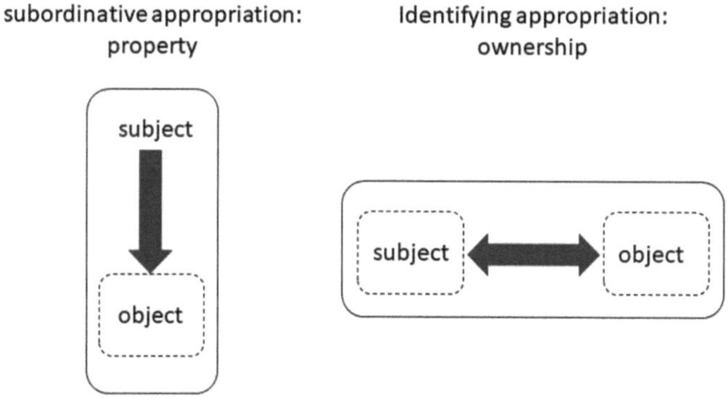

Fig. 7.7 Epitomized in classical Roman law versus contemporary Indigenous conceptions of appropriation of land, the former represents subordinative appropriation in which the appropriating subject of property establishes absolute domination over the appropriated object (left panel). In contrast, identifying appropriation establishes a mutual relationship of part and whole between the appropriating subject and object (right panel)

> What imposes obligation in the present received and exchanged, is the fact that the thing received is not inactive. Even when it has been abandoned by the giver, it still possesses something of him. (…) one must give back to another person what is really part and parcel of his nature and substance, because to accept something from somebody is to accept some part of his spiritual essence, of his soul. (Mauss, 1925/1990, pp. 15–16; see also, Godelier, 1996/1999, p. 15; Graeber, 2001, p. 151ff)

This also reveals deep connections to our treatment of money, since gifts of money, otherwise the medium *par excellence* of alienation, have a special status in many societies, subject to strong normative constraints (Zelizer, 1989, 1997).

Ownership, of course, is by no means limited to non-Western contexts:

> Here, I think we can say that Mauss' overall conclusions have been quite clearly confirmed. In every case, the most valuable objects in gift economies[21] are valued primarily because they embody some human quality, whether this be the creative potential of human action, or fertility, or the like, or particular histories and identities that have already been achieved. (Graeber, 2001, p. 2011)

Many forms of appropriation of everyday objects are ownership in the sense of establishing a relationship between subject and object that would not normally be eschewed through alienation. This certainly depends on the functional context: Mobile professionals will easily swap apartments with furniture according to their needs, while others may perceive their homes as inalienable, even to the extent of hoping to inherit them as family estate. Our homes are often filled with many items that have personal meanings, and fit our individual needs, such as a favorite sofa for relaxing and dreaming. Such arrangements embody the cognitive *Gestalt* effects of both subjective and intersubjective perception of the assemblage of persons and things that underscore the part-whole pattern of ownership (Schlicht, 2018): A person is seen as a *Gestalt* of body and belongings. This is the mere definition of self in James's parlance:

> Our fame, our children, the works of our hands, may be as dear to us as our bodies are, and arouse the same feelings and the same acts of reprisal if attacked. (...) a man's Self is the sum total of all that he CAN call his, not only his body and his psychic powers, but his clothes, and his house, his wife and children, his ancestors and friends, his reputation and works,

> his lands, and yacht and bank-account. All these things give him the same emotions. If they wax and prosper, he feels triumphant; if they dwindle and die away, he feels cast down. (James, 1890, p. 291)

Likewise, Simmel indicates about the self that: "Generally speaking, every possession is an extension of the self, a phenomenon within subjective life, and its whole meaning lies in the conscious and emotional reflexes that are the mind's response to the self's relations to objects" (Simmel, 1907/2004, p. 333).

However, there are also important cases of ownership that are different from property, even in a market context. One of these is the family business, which is a leading form of business organization in many countries and many trades. Family business often manifests a distinct relationship between family and business as embodied in factory sites, practices, and implicit tacit forms of knowledge. This has motivated distinct theoretical approaches, such as the theory of socio-emotional wealth (Berrone et al., 2012). Socio-emotional wealth (SEW) is a prominent example of embodied "property," in the sense that it imbues "capital" with a strong dose of ownership. Similarly, entrepreneurs often show a strong emotional attachment to the mission of the companies they found, especially when it comes to social and sustainable entrepreneurship (e.g., Krueger et al., 2011). There is a rich literature on measuring SEW and exploring its consequences in business, such as for competitive advantage (Zellweger, 2017). Family businesses are also rich in communicative actions, such as rituals that establish family identity as embodied in objects, even the products sold in markets, which may have iconic status in a company museum (Bruess, 2011; Massa et al., 2017).

Summarizing these observations, we define the first mode of appropriation as:

Mode A. Ownership: Belonging ⇔ Recognition

This mode refers to the Hegelian notion of self-actualization, and is characterized by the sense of mutuality conveyed by the verb "to belong." Following Hegel, ownership as an institutional action depends crucially on the recognition of others, while the law can articulate and protect ownership, but typically only in adjudication, since ownership is deeply embodied and, therefore, contextualized. Although Indigenous land is the case where we can observe the mode in its purest form as far as land is concerned, there are many manifestations of the "belonging

⇔recognition" nexus in all modern societies. Land is a set of places and relationships that often deeply implicate issues of identity for communities of different scopes and types. Three examples may suffice (Cooper, 1998). The first is the regulation of access to nature, since in most societies there are different ways of expressing identity (even national identity) in relating to nature. In England, for example, hunting remains a special right of the community that allows trespassing, whereas in other countries it is not. The second is the interface between private and public in urban settlements, for example when private actors want to construct a building with religious functions, that may be considered as sensitive by neighboring non-believers. Finally, another important example is the relationship between landlord and tenant: German constitutional law differs in important ways from German civil law in recognizing tenancy as a form of "*Eigentum*," which, in our conceptual scheme, clearly evokes notions of belonging and dwelling, that is, ownership (Alexander, 2003). However, German law does not have a specific term for this mode of appropriation, which is only recognized in court decisions.

Ownership is directly related to the second mode of appropriation that has been legally recognized since Roman times, possession, but must be seen as different, as is evident in the legal debates over Indigenous claims to land that is not actually occupied by the people. Possession is a medium of embodiment that refers to the actual physical relationship between subject and object, independent of the projection of a "right" onto it.

7.3.4 *Possession as Enacting Appropriation*

Possession is close to what economics refers to as "economic rights" (Barzel, 2015), which raises the question of whether the mere use or occupation of an object also constitutes a right. This is important in many respects, such as the question of whether animals possess their territories, which would directly imply that they must be regarded as proprietors with rights (Bradshaw, 2020). Indeed, when we think of land, all living beings on a piece of land are in fact exerting efforts to enjoy the benefits of the land, such as birds foraging and gathering twigs to build a nest. How is this different from human appropriation?

This points to the classical nineteenth-century legal debate between von Savigny and Jhering on "possession," which refers to the Roman notions of *corpus* and *animus*, hence quintessentially embodied concepts

(Emerich, 2017). The *corpus* account of possession refers to the view of the external observer who would ascertain facts about a subject who effectively uses and occupies an object, such as a squatter on a piece of land. Clearly, this would also apply to the bird. In light of the animus concept, this is not sufficient, since there must also be a "will" to use and occupy, and even more, this will must be expressed. The latter would also include the fact of use and occupation, if these are simultaneously seen as communication to the public (Rose, 2019, p. 267ff). We can interpret both views as embodied approaches to appropriation; taken together, possession must be enacted, that is, it is a type of action, and it must be accompanied by emotional and cognitive states that are expressed in these actions.

It is instructive to return to the example of birds. We argue that birds possess territory in the sense of *animus*. This follows from the observation that territorial claims do not arise primarily from ongoing struggles for access, but are expressed and negotiated in many forms of ritualized behaviors that, in most cases, avoid such struggles (Despret, 2019). In other words, the rituals manifest and communicate the "will" to claim a territory. In fact, we can also argue that many forms of communicating possession among humans are also ritual actions, most notably in the sacred status of territory among Indigenous peoples. Everyday rituals include practices such as seeing a closed gate as excluding and an open one as inviting, whether it has a lock or not.[22]

This constellation has been theorized in game-theoretic models christened "bourgeois" for the reason that they emerge from the analysis of the hawk and dove game as a simple model of direct conflict, where a third strategy, in addition to attack and retreat, leads to sustainable equilibria (Gintis, 2007). This third strategy is to attack when being the incumbent, and retreat when being the invader, which seems to establish possession because a necessary requirement is that the incumbent effectively communicates its status. The question remains, however, whether such a truce reflects a real advantage for the incumbent in the event of a real fight.

A possible factor that plays a prominent role in behavioral economics comes to mind here, namely the endowment effect (Kahneman et al., 1990; Knetsch, 1989; Thaler, 2016). This is often explained in terms of loss aversion, which can be regarded as a cross-species disposition (e.g., Santos & Hughes, 2009), that could explain why an incumbent takes a greater risk and spends more effort defending its turf. This would establish an ontological continuity across species, including humans, and thereby a naturalistic account of property.

However, various strands of research have shown that the loss aversion account is often weak (e.g., Gal & Rucker, 2018), or even that a substantial part (about half) of a representative sample of the US population is not loss averse, but loss tolerant (e.g., Chapman et al., 2022, 2023). Actually, the emerging empirical evidence converges and does not support a link between the endowment effect and loss aversion (e.g., Chapman et al., 2023; Fehr & Kübler, 2022). Several alternative explanations have been suggested in the literature (e.g., Morewedge & Giblin, 2015). Among them, interestingly, it appears that the endowment effect can arise from (psychological) ownership by physically assigning an object to a subject, thus creating an embodied association, whereas merely assigning a right may not be sufficient (e.g., Korobkin, 2014; Morewedge et al., 2009; Reb & Connolly, 2007). Most significantly, when considering contemporary human hunter-gatherer groups, such as the Hadza Bushmen of Northern Tanzania, the endowment effect emerges precisely in those groups that are closer to market societies and more familiar with markets, suggesting that the effect is not an endowed psychological mechanism that remains in continuity with animal behavior, but only materializes in a specific cultural environment that includes the possibility of alienation (Apicella et al., 2014). As a result, we avoid simplistic naturalistic approaches to the embodiment of possession: The endowment effect shows that appropriation involves enactive and embodied signs of appropriation. It follows that the endowment effect refers to ownership as arising from possession: The mode of possession leads to the extension of the self, described by James (1890), Simmel (1907/2004), or Belk (1988), and thus activates the mode of ownership.

An important consequence of this discussion is that the embodied approach to property can be extended beyond humans, but without falling into the trap of biological reductionism, which would relate possession to some "inner" biological dispositions, in the sense of evolutionary psychology. Even in the animal kingdom, and certainly in humans, possession as a "right" emerges as an enactive sign in the sense of Malafouris (2013). The birdsong that claims a territory as such is an enactive sign, and after all, in many bird species the songs are not genetically prescribed but culturally acquired and transmitted (Despret, 2019; Prum, 2017). In the human domain, enactive signs manifest themselves in a much wider variety, including in particular reflexive operations such as law. However, as we have seen, possession is also seen as an action that functions directly as an enactive sign, to which we can add many other items, such as facial expressions when encountering a stranger on one's premises or fences. This has to be neatly distinguished from legal documents that enshrine property, that is, that enable alienation through markets.

In summary, we define the second mode of appropriation as referring to the verb "to use" as a generic form of action that relates to others in terms of the action of "allowing," meaning that possession is recognized by others. This works in two directions (Serkin, 2016). One direction is the role of adverse possession which implies that if a person uses an object for a certain period of time without interference from the legal holder of the property, the person can acquire this legal right in the long run, as illustrated by the French "usucapion." The other direction is that, under certain circumstances, property holders must accede use rights ("easements"), hence a form of possession, to others, such as neighbors who need to access their own property by crossing a neighbor's property.

Mode B. Possession: Using ⇔ Allowing

Adding some detail to the notion of "allowing," a special topic of great significance is managerial possession or stewardship, which can include a very broad range of rights, including alienation, such as selling a unit of a business to another company. Yet, the manager does not hold property as a person: She is "allowed" to exert possession. In terms of embodiment, it is not the individual that counts, but the position as defined in an organization, such as CEO. By assuming this role, an individual also enters the mode of possessing the company. There are constructs, such as certain trusts, in which the holders of property are even explicitly barred from possession (Emerich, 2017, p. 180). Here, possession takes the form of a legal right.

Without going into the details here, the key observation in this more specific, though broadly applicable, context, is that property is defined by the structure of the legal person. Even though the shareholder of a public company is formally the holder of the property, her rights to interfere with managerial possession as defined by that structure are tightly circumscribed. What emerges here is a fact that was already discussed in medieval canon law, namely where exactly a legal person is materially incorporated. The solution offered was that even if all the monks had died, the legal person remained "encorporated" in the buildings of the monastery (Thomas, 2011, p. 207ff).

7.3.5 *Property: Disembodying Appropriation*

The discussion so far shows that a key aspect of disembodiment is the definition of a mode of appropriation, for which we will henceforth reserve the term "property." This goes back to Max Weber, who used the German word "*Eigentum*" (property) only for forms of appropriation that included both inheritability and the full right of alienation, the latter termed "*freies Eigentum*" (free property) (Ford, 2010): "*Chancen*[23] that are appropriated to individuals through inheritance, or to heritable communities or associations, will be called property (of the relevant individuals, communities, or associations), and where appropriated as an alienable *Chance*, free property" (Weber, 1922/2019, p. 124). Alienation means tradability on markets, thus reflecting the main concerns of nineteenth-century codifications. Most significantly, it also shows that property is not just a disembodied concept: Rather, it is also an institutionalized form of appropriation through the disembodiment of the relationship between people and things. This is one of the main reasons why property has been a key issue in ideological battles since the nineteenth century.

To understand disembodiment, it is essential to adequately address the role of monetary valuation as a means of abstraction. As noted above, the simplification of legal property rights pertaining to land was driven primarily by the need to streamline land valuation. The more potential claimants to land and its various uses, the more difficult it is to establish a specific market value. However, market value is not only important for trade and objects, but also for claiming the land as a creditor to repay a loan. Property is deeply connected with debt, for only when an object is exclusively owned by the borrower, can it be claimed unequivocally. This becomes clear when we look at legal history, where constructs of legal persons were created to clarify liability in debt relations.[24] As aforementioned, the legal battle against the *fidei commissum* was mainly driven by the concerns of creditors of aristocratic borrowers who might be prevented from foreclosing on the family estate.

Thus, we can also associate disembodiment with the direct rupture of modes of possession and ownership as embodied forms in the claiming of property to repay a debt. This is taken literally, since creditors' claims can be enforced by violent actions, such as imprisonment. Remarkably, in civil law codifications, the state assumes the role of ultimate enforcer. This differs from the role of communities in enforcing a claim through other sanctions, such as loss of reputation or ostracism, which are related to more abstract forms of defining equity. This is evident in home foreclosures where ownership relations that emerge from the contextualization of debtors' liabilities are excluded from the legal process.

We define the third mode of appropriation as follows:

Mode C. Property: Holding ⇔ Trading

We use the term "holding" here to point to the notion of "holding a right" (Honoré, 1961). The form of tradable legal rights which emerged in the nineteenth century, can be traced back to Roman law and was explicitly designed to enable alienation through the market. The important implication is that objects of property can also be valued at market prices.

This gives us an opportunity to discuss the relationship between our approach and the economics of property rights, which typically distinguishes between economic and legal rights. The former reflects the mode of possession, so the two modes are related as shown in the diagram (Fig. 7.8).

Economics focuses on the functions of appropriation, that is, the uses of an object of property. Thus, "economic property rights" are rights of possession, although we would avoid even the term "right" here, which would continue to confuse possession and property. We speak of property only in terms of legal rights, which may include possession when, as has been the case since Roman law, possession is legally defined as a right. However, in the form of a right, it also falls under property in our framework. Thus, as shown in Fig. 7.8, there is a continuum of rights that are not congruent with legal definitions of property, even though all of these rights are legally constituted. For example, the rights of possession of a CEO are legally constituted, but they are not property in the civil law sense.

Now, referring to property as a right is a direct form of disembodiment. Indeed, some legal systems, such as the German, even take the position that only material things can be objects of property, whereas Roman law distinguished between "*res corporeales*" and "*res incorporeales*" and asserted that both could be objects of property, a position maintained by the majority of legal systems (Gretton, 2007). As we have seen, the German system also recognizes ownership to some degree, thus apparently remaining in the shadow of Hegel.

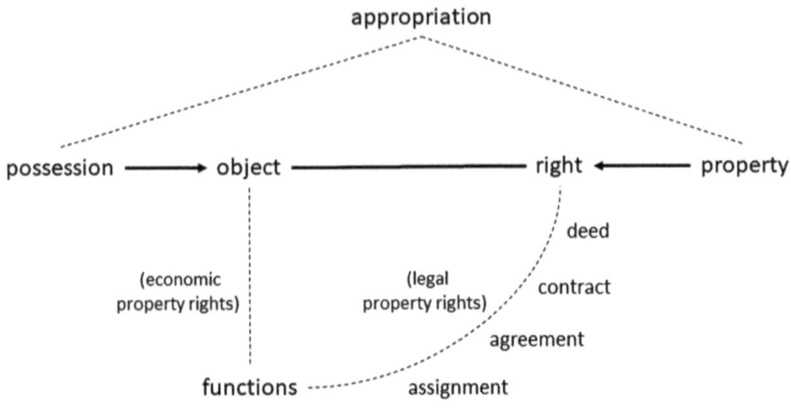

Fig. 7.8 The distinction between possession and property is related to the distinction between economic and legal property rights in institutional economics. Possession defines economic property rights that enable the realization of certain economic functions of the appropriated objects. Property as a legal right is established via various legal forms, which can include strong ones, such as the land deed, or weaker ones, such as an agreement in customary law or an assignment in the law of trusts

Legal rights are incorporated into linguistic constructs as "parole." This refers, among other things, to the phenomenon of contracts and to the domain of conflict resolution through courts or other media of dispute resolution. Thus, we can distinguish between the terms "transaction game" and "language game," where the use of the word "game" is not inspired by game theory but by Wittgenstein's (1953) meaning. The two terms relate to the two sides of interactions, their physical realization and their meaning. Transactions may be physically similar, such as handing over a watch to another person, but the meaning in terms of the "language game" can be very different, such as being a "sale" or a "gift." We encountered this difference in Chapter 6 when discussing framing effects in experimental economics where the experimenter tries to impose her definition of the game as a "transaction game" on the participants, while treating their interpretations as a "language game" as creating unwanted biases. This focuses attention on the various ways in which property comes to individuals in the first place. In the ownership mode, this is inheritance, but there are other transactions, most importantly, the gift, which we briefly discussed in Sect. 7.3.3. In contrast, acquiring an object by purchase means cutting off such a relationship altogether. This means, however, that this transformation is embodied in the form of the transaction, which can be analyzed in terms of Fiske's four modes of social relationships. Thus, despite the legal distinction between property law and contract law, the original contract embodies property as a legal right. This is obscured by the conventional distinction between property law and contract law, although it is systematically clear that a contractual claim is itself property (Wolff, 2020). Remarkably, in the early history of Roman law, for less valuable objects the simple transfer of a good (and thus a change of possession) was sufficient to legally conclude the property transaction—a tradition that is maintained in modern civil laws, such as that of France. For more valuable items, rituals were necessary in which the transfer was witnessed and obeyed sacred Roman traditions, and in which physical actions such as touching a slave were essential (Harke, 2016).

Accordingly, and continuing our discussion of debt, the institutionalized action of holding and trading an object builds directly on the disembodiment of the relationship between the subject and the object of appropriation. This is characterized by the fact that the endowment effect vanishes when experimental subjects frame the transaction game in the language game of trading (Kahneman, 2012, p. 297ff).

7.3.6 *Theft and Violence in Appropriation*

There is a primordial form of ownership that arises from elementary interactions, such as one individual grabbing an object and another individual saying "This is mine."[25] Or one individual gives an object away, but later changes her mind, claims it back, and now the other individual utters "This is mine."

In the pre-history of property, we cannot separate the concept from "brute" forms of appropriation, which we generically call "theft." Thus, the fourth mode is theft, which includes all kinds of violent and fraudulent appropriation. In a Hobbesian turn, theft would be seen as the primordial form of appropriation, which also requires violent means to protect the usurped objects. Advanced legal forms of property appear to be societal remedies against endemic violence, reviving the earlier argument about territoriality. As aforementioned, this has been systematized in North's new view of property and violence. At the same time, this implies that, from the earliest times, appropriation cannot only be understood as a relationship between the subject and the object of appropriation, including another subject with competing claims, but also as the result of a triangular structural condition in which the enforcers and protectors of appropriation participate directly, as is most visible in the arrangements of feudalism (Earle, 2017; Hicks, 1969). By implication, societal structures of control and the use of violent means of coercion are a primordial form of the embodiment of appropriation, including the corresponding language games, such as threats.

Mode D. Theft: Usurping ⇔ Disenfranchisement

Theft is a form of appropriation that has shaped global economic conditions from the earliest times to the present. Notorious examples include the colonial usurpation of land and resources and slavery. The institutional legacy casts a long shadow, as many postcolonial states continue to operate under the legal frameworks of colonialism (Acemoglu et al., 2001). This allows for two different forms of postcolonial theft. The first is where governments continue to control land and resources after nationalization, usurping the rights of local communities and allowing their possession by private actors through licensing schemes—for the example of Indonesian forests, see Larson and colleagues (2017). This often meets with community resistance and fuels violent conflicts. The second form takes this usurpation a step further: Private usurpation of government, especially in failed states (Wenar, 2017). This is a case of theft even under national law, but once resources such as oil and other commodities cross the border, they assume formal property status under the effectiveness doctrine of international law which is recognized by all national laws around the world:

> What all these specific national laws have in common is the structure of effectiveness. Every nation's laws will take the input of stolen minerals in the Congo and produce an output of perfect legal title at the point of final purchase. The laws of each country, that is, will turn a militia's might at one end of the sale into a pure legal right at the other. (Wenar, 2017, p. 104)

Given these examples, and following Searle, we must note that appropriation is to a considerable extent embodied in "brute facts" of violence, even if these are mostly shifted to background conditions. In modern societies, there are also acts of violence without a direct physical context, such as identity theft. A key aspect is the role of the state in controlling the monopoly of violence. Contrary to the mainstream position in institutional economics that the state is indispensable for securing property rights, there is no general presumption that this implies the absence of violent appropriation fully legitimized by property law, as in the case of the usurpation of land by white settlers in North America (Cai et al., 2020).

One of the most complex issues is that of the body as an object of appropriation. In most pre-modern societies and capitalist expansion until the mid-nineteenth century, slavery was a pillar of the economic system, hence the outright theft of bodies and the complete subordination of the individual to the proprietor, which also implied the suppression of all other modes of social relationships, albeit sometimes imperfectly, as in the case of the community mode. Marx argued that another form of theft is the expropriation of surplus value from workers. In our framework, this refers to the role of alienability. In the case of slavery, the proprietor of the slave also enjoys the right of alienation. In the case of the worker who does not own the means of production, that is, the tools of her labor, the market mode changes the form of appropriation by abstracting "labor power" from the body proper, thus creating the "labor market" as a supposedly free exchange between worker and employer. Here, the worker can be seen as both the owner of her body and the holder of the property rights of her labor power. In this peculiar construction, market exchange externalizes the relationship between the body and labor power. This means that even if market exchange were free, there could be externalities that would still count as theft in relation to the body. Examples abound: The externalization of the onerous costs of commuting onto workers without compensation, or the many kinds of work-related illnesses that often manifest themselves in later stages of life. We will return to these issues in the next section.

7.3.7 Conclusion

We have outlined the four modes of appropriation, which is the first step in a full-fledged embodied economics analysis of property that would deploy the full arsenal of tools such as conceptual blending analysis and the Aoki-Bourdieu model, as introduced in the case of money. A key aspect of institutional changes is the mediation of switches between modes through shifting conceptual blends. This is straightforward in the case of the shift from ownership to property, which can be understood as a shift between two generic spaces, using the example of the commons as a form of ownership (see Fig. 7.9). The reference to generic spaces is in turn embodied, here, materially anchored. The mode of possession is crucial: In the case of the commons, the anchor is the actual pattern of possession, such as the current uses of a forest by various people, who, once experiencing themselves as a community, would accordingly conceptualize the forest as a commons. If one form of possession becomes dominant, such as commercial logging by a powerful party, this may trigger a switch to the market as a cognitive frame, and drive actions towards privatization of the forest, and thus a transition from commons to private property.

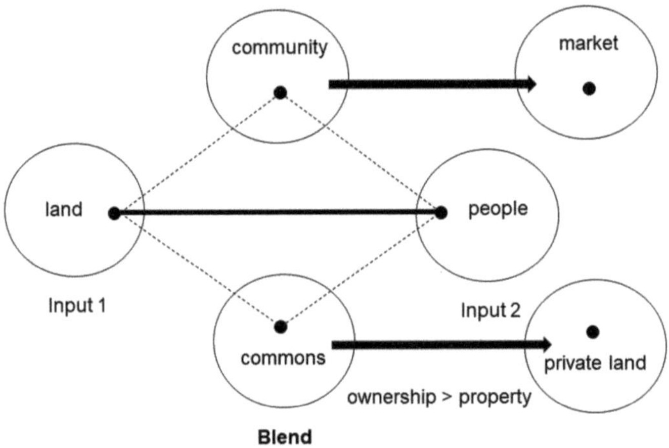

Fig. 7.9 In the mode of ownership, the counterparts of land and people are identified through the matching operation that takes place in the generic space of "community," and then projected into the blended space of "commons." As the notion and institution of the commons embrace certain forms of possession, more and more individuals may engage in market activities (e.g., legitimate private logging in commons forests). This evolving practice may trigger a shift towards the blending of private land rights, by matching "land" and "people" together in the generic space of "market." Ultimately, this interaction between evolving practices and cognitive transformations leads to the privatization of land and the destruction of commons

In the Aoki-Bourdieu model, we can add more details, such as that the approach to possession as a sign is associated with certain emotional and cognitive mechanisms that create ownership, while the simultaneous projection of an object onto a pricing scheme would trigger opposite feelings that foster the willingness to alienate the land for profit. These effects are part and parcel of the symbolic capital activated by various parties in pursuit of their goals in the fields of interactions such as the struggle for resources such as land. For example, a party pursuing business goals in the market may, even without deliberation (i.e., unintentionally), communicate pricing schemes that are also perceived by others, thus triggering shifts from the community mode to the market mode in the setting of a commons (e.g., a peasant enticed by profits from logging as done by a landlord). The community might counteract such developments by reinforcing solidarity through symbolic means such as seasonal festivals. In these cases, as discussed in Chapter 4, incongruencies between conceptual blends and (Fiske types as) vital relationships are drivers of social conflicts and contested discourses: The conceptual blend of property remains in tension with realized practices of community as vital relationship. Thus, the commons is only sustainable if viable institutional arrangements are found that contain the push towards the market as an alternative vital relationship, which ultimately triggers the collapse of the commons.

The embodied approach to property converges with the view developed by Dagan (2021), which has much in common with Hegel's view, although Dagan denies this. In both cases, property is seen as a medium of human flourishing. While Dagan adopts an explicitly individualistic view, an embodied economics of property, in the tradition of the commons, goes further by emphasizing community concerns, and thus the mutuality of individual and community flourishingin a similar vein, see Alexander and colleagues (2008). Ultimately, the notion of community takes on a more-than-human dimension, as our discussion of birds has already highlighted. Embodied property means shared, institutionalized actions of appropriation in ecosystems (Herrmann-Pillath, 2023a).

This is radically different from the institutional form of property that has emerged in capitalism. As we have seen, the core process is the abstraction of the ownership mode of appropriation to ensure the universality of alienation. This does not mean, however, that ownership does not exist as a living embodied relationship between people and objects, such as tenants in relation to their homes, or workers in relation to their workplaces. Let us now turn to labor in embodied economics.

7.4 Labor

7.4.1 *The Paradox of Labor in Disembodied Economics*

Of the three themes we discuss in this chapter, labor is most directly related to the body. Indeed, we observe a gradual rapprochement with the body: Money is an institutional action that is a medium of abstraction, and thus undergirds disembodiment in the market via assetification—though not necessarily when bounded by other social relational models. Property has historically developed into a similar abstraction, highlighting alienation via the market and legally, if not completely, obliterating the mode of ownership. Labor is what bodies do, and we have already noted how the labor market underpins the abstraction of labor power from bodies. In this section, we look closely at how labor is constituted as institutional action. Economics emphasizes markets as the relevant Fiske mode of social relationships. But this is a fiction: There are only a few labor activities that actually take place in markets, and these are often even sidelined in economic analysis, such as most notably trade. The labor market as such does not materialize human labor: People work in companies, on farms, in households, in government, or in any other kind of what economics would call "organization." The labor market is just the place where the terms are set under which people join such organizations and then start to work. This is true even of the closest thing to a "labor market," the spot markets for day workers: The daily wage is negotiated, and people move to the place where they work under supervision.

If we overview human labor historically, as Lucassen (2021) has done in his monumental contribution, work was originally governed in what he calls a regime of "reciprocity," and what in our categorization would mostly count as community or reciprocity. For example, most hunter-gatherer communities hunt in close cooperation, and large game is shared immediately, so the community mode applies (Bowles & Gintis, 2011). With the Neolithic transition to agriculture, the division of labor changed in many societies, and labor exchange was often realized following reciprocity. Yet, at the same time, the hierarchy mode emerged, reflecting increasing inequality due to the accumulation of surplus. One of the typical forms was slavery, especially in the emerging early empires. The market mode is the most recent transformation in the history of human labor, and in some ways quite special. Considering the situation since the rise of capitalism, even though labor markets have become a universal phenomenon, it means that human labor is organized in its context. Apart from the hierarchy mode in the legal form of the wage contract, which implies subordination to the hierarchy of the firm, a substantial part of human labor is still carried out in the community mode, namely in households and families, and in the reciprocity mode in neighborhoods. Even in the hierarchy mode of companies, much of the actual work is not directly controlled by the hierarchy (as in the case of the production line), but mainly by forms of reciprocity in groups of collaborating workers (Akerlof, 1982). The question, then, is how the hierarchy, market, and community modes interact, and what role the market plays.

In conventional economics, labor poses three paradoxical challenges, rooted in its disembodied conceptualization via the construct of a "labor market:"

- Labor is disutility.
- Labor is free but subject to hierarchical rule.
- Labor that reproduces labor power is unproductive.

The first paradox is that labor is conceived exclusively as cost and disutility, and thus even in an embodied metaphor, as "pain" (Lane, 1992). This reveals a powerful effect of conceptual blending on the seemingly "objective" analytical categories of economics. This conceptualization is a logical consequence of how the labor market is treated mathematically so that the marginalist theorems necessary to establish the notion of equilibrium in the labor market can hold. Beneath the surface of this formal reasoning, is the notion that labor is "free," in the sense that a worker voluntarily enters into a relationship with an employer. What is important is that the supply of labor is optimized in terms of perceived costs and benefits. The benefits are conceived solely in terms of the wage received and, ultimately, the consumer goods that can be purchased. These characterize the incentives to endure the pain of work.

This is paradoxical in the sense that this model actually recognizes Marx's critique of alienation in the capitalist market, since alienation is the abstract form of "pain" that results from being separated from the product of one's labor. Both the Marxian and the neoclassical workers suffer only from labor: We can interpret this as a direct rupture of the Lockean embodied relationship between a worker and the product of work, which constitutes property. In this sense, the labor market is indeed the institutional form of expropriating workers from the product of their work.

Moreover, the conventional economic model of the labor market would not work if the worker also received direct benefits from work, such as the pleasure (rather than pain) of doing and making, which is one of the key features of craftspersonship (Sennett, 2009). The assumption that work is all pain is certainly appropriate for the destitute proletarians that Marx had in mind, or for millions of migrant workers around the world today. But it also means that, under different conditions, work can become meaningful and even pleasurable, as can exhilarating sports activities that are voluntarily undertaken. In fact, some hunter-gatherer societies do not distinguish between work and play and other effortful activities (e.g., Sahlins, 1972, p. 64), and so the key criterion seems to be whether the work is done voluntarily or autonomously. Forced labor is painful.

The conventional view of economics is disembodied in two ways. First, although work is treated as "pain," the actual psychological state of pain is not considered (Spencer, 2009, p. 69ff). Hard work in the "satanic mills" of industrialization was truly painful, and this pain is one reason why this "free" relationship is morally flawed: No one is morally justified to inflict pain, analogous to torture, on others. This argument has far-reaching implications, as modern societies are rife with work-related illnesses and deaths. Second, the other aspect of disembodiment is the distinction between the person and her "labor power," the latter being commodified, and becoming the object of the labor market transaction. We have already noted that formally this means that the labor market externalizes costs onto the worker, with the boundary between internalization and externalization being set by the institutional actions of abstraction: Labor power is performed as disembodied, and the externalities are embodied by the worker (e.g., when commuting, or suffering from health issues).

This analysis relates to the second paradox of the "free labor market." This paradox is that in the labor contract that separates labor power from the person, the latter becomes subject to hierarchical rule and is formally deprived of her freedom (Anderson, 2019).[26] Indeed, in the early, still proto-industrialist stages of 18th-century capitalism, the liberal protagonists of the market had in mind the freeholder, both as farmer and as artisan, who would directly offer the product of his work in the marketplace. Here, work is indeed "free" in entering into contractual relations that remain spot transactions, and the key criterion is the Lockean relationship between labor and product, that is, property. This model was also implicit in certain forms of labor organization in early industrialization, such as labor gangs working on a short-term basis.

Conventional theory neutralizes this problem in much the same way as it deals with the pain of labor. The assumption is that workers voluntarily submit to hierarchical rule and can opt out at any time, so that the free labor market would entail autonomy in the hierarchical relationship. This view does not take into account real-world constellations such as an endemic oversupply of labor, or the actual embodied ties of workers to the company, such as embodied skills and tacit knowledge that are not reflected in market wages, creating a gap with the incumbent's salary and thus cementing the hierarchical relationship through market mechanisms. Therefore, as we will discuss in detail in this section, the question of labor is primarily about organizational life, and not about labor markets. The analysis of organizational life, in turn, suggests an embodied perspective. Indeed, this explains the curious separation between the disciplines of economics and management, with the former sticking to a set of abstract models of the market, sometimes applied to organizations as "managerial economics," and the latter being multidisciplinary and including references to embodied aspects such as the psychology of the workplace (aka industrial/organizational psychology).

The third paradox is the distinction between productive and unproductive work (Brooks et al., 1990). On the surface, this fell apart with the demise of classical economics, but only because the notion of "productive" was exclusively related to markets. Only products that are valued in markets are seen as the result of productive work. As is well known, this also underlies the measurement of GDP and excludes very substantial forms of labor in modern economies (Coyle, 2015). Here, we highlight the feminist theme of reproductive work which exposes the ideological and institutional conditions and relativity of this distinction, and directly reveals the disembodied nature of the conventional notion of "productive."

Marx did not adequately analyze a fundamental fact of the capitalist market economy, namely the gendered dissociation between the reproduction of the labor force in the domestic sphere and the labor market where labor power receives wages (Federici, 2004/2021; Fraser, 2016). The former is inherently embodied, not only in terms of the organic aspects of reproduction, but also in broader social contexts, such as emotional labor with children. Despite the rise of gender mainstreaming and equal opportunity policies, this separation between a predominantly feminized domestic sphere persists to this day, for example, in the form of unequal access to parental leave for men and women. Domestic reproductive work is systematically excluded from the market and thus considered "unproductive," even though (and perhaps because) it is clearly an expression of embodied production.

As we have already mentioned, these three paradoxes can be traced back to the analysis of Fiske's schemes of relational models, since labor is governed in different ways by both the market mode and the hierarchy mode. This can be analyzed in terms of what might be seen as a "blending indeterminacy," which means that in relation to a given type of action, in this case, work aimed at production, different generic spaces are simultaneously activated. As shown in Fig. 7.10, this means that the relationship between actors and activity, people and production, is seen differently in relation to the generic space, as "task" in hierarchy, as "labor" in reciprocity (cooperation in production), and "labor power" in the market. The intricate point is that "task" and "labor power" converge in a specific institutional regime that Max Weber (1922/2019, p. 279) dubbed "free labor," which effectively refers to the Marxian emphasis on the alienation of the relationship between worker and product in the hierarchical setting of the company ("task" is not "product"), which at the same time means the commodification of "labor power," that is, the transformation of the activity into a good that is priced in the market.

Hence, the conceptual problems in the treatment of labor in economics reflect the indeterminacy of conceptual blends in actual social practices, which in turn refer to complex interactions of Fiske types as vital relationships. This is illustrated by the highly contentious nature of labor relations, as well as the immense difficulties in finding consensual balances between political ideas of a free and liberal labor market and managerial ideals, such as the establishment of the firm as a kind of community—which often, if not mostly, turns out to be an ideological camouflage for the actual instituting of the hierarchical mode of operation.

Most significantly, hierarchy is manifested in the dominance of multi-person organizational units as the setting for work, and in the status differences between different groups which are endogenous to the market. The latter refers to the persistence of unequal power between employers and employees, aka capital and labor, resulting from different degrees of specificity based on disembodiment versus embodiment. Capital, as financial

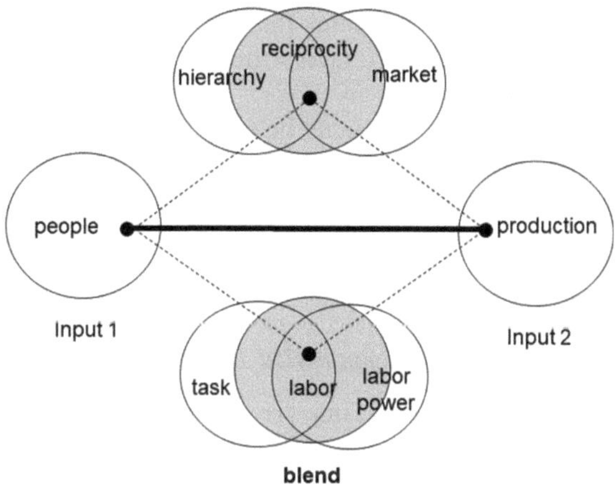

Fig. 7.10 In modern societies, productive work is materialized in a complex institutional form that manifests the indeterminacy of blending. When blending refers to the generic space of the market, the result is the notion of "labor power" results, which is highly disembodied because it is commodified. In the firm, blending refers to the generic space of hierarchy, which is the "task." Tasks are also disembodied, but in a different way: They are standardized. In the spheres of family, household, or civic engagement, work is blended in relation to the generic space of reciprocity (or even community), where it is highly embodied, as "labor." From the generic space of the market, however, this kind of work is considered "unproductive"

capital, is disembodied through a wider range of financial institutions and instruments, and can therefore move freely, whereas labor is often tied to places, such as social ties with friends and family. As we analyzed in the section on money, this creates asymmetric market power that undergirds the hierarchical dominance of employers in the firm. The other important case of unequal power is the gendered distinction between productive wage labor and reproductive work outside the market. As long as the latter is not internalized in the market, the asymmetry of power between men and women is maintained. However, internalizing reproductive work in the market (e.g., by paying someone to do domestic work) creates a dilemma, as this would also trigger (market) forces of disembodiment in the domestic sphere. Since avoiding this dilemma is largely the responsibility of women, another force favors the maintenance of the gendered hierarchies in society.

In light of this analysis, we focus below on the hierarchical mode of organizing labor in modern organizations, especially companies. Even when it comes to international trade, about half of it is intra-firm trade, that is, within organizations.[27] Thus, the distinctive form of work in capitalism takes place under the hierarchy mode.

7.4.2 Constructing Disembodied Labor in Economic Theory

Organizations are everywhere. They are ubiquitous. For example, when people go to work, they go from one organization to another: When they take the train, when they grab a cup of coffee on the way, and/or when they enter their office to work. In almost all cases, these organizations rely on the existence of a vertical metaphor: The hierarchical relationship between the employer, or its representatives (e.g., managers), and the employees, as illustrated by the POWERFUL IS UP, POWERLESS IS DOWN metaphor mentioned in Chapter 4.

Historically, the importance of organizations in the economy has grown steadily since the early nineteenth century (Perrow, 1991), and, it is now believed that "we do not live in a market economy, but in an organization economy, or at most, in an organization market economy, with a predominance of organizational over market activity" (Simon, 2000, p. 751). This means that labor is not only institutionalized, but also organized as an institutional action, performed by organizations and by the individuals who populate these organizations, be they employers or employees. This emphasizes the role of outward embodiment through organizational practices that are also inwardly embodied since "our social psychology, that is, our ways of constructing reality, is more and more forged by and accommodative to organizations" (Perrow, 1991, pp. 725–726).

Despite Smith's (1776/2005) analysis of the division of labor as the foundation of economic theory, the importance of organizations in contemporary economic life has not come easily to standard economics. This is not simply because organizations have not been studied (Lewis & Stewart, 1958). Rather, it is because organizations are far from obvious in conventional economics, where the market is the best way to coordinate economic agents. In standard economics, the mere existence of the market guarantees their individual freedom and the expression of their preferences thanks to the price mechanism. For instance, in theory, at least when markets are competitive, if consumers are not willing to pay the price for a good, they do not (have to) buy it. They can "exit" the market (Hirschman, 1970), which is supposed to reduce the demand for the good, and thus its price, until some more are willing to buy it. There is no planning, no central control (Hayek, 1937, 1945), and no authority: Relationships are assumed to be horizontal. This principle is also supposed to apply to production inputs, capital, and labor. Yet, as Coase pointed out,

> in the real world, we find that there are many areas where this does not apply. If a workman moves from department Y to department X, he does not go because of a change in relative prices, but because he is ordered to do so. (Coase, 1937, p. 387)

This means that economic exchanges do not always take place through horizontal market transactions, but also through vertical (power) relationships and that a large part of economic activity thus operates through hierarchies instead of markets. For labor, this is the primary mode.

The Coasean question that follows is: If markets are supposedly perfect, why do we have organizations? In other words, if markets are the best way to coordinate exchange in economic life, "why are not all the actors independent contractors?" (Simon, 1991, p. 25). Coase suggested that hierarchies are necessary because "there is a cost of using the price mechanism" when it comes to "discovering what the relevant prices are" (Coase, 1937, pp. 390), and when it comes to "negotiating and concluding a separate contract for each exchange transaction which takes place on a market" (Coase, 1937, pp. 390–391). So, the answer is economic: Forming an organization, by substituting authority relations for market relations, is a way of saving transaction costs.

Williamson's (1975, p. 40) framework of market failures identifies several reasons why transaction costs exist. We will focus mainly on those that pertain to "human factors" in his parlance: Opportunism and bounded rationality. These two assumptions, according to him, underlie the problem of economic organization, which is to "devise contract and governance structures that have the purpose and effect of economizing on bounded rationality while simultaneously safeguarding transactions against the hazards of opportunism" (Williamson, 1985, p. xiii).

This quote is quite explicit: It portrays hierarchical organizations as solutions to problems pertaining to bounded rationality and opportunism. This reflects mainstream economics' perspective on human behavior. Bounded rationality, as discussed in Chapter 3, is theoretically tolerated because it requires the existence of the neoclassical benchmark of substantive rationality (as provided by *Homo economicus*) against which decision-making appears "bounded" when compared to the all-seeing eye of an external observer. Opportunism perpetuates the idea that economic agents are self-interested, which maintains a very individualistic focus on economic activity.

As we shall see, the opportunism argument fails to explain the existence of hierarchies and leads to toxic and counterproductive managerial solutions. Although the bounded rationality explanation contributes to explaining hierarchies and the division of labor, it remains grounded in the computer metaphor of the mind, which disembodies knowledge and rationality (see Chapters 3 and 4), and fails to prevent the commodification and dehumanization of workers, leading to feelings of alienation. We will then show that human capital theory, despite its approach to knowledge as embodied in workers, expands the scope of commodification, dehumanization, and alienation in economic life. Against this background, the embodied economics perspective develops an alternative understanding of labor. We diagnose three "deadly sins" of the economics of organizations:

- First, opportunism is created, not controlled, by capitalist organizations.
- Second, the organizational division of labor expropriates embodied knowledge.
- Third, capitalist organizations assetify embodied knowledge.

Regarding the first sin, Williamson's idea is that, by moving away from horizontal transactions (market exchanges) and towards vertical relationships (hierarchies), organizations are assumed to prevent economic agents from engaging in opportunistic behaviors in economic life. Opportunism "includes but is scarcely limited to" self-interested behaviors such as "lying, stealing, and cheating" (Williamson, 1985, p. 47), and is thus "unconstrained by morality" (Ghoshal & Moran, 1996, p. 14). It can then take two main forms: A strong form, which involves the violation of explicit contractual obligations, such as cheating on the agreed terms and provisions written in a contract (Wathne & Heide, 2000); and a weak form, which involves the violation of a relational norm that is not explicit, but rather embedded in the common implicit understanding between economic actors (Lumineau & Quélin, 2012). In addition to these two forms, opportunism includes subtle forms of deceit that can occur before or after the conclusion of a contract, referring respectively to the mechanisms of adverse selection (ex-ante opportunism) and moral hazard (ex-post opportunism) (Wathne & Heide, 2000; Williamson, 1985). In any case, opportunism is considered "a subtle and pervasive condition of human nature" (Williamson, 1985, p. 6), or "a behavioral trait embodied in economic actors" (Lumineau & Quélin, 2012, p. 55). Accordingly, "the higher the external rewards from being dishonest, the higher is the extent to which an individual engages in dishonest behavior" (Mazar & Ariely, 2006, p. 118), and opportunism is a call for hierarchical control.

The first problem with this approach is striking: Although today's capitalism is claimed to be an "organization market economy" (Simon, 2000, p. 751), it is enough to read the news to see that opportunism still exists, especially within hierarchies, think of the Volkswagen emissions scandal. Or it is enough to read academic journals to see that, although opportunism is supposed to be addressed by hierarchies, it is common to find economic analyses of the manager-employee relationship, one of the most vertical in the economy, as subject to adverse selection (e.g., the employee knows her competence for the job she is applying for, but the employer does not) and moral hazard (e.g., the employee's behavior as desired by the employer is not freely observable) (Schmid, 2008).

More importantly, opportunism in economics is fundamentally conceptually flawed. By treating opportunism as a trait that is part and parcel of humanity, standard economics intrinsically links opportunism to individual decision-making and, as per usual, develops an a-social analysis that divorces behavior from the professional background and context of economic agents. However, evidence of opportunism is lacking (e.g., Tsang, 2006), and results from Prisoners' Dilemmas, Trust Games, and Ultimatum Games reviewed in previous chapters and sections do not lead to the conclusion that economic agents are fundamentally opportunistic (e.g., Benkler, 2011a, 2011b). Even when conducted with bank employees, who are supposed to be more self-interested, opportunistic behavior emerges only under certain circumstances. For instance, bank employees were found not to cheat more than employees from another industry or than students when they anonymously performed a coin toss task which allowed them to cheat and earn more money. Rather, they only started cheating when their social identity as bank employees was made salient (Cohn et al., 2014). This finding directly challenges Williamson's (1985) position: Opportunism is not inherent in human nature but subject to the business context. Opportunism, when it occurs, is socially situated, and likely socially created.

This is why opportunism is not only fundamentally conceptually flawed, but also dangerous: Its conceptualization actually contributes to the creation and generation of amoral, if not immoral, behavior in business contexts (Ghoshal, 2005; Ghoshal & Moran, 1996). Two mechanisms are of interest from the perspective of embodied economics. First, it is argued that the teaching of transaction cost theory and its associated opportunism in business schools "actively freed their students from any sense of moral responsibility," further feeding opportunism in business contexts (Ghoshal, 2005, pp. 75–76; see also, Dierksmeier, 2020; Ferraro et al., 2005; Holbrook, 2013; Racko, 2019; Trapp, 2024). Second, opportunism can become a "self-fulfilling prophecy" in that it is likely to increase with the rewards (incentives) and punishments (sanctions) intended to curb it, requiring the implementation of more incentives and sanctions (Ghoshal & Moran, 1996, p. 14). For instance, research shows that lack of autonomy (through excessive control) can be perceived as distrust and thus negatively impact people's motivation at work and increase opportunistic (deviant) behavior (Falk & Kosfeld, 2006). Ultimately, by assuming the existence of opportunistic behaviors, organizations increase their governance costs, which makes them uncompetitive by undermining motivation at work. Far from being a feature of (so-called) "human nature", opportunism seems to be, in part, the result of inward embodiment through the learning of economic theories (especially, but not only, in business schools) that pose it as normal behavior. Opportunism is then outwardly embodied, that is, performed, by economic actors through distrustful and controlling practices in business contexts (Herrmann-Pillath, 2016).

Overall, as Williamson himself acknowledges, opportunism as the reason for organizations "has turned out to be a controversial formulation," whereas "there is growing agreement that bounded rationality is the appropriate cognitive assumption for describing economic organization" (Williamson, 1993, p. 97; see also, Conner & Prahalad, 1996).

Let us now turn to the second sin: The organizational division of labor which "expropriates" embodied knowledge (Fumagalli et al., 2019; Moulier-Boutang, 2007, 2011). Consistent with Simon, the two main ingredients of bounded rationality, namely the cognitive limitations of human reasoning and uncertainty, are used to explain the existence of hierarchies: "Hierarchical organization and associated controls are traced to the limited capacities of human actors to cope with the complexity and uncertainty with which they are confronted" (Williamson, 1981, p. 551). The idea, fully in line with the problem-solving approach, is that despite the lack of substantive rationality, decisions can be rational as long as rationality is procedural.

Procedural rationality is "finding efficient procedures for computing actual solutions to concrete decision problems" (Simon, 1976, p. 139). As such, hierarchical organization is part and parcel of procedural rationality, along with other procedures such as satisficing and subgoals, because it is supposed to help transform intractable decision problems into tractable ones for economic agents to make rational decisions through cooperation (Simon, 1979).[28] An organization is then defined as a set of procedures that divides the task of decision-making among many specialists, and coordinates their work through a structure of communication and authority relations, which echoes the division of labor *à la* Adam Smith (1776, 2005).

Through the lens of embodiment, hierarchies serve, at least, two main functions in the division of labor: Disciplining the bodies of individual workers (e.g., Lawrence et al., 2023; Styhre, 2004), and detaching (abstracting) knowledge from their bodies (e.g., Sohn Rethel, 1978). In this respect, the division of labor echoes the division of knowledge. As described in Chapter 3, Hayek's (1982/2013) goal with the "Great Society" was to literally disembody the market. This disembodiment requires the discipline of the body: In Hayek, feelings, emotions, and anthropomorphism are derogated as forms of (so-called) "tribal" thinking and should be tamed because they underpin a social justice perspective which prevents markets from functioning properly. This disembodiment also requires that knowledge be conceptualized as separate from economic agents: Knowledge is distributed through the price system, and rationality is (supposedly) provided by the spontaneous order of the market. However, as Pasquinelli (2021, p. 165) observes:

> What escapes Hayek's assessment is that this decentralized and unconscious rationality is not only of markets but can be found in other forms of human organization and cooperation. Karl Marx, for example, recognized the division of labor in workshops and manufactories as a form of spontaneous and unconscious rationality.

Like the division of knowledge, the division of labor disciplines (workers') bodies. As Taylor's scientific management illustrates, gestures are measured, timed, maximized, and rationalized, arranged in the best way (Locke, 1982; Sohn-Rethel, 1978; Taylor, 1914). The division of labor also reflects the division of knowledge because rationality does not belong to the economic actors, but to the hierarchy: It is provided by the scientific management of their organization. Historically, the division of labor was a way of depriving workers of the mysteries (or "*mystères*") of their trade (Marx, 1867/1990, p. 616): Through the division of labor, workers lost their "*métier*;" a French word whose etymology comes from the Latin "*mysterium*." Once standardized to the greatest extent possible, knowledge can be detached from the bodies of workers, and transferred through procedures to the technocratic management of the hierarchical organization (Nelson, 1974).

Against this background, what embodied economics emphasizes is that beyond uncertainty as an environmental factor that could explain the existence of hierarchies (Coase, 1937),[29] especially in conjunction with bounded rationality (Williamson, 1975, 1985), the uncertainty that hierarchical organizations seek to address with scientific management is uncertainty as a human factor: When knowledge remains embodied in workers, workers are a source of uncertainty for any organization, such as when there is turnover or a strike. The Taylorian solution to tame this uncertainty is to extract knowledge from workers, and standardize that knowledge through procedures so that each worker becomes, to some extent, easily replaceable (Sohn-Rethel, 1978, p. 153ff). With the division of labor, workers are interchangeable; any form of knowledge they embody (or have embodied) no longer matters since it has been passed on to the organization, crystallized into procedures and practices within the hierarchy that separates the "head" from the "hand." Taylorism introduces a "new division of mental and manual labor:" "The workman has, as it were, handed over his mind to a new institution which has come into existence—the modern management in charge of the economy of time peculiar to monopoly capital" (Sohn-Rethel,

1978, p. 157). Interchangeable and replaceable, (factory) workers are commodified, objectified, dehumanized, and perceived as instruments that merely extend the machine (e.g., Andrighetto et al., 2017; Arendt, 1958/2018; Berger et al., 1973; Nussbaum, 1995; Pasquinelli, 2019). It is worth noting that treating workers as commodities is fully consistent with neoclassical theory (Bowles & Gintis, 1975), and that dehumanization associated with commodification has been documented in contexts beyond factory work (e.g., Harris et al., 2014; Henkel et al., 2018).

In economic life, the commodification of the workforce extends to emotions and feelings in the service industry through what the philosopher Berger and his colleagues (1973, p. 39) called "emotional management," and the sociologist Hochschild (1979, 1983) called "emotional labor." In the case of flight attendants, for instance, emotional style is inherent in the service itself (Hochschild, 1983, pp. 4–5), and feelings are managed and prescribed by hierarchies "to create a publicly observable facial and bodily display" (Hochschild, 1983, p. 7).[30] Feelings are incorporated into services, and ultimately sold as commodities by organizations in the marketplace (Hochschild, 1979, 1983; see also Grandey & Sayre, 2019). Similar illustrations of "emotional labor" can be found in any service industry: Sadness is expected in the funeral business, happiness in amusement parks, urgency in bill collection systems, excitement in the porn industry, relaxation in a wellness center, etc.

This means that hierarchical organizations distribute not only rationality, but also emotions and feelings through their standardized procedures to ensure a consistent facial and bodily display to be sold as a commodity in economic life. Because embodiment is so important in interactions with consumers,[31] none of its expressions, from gestures to feelings, can be left to uncertainty and escape hierarchy. However, it can be argued that although cognition and emotion are commodified in the workplace, workers' knowledge can never be completely disembodied. This leads us to consider the third sin: Namely, capitalist organizations assetify embodied knowledge.

As regularly pointed out in the literature, tacit knowledge, as defined by Michael Polanyi (1966/2009), resists the disembodiment of managerial procedures (e.g., Bazin, 2013).For instance, Amartya Sen observes that: "The importance of tacit knowledge has implications, Polanyi argues, for the impossibility of depersonalizing knowledge and the difficulty of seeking objectivity in the form of personal detachment" (Sen, p. xiii, in Polanyi, 1966, 2009). However, it can also be argued that scientific management *à la* Taylor actually increased the importance of embodying knowledge for a certain category of workers:

> The systematic application of scientific knowledge to production of goods has greatly increased the value of education, technical schooling, and on-the-job training as the growth of knowledge has become embodied in people – in scientists, scholars, technicians, managers, and other contributors to output. (Becker, 1994, p. 24)

The embodiment of knowledge in economic life was recognized decades ago by one of the most influential developments in conventional economics: Human capital theory (e.g., Becker, 1962, 1964; Lucas, 1988; Mincer, 1958; Schultz, 1961). Simply put, human capital is "knowledge embodied in people" (Becker et al., 1994, p. 326), such as education and experience, that is invested in people and yields a return in the labor market in the form of higher wages (Folbre, 2012). Interestingly, human capital theory introduces the distinction between "general" and "specific" capital (Becker, 1962). When the skills associated with a job position are very particular to that position and not transferable to another organization, human capital is specific. General human capital, on the other hand, includes abilities that can be transferred with people (e.g., education), when they move from one organization to another. From a mainstream economics perspective, under the influence of Milton Friedman, this justifies the privatization of education, as there is no reason why companies, and more largely taxpayers, should be charged for knowledge, which is a private good (Fleming, 2017; Schultz, 1961).[32] From an embodied economics perspective, the difference between specific and general human capital shows that the embodiment of knowledge bounds hierarchies: The boundaries of a given hierarchical organization are determined by the extent to which the knowledge of its workers remains embodied (i.e., general), that is, as long as their knowledge cannot be disembodied by procedures and technologies (i.e., specific).

Arguably, the embodiment of knowledge (through general human capital) further represents uncertainty as a human factor for any organization because when workers leave, they leave the organization with their knowledge. In fact, non-compete clauses illustrate that embodied knowledge in the form of specific human capital can also be a source of uncertainty as a human factor because it could not be fully extracted from employees and retained in the organization.

Three important points should be made here to highlight the difference between conventional and embodied economics when it comes to the embodiment of knowledge.[33]

First, from the perspective of embodied economics, the fact that human capital theory treats knowledge as embodied in workers does not mean that workers are not disembodied in this theory. The reason why human capital theory leads to the disembodiment of workers is quite simple: It relies on the PEOPLE ARE DURABLE GOODS metaphor, which is an illustration of the aforementioned form of "assetification" of economic agents that occurs in capitalist markets. This metaphor made some of the most famous proponents of the theory uncomfortable (e.g., Schultz, 1961), but it is deeply rooted in the concept of human capital. For instance, Becker argued that children are "a durable consumption and production good" (Becker, 1960, p. 210) because parents' expenditures on education, training, medical care, and so forth, are investments that produce human capital that cannot be separated from the knowledge, skills, health, or value of their children (Becker, 1992). This position is at odds with embodied economics, which, as we will see in the final chapter, argues strongly against the commodification and privatization of living beings.

This leads to our second point, which is conveyed by another (though related) metaphor that underpins human capital theory: PEOPLE ARE CORPORATIONS.[34] Again, this testifies to the "assetification" of economic agents that takes place in capitalist markets, as described by embodied economics. However, this metaphor is more radical than the PEOPLE ARE DURABLE GOODS metaphor. The PEOPLE ARE CORPORATIONS metaphor is not only about the "commodification" of human beings, but also about their "capitalization" (Feher, 2009). Indeed, human capital theorists tend to claim that their concept transcends the classic tension between capitalists and workers. For instance, one can read that "laborers have become capitalists (...) from the acquisition of knowledge and skill that have economic value" (Schultz, 1961, p. 3; see also, Bowles & Gintis, 1975; Fleming, 2017; Folbre, 2009). To understand the implications of this idea, it is necessary to depart from one of the classical interpretations of human capital in economics. Traditionally, it has been understood in economics as an echo of either the Smithian or Fisherian accounts of capital (Schultz, 1961), or the Marxian concept of labor power (e.g., Folbre, 2009). When human capital is read in light of Marx's concept of labor power, workers are those "free laborers" who do not own capital, and thus must sell their labor power as a commodity on the labor market (Feher, 2009). But this is only one aspect of human capital. As analyzed by Foucault (2004), what human capital theory conveys is that workers, and people more broadly, are "entrepreneurs" of, or "investors" in, themselves (Feher, 2009; see also, Guala, 2006). Each worker is a "mini-corporation" (Fleming, 2017, p. 699) that makes "speculative" decisions, the outcomes of which can be evaluated through their return on investment in terms of monetary, real, or psychic income (Feher, 2009). With the PEOPLE ARE CORPORATIONS metaphor, human capital theory is thus underpinned by a description of the "assetification" of people through the inward embodiment of the market logic that occurs under capitalism, which in Foucauldian terms would be described as neoliberal "governmentality." Therefore, economic rationality is not only imposed through hierarchical organization, it is also outwardly embodied through self-discipline as workers become entrepreneurs who invest in themselves. This means that market rationality is not distributed through the price mechanism, it is literally embodied: People market themselves. Of course, this did not happen out of the blue: People have inwardly embodied a form of thinking in terms of human capital, favored by public policies inspired and supported by human capital theories, which led to the creation of a market society in which public goods such as education and health are privatized, thus fostering a form of thinking in terms of speculative investment (e.g., Feher, 2009; Fleming, 2017). As we will see in the next section, this has important implications for (the lack of) meaning at work.

Beforehand, we shall conclude these developments on some of the key differences between human capital theory and embodied economics with this third point: Human capital is "a-social" in the sense that it transcends any social role and functioning (in Sen's sense) that people might perform as citizens, students, patients, or employees, for example, and is thus conceived as detached from their economic and social embeddedness (Fleming, 2017; see also, Bowles & Gintis, 1975; Folbre, 2012). According to human capital theory, "people are now monadic and self-contained enterprises rather than members of a wider group" (Fleming, 2017, p. 698). However, if knowledge is embodied, mechanically because the body is situated in the world, it is socially embedded. In contrast to human capital, the social embeddedness of workers is intrinsic to embodied economics, and is conceptualized, as the Aoki-Bourdieu model illustrates, with reference to Bourdieu's habitus, field, and forms of capital. This means that the embodiment of knowledge cannot be thought of only in terms of return on investment, and, as we will argue, that the understanding of work and labor should be expanded beyond the economic sphere.

7.4.3 *Alienation and the Capitalist Organization*

In addition to the issues we have already pointed out in relation to each theory, we shall now turn to the common limitation to opportunism, procedural rationality, and human capital: Their inability to address the causes of alienation because they neglect the question of the meaning of work in society.

The concept of alienation is deeply linked to the way the nature of labor is conceptualized. In standard economics, labor is merely a means to an end: Consumption and leisure. For Marx, however, it is not in the nature of labor to be a means. Labor can be a source of self-realization, "defined as the full and free actualization and externalization of the powers and abilities of the individual" (Elster, 1986, p. 43). In psychological terms, one might consider that there is no alienation if labor can lead to the satisfaction of the Maslow-type (1943) higher-order need for self-actualization (Kanungo, 1979). However, in contrast to this psychological approach, as well as managerial approaches that focus on involvement at work, the Marxian approach sees the lack of self-actualization as an individual responsibility (Buss, 1979; Lethbridge, 1986; see also, Compton, 2018). For Marx, the lack of self-realization is tied to the capitalist system, where labor is not an end in itself, but merely a means of production.

The concept of alienation conveys the idea that the worker "only feels himself outside his work, and in his work feels outside himself" (Marx, 1932/1988, p. 74). There are, at least,[35] two dimensions that characterize the alienation of labor. The lack of autonomy, or powerlessness because the worker's "labor is therefore not voluntary, but coerced; it is forced labor" (Marx, 1932/1988, p. 74). And the lack of self-realization, or meaninglessness because "labor is *external* to the worker, that is, it does not belong to his essential being" (Marx, 1932/1988, p. 74).[36] The causes of powerlessness and meaninglessness are twofold: The division of labor and the wage system, both of which reflect the capitalist hierarchical organization of work.

Powerlessness is understood as the feeling that expresses the lack of autonomy and agency experienced by the worker subject to the capitalist division of labor. In the division of labor, as exemplified by Taylor's scientific management, the worker has no discretion over the design and production of her work, which is under the hierarchical control of the employer (or capitalist or manager). Moreover, the wage system associated with capitalism is characterized by the establishment of a relationship of authority between the worker and the employer (e.g., Dolan, 1971; Supiot, 2009/2017). In capitalist plutocracy, the capitalist owns the means of production (private property), and thus has the power to decide.

The division of labor and the wage system also contribute to meaninglessness, understood as the feeling that expresses the lack of self-realization experienced by the worker. In the division of labor, tasks are too specialized, narrow, and disconnected from the rest of the activity: Workers cannot see the relationship between their work and larger processes in the organization. The wage system reinforces this feeling of meaninglessness: Since the power to make decisions belongs to the employer, it becomes difficult for the worker to understand the reasons why some decisions are made (Dolan, 1971).

The fundamental implication of alienation—through the division of labor and the wage system—is that work damages rather than promotes human dignity (Kanungo, 1992). They are dehumanized:

> under capitalism, workers are deprived of the "truly human" essence of their work. (…) Thus, they become 'specialized tools' (Fromm, 1974) that are exclusively judged (and valued) on the basis of their efficiency and productivity, while their human qualities are devalued. (Andrighetto et al., 2017, p. 26)

Having characterized alienation and its causes, let us now turn to the reasons why theories of opportunism, procedural rationality, and human capital fail to address it.

Through the lens of opportunism, workers are seen as inherently selfish and amoral, and must be controlled. However, "the alienating effects of authoritarian environments" are old news (Simon, 1997, p. 175): Increasing hierarchical control undermines people's feelings of autonomy, which contributes to alienation (e.g., Chiaburu et al., 2014). Autonomy and agency are key concepts in embodied economics that illustrate an important difference in perspective from standard economics. In the context of hierarchical organizations, autonomy and agency emphasize the role of self-determination rather than the role of self-interest, shifting the focus from extrinsic to intrinsic motivation, which is concerned with meaning. In other words, what self-determination highlights is that people are motivated not only (extrinsically) by rewards and punishments, but also (intrinsically) by meaningful work (e.g., Ariely et al., 2008; Deci et al., 2017). This, of course, raises the question of what constitutes meaningful work, which will be discussed later when we conclude this chapter with the conceptualization of labor in embodied economics. For now, suffice it to say, that meaningful work has an individual and a collective dimension: It is self-realization through contribution to community life.

Another question we need to address before going further is whether thinking about labor in terms of human capital overcomes (or not) the alienation of work through self-determination. After all, since human capital is about "self-assetification" (in our parlance), workers are viewed as capitalists (Schultz, 1961), and one might wonder whether they can still be considered exploited (Becker, 1992), and alienated.[37] There are certainly conceptual advantages to human capital theory (e.g., Bowles & Gintis, 1975; Folbre, 2009),[38] but it cannot be concluded that human capital brings autonomy and meaning, that is, self-determination, to workers.

With respect to autonomy, we will simply point to analyses showing that self-employment, portfolio careers, or the "gig economy," which "faithfully reflect the assumptions that inform human capital theory," are associated with less rather than more autonomy at work (Fleming, 2017, p. 691).

In terms of meaning, the return on investment in human capital may be economically rewarding, but it may not be meaningful, at either the individual or the community level.

At the individual level, a classic illustration is a student who would self-realize as an artist, but whose parents would only financially support his law studies, think of Franz Kafka or Gustave Flaubert. Needless to say, this perennial problem is exacerbated by the privatization of education inspired by human capital theory (Fleming, 2017), which favors the most lucrative job positions that help pay off student loans. Still, what is economically rewarding, for instance in terms of investment in education when it comes to job prospects, does not bring meaning to work or life. Without going into the debates surrounding the market account of meaningfulness, which posits that well-paid work is the most meaningful work, labor as a source of self-realization is beyond the scope of a means to achieve primarily an economic end (e.g., Deci et al., 2017; Herzberg, 2003; Kimiecik & Teas, 2020; Michaelson, 2021). As exemplified by the enthusiasm generated by the notion of "bullshit jobs" (Graeber, 2019), the literature points to reasons why money does not make work intrinsically meaningful: "Some work is undervalued economically by the market because it is seen to be meaningful, whereas other work is overvalued economically by the market because it is seen to be less meaningful (e.g., Nozick, 1974)" (Michaelson, 2021, pp. 420–421). Against this background, the (self-) assetification of labor as a return-on-investment in education, as conveyed by human capital theory, is alien to, if not an obstacle to, self-realization.

At the community level, while economic theory tells us that investment in human capital is essential for economic growth (e.g., Lucas, 1988), as Amartya Sen has pointed out, it does not tell us

> why economic growth is sought in the first place. If, instead, the focus is, ultimately, on the expansion of human freedom to live the kind of lives that people have reason to value, then the role of economic growth in expanding these opportunities has to be integrated into that more foundational understanding of the process of development as the expansion of human capability to lead freer and more worthwhile lives. (Sen, 1997, p. 1960)

In other words, Sen argues that seeing labor as human capital does not answer the question of its meaning at the collective level, because its goals remain fundamentally economic and thus only a means to an end which, in terms of human capabilities, should be to ensure that everyone in society is able to live a dignified life (Nussbaum, 2006).

We shall now conclude these points with Simon's procedural rationality. As discussed earlier, in his view organizations are reduced to procedures driven by a problem-solving approach underpinned by the computer metaphor of the mind and the theory of physical symbol systems. These disembodied theoretical underpinnings do not prevent any form of scientific management that commodifies workers through the division of labor. Moreover, as argued in embodied economics (see Chapter 4), activity in economic life is not limited to problem-solving: It is also fundamentally about meaning-making, since the world we inhabit, whether economic (Hayek, 1988), or natural (Merleau-Ponty, 1945/1962), is mysterious. In other words, embodied economics does not reject problem-solving per se, but it does not claim that the world is problematic to begin with. Rather, the world, and economic life in particular, is first and foremost mysterious—and uncertainty is an expression of this mystery. Because of its mystery, economic agents have to make sense of their economic environment, and this sense-making is subject to their embodiment, through metaphors, narratives, conceptual blends, and other forms of outward embodiment. Offering procedures such as the division of labor to solve problems of efficiency does not provide meaning at work (or in life), and so people try (unsuccessfully) to find meaning in some other economic activity: Consumption.

One of the main strengths of the Marxian analysis of labor is to link alienation at work to consumption (e.g., Allison, 1978; Elster, 1986; Hudson & Hudson, 2003; Singer, 2000). Consumers are alienated workers in search of lost meaning:

> people who have been deprived of their connection to the products of their own labors, having lost meaning as a result of loss of control of their own lives, and being alienated, turn to commodities to find the qualities that they have lost. (Firat, 2018, p. 20)

In fact, this is another illustration of the importance of mystery in economic life. According to Marx, in capitalist societies, commodities are more than objects that satisfy or fail to satisfy (some of) our needs, they are "mysterious" because social relations are hidden by the (mystical) "veil" of commodity production (Marx, 1867/1990, p. 173). Capitalism is an "immense collection of commodities" (Marx, 1867/1990, p. 125) in which labor is a commodity to produce commodities, people exchange commodities on the market, and people relate to each other through commodities. In Marx's words: "the definite social relation between men themselves which assumes here, for them, the fantastic form of a relation between things" (Marx, 1867/1990, p. 165). This means that as consumers, we tend to think that things have a life of their own: "Like religious believers bowing before an idol, we make a fetish of commodities by treating them as more than they really are" (Singer, 2000, p. 68). Commodity fetishism is a "cognitive illusion arising from market transactions" (Elster, 1986, p. 58), because commodities are presented by organizations as abstracted from the social, environmental, and historical relations that go into their production (Hudson & Hudson, 2003).

This is an important insight for embodied economics: When people are assetified, they are abstracted from their economic, social, and ecological environments; whereas when things are fetishized, they are abstracted from their economic, social, and ecological environments. Commodity fetishism also has fundamental implications for embodied economics: What Marx understood, unlike Hayek, is that capitalism cannot escape anthropomorphism (i.e., a form of outward embodiment) and indeed needs it to function properly:

> In this sense, the commodity has a life of its own, completely divorced from the process by which it was created. It becomes not a result of production on which people have worked under a wide variety of more or less acceptable conditions but an entity unto itself, with characteristics of its own. (Hudson & Hudson, 2003, p. 417)

Consumer research on possessions as an extension of the self (Belk, 1988), brand personality (Aaker, 1997), brand relationships (Fournier, 1998), brand love (Batra et al., 2012), or brand hate (Zarantonello et al., 2016) to name a few, attest to the fact that, under capitalism, commodities have a life of their own—see also, in anthropology, Appadurai (1988). The irony of alienation under capitalism is thus that workers end up anthropomorphizing commodities when they act as consumers, while the entire economic system is based on the assetification of the natural and social environment, and of living beings.

The problem, as Marx pointed out, is that: "The less you are, the more you *have*; the less you express your own life, the greater is your *alienated* life—the greater is the store of your estranged being" (Marx, 1932/1988, p. 119). Interestingly, this can be explained in terms of the subjective utility cherished by conventional economics:

> Activities of self-realization are subject to increasing marginal utility: They become more enjoyable the more one has already engaged in them. Exactly the opposite is true of consumption. To derive sustained pleasure from consumption, diversity is essential. Diversity, on the other hand, is an obstacle to successful self-realization, as it prevents one from getting into the later and more rewarding stages. (Elster, 1986, p. 45)

In the end, material consumption is an additional source of alienation (and ill-being) rather than a source of self-realization (Fromm, 2002; see also, Bradshaw et al., 2023; Kasser & Ryan, 1993; Zavestoski, 2002).

Unsurprisingly, Hayek, in keeping with his "Great Society" approach, and failing to understand the significance of commodity fetishism,[39] dismissed any analysis of labor in terms of alienation or estrangement by associating it with a form of embodied ("instinctive") thinking:

> Similarly the people who are described as alienated or estranged from a society based on the market order are not the bearers of a new moral but the non-domesticated or un-civilized who have never learnt the rules of conduct on which the Open Society is based, but want to impose upon it their instinctive, 'natural' conceptions derived from the tribal society. (Hayek, 1982/2013, p. 304)

Hayek's critique conveys the dichotomy identified by Tönnies between society (identified with capitalism) and community.

As we will argue in the next section, following Hegel and Arendt, embodied economics suggests that if we are to address alienation, the understanding of labor should be broadened and socially re-embedded. At the heart of alienation, lies the notion of estrangement: There is a disconnection between the worker and the by-product of her labor. This disconnection is not limited to the boundaries of the organization, but extends to the sense of contribution to the community. Autonomy and meaning (or sense-making) are central concepts to embodied economics, and they are inextricably linked to community because they cannot be understood in the abstraction of others. Labor becomes meaningful when it transcends organizational hierarchies and is understood as a fundamental part of community life.

7.4.4 Labor in Embodied Economics: From Hegel to Arendt

As discussed so far, it appears that the study of labor in economics, but also in law, sociology, or (industrial) psychology, for instance, involves the study of hierarchical organizations in economic life. However, the way in which labor is conceptualized will actually shape the understanding of hierarchical organizations. In conventional economics, we have already highlighted that labor is associated with pain and effort, and is classically understood in contrast to leisure which is associated with pleasure. This association runs deep in social representations. For example, in Roman antiquity, "*otium*" was the leisure time during which people could enjoy social activities such as eating, playing, relaxing, or contemplating, and was viewed positively. In contrast, "*negotium*", which is the negation of "*otium*," means business, occupation, or employment. Historically, this has been reinforced by the more systematic use of time-measurement under Industrial Capitalism:

> This measurement embodies a simple relationship. Those who are employed experience a distinction between their employer's time and their 'own' time. And the employer must *use* the time of his labour, and see it is not wasted: not the task but the value of time when reduced to money is dominant. Time is now currency: it is not passed but spent. (Thompson, 1967, p. 61)

When people are employed, they work to earn a wage, which is spent through consumption in their "free" or "own" time. In the standard economic model, labor is defined within the realm of economic life, is extrinsically rewarded, and is merely a means to an end. Unsurprisingly, it assumes that people are motivated at work by rewards and punishments. There is no room for autonomy and meaning in such an approach to labor: As emphasized earlier, self-interest (or opportunism) demands control and eschews self-determination.

That said, if we go back to the definition of labor, we find that labor does indeed stand for hard physical effort (hence productivity), but also for the pain that women experience when they give birth. Fundamentally, labor is not only about (economic) production, but also about (biological and social) reproduction. As Nancy Folbre explains in her feminist economic analysis of human capital and labor economics:

> Most economic research on human capital focuses entirely on 'value added' in the form of education and experience, without considering the basic cost of bearing and rearing children, or creating the basic substrate which education and experience may enhance. As I have argued elsewhere (Folbre, 2008, 2009), I believe that the costs of producing future workers, developing their skills, maintaining their health, and providing for them in old age should be construed as part of the costs of producing human capital (Folbre, 2012, p. 282)

Taking stock of this critique, the conceptualization of work and labor in embodied economics requires expanding the understanding of work and labor beyond the boundaries of hierarchical organization, for without families and communities, there would literally be no workforce. To be clear, we do not contend that labor does not take place within hierarchical organizations. Under capitalism, the workforce consists of people who have no capital to invest (other than their human capital), which is the vast majority of the population, and thus have only their own bodies to provide them with a source of income. Generally, they end up working under someone else's authority, that is, in a hierarchical organization. They are paid to do with their bodies what someone else tells them to do. Under capitalism, labor cannot be conceptualized without reference to hierarchical organizations. But, as argued here, the scope of labor is broader than that.

As a form of embodied activity, labor *grounds* and *bounds* markets and hierarchical organizations: It grounds them through the biological and social reproduction of the workforce, and it bounds them because labor is fenced off when it undermines family and community life, as the WORK-LIFE BALANCE metaphor illustrates.

However, this metaphor is misleading if it equates work with labor, because it would portray labor as something that is not life. But labor goes beyond work, for instance, by creating and sustaining life through reproduction. To put the argument in a crude and radical way: If in embodied economics one understands that LABOR IS LIFE through contributions to economic, social, and political life, then one understands that there is a WORK-LIFE BALANCE metaphor as long as labor is (misleadingly) understood as contained within the boundaries of hierarchical organizations. This is why, we emphasized at the beginning of this section that the way labor is understood shapes the way hierarchical organizations are conceived.

The LABOR IS LIFE metaphor is not new to economic thought. Consistent with Hegel, Marx, for instance, emphasized that labor should be conceptualized beyond work. From a Marxian point of view,

> man produces his means of subsistence. This productive labor is the essence of man's life. Through this labor man molds the objects of his world and, in this sense, shapes his own reality. In this way, labor is, ideally, an end in itself. This process of conscious production is man's expression of his life. However, under certain conditions, man's labor becomes merely a means

> of subsistence and is viewed as work as opposed to a creative life-activity. When these conditions exist, labor is alienated. (Lefever & Lefever, 1977, p. 41; see also Patterson, 2009, p. 65ff)

LABOR IS LIFE because it is creation. More specifically, LABOR IS LIFE because it is the creation and transformation of the conditions of human existence. Against this background, meaningful work has an individual and a collective dimension: It is self-realization through world-making as a contribution to community life.

Let us turn to Arendt and Hegel to develop this argument about labor and embodiment. Arendt proposed a distinction between three types of human activity, labor, work, and action, as "*vita activa*." These three terms differ from common meanings in ways that are highly suggestive of the development of embodied economics. In characterizing these distinctions, she refers to Marx, albeit critically, but does not discuss Hegel at length in *The Human Condition* (Arendt, 1958/2018). In fact, Hegel anticipates important aspects of her approach by treating labor as a fundamental medium for the realization of what he calls "spirit" as elaborated in Chapter 5, which unfolds via outward and inward embodiment. For Hegel, labor is a bodily activity through which the subject expresses itself, thereby objectifying spirit, while the products of labor also transform the subject—in our parlance, this is a performative loop between outward and inward embodiment. In a society with a division of labor, this means that many products enter into relations of exchange, thus orienting labor towards the needs of others, leading to Hegel's conception of the "system of needs." Productive labor also means that nature (resources) becomes subject to means-end rationality, which is also the governing principle in a society bound together by the exchange of goods. This state is not sustainable because of pathologies such as alienation and inequality, so eventually civil society as a market society becomes embedded in the ethical life of the family, the associations and estates of civil society, and the state. Thus, for Hegel, the fundamental challenge is how to create the conditions for meaningful labor as self-realization, while maintaining the benefits of the division of labor and markets. Yet, Hegel did not anticipate the emergence of large-scale organizations, hence the factory system that Marx confronted.

A solution to these quandaries can be found in Hannah Arendt, who proposes the comprehensive notion of *vita activa* with three different forms in which she suggests a new categorization of the terms labor and work (Arendt, 1958/2018). Labor is the activity of the *animal laborans* and is focused on sustaining life as a bodily process. In this sense, labor is the reproduction of life, and there is no product beyond life, aka the body itself. Inspired by Marx, Arendt argues that labor is still dominant in modern society in the sense that wage earners are dissociated from their product and earn income only for consumption:

> The industrial revolution has replaced all workmanship with labor, and the result has been that the things of the modern world have become labor products whose natural fate is to be consumed, instead of work products which are there to be used. (Arendt, 1958/2018, p. 124)

In other words, even if they are not concerned with brute survival as the proletarians were in Marx's time, people still reproduce as consumers, as far as advanced economies are concerned.

Work is the activity of *Homo faber*. Only *Homo faber* is a world-maker in the sense of adding durable objects to the furniture of the world. Arendt (1958/2018, p. 161ff) offers an intriguing argument for why this requires the market, which is again Hegelian: *Homo faber* is concerned with the quality of the product, and exchange allows quality to be compared publicly, and thus to gain recognition from others. *Homo faber* makes and uses tools in production, which has given rise to modern technology, a world of machines. In such a world, even *animal laborans* can lead to a less painful life of mere reproduction because machines increase productivity. But wage-earners are not workers in the sense of *Homo faber*, because they are alienated from their product.

Action is primarily communication, and becomes speech in the public arena. This distinction (as with Hegel) is grounded in Arendt's ideal-typical view of the Greek polis. In the Greek polis, the institution of slavery allowed citizens to detach themselves from labor (the slave is the *animal laborans*), and concentrate on their role in the public sphere, that is, debating the political issues of the polis. Action, then, is political action. Unlike the means-end logic of work, the outcomes of action are never predictable or controllable by the actor, since they are determined in public debate. As such, they become part of history, the publicly recognized flow of past actions.

These distinctions are inspiring for an embodied theory of labor (now in the ordinary sense). Arendt also discusses the intersections and ambiguities of the three modes, when she notes that modern politics is often approached as "fabricating" desired states of society in a means-end logic (Arendt, 1958/2018, p. 220ff). Furthermore, she argues that the marketplace shares features with action in that it is a public domain where arguments over products ultimately determine recognition. Hence, we employ her categories not as disjunctive, but as aspectual modes. An important insight from her view of the *vita activa* is underscored by a consideration of historical development. In hunter-gatherer societies, we observe a mixture of all three activities, without the special institutions of Greek slavery. The original *vita activa* is largely concerned with labor, with the addition of important components of work such as tool making. However, a substantial part of the activities was devoted to "action" in Arendt's sense, namely commitments to social interactions, rituals, and other forms of preparing the conditions for ongoing cooperation. These cannot be counted as mere leisure because they respond to a feeling of obligation to contribute to the community.

We draw inspiration from Arendt in the following ways.

We relate labor to the contemporary notion of "care" (Puig de la Bellacasa, 2017). Indeed, the feminist analysis of care work in the family bears many resemblances with Arendt's analysis of slavery as the "hidden" domain in the household. The labor of care—the "invisible heart" in economic life (Folbre, 2001)—is deeply embodied in its focus on the embodied person in the broadest sense, such as the sick child or daily cooking. Unlike Arendt, we would include care of things, such as do-it-yourself (DIY) repairs, or tending the garden, insofar as these are also reproductive activities, even though they involve tools and often produce things. This, of course, has to do with the well-known shortcomings of the Gross Domestic Product (GDP) measurements of social product. The status of repair work, such as the DIY construction of a garden terrace, or the infamous self-assembly of IKEA furniture, raises intricate questions, since some of them reflect work in the domestic sphere, while others reflect the externalization of costs to consumers by market actors. Often this domestic distinction is also gendered, with men assuming the role of *Homo faber*. Regardless, we note that the domestic sphere cannot be reduced to labor; on the contrary, a large part of the work that sustains the capital stock in modern economies is done through DIY in the broadest sense. Indeed, an intriguing aspect of the organization of modern capitalism is that a specific form of DIY involvement is increasingly governed by the market (e.g., Gabriel et. al., 2015), as in the example of self-assembly. Another striking manifestation is the planned obsolescence of goods and designs that do not allow for DIY repair. That is to say, the form and extent of DIY are no longer determined autonomously by the households.

On the other hand, we distinguish a type of labor that is exclusively oriented to the market. This establishes a direct conceptual link with the conception of the market as a medium of disembodiment. In this argument, we follow Marx in important respects since we interpret alienation as a disembodiment that breaks the performative loop of outward and inward embodiment. However, in organizations, embodiment can be reinstated via structures of implicit knowledge, skills, and routines, and forms of recognition alternative to the market. Hence, the organizational design of companies assumes the key role in mediating the relationship between work and the market. As we analyzed in the previous section, this cannot be understood independently of the role of consumers as wage earners. In both roles, the wage-earners are laboring insofar as both work and consumption have only reproductive functions, given the alienation from the product of their work.

This is also evident when we depart from Arendt's exclusive focus on material production, since in modern economies many forms of labor are directly mediated as services to consumers in the marketplace. For example, healthcare services may appear, at first sight, to be a form of labor, but they are mediated by the market. To some extent, we can say that here the body becomes the product.

In addition, there is labor in the public sphere, which is political in the most general sense. Arendt completely ignores the role of government, referring to the *polis* as a form of direct democracy, and thus falling short behind Hegel, who even recognized government officials as a separate estate. But modern societies operate with large governments, and so this kind of governing activity would not qualify as labor or work in Arendt's sense. In contrast, we think of government as a form of labor in the public sphere, along with all kinds of labor in the media, and so on. We can generally classify bureaucratic functions as labor in this sense. Most importantly, this includes the education sector, which is part of the reproduction of the body in developed societies, and is mostly organized by the state. This is an important example of how original labor is institutionally diversified during economic development, while the original function of reproduction is maintained.

In contrast, we follow Arendt in including artistic work in the category of action, that is, more generally, creative expression beyond means-end rationality. Creative work is political in the broad sense that it contributes to ongoing public reflection on identities and cultural meanings.

The third type of *vita activa* plays an important role in setting the stage for the other types, as envisioned in Hegel's notion of ethical life, "*Sittlichkeit*." In this sense, we approach political labor as a medium for re-embedding the market in the community, and thus sublating disembodiment, since ethical life is directly related to embodied valuations, such as emotions of pride, discrimination, honor, or suffering. As with the relationship between organization and market, modern societies manifest a much more complicated structure of the public sphere, but we strictly follow Tönnies' classical distinction in conceptualizing "society" as capitalism, that is, disembodied markets, and thus claim that the fundamental function of the political is to re-constitute community under the conditions of our time. We turn to this issue in Chapter 8.

We summarize and systematize our approach in Fig. 7.11. We understand *vita activa* as "ACTIVITY IS LIFE." We distinguish three societal domains the household or "domestic," the firms or "corporate," and government in the broadest sense, the "public," and identify forms of *vita activa* in each. Our diagnosis applies to capitalism: By implication, our task in Chapter 8 is to imagine an alternative institutional arrangement.

Labor in the domestic sphere is primarily care and consumption as the reproduction of the body, which includes all forms of inward and outward embodiment, such as the consumption of status goods (e.g., fashion). In the conventional approach, consumption is strictly distinguished from labor, whereas we treat it as a form of reproductive labor. In the corporate sphere, the corresponding activity is wage labor. There is also labor in the public sphere, mainly as education and welfare, both aspects of government that have grown enormously in the last century. Both imply a shift of labor from the domestic to the public sphere, which entails a different pattern of externalization of the costs of reproducing laboring bodies.

Work in the domestic domain is DIY in the broadest sense, such as gardening, home repair, or making all kinds of things. In the corporate domain, we use a term from Max Weber (1922/2019) who distinguishes dispositional work from subordinate work.[40] Roughly speaking, dispositional work is (supposedly) higher-level managerial work and engineering work. This distinction is convenient because wage labor generally does the "making" in the narrow sense. However, in the sense of autonomous work on the product, in large organizations, this is distributed among different positions at the top of the hierarchy, as distinct from subordinate

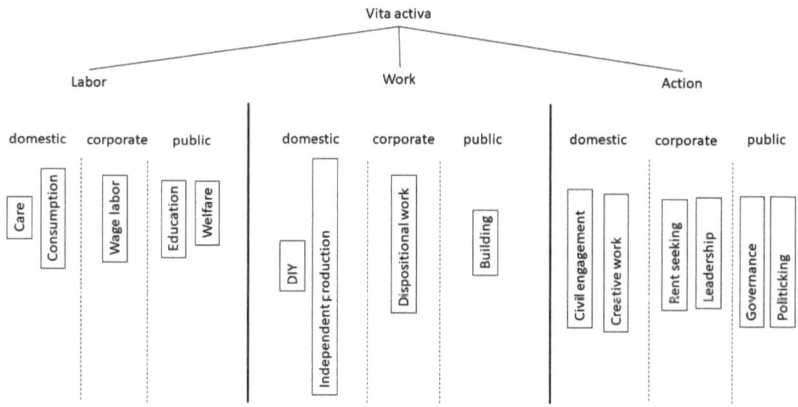

Fig. 7.11 *Vita activa* manifests the three forms of labor, work, and action in Arendtian terminology, as developed in the main text, which we project onto the three institutional domains of the domestic, the corporate, and the public. For each of the resulting combinations, we identify important types of institutionalized activity

work. In the public sphere, work is "building," that is, the construction of infrastructures.

Action in the domestic sphere is mainly engagement in civil society. We include creative work, such as that of artists, because in economic terms these are households. In the corporate sphere, action takes place at the top level, as corporate leadership, and as rent-seeking in general, or lobbying more specifically. In the public sphere, action is governance of all kinds (such as the judiciary) and politicking (such as election campaigns in democratic states).

The various forms of *vita activa* take on distinct expressions as institutional actions depending on the systemic contexts, as has been classically argued by feminist scholars about the gendered separation of care and wage labor in capitalism. If we consider the projection onto the four Fiske modes, additional aspects come to the fore, as we argued in the introduction. For example, wage labor is dominant in the hierarchy mode, which interacts with the market mode in the disembodiment of workers' knowledge ("deskilling"). However, there are also elements of the community mode when workers build countervailing informal structures.

This can overlap with political activism (and unionism), hence the intrusion of action into the organization of wage labor. Similarly, the modes can have different weights in gender relations: The domestic sphere under the rule of the *pater familias* might operate in the hierarchy mode, while a more modern couple with strong emotional commitments would ideally live in the community mode. As we have done in the previous sections, such phenomena can be analyzed in more detail using the analytical apparatus of conceptual blending. Yet, in the case of *vita activa*, it is important to use such tools within the full framework of the Aoki-Bourdieu model, since the interaction between power, symbolic capital, and dispositions is essential to understanding concrete forms of human activity in the economy.

7.5 Conclusion

The *vita activa* requires a radical transformation of the economic institutions of capitalism, which we discuss in the next chapter in developing a "concrete utopia" of embodied economics. In this chapter we have laid the conceptual groundwork in which labor is pivotal, effectively remaining in the tradition of Marx. Here, the body cannot be "abstracted away" except in a regime of robots. Changing the conditions of labor, here in both the generic and the Arendtian sense, requires institutional changes in the other two domains, money and property. As we have seen, money is the medium through which the market drives abstraction, and thus wage labor fundamentally alienates humans from their bodies. However, as the Fiske framework has shown, this is relative to various forms of embedding money practices in hybrids of types. The mere fact of receiving a wage does not necessarily imply abstraction because, for example, the embodied process of work takes place within organizations, not markets. Hence, changing the nature of the corporation is a means of de-abstracting labor. Similarly, the inherent potential for power asymmetries influences the way markets work, and so we can imagine countervailing institutional changes. In the domain of property, the Lockean formula opens up the prospect of creating institutional forms that reinforce the relationship between things and people as ownership, as in DIY. Ownership is also an important dimension in the relationship between employees and companies.

Marx did not offer a "concrete utopia," with the unfortunate result that the struggle against capitalism ended in socialist autocracies and dictatorships. With their partial demise, capitalism is seen by many as the only surviving institutional form of the economy (Fukuyama, 2020; Milanović, 2019; Plumpe, 2019). This conclusion, however, depends on whether we adopt the framework of conventional economics to analyze capitalism: We are caught in a performative vicious circle. Our analysis in this chapter allows us to break out of this circle.

Acknowledgements The section on property in this chapter builds on the results of a project supported by Deutsche Forschungsgemeinschaft (DFG, German Research Foundation)—Project-ID 424638267—TRR 294 "Structural change of property," Project C01: "Hybrid ownership structures in state capitalism: ownership-based society, socio-economic differentiation and governmentality analysed through the example of Shenzhen, China."

Notes

1. This is an important point because: "In societies based on commodity production the social synthesis is centred on the functions of money as the 'universal equivalent,' to use Marx's expression" (Sohn-Rethel, 1978, p. 6).
2. Simmel's contribution was almost entirely ignored in economics, despite a positive review when the English translation was published decades later (Laidler & Rowe, 1980). Note that Simmel's ideas about alienation in production and consumption as well as about money and exchange anticipated Marx's undiscovered *Paris Manuscripts* and *Grundrisse* (Frisby, p. lxii in Simmel, 1907/2004).
3. For related Marxian analyses, see Sohn-Rethel (1978, p. 6) who argues that: "The money abstraction can be more properly termed 'the exchange abstraction'."
4. Imagination is central to Adam Smith's thinking (Hankins & McDavid, 2023) but remains neglected in economics, with exceptions such as Shackle (1992).
5. The fairy tale relates to the rich literature on preferences in a dynamic context reviewed by Andreou (2020). A specific example is "money pumps" (e.g., Cubitt & Sugden, 2001), which would imply irrationality of the actor, as in the case of Hans, who adheres to a preference function that allows other players to continuously extract money from their interactions with him until he goes bankrupt.

6. For instance, Fiske observes: "In the United States, we apply market pricing in most of our labor, and communal sharing in our love life. Moose organize village labor primarily in the framework of communal sharing, and hardly ever according to market pricing. Moose working together to cultivate someone's field would generally be bewildered, if not shocked and insulted, to be paid for their time. On the other hand, a Moose woman would be equally offended if her lover ever did not offer her money for sleeping with him" (Fiske, 1990, p. 200).
7. For the fascinating case of the historical transformations of the Chinese God of Wealth, see Von Glahn (2004).
8. Our terminology follows Herrmann-Pillath and Hederer (2023). Recent literature in the sociology of finance uses the term "assetization" (e.g., Tellmann, 2022), but more narrowly refers to the transformation of certain objects into financial assets, such as buildings.
9. This is explored in Seaford's seminal analysis of the cultural and social consequences of money in ancient Greece (Seaford, 2004).
10. Wittgenstein argues that although feelings and sensations are irreducibly private, we cannot refer to them linguistically without recourse to a system of public rules of use that ultimately have no reference to these private sensations at all: "When one says 'He gave a name to his sensation' one forgets that a great deal of stage-setting in the language is presupposed if the mere act of naming is to make sense. And when we speak of someone's having given a name to pain, what is presupposed is the existence of the grammar of the word 'pain'; it shows the post where the new word is stationed" (Wittgenstein, 1953, §257).
11. For a complementary analysis on calculative reason through an anthropological lens, see Gudeman (2008).
12. Weyl (2019) argues that economics has even neglected earlier traditions of "price theory," such as the Chicago School represented by scholars like Stigler, and rooted in earlier contributions like Marshall's. Yet, as his review shows, the diagnosis of the economic sociologist Caliskan (2007) is still valid for his approach, namely that prices and pricing are not analyzed as institutional practices. Pricing remains determined by the abstract features of pricing as deduced from economic models such as models of imperfect

competition, which are then seen as a kind of analytical surrogate for understanding real-world pricing.

13. In his influential view, Haidt (2001) presented strong evidence that people initially rely on moral intuitions in making moral judgments, and only ex post, even introspectively, confirm them through rational reasoning.
14. Graeber (2011, p. 21ff) speaks of the "myth of barter." Alas, economists are stuck in their invented tradition.
15. For a similar economic approach, see Hicks (1989, p. 47ff).
16. In this article: "Holistic thinking (dominant thinking style for Easterners) is characterized by a focus on interrelationships between various objects. On the other hand, analytic thinking (dominant thinking style for Westerners) is characterized by a focus on the central object in a given context and a tendency to make rule- based decision" (Banerjee et al., 2019, p. 78).
17. In the original contribution to the theory, North and colleagues (2013) focus on the historical role of landed property which has been extended to other forms of wealth in the context of developing countries. The key point is that property rights are initially created and maintained to protect elite rights and rents, and are only universalized in certain forms of political systems, called "open access orders." In "limited access orders," violence is seen as endemic, both in the form of intra-elite struggles and the oppression of non-elites.
18. The emphasis on contextualized equity is also a defining feature of Chinese traditional law compared to Western civil law, see Huang (2006).
19. This is also supported by anthropologists (Strang & Busse, 2011). Weber defines "appropriation" as follows: "A closed social relationship can secure its monopolised *Chancen* to participants in a number of ways. Such allocation might be (a) freely arrived at, (b) regulated or rationed by degree and form, or (c) appropriated on a more or less permanent basis by specific individuals or groups. This represents internal closure. Appropriated *Chancen* can be called 'rights'" (Weber, 1922/2019, pp. 123–124).
20. In deep symbolism, George Washington was a leading figure in the land company business model that financialized land at the frontier, see Goetzmann (2017, p. 388ff).

21. Graeber discussed famous examples of Trobriand, Maori, and Kwakiutl "gift economies."
22. On the continuity of ritual across the human/non-human divide, see Stephenson (2015, p. 5ff).
23. "*Chancen*" means opportunities in German.
24. This was seminally developed in Max Weber's early work on medieval trading enterprises and their legal forms (Ford, 2010).
25. In Roman law, one of the rituals of property transfer creates the fiction that the receiver claims the object was already her property before the deal announcing "this is mine" (Harke, 2016).
26. Armbrüster (2005, p. 115ff) argues that the current form of the corporation poses a dilemma for a liberal theory of society in the Popperian sense confronting "open" versus "closed" societies: In a supposedly "open" society, corporations are "closed" social structures.
27. As Leamer observes: "In fact, there are very few exchanges that are mediated by 'markets.' There are very few 'commodities' whose value is transparent enough to allow the formation of a market. There are very few exchanges that take place at a frequency high enough and transparent enough to other potential participants that market prices can emerge. Most exchanges take place within the context of long-term relationships that create the language needed for buyer and seller to communicate, that establish the trust needed to carry out the exchange, that allow ongoing servicing of implicit or explicit guarantees, that monitor the truthfulness of both parties, and that punish those who mislead. Many exchanges occur between colleagues who work for the same firm. Indeed, about 40 percent of US imports are carried out internal to multinational enterprises" (Leamer, 2007, pp. 99–100).
28. With procedural rationality, Simon proposed that rationality be conceived not only as a product of thought, as is traditionally done in the standard economic model (e.g., maximizing), but also as a process, i.e. as deliberation that follows steps (Simon, 1978). This position is consistent with James' (1890, p. 325) definition of rationality as "the peculiar thinking process called reasoning," and with the embodied economics perspective that rationality is about reason and deliberation.
29. As Coase (1937, p. 392) points out: "It seems improbable that a firm would emerge without the existence of uncertainty."

30. This is perfectly illustrated by a 1971 advertisement from Delta Airlines, which featured the following message: "Delta is an airline run by professionals. Like Kris Conrad, stewardess. Pretty, alert, efficient, confident and sociable. Chosen from 25 applicants. You'll have a nice trip because we have 2,300 Kris Conrads! Delta is ready when you are."
31. Even more so when it comes to the experience economy, which aims to counteract the disenchantment of economic life, described by Weber, with fantasies, feelings, and fun (e.g., Holbrook & Hirschman, 1982). To reenchant economic life, one builds cathedrals of consumption (Kowinski, 1985), such as shopping malls, "to instil, maintain and reproduce a sense of enchantment and wonder" (Ostergaard et al., 2013, p. 338), and one sells feelings and emotions.
32. Note that the implications of human capital as a justification for public investment in education can actually be read differently. As Folbre points out, Becker's admission that "children depend on their parents and on society as a whole for the development of their human capital weakens the foundational meritocratic principle of neoclassical theory: that a market economy delivers to individuals what they deserve. James Heckman forthrightly describes the inability of children to choose their own parents as a market failure, far more binding than any mere credit constraint (Cunha & Heckman, 2010). Heckman has campaigned tirelessly in recent years for expansion of public investments in early childhood education (which he views as far more productive than public investments at the university level and above)" (Folbre, 2012, p. 285).
33. For further critical analyses of this theory, especially regarding its implications for schooling, education, family relations, or economic growth, see, for example, Bowles and Gintis (1975), Feher (2009), Fleming (2017), and Folbre (2009).
34. A clear expression of this metaphor can be found in Becker's writings with the FAMILY IS A FACTORY metaphor: "in recent years economists increasingly recognise that a household is truly a 'small factory' (Cairncross, 1958): it combines capital goods, raw materials and labour to clean, feed, procreate and otherwise produce useful commodities" (Becker, 1976, p.92 quoted in Sen, 1985/

1999, p. 10). As Sen indicates, reducing functionings to commodities is "misleading" because functionings are "features of the state of existence of a person, and not detached objects that the person or the household happens to 'product' and 'own'" (Sen, 1985/1999, p. 10). In that respect, human capital theory is individualistic and neglects that "many of the functionings (e.g., being free from malaria) are 'produced' at least as much outside the household as inside it (e.g., through anti-epidemic public policy)" (Sen, 1985/1999, p. 10).

35. Alienation can also take a social form through anomie (e.g., Kanungo, 1979; Seeman, 1959; Shantz et al., 2015), or a more psychological form through emotive dissonance (Hochschild, 1983).
36. Many other limitations to the division of labor have been pointed out. For instance, Smith, who described the division of labor in *The Wealth of Nations* was aware of its limitations: "The man whose whole life is spent in performing a few simple operations (…) generally becomes as stupid and ignorant as it is possible for a human creature to become" (Smith, 2005, p. 782; see also, Dolan, 1971).
37. As argued by Marx but also by Weber, exploitation leads to alienation. On the philosophical relationship between alienation and exploitation, see, for instance, Buchanan (1979).
38. Despite their Marxian critique of human capital, Bowles and Gintis acknowledge that: "Human capital theory allows fundamental insights not available to earlier versions of neoclassical economics. First, it returns to and extends the Ricardian and Marxian tradition in treating labor as a produced means of production, whose characteristics depend on the total configuration of economic forces. Second, it rejects the simplistic assumption of homogeneous labor and centers attention on the differentiation of the labor force. Third, it brings basic social institutions (such as schooling and the family), previously relegated to the purely cultural and superstructural spheres, into the realm of economic analysis" (Bowles & Gintis, 1975, p. 75).
39. This is somewhat ironic, given that the "information economy is the fetish form of the commodity in financial capitalism." (Prusik, 2018, p. 1611).

40. As Tribe notes: "there was no simple way to refer directly to managerial functions at the time Weber was writing. Literally, *disponierende Leistung* can be translated as 'work related to planning and arranging'" (Tribe, note 73 in Weber 1922/2019, p. 242). We do not follow Tribe here and use the expression "dispositional work" to translate "*disponierende Leistung*." This corresponds to Weber's German expression for the distinction between "dispositional work" and "subordinate work." Weber refers to subordinate work as "*Arbeit*," which is Arendt's "labor," fittingly.

References

Aaker, J. L. (1997). Dimensions of brand personality. *Journal of Marketing Research, 34*(3), 347–356. https://doi.org/10.2307/3151897

Acemoglu, D., Johnson, S., & Robinson, J. A. (2001). The colonial origins of comparative development: An empirical investigation. *American Economic Review, 91*(5), 1369–1401. https://doi.org/10.1257/aer.91.5.1369

Akerlof, G. A. (1982). Labor contracts as partial gift exchange. *The Quarterly Journal of Economics, 97*(4), 543–569. https://doi.org/10.2307/1885099

Alchian, A. A. (2018). Property rights. In *The new Palgrave dictionary of economics* (pp. 10892–10897). Palgrave Macmillan UK. https://doi.org/10.1057/978-1-349-95189-5_1814

Alexander, G. S. (2003). Property as a fundamental constitutional right—The German example. *Cornell Law Review, 88*, 733–778.

Alexander, G. S., Peñalver, E. M., Singer, J. W., & Underkuffler, L. S. (2008). A statement of progressive property. *Cornell Law Review, 94*, 743–744.

Allison, N. K. (1978). A psychometric development of a test for consumer alienation from the marketplace. *Journal of Marketing Research, 15*(4), 565–575.

Amir, O., Ariely, D., & Carmon, Z. (2008). The dissociation between monetary assessment and predicted utility. *Marketing Science, 27*(6), 1055–1064.

Anderson, E. (2019). *Private government: How employers rule our lives (and why we don't talk about it)*. Princeton University Press.

Andreou, C. (2020, Winter). Dynamic choice. In E. N. Zalta (Ed.), *The Stanford encyclopedia of philosophy*. Metaphysics Research Lab, Stanford University. https://plato.stanford.edu/archives/win2020/entries/dynamic-choice/

Andrighetto, L., Baldissarri, C., & Volpato, C. (2017). (Still) modern times: Objectification at work. *European Journal of Social Psychology, 47*(1), 25–35. https://doi.org/10.1002/ejsp.2190

Apicella, C. L., Azevedo, E. M., Christakis, N. A., & Fowler, J. H. (2014). Evolutionary origins of the endowment effect: Evidence from hunter-gatherers. *American Economic Review, 104*(6), 1793–1805. https://doi.org/10.1257/aer.104.6.1793

Appadurai, A. (1988). *The social life of things: Commodities in cultural perspective*. Cambridge University Press.

Arendt, H. (1958/2018). *The human condition*. University of Chicago Press. https://press.uchicago.edu/ucp/books/book/chicago/H/bo29137972.html

Ariely, D., Kamenica, E., & Prelec, D. (2008). Man's search for meaning: The case of Legos. *Journal of Economic Behavior & Organization, 67*(3–4), 671–677. https://doi.org/10.1016/j.jebo.2008.01.004

Armbrüster, T. (2005). *Management and organization in Germany*. Ashgate.

Bagehot, W. (1873/2017). *Lombard Street : A description of the money market* (Revised and updated new ed.). White Crane Publishing.

Banerjee, P., Chatterjee, P., Mishra, S., & Mishra, A. A. (2019). Loss is a loss, why categorize it? Mental accounting across cultures. *Journal of Consumer Behaviour, 18*(2), 77–88. https://doi.org/10.1002/cb.1748

Barzel, Y. (2015). What are "property rights", and why do they matter? A comment on Hodgson's article. *Journal of Institutional Economics, 11*(4), 719–723. https://doi.org/10.1017/S1744137415000181

Batra, R., Ahuvia, A., & Bagozzi, R. P. (2012). Brand love. *Journal of Marketing, 76*(2), 1–16. https://doi.org/10.1509/jm.09.0339

Bazin, Y. (2013). Understanding organisational gestures: Technique, aesthetics and embodiment. *Scandinavian Journal of Management, 29*(4), 377–393. https://doi.org/10.1016/j.scaman.2013.09.003

Becker, G. S. (1960). An economic analysis of fertility. In G. S. Becker (Ed.), *Demographic and economic change in developed countries* (pp. 209–240). Columbia University Press.

Becker, G. S. (1962). Investment in human capital: A theoretical analysis. *Journal of Political Economy, 70*, 9–49.

Becker, G. S. (1964). *Human capital: A theoretical and empirical analysis with special reference to education*. University of Chicago Press.

Becker, G. S. (1992). Education, labor force quality, and the economy. *Business Economics, 27*(1), 7–12.

Becker, G. S. (1994). Human capital revisited. In G. S. Becker (Ed.), *Human capital: A theoretical and empirical analysis with special reference to education* (3rd ed., pp. 15–28). University of Chicago Press.

Becker, G. S., Murphy, K. S., & Tamura, R. (1994). Human capital, fertility, and economic growth. In G. S. Becker (Ed.), *Human capital: A theoretical and empirical analysis with special reference to education* (3rd ed., pp. 323–350). University of Chicago Press.

Beckert, J. (2016). *Imagined futures: Fictional expectations and capitalist dynamics*. Harvard University Press.

Belk, R. (1988). Possessions and the extended self. *Journal of Consumer Research, 15*(2), 139–168.

Bellotti, V. M. E., Cambridge, S., Hoy, K., Shih, P. C., Handalian, L. R., Han, K., & Carroll, J. M. (2014). Towards community-centered support for peer-to-peer service exchange: Rethinking the timebanking metaphor. *Proceedings of the SIGCHI Conference on Human Factors in Computing Systems* (pp. 2975–2984). https://doi.org/10.1145/2556288.2557061

Benkler, Y. (2011a). *The penguin and the Leviathan: How cooperation triumphs over self-interest*. Crown.

Benkler, Y. (2011b). The unselfish gene. *Harvard Business Review, 89*(7/8), 76–85.

Berger, P. L., Berger, B., & Kellner, H. (1973). *The homeless mind: Modernization and consciousness*. Penguin Books.

Berrone, P., Cruz, C., & Gomez-Mejia, L. R. (2012). Socioemotional wealth in family firms: Theoretical dimensions, assessment approaches, and agenda for future research. *Family Business Review, 25*(3), 258–279. https://doi.org/10.1177/0894486511435355

Beunza, D., Hardie, I., & MacKenzie, D. (2006). A price is a social thing: Towards a material sociology of arbitrage. *Organization Studies, 27*(5), 721–745. https://doi.org/10.1177/0170840606065923

Binswanger, H. C. (2013). *The growth spiral: Money, energy, and imagination in the dynamics of the market process*. Springer.

Bioneers (Director). (2022, October 10). *The Rights of Nature movement in Indian country and beyond: From grassroots to mainstream | Bioneers*. https://www.youtube.com/watch?v=O6eUTqPzNmM

Blackstone, W. (1763/2001). *Blackstone's commentaries on the Laws of England. Volume II* (W. Morrison, Ed.). Cavendish Publishing.

Bloch, D. J. (2006). *Res sanctae* in Gaius and the Founding of the City. *Roman Legal Tradition, 3*, 48–62.

Bowles, S., & Gintis, H. (1975). The problem with human capital theory—A Marxian critique. *The American Economic Review, 65*(2), 74–82.

Bowles, S., & Gintis, H. (2011). *A cooperative species: Human reciprocity and its evolution*. Princeton University Press.

Bradshaw, E. L., Conigrave, J. H., Steward, B. A., Ferber, K. A., Parker, P. D., & Ryan, R. M. (2023). A meta-analysis of the dark side of the American dream: Evidence for the universal wellness costs of prioritizing extrinsic over intrinsic goals. *Journal of Personality and Social Psychology, 124*(4), 873–899. https://doi.org/10.1037/pspp0000431

Bradshaw, K. (2020). *Wildlife as property owners: A new conception of animal rights*. University of Chicago Press.

Bromley, D. W., & Chavas, J.-P. (2008). On the origins and evolving role of money. *Journal of Institutional and Theoretical Economics, 164*(4), 624. https://doi.org/10.1628/093245608786534631

Brooks, M. A., Heijdra, B. J., & Lowenberg, A. D. (1990). Productive versus unproductive labor and rent seeking: Lessons from history. *Journal of Institutional and Theoretical Economics (JITE) / Zeitschrift Für Die Gesamte Staatswissenschaft, 146*(3), 419–438.

Bruess, C. J. (2011). Family rituals and communication: The construction of family identity and social capital. In R. L. Sorenson (Ed.), *Family business and social capital*. Edward Elgar Publishing. https://doi.org/10.4337/9781849807388.0009

Buchanan, A. (1979). Exploitation, alienation, and injustice. *Canadian Journal of Philosophy, 9*(1), 121–139.

Buss, A. R. (1979). Humanistic psychology as liberal ideology: The socio-historical roots of Maslow's theory of self-actualization. *Journal of Humanistic Psychology, 19*(3), 43–55.

Cai, M., Murtazashvili, I., & Murtazashvili, J. (2020). The politics of land property rights. *Journal of Institutional Economics, 16*(2), 151–167. https://doi.org/10.1017/S1744137419000158

Cairncross, A. K. (1958). Economic schizophrenia. *Scottish Journal of Political Economy, 5*(1), 15–21. https://doi.org/10.1111/j.1467-9485.1958.tb00345.x

Caliskan, K. (2007). Price as a market device: Cotton trading in Izmir mercantile exchange. *The Sociological Review, 55*(2 suppl), 241–260. https://doi.org/10.1111/j.1467-954X.2007.00738.x

Candlish, S., & Wrisley, G. (2019, Fall). Private language. In E. N. Zalta (Ed.), *The Stanford encyclopedia of philosophy*. Metaphysics Research Lab, Stanford University. https://plato.stanford.edu/archives/fall2019/entries/private-language/

Chapman, J., Dean, M., Ortoleva, P., Snowberg, E., & Camerer, C. (2023). *Willingness to accept, willingness to pay, and loss aversion* (No. w30836). National Bureau of Economic Research. https://doi.org/10.3386/w30836

Chapman, J., Snowberg, E., Wang, S. W., & Camerer, C. (2022). *Looming large or seeming small? Attitudes towards losses in a representative sample* (No. w30243). National Bureau of Economic Research. https://doi.org/10.3386/w30243

Chiaburu, D. S., Thundiyil, T., & Wang, J. (2014). Alienation and its correlates: A meta-analysis. *European Management Journal, 32*(1), 24–36. https://doi.org/10.1016/j.emj.2013.06.003

Choy, Y. K. (2018). Cost-benefit analysis, values, wellbeing and ethics: An indigenous worldview analysis. *Ecological Economics, 145*, 1–9. https://doi.org/10.1016/j.ecolecon.2017.08.005

Coase, R. H. (1937). The nature of the firm. *Economica, 4*(16), 386–405. https://doi.org/10.1111/j.1468-0335.1937.tb00002.x
Coase, R. H. (1960). The problem of social cost. *The Journal of Law & Economics, 3*, 1–44.
Cohen, A. J., & Harcourt, G. C. (2003). Retrospectives: Whatever happened to the Cambridge capital theory controversies? *Journal of Economic Perspectives, 17*(1), 199–214. https://doi.org/10.1257/089533003321165010
Cohn, A., Fehr, E., & Maréchal, M. A. (2014). Business culture and dishonesty in the banking industry. *Nature, 516*(7529), 86–89. https://doi.org/10.1038/nature13977
Commons, J. R. (1996). *John R. Commons: Selected essays*. Routledge.
Compton, W. C. (2018). Self-actualization myths: What did Maslow really say? *Journal of Humanistic Psychology, 0022167818761929.*
Conner, K. R., & Prahalad, C. K. (1996). A resource-based theory of the firm: Knowledge versus opportunism. *Organization Science, 7*(5), 477–501. https://doi.org/10.1287/orsc.7.5.477
Cooper, D. (1998). *Governing out of order: Space, law, and the politics of belonging*. Distributed in the USA by New York University Press.
Coyle, D. (2015). *GDP: A brief but affectionate history* (Revised and expanded ed.). Princeton University Press.
Cubitt, R. P., & Sugden, R. (2001). On money pumps. *Games and Economic Behavior, 37*(1), 121–160. https://doi.org/10.1006/game.2000.0834
Cunha, F., & Heckman, J. J. (2010). Investing in our young people (NBER Working Paper No. 16201). National Bureau of Economic Research.
Dagan, H. (2021). *A liberal theory of property*. Cambridge University Press.
Davis, J. B. (2003). *The theory of the individual in economics: Identity and value*. Routledge.
De Moor, T. (2015). The dilemma of the commoners: Understanding the use of common-pool resources in long-term perspective. *Cambridge University Press*. https://doi.org/10.1017/CBO9781139135450
Deci, E. L., Olafsen, A. H., & Ryan, R. M. (2017). Self-determination theory in work organizations: The state of a science. *Annual Review of Organizational Psychology and Organizational Behavior, 4*(1), 19–43. https://doi.org/10.1146/annurev-orgpsych-032516-113108
Despret, V. (2019). *Habiter en oiseau*. Actes sud.
Dierksmeier, C. (2020). From Jensen to Jensen: Mechanistic management education or humanistic management learning? *Journal of Business Ethics, 166*(1), 73–87. https://doi.org/10.1007/s10551-019-04120-z
Dolan, E. G. (1971). Alienation, freedom, and economic organization. *Journal of Political Economy, 79*(5), 1084–1094. https://doi.org/10.1086/259816

Earle, T. (2017). Property in prehistory. In M. Graziadei & L. Smith (Eds.), *Comparative property law. A global perspective* (pp. 3–25). Edward Elgar Publishing. https://doi.org/10.4337/9781785369162.00008

Elster, J. (1986). *An Introduction to Karl Marx*. Cambridge University Press.

Emerich, Y. (2017). Possession. In M. Graziadei & L. Smith (Eds.), *Comparative property law: A global perspective* (pp. 171–191). Edward Elgar Publishing.

Falk, A., & Kosfeld, M. (2006). The hidden costs of control. *American Economic Review, 96*(5), 1611–1630. https://doi.org/10.1257/aer.96.5.1611

Federici, S. (2004/2021). *Caliban and the witch: Women, the body and primitive accumulation*. Penguin Books.

Feher, M. (2009). Self-appreciation; or, the aspirations of human capital. *Public Culture, 21*(1), 21–41. https://doi.org/10.1215/08992363-2008-019

Fehr, D., & Kübler, D. (2022). *The endowment effect in the general population* (CESifo Working Paper No. 10150). https://doi.org/10.2139/ssrn.4309201

Ferguson, N. (2009). *The ascent of money: A financial history of the world* (Publ. with updates). Penguin Books.

Ferraro, F., Pfeffer, J., & Sutton, R. I. (2005). Economics language and assumptions: How theories can become self-fulfilling. *Academy of Management Review, 30*(1), 8–24. https://doi.org/10.5465/AMR.2005.15281412

Firat, A. F. (2018). Marx, commodity and consumer culture. In S. Askegaard & B. Heilbrunn (Eds.), *Canonical authors in consumption theory* (pp. 15–22). Routledge.

Fiske, A. P. (1990). Relativity within Moose ("Mossi") culture: Four incommensurable models for social relationships. *Ethos, 18*(2), 180–204.

Fiske, A. P., & Tetlock, P. E. (1997). Taboo trade-offs: Reactions to transactions that transgress the spheres of justice. *Political Psychology, 18*(2), 255–297. https://doi.org/10.1111/0162-895X.00058

Fiske, A. P., Thomsen, L., & Thein, S. M. (2009). Differently embodying different relationships. *European Journal of Social Psychology, 39*(7), 1294–1297. https://doi.org/10.1002/ejsp.697

Fleming, P. (2017). The human capital hoax: Work, debt and insecurity in the era of Uberization. *Organization Studies, 38*(5), 691–709.

Folbre, N. (2001). *The invisible heart: Economics and family values*. New Press.

Folbre, N. (2008). *Valuing children: Rethinking the economics of the family*. Harvard University Press.

Folbre, N. (2009). *Greed, lust and gender: A history of economic ideas*. Oxford University Press.

Folbre, N. (2012). The political economy of human capital. *Review of Radical Political Economics, 44*(3), 281–292. https://doi.org/10.1177/0486613412440240

Ford, L. R. (2010). Max Weber on property: An effort in interpretive understanding. *SSRN Electronic Journal*. https://doi.org/10.2139/ssrn.1560042

Foucault, M. (2004). *Naissance de la biopolitique: Cours au Collège de France, 1978–1979*. Gallimard/Seuil.

Fournier, S. (1998). Consumers and their brands: Developing relationship theory in consumer research. *Journal of Consumer Research, 24*(4), 343–353. https://doi.org/10.1086/jcr.1998.24.issue-4

Fraser, N. (2016). Contradictions of capital and care. *New Left Review, 100*, 99–117.

Fromm, E. (1974). Is man lazy by nature? In E. Fromm (Ed.), *The pathology of normalcy*. Lantern Books.

Fromm, E. (2002). *The sane society*. Routledge.

Fukuyama, F. (2020). *The end of history and the last man*. Penguin Books.

Fumagalli, A., Giuliani, A., Lucarelli, S., & Vercellone, C. (2019). *Cognitive capitalism, welfare and labour: The commonfare hypothesis*. Routledge.

Furubotn, E. G., & Richter, R. (1997). *Institutions and economic theory: The contribution of the new institutional economics*. University of Michigan Press.

Gabriel, Y., Korczynski, M., & Rieder, K. (2015). Organizations and their consumers: Bridging work and consumption. *Organization, 22*(5), 629–643. https://doi.org/10.1177/1350508415586040

Gal, D., & Rucker, D. D. (2018). The loss of loss aversion: Will it loom larger than its gain? *Journal of Consumer Psychology, 28*(3), 497–516. https://doi.org/10.1002/jcpy.1047

Gallus, J., Reiff, J., Kamenica, E., & Fiske, A. P. (2022). Relational incentives theory. *Psychological Review, 129*(3), 586–602. https://doi.org/10.1037/rev0000336

Gasiorowska, A., & Zaleskiewicz, T. (2022). Can we get social assistance without losing agency? Engaging in market relationships as an alternative to searching for help from others. *Psychological Inquiry, 33*(1), 38–41. https://doi.org/10.1080/1047840X.2022.2037998

Gates, H. (1996). *China's motor: A thousand years of petty capitalism*. Cornell University Press.

Gesell, S. (1916/2022). *Die natürliche Wirtschaftsordnung durch Freigeld und Freiland (Classics reprint)*. Forgotten books.

Ghoshal, S. (2005). Bad management theories are destroying good management practices. *Academy of Management Learning & Education, 4*(1), 75–91. https://doi.org/10.5465/AMLE.2005.16132558

Ghoshal, S., & Moran, P. (1996). Bad for practice: A critique of the transaction cost theory. *Academy of Management Review, 21*(1), 13–47. https://doi.org/10.5465/AMR.1996.9602161563

Gintis, H. (2007). The evolution of private property. *Journal of Economic Behavior & Organization, 64*(1), 1–16. https://doi.org/10.1016/j.jebo.2006.02.002

Godelier, M. (1996/1999). *The enigma of the gift*. University of Chicago Press.

Goetzmann, W. N. (2017). *Money changes everything: How finance made civilization possible; with a new afterword by the author* (Third printing, and first paperback printing). Princeton University Press.

Graeber, D. (1997). Manners, deference, and private property in early modern Europe. *Comparative Studies in Society and History, 39*(4), 694–728. https://doi.org/10.1017/S0010417500020867

Graeber, D. (2001). *Toward an anthropological theory of value: The false coin of our own dreams*. Springer.

Graeber, D. (2011). *Debt: The first 5,000 years*. Melville House.

Graeber, D. (2019). *Bullshit jobs*. Penguin Books.

Grandey, A. A., & Sayre, G. M. (2019). Emotional labor: Regulating emotions for a wage. *Current Directions in Psychological Science, 28*(2), 131–137. https://doi.org/10.1177/0963721418812771

Graziadei, M. (2017). The structure of property ownership and the common law/civil law divide. In M. Graziadei & L. Smith (Eds.), *Comparative property law: A global perspective* (pp. 71–99). Edward Elgar Publishing. https://doi.org/10.4337/9781785369162.00012

Greer, A. (2017). *Property and dispossession: Natives, empires and land in early modern North America*. Cambridge University Press.

Gretton, G. L. (2007). Ownership and its Objects. *Rabels Zeitschrift Für Ausländisches Und Internationales Privatrecht, 71*(4), 802. https://doi.org/10.1628/003372507782419462

Guala, F. (2006). Critical notice: Naissance de la biopolitique: Cours au Collège de France, 1978–1979. *Michel Foucault. Economics and Philosophy, 22*(3), 429–439. https://doi.org/10.1017/S0266267106001052

Gudeman, S. (2008). *Economy's tension: The dialectics of community and market*. Berghahn Books.

Gupta, A. (2019). Foreclosure contagion and the neighborhood spillover effects of mortgage defaults. *The Journal of Finance, 74*(5), 2249–2301. https://doi.org/10.1111/jofi.12821

Haidt, J. (2001). The emotional dog and its rational tail: A social intuitionist approach to moral judgment. *Psychological Review, 108*(4), 814–834. https://doi.org/10.1037//0033-295X.108.4.814

Hamrick, W. S. (1987). *An existential phenomenology of law: Maurice Merleau-Ponty*. Springer, Netherlands. https://doi.org/10.1007/978-94-017-0707-7

Hankins, K., & McDavid, B. (2023). Adam Smith and the creative role of imagination. In *Adam Smith and modernity* (pp. 109–127). Routledge.

Harke, J. D. (2016). *Römisches Recht: Von der klassischen Zeit bis zu den modernen Kodifikationen (2., überarbeitete Auflage).* C.H. Beck.

Harris, L. T., Lee, V. K., Capestany, B. H., & Cohen, A. O. (2014). Assigning economic value to people results in dehumanization brain response. *Journal of Neuroscience, Psychology, and Economics, 7*(3), 151–163. https://doi.org/10.1037/npe0000020

Hase, P. H. (2013). *Custom, land and livelihood in rural south China: The traditional land law of Hong Kong's New Territories, 1750–1950.* Hong Kong University Press.

Hayek, F. A. (1937). Economics and knowledge. *Economica, 4*(13), 33–54.

Hayek, F. A. (1945). The use of knowledge in society. *American Economic Review, 35*(4), 519–530.

Hayek, F. A. (1988). *The fatal conceit: The errors of socialism.* Routledge.

Hayek, F. A. (1982/2013). *Law, legislation and liberty: A new statement of the liberal principles of justice and political economy* (New ed.). Routledge.

Helion, C., & Gilovich, T. (2014). Gift cards and mental accounting: Green-lighting hedonic spending. *Journal of Behavioral Decision Making, 27*, 386–393. https://doi.org/10.1002/bdm.1813

Heller, M. A. (1998). The tragedy of the anticommons: Property in the transition from Marx to markets. *Harvard Law Review, 111*(3), 621–688.

Hénaff, M. (2002). *Le prix de la vérité: Le don, l'argent, la philosophie.* Seuil.

Henkel, A. P., Boegershausen, J., Hoegg, J., Aquino, K., & Lemmink, J. (2018). Discounting humanity: When consumers are price conscious, employees appear less human. *Journal of Consumer Psychology, 28*(2), 272–292. https://doi.org/10.1002/jcpy.1023

Herrmann-Pillath, C. (2013). *Foundations of economic evolution: A treatise on the natural philosophy of economics.* Edward Elgar.

Herrmann-Pillath, C. (2016). Performative mechanisms. In I. Boldyrev & E. Svetlova (Eds.), *Enacting dismal science* (pp. 53–86). Palgrave Macmillan US. https://doi.org/10.1057/978-1-137-48876-3_3

Herrmann-Pillath, C. (2023a). The universal commons: An economic theory of ecosystem ownership. *Ecological Economics, 208*, 107822. https://doi.org/10.1016/j.ecolecon.2023.107822

Herrmann-Pillath, C. (2023b). *Towards a new language of property* (Working Paper No. 4), Sonderforschungsbereich/Transregio 294. Strukturwandel des Eigentums. https://sfb294-eigentum.de/de/working-paper/

Herrmann-Pillath, C., & Hederer, C. (2023). *A new principles of economics: The science of markets.* Routledge.

Herzberg, F. (2003, January). How do you motivate your employees? *Harvard Business Review*, 87–96.

Hicks, J. (1969). *A theory of economic history.* Clarendon Press.

Hicks, J. (1989). *A market theory of money.* Clarendon Press.

Hirschman, A. O. (1970). *Exit, voice, and loyalty: Responses to decline in firms, organizations and states*. Harvard University Press.
Hochschild, A. R. (1979). Emotion work, feeling rules, and social structure. *American Journal of Sociology, 85*(3), 551. https://doi.org/10.1086/227049
Hochschild, A. R. (1983). *The managed heart: Commercialization of human feeling*. University of California Press.
Hodgson, G. M. (2015). Much of the "economics of property rights" devalues property and legal rights. *Journal of Institutional Economics, 11*(4), 683–709. https://doi.org/10.1017/S1744137414000630
Hohfeld, W. N. (1917). Fundamental legal conceptions as applied in judicial reasoning. *The Yale Law Journal, 26*(8), 710–770.
Holbrook, M. B. (2013). The greedy bastard's guide to business. *Journal of Macromarketing, 33*(4), 369–385. https://doi.org/10.1177/0276146713491435
Holbrook, M. B., & Hirschman, E. C. (1982). The experiential aspects of consumption: Consumer fantasies, feelings, and fun. *Journal of Consumer Research, 9*(2), 132–140.
Honoré, A. M. (1961). Ownership. In A. G. Guest (Ed.), *Oxford essays in jurisprudence* (pp. 107–147). Oxford University Press.
Huang, P. C. C. (2006). Civil adjudication in China, past and present. *Modern China, 32*(2), 135–180. https://doi.org/10.1177/0097700405285397
Huang, Y., & Yu, R. (2019). Common and distinct neural substrates of the money illusion in win and loss domains. *NeuroImage, 184*, 109–118. https://doi.org/10.1016/j.neuroimage.2018.09.032
Hudson, I., & Hudson, M. (2003). Removing the veil? Commodity fetishism, fair trade, and the environment. *Organization & Environment, 16*(4), 413–430. https://doi.org/10.1177/1086026603258926
Hutchins, E. (2005). Material anchors for conceptual blends. *Journal of Pragmatics, 37*(10), 1555–1577. https://doi.org/10.1016/j.pragma.2004.06.008
Hutter, M. (1994). Communication in economic evolution: The case of money changing the primary distinction: From observer to observation. In *Evolutionary concepts in contemporary economics* (pp. 111–138). University of Michigan Press.
Ingham, G. (2000). "Babylonian Madness": On the historical and sociological origins of money. In J. Smithin (Ed.), *What Is Money?* (pp. 16–41). Routledge.
James, W. (1890). *The principles of psychology* (Vol. 2). Henry Holt.
Kahneman, D. (2012). *Thinking, fast and slow*. Penguin Books.
Kahneman, D., Knetsch, J. L., & Thaler, R. H. (1990). Experimental tests of the endowment effect and the Coase theorem. *Journal of Political Economy, 98*(6), 1325–1348.

Kanungo, R. N. (1979). The concepts of alienation and involvement revisited. *Psychological Bulletin, 86*(1), 119–138. https://doi.org/10.1037/0033-2909.86.1.119

Kanungo, R. N. (1992). Alienation and empowerment: Some ethical imperatives in business. *Journal of Business Ethics, 11*(5), 413–422. https://doi.org/10.1007/BF00870553

Kasser, T., & Ryan, R. M. (1993). A dark side of the American dream: Correlates of financial success as a central life aspiration. *Journal of Personality and Social Psychology, 65*(2), 410–422. https://doi.org/10.1037/0022-3514.65.2.410

Keenan, S. (2015). *Subversive property: Law and the production of spaces of belonging*. Routledge.

Kelton, S. (2020). *The deficit myth: Modern monetary theory and how to build a better economy*. PublicAffairs.

Kennedy, D. (2011). Some caution about property rights as a recipe for economic development. *Accounting, Economics, and Law, 1*(1). https://doi.org/10.2202/2152-2820.1006

Keynes, J. M. (1936/2018). *The general theory of employment interest and money*. Springer International Publishing. https://doi.org/10.1007/978-3-319-70344-2

Kimiecik, J., & Teas, E. (2020). Express your self: Exploring the nature of the expressive self and the health and well-being consequences of its restriction in a market society. *Journal of Humanistic Psychology, 0022167820966154*,. https://doi.org/10.1177/0022167820966154

Knetsch, J. L. (1989). The endowment effect and evidence of nonreversible indifference curves. *American Economic Review, 79*(5), 1277–1284.

Knutson, B., & Wimmer, G. E. (2007). Reward: Neural circuitry for social valuation. In E. Harmon-Jones & P. Winkielman (Eds.), *Social neuroscience: Integrating biological and psychological explanations of social behavior* (pp. 157–175). Guilford Press.

Korobkin, R. (2014). Wrestling with the endowment effect, or how to do law and economics without the Coase theorem. In E. Zamir & D. Teichman (Eds.), *The Oxford handbook of behavioral economics and the law* (pp. 299–334). Oxford University Press. https://doi.org/10.1093/oxfordhb/9780199945474.013.0012

Kowinski, W. S. (1985). *The malling of America: An inside look at the great consumer paradise*. William Morrow and Company.

Krippner, G. R. (2005). The financialization of the American economy. *Socio-Economic Review, 3*(2), 173–208. https://doi.org/10.1093/SER/mwi008

Krueger, N., Hansen, D. J., Michl, T., & Welsh, D. H. B. (2011). Thinking "sustainably": The role of intentions, cognitions, and emotions in understanding new domains of entrepreneurship. In G. T. Lumpkin & J. A. Katz (Eds.), *Social and sustainable entrepreneurship (Advances in entrepreneurship, firm emergence and growth, Vol. 13)* (pp. 275–309). Emerald Group Publishing Limited. https://doi.org/10.1108/S1074-7540(2011)0000013014

Laibson, D. (1997). Golden eggs and hyperbolic discounting. *The Quarterly Journal of Economics, 112*(2), 443–478. https://doi.org/10.1162/003355397555253

Laidler, D., & Rowe, N. (1980). George Simmel's philosophy of money: A review article for economists. *Journal of Economic Literature, 18*(1), 97–105.

Landreth, A., & Bickle, J. (2008). Neuroeconomics, neurophysiology and the common currency hypothesis. *Economics & Philosophy, 24*(3), 419–429. https://doi.org/10.1017/S0266267108002058

Lane, R. E. (1992). Work as "disutility" and money as "happiness": Cultural origins of a basic market error. *The Journal of Socio-Economics, 21*(1), 43–64. https://doi.org/10.1016/1053-5357(92)90025-3

Larson, A. M., Monterosso, I., Banjade, M. R., & Mwangi, E. (2017). Community rights to forests in the tropics. In M. Graziadei & L. Smith (Eds.), *Comparative property law: A global perspective* (pp. 435–457). Edward Elgar.

Lawrence, T. B., Schlindwein, E., Jalan, R., & Heaphy, E. D. (2023). Organizational body work: Efforts to shape human bodies in organizations. *Academy of Management Annals, 17*(1), 37–73. https://doi.org/10.5465/annals.2021.0047

Lea, S. E. G., & Webley, P. (2006). Money as tool, money as drug: The biological psychology of a strong incentive. *Behavioral and Brain Sciences, 29*(2), 161–209. https://doi.org/10.1017/S0140525X06009046

Leamer, E. E. (2007). A flat world, a level playing field, a small world after all, or none of the above? A review of Thomas L. Friedman's the world is flat. *Journal of Economic Literature, 45*(1), 83–126. https://doi.org/10.1257/jel.45.1.83

Lefever, D. M., & Lefever, J. T. (1977). Marxian alienation and economic organization: An alternate view. *The American Economist, 21*(2), 40–48. https://doi.org/10.1177/056943457702100206

Lenzerini, F. (2017). The land rights of indigenous peoples under international law. In M. Graziadei & L. Smith (Eds.), *Comparative property law: A global perspective* (pp. 393–411). Edward Elgar Publishing. https://doi.org/10.4337/9781785369162.00027

Lethbridge, D. (1986). A Marxist theory of self-actualization. *Journal of Humanistic Psychology, 26*(2), 84–103.

Levav, J., & McGraw, A. P. (2009). Emotional accounting: How feelings about money influence consumer choice. *Journal of Marketing Research, 46*(1), 66–80. https://doi.org/10.1509/jmkr.46.1.66

Lewis, R., & Stewart, R. (1958). *The boss: The life and times of the British business man*. Phoenix House.

Lichtenstein, S., Gregory, R., & Irwin, J. (2007). What's bad is easy: Taboo values, affect, and cognition. *Judgment and Decision Making, 2*(3), 169–188. https://doi.org/10.1017/S1930297500000838

Locke, E. A. (1982). The ideas of Frederick W. Taylor: An evaluation. *Academy of Management Review, 7*(1), 14–24. https://doi.org/10.5465/AMR.1982.4285427

Long, Q. (2009). Reinterpreting Chinese property law. *Southern California Interdisciplinary Law Journal, 19*, 55–72.

Lucas, R. E. (1988). On the mechanics of economic development. *Journal of Monetary Economics, 22*, 3–42.

Lucassen, J. (2021). *The story of work: A new history of humankind*. Yale University Press.

Lumineau, F., & Quélin, B. V. (2012). An empirical investigation of interorganizational opportunism and contracting mechanisms. *Strategic Organization, 10*(1), 55–84. https://doi.org/10.1177/1476127011434798

Malafouris, L. (2013). *How things shape the mind: A theory of material engagement*. MIT Press.

Marcoux, J. S. (2009). Escaping the gift economy. *Journal of Consumer Research, 36*(4), 671–685. https://doi.org/10.1086/600485

Martin, F. (2014). *Money: The unauthorized biography from coinage to cryptocurrencies*. Vintage Book.

Marx, K. (1932/1988). *The economic and philosophic manuscripts of 1844*. Prometheus Books.

Marx, K. (1867/1990). *Capital: A critique of political economy* (Vol. 1). Penguin Classics.

Maslow, A. H. (1943). A theory of human motivation. *Psychological Review, 50*(4), 370–396. https://doi.org/10.1037/h0054346

Massa, F. G., Helms, W. S., Voronov, M., & Wang, L. (2017). Emotions uncorked: Inspiring evangelism for the emerging practice of cool-climate winemaking in Ontario. *Academy of Management Journal, 60*(2), 461–499. https://doi.org/10.5465/amj.2014.0092

Mauss, M. (1925/1990). *The gift: The form and reason for exchange in archaic societies*. Routledge.

Mazar, N., & Ariely, D. (2006). Dishonesty in everyday life and its policy implications. *Journal of Public Policy & Marketing, 25*(1), 117–126. https://doi.org/10.1509/jppm.25.1.117

McNeil, K. (2017). Indigenous territorial rights in the common law. In M. Graziadei & L. Smith (Eds.), *Comparative property law: A global perspective* (pp. 412–434). Edward Elgar Publishing. https://doi.org/10.4337/9781785369162.00028

Merleau-Ponty, M. (1945/1962). *Phenomenology of perception*. Routledge.

Michaelson, C. (2021). A normative meaning of meaningful work. *Journal of Business Ethics, 170*(3), 413–428. https://doi.org/10.1007/s10551-019-04389-0

Milanović, B. (2019). *Capitalism, alone: The future of the system that rules the world*. The Belknap Press of Harvard University Press.

Mincer, J. (1958). Investment in human capital and personal income distribution. *Journal of Political Economy, 66*, 281–302.

Morewedge, C. K., & Giblin, C. E. (2015). Explanations of the endowment effect: An integrative review. *Trends in Cognitive Sciences, 19*(6), 339–348. https://doi.org/10.1016/j.tics.2015.04.004

Morewedge, C. K., Shu, L. L., Gilbert, D. T., & Wilson, T. D. (2009). Bad riddance or good rubbish? Ownership and not loss aversion causes the endowment effect. *Journal of Experimental Social Psychology, 45*(4), 947–951. https://doi.org/10.1016/j.jesp.2009.05.014

Moulier-Boutang, Y. (2007/2011). *Cognitive capitalism*. Polity Press.

Moyar, D. (2008). Self-completing alienation: Hegel's argument for transparent conditions of free agency. In D. Moyar & M. Quante (Eds.), *Hegel's phenomenology of spirit: A critical guide* (pp. 150–172). Cambridge University Press.

Nelson, D. (1974). Scientific management, systematic management, and labor, 1880–1915. *Business History Review, 48*, 479–500.

Nishibe, M. (2016). *The enigma of money: Gold, central banknotes, and bitcoin*. Springer.

North, D. C., Wallis, J. J., Webb, S. B., & Weingast, B. R. (Eds.). (2013). *In the shadow of violence: Politics, economics, and the problem of development*. Cambridge University Press.

North, D. C., Wallis, J. J., & Weingast, B. R. (2009). *Violence and social orders: A conceptual framework for interpreting recorded human history*. Cambridge University Press.

Nozick, R. (1974). *Anarchy, state, and utopia*. Basic Books.

Nussbaum, M. C. (1995). Objectification. *Philosophy & Public Affairs, 24*(4), 249–291. https://doi.org/10.1111/j.1088-4963.1995.tb00032.x

Nussbaum, M. C. (2006). *Frontiers of justice: Disability, nationality, species membership*. Harvard University Press.

Ostergaard, P., Fitchett, J., & Jantzen, C. (2013). A critique of the ontology of consumer enchantment. *Journal of Consumer Behaviour, 12*(5), 337–344. https://doi.org/10.1002/cb.1438

Padoa Schioppa, A. (2017). *A history of law in Europe: From the early middle ages to the twentieth century*. Cambridge University Press.

Pasquinelli, M. (2019). On the origins of Marx's general intellect. *Radical Philosophy, 206*, 43–56.

Pasquinelli, M. (2021). How to make a class: Hayek's neoliberalism and the origins of connectionism. *Qui Parle, 30*(1), 159–184. https://doi.org/10.1215/10418385-8955836

Patterson, T. C. (2009). *Karl Marx, anthropologist*. Berg.

Perrow, C. (1991). A society of organizations. *Theory and Society, 20*(6), 725–762. https://doi.org/10.1007/BF00678095

Perry, J., & Nölke, A. (2006). The political economy of International accounting standards. *Review of International Political Economy, 13*(4), 559–586. https://doi.org/10.1080/09692290600839790

Pierce, J. L., Kostova, T., & Dirks, K. T. (2003). The state of psychological ownership: Integrating and extending a century of research. *Review of General Psychology, 7*(1), 84–107. https://doi.org/10.1037/1089-2680.7.1.84

Phelps, E. A. (2009). The study of emotion in neuroeconomics. In P. W. Glimcher, C. F. Camerer, E. Fehr, & R. A. Poldrack (Eds.), *Neuroeconomics: Decision making and the brain* (pp. 233–250). Elsevier Academic Press. https://doi.org/10.1016/B978-0-12-374176-9.00016-6

Piketty, T. (2013). *Le capital au XXIe siècle*. Éditions du Seuil.

Pistor, K. (2019). *The code of capital: How the law creates wealth and inequality*. Princeton University Press.

Plumpe, W. (2019). *Das kalte Herz: Kapitalismus, die Geschichte einer andauernden Revolution* (1. Auflage). Rowohlt Berlin.

Polanyi, K. (1944/2001). *The great transformation: The political and economic origins of our time*. Beacon Press.

Polanyi, M. (1966/2009). *The tacit dimension*. University of Chicago Press.

Posner, E. A., & Weyl, E. G. (2018). *Radical markets: Uprooting capitalism and democracy for a just society*. Princeton University Press.

Prum, R. O. (2017). *The evolution of beauty: How Darwin's forgotten theory of mate choice shapes the animal world—and us*. Doubleday.

Prusik, C. (2018). Neoliberalism: Critical theory as natural-history. In B. Best, W. Bonefeld, & C. O'Kane (Eds.), *The SAGE handbook of Frankfurt school critical theory* (pp. 1601–1614). Sage. https://doi.org/10.4135/9781526436122.n97

Przybyszewski, K., & Tyszka, T. (2007). Emotional factors in currency perception. *Journal of Consumer Policy, 30*, 355–365. https://doi.org/10.1007/s10603-007-9047-0

Puig de la Bellacasa, M. (2017). *Matters of care: Speculative ethics in more than human worlds*. University of Minnesota Press.

Racko, G. (2019). The values of economics. *Journal of Business Ethics, 154*(1), 35–48. https://doi.org/10.1007/s10551-017-3442-5

Reb, J., & Connolly, T. (2007). Possession, feelings of ownership and the endowment effect. *Judgment and Decision Making, 2*(2), 107–114. https://doi.org/10.1017/S1930297500000085

Reinholtz, N., Bartels, D. M., & Parker, J. R. (2015). On the mental accounting of restricted-use funds: How gift cards change what people purchase. *Journal of Consumer Research, 42*, 596–614. https://doi.org/10.1093/jcr/ucv045

Richter, R. (1990). *Geldtheorie: Vorlesung auf der Grundlage der Allgemeinen Gleichgewichtstheorie und der Institutionenökonomik* (2., durchges. und erg. Aufl). Springer.

Ritter, J. (2004). Person and property in Hegel's Philosophy of right (§§34–81). In N. Walker, O. Höffe, & R. B. Pippin (Eds.), *Hegel on ethics and politics* (pp. 101–123). Cambridge University Press. https://doi.org/10.1017/CBO9780511498176.006

Rose, C. M. (2019). *Property and persuasion: Essays on the history, theory, and rhetoric of ownership*. https://www.taylorfrancis.com/books/e/9780429303227

Roth, A. E. (2007). Repugnance as a constraint on markets. *Journal of Economic Perspectives, 21*(3), 37–58. https://doi.org/10.1257/jep.21.3.37

Sandel, M. J. (2013). Market reasoning as moral reasoning: Why economists should re-engage with political philosophy. *Journal of Economic Perspectives, 27*(4), 121–140. https://doi.org/10.1257/jep.27.4.121

Santos, L. R., & Hughes, K. D. (2009). Economic cognition in humans and animals: The search for core mechanisms. *Current Opinion in Neurobiology, 19*(1), 63–66. https://doi.org/10.1016/j.conb.2009.05.005

Sassen, S. (2012). Global finance and its institutional spaces. *Oxford University Press*. https://doi.org/10.1093/oxfordhb/9780199590162.013.0002

Schlager, E., & Ostrom, E. (1992). Property-rights regimes and natural resources: A conceptual analysis. *Land Economics, 68*(3), 249–262. https://doi.org/10.2307/3146375

Schlicht, E. (2018). *On custom in the economy*. Clarendon Press.

Schmid, A. A. (2008). *Conflict and cooperation: Institutional and behavioral economics*. Wiley.

Schotter, A. (1981). *The economic theory of social institutions*. Cambridge University Press.

Schultz, T. W. (1961). Investment in human capital. *American Economic Review, 51*(1), 1–17.

Schwartz, B. (1967). The social psychology of the gift. *American Journal of Sociology, 73*(1), 1–11. https://doi.org/10.1086/224432

Seaford, R. (2004). *Money and the early Greek mind: Homer, philosophy, tragedy*. Cambridge University Press.

Searle, J. (2011). *Making the social world: The structure of human civilization*. Oxford University Press.

Seeman, M. (1959). On the meaning of alienation. *American Sociological Review, 24*(6), 783–791. https://doi.org/10.2307/2088565

Sen, A. K. (1997). Human capital and human capability. *World Development, 25*(12), 1959–1961.
Sen, A. K. (1985/1999). *Commodities and capabilities*. Oxford University Press.
Sennett, R. (2009). *The craftsman*. Penguin Books.
Serkin, C. (2016). *The law of property* (2nd ed.). Foundation Press.
Sahlins, M. (1972). *Stone age economics*. Aldine-Atherton.
Shackle, G. L. S. (1992). *Epistemics & economics: A critique of economic doctrines*. Transaction Publishers.
Shafir, E., Diamond, P., & Tversky, A. (1997). Money illusion. *The Quarterly Journal of Economics, 112*(2), 341–374.
Shantz, A., Alfes, K., Bailey, C., & Soane, E. (2015). Drivers and outcomes of work alienation: Reviving a concept. *Journal of Management Inquiry, 24*(4), 382–393. https://doi.org/10.1177/1056492615573325
Shell, M. (1980). Money and the mind: The economics of translation in Goethe's Faust. *MLN, 95*(3), 516–562. https://doi.org/10.2307/2906688
Simmel, G. (1907/2004). *The philosophy of money*. Routledge. https://doi.org/10.4324/9780203481134
Simon, H. A. (1976). From substantive to procedural rationality. In *Method and appraisal in economics*. Cambridge University Press. https://doi.org/10.1017/CBO9780511572203.006
Simon, H. A. (1978). Rationality as process and as product of thought. *American Economic Review, 68*(2), 1–16.
Simon, H. A. (1979). Rational decision making in business organizations. *American Economic Review, 69*(4), 493–513.
Simon, H. A. (1991). Organizations and markets. *Journal of Economic Perspectives, 5*(2), 25–44.
Simon, H. A. (1997). *Administrative behavior, 4th edition*. The Free Press.
Simon, H. A. (2000). Public administration in today's world of organizations and markets. *PS: Political Science & Politics, 33*(4), 749–756.
Singer, P. (2000). *Marx: A very short introduction*. Oxford University Press.
Skwara, F. (2023). Effects of mental accounting on purchase decision processes: A systematic review and research agenda. *Journal of Consumer Behaviour*, cb.2193. https://doi.org/10.1002/cb.2193
Smit, J. P., Buekens, F., & du Plessis, S. (2011). What is money? An alternative to Searle's institutional facts. *Economics and Philosophy, 27*(1), 1–22. https://doi.org/10.1017/S0266267110000441
Smith, A. (1776/2005). *The Glasgow edition of the works and correspondence of Adam Smith. Volume 2: An inquiry into the nature and causes of the wealth of nations*. Liberty Fund.
Smith, V. L. (1976). Experimental economics: Induced value theory. *American Economic Review*, *66*(2), 274–279. https://www.jstor.org/stable/1817233

Smith, V. L., & Walker, J. M. (1993). Monetary rewards and decision cost in experimental economics. *Economic Inquiry, 31*(2), 245–261. https://doi.org/10.1111/j.1465-7295.1993.tb00881.x

Sohn-Rethel, A. (1978). *Intellectual and manual labour: A critique of epistemology*. Humanities Press.

Soll, J. (2014). *The reckoning: Financial accountability and the making and breaking of nations*. Penguin Books.

Spencer, D. A. (2009). *The political economy of work*. Routledge.

Stephenson, B. (2015). *Ritual: A very short introduction*. Oxford University Pres.

Strang, V., & Busse, M. (Eds.). (2011). *Ownership and appropriation*. Berg Publishers.

Styhre, A. (2004). The (re)embodied organization: Four perspectives on the body in organizations. *Human Resource Development International, 7*(1), 101–116. https://doi.org/10.1080/1367886032000150578

Sundström, L. (1974). *The exchange economy of pre-colonial tropical Africa*. C. Hurst & Company.

Supiot, A. (2009/2017). *Homo juridicus: On the anthropological function of the law*. Verso Books.

Taylor, F. W. (1914). Scientific management: Reply from Mr. F. W. Taylor. *The Sociological Review, a7*(3), 266–269. https://doi.org/10.1111/j.1467-954X.1914.tb02387.x

Tellmann, U. (2022). The politics of assetization: From devices of calculation to devices of obligation. *Distinktion: Journal of Social Theory, 23*(1), 33–54. https://doi.org/10.1080/1600910X.2021.1991419

Thaler, R. H. (2016). *Misbehaving: The making of behavioural economics*. W. W. Norton.

Thomas, Y. (2011). *Les opérations du droit*. Gallimard Seuil.

Thompson, E. P. (1967). Time, work-discipline, and industrial capitalism. *Past & Present, 38*, 56–97.

Trapp,T. (2024). Business schools and inequality. In E. Rosier, A. Lindgreen, A. Erz, B. Marder & S. van Wallpach (Eds.), *Business Education in the 21st Century* (pp. 147-168). Edward Elgar Publishing.

Trentmann, F. (2017). *Empire of things: How we became a world of consumers, from the fifteenth century to the twenty-first*. Penguin Books.

Tripp, C. (2006). *Islam and the moral economy: The challenge of capitalism*. Cambridge University Press.

Tsang, E. W. K. (2006). Behavioral assumptions and theory development: The case of transaction cost economics. *Strategic Management Journal, 27*(11), 999–1011. https://doi.org/10.1002/smj.553

Tyran, J. R. (2007). Money illusion and the market. *Science, 317*(5841), 1042–1043. https://doi.org/10.1126/science.1143917

Tyszka, T., & Przybyszewski, K. (2006). Cognitive and emotional factors affecting currency perception. *Journal of Economic Psychology, 27*(4), 518–530. https://doi.org/10.1016/j.joep.2006.01.004

Vanuxem, S. (2022). *La propriété de la terre* (Nouvelle ed.). Wildproject.

Ver Eecke, W. (2008). *Ethical dimensions of the economy: Making use of Hegel and the concepts of public and merit goods*. Springer.

Von Glahn, R. (1996). *Fountain of fortune: Money and monetary policy in China, 1000–1700*. University of California Press.

Von Glahn, R. (2004). *The sinister way: The divine and the demonic in Chinese religious culture*. University of California Press.

Waldron, J. (2023, Fall). Property and ownership. In E. N. Zalta & U. Nodelman (Eds.), *The Stanford encyclopedia of philosophy*. Metaphysics Research Lab, Stanford University. https://plato.stanford.edu/archives/fall2023/entries/property/

Walsh, A. J., & Lynch, T. (2008). *The morality of money: An exploration in analytic philosophy*. Palgrave Macmillan.

Wang, X., Chen, Z., & Krumhuber, E. G. (2020). Money: An integrated review and synthesis from a psychological perspective. *Review of General Psychology, 24*(2), 172–190. https://doi.org/10.1177/1089268020905316

Wargo, D. T., Baglini, N. A., & Nelson, K. A. (2010). The new millennium's first global financial crisis: The neuroeconomics of greed, self-interest, deception, false trust, overconfidence and risk perception. In A. A. Stanton, M. Day, & I. M. Welpe (Eds.), *Neuroeconomics and the firm* (pp. 78–98). Edward Elgar Publishing.

Wathne, K. H., & Heide, J. B. (2000). Opportunism in interfirm relationships: Forms, outcomes, and solutions. *Journal of Marketing, 64*(4), 36–51. https://doi.org/10.1509/jmkg.64.4.36.18070

Weber, B., Rangel, A., Wibral, M., & Falk, A. (2009). The medial prefrontal cortex exhibits money illusion. *Proceedings of the National Academy of Sciences, 106*(13), 5025–5028. https://doi.org/10.1073/pnas.0901490106

Weber, M. (1922/2019). *Economy and society: A new translation* (K. Tribe, Ed. and trans.). Harvard University Press.

Wenar, L. (2017). *Blood oil: Tyrants, violence, and the rules that run the world*. Oxford University Press.

Weyl, E. G. (2019). Price theory. *Journal of Economic Literature, 57*(2), 329–384. https://doi.org/10.1257/jel.20171321

White, R. (2008). The mental accounting of gift card versus cash gift funds. In A. Y. Lee & D. Soman (Eds.), *ACR North American advances* (Vol. 35, pp. 722–723). Association for Consumer Research.

Williamson, O. E. (1975). *Markets and hierarchies*. The Free Press.

Williamson, O. E. (1981). The economics of organization: The transaction cost approach. *American Journal of Sociology, 87*(3), 548–577.

Williamson, O. E. (1985). *The economic institutions of capitalism: Firms, markets, relational contracting*. The Free Press.
Williamson, O. E. (1993). Opportunism and its critics. *Managerial and Decision Economics, 14*, 97–107.
Wittgenstein, L. (1953). *Philosophical investigations*. Macmillan.
Wolff, L.-C. (2020). The relationship between contract law and property law. *Common Law World Review, 49*(1), 31–55. https://doi.org/10.1177/1473779520903729
Woloson, W. A. (2012). *In hock: Pawning in America from independence through the Great Depression*. University of Chicago Press.
Zarantonello, L., Romani, S., Grappi, S., & Bagozzi, R. P. (2016). Brand hate. *Journal of Product & Brand Management, 25*(1), 11–25. https://doi.org/10.1108/JPBM-01-2015-0799
Zavestoski, S. (2002). The social–psychological bases of anticonsumption attitudes. *Psychology and Marketing, 19*(2), 149–165. https://doi.org/10.1002/mar.10007
Zelizer, V. A. (1989). The social meaning of money: "Special monies." *American Journal of Sociology, 95*(2), 342–377. https://doi.org/10.1086/229272
Zelizer, V. A. (1997). *The social meaning of money*. Princeton University Press.
Zellweger, T. M. (2017). *Managing the family business: Theory and practice*. Edward Elgar Publishing.

CHAPTER 8

Embodied Market Utopia: Human Flourishing in Economic Life

8.1 Introduction: Utopia as an Essential Dimension in Economic Thought

As famously illustrated by John Maynard Keynes' (1931/2010) essay *Economic Possibilities for Our Grandchildren*, utopianism is not foreign to theorizations of economic life. Historically, it ranges from one end of the political spectrum with what is now called the "utopian socialism" of Saint-Simon and Fourier in France and Robert Owen in England, who inspired the cooperative movement in the nineteenth century (Goodwin & Taylor, 1982/2009; Levitas, 1990/2011),[1] to the other end with Hayek's call for a "liberal utopia" (Levitas, 1985), and the "neoliberal utopianism" celebrated by the Mont Pèlerin Society (Mirowski & Plehwe, 2015). More recently, in the field of ecological economics (Ingebrigtsen & Jakobsen, 2012), the degrowth movement has made explicit reference to "concrete utopia" (e.g., Kallis & March, 2015; Latouche, 2009), and related "new commons" (D'Alisa et al., 2014), such as eco-communities, cooperatives, urban gardens, transition towns, timebanks, barter markets, or child- or healthcare associations, can be considered as alternative and transformative practices that fall within the scope of utopian thinking (Basso & Krpan, 2022). Green growth, which is one of the main theoretical alternatives to degrowth with the concept of decoupling (e.g., Jackson & Victor, 2019), can also be considered utopian (Hedrén & Linnér, 2009a). Likewise, geoengineering

F. Basso and C. Herrmann-Pillath, *Embodiment, Political Economy and Human Flourishing*, https://doi.org/10.1007/978-3-031-54971-7_8

(Augustine et al., 2019), "techno-fixes" (Segal, 2017), and the forms of "energetic utopias" described in relation to the "atomic society" and the hydrogen economy (Hultman, 2009), can be seen as an illustration of utopian techno-optimism in capitalist societies. Beyond industrial policies, empirical work shows that people's choices for fairly traded, ethical, or socially conscious products and services are also economic practices associated with visions of utopia and transformative social change in Western societies (Basso & Krpan, 2022; see also Bossy, 2014; Hedrén & Linnér, 2009b; Wright, 2013).

In this chapter, we unfold the vision of an embodied market utopia that unleashes transformative powers to change economic life. Transformative social change requires interrogating the "underpinning values, goals and world views of actors that shape the emergent direction to which a system is oriented" in addition to the "social structures and institutions" that express these values (Abson et al., 2017, p. 32). Whether behavioral, experimental, or in its more standard blackboard form, neoclassical economics takes for granted and contributes to reproducing, the values, goals, and worldviews of the Western economic system, largely inherited from deep-seated religious beliefs (Graeber, 2001, p. 257; Sahlins et al., 1996): Namely, individual freedom as a cardinal value, economic growth as a main goal, and anthropocentrism as a worldview.[2] These three concepts are linked to each other. Economic growth and anthropocentrism stem from individual freedom: Curbing economic growth would threaten the individual freedom of ever-more consumption and production, and an "ecocentric" worldview would stand in the way of satisfying human aspirations and the human capacity to ascribe economic value to the world, and to commodify it.

Embodied economics rejects such a mainstream (behavioral and experimental) economic approach because we contend that knowledge, *as well as* values, goals, and worldviews, cannot be analyzed in isolation from economic actors in their material, economic, social, and ecological environments. Karl Marx and John Stuart Mill pointed this out in their writings on political economy (Gillig, 2016) as did Vilfredo Pareto (1935, §142) for instance:

> The man entirely unaffected by sentiments and free from all bias, all faith, does not exist; and to regard that freedom as an essential prerequisite to profitable study of the social sciences would amount to saying that such study is impossible.

Against this background, embodied economics proposes that autonomy should replace individual freedom as the cardinal value, that flourishing rather than economic growth should be the main goal, and that ecocentrism rather than anthropocentrism should become the worldview. Autonomy is one of the cornerstones of embodiment (e.g., Thompson & Stapleton, 2009). Biologically, it allows us to distinguish living beings from machines, as Jakob von Uexküll, and Francisco Varela and Humberto Maturana have pointed out (Thompson, 2010, p. 57ff), and, politically, it allows us to incorporate institutions as "second nature" *à la* Hegel. Contrary to how autonomy is sometimes understood in the literature (e.g., Brand-Correa & Steinberger, 2017), it does not stand in opposition to the concept of community. Rather, as Hegel argued, and as discussed in Chapter 5, agency and personal autonomy can only be achieved through belonging to and participating in a community (e.g., Luther, 2009). Connected to the concept of community, autonomy is deeply associated with flourishing through the capability approach (Nussbaum & Sen, 1993). Importantly, flourishing is a key concept that aims to structure the opposition with economic value (Naess & Sessions, 1986).[3] In this respect, flourishing means moving beyond anthropocentrism in favor of ecocentrism, and abandoning the logic of control over the environment that underlies the mainstream economics approach (e.g., Malm & Hornborg, 2014; Washington et al., 2021).

What does it mean, then, for social and political design and policy if embodied economics is the guiding insight? In developing our argument, we begin with analytical steps: The key idea, as conveyed by the concept of forward embodiment, is that embodied and transformative processes in economic life are the hallmarks of utopian thinking. Embodied economics offers a radical and concrete utopian alternative that aims to reinvent markets as communities. We show that these embodied and transformative processes are necessary for public policy to address "externalities," since their very existence is a direct recognition that embodiment *grounds* and *bounds* economic life. We develop a critical reflection on market failures and externalities as conceptualized in the standard model, and discuss the limits of potentially embodied developments, through behavioral economics, Ostrom's institutionalism, and happiness studies. Building on these insights, we present reflections on how embodiment can *transform* markets by disentangling them from capitalism with solutions that promote flourishing: We follow the eudaimonic approach to well-being as flourishing, characterized in terms of Well-being, Inclusivity, Sufficiency,

Empowerment, and Resilience (WISER framework). In doing so, we make a clear distinction between markets and capitalism and challenge the "Tönnies duality." In a nutshell, this means that we approach markets as forms of community, and capitalism as a de-ecologized and toxic form of markets.[4] We focus on two related themes: The nature of labor, echoing a key theme in Marx's thought, and the reconciliation of markets with community in order to overcome the tension between different forms of sociality outlined in the previous chapters. This is feasible because there is much scope for combining the four relationships of community, reciprocity, hierarchy, and market in new institutional designs that safeguard the flourishing of all life. Both themes explore concrete and practical measures for re-embodying economic action and markets. Finally, we consider the broader institutional framework as it relates to the key institutions of capitalist markets, such as money and property. We contend that a sustainable and humane economy cannot be achieved without radical social and institutional transformations of the scope of a truly revolutionary movement similar to the long century from the French Revolution to World War I. In this regard, we suggest that proposals that can gain consensus such as Universal Basic Income, personal liability, or de-financialization, are key to flourishing by creating autonomy in and from the market.

Approaching markets as a form of community is an idea that has persisted in economics since its inception. A systematic approach was seminally developed in Hegel's "system of needs" in which market society is seen as institutionalized in associations (Hegel, 1820/2009, §189ff).[5] Hegel extended the famous "*doux commerce*" thesis to a more abstract level by emphasizing that markets require the mutual recognition of market actors as persons. For example, a businessperson who wants to sell a product to a customer would have to accept the customer's views and preferences as given, and not discriminate against them because they do not coincide with her own. If the businessperson wants to convince a customer of her own preferences, this would amount to forming a community by engaging in a constructive dialogue. In modern economics parlance, in the Hegelian view, markets systematically build on and foster the formation of social preferences and experiences, and do not just process individual preferences (Stehr, 2007). It follows, as we will argue, that markets could be a powerful means of transforming consumer habits towards ecologically conscious norms, if communities of consumption undergird them. Questions like these define a future research agenda in embodied economics to address some of the limitations of our book and to transform economic life, with which we conclude this chapter.

8.2 Embodied Market Utopia as Transformative Political Economy

As per Thomas More's (1516) pun, "Utopia" is both "Eutopia," meaning the "good place," and "Outopia," meaning "no place" in Greek. Since then, the colloquial definition of utopia has been associated with a good place that is no place: An ideal and perfect society, but completely unrealistic (Levitas, 1990/2011). This association remains popular in both economics and psychology, as illustrated by famous quotes from Adam Smith[6] and Karl Marx,[7] or, more recently, the American Psychological Association's (APA) definition of utopia.[8] The problem with this understanding of utopia, aside from suggesting unrealism, is that it is conceptually inappropriate to equate utopia with perfection, since "perfection" does not seem to be a key characteristic of utopia in the literature (Bell, 2017; Sargent, 1994), and may even appear as a way of dismissing utopia: "nothing is finished, complete, or unchangeable, so the equation makes utopia look foolish or at least foolhardy" (Sargent, 2010, p. 103). More importantly, perfection, by definition, is flawless, correct in every way, and cannot be improved.

Rather than considering utopia as a perfect society, embodied economics adopts a different perspective based on the association between utopia and progress, celebrated by Oscar Wilde (1891, p. 304) who claimed that "progress is the realization of utopias," or illustrated by Keynes (1931/2010) who envisioned the future as progress towards an age of abundance and unprecedented leisure (Magness & Harrigan, 2020). Indeed, historically, it is the idea of progress or improvement, which emerged in the seventeenth century, rather than the idea of perfection, which, by definition, can no longer progress, that has inspired social change (Davis, 1981; Hansot, 1974; Morton, 1969; Negley & Patrick, 1971). This approach implies a different definition of utopia, conceived as "the expression of the desire for a better way of being and living" (Levitas, 1990/2011, p. 8). This definition has several strengths (Stillman, 1991).[9] As we will see later in this chapter, an important one for embodied economics is that this definition of utopia is conceptually linked to the capabilities approach which focuses on what people are capable of *being* and *doing*, and the opportunities that society gives them to do so and move forward. Another important strength is that this definition does not portray utopia as a (Western)[10] literary genre (Kumar, 1987, 1991),[11] but instead characterizes it as an "analytical" (Bradley & Hedrén, 2014, p. 7) and "transformative" category (Levitas, 1990), following the lead of those who have explored the utopian impulse (e.g., Bloch, 1959/1986; Jameson, 2005; Levitas, 1990/2011).

The term "utopian impulse" is classically associated with the utopian scholarship of Ernst Bloch (1959/1986) and Fredric Jameson (2005):

> Bloch posited the existence of a utopian impulse, an anthropological given that underpins the human propensity to long for and imagine a life otherwise. The origins of this impulse lie in the human experience of a sense of hunger, loss and lack: A deep sense that something's missing. Crucially, Bloch argues that this lack cannot be articulated other than through imagining its fulfilment. Everything that reaches to a transformed existence is, in this sense, utopian. (Levitas, 2013, p. 5)

Interestingly, the concept of "utopian impulse" is a reflection of the *criticism* and the *change* functions of utopia (Levitas, 1990/2011), as it characterizes "a desire for a better world" (Moylan, 2020, p. 191).[12] Arguably, "most utopias compare life in the present and life in the utopia and point out what is wrong with the way we now live, thus suggesting what needs to be done to improve things" (Sargent, 2010, p. 5): This means that virtually every utopia is a constructive criticism of the present world in light of a hypothetical future world (Goodwin, 1978), and indicates that people believe that the present is unfinished and can be improved (Levitas, 1990/2011). Beyond criticism, utopia then fulfills the change function because it suggests that *another* and *better* way of being and living is *possible*. In other words, through its difference from perfection, which precludes the possibility of change, progress as an improvement over an unsatisfactory present conveys the transformative function of utopia.

Importantly, this conceptualization of the utopian impulse also encompasses three dimensions: an embodied, a temporal, and a collective dimension (Jameson, 2005, p. 4), which are essential to embodied economics. Regarding embodiment, the utopian impulse is the expression of a desire, which can be defined as something that one strongly wants (Cambridge Dictionary, n.d.). In this sense, the utopian impulse is thus fundamentally about motivation, affect, and action (Basso & Krpan, 2022): It is the expression of "will-full thinking" that articulates reflection and action to make utopia concrete by creating a new future world (Bloch, 1959/1986; Marvakis, 2007; Webb, 2007).[13] Ultimately, this means that the utopian impulse involves a future orientation, which is why it pertains to what is "not yet," and expresses the "hope of possible" (Bloch, 1959/1986; see also Boldyrev, 2023; Jovchelovitch & Hawlina, 2018; Levitas, 1990/2011; Webb, 2007).

Let us elaborate on this point. One of the main characteristics of utopia is its "non-existence" (Claeys & Sargent, 1999). But if utopia is a nonexistent place, and therefore something that is "not," this does not mean that what is utopian will never be. Rather, as the expression of will-full thinking, utopia can be thought of as concrete because it can be understood as that which is "not yet" existing (Bloch, 1959/1986). This reference to "not yet" conveys the aforementioned deep-seated association between utopia and progress as social improvement, and is a "mode of hoping" that another and better way of being and living in society is possible in the future (Webb, 2007). In relation to its collective aspect, the utopian impulse emphasizes or implies that the transformation of the world must benefit people universally within the community, because the utopian impulse cannot be dissociated from "the values of social and economic equality and the universal right to food, lodging, medicine, education and work" (Jameson, 2005, p. 197), the purpose of which is to achieve happiness and dignity and to avoid suffering and degradation (e.g., Bloch, 1959/1986; Goodwin, 1978). In other words, what is utopian is "transformative as it moves social reality toward a horizon comprehensively better for all human beings and nature itself" (Moylan, 2018, p. 309): The utopian impulse is the We-mode of hoping.

Taken together, these several dimensions characterize the utopian impulse as a desire for transformative social change projected into a concrete and possible better future. Therefore, in embodied economics, utopia is an enactment of the future: The projection of a better experience of inhabiting the world into the future. Utopia is both a comparison and a metaphor: It compares (criticism) and transports (metaphor, change).[14] The utopian impulse thus involves future-oriented imagination, motivation, emotion, and action, and, as such, transcends both *inward* and *outward* embodiment in embodied economics. Indeed, because of its future-orientedness, the utopian impulse characterizes *forward* embodiment. Forward embodiment specifies the conceptual move from sense-making to world-making that undergirds utopia through the coupling of perception and action: It is the critical *perception* that "something is missing" in the present world, coupled with the *action* of changing this world to shape a better future (Bloch, 1988). Conceptually then, utopia emphasizes the importance of moving beyond "adaptation:" It is about transformation and has implications for the conceptualization of embodied economics. In essence, embodiment could remain at an adaptive level, with approaches such as homeostasis, whereby we could learn to adapt to changes in the environment. Transformation, however, is more than adaptation, as it changes the environment. A key point here is that, through forward embodiment, world-making is meaningful because it does not rely on an abstract space that escapes embodiment and social justice, such as Hayek's "Great Society" described in Chapter 3. Rather, forward embodiment entails the transformation of the current society into a place that is better for everyone in the future, with concrete possible solutions. In this light, by acknowledging the utopian impulse with the concept of forward embodiment, embodied economics is a transformative Political Economy.[15]

The utopian impulse is now seen as essential for implementing the economic and social transformations put forward by the United Nations (UN) 2030 Agenda, which are urgently needed to live in a more sustainable society in the future (e.g., Basso & Krpan, 2022; Fazey et al., 2018; Krpan & Basso, 2021). However, just as someone's utopia may turn out to be someone else's dystopia, the concept of "transformation" itself can be understood in a variety of ways, and it is believed that there is no "single agreed definition" of it in the literature (Fazey et al., 2018, p. 198; Stillman, 1991), and that "no particular perspective owns the notion of transformation" (Blythe et al., 2018, p. 1218). For instance, although the concept of transformation classically refers to "major, fundamental change" as "opposed to minor, marginal and incremental change" (Feola, 2015, p. 377), some authors argue that sustainability transformations also require a form of incrementalism with "a strategy of incremental change with a transformative agenda" (Patterson et al., 2017, p. 4), or an approach in terms of "radical incremental transformation strategies" (Göpel, 2016, p. 2). Alternatively, the concept of transformation may or may not be contrasted with other classical concepts in the academic literature on sustainability. For example, unlike "transition," which pertains to technological systems, societal transformation encompasses a broader range of social practices and knowledge (e.g., Linnér & Wibeck, 2019, 2020).

Against this background, in this chapter, we will understand transformation in economic life as the implementation of significant and fundamental changes in the way society, in particular working conditions and markets, operates in order to live in a more sustainable world in the future. Obviously, we are aware that people's judgments may diverge when it comes to deciding why and what should be transformed (O'Brien, 2012), or when it comes to assessing whether something has actually been transformed (Fazey et al., 2018). In other words, what is seen as an object or result of transformation by some, might not be seen as such by others, and this may also vary across cultures (Linnér & Wibeck, 2019, 2020). This is why, before describing some of the transformative solutions in line with embodied economics, in the next sections, we shall first explain why the problem of sustainability cannot be adequately addressed by disembodied economic models, and then why their limitations actually point to the recognition of the need for embodiment in economic life. To demonstrate this idea, we must begin with a critique of the Gross Domestic Product (GDP) and the concept of externalities. Tellingly, in the standard model of economics, externalities are mostly treated as "imperfections" of markets, reflecting the idea that, under very specific and restrictive conditions, markets are envisioned by mainstream economics as a utopia—here, understood in the narrow sense of a perfect state of affairs.

8.3 Externalities and Embodiment

8.3.1 The Problem of GDP

The expansive nature of capitalism has traditionally been legitimized by the idea that the expansion of markets contributes to the growth of the general welfare of society. This is usually measured by GDP, which is based on the sum of all value added by production processes measured in monetary prices in a given economy, thus measuring the material extent of the market (Stiglitz et al., 2009). However, several limitations of GDP are regularly pointed out (e.g., Costanza et al., 2014; Mazzucato, 2018). One of them, which is widely acknowledged in the literature, is the existence of negative externalities associated with increased economic activity. A negative externality can be defined as any action, such as pollution, that is "costly to other individuals and takes place without their consent and compensation" (Herrmann-Pillath & Hederer, 2023, p. 51). As such, a negative externality occurs outside the market and thus escapes monetary prices, which implies that its (financial) costs are neglected by actors in the economic system. Therefore, given the existence of negative externalities, higher GDP is not always good news, and can be associated with economic activities that threaten the habitat and the lives of human and non-human beings (e.g., Hickel, 2020a). As mentioned in the previous chapter, the classic solution proposed by neoclassical environmental economics (or "market environmentalism") is to "internalize" these negative externalities by creating markets to associate them with a monetary price thanks to well-defined property rights (Gómez-Baggethun & Muradian, 2015).

The problems associated with this anthropocentric economic perspective—whether ideological, ethical, technical, institutional, or biophysical, among others—have been extensively discussed in the literature (e.g., Brand-Correa et al., 2022; Gómez-Baggethun & Muradian, 2015; Herrmann-Pillath, 2021), and it is not our purpose to review them here. Even some of the most prominent neoclassical proponents of environmental economics recognize that the commodification of human life and the environment, which underlines this approach and characterizes a process of disembodiment, is questionable. For instance, William Nordhaus, who has developed models to estimate the damages (i.e., costs) to GDP of future climate change, indicates in his Nobel lecture:

> A deeper critique is that damage functions monetize all human and non-human activities, which is correct. People (...) have firmer grounds for moral objections when studies put a price on human health impairments or monetize the submergence of entire island cultures. The economists' response is usually that we attempt to put all costs and benefits in a common metric so that we can balance the losses in one area with losses in others. We should be attentive to imputing appropriate prices, but it is better to include some values on health damages than to omit them from the analysis. (Nordhaus, 2019, p. 2000)

This kind of disembodied perspective, classically adopted in mainstream economics, leads to the conclusion that, although "controversial" in light of current international goals, average global warming above +3 °C in 2100 is the "optimal" scenario in terms of cost–benefit analysis to minimize the joint costs of damage to economic output (GDP) and abatement—that is, reducing emissions of CO_2 and other greenhouse gases

(GHGs) primarily by reducing the combustion of carbon fuels (Nordhaus, 2019, p. 2003).

Needless to say, this conclusion is bleak from an embodied economics perspective, as well as from pretty much any perspective that does not stem from the neoclassical economic model. Without going into the conceptual and methodological issues that underpin these neoclassical models and their conclusions (see Keen, 2021), one might ask how it is possible to conclude that global warming above +3 °C in 2100 is optimal, given the devastating effects such a temperature would have on living beings around the world.[16]

Let us take a very embodied, albeit anthropocentric, illustration of the implications of the so-called "optimal" temperature by GDP standards, identified by Nordhaus (2019), with scenarios that focus not on GDP but on deadly heat, that is, the combination of heat and humidity that reaches the lethal level for humans. As Mora and colleagues (2017) showed years ago, the Representative Concentration Pathway (RCP) 4.5, a scenario presented by the Intergovernmental Panel on Climate Change (IPCC) that would amount to global warming of +2 °C to +3 °C,[17] would lead to the risk of deadly heat for more than 100 days per year in Amazonia, India, Southeast Asia, and the west coast of Africa, to name a few, threatening the lives of billions of people (see also Domeisen et al., 2023; Lüthi et al., 2023). Ironically, this deadly heat will have a much smaller impact on rich countries (Mora et al., 2017), even though they are responsible for more than 90% of the post-1850 GHG emissions that have contributed to climate breakdown (Hickel, 2020b). The moral of this study is clear from an embodied economics standpoint: Minimizing the impact of global warming on disembodied measures like GDP is misleading[18] and, as alternative (and embodied) measures like deadly heat show, very far from "optimal." What would be "welfare" if almost every other day people risk dying from a deadly heat wave? Moreover, in the standard model, externalities are fundamentally fueled by an anthropocentric perspective and thus considered only in terms of their effects on humans. For example, Nordhaus' model excludes from the impact of global warming on GDP any economic activity that takes place "indoors," where people can be protected from the heat (Keen, 2021). However, deadly heat will not only affect humans, but it will also further impact other living beings—as we witness the sixth mass extinction, global warming is already severely impacting them (e.g., Cowie et al., 2022) and their ecosystems (e.g., soil erosion, ocean acidification).

Therefore, it is not an optimal neoclassical scenario in terms of GDP that should set targets for global warming, but rather what could be (at least) "tolerated" by living beings that should set limits on GDP as a source of global warming. In other words, embodiment should *bound* the market processes, and place limits on GDP. As we shall see, the epistemological critique of externalities extends to the *grounding* of market processes. As aforementioned, in the standard model of economics, externalities are mostly treated as "imperfections" of markets, and these imperfections can be remedied in two ways: By lowering transaction costs in markets, and creating new property rights as objects of transactions. The general idea is that people will receive sufficient monetary compensation for any negative impact on their interests if they reveal this preference when entering into negotiations. If they do not, it is argued that the gains are less than the costs of individual effort, so everyone ends up satisfied with the *status quo*. For example, noise in the neighborhood will be considered to be accepted if it requires too much effort on the part of those who are affected to negotiate it away. The problem with the mainstream economic approach to externalities is that it neglects the embodied nature of externalities. Labeling them as market imperfections is misleading, and actually further reveals the disembodied approach that inspires the standard economic model.

8.3.2 Externalities as "Market Feelings"

The thrust of our argument is that externalities are pervasive, and even constitutive of markets. Hence, labeling them as manifestations of imperfection misrepresents what externalities actually are. Let us turn to the insights of the jurisprudence that has emerged as economic ideas have been put into practice, particularly in the US common law context. The treatment of externalities in standard economics tends to overlook an aspect that lawyers emphasize in the context of nuisance, namely, that causation is ambivalent: At common law, if a factory causes pollution and harm to neighbors, we can also say that the neighbors cause the harm by staying. From a legal perspective, the resolution of the conflict aims to maximize the joint product for society (Serkin, 2016).

Intuitively, for many people, the two interpretations are associated with different emotional judgments, such as regarding the latter as unfair. However, there are many examples where this reasoning applies, such as when a job-creating construction project harms neighbors, but they may even willingly accept and stay because the project is valued as contributing to local development; otherwise, they are seen as free to move away. In legal scholarship, this is linked to notions of justice and equity that go beyond the mere analysis of causation, and is often referred to the judge, as an essential form of embodiment of the law, as famously expressed in the metaphor of "Solomonic judgments." These are judgments that deeply contextualize the decision and take into account the emotionally grounded valuations of the parties involved.

Externalities are a key concept in the embodiment approach to economics, but the standpoint from which they are judged is reversed. What embodied economics claims is the following: When externalities are internalized, that is, valued in monetary terms through market processes, they are transformed through a process of disembodiment because, in the first place, externalities have no price at all. This means that if we want to assess the subjective value of the externality, we cannot but consider it in its embodied form, and this in, at least, two senses. One is its materiality, which is the physical form it takes. For example, if construction causes a lot of noise in the neighborhood, we can measure its loudness. The other is how people feel about the noise, which we can assess in a number of ways, including indirect ways of assessing the health effects of noise that people may not even be aware of.

If we generalize this argument to externalities, they can be thought of as "market feelings," as opposed to the market rationality that governs their internalization. Indeed, the conventional idea in mainstream economics is that once people negotiate over externalities and agree on a price, this neutralizes all other kinds of feelings about the externalities. That said, this would be the same as assuming that receiving a life insurance premium for the death of a beloved partner neutralizes grief, especially if the partners agreed on the amount. If the construction company pays a settlement to the neighborhood for noise, that does not neutralize the adverse health effects. Or the company may not have to pay at all, because the neighbors are proud of the symbol of progress. Internalizing externalities does not suppress the feelings experienced: Rather, it suppresses their public expression. It is, therefore, a *process* of disembodiment, because externalities cannot be completely disembodied; their expression (voice) may be muted, but their feelings do not cease to exist.

In essence, internalizing externalities is moving from "voice," as defined by Albert Hirschman (1970), to "silence," adding a fourth dimension to his typology. Hirschman distinguished between exit, voice, and loyalty in economic life. When economic actors are satisfied with a product, they continue to buy, they are loyal. If they are dissatisfied, the solution is either "exit," or "voice." Exit is the outcome traditionally envisaged in economics: It is neat, in that one either exits or one does not; it is impersonal, in that there is no face-to-face confrontation between customer and firm, success and failure being communicated only through a set of statistics such as market share or profit; and it is indirect, in that the decline of the firm comes through the market, which is the unintended by-product of the consumer's decision to switch. The alternative is voice, through which economic actors enter the political sphere, as exemplified by consumer resistance and political consumerism (e.g., Bouillé et al., 2016; Micheletti, 2003). In contrast to exit, voice is "messy," in that it can range from quiet grumbling to violent protest; it is also personal, in that it implies the expression of one's critical opinion; and it is direct and straightforward (Hirschman, 1970, pp. 15–16). Arguably, because voice involves the expression of feelings and emotions and face-to-face communication, it is embodied and thus traditionally neglected by standard economic models. In contrast to exit and voice, we propose that when it comes to silence, economic action becomes negation: People must suppress the expression of their feelings because they are given money to do so. The expression of their feelings is "silenced," not neutralized, because people rationalize their suppression: It is no longer necessary to express a feeling of discontentment, although it can still be experienced, because they are given money to compensate for their experience.

There is no economic activity that does not involve externalities, whether positive or negative. Externalities are key aspects of how people value a market transaction, in terms of market feeling. Consider a few examples. First, the construction case again. People will feel very differently about the noise if they perceive the project as important for the development of their community, or if they see it as usurpation by an aggressive developer. They will feel differently if they are poor and powerless, or if they are well-off citizens who know they can take action against the nuisance. Second, as the literature on social capital emphasizes, trust is generated by many activities that have nothing to do with the market, such as religious associations. However, by maintaining trust, market actors enjoy positive externalities by reducing transaction costs. In the absence of trust, every transaction could be interpreted as a struggle for advantage. Third, consider the case of knowledge transfer: For example, a company that trains an employee who leaves for another job and transfers knowledge to the new company. Even if neither actor intentionally pursues this transfer (e.g., the new company lures the worker away), the externality contributes to the productivity of the receiving company without compensation. In fact, this type of knowledge transfer is ubiquitous in the economy. When the economy has a strong regional identity, there is a cooperative spirit in the business community which takes such transfers for granted and generally assumes that reciprocity will hold, on balance, and in the long run.[19]

In all these cases, by internalizing externalities, mainstream economics would claim that it is possible to neutralize these feelings, that is, the way economic actors interpret these activities, whereas they can be essential for the smooth functioning of markets. The simplest example is trust: Can we pay for trust? Not at all, because if we really believed that trust could be bought, we would lose the primordial form of trust. Even seemingly obvious cases, like construction, fit this point if we consider the standard problem of reconciling divergent interests in construction. Noise affects many different people in various ways, and even in the standard model of internalization, they would have to agree on a common standard when negotiating with the construction company. Imagine that the company is faced with an injunction to stop construction until the internalization negotiations are completed. Since compensation is perceived differently by individuals with different income levels, this could lead to a stalemate, either in the form of a failure to reach a collective agreement, or isolated individuals blocking the conclusion of sequential negotiations. That is, the problem of noise requires the emergence of a common view of the feelings of nuisance and the equitable arrangements of the different ways of feeling concerned: As we will detail later, instead of a market-based solution in the form of internalizing externalities, embodied economics argues that a political solution, implemented in the affected community and engaging all stakeholders who aim for a consensus, is needed to allow this shared view to emerge.

Before elaborating on this point, we shall supplement this analysis of the impossibility of internalization with arguments of principle. There are several reasons, but we choose only two, which also show that externalities are pervasive and a necessary element in any form of market. Moreover, we invert the argument by showing that it is not prices that reveal scarcity, but externalities, which are by definition beyond prices.

8.3.3 Social Preferences and Identity

The first argument relates to an important contribution by Amartya Sen (1970), the "impossibility of the Paretian liberal" (see also Chung, 2019). In a nutshell, this is the story of someone who loathes another person reading a pornographic novel. The question is whether there is a solution that makes both of them better off. There is not. We generalize this result to the problem of externalities across consumers arising from social preferences. Most often, consumption externalities refer to the direct effects of an action on others, such as me enjoying a heavy metal song at its highest pitch, and thereby annoying my neighbors. The Senian case, however, is different in that people have preferences about the preferences of others. This is universal in education and socialization: All societies have institutionalized forms of shaping the preferences of children and even adults, resulting in adaptive conformism. Conformism triggers emotions of moral outrage and aggression when people observe others behaving differently even if it does not physically affect their well-being (Bowles et al., 2003). In the standard model of economics, this has been systematically treated in what is known as identity economics. This approach posits that utility functions include a social preference to be recognized as a member of a group. If these preferences are shared in the group, externalities become universal as individual actions always affect the identity of the other members of the group and vice versa (Akerlof & Kranton, 2000; Kranton, 2016). For instance, if I belong to a group where everyone wears red trousers and I happen to deviate by choosing blue trousers, this creates an externality for the others because the importance of red trousers in defining their identity is now in question.

Preferences over the preferences of others are universal because humans are social beings. To internalize them in markets is a contradiction in terms: It would mean that people trade their identities in markets. In a positive sense, this means that markets are always embedded in moral norms that govern preferences. The reason for this is that externalities manifest themselves as feelings and emotional actions about consumption. This brings us back to Pierre Bourdieu's argument, which challenges the "*de gustibus non est disputandum*" adage, discussed in previous chapters (e.g., Chapter 4): Preferences are also defined against the preferences of others, in the form of a feeling of disgust, taste being distaste (Bourdieu, 1979/1984). This applies to moral consumption in general. A vegan expresses a self-perception of moral responsibility towards nature, her disgust at the consumption of animal-based products also suggests the moral failure of meat-eaters.

Another form of consumption externality is the fact that much consumption is done in community with others. Of course, there are the solitary Bach aficionados who stay in their rooms with their headphones on and their eyes closed. But most activities certainly gain individual value when they are done in communion with others, such as enjoying a delicious meal at home with friends or in a restaurant (Kavedžija, 2021). People enjoy the "fellow feeling" of consuming together, which does not necessarily imply cooperation (e.g., Boothby et al., 2014). This can be generalized in terms of the "social network markets" approach, which points out that for many consumer goods, such as music or movies, individual preferences are directly shaped by interaction with others, leading to frequency-dependent phenomena such as the blockbuster phenomenon (Potts et al., 2008).

A third example is ritual consumption (Collins, 2005). For example, in traditional societies, the consumption of status goods is highly ritualized. This persists in the rituals of haute couture. Yet, there are other distinct forms of ritualized consumption in the Durkheimian sense of expressing community and even sacred values, especially if we include secular forms of sanctity, such as the American Super Bowl event. One major form is gift-giving. The consumption of luxury goods in East Asia, for example, is deeply shaped by gift-giving rituals, and many product lines would not be maintained without them, such as extremely expensive mushrooms in Japan (Rupp, 2003).

From the perspective of standard economics, all of these consumption activities involve externalities. But this is an artificial construct that focuses on individualized market transactions. On the contrary, what is called "externalities" means that market transactions are grounded in, and bounded by, shared feelings and valuations. As we will see later, one of the main purposes of embodied economics is to acknowledge these feelings and their political expression within the community.

8.3.4 *Externalizing the Costs of Sustaining Markets: The Paradox of Capitalism*

There is another type of externality that is constitutive of markets and that feminist scholars have identified early on, also criticizing the limitations of Marxian thinking. This is the externalization of costs to the family and to women, such as raising children, providing retreat and recreation for (male) workers, taking care of basic services such as nutrition, hygiene, and so on (Fraser, 2016; Power, 2004). This is interesting because it reveals the asymmetrical nature of externalization processes. Externalization is often an expression of inequalities in social and political power in society. Remarkably, these inequalities can be fully justified by the standard economic model. A striking illustration of this is the famous 1991 memorandum signed by Lawrence Summers, when he was Chief Economist of the World Bank, according to which "the economic logic behind dumping a load of toxic waste in the lowest wage country is impeccable," since, according to the standard economic model, human life is (supposedly) "worth" more in a rich country than in a poor one (e.g. Petri, 2021, p. 1287ff). Needless to say, such a conclusion is highly problematic and raises many issues,[20] but it illustrates the kind of solutions that are reached when disembodied models inspire economic analysis.[21]

Beyond the obvious ethical issues that arise here, one of the key observations we want to highlight here is that markets incentivize externalization. This is another way in which the notion of "imperfect markets" is grossly misleading. Market competition creates incentives for externalization, such as externalizing the costs of production by polluting land and rivers (especially in poor countries). The more imperfect markets are, in this sense, the higher the profits that economic agents can reap. This also applies to the beneficiaries of positive externalities, so it is universal. However, in the case of positive externalities, there is also the possibility that internalization would undermine their sources. This is the famous diagnosis of the social capital literature: Markets depend on social capital, but at the same time they undermine it (Putnam, 2020). There are two steps in this argument. The first is to note that markets often weaken communities, which are embodied forms of social capital, for example by incentivizing greater labor mobility. Indeed, mere spatial mobility erodes many forms of social capital that are situated in places, such as religious communities. The second step is whether this can be solved through internalization. But market logic cannot accommodate such collective forms of producing a social good. For example, compensating a community for the loss of people due to mobility does not stop the erosion of that community.

The externalization of the costs of making markets work is a deep paradox of capitalism first identified by Karl Polanyi (1944/2001). We can resolve it by stating that these externalities as "market feelings" reveal the true information about what is "scarce" in society, completely inverting the standard economic model's argument about prices as indicators of scarcity. In the equilibrium view, prices do not really reflect any kind of scarcity since market agents are assumed to be satisfied with the resulting status quo. But this status quo may be accompanied by a feeling that something important is missing: For example, parents who earn sufficient income to maintain a prosperous family life may actually lament the lack of time they have to spend with their children.[22] They discover the value of this time precisely because they are apparently successful in the market. Similarly, a wealthy industrial society learns the value of nature as it faces the consequences of pollution, and so on. Polanyi recognized early on that many of these externalities refer to phenomena that are essential to the functioning of markets.

But this points to another fundamental issue with externalities. The economic concept of internalization refers only to negotiations between human agents as market participants, or, externalities are conceived in anthropocentric terms (Herrmann-Pillath, 2021). This means that externalities affecting non-humans are only considered in terms of their impact on humans. This is particularly problematic for environmental issues and is reflected in concepts such as "ecosystem services" and "nature capital" which involve valuation at market prices (Dasgupta, 2021). In this view, a positive externality of nature on the human economy is valued in terms of its indirect contribution to market outcomes, including public goods as market infrastructure (Gomez-Baggethun, 2018). A negative externality would only refer to direct and indirect harm to humans.

From the embodied perspective, this raises the general issue of inclusion in markets. This must be distinguished from the internalization of externalities. Inclusion also concerns the human domain and is increasingly discussed under the heading of "vulnerable groups." Processes of internalization can actually harm such groups. For example, ecological and environmental improvements in cities may exclude poorer groups through "green gentrification" (Anguelovski et al., 2022; Cousins, 2021). These problems are endemic when it comes to non-humans, even though environmental externalities affect all living systems. This can only be remedied by broadening the scope of feelings to include non-human feelings, which requires an empathetic extension of human feelings, and a challenge to speciesism. The path to internalization is blocked because non-humans cannot enter into negotiations with humans. Indeed, ecological economists have criticized indirect approaches, such as the monetary valuation of natural capital, for actually undermining the commitment to its preservation since market valuation, even if imputed, suggests that the good in question is in principle open to substitution (Spash, 2013).

In sum, the paradox of capitalism is that it is based on conditions that cannot become the object of capitalism. There are principled limits to internalization, and these limits should be recognized and presented as the starting point of the solutions to be envisioned when it comes to dealing with externalities, rather than being presented as a so-called "imperfection" in light of an abstract and unrealistic (neoclassical) model. In this context, it could be argued that the development of behavioral interventions such as nudging, the New Institutional Economics literature on the commons, and subjective well-being studies, can be seen conceptually as solutions to overcome the limitations of internalizing externalities without market mechanisms. As we shall see in the next section, while these developments are certainly worth considering, they do not mechanically challenge the neoclassical model as a benchmark for understanding human behavior in economic life. In doing so, although they may pave the way for some form of embodiment in the conceptualization of economic life, this embodiment remains bounded by the market. In embodied economics, as discussed so far, the whole argument is reversed: The market is grounded in and bounded by embodiment, which means that embodiment, not the market, is the principle of economic life.

8.4 Limits to Embodiment in Recent Economic Thinking About Externalities and Well-Being

Let us begin with a disclaimer: We are conscious that the literature on nudging, the commons, and well-being is rich, subtle, and complex. We do not claim that our analysis is exhaustive and that every researcher in these fields would share our interpretation of them. However, if we look at the positions taken by some of their main proponents, or at some of the conceptual and methodological tools they use in economics, it seems that the neoclassical model remains *a*—if not *the*—reference point for defining their approach. For this reason, although some of their perspectives could be considered as aligned with embodied economics, in these approaches, embodiment remains conceptually bounded by the neoclassical model of the rational actor and/or the market. In other words, unlike embodied economics, these approaches do not posit as a principle of their analyses that embodiment grounds and bounds market processes, and, more broadly, economic life.

8.4.1 Externalities and Behavioral Interventions

Nudging is one of the main illustrations of the use and application of behavioral economics in economic life (e.g., Kahneman, 2012). At first sight, nudging could be seen as an inspiration for public policy interventions rather well aligned with embodied economics when it comes to dealing with externalities. It is associated with the claim that people "are not *Homo economicus*; they are *Homo sapiens*" (Thaler & Sunstein, 2008, p. 7), and, in principle, it relies on solutions that would not matter to rational economic agents (Thaler, 2018). For instance, a nudge is neither a mandate nor a monetary incentive. It is defined as

> any aspect of the choice architecture that alters people's behavior in a predictable way without forbidding any options or significantly changing their economic incentives. To count as a mere nudge, the intervention must be easy and cheap to avoid. Nudges are not mandates. Putting the fruit at eye level counts as a nudge. Banning junk food does not. (Thaler & Sunstein, 2008, p. 6)[23]

Thus, to deal with externalities, nudge-based solutions to pollution and its impact on climate change include, for instance, an "environmental blacklist" that would publish the names of the biggest polluters (Thaler & Sunstein, 2008, p. 191), and green default rules such as double-sided printing, or a green energy provider by default (Sunstein & Reisch, 2014; see also, Oullier et al., 2010; Sunstein, 2018).[24] More generally, in principle, nudge-based solutions do not require the internalization of externalities through market mechanisms, as conventional economics would recommend. Rather, as illustrated, they locate human action in the material (e.g., default) and social environment (e.g., blacklisting), which may seem consistent with the embodied economics approach. Indeed, it is quite striking that the concept of assemblage, which is part and parcel of embodied economics, strongly evokes some nudge solutions, as exemplified by this quote from Bruno Latour, years before the concept of nudging was coined:

> Consider a tiny innovation commonly found in European hotels: attaching large cumbersome weights to room keys in order to remind customers that they should leave their key at the front desk every time they leave the hotel instead of taking it along on a tour of the city. An imperative statement inscribed on a sign – 'Please leave your room key at the front desk before you go out' – appears to be not enough to make customers behave according to the speaker's wishes. Our fickle customers seemingly have other concerns, and room keys disappear into thin air. But if the innovator, called to the rescue, displaces the inscription by introducing a large metal weight, the hotel manager no longer has to rely on his customers' sense of moral obligation. Customers suddenly become only too happy to rid themselves of this annoying object which makes their pockets bulge and weighs down their handbags: they go to the front desk on their own accord to get rid of it. Where the sign, the inscription, the imperative, discipline, or moral obligation all failed, the hotel manager, the innovator, and the metal weight succeeded. And yet, obtaining such discipline has a price: the hotel manager had to ally himself with an innovator, and the innovator had to ally herself with various metal weights and their manufacturing processes. (Latour, 1990, p. 104)

In nudging, however, embodiment is not paradigmatic, at either the conceptual or the practical level. At the conceptual level, nudging inherits directly from the biases-and-heuristics research program developed by Kahneman who, as argued in previous chapters, maintained *Homo economicus* as the definition of rationality (e.g., Kahneman, 2003). Following this line of argument, one of the main proponents of nudging claims that

> we do not need to throw away everything we know about how economies and markets work. Theories based on the assumption that everyone is an Econ [rational actor] should not be discarded. They remain useful as starting points for more realistic models. (Thaler, 2015, p. 7)

Mechanically, to the extent that market trends and human behavior are considered outside of neoclassical benchmarks, such as the behavior expected of *Homo economicus*, interventions in the architecture of choice will be necessary. Behavioral economics in the form of nudging should therefore be seen as an extension of, rather than an alternative to, neoclassical economics which contributes to the promotion of "processes of commodification:"

> The problems of bounded rationality are to be dealt with the design of 'choice architectures' to help individuals calculate the costs and benefits associated with available options, or to 'nudge' them in directions considered welfare-improving. The ultimate goal is to improve the functioning or the expansion of markets. The more consumers make the right choices, the more markets become competitive and indeed legitimate. (Santos & Rodrigues, 2014, p. 517)

In other words, under the auspices of nudging, interventions are intended to shape the context of decision-making in such a way that people make decisions that are deemed more rational, by the standards of *Homo economicus*.[25]

At the practical level, it follows that interventions in the environment of economic actors focus on the material and social context of individual choices in the market, but nudging does not intend to challenge the market as envisioned in neoclassical economics. Instead of being challenged, the neoclassical vision of the market remains posited as one, if not the main, solution to the societal problems associated with economic activity. Externalities, such as CO_2 emissions, which are one of the main sources of GHG generated by economic activity (e.g., Hickel, 2020b), should be addressed by creating rights to pollute that are then traded in dedicated markets, as illustrated by the cap-and-trade systems celebrated by Richard Thaler and Cass Sunstein (Thaler & Sunstein, 2008, pp. 187, 197). In this respect, the behavioral economics of nudging works in tandem with the experimental economics of market design (see also Santos & Rodrigues, 2014).

Importantly, and this is another major difference between nudging and embodied economics, the two economist-as-architect approaches, whether in charge of designing markets, inspired by experimental economics, or in charge of the architecture of choice, inspired by behavioral economics, thus rely on the fundamental hypothesis that (behavioral and experimental) economists are the ones who possess the knowledge needed to behave rationally in economic life.[26] According to this technocratic approach, knowledge about the economic system and economic behavior belongs to scientists. As technocrats and experts (Earle et al., 2016), these economists posit that they know what economic life is and what it should be, since they are guided by models of perfect markets and substantive rationality that serve as benchmarks. As can be inferred from the previous chapters, this position is firmly rejected by embodied economics. If knowledge is embodied and situated, as embodied economics posits, then neoclassical models of substantive rationality and market perfection can no longer serve as benchmarks. Indeed, these models define standards divorced from economic actors and their environments, and inevitably recommend interventions whose guiding principles have been conceptualized in isolation from them. In other words, from the perspective of embodied economics, what is needed are not neoclassically inspired solutions to problems defined *in abstracto* by economists or behavioral scientists.[27] Rather, what is needed is guidance on how to meaningfully approach solutions to problems experienced by economic actors in their material, economic, social, and ecological environments. This leads us to another stream of research with which embodied economics shares several positions: the New Institutional Economics of Elinor Ostrom and her colleagues.

8.4.2 Externalities and the Commons

One of the reasons why conventional economics suggests market-based solutions to externalities is usually supported by the narrative revolving around the tragedy of the commons where non-cooperative self-serving individuals over-exploit shared resources (Hardin, 1968). The alleged "tragedy" has been challenged by a wide range of field and experimental studies of common-pool resources (Ostrom, 2010). As in the previous section, our intention here is not to detail the richness of these studies, but rather to highlight how some of their key findings could further inform and position embodied economics in relation to externalities. Ostrom and her colleagues have shown that there are alternatives to internalizing externalities with neoclassical market-based solutions and some form of nudging to address common-pool resource management problems:

> Unfortunately, policy analysts, public officials, and scholars who still apply simple mathematical models to the analysis of field settings have not yet absorbed the central lessons articulated here. All too often a single policy prescription – such as Individual Transferable Quotas (ITQs) – is recommended for all resources of a particular type, such as all fisheries. (…) Designing institutions to force (or nudge) entirely self-interested individuals to achieve better outcomes has been the major goal posited by policy analysts for governments to accomplish for much of the past half century.

> Extensive empirical research leads me to argue that, instead, a core goal of public policy should be to facilitate the development of institutions that bring out the best in humans. (Ostrom, 2010, pp. 664–665)

The question that comes to mind after reading this quote is: What then should be facilitated to "bring out the best in humans?" An essential part of the answer is very embodied: Face-to-face communication within the rules crafted by the community. Indeed, as Ostrom and colleagues have found, people tend to behave as expected from the rational choice model, that is, non-cooperatively, notably when they cannot communicate in a common-pool resource dilemma. However, when face-to-face communication is allowed, cooperation emerges between people: "Simply allowing communication, or 'cheap talk,' enables participants to reduce overharvesting and increase joint payoffs contrary to game theoretical predictions" (Ostrom, 2010, p. 641). Such findings have significant implications from the perspective of embodied economics: If face-to-face communication helps to foster cooperation, then facilitating embodied interactions in economic life should be encouraged, as this could help institutions address some societal problems and deal with externalities. Obviously, designing markets to deal with externalities with a pricing system that favors anonymity would hinder embodied interactions such as face-to-face communication and thus prevent the emergence of constructive solutions to societal issues.

Beyond this fundamental point, there are, at least, two other important elements that Ostrom mentions in light of her research that resonate with embodied economics.

First, her work demonstrates the need to think about interventions based on the knowledge of economic actors engaged in linguistically mediated exchanges in their material, economic, social, and ecological environments. This position departs radically from the conventional technocratic approach of (behavioral and experimental) economics. As explained:

> When analysts perceive the human beings they model as being trapped inside perverse situations, they then assume that other human beings external to those involved – scholars and public officials – are able to analyze the situation, ascertain why counterproductive outcomes are reached, and posit what changes in the rules-in-use will enable participants to improve outcomes. Then, external officials are expected to impose an

> optimal set of rules on those individuals involved. It is assumed that the momentum for change must come from outside the situation rather than from the self-reflection and creativity of those within a situation to restructure their own patterns of interaction. (Ostrom, 2010, p. 648; see also, Sugden, 1986)

Contrary to the conventional view of economics, her Nobel lecture asserts that people are not "rational individuals helplessly trapped in social dilemmas" (Ostrom, 2010, p. 648), whose only hope is to expect market-based solutions implemented by government and/or designed by a bunch of economists-as-architects espousing some form of methodological fundamentalism.[28] Rather, Ostrom demonstrated that the ability of people to transform a deleterious situation and find a collective solution is subject to the context of their collective action, and fundamentally depends on their ability to engage in face-to-face communication.

Second, in this perspective, Ostrom argues for the importance of self-organized mechanisms that are not market-based—as Hayek would prefer—but embodied and situated at the community level, if we are to find solutions to societal issues. Along this line of argument, Ostrom developed a theory of institutional *crafting* which emphasizes autonomy along with the embodied and situated dimensions of the knowledge needed to address issues affecting the local community (e.g., Sinner et al., 2022; see also, Ostrom, 1980; Ostrom et al., 1992), and which can extend views and analyses of "real" utopias (Ostrom, 1998a).[29] Rules to address these issues are crafted as tools:

> Humans are viewed as fallible, boundedly rational, and norm-using. In complex settings, no one is able to do a complete analysis before actions are taken, but individuals learn from mistakes and are able to craft tools – including rules – to improve the structure of the repetitive situations they face. (Ostrom, 1999, p. 496)[30]

This RULES ARE TOOLS metaphor introduces a new way of thinking about economic interventions: The rules are not set in stone by mainstream economics, but rather are tools that are collectively crafted through trial and error, and empower economic actors as change agents to tackle the collective issues they face in the context of a given local community (e.g., Caggiano et al., 2023). In that regard:

> The Ostroms join the company of those who reject the notion that institutional design should be the exclusive object of a profession, a specialization, and expertise; on the contrary they consider it a core element of citizens' competence and as such a basic ingredient of self-governance and democracy. (Aligica, 2003, p. 165)

Ostrom's approach shifts the focus away from interventions based on the market, the government, or the ECONOMISTS ARE ARCHITECTS metaphor underlying mainstream (experimental and behavioral) economics. Rather, her work emphasizes that knowledge belongs to the local people who are responsible for change, at the community level, where the "rules-in-use are not formally written by those using them to structure their daily interactions" (Ostrom & Basurto, 2011, p. 322). This knowledge is embodied: It is implicit in people's actions and situated in their communities, and its expression requires empowerment through participatory and democratic processes. This leads Ostrom to criticize "institutional monocropping" and, instead, to move beyond the panacea problem of overly general theories and excessively precise models, and to celebrate institutional diversity (Ostrom & Cox, 2010) rather than market or methodological fundamentalism (e.g., Labrousse, 2016; May & Summerfield, 2012; see also, Deaton & Cartwright, 2018; Kabeer, 2020). Empirical evidence shows that governance arrangements that are locally (rather than externally) controlled by the Indigenous peoples and local communities, and thus incorporate local informal and unwritten customary systems of use, control, and authority over natural resources, have positive outcomes for both well-being and environmental conservation (Dawson et al., 2021).

Despite the several positions that embodied economics shares with Ostrom, particularly when it comes to the question of empowering local communities in sustainability decision-making, we contend that the main issue with her approach is that it limits the mechanisms she presents to the management of common-pool resources, thereby adopting the neoclassical typology of public goods (Dardot & Laval, 2019; Ostrom, 2010). In this way, the market bounds embodiment, whereas the exact opposite is suggested by embodied economics: Embodiment bounds the market. It is worthwhile to indicate, however, that she acknowledges that her findings can "have a wider range of application than CPR [common-pool resources] groups and are relevant to nearly any situation where people must cooperate and coordinate to achieve shared goals" (Wilson et al.,

2013, p. S21). In this sense, the importance of face-to-face communication in cooperation, which is usually neglected in experimental markets (e.g., Williams, 1980),[31] has also been pointed out when it comes to political behavior, since "the direct interaction of the citizens in the form of communication accounts for one specific feature of a viable democracy: it increases 'other-regarding behaviour'" (Frey & Bohnet, 1997, p. 25), such as cooperation and fairness. Moreover, in embodied economics, economic theory cannot be disentangled from political economy, so embodiment, including face-to-face communication, is relevant to every sphere of economic life.

Finally, Ostrom's analysis remains anthropocentric because the ecological system is conceptualized from a human perspective as a resource system (e.g., water, forest) and corresponding resource units (e.g., water volume, tree) (Binder et al., 2013; see further critiques in Cumming et al., 2020). In contrast, embodied economics is fundamentally ecocentric. Indeed, in keeping with its phenomenological and enactive roots, embodied economics does not posit that humans are, *in the first place*, "users," "consumers," or more largely "economic agents (or actors)" who view nature as a resource system. Rather, human beings, like *other living beings*, are first and foremost "inhabitants" of a world that they make sense of (e.g., Thompson & Stapleton, 2009; Varela et al., 2016). This posits the fundamental imperative to be sustainable by default and does not limit economic analysis to the problem-solving approach conveyed by a user-centric approach (e.g., Gee, 1994). When humans are thought of only as users, consumers, or *economic* agents (actors), the world is seen as an instrument, with a mere function that serves primarily, if not exclusively, human needs and other (advertising-induced) desires beyond them. Limiting embodied economics to such a user-centric perspective would foster the dark side of embodiment, since it would imply that the world revolves around the human body, and that nature is just a tool, a mere extension of the human hand.

Overall, despite some differences with embodied economics, Ostrom's approach is considered fundamental because it showed that there are solutions to externalities that are neither market-based nor government-led, and that these solutions require recognizing the embodied and situated aspects of the knowledge of economic actors empowered in their communities. This is an important conceptual move, as it shifts the focus of analysis away from the neoclassical model conceptualized in the abstraction of people's material, economic, social, and ecological environments.

8.4.3 *Externalities and Well-Being*

Well-being has traditionally been celebrated as a way to overcome the well-known limitations of GDP, even recognized in the mainstream economic literature, and to develop an argument beyond welfare and economic utility (Taylor, 2011). At first sight, the concept of well-being might be considered mechanically embodied, since it usually pertains to *feelings* of happiness (e.g., Kövecses, 1991). However, as we shall see, depending on its definition, well-being, whether understood as eudaimonic or hedonic, will be more or less aligned with embodied economics.

Let us start here with the hedonic school of thought—the eudaimonic school will be discussed in the next section. The hedonic approach conceptualizes well-being primarily as the maximization of pleasure (and minimization of pain) and is mostly aligned with the utility theory of neoclassical economics (e.g., Konow & Earley, 2008). It inspires research on subjective well-being (Layard, 2010), is exemplified by the World Happiness Report (e.g., Helliwell et al., 2022), and can fairly be said to dominate "ongoing popular and policy discourses" (Brand-Correa & Steinberger, 2017, p. 43). The implications of this perspective at the policy level are closely linked to the measurement of subjective well-being, which comprises measures of positive and negative affect along with life satisfaction (Ryff et al., 2021). Defined as "a global assessment of a person's quality of life according to his chosen criteria" (Shin & Johnson, 1978, p. 478), "life satisfaction judgments are based on one's own subjective criteria, rather than necessarily reflecting outward conditions" (Margolis et al., 2019, p. 621). Consistently, because such "outward conditions" are not the main issue, from the perspective of hedonic well-being research, improving people's well-being remains mostly focused at the psychological or cognitive level, either by "improving a person's state of mind" or by "changing their understanding of what contributes to well-being (i.e. their utility function)" (Brand-Correa & Steinberger, 2017, p. 43; see also O'Neill, 2008; Walton, 2014; Walton & Wilson, 2018). For instance, in light of empirical evidence showing that the typical association between meaning and well-being is weakened in consumption contexts compared to non-consumption ones (e.g., hanging out with close ones, helping others), interventions targeting consumers at the psychological level are suggested to "reframe purchases as intrinsically rewarding, change (erroneous) lay theories that profit necessarily comes at the expense of the social good, or highlight the future, enduring benefits of consumption" (Mead & Williams, 2022, p. 1).

This kind of individualistic perspective, fueled by the hedonic approach, is consequential when it comes to dealing with issues related to the economic, social, and ecological environment. It can influence the scope of analysis: For instance, the focus on social justice, which highlights economic and social inequalities and questions societal structures and organization, seems to be "conspicuously absent" from the "psychology and behavioral economics" of (hedonic) well-being (Prilleltensky, 2012, p. 2). This may also influence the scope of the solutions envisioned. On the one hand, from a top-down perspective, for example, a sufficiency-led policy that challenges overconsumption in Western societies, and thus intends to set "limits to consumption (e.g. limits on resource use, on environmental impacts or economic growth), can be immediately perceived as limits to HW [hedonic well-being] from a mainstream economic perspective" (Brand-Correa & Steinberger, 2017, p. 43). Indeed, the standard approach posits unlimited wants, despite contrary evidence supporting limited ideals of wealth and ways of being, such as happiness, freedom, and pleasure (e.g., Bain & Bongiorno, 2022; Hornsey et al., 2018; Sahlins, 1972). On the other hand, from a bottom-up perspective, for example, as illustrated by positive psychology, which shares an individualistic perspective on well-being similar to the hedonic school (Adams et al., 2019), considering economic actors as empowered actors of societal change is not taken seriously as an option: "Positive psychologists (…) shy away from creating alternative social settings or engaging grassroots organizations" (Montiel et al., 2021, p. 3).

In contradistinction with this approach, embodied economics considers outward economic, social, and ecological conditions as well as psychological dimensions as essential to approaching happiness and well-being. Take, for example, Chinese happiness data for two decades after 1990 (Helliwell et al., 2017). Despite extremely high economic growth, most surveys converge on the finding that indicators initially plummeted and recovered only slowly, with some, such as the World Values Survey, still below baseline at the end of this period. Clearly, growth has not contributed to feelings of happiness.[32] There are a couple of explanations, and we mention just one: Unemployment rose, which favored heightened feelings of insecurity even among those who were still employed. The Chinese felt increasingly threatened, even though their incomes were generally rising. The heightened sense of insecurity among the Chinese may have manifested itself in rising rates of depressive anxiety and other feelings of distress.

Feelings relate to what philosophers have labeled "thick concepts" (Väyrynen, 2021). These are terms, such as "greedy," "brutal," or "amicable," that have both descriptive and evaluative meanings. When we say, "bankers are greedy," we are primarily describing them, but we are also suggesting that we disapprove of such behavior. This is more than a subjective and arbitrary attribution: When I say, "I am hungry," this is a description that also involves a valuation that invites some action, such as motivating another person to offer me a snack. Thick ethical concepts are embodied in the linking of feelings, valuations, and drives for action at the individual and collective levels. We argue that such phenomena provide the grounding for "interests" which are merely rational reconstructions in a specific context, such as bargaining over subsidies for farmers. The example of farmers also reveals the importance of feelings: In many countries, farmers express their policy preferences in highly emotional terms, such as at public rallies.

Against this background, embodied economics refers directly to the valuations that people express, and which are emotionally grounded, when they assess certain economic states or institutional designs. This has long been known in the social sciences (e.g., Simmel, 1908/1965); consider unemployment, for instance: Even with generous unemployment benefits, the feelings associated with unemployment are essential elements in valuing this state, such as the loss of self-esteem or the rupture of social relationships at work (e.g., Gedikli et al., 2023; Viney, 1985). To reduce unemployment only to the loss of monetary income, which can theoretically be compensated by insurance schemes, would seriously distort the true damage to society and individuals. On the other hand, as the Chinese case shows, simply asking people about changes in "happiness" does not reveal which specific emotions are driving this response, and thus does not provide concrete guidance for necessary policies and other interventions.

The implication of all these observations is that when comparing different economic states resulting from institutional settings, emotional valuations are primordial, and "interests" are transformations of these valuations in the context of settings where pecuniary valuations prevail.

This is salient in social and political conflicts over economic issues, such as public resentment over perceived injustice in energy pricing and windfall profits, or civil society initiatives against trade agreements. Overall, the importance of outward living conditions in conjunction with psychological dimensions for understanding happiness and subjective well-being, as illustrated by the Chinese case, leads embodied economics to support the creation of alternative social settings that allow for collective discussions about feelings pertaining to societal issues (e.g., Curato et al., 2017, p. 30).

8.5 Human Flourishing in Embodied Economics

Our previous discussions of the GDP problem and the existence of externalities, and how these are dealt with in the literature on nudging, the commons, and subjective well-being, further point to the importance of embodiment and lead us to a key question: What then corresponds to general welfare in embodied economics? There are two answers. One is that a notion of general good emerges from public discourse about desirable realizations (Sen, 2009). This raises complicated questions about the inclusiveness of this discourse and how participants can agree on a shared view, especially if they would have to accept negative consequences for themselves (Haug, 2015). We do not cover this important point here, but concentrate on the second answer which moves toward our utopian perspective on mindful human flourishing, and its connection to the other approach to well-being, the eudaimonic school. As we shall see, well-being means flourishing, but flourishing means more than well-being: It includes dignity as well as inclusivity, sufficiency, empowerment, and resilience.

8.5.1 Well-Being Means Flourishing

In political economy (Sen, 2009) and political philosophy (Nussbaum, 2006), the eudaimonic school of well-being is concerned with social justice (Prilleltensky, 2012), and "sees well-being as the enabling of humans to reach their highest potential within the context of their society" (Brand-Correa & Steinberger, 2017, p. 43). Following this literature, the concept that corresponds to "welfare" in embodied economics is "flourishing." Eudaimonia in Greek can be translated as "human flourishing" and is inherited from Aristotle, whose analysis of the human good is deeply connected to the capability approach discussed in Chapter 5: "it is interesting to note that the Greek word *dunamin*, used by Aristotle to discuss an aspect of the human good, which is sometimes translated as 'potentiality,' can be translated also as 'capability of existing or acting'" (Nussbaum & Sen, 1993, p. 30). Potentiality is an essential feature of capability, which represents "the alternative combinations of things a person is able to do or be – the various 'functionings' he or she can achieve" (Nussbaum & Sen, 1993, p. 30). Importantly, Aristotle's analysis of eudaimonia "in terms of valued activities" is consequential because it contrasts with the hedonic approach which is rather "relying on readings of mental states, as in some utilitarian procedures" (Nussbaum & Sen, 1993, p. 47). This is reflected in the psychological approach of eudaimonia, which, unlike the life-satisfaction approach and related subjective well-being, is "not conceived of as a mental state, a positive feeling, or a cognitive appraisal of satisfaction, but rather as a way of living" (Ryan et al., 2008, p. 143). In other words, (eudaimonic) "well-being is not just a matter of subjective experiences, it is a matter of what one can do or be in one's life" (O'Neill, 2006, p. 165). In this perspective, well-being as flourishing resonates with utopia, which is defined as the expression of a better way of being and living. Consistently, eudaimonic well-being "allows for the inclusion in the analysis of a sense of social belonging to our community both in the past and future, hence it opens the space for intergenerational citizenship through the sharing of common projects and places" (Brand-Correa & Steinberger, 2017, p. 45).

Therefore, whereas the concept of "welfare" focuses on realized states, "flourishing" refers to a dynamic process of creating and realizing opportunities for realizing one's aspirations in life. In embodied economics, through the concept of forward embodiment, consistent with our argument developed in Chapter 5, we refer flourishing to agential power as the creation of the means for flourishing. The question, then, is how the economy can contribute to the enhancement of agential powers, which differs from the conventional view in which the economy is seen as providing for the fulfillment of consumer preferences. In other words, in embodied economics, the market is a means that exists to serve human beings within planetary boundaries, not an end in itself that human beings should serve. This view transcends the conventional economic approach in a fundamental way: Flourishing is not only about means, but also about ends. Economists focus on the availability of resources in the broadest sense and the freedom to employ them to satisfy subjective preferences.

Flourishing includes the future, which refers to the aspirations and hopes of individuals, that is, ends beyond means. The question is whether individuals can set goals for themselves and pursue them effectively. However, this could still mean that goals can be reduced to mere subjective preferences. In our conception of agential power, ends require the approval and recognition of others, since agential power is always relational.

This leads us to the Kantian approach as the most abstract way of expressing this, which is regarding individuals as ends in themselves, which means recognizing their dignity as persons and preventing their dehumanization through the process of commodification. Kant distinguished between two ways of valuing a person or an object, one is the price, and the other is dignity. A price suggests that the reference object can be substituted, whereas dignity implies that it cannot, because it is valued as such. Embodied economics puts dignity at the center of valuing people and things—in the latter case, integrity is perhaps a better companion term, also used in ecology. Flourishing and dignity are closely related. As we will see later, one issue where this is most evident in economic life is work. Beforehand, we shall develop the other concepts implied by the embodied economics approach to flourishing in economic life.

8.5.2 Flourishing Beyond Well-Being: The WISER Framework

The capability approach, which translates some of the principles of the eudaimonic school of well-being into theoretical analyses of economic life, has inspired the work of the United Nations (UN) on sustainable development. For instance, since the 1990s, the UN Human Development Report has been based in part on the capability approach (e.g., Fukuda-Parr, 2003; Pedersen, 2020), and Sen directly contributed to the elaboration of the Human Development Index (HDI) which goes beyond a GDP approach by taking into account education, life expectancy, and income (Nussbaum & Sen, 1993). More recently, the capability approach has influenced the UN Millennium Development Goals and the subsequent Sustainable Development Goals (SDGs) (Robeyns, 2017).

Interestingly, the 17 interlinked SDGs, unanimously adopted by 193 UN members in 2015 (United Nations, 2015), encompass a wide range of fundamental issues that go beyond GDP metrics, such as poverty (SDG 1), climate action (SDG 13), or peace and justice (SDG 16). One of the key strengths of these goals is the breadth of their scope and ambition. They are considered progressive and utopian (e.g., Kuenkel, 2019; Linnér & Wibeck, 2019), and they are appropriate for defining which concrete utopia is envisioned for the future by today's standards (Basso & Krpan, 2022). However, the scope of these goals is so broad that they lack focus and principles, and may appear incoherent (e.g., Coscieme et al., 2020, 2021). The WISER framework, whose acronym stands for Well-being, Inclusivity, Sufficiency, Empowerment, and Resilience, reorganizes the SDGs into five main overarching categories (Basso & Krpan, 2023).[33] For this reason, in embodied economics, flourishing goes beyond well-being. Our aim here is not to review the literature that revolves around each of these categories, but rather to demonstrate their relevance to embodied economics if we are to conceptualize an embodied market utopia that contributes to flourishing within communities, and overcomes some of the limitations of the approaches discussed in previous sections.

Well-being is the degree to which people can flourish as a whole, characterized by being and feeling happy and surrounded by the resources necessary to ensure an optimal life expectancy, and to meet needs for nutrition (SDG 2), health (SDG 3), sanitation (SDG 6), and energy (SDG 7). This definition is consistent with a perspective that aims to articulate both the subjective dimension and the outward conditions of well-being. Its main limitation is that it portrays the natural environment—that is, the planet and other living beings—as a main provider of "resources" for humans as its users. This is consistent with the anthropocentrism that inspires the SDGs, although in embodied economics this can be overcome thanks to the concepts of inclusivity, sufficiency, empowerment, and resilience.

Inclusivity is the extent to which a society provides equal participation for all and ensures freedom, equal opportunity, and diverse values by tackling poverty (SDG 1), achieving gender equality (SDG 5), reducing inequalities within and between countries (SDG 10), and promoting peace and justice (SDG 16). Inclusivity is linked to embodiment. For instance, when it comes to economic life, as pointed out in feminist economics: "Gender matters because men and women have bodies that differ in significant ways" (Nelson, 2016, p. 1365). This illustrates the idea that embodiment restores the political aspects of economics. This is not surprising because embodiment is political:

> those with stigmatized bodies, to borrow Goffman's phrase, are fully aware that the body is political, central to personal identity and life-chances. People judged by their bodies do not take them for granted, and may love or hate their bodies – not for philosophical but for political and very practical reasons, whether they are judged by their physical handicaps, age, colour, gender, aesthetics. (Synnott, 1992, pp. 100–101)

We argue that it is precisely because embodiment is political that it was rejected by Hayek in his utopian vision of the "Great Society." For embodiment underpins and nurtures social justice aspirations in economic life, whether in terms of emotions (e.g., anger, disgust), actions (e.g., voice, protests), or metaphors, such as the CONTAINER metaphor to represent social exclusion as being "left out," the BALANCE metaphor to represent justice between two parties, or ontological metaphors to represent market mechanisms (e.g., "overconsumption is killing the planet").

As discussed in Chapter 3, Hayek's critique of anthropomorphism actually denounced the use of ontological metaphors to think about social justice in the marketplace. Nevertheless, it is precisely anthropomorphism that is needed to escape the commodification of nature that underpins the anthropocentrism of standard economic models, and to develop an alternative ecocentric view in economics. Anthropomorphism is one of the mechanisms, an embodied one, that undergirds ecojustice, and helps overcome the Cartesian rationalist view that animals are machines and that humans should behave as masters and possessors of nature. Indeed, anthropomorphism allows us to extend the conceptualization of "inclusivity" beyond human beings to understand the community as a "community of life," that is as a container of the living beings that *inhabit* the world. Embodiment emphasizes what human beings share with every other living being in the ecosystem. For instance, to think that an animal suffers "like us" does not mean that it is necessarily humanized, but we humans recognize that we are like the animal because we all have bodies. In the case of ecojustice, Mother Earth,[34] which is an anthropomorphization of nature and the planet, is the key ontological metaphor commonly employed to grant rights to nature, and enable it to act in justice to defend the rights of living beings (Lockwood, 2023). This ecocentric worldview, although grounded in outward embodiment and thus in a human point of reference, is in full alignment with the very first principle (1a) of the Earth Charter, which recognizes that "all beings are interdependent and every form of life has value regardless of its worth to human beings" (Earth Charter, 2000). More largely, an ecocentric worldview is consistent with traditional stories, myths, and spiritual traditions across cultures and human history (Cutanda, 2020). By challenging the anthropocentric worldview, inclusivity challenges the user-centric and instrumental view of nature and leads to a conceptual shift from *efficiency* to *sufficiency*.

Sufficiency means living within planetary boundaries by limiting the consumption and production of environmentally unsustainable goods and services, and preserving the environment. This perspective is more ambitious than green growth (SDG 12), and user-centric protection of terrestrial and marine ecosystems (SDGs 14 and 15), as initially conveyed by the SDGs. By emphasizing the concept of sufficiency, embodied economics acknowledges that degrowth is a necessity in rich countries, especially in the name of climate justice (e.g., Hickel, 2020a, 2020b; Rodríguez-Labajos et al., 2019). The concept of sufficiency also further illustrates the difference between embodied economics and the hedonic school of well-being, or the libertarian paternalism that underpins nudging, which, as aforementioned, would not welcome any form of limitation on economic growth. Of course, the concept of "sufficiency" raises the question of what is considered "sufficient" to satisfy human needs within planetary boundaries (Smith & Max-Neef, 2011). According to Manfred Max-Neef (1991), who developed the Human Scale Development (HSD) approach to studying how basic human needs can be fulfilled, "fundamental human needs are finite, few and classifiable," and they "are the same in all cultures and in all historical periods" while "the way or the means by which the needs are satisfied" change through time (Max-Neef, 1991, p. 18).[35] Our aim is not to give a detailed presentation of the HSD approach, but to highlight two important points. First, in contrast to psychological approaches to fundamental needs, which remain very anthropocentric (e.g., Maslow, 1943), the HSD approach can be extended to include non-human needs in sustainable development strategies (Jolibert et al., 2011), which is conducive to conceiving the satisfaction of human needs within the planetary boundaries set by other living beings. Second, in contrast to the technocratic tendencies of conventional economics, participatory workshops, allow people to identify the destructive elements (negative satisfiers) that threaten the future of their community, and the constructive elements (positive satisfiers) that will enable their community to move towards their Utopia (Jolibert et al., 2011). This means, in line with inclusivity, that sufficiency cannot be thought of without considering empowerment.

Empowerment is the capability to maintain determination over one's life, and to participate in the life of one's community through involvement in the functioning of institutions such as schools, churches, and other voluntary organizations. Thus, empowerment is a very broad concept that is linked to autonomy, agency, and democratic and participatory processes that allow for the expression of feelings through realization-focused comparisons. It encompasses education and lifelong learning (SDG 4), work opportunities and economic security (SDG 8), and partnerships between communities (SDG 17), which contribute to providing control over one's economic, social, and ecological environments. These various aspects of empowerment overlap with the capability to gain control over one's environment identified by Martha Nussbaum (2006) in her objective list of capabilities,[36] and with the emotional, cognitive, relational, and behavioral dimensions of empowerment in community psychology (Christens, 2012).

Empowerment in embodied economics should be distinguished from another approach developed in economic psychology through the concept of "boosting." This concept is derived from Gerd Gigerenzer's reading of Herbert Simon's bounded and ecological rationality, which stands in opposition to Kahneman's biases-and-heuristics approach to people as cognitive misers discussed in Chapters 2, 3, and 4, and has emerged in the literature as a solution to overcome some of the limitations of nudging (Hertwig & Grüne-Yanoff, 2017). Within the scope of the ecological approach, the perspective is different: The purpose of interventions based on the model of ecological rationality is to analyze the context of decision-making and to provide economic actors with solutions that should foster their skills and competences, so that they can exercise their own *agency*, get more *autonomy*, and be *empowered*. In this sense, through their skills and competences, economic actors can *embody* some knowledge. Moreover, because they are expected to learn new heuristics, their *cooperation* is required, which overcomes the ethical limitations pertaining to nudging (e.g., Lades & Delaney, 2022). As such, boosting represents a change in thinking compared to nudging, and *ipso facto* leads to interventions of a very different nature, aiming, for instance, at risk literacy or uncertainty management. The implicit or explicit references to agency, autonomy, empowerment, embodiment, and cooperation in the boosting literature resonate with the embodied economics approach. That said, like nudging, boosting rests on a fundamental hypothesis: Knowledge comes primarily from the economist or behavioral scientist, and thus the approach remains technocratic. More importantly, although boosting does not focus on (so-called) cognitive biases, like nudging, it still contributes to promoting interventions that favor an individualistic view of societal problems and their potential solutions, in lieu of interventions that take a more "systemic" perspective on these issues (Chater & Loewenstein, 2023). In boosting, people are trained, coached, or educated to adapt to the current socio-economic system, not to change it, or to question the value, goal, and worldview it conveys. If not critical, boosting remains essentially compatible with the neoliberal agenda that inspires individualistic interventions (e.g., Andreas & Jabakhanji, 2023; Whitehead et al., 2017). In contrast, empowerment in embodied economics calls for boosting critical thinking,[37] and more importantly relies on planetary health education (e.g., Baena-Morales & Fröberg, 2023; Guzmán et al., 2021; Spínola, 2023) and institutional mechanisms, such as face-to-face communication and participatory processes, which enable criticism and change at the individual and community levels (e.g., Curato et al., 2017; Maiese & Hanna, 2019; Ostrom, 2010). This brings us to the concept of resilience.

Resilience is much needed to bring stability: "Economies that collapse threaten human flourishing immediately" (Jackson, 2014, p. 179). Resilience is the ability of communities to successfully adapt to difficult situations, adversity, and crises. In essence, resilience emphasizes the temporal dimensions of the transformative processes that should take place in our current ways of being and living, whether in the short or long term. Of course, this entails urgent climate action (SDG 13) as well as technological innovation and better infrastructure (SDGs 9 and 11), but resilience also requires the consideration of a wide range of social processes including visioning and scenario building, social networks, and governance (Folke, 2006). Social networks and governance echo our earlier developments in this book, and are closely linked to inclusivity, sufficiency, and empowerment. Importantly, visioning and scenario-building connect resilience to utopia. Visioning because "utopia is as much about the quest as resilience is about a dynamic process. It is a critical social quest to galvanise change" (Beilin & Wilkinson, 2015, p. 1215). Scenario building because narratives, that reflect forward embodiment, are "a way to express the subjective and symbolic meaning of resilience, enhancing our ability to engage multiple voices and enable self-organising processes to decide what should be made resilient and for whose benefit" (Goldstein et al., 2015, p. 1295).

In the next section, we turn to how human flourishing as understood in embodied economics would transform work and markets.

8.6 Dignified Work and Communities in Embodied Market Utopia

We argued in Chapter 7 that labor in modern capitalism is subject to various forces of abstraction that disembody human effort and creativity in the form of "labor power." Accordingly, embodied economics proposes various institutional arrangements that heal this pathology of capitalism. This amounts to an approach to flourishing as *vita activa*. As we have seen, *vita activa* encompasses three dimensions, *labor* as the reproduction of the body embedded in social relationships, *work* as the crafting of the external world and the creation of objects that become constitutive of a flourishing life, and *action* as active participation in the political life of communities. We have also shown that the dilemma lies in the fact that the current institutional regime contains three paradoxes: That labor in the generic sense is pain; that it is subject to hierarchical rule; and that reproductive labor is viewed as unproductive. These three paradoxes break the link between capitalist labor and flourishing, what Karl Marx called alienation. As we shall see, there are simple institutional solutions that offer a way out. The most fundamental one is Universal Basic Income.[38]

8.6.1 Reclaiming Dignity in Work: Universal Basic Income in Market Utopia

The enhancement of agential powers has been suggested as an effect of markets in the sense that markets are supposed to increase the range of choices and, despite the experience of choice overload, make individual choices more independent of the control of others. Markets can create areas of freedom. But this is only one possibility; for markets can also have the opposite effect, enforcing certain economic activities without leaving much room for choice. This implies that one aspect of agential power (hence empowerment) is whether people can approach markets in an instrumental way, in the sense that they have the power to choose for or against engaging in market exchange, thus subjecting participation in markets to their autonomous choices about how to flourish (hence well-being). The question is whether markets themselves can contribute to enhancing this power of enter and exit. This is certainly the case for those who succeed in markets to the extent that they accumulate enough wealth to be able to withdraw, like the ideal–typical investment banker who sacrifices 20 years of restless trading and then retires. But this is a tiny minority of people.

The general assumption in capitalist societies is that individuals must work in the sense of participating in the labor market, with the only alternative being to join the public sector in the broadest sense, such as civil and military service or religious organizations. This assumption also underlies the notion of the welfare state, even socialism. The welfare state, in principle, benefits only those who, for some "legitimate" reason, cannot participate in the market, such as those who are unemployed, sick, and older adults—where "legitimate" is defined here as legality in the sense of recognized reasons for not being able to work. There are two problems with this: First, it implies that work is a universal human value that must be obeyed; and second, that a certain kind of work is valued more than others, namely wage labor. The latter is also implicit in the notion of social support through the welfare state, as compensation is typically for lost market income, as opposed to other losses.

As we have seen in Chapter 7, this appreciation of work is paradoxical, since, at the same time, economic theory treats work as disutility, that is, as pure suffering. People work only to earn a monetary income to spend on goods of positive utility. Work is a means; consumption is an end. Obviously, this picture is deeply shaped by Judeo-Christian religious conceptions of necessary suffering after the fall from paradise. There is no systematic recognition of work as a meaningful and possibly gratifying activity. In contrast, it is precisely this conception of meaningful work that follows from the notion of agential power and flourishing, because agential power is expressed in action, especially "productive" action, albeit entirely independent of the market context. Production means flourishing, in the literal sense, just as trees produce nuts and fruits, which in turn produce new trees. As said, in the embodied economics view, the ends of work must be included in the scope of agential power. This is commonly called "self-determination:" Alas, for most people, self-determination in work is rarely achieved. This can be summed up in the question of whether their dignity is respected and recognized, even enhanced, in the workplace. This is rarely the case, even in rich countries. For most people in the world, entering into capitalist labor relations means a lack of recognition of their dignity as persons. Even if this is not directly expressed in the form of degrading and disrespectful treatment at work, it is universally reflected in the lack of autonomy people have in deciding whether to enter the labor market, and often what kind of activity they pursue, beyond general orientations such as the field of their education and training.

There is one policy issue that encapsulates all these themes, namely the debate on Universal Basic Income (UBI; van Parijs & Vanderborght, 2019). In our approach, UBI is an essential element of the embodied market utopia because it is a way of transforming markets to contribute to human flourishing and the enhancement of people's agential powers. As said, in the welfare state model, individuals are ultimately forced into the market. In the UBI model, the fiscal apparatus of the welfare state is overhauled to finance UBI, which effectively creates the freedom to choose whether or not to participate in markets. In other words, UBI is the key measure to subject markets to people's agential powers, as it enables them to autonomously judge whether market action contributes to their own flourishing.

We do not delve into the details of financing UBI, as this depends on many factors and cannot be seen as independent of other policy areas (Herrmann-Pillath & Bannas, 2021). Suffice it to say that UBI must be designed as a comprehensive substitute for all other welfare state expenditures related to the replacement of lost market income, thus freeing up a very substantial amount of taxes to finance UBI. In addition, tax reforms that take into account environmental costs and damages, in the widest sense of resource use taxation, as in the earliest UBI conceptions by Thomas Paine (1797/2008, p. 418ff), can also contribute substantially. Finally, there are models of UBI that reduce the need for current spending by only creating entitlements that can be allocated over an individual's life cycle. In other words, financing issues are not a principled constraint in our market utopia, but merely a technical one.

The essential role of UBI results from the fact that it frees people from compulsory market participation, and thus puts all kinds of work on an equal footing. Someone is free to choose between market activity and community service, for example, paving the way to sufficiency. Moreover, as a form of enhancement of agential power, UBI is truly transformative with respect to the labor market and the organization of firms. UBI resolves all three paradoxes of labor under capitalism that we pointed out in the previous chapter (Sect. 7.4).

First, since the decision to enter the labor market is now autonomous, the common assumption of economics that freedom of decision-making implies individual benefits from positive choices holds. This resolves the paradox of labor as pain. However, this argument now transcends markets, and in this, it even radicalizes the economic view: With UBI, participation in markets becomes voluntary. This is a fundamental condition for turning them into institutions that benefit everyone, and promote inclusivity. At the individual level, the important implication is that work is no longer disutility per se, as people autonomously make sense of their decision to enter the labor market.

Second, UBI shifts the balance between market and hierarchy modes of organizing work, thus resolving the paradox of free markets versus hierarchical domination as the default institutional setting for work. Again, we are simply transforming an argument from standard economics, this time from game theory (Elster, 2015, p. 417ff): UBI creates a radically different pattern of external options, thereby directly altering power structures in organizations (hence empowerment). In simplest terms, UBI removes the institutionalized threat of "unemployment" at a stroke, which is a major determinant of power asymmetries in both the labor market and organizations.

Third, UBI offers a free choice between the allocation of individual activities across the spectrum of wage employment, entrepreneurship, and care, thereby neutralizing many fault lines in the current organization of labor, such as gender discrimination against care. UBI enables *vita activa* in a coherent institutional form without discriminating between its three aspects, thus offering a resilient solution to the paradox of considering essential forms of work as "unproductive."

One effect of resolving the second paradox is that, in a market environment conditioned by UBI, companies must adapt by enriching, if not shifting, the hierarchy mode by strengthening the community and reciprocity modes.

8.6.2 Purpose and the Corporation

Universal Basic Income radically changes the setting of companies in markets, as it creates a wide space of outside options for employees, freeing them from the stigma of being unemployed (hence inclusivity). People are free to subordinate themselves to the hierarchy, which means that they now have the countervailing power to leave ("exit"). In the welfare state, unemployment benefits usually do not cover voluntary unemployment: Under the UBI regime, the category of "unemployed" becomes meaningless, since there is a wide range of types of work, some of which involve "employment" and some of which do not.

The implications for business organizations are far-reaching and can be envisioned if one considers current workplaces where skilled workers are in high demand and where work is not easily controlled and depends mainly on personal motivation, such as in certain high-tech companies (Roberts, 2007). The organization of companies would converge on a cooperative model that focuses on the collective flourishing of all members of the organization (Holz, 2018). This has important consequences for defining the goal of the corporation, which in capitalism is to maximize "profit." Looking again at the distinction between means and ends, UBI allows people to choose between different kinds of work, in the market and in other domains. Once you join a company, the means are determined. However, the specific ends of work remain undefined. Can individuals also determine these ends in the corporation? Embodied economics considers three possibilities.

The first is increasingly discussed in public debates, namely the role of the "purpose" of the corporation (Henderson, 2020, p. 85ff; Henderson & Steen, 2015). Even if a worker performs a boring and tedious task in order to earn money, she might feel that she is contributing to a purpose that she endorses, and may therefore regard it as an aspect of her own aspirations—the work itself is "worth the pain." In addition, UBI allows people to freely choose among purposes, including sufficiency, and not just opportunities to earn monetary income. On the other hand, it forces corporate leaders to clearly communicate these purposes and express their commitment to them. This also allows for the development of organizational discourses about purpose that go beyond formal schemes of worker participation.

The second way is to take up a profession. This is a Hegelian turn that has deep historical roots in conceptions of craft as individual vocation (Sennett, 2009). Professions can be defined as a type of purpose to which an individual is committed as an aspect of flourishing. This is independent of corporate goals, but combines purpose with a meaningful personal goal in doing one's profession. An important implication is that the corporation is also a place where individuals can practice their profession as a form of individual flourishing (hence including well-being).

The third way is that UBI neutralizes the personal risks (e.g., job loss) of expressing ethical concerns about corporate practices and whistle-blowing, thus empowering by enhancing agential powers in ethical judgments and actions. This is an important participatory mechanism that subjects corporate governance, as expressed in purposes, to the control of all members of the organization, thereby also promoting inclusivity.

All of these considerations converge on the idea that embodied markets center on the notion of dignified work as an essential element of flourishing and well-being, through inclusivity and empowerment, and enabling sufficiency. Markets are one domain where this is possible, but their productivity allows for the universal recognition of all other kinds of work that people deem important for their flourishing, institutionalized in the form of UBI.

8.6.3 Re-embodying and Re-embedding Market Communities

The Tönnies distinction between community and society diagnoses that, under capitalism, markets are media of disembodiment, defining a domain in which human relations are reduced to instrumental dimensions. This has never been entirely true, but the market ideology of the "Great Society," radically posited by Hayek, certainly suggests and encourages it. In embodied economics, markets can be re-conceptualized as a form of community. The key point is to conceive of markets less as a regime of competition than as a form of cooperation (Herrmann-Pillath & Hederer, 2023). In a regime of cooperation, competition is like a contest for a common good: Consider the National Basketball Association league. The league is a cooperative business venture that stages and performs basketball tournaments for the enjoyment of fans and spectators. It is fiercely competitive, but with well-defined rules. Similarly, we can think of markets as institutional settings in which economic actors compete, but take seriously the economic theorists' adage that this serves a common good. This is neither the "invisible hand" nor the planned economy: It is a "community of advantage" in which economic actors view their competition as a form of cooperation for the common good. Such views are not uncommon. A fascinating example is the "father of Japanese capitalism" Shibusawa Eiichi who famously argued that the main concern of the businessman should be whether his fellow businessmen make profits, because if they do, he will also prosper (Fridenson & Takeo, 2017).

The Polanyian view of re-embedding markets has been interpreted mainly in terms of the welfare state, as in Ruggie's notion of "embedded liberalism" (Ruggie, 1982). Embodied economics opens up the possibility of reinventing markets as communities that contribute to each other's well-being.[39] This is clearly on the public agenda in some places: Organic farming movements, for example, emphasize the local and regional embeddedness of their trade, and this is now even reflected in the marketing campaigns of some large retail chains (e.g., Thompson & Coskuner-Balli, 2007). The idea is to reduce the distance between producer and consumer so that consumers are better informed about the conditions under which food is produced (thereby de-fetishizing commodities; Hudson & Hudson, 2003), and can even identify with their region (Balzano & Vianelli, 2022; Reich et al., 2018). This also enables informed choices about food, for example, in terms of animal welfare. This form of localizing production even allows consumers to experience the life-worlds of producers and other market actors, fostering feelings of inclusivity. With modern social media, such forms of "regionalization" could be virtualized (Holloway, 2002; Schneider et al., 2017).

There are various forms of communities in which markets could be re-embodied and re-embedded. To give an incomplete list, we can think of local and regional markets, which can be extended to virtual marketplaces (e.g., connecting consumers virtually with a coffee-growing community); product- and industry-based user and consumer groups; (producer and consumer) cooperatives; commons; all forms of associations; or the firm as a cooperative enterprise.

Let us briefly discuss some examples that relate to the re-embodiment of labor as mediated by market communities.

The focus on regional markets reflects the special nature of space and place in human life, which is deeply embodied and interactional (Tuan, 2011). The revitalization of regional markets is most often an issue in agriculture, tourism, and other forms of spatially bound economic activity, including regionalized food industries, such as breweries. Obviously, this also points to limitations: Can we imagine the regionalization of smartphone production? This question shows that we cannot discuss single aspects without complementary changes in other domains and economic practices. Regionalization is also widespread in crafts and related services that often resist economies of scale and standardization, such as roofing. One way to broaden the scope of regionalization is to change the way industrial products are designed, in two senses.

First, standardized products may allow for modification and individualization. This combines regionalization with the trend towards individualization of consumption. A fascinating example of this is the individualization of smartphone production in the Shanzhai production model in Shenzhen, which is mostly shunned as intellectual property (IP) theft, but actually shows how even smartphone production allows for artisanal production in small batches (Chubb, 2015; Qin et al., 2019). One technical approach, as in the case of smartphones, is the modularization of technical components, which can be commodified and standardized, but the final assembly according to individual tastes and needs could be done locally. Even if the value chains of the modules are commoditized and globalized, the final production can be localized involving a more direct interaction between skilled craftspeople and consumers. In fact, many products have this potential, but it is stifled by the hegemonic regime of intellectual property (IP) and branding. As we argue in the next section, if IP protection is dismantled, producers' creativity is empowered and can satisfy consumers' apparent desire for product customization, which in turn creates a stronger sense of ownership (and extended self).

Second, standardized products should allow for all kinds of repairs and upgrades that prolong product life—as exemplified by products like FairPhone, places like repair cafés, or websites like iFixit—and can lead to sufficiency (e.g., Beyeler & Jaeger-Erben, 2022; Nesterova & Buch-Hansen, 2023). This has long been called for to reduce waste and resource consumption (e.g., Higgs, 2014) and move away from the Western throwaway lifestyle (e.g., Newman, 2023), but will also contribute to regionalization, since repairs, like cars, are mostly done locally. It also fosters emotional attachments to products as expressions of embodied identity, even as expressions of caring for things (Corwin & Gidwani, 2021; Tronto, 1993). Of course, such examples also show that regionalization goes hand in hand with the strengthening of small and medium-sized enterprises (SMEs) relative to the role of multinational corporations. We will return to this aspect in the next section.

Another form of re-embodying and re-embedding markets is user and consumer communities, which are already much emphasized in the IT sector, where this is partly a means of externalizing the costs of customer support. However, there is also a lot of scope for cooperation among users, which can lead to a rebalancing of agential powers *vis-à-vis* companies, for example when a user community starts to complain publicly about product flaws on a dedicated website (Cova & Pace, 2006). A specific form of consumer community can be found in the (so-called) "sharing economy" (e.g., Belk, 2014). So far, this has mostly been dominated by corporate services, where "sharing" simply means making a product accessible to more people for temporary use, without any real "sharing" among them. This is different when a group of consumers actively cooperates to share a product, such as a neighborhood that owns cars for shared use among its members. Compare, for instance, Zipcar with the car-sharing organization of the Majorna residential district in Göteborg (Bardhi & Eckhardt, 2012; Jonsson, 2007).

Cooperatives are a well-established, institutionalized form of such communities (e.g., Levi & Pellegrin-Rescia, 1997; Parker et al., 2008, p. 61ff). Producer cooperatives combine competition with joint investment and resource sharing (e.g., Bijman & Wijers, 2019). Consumer cooperatives, such as neighborhoods that collectively buy goods from wholesalers and distribute them to their members, have become almost obsolete. Yet they are an effective form of community in two senses (Honneth, 2015, p. 384ff). First, they enhance agential powers, for example, in negotiating with producers, and second, they require deliberative processes in consumer choice, for example, in choosing certain types of products. Beyond cooperatives, an important form of embedding markets is the commons, which can also be seen as a historical origin of cooperatives (e.g., De Moor, 2015), and which we discussed when reflecting on Ostrom's approach. A commons combines various aspects of local resources in a regime of joint management and multiple ownership. For example, when a fishery is institutionalized as a commons, fishing rights are still individualized and fishers compete individually, but they are constrained by rules and quotas set by the community that ultimately owns the commons. The important corollary is that market activity is also monitored and bound by the community.

In sum, as illustrated, there are many ways in which markets can become communities, both in the sense of being embedded in communities and in the sense of operating as communities. Indeed, this has long been recognized theoretically in the context of network analysis of markets, for example, in relation to international ethnic traders (e.g., Landa, 1994), as well as in studies of the role of African American communities in the formation of cooperatives (e.g., Nembhard, 2015; Prieto et al., 2021), or studies of Indigenous management and organization (e.g., Salmon et al., 2023). Nevertheless, mainstream economists have mostly treated community economies as manifestations of market failure (e.g., Gudeman, 1998), characterized by a lack of formal institutions that could sustain a more efficient anonymous market. We turn this argument on its head. But the general argument still holds: The re-embodiment of markets as communities is bound to fail and will not be resilient unless the general institutional framework of markets is radically adjusted.

8.7 Fundamental Institutions of Embodied Market Utopia

As the example of localized production and repair has shown, we cannot analyze institutions in isolation from other institutions, in this case Intellectual Property Rights (IPR) and brands. The current existence of IPRs enshrines the power of corporations globally, and thereby builds formidable obstacles to localization, especially with respect to a key form of economic action in markets: entrepreneurship. Local entrepreneurs are systematically excluded from the use of knowledge, which is free and public by nature, but is enclosed by IPR, whose owner appropriates the rents from that knowledge. The argument that IPRs are necessary to create incentives for innovative entrepreneurship is grossly misleading and contradicted by both theory and historical evidence (Boldrin & Levine, 2008). For example, the Industrial Revolution took place without a fully developed IPR system, and many entrepreneurs were even highly critical of its introduction, which was promoted as a reform of the traditional system of royal privileges to incentivize industrial innovation, but retained the feature of monopolizing markets (Mokyr, 2009a, 2009b). In a cross-country comparison, many industries flourished without IPR protection, such as the chemical and pharmaceutical industries in the late nineteenth and early twentieth centuries, and even the early stages of the rise of the software and digital industries in the late twentieth century. In his famous study of patents commissioned by the US Congress, the liberal economist Fritz Machlup noted that:

> If we did not have a patent system, it would be irresponsible, on the basis of our present knowledge of its economic consequences, to recommend instituting one. But since we have had a patent system for a long time, it would be irresponsible, on the basis of our current knowledge, to recommend abolishing it. (Machlup, 1958, p. 80)

Machlup's argument captures the spirit of many of our subsequent arguments: Our existing institutional regime has been shaped by deep path dependencies over two centuries and is now supported by a dense web of political and economic interests, so changing it seems utterly unrealistic. However, as Machlup's statement shows, this does not mean that an alternative institutional regime, even in the mainstream sense (e.g., Slobodian, 2020), would not be economically feasible. In this respect, we are describing a concrete utopia, such as a world without IPRs as they are currently designed. We live in the institutional regime of capitalism. The embodied market utopia is defined by a set of fundamental institutions and institutional transformations that amount to nothing less than the revolution of capitalism. Since our book focuses on the theoretical foundations and principles of embodied economics, we will not explore these institutional transformations in detail. We will simply present them in a nutshell.[40]

As we have seen, one of these transformations is the introduction of UBI. In essence, UBI requires the radical transformation of the welfare state in terms of (a) unemployment benefits, and (b) the pension system. The healthcare system is only affected by UBI in situations where there are transfer payments because of inability to work due to disability, which is another mechanism to replace lost income. This transformation is motivated by two reasons. First, the welfare state treats welfare in the hierarchy mode and enforces participation in the labor market. Second, resources are needed to finance UBI.

This raises the question of whether and how the tax system needs to be overhauled, if only to ensure the fiscal power to restructure the role of the market in society: Basically, all tax revenues depend on GDP, which makes modern states reliant on economic growth. This link must be severed. As mentioned above, the classical solution was already presented by Paine, at that time referring to land rent (Paine, 1797/2008, p. 416ff). This shows that taxation is important not only in terms of the relative shares in the allocation and appropriation of economic resources between the government and the private sector, but also in terms of directly shaping the institutional forms of the economy and related real activities.[41]

Land represents natural resources in general. Accordingly, a fundamental transformation is to shift the tax base from one based on market income to one based on resource use, which is itself an expression of the re-embodiment of markets. The new tax system rests on two pillars. With the transition to capitalism, modern tax systems focused on income as a monetary category, reflecting the central role of the rate of return on capital: Even wages can be considered in this framework as a return on human capital. The new tax system we propose shifts from an income tax to a consumption tax, which focuses directly on the consumption of resources through monetary expenditures.[42] The consumption tax leaves savings tax-free until they are spent on consumption, and correspondingly leaves investment tax-free, until the resulting returns are spent on final consumption. The consumption tax has been advocated by many economists: An important argument is that it directly dampens incentives for wasteful status competition through luxury goods, since it can also be designed as a progressive tax. In designing the tax, a key measure is the legal definition of a clear distinction between consumption and investment goods, so that items such as luxury cars are not declared as "investment goods" by companies that purchase vehicles for business purposes, as is the case today. Here, as in many other cases, the detailed design of the institutions ultimately depends on political decisions and thus on the involvement of the empowered community.

The second pillar is a tax on resource use, as envisaged by Paine. This reinstates the physiocratic doctrine that only agriculture can be taxed, since this can be conceptualized in terms of the modern view that all life on Earth and all human activity is ultimately based on the continuous inflow of solar energy, which is, therefore, the ultimate source of value in the material sense.[43] Every other source of energy is dependent on it, except nuclear energy in all its forms. This is especially true of carbon-based energy, which is a storage of past inflows of solar energy. Since all other forms of human resource use involve material transformations that consume energy, the simplest form of resource-use tax is a universal energy tax that treats all forms of energy equally, including renewables and nuclear. This reflects the insight that economic growth, as an expansion of human appropriation of the planet, ultimately depends on energy throughput (Herrmann-Pillath, 2015). Unlike the consumption tax, the energy tax also covers investments. Energy cannot be substituted; it can only be saved in relative terms. Therefore, the tax base is stable and reliable, although it also incentivizes less resource use in the economy. Note that here we are emphasizing resource use in general, not distinct forms of energy use. Indeed, different sources of energy (e.g., solar, nuclear) may be used in the production process. This means that, in addition to the resource-use tax, a tax on carbon emissions can be applied to non-renewable energy sources.

A very important implication of the energy tax is that the relative prices of energy and labor are shifted in favor of labor, since capital also becomes relatively more expensive, as capital formation also requires energy throughput: Capital is not a substitute for energy. By comparison, the direct energy consumption of human labor is minuscule. Thus, the energy tax drives the intensification of labor in the market-based domains of the economy, in all its forms, with implications for the social status and appreciation of human work. For example, mass production with huge capital and energy expenditures is disincentivized, while craftspersonship is favored.[44] We are familiar with such economies, such as Japan on the eve of the transition to capitalism, where crafts flourished to an admirable degree. The "Great Divergence" between Imperial China and Europe can be explained mainly by the price differences of energy and labor (Allen, 2009).

The re-embodiment of the economy focuses on the role of human beings within planetary boundaries. This must be reinforced by key institutional transformations that place human beings at the center of economic action.[45] In this regard, a defining feature of capitalism was the rise of a peculiar form of investment channeled through the modern corporation. This was accompanied by two major legal transformations: First, the creation of the public corporation as a legal person[46]; second, the limited liability that protects the private wealth of investors in such a corporation (Pistor, 2019), the fundamental importance of which should not be underestimated. As emphasized by Nicholas Murray Butler (1912, p. 82):

> I weigh my words, when I say that in my judgment the limited liability corporation is the greatest single discovery of modern times, whether you judge it by its social, by its ethical, by its industrial, or, in the long run – after we understand it and know how to use it, – by its political effects. Even steam and electricity are far less important than the limited liability corporation, and they would be reduced to comparative impotence without it. (cited in Foster, 2017, p. 111)

Corporate legal personality and limited liability are legal means of abstracting the investment process, creating a duality between original entrepreneurship and the role of financial investors (Ireland, 2010; Preda, 2005). The latter are primarily interested in the rate of return on capital, while the former are Schumpeterian actors driven by many other human motivations, with the desire for monetary profit often secondary (Schumpeter, 1912/2006). Thus, the embodied economy restores the role of the entrepreneur and dismantles the construct of the financial investor, or, in other words, the "capitalist" as a form of institutional action in the economy.

This transformation involves several measures. The first is to abolish the legal form of limited liability as such: Full personal liability means individual responsibility for economic action, which in turn implies embodiment, that is closing the loop between action and outcome, cognitively and emotionally.[47] Limited liability is always defended as a means to incentivize risk-taking that supposedly creates beneficial outcomes for society, but is in fact nothing more than a socialization of the costs of individual risk-taking, which is seen as legitimate even in anti-socialist capitalism. However, this is only an ideologically motivated belief and is certainly questionable, given the destructive impact of risk-taking economic growth on all life on Earth. Full personal liability is the key legal form for the re-embodiment of economic action, as the entrepreneur must consider all possible outcomes of her action in terms of her personal situation—consider, for instance, how risk feels different when one is personally liable.

With full personal liability, the pillar on which the modern corporation and its associated capital market rest is toppled. This is the aspect that seems the most transformative, given current widespread assumptions about how an economy works, even though it is formally a simple step that can be accomplished with a single stroke of the pen that annuls the laws that define limited liability. It is not unrealistic, however, since such economies have existed for most of human history, including in Europe and the United States until the mid-nineteenth century. Limited liability and the modern corporation are pathological forms of disembodied markets that have grown in importance for less than two centuries, perhaps even less than one century as they became dominant with the hegemony of the US in the global economy. This is evident in the strength of the family business in all advanced economies, which often retains the institutional form of full personal liability as a means of cementing family ownership of the business.

There is still a strong argument that limited liability is necessary to encourage innovation with beneficial outcomes. This is straightforward to refute, since limited liability in its current form is designed to protect the interests of capitalist investors (Standing, 2016), paving the way for managerial feudalism (Graeber, 2020). On the contrary, the instrument of limited liability can be used in the public interest.[48] That is, the concept of the "public corporation" can be taken seriously in the sense that there are public corporations with a public purpose: The socialization of risk in the form of limited liability is reciprocally justified by, and must be legally tied to, the satisfaction of the public interest as determined by a participatory political process. In principle, this follows the legal form of a foundation with a public purpose, which would include the possibility of participation in the form of limited liability investments.[49]

The abolition of limited liability is a powerful means of de-financialization, since all forms of derivatives and other legal constructs for financial investment would simply implode, along with the corporate forms associated with them, such as investment banks and hedge funds.[50] De-financialization reinstates the role of classical banking, personified by the private banker. Banks would mainly play the role of loan agencies financed by deposits, and of intermediaries between entrepreneurial actors for joint and cooperative projects. This implies a revival of the regional role of banks, which is still vigorous in American community banks or German savings banks. Regionalization is a form of re-embodying finance in the sense of re-embedding it regionally and locally. It also promotes institutional diversity in banks, such as a renewal of the cooperative movement.

Rethinking the role of banks raises the issue of the reform of the monetary system. Embodied economics aligns with a long tradition of monetary reform proposals put forward by leading economists over the past century, such as the Graham Plan.[51] Details differ and do not matter here, as all of these proposals aim to contain or abolish private money creation in the banking sector and favor a narrow banking system. These reforms also revive the role of the state in issuing money as a public good.

This is just one aspect of the restructuring of the role of the distinction between private and public in the economy, which is not congruent with the distinction between market and government, as is often done in the mainstream economics tradition. The "public" encompasses a wide range of institutional forms, from cooperatives to local governments, national governments, and supranational entities. Public actors may operate in markets or through other institutional forms.

This brings us to another key element in the re-embodiment of the economy, which is a radical reform of the property system, as adumbrated in the section on property (Chapter 7). The distinction is not simply between private and public, but between the four modes of appropriation, which allows for flexible adaptation of institutional forms. The general rule is to "de-abstract" the relationship between people and objects of appropriation. There are several key concerns, focusing mainly on the complexity of certain classes of objects. We assess this complexity in terms of actual patterns of resource use by various actors, that is, in terms of the mode of possession. For many and important resources, possession is often highly diversified, and in general, the current property regime tends to dispossess most actors in favor of one single proprietor (so-called private ownership). In general, the goal of transformation is to protect the interests and needs of all possessors by transforming the shared key resource into an inalienable good, that is, by removing it from the scope of market transactions. In principle, this means creating commons in the sense of Ostrom (1990; see also, Dardot & Laval, 2019). Hence, a fundamental difference between the embodied market economy and the capitalist market is that the latter is based on private property in the sense outlined in the previous chapter, while the former is grounded in commons as a fundamental institutional form of appropriation. This reflects the fact that in order for markets to operate efficiently for the common good, it is necessary to have a wide range of public goods that are enshrined in the institution of the commons.[52] The concept of commons leaves much room for the detailed institutional design of individual rights of resource use, including rights of alienation through markets (Schlager & Ostrom, 1992).

One of the most important cases is land, as it is the universal resource needed for all economic action, and even the use of solar energy inflows is constrained by the availability of land (Herrmann-Pillath, 2023). Land is factually possessed by all members of the local ecosystem, including its use by migratory species such as some birds. From the perspective of embodiment and flourishing, the institutional design must recognize these various uses and their associated needs. The appropriate institutional form is the commons, in which the dimensions of ownership, property, and possession are arranged on the basis of mutual agreement among all members of the commons. A fundamental condition, however, is that alienability through markets, as enabled by property, is bounded by ownership: The ultimate owner of the commons is the local ecosystem, and it cannot be alienated. That is, the commons should determine which sub-rights can be subject to institutional forms of property and possession. This includes the possibility that some rights of possession, that is, the right to use the resource in a certain way, may also become alienable property rights, a constellation known from many commons—for example, fishing rights in a fishery commons may be alienable via markets, but not the fishery as such.

There are other important resources that manifest the complexity of resource use, and where the legal form of property has been deployed to drive a process of abstraction that is expropriating. This is true of a central area of modern capitalism, the system of intellectual property, as discussed at the beginning of this section. Knowledge and ideas are complex resources, both in their production and use, and mostly qualify as so-called "public goods" (e.g., Foray, 2004). In embodied economics, IPR are viewed as an artificial institutional form that reduces this complexity for profitable use. Re-embodiment requires the radical abolition of such rights and the transformation of the system into a regime of sharing and mutual recognition, as it is mostly applied in modern academia. This position has been defended by many mainstream economists, so, on second thought, it seems less radical than it appears (Boldrin & Levine, 2008). The defense of the existing IPR system rests primarily on the argument that monetary incentives are necessary to sustain high rates of innovation, including the need for financing, as in the case of pharmaceuticals. In our embodied market utopia, these financing needs must be justified in the public interest and are met by public corporations, as sketched above. For innovation in general, the same argument applies, as in today's open-source digital industries: Dismantling the IPR system unleashes the dynamics of diverse individual and collective creativity. There are related arguments or other cases, involving education, health care, and basic infrastructure (Uzawa, 2009). In all these areas, the commons framework can be used to create flexible institutional arrangements while keeping the basic resources inalienable.

Our embodied market utopia needs to be fleshed out in many ways. That said, the sketch so far highlights two main points. The first is that the utopia is reachable and concrete, because the legal framework is what matters. Changing the law changes the way the economy is performed.[53] This was also true of capitalism as an alternative utopia in the past. Capitalism succeeded mainly through legal transformations, so why should our market utopia fail? Failure is an expression of political power structures: Capitalism was a project of powerful elites who subjugated the majority of people to the new regime, and did not anticipate all the consequences for them, even though many resisted feeling the immediate impact on their lives. Our market utopia can succeed if it is endorsed by a democratic movement that overcomes capitalism (Curato et al., 2017), and creates the political consensus for legal transformations,[54] such as a gradual transition to full personal liability—for concrete measures of transformation such as changing the tax code, see Bannas and Herrmann-Pillath (2020).

The second point is that this is an embodied market utopia in the sense that the various institutional forms complement and reinforce each other in their performative effects. Reforming individual institutions while maintaining the capitalist system in other respects cannot work. For example, Islamic finance is a de-financialized regime because Sharia law prohibits the charging of interest and the use of financial instruments that do not relate to real transactions, which resembles some aspects of our recommended institutional "crafting." However, it is not competitive in the current financial system, which is biased against such alternatives.

In sum, the embodied market utopia is a political utopia, that is, given our current political conditions. But while the political obstacles may seem insurmountable, "political" actually means that we are free to choose. We are not talking about a desire for paradise, quite the contrary: The embodied economy remains a world of hard work and challenges for the material improvement of our lives and or those of other creatures. Yet, we toil together, driven by the spirit of making the world a place where every living being can flourish.

8.8 Conclusion

A striking feature of the embodied market utopia is that most of our proposals are familiar from the work of eminent economists, often even from the mainstream of their time. For example, variants of UBI have been proposed by economists of all political leanings, albeit for different reasons (van Parijs & Vanderborght, 2019, p. 70ff). In this respect, our utopia is "concrete" because there is this potential for agreement with economists across the board, so there is a "hope of possible" (Bloch, 1959/1986). The "utopian" dimension is inherent in the comprehensive transformative change of the entire economic system that we propose: Someone who welcomes UBI does not necessarily endorse our recommendations when it comes to abolishing the IPR system. But the utopian impulse is "transgressive" (criticism), "transformative" (change), and "totalizing" (Moylan, 2020): The simultaneous implementation of all elements is what qualifies our thinking as utopian, and this utopia is fundamentally concrete because the adoption of these measures as such is feasible and doable. There are no flying horses in our embodied market utopia, not even fancy visions of fetishized technologies-to-come that would help build net-zero castles in the air.

This observation leads us to consider what defines the essential difference between our approach to economics and the conventional view, also in the specific sense of asking, what defines the role of economists, and more broadly of social and behavioral scientists, in practice, and what is taught to students who want to understand economic life? What would teachers do if they followed our prescriptions? This also motivates us to reflect on some of the limitations of our work, and to envision future research agendas.

The defining feature of our approach is embodiment, for sure. The question is how this view changes the performative role of economic concepts in shaping the way we see and do the economy. Why does it matter if we know about conceptual blending or Fiske's typology of social relational models? Let us look at the example of surrogate motherhood, which stands for the many examples of contested and repugnant markets showcased in economics. In doing so, we should not forget that what is considered "repugnant" in the first place is open to interpretation and social framing: Why isn't a market in animal body parts universally repugnant, but only to a minority of vegetarians? We can approach the market for surrogate motherhood in terms of standard market design, emphasizing the role of information, efficiency, free individual choice, and so on. Typically, this will lead to recommendations to liberalize this market. Some, if not many, economists, will criticize the interference of other considerations, probably as misguided moral traditions, and, therefore, even justify their view as "liberal" in both the economic and political sense.[55]

Embodied economics takes a different approach because the very notion of embodiment is transdisciplinary in the first place. This means that we do not approach the market *in abstracto*, treating the different parties as rational economic agents, but as flesh-and-blood actors. Thus, embodied economics directly integrates various disciplinary knowledge from psychology, sociology, anthropology, and so on when looking at the surrogacy market. All of this can be combined to approach the market in terms of the market feelings that accompany the institutional actions of various actors. This requires research methods that are usually neglected in conventional economics, such as qualitative research involving participant observation and in-depth interviews as used by Ostrom, for example. At the end of the day, what matters is how real human actors feel about the market for surrogate motherhood, how human dignity can be defended, and how human flourishing can be promoted. This inclusion of real-world actors in the picture is defined not only in methodological terms, but also, and even predominantly, in political terms: Embodied economics does not celebrate markets as markets designed by experts pretending to have an all-seeing view from nowhere, but aims to engage in the political processes of crafting markets. In fact, this is already best practice in areas such as ecological transformation. In this field, stakeholder engagement and the integration of diverse knowledge systems, both expert and Indigenous, as illustrated by the "Two-Eyed Seeing" approach described by Elder Albert Marshall (e.g., Redvers et al., 2022), are a must, even in public calls for research projects (IUCN, 2020). To return to the question of surrogacy, the embodied economics approach rejects the "womb-as-capital metaphor" whereby the embodied subject (here, the mother) is replaced by the "masculine subject position of contracting agent" essential to the neoclassical conception of such commercial arrangements (Hewitson, 2001, p. 223). Rather, embodied economics contends that we must systematically recognize that the neoclassical theoretical distancing abstracted from the moral and political realities of economic life is not possible. The moral and political dimensions of economic life are an integral part of the theory.

This example reveals that one limitation of our book is that we did not go into the details of how embodied economics is actually done, in terms of specific research methods. We have shown that, to a large degree, the performativity of conventional economics is mediated by research methods, such as behavioral economics, which defines empirical topics as "anomalies," or experimental economics, which decontextualizes the setting of action in the laboratory. How do the research methods of embodied economics contribute to performing the economy differently from the forces of disembodiment that emanate from the neoclassical model? This is an important direction for future research. As said, this is not reinventing the wheel, as the methods are readily available in the disciplines of the social and behavioral sciences, extending into fields such as biology and ecology. Indeed, a key difference between the conventional view and embodied economics is that the latter does not define itself in terms of a specific set of methods, as the former tends to do, for example in distinguishing behavioral economics from experiments in economic psychology with the use of monetary payoffs. If not method, what else defines disciplinary identity? In the embodied view, it must be the specific material and social context in which embodied human action unfolds. As our discussion of Hayek made clear, this is the market (Herrmann-Pillath & Hederer, 2023). The difference between embodied economics and the conventional view is that markets are treated as real-world institutional entities and networks of contextualized actions involving specific artifacts, including money.

Here we diagnose another limitation of our book: We have not given much detail to the workings of markets in this sense, since our focus has been on preparing the fundamentals for reframing them analytically. However, the potential is obvious: Take, for example, the discussion of trader Bill in relation to our new view of money. There are rich implications for thinking about the institutions and regulations of financial markets, for instance when it comes to risk-taking.[56] The method of embodied economics can be "mechanistical" as defined in Chapter 2, eschewing abstract models of markets and inquiring into specific mechanisms that explain particular actions and their consequences. In our book, we have only introduced general types of mechanisms, such as cognitive blending, and shown exemplary applications. For example, assetification is one type of mechanism in real-world markets which may result from introducing certain kinds of incentives and accounting procedures in a social field, such as health care. Embodied economics approaches this not in terms of standard notions of efficiency, but in terms of effects on actor identities and agential powers, and eventually in terms of flourishing. The mechanism of assetification needs to be contextualized as it works differently in this field than in, say, finance, or art. In this sense, our book often operates in its own modus of abstraction, focusing on generic mechanisms. Ultimately, doing embodied economics brings us closer to the methods of the anthropology of economic life (Stafford, 2020; see also, Lahlou, 2017).

One issue where embodiment is extremely important to consider is inequality. After Thomas Piketty (2013) published his book on inequality in 2013, economics became aware of the benign neglect of inequality and all related social issues in the hegemonic view of the discipline that emerged after the 1970s (Boushey et al., 2017). Inequality was normatively neutralized, and mostly seen as a necessary property of an economic system that was incentive-compatible in reference to universal goals such as growth and innovation. The fact that inequality is endogenous in the important sense that it also defines the agential powers of actors participating in the economy was obscured by the disembodied models of standard economics. As we have seen, the institution of money implies that even in the simplest and most abstract toy model of an integrated market system, inequality in the form of power differentials is a necessary feature. These power differentials interact with other determinants of inequality in a social field, which often even leverage the market mechanisms, and cement inequalities in the form of persistent stratification. Just think of how wealth affects patterns of enrollment at US Ivy League universities, and how the (so-called) "human capital" acquired there impacts future income and social status (Chetty et al., 2023).

Embodied economics approaches inequality in relation to markets and market mechanisms, and how these imply the institutionalization of inequality, analyzed in terms of the Aoki-Bourdieu model.[57] This view reinstates a classical category of political economy; social class. There are many forms of social stratification, and we interpret social class as a stratification deeply implicated in market processes and outcomes. This is only hinted at in our book and is certainly a major topic for future research. However, there is already a rich body of research in other areas, especially when it comes to issues such as discrimination and stigma, where the relationship between social class and embodiment has long been investigated. Economic models have almost systematically ignored this intersectionality of inequality—even Marx did not discuss gender in relation to social class (Federici, 2004/2021). In this sense, the first challenge is simply to integrate this research into the embodied economic library of established knowledge.

This is also an example relevant to our initial question: What does embodied economics teach? This is a very serious and challenging question. Our modern market system is deeply shaped by the economic knowledge of the past, and so people who want to study economic life and work as economists, or more broadly as social and behavioral scientists, would be well advised to have some understanding of conventional economics. As many students know, this is not an easy task. How can you free up your mind and time to expand that knowledge through embodied economics, or better yet, how can you include it as a technical and historical part of embodied economics? For example, in assessing the effects of markets on human well-being, embodied economics focuses on flourishing which can be methodologically substantiated by various approaches, such as the capability approach. However, students need to know how GDP is calculated, and be able to suggest specific improvements, such as accounting, for finance. Moreover, embodied economics approaches GDP in the wider institutional context, for instance by exploring the performative effects of GDP narratives in explaining business cycles (Herrmann-Pillath & Hederer, 2023, p. 344ff). In other words, students will learn not only about GDP as a statistical system, but also about its institution, that is, the political economy of the institutional action of national accounting. Again, there is no need to reinvent the wheel, as this is well-known from other disciplines such as political science. The point will be to think about GDP in light of the impact of economic growth on living beings, for instance. As discussed in this chapter, it would be hard to accept that +3 °C of global warming could be "optimal" in terms of GDP, unless one looks at economic life through the lens of disembodied and abstract neoclassical models.

As we can see, embodied economics can build its canon and curriculum to a considerable extent by receiving and organizing contributions to the study of markets from other disciplines, as we have already done in this book, and as is reflected in textbooks such as Carsten Herrmann-Pillath and Christian Hederer (2023), and Neva Goodwin and colleagues (2023a, 2023b).[58] This is not an isolated claim: It can be illustrated by the work and claims of George Akerlof and Robert Shiller (2009), Deidre McCloskey (2016), Elinor Ostrom (2010), or Vernon Smith and Bart Wilson (2019), to name a few. One of the fundamental differences between their (diverse) perspectives and ours is that, in embodied economics, the unifying focus is on markets as real-world institutional assemblages, combined with the principles of embodiment as outlined in Chapters 4 and 5 of this book. The latter has a strong systematizing epistemic power, as we can often reformulate and perhaps develop other disciplinary views. For example, many approaches to performativity adopt another form of abstraction, which might be called the "language fallacy," treating language and other symbolic systems, or even culture in general, as disembodied. We argue for an embodied approach to performativity, as our discussion of Searle in Chapter 6 has shown. Here, foundational research in embodied economics proves remarkably constructive.

In addition to this, we must also acknowledge that some aspects of this performativity may be difficult to explain in terms of embodiment alone: For instance, in Chapter 7, we argued that workers are commodified (and dehumanized) on the one hand, and commodities are anthropomorphized (and fetishized) on the other. In both cases, this is the result of embodiment, which can be analyzed in terms of metaphor or conceptual blending, whereby "people are commodities," and "commodities are people." Here, however, embodiment leads to a reverse process: People commodify other people but would anthropomorphize (some) commodities. This is an insight that we point out in the book, but, beyond sense-making, as people who feel commodified (or alienated at work) might look for meaning in their consumption, the whole process is not yet fully conceptualized because we do not have a complete theory of consumption in embodied economics as outlined so far in this book. This may require an analysis of the performative aspects of markets beyond their monetary aspects: It is very likely, for example, that the anthropomorphization of commodities is the by-product of the advertising and marketing techniques we have mentioned, such as brand personality, and that these are inwardly embodied.[59] Nonetheless, this leaves open the question of the extent to which people would anthropomorphize commodities, if they did not find themselves commodified (or alienated). In other words, it remains to be clarified whether "people are commodities" and "commodities are people" are metaphors and blends that come together, and balance each other out within the market, or whether they could exist independently of each other.[60]

Incidentally, this question raises another issue: In this chapter, we argue that markets should be grounded in communities, so as to restore economic exchange as a means of serving other people's needs in order for them to flourish, rather than as an end that people must serve for the sake of growing profits. That said, markets are still part of our embodied market utopia, and while some of the proposals we offer, such as UBI, might ring-fence their performative effects when it comes to commodifying people at work, we have to acknowledge that commodification can reach into every sphere of human activity, even when these are inspired by progressive ideas: From sustainability to "wokism" to activism and feminism, everything can be commodified and co-opted by the market (e.g., Banet-Weiser et al., 2020; Bhagwat et al., 2020; Mirzaei et al., 2022; Mukherjee & Banet-Weiser, 2012). This means that although these social movements are community-based, they have nonetheless become a business, shedding their radicalism, and diluting it, more or less subtly, in advertising and marketing techniques. This could be due to the capitalist aspect of markets, but this remains to be proven; after all, propaganda and manipulation techniques have a long history, older than capitalism.

This leads us to an additional observation: We identify capitalism, especially its neoliberal aspects, as one of the main underpinnings of disembodiment. This is in full alignment with embodiment theories. Although most of them remain a-political, especially those on embodied cognition, which seem to develop in a political vacuum, embodiment theories emphasize the situated aspects of cognition, so it is not surprising that the way we think reflects the way we live: When everything around us can be seen as a commodity, people tend to be seen as commodities. One issue, of course, is to characterize whether embodiment and disembodiment are discrete, or whether there are some degrees of embodiment and disembodiment on a continuum, like the difference between concrete and abstract, which is relative, not absolute—something is more concrete, or less abstract, than something else. Another question is to specify whether disembodiment operates only under the influence of economic artifacts such as money, or whether it can operate by other means. For instance, the "male gaze" that objectifies and commodifies women, does not only occur in advertisements and movies, but is also part of their daily lives, including in non-economic environments (e.g., King, 2020). The dehumanization of women, when exchanged like goods between families, has been a historical feature of societies, capitalist or not, Western as well as non-Western, as illustrated by the debates surrounding Claude Lévi-Strauss' (1949/1969) analysis of kinship (e.g., Rubin, 1975). Embodiment, as we have said, is political and lies at the heart of society, economic life being in many ways a magnifier of the issues involved.[61]

This discussion also reveals that the critique of capitalism does not imply that alternatives are necessarily better. Thinkers such as Georg Simmel already pointed to the ambivalences of capitalism, and judged phenomena such as the increasing areas of individual freedom as a positive achievement. This connects to the general idea of "progress" that is often invoked when discussing the past three centuries of transformations and revolutions (for such a "neo-Whiggish" account, see Pinker, 2018).[62] At a time when populism, obscurantism, and demagoguery are infecting the liberal democracies that have been hailed as the pinnacle of this development, disorientation is growing and being exploited by phenomena such as the rise of China and the increasing distance of non-Western political elites from the claims of civilizational leadership by the so-called "West." Yet, the challengers themselves, of course, are often authoritarian and populist of their own making. Embodied economics retreats from the claim that "experts" (a modern variant of Plato's philosopher-kings) have privileged knowledge of what is best for society and cedes ground to "the political," idealized as the inclusive and deliberative discourse in communities of actors who autonomously determine their own fate. Alas, this ideal of the political in *vita activa* is itself a utopian goal pursued in the current political struggles of real-world societies. Who is included, who can self-determine, or who gets access to the resources for participation in deliberation, such as education, is mostly decided by endemic conflicts over political power. In this situation, science in general, and embodied economics in particular, has a responsibility to engage in these struggles with a critical voice. We cannot claim privileged knowledge, but we can do our best to adopt the virtue of impartiality that was highlighted in Adam Smith's (1759/2002) *Theory of Moral Sentiments*.[63]

Finally, let us take stock of embodiment by applying some of its lessons to ourselves: This book was written by two white, heterosexual, cisgender European male scholars who do not experience motor disability and who are both well past their late twenties. This is common in academia, and we believe it also influences the way we think, in at least two ways.

First, the content of this book outwardly embodies what we have inwardly embodied in Western scholarship: Many of our references are Western-centric, collected on Western samples by Western scholars in rich countries, and many of our concepts were coined by German (e.g., Arendt, Hegel, Marx, Simmel, Tönnies, Weber) and French thinkers (e.g., Bourdieu, Foucault, Merleau-Ponty) from the last century (or earlier), which somewhat says as much about us, a German and a French academic trained in culturally and socially shaped educational systems, as it does about economic life. Despite our interest (FB) and expertise (CHP) in non-Western thought (e.g., China), we have not integrated non-Western theories of embodiment, and in the future, embodied economics will have to refer to them as well. As exemplified by Varela and colleagues (2016) in *The Embodied Mind*, embodiment as understood by some phenomenologists such as Merleau-Ponty, can converge with readings on Buddhism.

Second, growing up in Europe as white, heterosexual, cisgender males who do not experience motor disability, our bodies have largely remained "transparent" to us in economic and social life, in the sense that we have not been victims of gender discrimination, or racism, for instance. Given that most economic models have been developed by white male Western scholars who are celebrated by capitalist patriarchal societies,[64] it is not surprising that embodiment does not seem to matter much to them. Perhaps their disembodied models reflect the "transparency" of their bodies in economic and social life. This is why embodied economics is a political economy, a gentle reminder of our privileges, and a call for more self-reflexivity, which is not possible without our bodies and the bodies of others.

Notes

1. Like Marx, Saint-Simon, Fourier, and Owen rejected the term "utopia" because at the time it was associated with the idea of impossibility (Levitas, 1990/2011).
2. See Nelson (1992, 1997) for a complementary critique from a feminist perspective.
3. For instance, the first basic principle of deep ecology states: "The well-being and flourishing of human and nonhuman Life on Earth have value in themselves (synonyms: intrinsic value, inherent value). These values are independent of the usefulness of the nonhuman world for human purposes" (Naess & Sessions, 1986).
4. In mainstream thinking, this idea has been ventilated in Mill's notion of markets as "communities of advantage," which has recently been taken up by Sugden (2018), where he takes a step towards embodiment in relation to behavioral economics.
5. For a brief overview, see Schnädelbach (2000, p. 271ff), and on Hegel's economic thought, see Priddat (1990).
6. "To expect, indeed, that the freedom of trade should ever be entirely restored in Great Britain, is as absurd as to expect that an Oceana or Utopia should ever be established in it" (Smith cited in Viner, 1949, p. 361).
7. "They still dream of experimental realization of their social utopias, of founding isolated 'phalanstères,' of establishing 'Home Colonies,' of setting up a 'Little Icaria' (…) and to realize all these castles in the air they are compelled to appeal to the feelings and purses of the bourgeois" (Marx & Engels, 1848/1988, p. 241). On Marx's "utopophobia," see Wolff and Leopold (2021).
8. "Utopia. *n.* an idealized, perfect society. Coined by English statesman and author Thomas More (1478–1535) in his speculative political fiction *Utopia* (1516), the term is of Greek derivation (literally, 'no place'). By contrast, the term dystopia, coined in

about 1950, refers to an imaginary society of nightmarish conditions" (APA, 2023).

9. Of course, this does not mean that the definition of utopia proposed by Levitas (1990/2011) is not without limitations. For instance, Stillman (1991, p. 221) points out that this definition is "consciously broad" "in order to allow for historical variability as well as to encourage scholarly diversity," but this desire could be seen as "too broad," "including as it does almost every particular feeling of dissatisfaction each individual has," while it could also be seen as "too narrow," "downplaying reason too much and ignoring the dreaming and play, the complex logic and intricately-articulated ideals, that can go into creating an extensively-described model society" (Stillman, 1991, p. 221). The implications of Levitas' (1990/2011) broad definition have also been criticized by Kumar (2010) who questions whether such an approach is sometimes still useful when applied to some cultural artifacts. As many utopian scholars have pointed out, it is very likely that there is no conclusive definition of utopia that could exhaust all its subtleties (Bell, 2017): "anyone who attempts to define Utopia quickly learns that conundra, ambiguities, and ideological differences surface at every turn. How descriptively complete must something be to be a Utopia? From whose point of view is it to be evaluated as a 'good' or 'better' place? Must it be realizable (and, if so, on whose view of how the world functions)?" (Stillman, 1991, p. 220).
10. See contra for its Western aspects: Claeys and Sargent (1999), Dutton (2010), Longxi (2002), and Sargent (2010).
11. Kumar (1991) also developed the concept of utopian thought to analyze some utopian dimensions of social life beyond the literary genre *à la* Thomas More. In this respect, utopian thought is more common and fragmentary, as it does not describe a society in full operation, and takes the form of visionary expressions ranging from abstract principles to more concrete implementations. According to him, the "territory of utopia" need not "be restricted to utopia as a form of writing, imaginative or theoretical" (Kumar, 2010, p. 562). In light of the existence of "glocalized" or "local" utopia, he concluded that "More's project – an imaginative rendering of a whole society – was not perhaps that of today's local activists" (Kumar, 2010, p. 564), and added that "what we might call their 'banal utopianism,' the utopianism of mundane,

everyday existence, thought through in the form of a whole way of life, must surely have a place in the utopian tradition" (Kumar, 2010, p. 564). Kumar's position in this article inspired Schiffer's (2018) empirical work on "glocalized utopia" (here, an ecovillage) as a form of everyday utopianism that emerges "in the face of an agency- and imagination-limiting globalizing neoliberalism" (Schiffer, 2018, p. 67).

12. The third function of utopia identified by Levitas (1990/2011) is the compensation function. When it is compensatory, utopia is associated with daydreaming and escapism which may actually disengage people from their society and encourage inaction (Fernando et al., 2018; Levitas, 1990/2011). Nevertheless, empirical findings suggest that utopia is more likely to be a catalyst for social change than a source of escapism (Fernando et al., 2018).
13. According to Bloch (1986), who coined the distinction between abstract and concrete utopia, when abstract, utopia is the realm of "wishful thinking" and is confined to fantasies or inner (day-)dreams of ideal alternative worlds. Note that, as Kumar (2010, p. 562) indicates, for Bloch "wishful thinking" "does not carry the usual pejorative overtones." See also Boldyrev (2023).
14. In Greek, "metaphora" means "transport," and metaphors can be seen as transporting an experience which is mapped onto another. Narratives also transport, but in a different way: They transport into a story, which is called narrative transportation (Gerrig, 1993; Green & Brock, 2000).
15. As Polanyi (1944/2001) has argued, capitalism is already a form of utopia, but disembodied. There is even an aspect of "concreteness," as Beckert (2016) has shown in detail. Entrepreneurial action in capitalism is driven by visions of techno-economic transformations of society in the name of progress.
16. Research shows that the mainstream "top" journals in economics—and the same is true for management and finance—do not really consider sustainability-related issues (e.g., Diaz-Rainey et al., 2017; Harley & Fleming, 2021; Oswald & Stern, 2019; van 't Klooster, 2023): "We point out in this paper that academic economists have contributed disturbingly little to discussions about climate change. We suggest that economists are failing the world – and their own grandchildren. As one example, the Quarterly Journal of Economics, which is currently the most-cited journal in the field

of Economics, has never published an article on climate change" (Oswald & Stern, 2019).

17. At the time, this was "the most probable baseline scenario (no climate policies) taking into account the exhaustible character of non-renewable fuels" and which was "more likely than not to result in global temperature rise between 2 °C and 3 °C by 2100" (Wikipedia, n.d.).
18. For a similar debate on the economic impact of tipping points in the climate system, see Dietz and colleagues (2021, 2022) and Keen and colleagues (2022).
19. There is a huge literature in regional economics and economic geography which analyzes all these forms of embeddedness of business and presents many insights on embodiment (e.g., Rutten & Boekema, 2007). A classic is Storper (1995) who highlighted the essential point that the competitive advantage of regions is incorporated in non-traded externalities.
20. For a critical perspective on these issues, see, for instance, Bebbington and colleagues (2007), Boyce (2021), Bressler and Heal (2022), Davidson (2013), Martinez-Alier (1995), and Petri (2021).
21. Another famous debate generated by one of Summers' positions is the conclusion, also in line with the standard economic model, that the logic of the market explains why (gender) discrimination cannot exist (May, 2006).
22. Despite their differences, Marx and Keynes both concluded that society would benefit from a reduction in working time, and a reciprocal increase in free time (Spencer, 2023).
23. Thaler and Sunstein are cautious about using nudges to tackle externalities, such as pollution and its impact on climate change. For instance, they indicate: "We are all too aware that for environmental problems, gentle nudges may appear ridiculously inadequate – a bit like an effort to capture a lion with a mousetrap" (Thaler & Sunstein, 2008, p. 184).
24. Nudging does not only aim to address environmental externalities. Beyond sustainability, it can be argued that nudges intend to reduce externalities when they aim to address, for instance, the "obesity problem" (e.g., Rozin et al., 2011), because according to the mainstream model, and under certain circumstances, it is considered that people who are obese "impose a negative

externality on normal weight individuals in their insurance pool" (Bhattacharya & Sood, 2006, p. 279).

25. Note that, according to nudging, the environment is considered the basis for these interventions because people are supposed to be cognitively biased (e.g., Thaler, 2015, 2018; Thaler & Sunstein, 2008). This leads to a curious position: Although nudge-based interventions are inspired by the biases-and-heuristics research program, which is abstracted from the social and economic environment, because it is based on laboratory studies that test hypothetical scenarios in controlled settings far removed from everyday life (e.g., Gigerenzer, 2015; Rossiter, 2019), it concludes that the environment is what should be changed to overcome people's cognitive biases, which means that people should behave as much as possible as expected from the economic model of substantive rationality, namely *Homo economicus*.
26. For an extension of this critique to Esther Duflo's work on poverty, in contrast to Elinor Ostrom's approach, see Labrousse (2016).
27. Cognitive biases are part and parcel of such problems defined *in abstracto* by economists.
28. Paradoxically, and ironically, some of the main proponents of market design (Smith, 2008) and nudging (Sunstein, 2023) claim their affiliation with Hayek, yet end up with market-based solutions at odds with his approach of the spontaneous order (e.g., Hayek, 1989).
29. "Real" utopias, in Wright's (2010, 2013) parlance, are utopias that actually exist. For this reason, "real" utopias differ from "concrete" utopias as conceptualized by Bloch (1986; see, for instance, Levitas, 2013, p. 141ff).
30. Ostrom (1998b, pp. 9–10) distinguishes between heuristics (rules of thumb), norms ("the individual attaches an internal valuation-positive or negative-to taking particular types of action"), and rules ("a group of individuals has developed shared understandings that certain actions in particular situations must, must not, or may be undertaken and that sanctions will be taken against those who do not conform"). Ostrom and colleagues have identified, at least, seven "clusters" or "types" of rules in her field studies (e.g., see Ostrom, 1999, 2010).
31. Williams observed that, in contrast to computerized double-auction markets, in oral markets, in which face-to-face interactions

occur: "First, participants who orally enter or accept a price quote which is unusually favorable to the other side of the market often spur their fellow functionaries to express their displeasure through frowns, moans, groans, sighs, and other less subtle vocalizations. Such occurrences are against the rules of the experimental market but seem to be unavoidable in the face-to-face interaction of the oral double auction. (…) Second, bids (offers) from buyers (sellers) which are unusually high (low) often generate multiple acceptance responses from sellers (buyers). This verbal feedback is public information in the oral double auction, with a coin toss or some other random device used to determine the accepter if no one was clearly the first to accept. Such feedback may help to bring deviant price makers back into line with others in the market" (Williams, 1980, pp. 256–257).

32. This point echoes the larger debate about the Easterlin paradox according to which growth rates of happiness and income are not significantly related in the long run (e.g., Easterlin & O'Connor, 2020).
33. This section builds on Basso and Krpan (2023), adopting and adapting their definitions of Well-being, Inclusivity, Sufficiency, Empowerment, and Resilience.
34. The Rights of Nature have been formally recognized in the 2008 Constitution of Ecuador, Article 71 of which states that: "Nature, or *Pacha Mama*, where life is reproduced and occurs, has the right to integral respect for its existence and for the maintenance and regeneration of its life cycles, structure, functions and evolutionary processes. All persons, communities, peoples and nations can call upon public authorities to enforce the rights of nature." One of the landmark articles on the Rights of Nature is Stone (1972/2012). See also Boyd (2017) and Chapron and colleagues (2019) for further discussion and illustrations of the Rights of Nature.
35. In this approach, human needs are divided into two categories, existential and axiological, which interact to form a matrix. The axiological needs are those of Subsistence, Protection, Affection, Understanding, Participation, Idleness, Creation, Identity, and Freedom. The existential needs are Being, Having, Doing, and Interacting (Max-Neef, 1991; Smith & Max-Neef, 2011).
36. Unlike Sen, who refused to provide an objective list of capabilities (Nussbaum, 1988; Nussbaum & Sen, 1993), Nussbaum

(2006) identified the most important capabilities that ensure a life with dignity. As she shows, many of these capabilities are already enshrined in the UN Declaration of Human Rights and in the constitutions of several countries (see also Pedersen, 2020, p. 97).

37. To some extent, this is emerging with the use of inoculation theory to boost cognitive resilience to misinformation and (online) manipulation (Kozyreva et al., 2020).
38. Some proposals add universal public services to the implementation of UBI (e.g., Hickel et al., 2022). We do not develop this argument here and follow Herrmann-Pillath and Bannas (2021). In their view, UBI opens up the freedom for communities to develop public services autonomously, and to get recognition for such work.
39. Latouche's (2009) "eight Rs," namely, re-evaluate, reconceptualize, restructure, redistribute, re-localize, reduce, reuse, and recycle, can be seen as ways to re-embody and re-embed markets.
40. One of the authors, together with Stefan Bannas, has published a manifesto in German that presents many of our ideas with detailed explanations (Bannas & Herrmann-Pillath, 2020). This section builds on the chapter on "realistic utopia" in Herrmann-Pillath (2018).
41. This view was originally developed by Schumpeter in his concept of the "tax state" (Swedberg, 2022).
42. The consumption or expenditure tax was systematically elaborated by Kaldor (1955/2003). Later it was proposed by Robert Frank as an institutional means to dampen status competition as a driver of unsustainable growth (Frank, 1985, 1997). We do not discuss inheritance tax here, although it is essential to reduce intergenerational forces of inequality (Piketty, 2015). A specific proposal relating this tax to the financing of UBI is made by Herrmann-Pillath and Bannas (2021). It is important to emphasize that such institutions can only be assessed in a systemic context, that is, taking into account interdependencies with other institutions. Keeping investment tax free would cement and widen economic inequalities across generations, unless combined with a very substantial inheritance tax, because rich individuals would be able to postpone consumption indefinitely, and thus accumulate wealth, as Piketty famously demonstrated.
43. An influential early contribution to this view is Soddy (1922/2012) which is considered a precursor to ecological economics, with

the next milestone being the work of Georgescu-Roegen (1971/2013). For an advanced view of thermodynamics and economics, see Kümmel (2011). For the role of photosynthesis in particular, see Smil (2008). There are ramifications in philosophy and the humanities, such as the debates following Bataille (1949/1988).

44. The role of crafts has been emphasized by many contributions following Ruskin's classic (Ruskin, 1985). Sennett (2009) is a comprehensive treatment of the possible revival of craft in the contemporary world. We emphasize that our argument is not primarily about an ideological movement, but about changes in the relative prices of labor and energy, as argued in Kümmel (2011).
45. For complementary views, see for instance, D'Alisa and colleagues (2014), Fioramonti and colleagues (2022), Fitzpatrick and colleagues (2022), Hickel and colleagues (2022), Kothari and colleagues (2019), Sutterlütti and Meretz (2023), and Villamayor-Tomas and Muradian (2023).
46. As can be inferred from Dewey, corporate legal personality is a metaphor with radical implications: "Dewey (1926, p. 668) noted that assimilating a corporation to a singular person, even if deemed a limited creature of the state, might end up enlarging the corporation's rights, privileges and immunities: "In an 'individualistic' period – that is, an era chiefly concerned with rights of private property and contract – it is pretty sure to do so. Consider, for example, the court decisions that a business corporation is a 'person' in the sense covered by the Fourteenth Amendment, and the effects of this decision." In other words, the corporate-person metaphor can have unintended effects (...)" (Foster, 2017, p. 125).
47. The argument against limited liability is a key point in German Ordoliberalism as represented by scholars such as Eucken and Rüstow (e.g., Eucken, 1952/2004, p. 279ff). Eucken opposed the new German law on public corporations, an opinion which was already considered outdated at the time.
48. This view was systematically developed by the so-called "father of Japanese capitalism" Shibusawa Eiichi, who also coined another Japanese word for this type of capitalism (Fridenson & Takeo, 2017). Shibusawa argued that private businesses should be run with full liability and without public investment. Even for the public corporation, he argued that investors should be transparently identified, to strengthen moral commitment to both the

corporation and the public, despite limited liability in the legal sense.

49. There are a number of related ideas in the literature today, such as the notion of "ethical firm" promoted by Collier (2019), and the purpose-driven corporation advocated by Henderson (2020).
50. Definancialization does not destroy value even according to the standard measure of GDP: It is only a matter of accounting conventions that finance shows up in GDP at all (Coyle, 2015), and this does not include externalities, such as crises caused by the financial sector (Zingales, 2015). An important real alternative in this sense is Islamic finance, if we ignore specific religious aspects and focus on the technical ones—as outlined in Hayat and Malik (2014). However, in an environment of capitalist financial institutions, such alternatives cannot be competitive because they are less profitable. Tripp (2006) reviews Islamic debates on capitalism and contextualizes Islamic finance.
51. We cannot even begin to sketch this long and rich history. This is an issue on which capitalism has proven resilient, even against the advice of its leading ordo- and neo-liberal theorists who may seem "utopian" here. Although it is very clear that we do not associate ourselves with the Ordo- and Neo-liberal views, let us quote one of the less usual suspects, Maurice Allais: "*En fait, sans aucune exagération, le mécanisme actuel de la création de monnaie par le crédit est certainement le 'cancer' qui ronge irrémédiablement les économies de marchés de propriété privée*" (Allais, 1999, p. 74), which can be translated as follows: "In fact, without any exaggeration, the present mechanism of money creation through credit is certainly the 'cancer' that is irremediably eating away at the economies of private property markets." His fellow German Ordoliberal, Walter Eucken, expressed the same view. All agree that the production of money should not be subject to market mechanisms, i.e. private. We cite these two because they were both members of the Mont-Pèlerin society, along with Hayek. Hayek opted for a radical privatization of money. For more recent views on this issue, see, for example, Martin (2014) or Admati and Hellwig (2014).
52. This is the argument of Polanyi (1944/2001). For an economic perspective, see Uzawa (2009).

53. The central role of law was clearly recognized by German Ordoliberals, such as Franz Böhm. Modern economic sociologists have added the theoretical concept of performativity (Çalışkan & Callon, 2009, 2010).
54. For a discussion of the limits of consensus when it comes to economic and sustainability issues, see Banerjee (2022).
55. This is the position of the influential liberal newspaper *The Economist*. With regard to the current topic, see *The Economist* (2023).
56. For example, Herrmann-Pillath (2019) argues that, in analogy to the "Oath of Hippocrates" in medicine an "Oath of Aristotle" should become mandatory for professionals in the financial sector, and that any form of contingent financial incentives should be abolished, reflecting the enormous potential damage that irresponsible behavior can inflict on society.
57. Analyses of inequality in terms of cognitive biases seem limited in explaining their reproduction: "This study aimed to determine if rates of cognitive biases were different between positive deviants and low-income adults in a way that might explain some elements of what impedes or facilitates upward economic mobility. We anticipated finding small-to-moderate effects between groups indicating positive deviants were less prone to biases involving risk and uncertainty in financial choices. However, across a sample of nearly 5000 participants from 27 countries, of which 1458 were low-income or positive deviants, we find no evidence of any difference in the rates of cognitive biases – minor or otherwise – and no systematic variability to indicate patterns vary globally" (Ruggeri et al., 2023, p. 5).
58. Likewise, the Core project (https://www.core-econ.org/) aims to bring pluralism to economics. Hopefully, this will help alleviate the long-standing fear "that graduate programs may be turning out a generation with too many *idiots savants*, skilled in technique but innocent of real economic issues" (Krueger, 1991, pp. 1044–1045).
59. Similar forms of inward embodiment can operate on a larger scale: For instance, the growth ideology, which pervades Western societies, transforms into (and is thus outwardly embodied as) perfectionism and its associated pathologies (e.g., Curran, 2023).

60. Perhaps one solution is to turn to the anthropological literature, following Gregory's (1982) approach, which contrasts gift-giving and commodity exchange when it comes to personification. See also, Graeber (2001, p. 35ff).
61. For instance, as Gayle Rubin argues: "If Lévi-Strauss is correct in seeing the exchange of women as a fundamental principle of kinship, the subordination of women can be seen as a product of the relationships by which sex and gender are organized and produced. The economic oppression of women is derivative and secondary. But there is an 'economics' of sex and gender, and what we need is a political economy of sexual systems. We need to study each society to determine the exact mechanisms by which particular conventions of sexuality are produced and maintained. The 'exchange of women' is an initial step toward building an arsenal of concepts with which sexual systems can be described" (Rubin, 1975, p. 177).
62. For a critique of the Western-centric view that generally inspires the literature on progress, see Graeber and Wengrow (2021).
63. Following Smith, impartiality is the pivotal concept in Amartya Sen's (2009) approach to justice. For more on the role of impartiality in economics as applied to policy advice, see Herrmann-Pillath and Hederer (2023, p. 482ff).
64. At least, this is true of the economic models developed by Nobel laureates, 90 out of 93 of whom are men, and the vast majority of whom are white and from the "West." However, this does not mean that women have not contributed to economic thought, as Kuiper (2022) shows.

References

Abson, D. J., Fischer, J., Leventon, J., Newig, J., Schomerus, T., Vilsmaier, U., von Wehrden, H., Abernethy, P., Ives, C. D., Jager, N. W., & Lang, D. J. (2017). Leverage points for sustainability transformation. *Ambio, 46*(1), 30–39. https://doi.org/10.1007/s13280-016-0800-y

Adams, G., Estrada-Villalta, S., Sullivan, D., & Markus, H. R. (2019). The psychology of neoliberalism and the neoliberalism of psychology. *Journal of Social Issues, 75*(1), 189–216. https://doi.org/10.1111/josi.12305

Admati, A. R., & Hellwig, M. (2014). *The bankers' new clothes: What's wrong with banking and what to do about it*. Princeton University Press.

Akerlof, G. A., & Kranton, R. E. (2000). Economics and identity. *The Quarterly Journal of Economics, 115*(3), 715–753.

Akerlof, G. A., & Shiller, R. J. (2009). *Animal spirits: How human psychology drives the economy, and why it matters for global capitalism.* Princeton University Press.

Aligica, P. (2003). *Rethinking institutional analysis and development: The Bloomington School. Interviews with Vincent and Elinor Ostrom.* George Mason University.

Allais, M. (1999). *La crise mondiale d'aujourd'hui: Pour de profondes réformes des institutions financières et monétaires*. Juglar.

Allen, R. C. (2009). *The British industrial revolution in global perspective*. Cambridge University Press.

Andreas, M., & Jabakhanji, S. B. (2023). The I-frame vs. S-frame: How neoliberalism has led behavioral sciences astray. *Frontiers in Psychology, 14*, 1247703. https://doi.org/10.3389/fpsyg.2023.1247703

Anguelovski, I., Connolly, J. J. T., Cole, H., Garcia-Lamarca, M., Triguero-Mas, M., Baró, F., Martin, N., Conesa, D., Shokry, G., del Pulgar, C. P., Ramos, L. A., Matheney, A., Gallez, E., Oscilowicz, E., Máñez, J. L., Sarzo, B., Beltrán, M. A., & Minaya, J. M. (2022). Green gentrification in European and North American cities. *Nature Communications, 13*(1), Article 1. https://doi.org/10.1038/s41467-022-31572-1

APA. (2023). *Utopia*. In American Psychological Association (APA) Dictionary of psychology. https://dictionary.apa.org/utopia

Augustine, G., Soderstrom, S., Milner, D., & Weber, K. (2019). Constructing a distant future: Imaginaries in geoengineering. *Academy of Management Journal, 62*(6), 1930–1960. https://doi.org/10.5465/amj.2018.0059

Bain, P. G., & Bongiorno, R. (2022). Evidence from 33 countries challenges the assumption of unlimited wants. *Nature Sustainability, 5*(8), 669–673. https://doi.org/10.1038/s41893-022-00902-y

Balzano, M., & Vianelli, D. (2022). What contributes to locavorism as a consumer ideology? *British Food Journal, 124*(13), 460–477. https://doi.org/10.1108/BFJ-02-2022-0164

Banerjee, S. B. (2022). Decolonizing deliberative democracy: Perspectives from below. *Journal of Business Ethics, 181*(2), 283–299. https://doi.org/10.1007/s10551-021-04971-5

Banet-Weiser, S., Gill, R., & Rottenberg, C. (2020). Postfeminism, popular feminism and neoliberal feminism? Sarah Banet-Weiser, Rosalind Gill and Catherine Rottenberg in conversation. *Feminist Theory, 21*(1), 3–24. https://doi.org/10.1177/1464700119842555

Bannas, S., & Herrmann-Pillath, C. (2020). *Marktwirtschaft: Zu einer neuen Wirklichkeit: 30 Thesen zur Transformation unserer Wirtschaftsordnung* (1. Aufl.). Schäffer-Poeschel Verlag.

Bardhi, F., & Eckhardt, G. M. (2012). Access-based consumption: The case of car sharing. *Journal of Consumer Research, 39*(4), 881–898. https://doi.org/10.1086/666376

Basso, F., & Krpan, D. (2022). Measuring the transformative utopian impulse for planetary health in the age of the Anthropocene: A multi-study scale development and validation. *The Lancet Planetary Health, 6*(3), e230–e242. https://doi.org/10.1016/S2542-5196(22)00004-3

Basso, F., & Krpan, D. (2023). The WISER framework of behavioural change interventions for mindful human flourishing. *The Lancet Planetary Health, 7*(2), e106–e108. https://doi.org/10.1016/S2542-5196(22)00336-9

Bataille, G. (1949/1988). *The accursed share*. Zone Books.

Baena-Morales, S., & Fröberg, A. (2023). Towards a more sustainable future: Simple recommendations to integrate planetary health into education. *The Lancet Planetary Health, 7*(10), e868–e873. https://doi.org/10.1016/S2542-5196(23)00194-8

Bebbington, J., Brown, J., & Frame, B. (2007). Accounting technologies and sustainability assessment models. *Ecological Economics, 61*(2), 224–236. https://doi.org/10.1016/j.ecolecon.2006.10.021

Beckert, J. (2016). *Imagined futures: Fictional expectations and capitalist dynamics*. Harvard University Press.

Beilin, R., & Wilkinson, C. (2015). Introduction: Governing for urban resilience. *Urban Studies, 52*(7), 1205–1217. https://doi.org/10.1177/0042098015574955

Belk, R. W. (2014). Sharing versus pseudo-sharing in Web 2.0. *Anthropologist, 18*(1), 7–23.

Bell, D. M. (2017). *Rethinking utopia: Place, power, affect*. Routledge. https://doi.org/10.4324/9781315709697

Beyeler, L., & Jaeger-Erben, M. (2022). How to make more of less: Characteristics of sufficiency in business practices. *Frontiers in Sustainability, 131*. https://doi.org/10.3389/frsus.2022.949710

Bhagwat, Y., Warren, N. L., Beck, J. T., & Watson, G. F. (2020). Corporate sociopolitical activism and firm value. *Journal of Marketing, 84*(5), 1–21. https://doi.org/10.1177/0022242920937000

Bhattacharya, J., & Sood, N. (2006). Health insurance and the obesity externality. In K. Bolin & J. Cawley (Eds.), *The Economics of obesity* (Vol. 17, pp. 279–318). Emerald Group. https://doi.org/10.1016/S0731-2199(06)17011-9

Bijman, J., & Wijers, G. (2019). Exploring the inclusiveness of producer cooperatives. *Current Opinion in Environmental Sustainability, 41*, 74–79. https://doi.org/10.1016/j.cosust.2019.11.005

Binder, C. R., Hinkel, J., Bots, P. W. G., & Pahl-Wostl, C. (2013). Comparison of frameworks for analyzing social-ecological systems. *Ecology and Society, 18*(4). https://www.jstor.org/stable/26269404

Bloch, E. (1959/1986). *The principle of hope*. The MIT Press.

Bloch, E. (1988). Something's missing: A discussion between Ernst Bloch and Theodor W. Adorno on the contradictions of utopian longing. In E. Bloch (Ed.), *The utopian function of art and literature: Selected essays* (pp. 1–17). MIT Press.

Blythe, J., Silver, J., Evans, L., Armitage, D., Bennett, N. J., Moore, M.-L., Morrison, T. H., & Brown, K. (2018). The dark side of transformation: Latent risks in contemporary sustainability discourse. *Antipode, 50*(5), 1206–1223. https://doi.org/10.1111/anti.12405

Boldrin, M., & Levine, D. K. (2008). *Against intellectual monopoly*. Cambridge University Press.

Boldyrev, I. (2023, Spring). Ernst Bloch. In E. N. Zalta & U. Nodelman (Eds.), *The Stanford encyclopedia of philosophy*. Metaphysics Research Lab, Stanford University. https://plato.stanford.edu/archives/spr2023/entries/bloch/

Boothby, E. J., Clark, M. S., & Bargh, J. A. (2014). Shared experiences are amplified. *Psychological Science, 25*(12), 2209–2216. https://doi.org/10.1177/0956797614551162

Bossy, S. (2014). The utopias of political consumerism: The search of alternatives to mass consumption. *Journal of Consumer Culture, 14*(2), 179–198. https://doi.org/10.1177/1469540514526238

Bouillé, J., Basso, F., & Robert-Demontrond, P. (2016). The embodied rhetoric of consumerist activism through the lens of conceptual metaphor theory: An exploratory study and research perspectives. *Recherche et Applications En Marketing (English Edition), 31*(2), 81–104. https://doi.org/10.1177/2051570716644544

Bourdieu, P. (1979/1984). *Distinction: A social critique of the judgement of taste*. Routledge & Kegan Paul.

Boushey, H., DeLong, J. B., & Steinbaum, M. (Eds.). (2017). *After Piketty: The agenda for economics and inequality*. Harvard University Press.

Bowles, S., Choi, J.-K., & Hopfensitz, A. (2003). The co-evolution of individual behaviors and social institutions. *Journal of Theoretical Biology, 223*(2), 135–147. https://doi.org/10.1016/S0022-5193(03)00060-2

Boyce, J. K. (2021). Political economy of the environment. In É. Laurent & K. Zwickl (Eds.), *The Routledge handbook of the political economy of the environment* (1st ed., pp. 13–25). Routledge. https://doi.org/10.4324/9780367814533-2

Boyd, D. (2017). *The rights of nature*. ECW Press.

Bradley, K., & Hedrén, J. (Eds.). (2014). *Green utopianism: Perspectives, politics and micro-practices*. Routledge. https://doi.org/10.4324/9780203067215

Brand-Correa, L. I, Brook, A., Büchs, M., Meier, P., Naik, Y., & O'Neill, D. W. (2022). Economics for people and planet—Moving beyond the neoclassical paradigm. *The Lancet Planetary Health, 6*(4), e371–e379. https://doi.org/10.1016/S2542-5196(22)00063-8

Brand-Correa, L. I., & Steinberger, J. K. (2017). A framework for decoupling human need satisfaction from energy use. *Ecological Economics, 141*, 43–52. https://doi.org/10.1016/j.ecolecon.2017.05.019

Bressler, R. D., & Heal, G. (2022). *Valuing excess deaths caused by climate change* (w30648). National Bureau of Economic Research. https://doi.org/10.3386/w30648

Butler, N. M. (1912) *Why should we change our form of government? Studies in practical politics*. Charles Scribner's Sons.

Caggiano, H., Constantino, S. M., Lees, J., Majumdar, R., & Weber, E. U. (2023). Community-engaged research is best positioned to catalyze systemic change. *Behavioral and Brain Sciences, 46*, e152. https://doi.org/10.1017/S0140525X23001024

Çalışkan, K., & Callon, M. (2009). Economization, part 1: Shifting attention from the economy towards processes of economization. *Economy and Society, 38*(3), 369–398. https://doi.org/10.1080/03085140903020580

Çalışkan, K., & Callon, M. (2010). Economization, part 2: A research programme for the study of markets. *Economy and Society, 39*(1), 1–32. https://doi.org/10.1080/03085140903424519

Cambridge Dictionary. (n.d.). *English dictionary, translations & thesaurus*. https://dictionary.cambridge.org/

Chapron, G., Epstein, Y., & López-Bao, J. V. (2019). A rights revolution for nature. *Science, 363*(6434), 1392–1393. https://doi.org/10.1126/science.aav5601

Chater, N., & Loewenstein, G. (2023). The i-frame and the s-frame: How focusing on individual-level solutions has led behavioral public policy astray. *Behavioral and Brain Sciences, 46*(e147), 1–84. https://doi.org/10.1017/S0140525X22002023

Chetty, R., Deming, D. J., & Friedman, J. N. (2023). *Diversifying society's leaders? The causal effects of admission to highly selective private colleges* (Working Paper 31492). National Bureau of Economic Research. https://doi.org/10.3386/w31492

Christens, B. D. (2012). Toward relational empowerment. *American Journal of Community Psychology, 50*(1–2), 114–128. https://doi.org/10.1007/s10464-011-9483-5

Chubb, A. (2015). China's *Shanzhai* culture: "Grabism" and the politics of hybridity. *Journal of Contemporary China, 24*(92), 260–279. https://doi.org/10.1080/10670564.2014.932159

Chung, H. (2019). The impossibility of liberal rights in a diverse world. *Economics & Philosophy, 35*(1), 1–27. https://doi.org/10.1017/S0266267118000044

Claeys, G., & Sargent, L. T. (1999). *The utopia reader*. New York University Press.

Collier, P. (2019). *The future of capitalism: Facing the new anxieties*. Penguin Books.

Collins, R. (2005). *Interaction ritual chains*. Princeton University Press.

Corwin, J. E., & Gidwani, V. (2021). Repair work as care: On maintaining the planet in the Capitalocene. *Antipode*. https://doi.org/10.1111/anti.12791

Coscieme, L., Mortensen, L. F., Anderson, S., Ward, J., Donohue, I., & Sutton, P. C. (2020). Going beyond Gross Domestic Product as an indicator to bring coherence to the Sustainable Development Goals. *Journal of Cleaner Production, 248*, 119232. https://doi.org/10.1016/j.jclepro.2019.119232

Coscieme, L., Mortensen, L. F., & Donohue, I. (2021). Enhance environmental policy coherence to meet the Sustainable Development Goals. *Journal of Cleaner Production, 296*, 126502. https://doi.org/10.1016/j.jclepro.2021.126502

Costanza, R., Kubiszewski, I., Giovannini, E., Lovins, H., McGlade, J., Pickett, K. E., Ragnarsdóttir, K. V., Roberts, D., De Vogli, R., & Wilkinson, R. (2014). Development: Time to leave GDP behind. *Nature, 505*(7483), Article 7483. https://doi.org/10.1038/505283a

Cousins, J. J. (2021). Justice in nature-based solutions: Research and pathways. *Ecological Economics, 180*, 106874. https://doi.org/10.1016/j.ecolecon.2020.106874

Cova, B., & Pace, S. (2006). Brand community of convenience products: New forms of customer empowerment—The case "my Nutella The Community." *European Journal of Marketing, 40*(9/10), 1087–1105. https://doi.org/10.1108/03090560610681023

Cowie, R. H., Bouchet, P., & Fontaine, B. (2022). The Sixth Mass Extinction: Fact, fiction or speculation? *Biological Reviews, 97*(2), 640–663. https://doi.org/10.1111/brv.12816

Coyle, D. (2015). *GDP: A brief but affectionate history* (Revised and expanded ed.). Princeton University Press.

Cumming, G. S., Epstein, G., Anderies, J. M., Apetrei, C. I., Baggio, J., Bodin, Ö., Chawla, S., Clements, H. S., Cox, M., Egli, L., Gurney, G. G., Lubell, M., Magliocca, N., Morrison, T. H., Müller, B., Seppelt, R., Schlüter, M., Unnikrishnan, H., Villamayor-Tomas, S., & Weible, C. M.

(2020). Advancing understanding of natural resource governance: A post-Ostrom research agenda. *Current Opinion in Environmental Sustainability, 44*, 26–34. https://doi.org/10.1016/j.cosust.2020.02.005

Curato, N., Dryzek, J. S., Ercan, S. A., Hendriks, C. M., & Niemeyer, S. (2017). Twelve key findings in deliberative democracy research. *Daedalus, 146*(3), 28–38. https://doi.org/10.1162/DAED_a_00444

Curran, T. (2023). *The perfection trap: Embracing the power of good enough*. Simon and Schuster.

Cutanda, G. A. (2020). Changing world-views through a stories collection and the Earth Charter. In P. Molthan-Hill, H. Luna, T. Wall, H. Puntha, & D. Baden (Eds.), *Storytelling for sustainability in higher education: An educator's handbook* (1st ed., pp. 29–37). Routledge. https://doi.org/10.4324/9780429291111

D'Alisa, G., Demaria, F., & Kallis, G. (2014). *Degrowth. A vocabulary for a new era*. Routledge.

Dardot, P., & Laval, C. (2019). *Common: On revolution in the 21st Century*. Bloomsbury Publishing.

Dasgupta, P. (2021). *The economics of biodiversity: The Dasgupta review*. HM Treasury.

Davidson, M. D. (2013). On the relation between ecosystem services, intrinsic value, existence value and economic valuation. *Ecological Economics, 95*, 171–177. https://doi.org/10.1016/j.ecolecon.2013.09.002

Davis, J. C. (1981). *Utopia and the ideal society: A study of English utopian writing, 1516–1700*. Cambridge University Press.

Dawson, N. M., Coolsaet, B., Sterling, E. J., Loveridge, R., Gross-Camp, N. D., Wongbusarakum, S., Sangha, K. K., Scherl, L. M., Phan, H. P., Zafra-Calvo, N., Lavey, W. G., Byakagaba, P., Idrobo, C. J., Chenet, A., Bennett, N. J., Mansourian, S., & Rosado-May, F. J. (2021). The role of Indigenous peoples and local communities in effective and equitable conservation. *Ecology and Society, 26*(3), Article 19. https://doi.org/10.5751/ES-12625-260319

Deaton, A., & Cartwright, N. (2018). Understanding and misunderstanding randomized controlled trials. *Social Science & Medicine, 210*, 2–21. https://doi.org/10.1016/j.socscimed.2017.12.005

De Moor, T. (2015). *The dilemma of the commoners: Understanding the use of common-pool resources in long-term perspective*. Cambridge University Press. https://doi.org/10.1017/CBO9781139135450

Dewey, J. (1926). The historic background of corporate legal personality. *Yale Law Journal, 35*(6), 655–673.

Diaz-Rainey, I., Robertson, B., & Wilson, C. (2017). Stranded research? Leading finance journals are silent on climate change. *Climatic Change, 143*(1), 243–260. https://doi.org/10.1007/s10584-017-1985-1

Dietz, S., Rising, J., Stoerk, T., & Wagner, G. (2021). Economic impacts of tipping points in the climate system. *Proceedings of the National Academy of Sciences, 118*(34), e2103081118. https://doi.org/10.1073/pnas.2103081118

Dietz, S., Rising, J., Stoerk, T., & Wagner, G. (2022). Reply to Keen et al.: Dietz et al. modeling of climate tipping points is informative even if estimates are a probable lower bound. *Proceedings of the National Academy of Sciences, 119*(21), e2201191119. https://doi.org/10.1073/pnas.2201191119

Domeisen, D. I., Eltahir, E. A., Fischer, E. M., Knutti, R., Perkins-Kirkpatrick, S. E., Schär, C., Seneviratne, S. I., Weisheimer, A., & Wernli, H. (2023). Prediction and projection of heatwaves. *Nature Reviews Earth & Environment, 4*(1), 36–50. https://doi.org/10.1038/s43017-022-00371-z

Dutton, J. (2010). "Non-western" utopian traditions. In G. Claeys (Ed.), *The Cambridge companion to utopian literature* (1st ed., pp. 223–258). Cambridge University Press. https://doi.org/10.1017/CCOL9780521886659.010

Earle, J., Moran, C., & Ward-Perkins, Z. (2016). *The econocracy: The perils of leaving economics to the experts*. Manchester University Press.

Earth Charter. (2000). Earth Charter. https://earthcharter.org/

Easterlin, R. A., & O'Connor, K. J. (2020). The Easterlin paradox. In K. F. Zimmermann (Ed.), *Handbook of labor, human resources and population economics* (pp. 1–25). Springer. https://doi.org/10.1007/978-3-319-57365-6_184-2

Elster, J. (2015). *Explaining social behavior: More nuts and bolts for the social sciences* (Revised ed.). Cambridge University Press.

Eucken, W. (1952/2004). *Grundsätze der Wirtschaftspolitik* (7. Aufl.). Mohr Siebeck.

Fazey, I., Moug, P., Allen, S., Beckmann, K., Blackwood, D., Bonaventura, M., Burnett, K., Danson, M., Falconer, R., Gagnon, A. S., Harkness, R., Hodgson, A., Holm, L., Irvine, K. N., Low, R., Lyon, C., Moss, A., Moran, C., Naylor, L., ... Wolstenholme, R. (2018). Transformation in a changing climate: A research agenda. *Climate and Development*, *10*(3), 197–217. https://doi.org/10.1080/17565529.2017.1301864

Federici, S. (2004/2021). *Caliban and the witch: Women, the body and primitive accumulation*. Penguin Book.

Feola, G. (2015). Societal transformation in response to global environmental change: A review of emerging concepts. *Ambio, 44*(5), 376–390. https://doi.org/10.1007/s13280-014-0582-z

Fernando, J. W., Burden, N., Ferguson, A., O'Brien, L. V., Judge, M., & Kashima, Y. (2018). Functions of utopia: How utopian thinking motivates societal engagement. *Personality and Social Psychology Bulletin, 44*(5), 779–792. https://doi.org/10.1177/0146167217748604

Fioramonti, L., Coscieme, L., Costanza, R., Kubiszewski, I., Trebeck, K., Wallis, S., Roberts, D., Mortensen, L. F., Pickett, K. E., Wilkinson, R., Ragnarsdottír, K. V., McGlade, J., Lovins, H., & De Vogli, R. (2022). Wellbeing economy: An effective paradigm to mainstream post-growth policies? *Ecological Economics, 192*, 107261. https://doi.org/10.1016/j.ecolecon.2021.107261

Fitzpatrick, N., Parrique, T., & Cosme, I. (2022). Exploring degrowth policy proposals: A systematic mapping with thematic synthesis. *Journal of Cleaner Production, 365*, 132764. https://doi.org/10.1016/j.jclepro.2022.132764

Folke, C. (2006). Resilience: The emergence of a perspective for social–ecological systems analyses. *Global Environmental Change, 16*(3), 253–267. https://doi.org/10.1016/j.gloenvcha.2006.04.002

Foray, D. (2004). *Economics of knowledge*. MIT Press.

Foster, R. J. (2017). The corporation in anthropology. In A. Spicer & G. Baars (Eds.), *The corporation: A critical, multi-disciplinary handbook* (pp. 111–133). Cambridge University Press. https://doi.org/10.1017/9781139681025.006

Frank, R. H. (1985). *Choosing the right pond: Human behavior and the quest for status*. Oxford University Press.

Frank, R. H. (1997). The frame of reference as a public good. *The Economic Journal, 107*(445), 1832–1847. https://doi.org/10.1111/j.1468-0297.1997.tb00086.x

Fraser, N. (2016). Contradictions of capital and care. *New Left Review, 100*, 99–117.

Frey, B. S., & Bohnet, I. (1997). Identification in democratic society. *The Journal of Socio-Economics, 26*(1), 25–38.

Fridenson, P., & Takeo, K. (Eds.). (2017). *Ethical capitalism: Shibusawa Eiichi and business leadership in global perspective*. University of Toronto Press.

Fukuda-Parr, S. (2003). The human development paradigm: Operationalizing Sen's ideas on capabilities. *Feminist Economics, 9*(2–3), 301–317. https://doi.org/10.1080/1354570022000077980

Gedikli, C., Miraglia, M., Connolly, S., Bryan, M., & Watson, D. (2023). The relationship between unemployment and wellbeing: An updated meta-analysis of longitudinal evidence. *European Journal of Work and Organizational Psychology, 32*(1), 128–144. https://doi.org/10.1080/1359432X.2022.2106855

Gee, M. (1994). Questioning the concept of the "user." *Journal of Environmental Psychology, 14*(2), 113–124. https://doi.org/10.1016/S0272-4944(05)80165-3

Georgescu-Roegen, N. (1971/2013). *The entropy law and the economic process*. Harvard University Press.

Gerrig, R. J. (1993). *Experiencing narrative worlds: On the psychological activities of reading*. Yale University Press.

Gigerenzer, G. (2015). On the supposed evidence for libertarian paternalism. *Review of Philosophy and Psychology, 6*(3), 361–383. https://doi.org/10.1007/s13164-015-0248-1

Gillig, P. (2016). Marx's critique of "eternal" political economy: How Mill is alien to Marx's attacks. *The European Journal of the History of Economic Thought, 23*(3), 378–399. https://doi.org/10.1080/09672567.2014.916732

Goldstein, B. E., Wessells, A. T., Lejano, R., & Butler, W. (2015). Narrating resilience: Transforming urban systems through collaborative storytelling. *Urban Studies, 52*(7), 1285–1303. https://doi.org/10.1177/0042098013505653

Gomez-Baggethun, E. (2018). Ecosystem services. In C. L. Spash (Ed.), *Routledge handbook of ecological economics: Nature and society* (pp. 445–454). Routledge.

Gómez-Baggethun, E., & Muradian, R. (2015). In markets we trust? Setting the boundaries of market-based Instruments in ecosystem services governance. *Ecological Economics, 117*, 217–224. https://doi.org/10.1016/j.ecolecon.2015.03.016

Goodwin, B. (1978). *Social science and utopia*. Harvester.

Goodwin, N., Harris, J. M., Nelson, J. A., Rajkarnikar, P. J., Roach, B., & Torras, M. (2023a). *Macroeconomics in context*. Routledge.

Goodwin, N., Harris, J. M., Nelson, J. A., Rajkarnikar, P. J., Roach, B., & Torras, M. (2023b). *Microeconomics in context*. Routledge.

Goodwin, B., & Taylor, K. (1982/2009). *The politics of utopia: A study in theory and practice*. Peter Lang.

Göpel, M. (2016). *The great mindshift*. Springer. https://doi.org/10.1007/978-3-319-43766-8

Graeber, D. (2001). *Toward an anthropological theory of value: The false coin of our own dreams*. Springer.

Graeber, D. (2020). Policy for the future of work. In R. Skidelsky & N. Craig (Eds.), *Work in the future* (pp. 157–173). Palgrave Macmillan. https://doi.org/10.1007/978-3-030-21134-9_16

Graeber, D., & Wengrow, D. (2021). *The dawn of everything: A new history of humanity*. Penguin.

Green, M. C., & Brock, T. C. (2000). The role of transportation in the persuasiveness of public narratives. *Journal of Personality and Social Psychology, 79*(5), 701–721. https://doi.org/10.1037//0022-3514.79.5.701

Gregory, C. A. (1982). *Gifts and commodities*. Academic Press.

Gudeman, S. (1998). Banishing the other from the market: The development economics of W. Arthur Lewis. *Paideuma, 44*, 125–137.

Guzmán, C. A. F., Aguirre, A. A., Astle, B., Barros, E., Bayles, B., Chimbari, M., El-Abbadi, N., Evert, J., Hackett, F., Howard, C., Jennings, J., Krzyzek,

A., LeClair, J., Maric, F., Martin, O., Osano, O., Patz, J., Potter, T., Redvers, N., … Zylstra, M. (2021). A framework to guide planetary health education. *The Lancet Planetary Health, 5*(5), e253–e255. https://doi.org/10.1016/S2542-5196(21)00110-8

Hansot, E. (1974). *Perfection and progress: Two modes of utopian thought*. MIT Press.

Hardin, G. (1968). The tragedy of the commons. *Science, 162*(3859), 1243–1248. https://doi.org/10.1126/science.162.3859.1243

Harley, B., & Fleming, P. (2021). Not even trying to change the world: Why do elite management journals ignore the major problems facing humanity? *The Journal of Applied Behavioral Science, 57*(2), 133–152. https://doi.org/10.1177/0021886321997189

Haug, C. (2015). What is consensus and how is it achieved in meetings?: Four types of consensus decision making. In J. A. Allen, N. Lehmann-Willenbrock, & S. G. Rogelberg (Eds.), The Cambridge Handbook of Meeting Science (1st ed., pp. 556–584). Cambridge University Press. https://doi.org/10.1017/CBO9781107589735.024

Hayat, U., & Malik, A. (2014). *Islamic finance: Ethics, concepts, practice*. CFA Institute Research Foundation.

Hayek, F. A. (1989). The pretence of knowledge. *American Economic Review, 79*(6), 3–7.

Hedrén, J., & Linnér, B.-O. (2009a). Utopian thought and sustainable development. *Futures, 41*(4), 197–200. https://doi.org/10.1016/j.futures.2008.09.002

Hedrén, J., & Linnér, B.-O. (2009b). Utopian thought and the politics of sustainable development. *Futures, 41*(4), 210–219. https://doi.org/10.1016/j.futures.2008.09.004

Hegel, G. W. F. (1820/2009). *Grundlinien der Philosophie des Rechts oder Naturrecht und Staatswissenschaft im Grundrisse* (Nachdr.). Reclam.

Helliwell, J. F., Layard, R., & Sachs, J. D. (2017). *World Happiness Report 2017*. https://worldhappiness.report/ed/2017/

Helliwell, J. F., Layard, R., Sachs, J. D., De Neve, J.-E., Aknin, L. B., & Wang, S. (2022). *World Happiness Report 2022*. https://worldhappiness.report/ed/2022

Henderson, R. (2020). *Reimagining capitalism in a world on fire*. PublicAffairs.

Henderson, R., & den Steen, E. V. (2015). Why do firms have "purpose"? The firm's role as a carrier of identity and reputation. *American Economic Review, 105*(5), 326–330. https://doi.org/10.1257/aer.p20151072

Herrmann-Pillath, C. (2015). Energy, growth, and evolution: Towards a naturalistic ontology of economics. *Ecological Economics, 119*, 432–442. https://doi.org/10.1016/j.ecolecon.2014.11.014

Herrmann-Pillath, C. (2018). *Grundlegung einer kritischen Theorie der Wirtschaft*. Metropolis-Verlag.

Herrmann-Pillath, C. (2019, April 1). *The case for an Aristotelian oath in finance*. INSOSCI Blog. https://www.insosci.eu/the-case-for-an-aristotelian-oath-in-finance/

Herrmann-Pillath, C. (2021). A Copernican moment: Engaging economic ethics in orchestrating the geocentric turn in economics. In M. Bohle & E. Marone (Eds.), *Geo-societal narratives* (pp. 105–126). Springer. https://doi.org/10.1007/978-3-030-79028-8_8

Herrmann-Pillath, C. (2023). The universal commons: An economic theory of ecosystem ownership. *Ecological Economics, 208*, 107822. https://doi.org/10.1016/j.ecolecon.2023.107822

Herrmann-Pillath, C., & Bannas, S. (2021). Community money COMMON. The alternative to Universal Basic Income. *Zeitschrift Für Wirtschafts- Und Unternehmensethik, 22*(2), 332–348. https://doi.org/10.5771/1439-880X-2021-2-332

Herrmann-Pillath, C., & Hederer, C. (2023). *A new principles of economics: The science of markets*. Routledge.

Hertwig, R., & Grüne-Yanoff, T. (2017). Nudging and boosting: Steering or empowering good decisions. *Perspectives on Psychological Science, 12*(6), 973–986. https://doi.org/10.1177/1745691617702496

Hewitson, G. (2001). The disavowal of the sexed body in neoclassical economics. In J. Cullenberg, S. E. Amariglio, & D. F. Ruccio (Eds.), *Post-modernism, economics and knowledge* (pp. 221–245). Routledge. https://doi.org/10.4324/9780203410707-19

Hickel, J. (2020a). *Less is more*. William Heinemann.

Hickel, J. (2020b). Quantifying national responsibility for climate breakdown: An equality-based attribution approach for carbon dioxide emissions in excess of the planetary boundary. *The Lancet Planetary Health, 4*(9), e399–e404. https://doi.org/10.1016/S2542-5196(20)30196-0

Hickel, J., Kallis, G., Jackson, T., O'Neill, D. W., Schor, J. B., Steinberger, J. K., Victor, P. A., & Ürge-Vorsatz, D. (2022). Degrowth can work—Here's how science can help. *Nature, 612*(7940), 400–403. https://doi.org/10.1038/d41586-022-04412-x

Higgs, K. (2014). *Collision course: Endless growth on a finite planet*. MIT Press.

Hirschman, A. O. (1970). *Exit, voice, and loyalty: Responses to decline in firms, organizations and states*. Harvard University Press.

Holloway, L. (2002). Virtual vegetables and adopted sheep: Ethical relation, authenticity and Internet-mediated food production technologies. *Area, 34*(1), 70–81. https://doi.org/10.1111/1475-4762.00058

Holz, P. (2018). *Towards a new social order? Real democracy, sustainability & peace*. Vernon Press.

Honneth, A. (2015). *Das Recht der Freiheit: Grundriß einer demokratischen Sittlichkeit* (2. Aufl.). Suhrkamp.

Hornsey, M. J., Bain, P. G., Harris, E. A., Lebedeva, N., Kashima, E. S., Guan, Y., González, R., Chen, S. X., & Blumen, S. (2018). How much is enough in a perfect world? Cultural variation in ideal levels of happiness, pleasure, freedom, health, self-esteem, longevity, and intelligence. *Psychological Science, 29*(9), 1393–1404. https://doi.org/10.1177/0956797618768058

Hudson, I., & Hudson, M. (2003). Removing the veil? Commodity fetishism, fair trade, and the environment. *Organization & Environment, 16*(4), 413–430. https://doi.org/10.1177/1086026603258926

Hultman, M. (2009). Back to the future: The dream of a perpetuum mobile in the atomic society and the hydrogen economy. *Futures, 41*(4), 226–233. https://doi.org/10.1016/j.futures.2008.09.006

Ingebrigtsen, S., & Jakobsen, O. (2012). Utopias and realism in ecological economics—Knowledge, understanding and improvisation. *Ecological Economics, 84*, 84–90. https://doi.org/10.1016/j.ecolecon.2012.09.015

Ireland, P. (2010). Limited liability, shareholder rights and the problem of corporate irresponsibility. *Cambridge Journal of Economics, 34*(5), 837–856. https://doi.org/10.1093/cje/ben040

IUCN. (2020). *Global standard for nature-based solutions. A user-friendly framework for the verification, design and scaling up of NbS* (1st ed.). IUCN.

Jackson, T. (2014). New economy. In G. D'Alisa, F. Demaria, & G. Kallis (Eds.), *Degrowth: A vocabulary for a new era* (p. 179). Routledge.

Jackson, T., & Victor, P. A. (2019). Unraveling the claims for (and against) green growth. *Science, 366*(6468), 950–951. https://doi.org/10.1126/science.aay0749

Jameson, F. (2005). *Archaeologies of the future. The desire called utopia and other science fictions*. Verso. https://www.jstor.org/stable/466409

Jolibert, C., Max-Neef, M., Rauschmayer, F., & Paavola, J. (2011). Should we care about the needs of non-humans? Needs assessment: A tool for environmental conflict resolution and sustainable organization of living beings. *Environmental Policy and Governance, 21*(4), 259–269. https://doi.org/10.1002/eet.578

Jonsson, P. (2007). A tale of a car sharing organization (CSO) monster. In H. Brembeck, K. M. Ekstrom, & M. Morck (Eds.), *Little Monsters: (De)coupling assemblages of consumption* (pp. 149–164). Transaction Publishers.

Jovchelovitch, S., & Hawlina, H. (2018). Utopias and world-making: Time, transformation and the collective imagination. In C. de Saint-Laurent, S. Obradović, & K. R. Carriere (Eds.), *Imagining collective futures* (pp. 129–151). Springer. https://doi.org/10.1007/978-3-319-76051-3_7

Kabeer, N. (2020). Women's empowerment and economic development: A feminist critique of storytelling practices in "randomista" economics. *Feminist Economics, 26*(2), 1–26. https://doi.org/10.1080/13545701.2020.1743338

Kahneman, D. (2003). Maps of bounded rationality: Psychology for behavioral economics. *American Economic Review, 93*(5), 1449–1475.

Kahneman, D. (2012). *Thinking, fast and slow*. Penguin Books.

Kaldor, N. (1955/2003). *An expenditure tax*. Routledge.

Kallis, G., & March, H. (2015). Imaginaries of hope: The utopianism of degrowth. *Annals of the Association of American Geographers, 105*(2), 360–368. https://doi.org/10.1080/00045608.2014.973803

Kavedžija, I. (2021). The process of wellbeing: Conviviality, care, creativity. *Elements in Psychology and Culture*. https://doi.org/10.1017/9781108935616

Keen, S. (2021). The appallingly bad neoclassical economics of climate change. *Globalizations, 18*(7), 1149–1177. https://doi.org/10.1080/14747731.2020.1807856

Keen, S., Lenton, T. M., Garrett, T. J., Rae, J. W. B., Hanley, B. P., & Grasselli, M. (2022). Estimates of economic and environmental damages from tipping points cannot be reconciled with the scientific literature. *Proceedings of the National Academy of Sciences, 119*(21), e2117308119. https://doi.org/10.1073/pnas.2117308119

Kuiper, E. (2022). *A Herstory of economics*. Polity.

Keynes, J. M. (1931/2010). Economic possibilities for our grandchildren. In J. M. Keynes (Ed.), *Essays in persuasion* (pp. 321–332). Palgrave Macmillan. https://doi.org/10.1007/978-1-349-59072-8_25

King, C. S. (2020). The male gaze in visual culture. In M. N. Goins, J. F. McAlister, & B. K. Alexander (Eds.), *The Routledge handbook of gender and communication* (pp. 120–132). https://doi.org/10.4324/9780429448317-10

Konow, J., & Earley, J. (2008). The hedonistic paradox: Is homo economicus happier? *Journal of Public Economics, 92*(1), 1–33. https://doi.org/10.1016/j.jpubeco.2007.04.006

Kothari, A., Salleh, A., Escobar, A., Demaria, F., & Acosta, A. (Eds.). (2019). *Pluriverse: A post-development dictionary*. Tulika Books and Authorsupfront.

Kövecses, Z. (1991). Happiness: A definitional effort. *Metaphor and Symbolic Activity, 6*(1), 29–47. https://doi.org/10.1207/s15327868ms0601_2

Kozyreva, A., Lewandowsky, S., & Hertwig, R. (2020). Citizens versus the internet: Confronting digital challenges with cognitive tools. *Psychological Science in the Public Interest, 21*(3), 103–156. https://doi.org/10.1177/1529100620946707

Kranton, R. E. (2016). Identity economics 2016: Where do social distinctions and norms come from? *American Economic Review, 106*(5), 405–409. https://doi.org/10.1257/aer.p20161038

Krpan, D., & Basso, F. (2021). Keep degrowth or go rebirth? Regulatory focus theory and the support for a sustainable downscaling of production and consumption. *Journal of Environmental Psychology, 74*, 101586. https://doi.org/10.1016/j.jenvp.2021.101586

Krueger, A. O. (1991). Report of the commission on graduate education in economics. *Journal of Economic Literature, 29*(3), 1035–1053.

Kuenkel, P. (2019). *Stewarding sustainability transformations: An emerging theory and practice of SDG implementation*. Springer. https://doi.org/10.1007/978-3-030-03691-1

Kumar, K. (1987). *Utopia and anti-utopia in modern times*. Basil Blackwell.

Kumar, K. (1991). *Utopianism*. Open University Press.

Kumar, K. (2010). The ends of utopia. *New Literary History, 41*(3), 549–569.

Kümmel, R. (2011). *The second law of economics: Energy, entropy, and the origins of wealth*. Springer.

Labrousse, A. (2016). Not by technique alone. A methodological comparison of development analysis with Esther Duflo and Elinor Ostrom. *Journal of Institutional Economics, 12*(2), 277–303. https://doi.org/10.1017/S1744137415000429

Lades, L. K., & Delaney, L. (2022). Nudge FORGOOD. *Behavioural Public Policy, 6*(1), 75–94. https://doi.org/10.1017/bpp.2019.53

Lahlou, S. (2017). *Installation theory: The societal construction and regulation of behaviour*. Cambridge University Press.

Landa, J. T. (1994). *Trust, ethnicity, and identity: Beyond the new institutional economics of ethnic trading networks, contract law, and gift-exchange*. University of Michigan Press.

Latouche, S. (2009). *Farewell to growth*. Polity Press.

Latour, B. (1990). Technology is society made durable. *The Sociological Review, 38*(1_suppl), 103–131. https://doi.org/10.1111/j.1467-954X.1990.tb03350.x

Layard, R. (2010). Measuring subjective well-being. *Science, 327*(5965), 534–535.

Levitas, R. (1985). New right utopias. *Radical Philosophy, 39*, 2–9.

Levitas, R. (1990a). Educated hope: Ernst Bloch on abstract and concrete utopia. *Utopian Studies, 1*(2), 13–26.

Levitas, R. (1990/2011). *The concept of utopia* (2nd ed.). Peter Lang.

Levitas, R. (2013). *Utopia as method: The imaginary reconstitution of society*. Palgrave Macmillan.

Lévi-Strauss, C. (1949/1969). *The elementary structures of kinship*. Beacon Press.

Levi, Y., & Pellegrin-Rescia, M. L. (1997). A new look at the embeddedness/disembeddedness issue: Cooperatives as terms of reference. *The Journal of Socio-Economics, 26*(2), 159–179. https://doi.org/10.1016/S1053-5357(97)90031-7

Linnér, B.-O., & Wibeck, V. (2019). *Sustainability transformations: Agents and drivers across societies* (1st ed.). Cambridge University Press. https://doi.org/10.1017/9781108766975

Linnér, B.-O., & Wibeck, V. (2020). Conceptualising variations in societal transformations towards sustainability. *Environmental Science & Policy, 106*, 221–227. https://doi.org/10.1016/j.envsci.2020.01.007

Lockwood, R. (2023). Anthropomorphism and anthropocentrism in the Anthropocene. In A. H. Fine, M. K. Mueller, Z. Y. Ng, A. M. Beck, & J. M. Peralta (Eds.), *The Routledge handbook on human animal interactions and anthrozoology* (16 p.). Routledge.

Longxi, Z. (2002). The utopian vision, east and west. *Utopian Studies, 13*(1), 1–20.

Luther, T. C. (2009). *Hegel's critique of modernity: Reconciling individual freedom and the community*. Lexington Books.

Lüthi, S., Fairless, C., Fischer, E. M., Scovronick, N., Armstrong, B., Coelho, M. D. S. Z. S., Guo, Y. L., Guo, Y., Honda, Y., Huber, V., Kyselý, J., Lavigne, E., Royé, D., Ryti, N., Silva, S., Urban, A., Gasparrini, A., Bresch, D. N., & Vicedo-Cabrera, A. M. (2023). Rapid increase in the risk of heat-related mortality. *Nature Communications, 14*(1), 4894. https://doi.org/10.1038/s41467-023-40599-x

Machlup, F. (1958). *An economic review of the patent system*. US Government Printing Office.

Magness, P. W., & Harrigan, J. R. (2020). John Maynard Keynes, HG Wells, and a problematic utopia. *History of Political Economy, 52*(2), 211–238.

Maiese, M., & Hanna, R. (2019). *The mid-body politic*. Palgrave.

Malm, A., & Hornborg, A. (2014). The geology of mankind? A critique of the Anthropocene narrative. *The Anthropocene Review, 1*(1), 62–69. https://doi.org/10.1177/2053019613516291

Margolis, S., Schwitzgebel, E., Ozer, D. J., & Lyubomirsky, S. (2019). A new measure of life satisfaction: The Riverside Life Satisfaction Scale. *Journal of Personality Assessment, 101*(6), 621–630. https://doi.org/10.1080/00223891.2018.1464457

Martin, F. (2014). *Money: The unauthorized biography from coinage to cryptocurrencies*. Vintage Book.

Martinez-Alier, J. (1995). Distributional issues in ecological economics. *Review of Social Economy, 53*(4), 511–528.

Marvakis, A. (2007). The utopian surplus in human agency: Using Ernst Bloch's philosophy for psychology. In V. Van Deventer, M. Terre Blanche,

E. Fourie, & P. Segaalo (Eds.), *Citizen city: Between constructing agent and constructed agency* (pp. 278–288). Captus University Publications.

Marx, K., & Engels, F. (1848/1988). Manifesto of the communist party. In K. Marx (Ed.), *The economic and philosophic manuscripts of 1844* (pp. 203–243). Prometheus Books.

Maslow, A. H. (1943). A theory of human motivation. *Psychological Review, 50*(4), 370–396. https://doi.org/10.1037/h0054346

Max-Neef, M. (1991). *Human scale development*. The Apex Press.

May, A. M. (2006). "Sweeping the heavens for a comet": Women, the language of political economy, and higher education in the US. *Feminist Economics, 12*(4), 625–640. https://doi.org/10.1080/13545700600885321

May, A. M., & Summerfield, G. (2012). Creating a space where gender matters: Elinor Ostrom (1933–2012) talks with Ann Mari May and Gale Summerfield. *Feminist Economics, 18*(4), 25–37. https://doi.org/10.1080/13545701.2012.739725

Mazzucato, M. (2018). *The value of everything: Making and taking in the global economy*. PublicAffairs.

McCloskey, D. N. (2016). Adam Smith did Humanomics: So should we. *Eastern Economic Journal, 42*(4), 503–513. https://doi.org/10.1057/s41302-016-0007-8

Mead, N. L., & Williams, L. E. (2022). Can't buy me meaning? Lay theories impede people from deriving meaning and well-being from consumption. *Current Opinion in Psychology, 46*, 101332. https://doi.org/10.1016/j.copsyc.2022.101332

Micheletti, M. (2003). *Political virtue and shopping: Individuals, consumerism and collective action*. Palgrave Macmillan. http://link.springer.com/10.1057/9781403973764_5

Mirowski, P., & Plehwe, D. (Eds.). (2015). *The road from Mont Pèlerin: The making of the neoliberal thought collective*. Harvard University Press. https://doi.org/10.4159/9780674495111

Mirzaei, A., Wilkie, D. C., & Siuki, H. (2022). Woke brand activism authenticity or the lack of it. *Journal of Business Research, 139*, 1–12. https://doi.org/10.1016/j.jbusres.2021.09.044

Mokyr, J. (2009a). Intellectual property rights, the industrial revolution, and the beginnings of modern economic growth. *American Economic Review, 99*(2), 349–355. https://doi.org/10.1257/aer.99.2.349

Mokyr, J. (2009b). *The enlightened economy: Britain and the industrial revolution, 1700–1850*. Yale University Press.

Montiel, C., Radziszewski, S., Prilleltensky, I., & Houle, J. (2021). Fostering positive communities: A scoping review of community-level positive psychology interventions. *Frontiers in Psychology, 12*, 720793. https://doi.org/10.3389/fpsyg.2021.720793

Mora, C., Dousset, B., Caldwell, I. R., Powell, F. E., Geronimo, R. C., Bielecki, C. R., Counsell, C. W. W., Dietrich, B. S., Johnston, E. T., Louis, L. V., Lucas, M. P., McKenzie, M. M., Shea, A. G., Tseng, H., Giambelluca, T. W., Leon, L. R., Hawkins, E., & Trauernicht, C. (2017). Global risk of deadly heat. *Nature Climate Change, 7*(7), Article 7. https://doi.org/10.1038/nclimate3322

More, T. (1516). *Utopia*. Dover.

Morton, A. L. (1969). *The English utopia*. Lawrence & Wishart.

Moylan, T. (2018). Transgressive, totalizing, transformative: Utopia's utopian surplus. *Utopian Studies, 29*(3), 309–324.

Moylan, T. (2020). The necessity of hope in dystopian times: A critical reflection. *Utopian Studies, 31*(1), 164–193. https://doi.org/10.5325/utopianstudies.31.1.0164

Mukherjee, R., & Banet-Weiser, S. (2012). *Commodity activism: Cultural resistance in neoliberal times*. New York University Press.

Naess, A., & Sessions, G. (1986). The basic principles of deep ecology. *The Trumpeter, 3*(4).

Negley, G., & Patrick, J. M. (1971). *The quest for utopia*. McGrath.

Nelson, J. A. (1992). Gender, metaphor, and the definition of economics. *Economics & Philosophy, 8*(1), 103–125. https://doi.org/10.1017/S026626710000050X

Nelson, J. A. (1997). Feminism, ecology and the philosophy of economics. *Ecological Economics, 20*(2), 155–162. https://doi.org/10.1016/S0921-8009(96)00025-0

Nelson, J. A. (2016). Male is a gender, too: A review of *Why gender matters in economics* by Mukesh Eswaran. *Journal of Economic Literature, 54*(4), 1362–1376. https://doi.org/10.1257/jel.20151398

Nembhard, J. G. (2015). *Collective courage: A history of African American cooperative economic thought and practice*. Penn State University Press.

Nesterova, I., & Buch-Hansen, H. (2023). Degrowth and the circular economy: Reflecting on the depth of business circularity. *Journal of Cleaner Production*. https://doi.org/10.1016/j.jclepro.2023.137639

Newman, S. (2023). *Unmaking waste: New histories of old things*. University of Chicago Press.

Nordhaus, W. (2019). Climate change: The ultimate challenge for economics. *American Economic Review, 109*(6), 1991–2014. https://doi.org/10.1257/aer.109.6.1991

Nussbaum, M. C. (1988). Nature, function and capability: Aristotle on political distribution. In J. Annas & R. H. Grimm (Eds.), *Oxford studies in ancient philosophy (supplementary volume)* (pp. 145–184). Oxford University Press.

Nussbaum, M. C. (2006). *Frontiers of justice: Disability, nationality, species membership*. Harvard University Press.

Nussbaum, M., C. & Sen, A. (Eds.). (1993). *The quality of life*. Oxford University Press.
O'Brien, K. (2012). Global environmental change II: From adaptation to deliberate transformation. *Progress in Human Geography, 36*(5), 667–676. https://doi.org/10.1177/0309132511425767
O'Neill, J. (2006). Citizenship, well-being and sustainability: Epicurus or Aristotle? *Analyse & Kritik, 28*(2), 158–172. https://doi.org/10.1515/auk-2006-0203
O'Neill, J. (2008). Happiness and the good life. *Environmental Values, 17*(2), 125–144.
Ostrom, E. (1990). *Governing the commons: The evolution of institutions for collective action*. Cambridge University Press.
Ostrom, E. (1998a). Norms and efficiency. In S. Bowles, H. Gintis, & H. Brighouse (Eds.), *Recasting egalitarianism: New rules for communities, states and markets* (pp. 113–120). Verso.
Ostrom, E. (1998b). A behavioral approach to the rational choice theory of collective action: Presidential address, American Political Science Association, 1997. *American Political Science Review, 92*(1), 1–22.
Ostrom, E. (1999). Coping with tragedies of the commons. *Annual Review of Political Science, 2*(1), 493–535. https://doi.org/10.1146/annurev.polisci.2.1.493
Ostrom, E. (2010). Beyond markets and states: Polycentric governance of complex economic systems. *American Economic Review, 100*(3), 641–672. https://doi.org/10.1257/aer.100.3.641
Ostrom, E., & Basurto, X. (2011). Crafting analytical tools to study institutional change. *Journal of Institutional Economics, 7*(3), 317–343. https://doi.org/10.1017/S1744137410000305
Ostrom, E., & Cox, M. (2010). Moving beyond panaceas: A multi-tiered diagnostic approach for social-ecological analysis. *Environmental Conservation, 37*(4), 451–463. https://doi.org/10.1017/S0376892910000834
Ostrom, E., Walker, J., & Gardner, R. (1992). Covenants with and without a sword: Self-governance is possible. *American Political Science Review, 86*(2), 404–417.
Ostrom, V. (1980). Artisanship and artifact. *Public Administration Review, 40*(4), 309–317.
Oswald, A., & Stern, N. (2019, October). *Why does the economics of climate change matter so much—And why has the engagement of economists been so weak?* Royal Economic Society, newsletter. https://res.org.uk/newsletter/october-2019-newsletter-why-does-the-economics-of-climate-change-matter-so-much-and-why-has-the-engagement-of-economists-been-so-weak/
Oullier, O., Cialdini, R., Thaler, R. H., & Mullainathan, S. (2010). Improving public health prevention with a nudge. In O. Oullier & S. Sauneron (Eds.), *Improving public health prevention with behavioural, cognitive and neuroscience* (pp. 38–46). Centre for Strategic Analysis. Rapports et documents.

Paine, T. (1797/2008). *Rights of man: Common sense and other political writings*. Oxford University Press.
Pareto, V. (1935). *The mind and society—Volume 1—Non-logical conduct*. Harcourt, Brace and Company.
Parker, M., Fournier, V., & Reedy, P. (2008). *The dictionary of alternatives: Utopianism and organization*. Bloomsbury.
Patterson, J., Schulz, K., Vervoort, J., van der Hel, S., Widerberg, O., Adler, C., Hurlbert, M., Anderton, K., Sethi, M., & Barau, A. (2017). Exploring the governance and politics of transformations towards sustainability. *Environmental Innovation and Societal Transitions, 24*, 1–16. https://doi.org/10.1016/j.eist.2016.09.001
Pedersen, J. (2020). *Distributive justice and taxation*. Routledge.
Petri, F. (2021). *Microeconomics for the critical mind: Mainstream and heterodox analyses*. Springer. https://doi.org/10.1007/978-3-030-62070-7
Piketty, T. (2013). *Le capital au XXIe siècle*. Éditions du Seuil.
Piketty, T. (2015). About *Capital in the twenty-first century*. *American Economic Review, 105*(5), 48–53. https://doi.org/10.1257/aer.p20151060
Pinker, S. (2018). *Enlightenment now: The case for reason, science, humanism, and progress*. Viking.
Pistor, K. (2019). *The code of capital: How the law creates wealth and inequality*. Princeton University Press.
Polanyi, K. (1944/2001). *The great transformation: The political and economic origins of our time*. Beacon Press.
Potts, J., Cunningham, S., Hartley, J., & Ormerod, P. (2008). Social network markets: A new definition of the creative industries. *Journal of Cultural Economics, 32*(3), 167–185. https://doi.org/10.1007/s10824-008-9066-y
Power, M. (2004). Social provisioning as a starting point for Feminist Economics. *Feminist Economics, 10*(3), 3–19. https://doi.org/10.1080/1354570042000267608
Preda, A. (2005). The investor as a cultural figure of global capitalism. In K. Knorr Cetina & A. Preda (Eds.), *The sociology of financial markets* (pp. 141–161). Oxford University Press.
Priddat, B. P. (1990). *Hegel als Ökonom*. Duncker & Humblot.
Prieto, L., Phipps, S., Giugni, L., & Stott, N. (2021). Teaching (cooperative) business: The "Bluefield experiment" and the future of black business schools. *Academy of Management Learning & Education, 20*(3), 320–341. https://doi.org/10.5465/amle.2020.0127
Prilleltensky, I. (2012). Wellness as fairness. *American Journal of Community Psychology, 49*(1–2), 1–21. https://doi.org/10.1007/s10464-011-9448-8
Putnam, R. D. (2020). *Bowling alone: The collapse and revival of American community* (Revised and updated ed.). Simon & Schuster Paperbacks.

Qin, Y., Shi, L. H., Stöttinger, B., & Cavusgil, E. (2019). Neither an authentic product nor a counterfeit: The growing popularity of Shanzhai products in global markets: consumers' motives of buying Shanzhai vs. counterfeit products. *Canadian Journal of Administrative Sciences/Revue Canadienne Des Sciences de l'Administration, 36*(3), 306–321. https://doi.org/10.1002/cjas.1501

Redvers, N., Celidwen, Y., Schultz, C., Horn, O., Githaiga, C., Vera, M., Perdrisat, M., Plume, L. M., Kobei, D., Kain, M. C., Poelina, A., Rojas, J. N., & Blondin, B. (2022). The determinants of planetary health: An Indigenous consensus perspective. *The Lancet Planetary Health, 6*(2), e156–e163. https://doi.org/10.1016/S2542-5196(21)00354-5

Reich, B. J., Beck, J. T., & Price, J. (2018). Food as ideology: Measurement and validation of locavorism. *Journal of Consumer Research, 45*(4), 849–868. https://doi.org/10.1093/jcr/ucy027

Roberts, J. (2007). *The modern firm: Organizational design for performance and growth*. Oxford University Press.

Robeyns, I. (2017). *Wellbeing, freedom and social justice*. Open Book Publishers.

Rodríguez-Labajos, B., Yánez, I., Bond, P., Greyl, L., Munguti, S., Ojo, G. U., & Overbeek, W. (2019). Not so natural an alliance? Degrowth and environmental justice movements in the Global South. *Ecological Economics, 157*, 175–184. https://doi.org/10.1016/j.ecolecon.2018.11.007

Rossiter, J. R. (2019). A critique of prospect theory and framing with particular reference to consumer decisions. *Journal of Consumer Behaviour, 18*(5), 399–405. https://doi.org/10.1002/cb.1779

Rozin, P., Dingley, M., Urbanek, J. K., Jiang, H., & Kaltenbach, M. (2011). Nudge to nobesity I: Minor changes in accessibility decrease food intake. *Judgment and Decision Making, 6*(4), 323–332.

Rubin, G. (1975). The traffic in women: Notes on the "political economy" of sex. In R. R. Reiter (Ed.), *Toward an anthropology of women* (pp. 157–210). Monthly Review Press.

Ruggeri, K., Ashcroft-Jones, S., Abate Romero Landini, G., Al-Zahli, N., Alexander, N., Andersen, M. H., Bibilouri, K., Busch, K., Cafarelli, V., Chen, J., Doubravová, B., Dugué, T., Durrani, A. A., Dutra, N., Garcia-Garzon, E., Gomes, C., Gracheva, A., Grilc, N., Gürol, D. M., … Stock, F. (2023). The persistence of cognitive biases in financial decisions across economic groups. *Scientific Reports, 13*(1), 10329. https://doi.org/10.1038/s41598-023-36339-2

Ruggie, J. G. (1982). International regimes, transactions, and change: Embedded liberalism in the postwar economic order. *International Organization, 36*(2), 379–415.

Rupp, K. (2003). *Gift-giving in Japan: Cash, connections, cosmologies*. Stanford University Press.

Ruskin, J. (1985). *Unto this last, and other writings*. Penguin Books.

Rutten, R., & Boekema, F. (Eds.). (2007). *The learning region: Foundations, state of the art, future*. Edward Elgar.

Ryan, R. M., Huta, V., & Deci, E. L. (2008). Living well: A self-determination theory perspective on eudaimonia. *Journal of Happiness Studies, 9*(1), 139–170. https://doi.org/10.1007/s10902-006-9023-4

Ryff, C. D., Boylan, J. M., & Kirsch, J. A. (2021). Eudaimonic and hedonic well-being: An integrative perspective with linkages to sociodemographic factors and health. In M. T. Lee, L. D. Kubzansky, & T. J. VanderWeele (Eds.), *Measuring well-being* (1st ed., pp. 93–135). Oxford University Press. https://doi.org/10.1093/oso/9780197512531.003.0005

Sahlins, M. (1972). *Stone age economics*. Aldine-Atherton.

Sahlins, M., Bargatzky, T., Bird-David, N., Clammer, J., Hamel, J., Maegawa, K., & Siikala, J. (1996). The sadness of sweetness: The native anthropology of Western cosmology [and comments and reply]. *Current Anthropology, 37*(3), 395–428.

Salmon, E., Chavez R, J. F., & Murphy, M. (2023). New perspectives and critical insights from Indigenous peoples' research: A systematic review of Indigenous management and organization literature. *Academy of Management Annals, 17*(2), 439–491. https://doi.org/10.5465/annals.2021.0132

Santos, A. C., & Rodrigues, J. (2014). Neoliberalism in the laboratory? Experimental economics on markets and their limits. *New Political Economy, 19*(4), 507–533. https://doi.org/10.1080/13563467.2013.829433

Sargent, L. T. (1994). The three faces of utopianism revisited. *Utopian Studies, 5*(1), 1–37.

Sargent, L. T. (2010). *Utopianism: A very short introduction*. Oxford University Press.

Schiffer, S. J. (2018). "Glocalized" utopia, community-building, and the limits of imagination. *Utopian Studies, 29*(1), 67–87.

Schlager, E., & Ostrom, E. (1992). Property-rights regimes and natural resources: A conceptual analysis. *Land Economics, 68*, 249–262.

Schnädelbach, H. (2000). *Hegels praktische Philosophie: Ein Kommentar der Texte in der Reihenfolge ihrer Entstehung* (1. Aufl.). Suhrkamp.

Schneider, T., Eli, K., Dolan, C., & Ulijaszek, S. (Eds.). (2017). *Digital food activism*. Routledge.

Schumpeter, J. A. (1912/2006). *Theorie der wirtschaftlichen Entwicklung* (J. Röpke & O. Stiller, Eds.; Nachdruck der 1. Auflage von 1912). Duncker & Humblot.

Segal, H. P. (2017). Practical utopias: America as techno-fix nation. *Utopian Studies, 28*(2), 231–246. https://doi.org/10.5325/utopianstudies.28.2.0231

Sen, A. (1970). The impossibility of a Paretian liberal. *Journal of Political Economy, 78*(1), 152–157.
Sen, A. (2009). *The idea of justice*. Belknap Press of Harvard University Press.
Sennett, R. (2009). *The craftsman*. Penguin Books.
Serkin, C. (2016). *The law of property* (2nd ed.). Foundation Press.
Shin, D. C., & Johnson, D. M. (1978). Avowed happiness as an overall assessment of the quality of life. *Social Indicators Research, 5*, 475–492.
Simmel, G. (1908/1965). The poor. *Social Problems, 13*(2), 118–140. https://doi.org/10.2307/798898
Sinner, J., Tadaki, M., Challies, E., Kilvington, M., Tane, P., & Robb, C. A. (2022). Crafting collective management institutions in messy real-world settings: A call for action research. *International Journal of the Commons, 16*(1), 1–13.
Slobodian, Q. (2020). The law of the sea of ignorance: F. A. Hayek, Fritz Machlup and other neoliberals confront the intellectual property problem (pp. 70–92). In D. Plehwe, Q. Slobodian, & P. Mirowski (Eds.), *Nine lives of neoliberalism*. Verso.
Smil, V. (2008). *Energy in nature and society: General energetics of complex systems*. MIT Press.
Smith, A. (1759/2002). *The theory of moral sentiments*. Cambridge University Press.
Smith, P. B., & Max-Neef, M. (2011). *Economics unmasked: From power and greed to compassion and the common good*. Green Books.
Smith, V. L. (2008). *Rationality in economics: Constructivist and ecological forms*. Cambridge University Press. http://www.loc.gov/catdir/toc/ecip079/2007002899.html
Smith, V. L., & Wilson, B. J. (2019). *Humanomics: Moral sentiments and the wealth of nations for the twenty-first century*. Cambridge University Press.
Soddy, F. (1922/2012). *Cartesian economics: The bearing of physical science upon state stewardship*. Cosimo Books.
Spash, C. (2013). The shallow or the deep ecological economics movement? *Ecological Economics, 93*, 351–362.
Spencer, D. A. (2023). Marx, Keynes and the future of working time. *Cambridge Journal of Economics*. https://doi.org/10.1093/cje/bead046
Spínola, H. (2023). Environmental education in the light of Paulo Freire's pedagogy of the oppressed. *PLOS Sustainability and Transformation, 2*(7), e0000074. https://doi.org/10.1371/journal.pstr.0000074
Stafford, C. (2020). *Economic life in the real world: Logic, emotion and ethics*. Cambridge University Press.
Standing, G. (2016). *The corruption of capitalism: Why rentiers thrive and work does not pay*. Biteback.

Stehr, N. (2007). *Die Moralisierung der Märkte: Eine Gesellschaftstheorie* (1. Aufl.). Suhrkamp.

Stiglitz, J. E., Sen, A., & Fitoussi, J. P. (2009). *Report by the commission on the measurement of economic performance and social progress*.

Stillman, P. (1991). Review of *The concept of utopia*, by R. Levitas. *Utopian Studies, 2*(1/2), 220–222.

Stone, C. D. (1972/2012). Should trees have standing? Toward legal rights for natural objects. *Journal of Human Rights and the Environment, 3*, 4–55. https://doi.org/10.4337/jhre.2012.02.02

Storper, M. (1995). The resurgence of regional economies, ten years later: The region as a nexus of untraded interdependencies. *European Urban and Regional Studies, 2*(3), 191–221. https://doi.org/10.1177/096977649500200301

Sugden, R. (1986). *The economics of rights, co-operation and welfare*. Blackwell.

Sugden, R. (2018). *The community of advantage: A behavioural economist's defence of the market*. Oxford University Press.

Sunstein, C. R. (2018). "Better off, as judged by themselves": A comment on evaluating nudges. *International Review of Economics, 65*(1), 1–8. https://doi.org/10.1007/s12232-017-0280-9

Sunstein, C. R. (2023). Hayekian behavioral economics. *Behavioural Public Policy, 7*(1), 170–188. https://doi.org/10.1017/bpp.2021.3

Sunstein, C. R., & Reisch, L. A. (2014). Automatically green: Behavioral economics and environmental protection. *Harvard Environmental Law Review, 38*(1), 127–158.

Sutterlütti, S., & Meretz, S. (2023). *Make capitalism history: A practical framework for utopia and the transformation of society*. Springer. https://doi.org/10.1007/978-3-031-14645-9

Swedberg, R. (2022). *Joseph A. Schumpeter: The economics and sociology of capitalism*. Princeton University Press.

Synnott, A. (1992). Tomb, temple, machine and self: The social construction of the body. *The British Journal of Sociology, 43*(1), 79–110. https://doi.org/10.2307/591202

Taylor, D. (2011). Wellbeing and welfare: A psychosocial analysis of being well and doing well enough. *Journal of Social Policy, 40*(4), 777–794. https://doi.org/10.1017/S0047279411000249

Thaler, R. H. (2015). *Misbehaving: The making of behavioural economics*. W. W. Norton.

Thaler, R. H. (2018). From cashews to nudges: The evolution of behavioral economics. *American Economic Review, 108*(6), 1265–1287.

Thaler, R. H., & Sunstein, C. R. (2008). *Nudge: Improving decisions about health, wealth, and happiness*. Yale University Press.

The Economist. (2023). Making babymaking better. *The Economist*. Retrieved 23 August 2023, from https://www.economist.com/leaders/2023/07/20/making-babymaking-better

Thompson, C. J., & Coskuner-Balli, G. (2007). Countervailing market responses to corporate co-optation and the ideological recruitment of consumption communities. *Journal of Consumer Research, 34*(2), 135–152. https://doi.org/10.1086/519143

Thompson, E. (2010). *Mind in life: Biology, phenomenology, and the sciences of mind*. Harvard University Press.

Thompson, E., & Stapleton, M. (2009). Making sense of sense-making: Reflections on enactive and extended mind theories. *Topoi, 28*(1), 23–30. https://doi.org/10.1007/s11245-008-9043-2

Tripp, C. (2006). *Islam and the moral economy: The challenge of capitalism*. Cambridge University Press.

Tronto, J. C. (1993) *Moral boundaries: A political argument for an ethic of care. Routledge*

Tuan, Y.-F. (2011). *Space and place: The perspective of experience*. University of Minnesota Press.

United Nations. (2015). *Transforming our world: The 2030 agenda for sustainable development*. Department of Economic and Social Affairs. https://sdgs.un.org/2030agenda

Uzawa, H. (2009). *Economic analysis of social common capital*. Cambridge University Press.

van Parijs, P., & Vanderborght, Y. (2019). *Basic income: A radical proposal for a free society and a sane economy*. Harvard University Press.

van 't Klooster, J. (2023). Reflections on the 2022 Nobel Memorial Prize awarded to Ben Bernanke, Douglas Diamond, and Philip Dybvig. *Erasmus Journal for Philosophy and Economics, 16*(1), Article 1. https://doi.org/10.23941/ejpe.v16i1.745

Varela, F. J., Thompson, E., & Rosch, E. (2016). *The embodied mind* (revised). MIT Press.

Väyrynen, P. (2021). Thick ethical concepts. In E. N. Zalta (Ed.), *The Stanford encyclopedia of philosophy*. https://plato.stanford.edu/archives/spr2021/entries/thick-ethical-concepts/

Villamayor-Tomas, S., & Muradian, R. (Eds.). (2023). *The Barcelona school of ecological economics and political ecology: A companion in honour of Joan Martinez-Alier* (Vol. 8). Springer. https://doi.org/10.1007/978-3-031-22566-6

Viner, J. (1949). Bentham and J. S. Mill: The utilitarian background. *American Economic Review, 39*(2), 360–382.

Viney, L. L. (1985). "They call you a dole bludger": Some experiences of unemployment. *Journal of Community Psychology, 13*(1), 31–45.

Walton, G. M. (2014). The new science of Wise psychological interventions. *Current Directions in Psychological Science, 23*(1), 73–82. https://doi.org/10.1177/0963721413512856

Walton, G. M., & Wilson, T. D. (2018). Wise interventions: Psychological remedies for social and personal problems. *Psychological Review, 125*(5), 617–655. https://doi.org/10.1037/rev0000115

Washington, H., Piccolo, J., Gomez-Baggethun, E., Kopnina, H., & Alberro, H. (2021). The trouble with anthropocentric hubris, with examples from conservation. *Conservation, 1*(4), 285–298. https://doi.org/10.3390/conservation1040022

Webb, D. (2007). Modes of hoping. *History of the Human Sciences, 20*(3), 65–83. https://doi.org/10.1177/0952695107079335

Whitehead, M., Jones, R., Lilley, R., Pykett, J., & Howell, R. (2017). *Neuroliberalism: Behavioural government in the twenty-first century*. Routledge.

Wikipedia. (n.d.). *Representative concentration pathway*. https://en.wikipedia.org/w/index.php?title=Representative_Concentration_Pathway&oldid=1167054232

Wilde, O. (1891, February). The soul of man under socialism. *Fortnightly Review, 291*, 292–319.

Williams, A. W. (1980). Computerized double-auction markets: Some initial experimental results. *The Journal of Business, 53*(3), 235–258.

Wilson, D. S., Ostrom, E., & Cox, M. E. (2013). Generalizing the core design principles for the efficacy of groups. *Journal of Economic Behavior & Organization, 90*(Supplement), S21–S32. https://doi.org/10.1016/j.jebo.2012.12.010

Wolff, J., & Leopold, D. (2021, Spring). Karl Marx. In E. N. Zalta (Ed.), *The Stanford encyclopedia of philosophy*. Metaphysics Research Lab, Stanford University. https://plato.stanford.edu/archives/spr2021/entries/marx/

Wright, E. O. (2010). *Envisioning real utopias*. Verso.

Wright, E. O. (2013). Transforming capitalism through real utopias. *American Sociological Review, 78*(1), 1–25. https://doi.org/10.1177/0003122412468882

Zingales, L. (2015). Presidential address: Does finance benefit society? *Journal of Finance, 70*(4), 1327–1363. https://doi.org/10.1111/jofi.12295

Index

F. Basso and C. Herrmann-Pillath, *Embodiment, Political Economy and Human Flourishing*, https://doi.org/10.1007/978-3-031-54971-7

R

MIX
Papier aus verantwortungsvollen Quellen
Paper from responsible sources
FSC® C105338

If you have any concerns about our products,
you can contact us on
ProductSafety@springernature.com

In case Publisher is established outside the EU,
the EU authorized representative is:
Springer Nature Customer Service Center GmbH
Europaplatz 3, 69115 Heidelberg, Germany

Printed by Libri Plureos GmbH
in Hamburg, Germany